CLINICAL
MENTAL HEALTH
COUNSELING

We dedicate this book to the brilliant souls who authored chapters. This project has been a long and winding road from start to finish, and it is only through your talents, patience, professionalism, and perseverance that this book became a reality.

JSY *and* CSC

SAGE was founded in 1965 by Sara Miller McCune to support the dissemination of usable knowledge by publishing innovative and high-quality research and teaching content. Today, we publish over 900 journals, including those of more than 400 learned societies, more than 800 new books per year, and a growing range of library products including archives, data, case studies, reports, and video. SAGE remains majority-owned by our founder, and after Sara's lifetime will become owned by a charitable trust that secures our continued independence.

Los Angeles | London | New Delhi | Singapore | Washington DC | Melbourne

CLINICAL MENTAL HEALTH COUNSELING

Elements of Effective Practice

Edited by

J. Scott Young
Craig S. Cashwell
The University of North Carolina at Greensboro

Los Angeles | London | New Delhi
Singapore | Washington DC | Melbourne

FOR INFORMATION:

SAGE Publications, Inc.
2455 Teller Road
Thousand Oaks, California 91320
E-mail: order@sagepub.com

SAGE Publications Ltd.
1 Oliver's Yard
55 City Road
London, EC1Y 1SP
United Kingdom

SAGE Publications India Pvt. Ltd.
B 1/I 1 Mohan Cooperative Industrial Area
Mathura Road, New Delhi 110 044
India

SAGE Publications Asia-Pacific Pte. Ltd.
3 Church Street
#10-04 Samsung Hub
Singapore 049483

Acquisitions Editor: Nathan Davidson
Development Editor: Abbie Rickard
Production Editor: Jane Haenel
Copy Editor: Mark Bast
Typesetter: Hurix Systems (P) Ltd.
Proofreader: Laura Webb
Indexer: Nancy Fulton
Cover Designer: Janet Kiesel
Marketing Manager: Shari Countryman

Library of Congress Cataloging-in-Publication Data

Names: Young, J. Scott, editor. | Cashwell, Craig S., editor.

Title: Clinical mental health counseling: elements of effective practice / [edited by] J. Scott Young, Craig S. Cashwell.

Description: Los Angeles: Sage Publications, [2017] | Includes bibliographical references and index.

Identifiers: LCCN 2016010158 | ISBN 9781506305639 (pbk.)

Subjects: | MESH: Counseling | Mental Health | Case Reports

Classification: LCC RC466 | NLM WM 55 | DDC 362.2/04256—dc23

LC record available at http://lccn.loc.gov/2016010158

16 17 18 19 20 10 9 8 7 6 5 4 3 2 1

Brief Contents

Detailed Contents

3 Advocacy and Social Justice   53

4 Continuum of Care   81

SECTION II PROCESSES AND PROCEDURES OF CLINICAL MENTAL HEALTH COUNSELING

5 Assessing Client Concerns

CASEY BARRIO-MINTON

10 Crisis Management and Disaster Relief   255

AMBER L. POPE AND ALLISON MARSH POW

SECTION III MAXIMIZING YOUR EFFECTIVENESS AS A CLINICAL MENTAL HEALTH COUNSELOR

11 The Importance of Clinical Supervision to Effective Practice   287

DIANNE BORDERS

12 Wellness, Self-Care, and Burnout Prevention

313

GERARD LAWSON AND JENNIFER M. COOK

13 Using Research to Improve Clinical Practice

337

KELLY L. WESTER AND TAMARINE FOREMAN

SECTION IV CURRENT AND FUTURE TRENDS IN CLINICAL MENTAL HEALTH PRACTICE

14 The Applications of Neuroscience to Clinical Mental Health Counseling

JANE E. MYERS AND LAURA JONES

15 Emerging Approaches to Clinical Mental Health Counseling

AMANDA L. GIORDANO, PHILIP B. CLARKE, CHERYL L. FULTON, AND TAMMY H. CASHWELL

Preface

*C*linical Mental Health Counseling: Elements of Effective Practice was written to provide a comprehensive overview of the field of clinical mental health counseling for counselors in training. Our interest in creating this text grew out of classroom experiences teaching introductory courses in clinical mental health counseling and struggling to identify what we believed was a text that covered the range of topics and issues that counselors face in the current practice environment. Therefore, this book was designed to serve as the text for courses that introduce students to clinical mental health counseling by exploring both the foundational elements of the field and real-world topics that directly impact clinical practice.

As such, this book includes a practical and applied focus. Throughout the book **key words are bolded** to help students focus their learning and case studies and discussion questions afford students opportunities to apply what they are reading and translate content to real-world scenarios. In addition, the book includes a section on emerging models for clinical intervention. This is a feature we hope will allow both instructors and students to explore approaches to clinical mental health counseling that are cutting edge and that will serve students well as they move into a practicum or internship setting and ultimately into full-time practice.

Chapter authors were carefully selected from among leading figures in the counseling field, so that each chapter presents the perspective of luminary writers and researchers working today. Chapter authors were asked to focus on two areas, (1) the counselor in training who is learning about the range of activities within clinical mental health practice and (2) the application of the material to clinical practice. Our aim was to create a text that is both theoretical *and* applied, a feature we believe makes this book unique in the marketplace.

This text is designed to assist instructors in providing students with an outstanding learning experience. To this end, the required 2016 CACREP standards for clinical mental health counseling programs are covered. Our hope is that our approach to the text will help to ensure your success in teaching this content by laying a pedagogical foundation that you may easily build on.

This book could not have been created without the assistance of many individuals. The chapter authors were wonderful to work with, grasping our vision for this text, and demonstrated incredible professionalism and flexibility with challenges that emerged along the way. Additionally, the individuals who served as reviewers for the draft of this book provided invaluable feedback in their thoughtful reviews—thank you. Further, the staff of SAGE Publishing was a joy to have along on this writing adventure. Your enthusiasm about the project and your warm support are deeply appreciated. Finally, our deepest and most heartfelt regards go to our colleagues in the Department of Counseling and Educational Development at the University of North Carolina at Greensboro for daily embodying what it means to be a professional counselor.

About the Editors and Contributors

EDITORS

J. Scott Young, PhD, NCC, LPC, is professor and chair of the Department of Counseling and Educational Development at The University of North Carolina at Greensboro (UNCG). His leadership in the field has included service as past president of the Association for Spiritual, Ethical, and Religious Values in Counseling (ASERVIC) and as a member of the Governing Council and Executive Committee for the American Counseling Association. He has served as an editorial board member for numerous journals, including the *Journal of Counseling & Development*, *Counseling and Values*, and *Counselor Education and Supervision*. He is coeditor of the book *Integrating Spirituality Into Counseling: A Guide to Competent Practice* and the text *Counseling Research: Quantitative, Qualitative, and Single Subject Design*. He has published numerous articles on the interface of clinical practice with spirituality and religion. Awards Dr. Young has received include selection as an ACA Fellow, the Meritorious Service Award from the Association for Spiritual, Ethical, and Religious Values in Counseling, the Alumni Excellence Award from the Department of Counseling and Educational Development at UNCG, and the Administrator of the Year from the North Carolina Counseling Association.

Craig S. Cashwell, PhD, LPC, NCC, ACS, CSAT-S, is professor in the Department of Counseling and Educational Development at The University of North Carolina at Greensboro (UNCG). He has served as president of Chi Sigma Iota International; president of the Association for Spiritual, Ethical, and Religious Values in Counseling (ASERVIC); CACREP board chair; and ACES representative to the ACA Governing Council. Craig has received numerous awards, including the CSI International Thomas J. Sweeney Professional Leadership Award, the American Counseling Association David K. Brooks Distinguished Mentor Award, and the ASERVIC Lifetime Service Award. In 2011, Craig received designation as an ACA Fellow. He has contributed to more than 125 publications and has received multiple research awards, including an ACA Best Practices Award and twice receiving the Association for Counselor Education and Supervision Outstanding Counselor Education and Supervision Article Award. Craig values mentoring relationships and has been recognized with mentoring awards from the UNCG Graduate School, the North Carolina Counseling Association, the Conference of Southern Graduate Schools, and the ACA. Additionally, he has been recognized with a UNCG School of Education Teaching Excellence Award.

CONTRIBUTORS

Amy T. Banner, PhD, NCC, is a counselor and counselor educator. She earned her PhD in counseling and counselor education at The University of North Carolina at Greensboro.

Casey A. Barrio-Minton, PhD, NCC, is an associate professor in the Department of Educational Psychology and Counseling at the University of Tennessee, Knoxville. She has specialty interest in clinical mental health counseling and teaches a range of courses, including those focused on professional issues and diagnosis and treatment planning. A past president of Chi Sigma Iota and the Association for Assessment and Research in Counseling (AARC), Casey has published multiple journal articles focused on assessment issues, crisis intervention, and teaching in counselor education. She is lead author of *Evaluating Student Learning Outcomes in Counselor Education* and coauthor of *DSM-5 Learning Companion for Counselors*.

L. DiAnne Borders, PhD, LPC, NCC, ACS, is the Burlington Industries Excellence Professor in the Department of Counseling and Educational Development at The University of North Carolina at Greensboro, where she teaches the doctoral clinical supervision course and supervises doctoral students' supervision internships. Dr. Borders has published extensively on supervision topics, including the supervisory relationship, counselors' and supervisors' cognitions and cognitive complexity, and new supervisors' challenges, such as giving corrective feedback. She has presented supervision workshops in several countries and hosted postdoctoral fellows from Turkey, Romania, and Australia. Dr. Borders currently serves as editor of *The Clinical Supervisor*.

Tammy H. Cashwell, PhD, LPC, NCC, is an assistant teaching professor in the Department of Counseling at Wake Forest University (WFU). She has experience as a school counselor at both the elementary and high school levels, as well as experience in college counseling and mental health settings.

Catherine Y. Chang, PhD, LPC, NCC, CPSC, is a professor at Georgia State University and program coordinator for the Counselor Education and Practice doctoral program. She is the director of International Programs for the College of Education and Human Development. Dr. Chang's primary areas of interest include social justice and advocacy, multicultural counseling competence, supervision, and counseling implications related to Asian American and Korean American clients.

Philip B. Clarke, PhD, LPC, NCC, is an assistant professor in the Department of Counseling at Wake Forest University. Dr. Clarke has worked in outpatient hospital, group practice, and addiction treatment settings. He has published on clinical mental health approaches as well as teaching and supervision.

Jennifer M. Cook, PhD, LPC, NCC, is an assistant professor of counselor education and counseling psychology at Marquette University in Milwaukee, Wisconsin. Jennifer identifies strongly with a client/student-centered, strength-based approach and teaches clinical mental health–focused counseling courses. Her research interests focus on counselor multicultural development, with emphasis on social class and identity intersectionality, counselor preparation, and supervision.

Jamie E. Crockett, PhD, LPCA, NCC, is an assistant professor in the Department of Counseling at Wake Forest University. She is also in part-time private practice at Triad Counseling and Clinical Services in Greensboro, North Carolina. Her clinical and research interests include ethics, attachment theory, emotion regulation, mindful and breath-based approaches, holistic wellness, multicultural competence, and high-risk populations.

John R. Culbreth, LPC-S, LCAS, CCS, NCC, MAC, ACS, is a professor in the Department of Counseling at the University of North Carolina, Charlotte. His research and training interests are in the areas of clinical supervision, addiction counseling, and the development of professional counselors. His clinical experience includes work as a mental health counselor and chemical dependency counselor working for agencies and in private practice.

Tamarine Foreman, PhD, NCC, LPCC-S, is an assistant professor of counselor education at Ohio University. Dr. Foreman's research is centered on understanding the impact of working with people who have experienced trauma while also inspiring commitment to wellness and supporting the developmental journey of counselors. Dr. Foreman earned her doctorate in counseling and counselor education, along with doctoral minors in educational research methodology and human development and family systems from the University of North Carolina at Greensboro.

Kerrie K. Fuenfhausen, PhD, LPC, NCC, ACS, is an associate professor in the Counseling Program at Lenoir-Rhyne University, Asheville Campus. She has been program coordinator of the Asheville Counseling Program since its inception in August 2012. Dr. Fuenfhausen has experience working with individuals, couples, and families in private practice, community agency, and hospital settings. She enjoys mentoring counselors in training as they develop their professional identity and embark on their counseling careers.

Cheryl L. Fulton, PhD, MBA, LPC, is an assistant professor in the Department of Counseling, Leadership, Adult Education, and School Psychology at Texas State University. She conducts research and frequently presents on the topic of mindfulness and its integration into counseling and counselor training. Her professional interests also include gender issues, leadership, and counselor entrepreneurship.

Gary G. Gintner, PhD, LPC, is an associate professor and program leader of the Counseling Program at Louisiana State University in Baton Rouge. He is a nationally recognized trainer on the *DSM-5* and best-practice guidelines. He is a Fellow of the American Counseling Association and was the 2007–2008 president of the American Mental Health Counselors Association (AMHCA).

Amanda L. Giordano, PhD, LPC, NCC, is an assistant professor in the Department of Counseling and Higher Education at the University of North Texas. Giordano specializes in addictions counseling and spiritual/religious issues in counseling.

Emily Goodman-Scott, PhD, LPC, NBCC, NCSC, ACS, is an assistant professor and school counseling coordinator in Old Dominion University's Department of Counseling and Human Services. Her research interests include a range of school counseling topics (e.g., preparation, schoolwide prevention, elementary school issues) and counseling children with exceptional needs in and out of the schools. Before her present position,

Dr. Goodman-Scott enjoyed working as a school counselor, licensed professional counselor primarily serving youth, and special education autism teacher.

Paige Bentley Greason, PhD, LPC-S, is the director of Counseling & Wellness Services and an assistant professor in the Department of Psychiatry at Wake Forest University School of Medicine. Her counseling experience spans community mental health, private practice, and university settings, and she teaches as an adjunct assistant professor in the Department of Counseling at Wake Forest University. In addition to her background and interest in mindfulness-based therapy and research, she is a registered yoga teacher.

Laura K. Jones is a lecturer in the Department of Health and Wellness at the University of North Carolina, Asheville. She holds a PhD in counseling and counselor education as well as a MS in psychology–cognitive neuroscience and uses her training in both disciplines to inform her research, clinical, and pedagogical practices. As such, Dr. Jones's primary interest lies in the confluence of neuroscience and counseling, with specific interests in the intentional and informed integration of neuroscience into the counseling field and counselor training programs as well as in the neuroscience of trauma and recovery as it relates to elucidating the impact of trauma on interpersonal relationships, perceptions of safety following trauma, and efficacious interventions for survivors. She also serves as the chair of the Association for Counselor Education and Supervision Neuroscience Interest Network and as a coeditor of the monthly column "Neurocounseling: Bridging Brain and Behavior" in *Counseling Today*.

Simone F. Lambert, PhD, LPC, NCC, is an associate professor in the Department of Counseling at Argosy University, Washington, DC. She has worked as a professional counselor in nonprofit, clinical mental health agency, and private practice settings. Dr. Lambert is a past president of the International Association of Addiction and Offender Counselors (IAAOC), a division of the American Counseling Association (ACA), and she currently serves as the IAAOC representative on the ACA Governing Council.

Gerard Lawson, PhD, LPC, NCC, ACS, is an associate professor in the Counselor Education program at Virginia Tech. Gerard has conducted research and has published on issues of counselor wellness. He chaired the ACA Task Force on Counselor Wellness and Impairment and, with Jane Myers, founded the ACA Wellness Interest Network. Gerard was elected the 66th president of the American Counseling Association.

Todd F. Lewis, PhD, NCC, LPC, is an associate professor of counseling and counselor education at North Dakota State University. Throughout his career, he has taught graduate-level students in motivational interviewing, substance abuse counseling, assessment, diagnosis and treatment planning, and quantitative research. He has presented on these topics at numerous local, state, national, and international venues. Dr. Lewis has published extensively on topics related to substance abuse, collegiate drinking, and theoretical approaches to addictions treatment.

A. Keith Mobley, PhD, LPC-S, NCC, ACS, is a clinical professor in the Department of Counseling and Educational Development at The University of North Carolina at Greensboro. He teaches professional orientation and ethics and serves as the clinic director for the departmental training clinic, supervising master's and doctoral practicum students and providing supervision for doctoral students at supervision internships. He engages in grant activities and supervises doctoral research in a variety of topics. He has received numerous recognitions for his leadership to the department and profession.

Muthoni Musangali, PhD, NCC, is an associate professor and chair of the Department of Professional Counseling at Webster University. She earned her PhD in counselor education from the University of Central Florida. She holds a MA in counseling from Heidelberg College and a B.Ed. (Arts) from Kenyatta University, Kenya. She is a member of the American Counseling Association (ACA); the Association for Counselor Education and Supervision (ACES), North Central ACES; and the Association for Assessment and Research in Counseling (AARC).

Jane E. Myers (deceased), LPC, NCC, NCGC, was a professor in the Department of Counseling and Educational Development at The University of North Carolina at Greensboro and executive director of Chi Sigma Iota International. She authored more than 175 publications and was recognized with numerous national and international awards.

Daniel M. Paredes, PhD, NCC, LPC-S, is assistant director for clinical services at the Wake Forest University Counseling Center. His professional interests include college/university counseling, counselor training, crisis counseling, identity development, multi/cross-cultural counseling, substance abuse counseling, the use of technology in counseling, and wellness.

Maria A. Brunelli Paredes, PhD, LPC-S, CEDS, is visiting assistant professor in the Department of Counseling and Educational Development at The University of North Carolina at Greensboro and a private practitioner specializing in eating disorders, body image, grief, and anxiety.

Amber L. Pope, PhD, LMHC, NCC, is the program chair and an associate professor in the Clinical Mental Health Counseling Department at Hodges University. She has worked in various clinical mental health settings, including private practice, college campus counseling centers, outpatient mental health at community agencies, and pastoral care services at a hospital treating a variety of presenting issues. Dr. Pope specializes in the areas of couples counseling, sexuality concerns, gender and sexuality development, and LGBTQ-related counseling.

Allison Marsh Pow, PhD, LPC, NCC, is an assistant professor of clinical mental health counseling at the University of Texas at San Antonio. Her research interests include trauma and the mental health implications of disaster, terrorism, and violence. She has worked for many years as a licensed professional counselor, specializing in trauma and crisis intervention in community outpatient and inpatient settings.

Laura E. Welfare, PhD, LPC, NCC, ACS, is an associate professor in the Counselor Education Program at Virginia Tech in Blacksburg, Virginia. Dr. Welfare has worked with children and adults in outpatient and inpatient mental health settings.

Kelly L. Wester, PhD, LPC, NCC, is a professor in the Department of Counseling and Educational Development at The University of North Carolina at Greensboro. Her research interests include nonsuicidal self-injury as well as researcher identity and training in counseling. She has mentored and taught others in research and has developed research competencies for the field of counseling.

Framework of Clinical Mental Health Counseling

CHAPTER 1

History and Evolution of Clinical Mental Health Counseling

Kerrie K. Fuenfhausen, Scott Young, Craig Cashwell, and
Muthoni Musangali

Learning Goals

Upon completion of this chapter, you will be able to do the following:

1. Define the practice of clinical mental health (CMH) counseling and the unique elements of this counseling specialty

2. Understand the history and development of CMH counseling as a specialty practice

3. Describe the foundational principles and philosophy of the CMH specialty

4. Understand the range of services provided by CMH counselors

5. Identify the training, certification, and licensure required to practice as a CMH counselor

6. Communicate effectively about models of CMH counseling

CMH counseling is a vibrant and dynamic field of practice that affords counselors rich potential to impact the lives of clients. The Bureau of Labor Statistics indicated that there were over 128,000 CMH counselors practicing in the United States in May 2015 (Bureau of Labor Statistics, 2016). Current estimations suggest significant growth in the number of CMH counselors needed, with a projected growth rate of 24%, which is much higher than average for most professions. The anticipated growth in the field provides job security and rich opportunities for CMH counselors into the future. In 2012, the earning potential for CMH counselors ranged from $32,000 to $48,000 in the top industries in which these counselors worked, with a median income of about $40,000 (Bureau of Labor Statistics, 2013). This range primarily applies to work within mental health agencies, and the earning potential within private practice is significantly higher. There is good potential for employment and meaningful work as a CMH counselor, which is shaped by the unfortunate reality that there are many individuals who suffer from mental disorders and are in need of treatment to cope with the debilitating effects of mental illness as well as the normal developmental challenges and struggles of life. To understand how the field of CMH counseling fits within the scope of the helping professions and the field of counseling specifically, it is helpful to begin with an overview of the counseling field and the foundational orientations upon which the field is built.

FOUNDATIONAL PRINCIPLES OF COUNSELING

The mental health field includes different types of helping professionals: counselors, social workers, psychologists, psychiatrists, mental health technicians, and marriage and family therapists, to name a few. Each of these professions has its own training standards, licensure and certification requirements, ethical codes, and standards of practice, as well as organizations that serve to define the profession and support practitioners. Perhaps more importantly, however, each field has a unique professional identity, a shared philosophy of helping that distinguishes it from the other mental health professions. In the profession of counseling, that identity is characterized by the following:

1. A wellness model of mental health

2. A developmental perspective

3. A focus on prevention and early intervention

4. The empowerment of clients (Remley & Herlihy, 2010)

5. An ongoing commitment to multicultural considerations

These principles are embodied in the definition approved by the ACA Governing Council and posted on the ACA website (www.counseling.org): "Counseling is a professional relationship that empowers diverse individuals, families, and groups to accomplish mental health, wellness, education, and career goals."

The designation of counseling as a profession, of which CMH counseling is a subspecialty, is important because such a status gives legitimacy to the work and makes it a specific vocation in which not just anyone can claim membership. Technically, for an occupation to qualify as a profession, a definitional set of criteria must be met (Greenwood, 1962; Gross, 1958). When these criteria are considered within the context of professional counseling, it quickly becomes evident that counseling indeed meets the criteria of a unique profession.

1. *A specialized body of knowledge.* Counseling is clearly a field that produces a unique body of knowledge. This is evident from the fact that there are scientific journals that addresses the broad continuum of work that counselors do (e.g., *The Journal of Counseling and Development*).

2. *Systematic theory.* A theory is an explanation of a certain set of observed phenomenon in terms of a system of constructs or laws that relate to one another. Counseling uses a range of theories that inform practice, including traditional theories of individual psychology (such as psychoanalytic, behavioral, and existential humanistic models) and theories of group interactions (such as family systems and group theory). More recent are emerging models of the most effective treatment of specific mental health concerns, such as trauma focused cognitive behavioral therapy to treat the effects of trauma.

3. *Special relationship between practitioner and client.* Legal statutes and ethical standards make it clear that the work of CMH counselors exists within a specialized professional relationship that provides protection to the client. Accordingly, licensed counselors work under a set of unique legal and ethical responsibilities that are outlined both by licensure bodies with individual states and by professional association (e.g., The American Counseling Association).

4. *Societal approval.* That counseling is recognized broadly as a profession is evidenced by state licensure, national credentialing, accreditation standards, and legal precedence. Furthermore, the fact that the services of counselors are reimbursed by both public and private payers makes it clear that there is broad social acceptance of the important role that counselors play in society. See Table 1.1 for an overview of counselor national certification and licensure.

Table 1.1   National Counselor Certification and State Counseling Licensure

	National Certification	**State Licensure**
Name of Credential	National Certified Counselor (NCC) Issued by NBCC. NBCC also offers three specialty certifications for NCCs in addictions, clinical mental health, and school counseling.	Differs from state to state. Most common titles are licensed professional counselor (LPC), licensed mental health counselor (LMHC), licensed clinical professional counselor (LCPC), and licensed professional clinical counselor (LPCC). Issued by each state regulatory board.
Purpose	To promote and represent the counseling profession through a national certification program where the standards are set by members of the counseling profession. Compliance with continuing education requirements and the NBCC Code of Ethics ensure that NCCs stay current with the profession's best practices.	To protect the public by defining practitioners who can legally use the title of a licensed counselor and/or who can provide counseling services in a particular state. These standards are set by state legislatures.

(Continued)

Table 1.1 (Continued)

	National Certification	State Licensure
Examinations	The National Counselor Examination for Licensure and Certification (NCE)	NCE and/or NCMHCE State counselor licensure boards contract with NBCC to use one or both of these examinations.
Requirements	• Master's degree in counseling or with a major study in counseling from a regionally accredited institution • 3,000 hours of counseling experience and 100 hours of supervision both over a 2-year postmaster's time period • Postmaster's experience and supervision requirements are waived for graduate students who have completed CACREP accredited tracks. • Passing score on NCE	Varies from state to state. All require some combination of • Master's degree • Counseling experience and supervision • Passing score on NCE and/or NCMHCE. Some require mental health laws exam of that state.

5. *Standards for admitting and policing practitioners.* Individuals can join the counseling profession only after completing a minimum of a master's degree in counseling. Additionally, licensure by a state licensing board is required for independent practice. Each of the 50 U.S. states has licensure laws regulating the title and scope of practice of professional counselors. Typically, licensure laws govern title (who may use a title such as *professional counselor*) and practice (what a professional counselor can do). Once a counseling professional begins practicing, he or she can be charged for ethical violations of professional standards and be sanctioned by or dismissed from professional societies or from practice by licensure boards.

6. *Code of ethics.* A unique code of ethics guides the decision making and professional practice of its members. At a minimum, CMH counselors operate under the ethical standards used by the appropriate state licensing board. If the CMH counselor holds additional professional memberships (e.g., American Counseling Association [ACA] or American Mental Health Counselors Association [AMHCA]) or credentials (e.g., National Certified Counselor), he or she is subject to additional ethical standards and codes of practice.

7. *Professional organizations and similar evidence of a professional culture.* Many counselors belong to professional organizations such as the ACA and AMHCA. Additionally, many counselors are members of Chi Sigma Iota, the international

counseling academic and professional honor society. CMH counselors also join specialty groups, such as the Society for the Study of Trauma and Dissociation, or attain specialty credentials, such as certified sex addiction therapist, that focus on more discrete populations and issues.

Table 1.2 lists the divisions of the American Counseling Association and related journals.

Table 1.2   National Counselor Certification and State Counseling Licensure

American Counseling Association (ACA)   *Journal of Counseling and Development*
Association for Assessment in Counseling and Education (AACE)   *Measurement and Evaluation in Counseling and Development*   *Counseling Outcome Research and Evaluation*
Association for Adult Development and Aging (AADA)   *Adultspan*
Association for Creativity in Counseling (ACC)   *Journal of Creativity in Mental Health*
American College Counseling Association (ACCA)   *Journal of College Counseling*
Association for Counselors and Educators in Government (ACEG)
Association for Counselor Education and Supervision (ACES)   *Counselor Education and Supervision*
Association for Humanistic Counseling (AHC)   *Journal of Humanistic Counseling*
Association for Lesbian, Gay, Bisexual and Transgender Issues in Counseling (ALGBTIC)   *Journal of LGBT Issues in Counseling*
Association for Multicultural Counseling and Development (AMCD)   *Journal of Multicultural Counseling and Development*
American Mental Health Counselors Association (AMHCA)   *Journal of Mental Health Counseling*
American Rehabilitation Counseling Association (ARCA)   *Rehabilitation Counseling Bulletin*
American School Counselor Association (ASCA)   *Professional School Counseling*
Association for Spiritual, Ethical, and Religious Values in Counseling (ASERVIC)   *Counseling and Values*

(Continued)

Table 1.2 (Continued)

Association for Specialists in Group Work (ASGW) *Journal for Specialists in Group Work*
Counselors for Social Justice (CSJ) *Journal for Social Action in Counseling and Psychology*
International Association of Addictions and Offender Counselors (IAAOC) *Journal of Addictions and Offender Counseling*
International Association of Marriage and Family Counselors (IAMFC) *Family Journal: Counseling and Therapy for Couples and Families*
National Career Development Association (NCDA) *Career Development Quarterly*
National Employment Counseling Association (NECA) *Journal of Employment Counseling*

Wellness Model of Mental Health

All counselors, regardless of specialty, operate from the perspective that the goal of counseling is to promote general wellness, rather than to focus solely on curing an illness or fixing a problem. The **wellness model of mental health** emphasizes the importance of helping clients work toward optimal mental and emotional health. The wellness perspective is an alternative to the medical or illness model used by most other helping professions, which approaches client concerns by isolating the problem, diagnosing an illness, and treating the symptoms in an attempt to cure the problem and return the client to his or her prior level of functioning. From this perspective, health is equated with the absence of problems or symptoms. This perspective is also referred to as the deficit model, because it is focused on what is *wrong* or *lacking* in an individual.

Professional counselors, on the other hand, help clients focus on their strengths and how those strengths can assist them in moving toward optimal well-being of body, mind, and spirit. This perspective emphasizes a holistic view of wellness across many areas of life, including the physical, emotional, mental, spiritual, relational, vocational, financial, and sexual realms. Based on an understanding that each of these areas can affect one another, as well as one's overall wellness, counselors support clients in evaluating which areas may need attention in order to improve one's general health and well-being (Myers, Sweeney, & Witmer, 2000). For example, a client may be struggling with depression or anxiety (emotional/psychological) and job-related stress (vocational), but through a strength-based assessment of wellness, the counselor discovers that the client has a passion for running (physical) and a meaningful spiritual practice. The counselor would help the client to draw on these physical and spiritual strengths and resources as a way of coping with and managing the current experience of emotional and vocational struggles.

The importance of the wellness paradigm in counseling is evident in the number of wellness models that have been developed, including but not limited to the following: Zimpfer's (1992) wellness model; Hettler's (1984) hexagonal model of wellness; the lifespan model of wellness, which is known for the Wheel of Wellness (Witmer & Sweeney, 1992); and the indivisible self wellness model (Myers & Sweeney, 2005). Granello and Witmer (2012) presented 11 themes that characterize the wellness approach to counseling:

- *Striving for wellness and well-being.* Helping clients strive for their healthiest potential; this includes improving the overall quality of life for individuals who are struggling with physical, emotional, or mental difficulties.

- *Unity of all dimensions of human existence.* Consideration of the range of human experience, including physical, emotional, cognitive, social, sexual, cultural, spiritual, and vocational spheres.

- *Concern for both quality and longevity of life.* "The wellness counseling model values *adding more life to living* as much as extending the life that one lives" (p. 30).

- *Person-oriented rather than disease-oriented.* Focus on the unique needs of the individual and approach each client with genuineness, positive regard, and respect for the whole person.

- *Developmentally all-inclusive.* Recognition that clients of any age or level of health can benefit from positive lifestyle changes and improve their quality of life.

- *Cross-cultural universal qualities.* The belief that "the opportunity to pursue high level wellness is a fundamental right of all human beings" (p. 30).

- *Sensitivity to context.* Consideration of the impact of environmental, economic, social, and political variables on individual health along with interventions that are culturally relevant and realistic.

- *Integrated multidisciplinary approaches and methods.* A holistic approach to wellness includes an openness to a wide range of perspectives and sources of knowledge.

- *Personal responsibility and self-care.* An emphasis on personal control, empowerment, and self-efficacy in the pursuit of healthy living. **Self-care** strategies refer to the ways one nurtures the self and ensures that one's needs are being met. Self-care includes addressing physical needs, such as sufficient sleep, nutrition, and exercise. It also includes psychological needs, such as setting healthy boundaries, having realistic expectations of oneself, and willingness to seek support from others when needed.

- *Proactive rather than reactive.* Advocacy for prevention efforts in families, schools, and communities that promote healthy lifestyle behaviors.

- *Social connectivity.* An emphasis on the importance of social support systems.

Developmental Perspective

All counselors share a belief that the majority of challenges people face are developmental in nature and that an understanding of human growth and development can help counselors conceptualize and work effectively with client issues. Developmental theorists suggest that humans grow and develop in predictable ways by moving through a series of physical, psychosocial, or cognitive stages or phases over the life span. When issues are viewed within a developmental perspective, they are seen as a normal part of transitioning through life, rather than an indication of pathology. Counselors believe that most mental health issues or emotional difficulties are understandable within a developmental context. For example, consider the developmental aspects of the following concerns:

- A newly married couple struggling to communicate effectively

- An 8-year-old acting out in the months following his parents' separation

- A middle-aged man experiencing depression after being laid off from his job

- A new mother experiencing loneliness, isolation, and sadness

- A teenager experimenting with alcohol and other risky behaviors

- A recent retiree struggling with issues of identity and loss

- A grieving person grappling with spiritual beliefs following the unexpected death of a close friend or family member

The commitment to a developmental perspective is evident in the preamble of the American Counseling Association (2014) Code of Ethics, which states that ACA members are "dedicated to the enhancement of human development throughout the life span." This developmental focus has deep historical roots in the counseling profession. Developmental models include theories focused on attachment (e.g., Bowlby, 1969), psychosocial development (e.g., Erikson, 1963), cognitive development (e.g., Piaget, 1955), moral development (e.g., Kohlberg, 1981), ego development (e.g., Loevinger, 1976), evolution of the self (e.g., Kegan, 1982), gender development (e.g., Gilligan, 1982; Neugarten, 1979), developmental needs (e.g., Maslow, 1968), transitions (e.g., Schlossberg, 1984), career development (e.g., Lent, Brown, & Hackett, 1994; Super, 1990), sexual identity development (e.g., Cass, 1979; McCarn & Fassinger, 1996), multicultural identity development (e.g., Helms, 1995; Root, 1998), and spiritual development (e.g., Fowler, 1981). The developmental perspective is consistent with the wellness model, in that developmental issues are less stigmatizing than models that emphasize pathology or abnormality. In addition, the developmental approach allows for the normalization and validation of client experiences, which instills hope and serves to empower clients.

Prevention and Early Intervention

In addition to wellness and developmental approaches, **prevention** is a defining principle of the counseling profession (Albee & Ryan-Finn, 1993; Hershenson & Strein, 1991; Myers, 1992; Spruill & Fong, 1990). When possible, counselors share a preference for prevention and early intervention on mental and emotional problems, rather than remediation. Although counselors have the training and skills to address more severe mental health problems (and many work in settings in which this is necessary), there is a general belief that early intervention and prevention is a more effective way of managing emotional and mental health challenges. Prevention efforts are time-efficient and cost-effective; they allow for the promotion of mental health among the largest amount of people (Gladding & Newsome, 2010).

According to Granello (2000), counselors have a unique combination of education and skill sets conducive to offering preventive care for clients, including cognitive and behavioral change techniques, psychoeducation, social skills training, stress management training, and self-care strategies. Counselors also are trained in group counseling skills, an effective forum for many prevention efforts. Some of the topics that are often the focus of prevention programs include relationship preparation and enrichment, parenting, stress management, general wellness and self-care, career exploration, eating disorders, substance abuse, relationship violence, self-injury, and sexual health.

An emphasis on prevention and early intervention fits nicely with the wellness model and the developmental perspective. The focus is on helping clients seek and maintain a high level of mental and emotional well-being, rather than merely treating what is "wrong" (remediation). With an understanding of human development, counselors can help clients anticipate and prepare for challenges they may face during certain life transitions or circumstances, which connects directly to the foundational principle of empowering clients.

Empowerment

All counselors share a belief that the most effective methods of helping clients to work toward optimal wellness include an emphasis on empowerment. In other words, counselors seek to help clients identify and use their own strengths and resources in order to manage life challenges and developmental transitions. Rather than providing clients with answers or solutions to their problems, counselors see their role as one of supporting clients in their quest for personal growth. Counselors believe that the potential for growth is much greater when clients are empowered to use their own voice, set their own goals, and uncover their own insights. This is consistent with the philosophy of Carl Rogers who developed person-centered counseling and is considered one of the founding fathers of counseling. Part of Rogers's legacy is the counseling value that clients have the potential and the innate ability to solve their own problems when certain conditions are present in the counseling relationship. He introduced the concept of the **core conditions** of empathy, genuineness, and unconditional positive regard as essential to the helping relationship.

The concept of empowerment is consistent with the ethical principle of autonomy. Although clients may seek help, they have the right to make their own choices and come to their own conclusions about what paths to choose for their life. This can be a challenge when clients make choices that are counter to what counselors might wish for them therapeutically (e.g., risky behaviors, such as choosing to continue drinking excessively, or self-defeating behaviors, such as repeated absences that result in lower academic performance). Counselors walk alongside clients for part of their journey, offering a therapeutic relationship within which insight and personal growth can be sought. Ultimately, however, the goal of counseling is for clients to discover that they no longer need counseling.

Multicultural Worldview

The importance of a multicultural perspective in counseling practice has been a consistent topic in counseling literature over the past several decades. The preamble to the ACA (2014) Code of Ethics states that ACA members "enhance the quality of life in society by promoting the development of professional counselors, advancing the counseling profession, and using the profession and practice of counseling to promote respect for human dignity and diversity." The Association for Multicultural Counseling and Development (AMCD) was chartered as a division of the ACA in 1972 (originally the Association of Non-White Concerns in Personnel and Guidance). In response to the growing efforts of the counseling profession to respond more effectively to the needs of a diverse society, multicultural counseling competencies were developed (Sue, Arredondo, & McDavis, 1992). These competencies included relevant standards regarding the awareness, knowledge, and skills that characterize the culturally competent counselor.

For most of the 20th century, the theory and practice of counseling reflected the assumption that clients were somewhat homogenous and that universal methods of conceptualization and treatment would be effective. This assumption characterized the first three forces of psychotherapy: psychodynamic, behaviorism, and existentialism/humanism. Due to demographic and sociocultural trends in the United States and Europe, counseling professionals have been challenged to broaden their focus in order to respond effectively to the rapidly changing needs of clients. This shift in focus has led to the emergence of multiculturalism as the fourth force of counseling (Hays & McLeod, 2009). Multicultural counseling refers to the integration of cultural context into the counseling process and therapeutic relationship. Counselors actively seek to understand and respond effectively to all aspects of a client's cultural context, including race, ethnicity, age, gender, sexual orientation, disability, socioeconomic status, spirituality, and any other aspect of cultural identity that contributes to the client experience.

The principles of wellness, prevention, empowerment, and multicultural development have been discussed separately, but there is considerable overlap among these concepts. Counselors help clients seek optimal well-being by conceptualizing client issues through a multicultural and developmental lens, using educational and preventive interventions and empowering clients to make healthy choices that promote their own wellness. These foundational values characterize the identity of the professional counseling field, regardless of specialty area, work setting, or theoretical orientation. CMH counseling is a specialty within counseling that focuses both on the treatment of mental disorders and normal developmental concerns across the life span.

HISTORY OF CMH COUNSELING

CMH counseling arose out of a range of historical influences into its current role as a vital component of the mental health treatment continuum that exists today. A description of CMH counseling is provided by the American Mental Health Counselors Association (AMHCA), a division of the American Counseling Association. AMCHA (2013) defines clinical mental health counseling as

> a distinct profession with national standards for education, training and clinical practice. Clinical mental health counselors are highly skilled professionals who provide flexible, consumer-oriented therapy. They combine traditional psychotherapy with a practical, problem-solving approach that creates a dynamic and efficient path for change and problem resolution.

This description is rich with meaning, so let us consider it in greater detail.

First, the AMHCA description emphasizes the uniqueness of the counseling specialization known as clinical mental health counseling. This distinctiveness is important in providing a clear identity for CMH counselors and is evidenced by the fact that the education and training CMH counselors receive before entering the field is well established and informed by accrediting bodies, licensure laws, and best-practice research. In other words, although CMH counseling training and practice shares common elements with other helping professions (such as psychology, social work, and marriage and family therapy), there are a unique core set of training approaches for CMH counselors. Additionally, CMH counselors practice from a **developmental perspective** that emphasizes the strengths, adaptability, and resilience of clients; this developmental and strength-based focus is unique to the counseling profession. For those training programs that are accredited by the Council for Accreditation of Counseling and Related Educational Programs (CACREP), there are training standards for CMH counseling preparation that further distinguish mental health counselors from other helping professionals.

Second, the description stresses that CMH counselors are highly skilled and flexible in their delivery of client care. To practice effectively as a CMH counselor requires mastery of a nuanced set of skills that include the ability to assess client concerns, diagnose mental disorders, create treatment plans, advocate for client needs, make appropriate referrals, coordinate medical care, manage client crises, implement interventions, document treatment, navigate billing systems, keep abreast of emerging science and new treatment approaches, and communicate effectively with multiple professionals, all while practicing in an ethical manner to bring about change for clients. Although this may sound like a daunting number of activities and skills to manage, CMH counselors are called on to have command of this range of skills to deliver meaningful client care. Throughout your training program, you will begin developing all of these skills, and, through continuing education, clinical supervision, and ongoing self-reflection on your work, you will continue to grow in your skills throughout your career as a CMH counselor.

Third, the description indicates that CMH counselors deliver both traditional psychotherapeutic services *and* focus on practical problem solving with clients so that change occurs.

In other words, CMH counselors use a range of techniques driven by a set of well-known theories, while at the same time remaining pragmatic in focus, such that talking about change should never be confused with *making* change. Needless to say, the AMHCA description makes it clear that to practice as a CMH counselor is to join a profession that is based on a rich and complex approach to helping.

Historical Influences

Any discussion of the history of CMH counseling must in essence be a discussion of the history of counseling in general. In the early 20th century, there was great interest in vocational guidance fueled in part by a pivotal book, *Choosing a Vocation*, published in 1909 by Frank Parsons, who is widely regarded as the father of vocational guidance. Parsons put forward a theory that came to form the basis of many subsequent career theories that included understanding of the self, understanding the world of work, and matching people to the occupation deemed the best fit for their particular personal traits. Vocational planning gained importance and gave rise to vocational counselors in many states. At about the same time, a similar development was taking place in the field of testing with Alfred Binet's development of assessments geared toward intellectual capabilities. The two world wars (World War I from 1914 to 1918 and World War II from 1939 to 1945) further highlighted the need for efficient use of human resources and advanced the movement toward psychological testing in counseling. During the First World War, the United States Army commissioned intelligence tests to facilitate placement decisions for army personnel. In the Second World War, vocational guidance was an important tool in helping to match soldiers to positions within the military.

The National Defense Education Act of 1958 was a major influence in the development of guidance and counseling programs, particularly in the school setting (Gladding & Newsome, 2010). This legislative act was a response to the Soviet Union's advances in space technology with the launch of Sputnik, which set off what became known as the space race. The United States government pushed for more students to get into the science and engineering fields so that America could compete on the world stage (Sweeney, 2001). This legislation funded the training of school counselors who would encourage students to explore careers in math, science, and engineering in an effort to advance national interests. This resulted in a proliferation of training programs for counselors as well as the introduction of guidance counselors in schools across the nation.

As a result of the early influences of vocational guidance, much early counselor preparation was focused on training school counselors. This would begin to change, however, with the emergence of theorists such as Carl Rogers (1942) whose publication, *Counseling and Psychotherapy*, helped to shape the future of the counseling profession. In addition, Rogers helped to shift the focus of counseling away from the standardized tests that had been popularized by the world wars to a more humanistic view of counseling that valued the counseling relationship and regarded the client as a partner in treatment rather than a passive participant (Gladding & Newsome, 2010).

Traditionally, much clinical mental health care was provided in institutions for the mentally ill, where both the services offered and the facilities were grossly inadequate

(Rochefort, 1984). These facilities were regarded as insane asylums, and individuals who were institutionalized had little hope of recovery. In 1946, Congress passed the National Mental Health Act of 1946 (PL 79–487) that established the National Institute of Mental Health (NIMH). The NIMH sought to develop and expand mental health care, and it established community mental health clinics around the United States. There was also a move toward more humane care for the mentally ill, and the Community Mental Health Centers Act of 1963 was significant in altering the delivery of mental health services. This act provided funding for community mental health centers and led to mass deinstitutionalization of individuals with mental disorders. As many of these individuals reentered their respective communities, there was a surge in demand for mental health counselors to staff the community mental health centers in order to serve this population. This resulted in the growth of outpatient delivery of mental health services. A 1965 amendment to the Community Mental Health Centers Act provided grants to fund salaries for professional staff to work at the community centers. Further, the passage of Medicaid and Medicare in 1965 led to an expansion of services to individuals who previously may not have had access to mental health services.

In 1952, the American Personnel and Guidance Association (APGA) was formed. At that time, counselors worked chiefly in educational settings and much of their work was career guidance. The Community Mental Health Centers Act of 1965 had led to a significant increase in the number of counselors working in community counseling centers. Because the APGA had a diverse membership and was charged with many tasks, mental health counselors felt the need to form an organization that catered specifically to the unique needs of mental health counselors. To this end, the American Mental Health Counselors Association was formed in 1976 (Sweeney, 2001). AMHCA became a division of the APGA in 1978 and remains one of the largest divisions of the ACA. With the increasing numbers of community counselors working in community health settings and the expansion of counseling beyond educational settings, the APGA sought to redefine its role and was renamed the American Association for Counseling and Development (AACD) in 1983 to better reflect the expanded nature of its membership. This organization eventually became the American Counseling Association (ACA) in 1992.

The impact of veteran mental health concerns on the growth of clinical mental health dates back to World Wars I and II. This trend continued over the years, notably during the Vietnam War in the 1960s through 1975 when American troops withdrew from Vietnam. During this period, a large number of Vietnam War veterans returned from the war with mental health problems that included post-traumatic stress disorder and addictions. The federal government increased its efforts to address these growing problems. For example, the Narcotic Addict Treatment Act of 1974 established the National Institute on Drug Abuse (NIDA) as an independent institute to determine appropriate standards for drug abuse treatment.

The Medicare and Medicaid Act provided insurance coverage for mental health services, thereby pressuring other insurance providers to do the same. Over time, many states came to require that private medical insurance providers have a minimum provision for mental health services. Even then, individuals on Medicare were required to pay half the cost for outpatient services, though they only paid 20% of the costs for all other services and there was an annual spending limit of $500 that applied to mental health care only. This was a significant hindrance to many middle-class people who could not afford the copay. Additionally, mental health care continued to be inaccessible for more than half the population who did not have private health insurance and did not qualify for either Medicare or Medicaid (Frank & Glied, 2006). The Mental Health Parity Act of 1996, which required parity between medical coverage and mental health coverage, as well as the Mental Health Parity and Addiction Act of 2008, which disallowed higher deductibles for mental health services, helped to address some of these challenges. The 1990s also saw a concerted effort by insurance providers to contain costs by setting limits to the amount of benefits that would be paid out to service providers, resulting in managed care behavioral health. Unfortunately, managed care adversely affected the provision of services by increasing client loads, dictating treatment options, and limiting the number of sessions and services for which a counselor could obtain reimbursement (Granello & Young, 2012). This continues to pose significant challenges for counselors, particularly those in community settings and private practice.

As the number of counselors and counselor training programs increased, there was a need to regulate the practice and training of the profession. Licensure requirements soon followed, with the state of Virginia being the first to introduce licensing in 1976, followed thereafter by Arkansas and Alabama. In 2009, California became the final U.S. state to adopt licensure for professional counseling.

In the 1980s, the number of counselor training programs increased. There were a large number of school counselors working primarily in educational settings and an equally large number of community counselors (Lewis & Lewis, 1977) who worked in a variety of settings such as community mental health clinics, hospitals, and substance abuse treatment centers. It became necessary to institute standards for the specialty areas of counselor training, and the Council for Accreditation of Counseling and Related Educational Programs (CACREP) was formed in 1981 as an offshoot of the APGA (now ACA) to oversee training standards within counselor preparation programs (Gladding & Newsome, 2010). CACREP now operates independent of the ACA to promote the counseling profession, establish and maintain accreditation standards, and accredit training programs. In 1982, the National Board for Certified Counselors (NBCC) was formed, and CACREP and the NBCC worked together to unify counselor training. Eight core areas were defined for counselor training regardless of specialty area; these now form the core curriculum requirements for CACREP accreditation and are also the eight areas tested on the National Counselor Exam (NCE).

Given the various historical influences that have contributed to the development of CMH counseling, it is a subspecialty with a rich collection of theoretical orientations, work settings, and focus areas. The current approach to training CMH counselors evolved from the merger by CACREP in 2009 of two program areas that historically viewed themselves as unique (clinical mental health counseling and community counseling). Although this merger highlighted tensions between those who identified more strongly with either community counseling or mental health counseling, there is much more that unites the two areas than divides them. Literature from both areas highlights the general counseling foundations of wellness, development, prevention, empowerment, and multicultural considerations. The philosophy that underlies CMH counseling is provided in the most recent definition of CMH counseling from the American Mental Health Counseling Association website (www.amhca.com):

> Clinical mental health counseling is the provision of professional counseling services involving the application of principles of psychotherapy, human development, learning theory, group dynamics, and the etiology of mental illness and dysfunctional behavior to individuals, couples, families and groups, for the purpose of promoting optimal mental health, dealing with normal problems of living and treating psychopathology. The practice of clinical mental health counseling includes, but is not limited to, diagnosis and treatment of mental and emotional disorders, psycho-educational techniques aimed at the prevention of mental and emotional disorders, consultations to individuals, couples, families, groups, organizations and communities, and clinical research into more effective psychotherapeutic treatment modalities. Clinical Mental Health Counselors have always understood that their professional work encompasses a broad range of clinical practice, including dealing with normal problems of living and promoting optimal mental health in addition to the prevention, intervention and treatment of mental and emotional disorders. This work of Clinical Mental Health Counselors serves the needs of socially and culturally diverse clients (e.g., age, gender, race/ethnicity, socioeconomic status, sexual orientation) across the lifespan (i.e., children, adolescents and adults including older adults and geriatric populations).

PROFESSIONAL PRACTICE IN CMH COUNSELING

Professional Identity

You may hear your professors and mentors emphasize the importance of professional identity and wonder why it is such an important concept. The emphasis on professional identity is due, in part, to the number of other professions in the mental health field and the need for counselors to distinguish themselves from other mental health practitioners. The concept of professional identity has a much richer meaning, however, for most counselors. Becoming a counselor is more than simply learning the skills associated with *doing* counseling. It is a personal journey that requires considerable reflection and self-examination. Over the course of your training, you will grapple with questions about your own identity, your personal strengths and challenges, the way you receive and use feedback, your blind spots (yes, we all have them), your own theoretical orientation, and personal issues that may stand in the way of effectively working with clients. Unlike the majority of other skills-based professions, a counselor's personal development is very closely tied to her or his professional development. As a result, counselors tend to have a great deal of pride and ownership in the shared values and philosophical foundations that help to define *who we are* as counseling professionals.

This is not to say that all counselors have identical theoretical orientations and approaches to working with clients. On the contrary, there are a myriad of conceptual frameworks, strategies, and tools. Part of your professional development will include figuring out what style works for you, your work setting, your clientele, and the specific issues your clientele bring to counseling. Beyond the primary professional identity of *professional counselor*, counselors may identify themselves based on their work setting or population of clientele, such as clinical mental health counselors, school counselors, college counselors, or family counselors. They may further identify themselves according to areas of expertise, such as substance abuse, trauma, eating disorders, parenting issues, or spiritual concerns. Additionally, counselors often include their theoretical approaches in a description of professional identity.

There are a number of ways for CMH counselors to develop and strengthen their professional identity.

- Attending a CACREP-accredited program in clinical mental health counseling ensures the receipt of training consistent with standards of curriculum, faculty, and educational experiences, all of which serve to foster a strong connection with the history, philosophy, and foundations of the profession. Furthermore, faculty members who share a strong sense of professional identity are more likely to model this for counseling trainees.

- Professional organizations offer many opportunities for CMH counselors to be involved through membership or leadership positions. Each organization has committees, interest groups, and task forces focused on specific areas of clinical practice, advocacy, and professional development. Involvement with the counseling profession is an important step in the development of professional identity.

- *Professional conferences* are a meaningful way to network with other professionals, obtain continuing education credits (required for certification and licensure), and learn from other practitioners. Many counselors find conferences to be an energizing boost to their professional identity, by reminding them that they are part of something bigger, a profession filled with individuals who are passionate about helping people work toward change, growth, and wellness.

- Membership in most professional organizations comes with the benefit of receiving the *monthly or quarterly journal* published by the organization. This is a valuable way for CMH counselors to stay abreast of current scholarly research in the field. Journal articles may include empirical research findings, theoretical discussions, case studies, and application pieces, all of which may help to inform clinical practice, teaching strategies, and dialogue about current issues in the field.

- Many CMH counselors nurture their professional identity through *communication and dialogue* with other counselors via listservs, newsletters, and local or regional meetings. This may involve consultation with respected colleagues about clinical or ethical issues, the exchange of helpful tools and resources, and the sharing of information about current topics in the field.

- The counseling profession encourages an attitude of lifelong learning, which means that one does not stop learning once a degree is earned, licensure obtained, or a person has practiced for a number of years. This philosophy is built into the certification and licensure requirements, which mandate specific numbers of *continuing education units* (CEUs) in order to be renewed. The master's degree is designed to provide you with a solid foundation with which to *begin* your career, however it would be impossible for you to learn everything you need to know by the end of your training period. CEUs are a means to participate in lifelong learning at professional conferences, at local workshops or trainings, and even through online sources.

- Involvement in professional service through *leadership positions or advocacy efforts* for clients, communities, and the counseling profession is a powerful way of enhancing professional identity. Advocacy efforts are also a way of networking with other professionals around issues that are particularly meaningful for you.

Qualifications

A graduate education and clinical training prepare CMH counselors to provide a full range of services for individuals, couples, families, adolescents, and children. Typically, CMH counseling programs require 60 semester hours to meet the requirements of state licensing boards and accreditation standards. Training to become a CMH counselor includes the same core areas of training required for other counselor specializations. Specifically, CACREP requires that all accredited programs train counselors in eight core areas: (1) professional orientation and ethical practice, (2) social and cultural diversity, (3) human growth and development, (4) career development, (5) helping relationships, (6) group work, (7) assessment, and (8) research and program evaluation.

In addition to these core areas, AMHCA (2013) requires specialized training for CMH counselors in diagnosis and psychopathology. There is an expectation that knowledge of and skill in clinical assessment will include the ability to select, use, and interpret psychological tests, including personality tests. Finally, an aspect of training as a CMH counselor is field-based practicum and internship training while receiving clinical supervision.

Beyond completion of a graduate degree in counseling, those individuals interested in attaining state licensure also are required to complete a set number of hours of supervised clinical practice while working as a counselor and pass a standardized exam, most often the National Certified Counselor (NCC) exam, although this varies by state. Currently, there are more than 55,000 national certified counselors (NCCs), making it the most widely held credential by professional counselors. Some CMH counselors also choose to obtain the specialty certification of certified clinical mental health counselor (CCMHC), which requires passing an additional exam focused closely on CMH counseling practice as well as 3,000 hours of clinical practice (NBCC, 2013).

Models of Change

Many models of CMH counseling focus on the individual as the unit of change, meaning that the problems that bring a client into counseling exist within that individual and are relieved within that individual. In fact, many practitioners and theorists share this focus. Such models prepare the practitioner to consider the client in distress as the point at which the therapeutic energies must be rallied. For example, Hershenson and Power (1987) present a model that consists of four broad phases of treating the individual in distress: (1) appraisal, (2) planning, (3) intervention, and (4) evaluation.

Appraisal. According to Hershenson and Power (1987), the counselor, regardless of the complaint, must initiate the therapeutic relationship with a process of systematic appraisal of the exact nature of the client's concerns. This can occur through the use of formal assessments, informal questionnaires, and therapeutic interviews. Furthermore, appraisal should entail discernment of the client's individual strengths, skills, and environmental resources. Client strengths are individual capacities that a client possesses (e.g., physical fitness, ability to work hard, intelligence). Skills are abilities that one has accumulated over a lifetime (e.g., effective communicator, excellent interpersonal intelligence, or resourcefulness). Environmental resources are connections one has within the domains of life and work (or school for a child or adolescent), for example, a strong family network, a stable job, or a supportive religious community.

Planning. Following appraisal, the planning phase involves reaching agreement between counselor and client as to the approaches to treatment that will be employed. In most instances, there are a range of alternatives that could be considered to effect change. For example, a client with depressive symptoms could be treated by medication, inpatient hospitalization, electroconvulsive therapy, a support group for people with depression, individual counseling, group counseling, family counseling, inpatient hospitalization, and partial hospitalization, among other options. It is the role of the counselor to guide the client in considering the multiple options and arrive at a plan for treatment that is mutually acceptable. Until this occurs, no progress can be made.

Intervention. Intervention begins once the problem has been defined in a manner in which it can be addressed. This might involve specific behaviors to be targeted for change, environmental factors that need to be attended to, beliefs and feelings thought to be the source of unhappiness, or a combination of all of these. In any case, the intervention emerges as a process of reaching agreements about where and how the focus of treatment should occur, implementing the intervention, and some evaluation of effectiveness.

Evaluation. Evaluation may occur along with intervention or after it, but in either case the focus is to determine the effectiveness of treatment and, if necessary, to modify the existing treatment protocol or substitute another treatment if change is not occurring, is occurring in an undesirable direction, or is occurring too slowly. This evaluation is discussed in more detail in Chapter 13. Demonstration that counseling interventions are, in fact, bringing about change is an important focus in most settings. For example, federal payers such as Medicaid require the use of intervention and specific documentation aimed at providing evidence that therapeutic progress is being made. Similarly, many insurance companies emphasize the provision of evidence of client improvement. Beyond these external pressures, a counselor's professional efficacy should drive him or her to make every effort to ensure that clients are benefiting in tangible ways from counseling services. Methods such as regularly obtaining completed clinical assessments (e.g., the Beck Depression Inventory) or seeking reports from individuals who live with or interact with a client, use and documentation of scaling questions ("On a scale of 1–10, with 10 being the most severe, how much anxiety are you experiencing today?"), and consultation with other practitioners are among the many possible means that can be used to evaluate clinical change.

ROLES AND FUNCTIONS OF CMH COUNSELORS

CMH counselors work in a wide variety of settings. During the 1960s and into the 1970s, CMH counselors (at the time referred to as community counselors or community agency counselors) were employed largely in community mental health centers as the demand for their services grew due to federal investment of funds into the provision of mental health services within the community and the release of large numbers of individuals from long-term inpatient psychiatric hospitals. Over time, however, as both societal needs and funding patterns changed, CMH counselors began to expand the range of their work settings.

Today CMH counselors are found in settings that include private practice, community agencies, managed behavioral health care organizations, integrated delivery systems, hospitals, employee assistance programs, and substance abuse treatment centers. Although less common, CMH counselors also may work in colleges or universities, military settings, prisons and correctional agencies, settings for geriatric individuals, and domestic violence and child abuse shelters (Hershenson and Powers, 1987). CMH counselors may work with adults, children, adolescents, or families with a multitude of issues, including school problems, trauma, career counseling, mental health disorders, addiction, and disability. Often, CMH counselors work in an office setting in which clients are scheduled throughout the day, but others may provide services within the community, working as in-home counselors, in schools, or in other community-based settings.

Within these diverse settings, the continuum of care provided by mental health counselors is discussed more fully in Chapter 4. Depending on the setting and job description, the roles or "hats" a CMH counselor wears may vary. Within each of these roles, the counselor may serve multiple functions. It may help to think of the role as the position being filled, and the function as the tasks related to that position. Because there is a great deal of overlap of functions across roles, we first describe the common functions that CMH counselors serve, followed by a description of some common counseling roles.

CMH Counselor Functions

The CMH counselor must provide specific functions regardless of the setting in which he or she works. These tasks can be conceptualized as foundational skills that all CMH counselors must execute to fulfill their responsibilities to their clients and other constituencies.

Relationship Building. First and foremost, a counselor builds relationships. The therapeutic relationship provides the space in which all other counseling functions occur, and a strong relationship has been shown to be more predictive of client change than any other counselor skills or theoretical approach (Young, 2009).

Assessment. Regardless of setting or clientele, all counselors engage in some type of formal or informal assessment of clients, which informs the goal-setting and treatment planning processes. **Assessment** involves gathering information about the client, including presenting concerns, strengths, challenges, and contextual factors that may be relevant to the counseling process. Informal assessment consists of interviews, observations, and consultation with other service providers. Formal assessment refers to standardized instruments with specific administration and scoring instructions. Thorough and accurate assessment is essential for effective and ethical counseling practice.

Diagnosis. **Diagnosis** is a process by which mental health professionals use a standard categorical system for identifying and classifying mental disorders. The *Diagnostic and Statistical Manual for Mental Disorders* is published by the American Psychiatric Association (the most recent edition is the *DSM-5*, published in 2013) and is the most common tool used by mental health professionals for diagnostic purposes. The *DSM-5* provides information about the diagnostic criteria for each disorder, development and etiology, and possible treatment strategies. Although diagnosis is a process that is more consistent with the medical model than the wellness model, a working knowledge of the *DSM-5* allows CMH counselors to compete for and work effectively in managed care settings where diagnosis is a requirement. Even in these settings, counselors can approach the diagnostic process in a collaborative manner, empowering clients to be an active part of their treatment decisions.

Goal Setting. Goal setting ensures that client and counselor are on the same page and working toward the same outcome. The acronym SMART often is used to inform goal setting: goals should be specific, measurable, attainable, realistic, and timely (i.e., attention given to appropriate short-term and long-term goals). Additionally, goals should be collaborative by involving the client in the goal-setting process and ensuring that goals are "owned" by the client rather than imposed by the counselor. The goal-setting process promotes clarity, accountability, and a way to determine if progress is being made. Facilitation of effective goal setting is also a process through which clients can learn to set more effective goals for themselves outside of the counseling relationship.

Treatment Planning. Once goals are set, the counselor determines the best course of action to help the client meet those goals. This process should include consideration of the assessment information that was gathered, such as client strengths, resources, contextual factors, personality factors, and the client's ideas about what would be helpful. Depending on the work setting, there may be a required format for treatment plans.

Consultation. **Consultation** involves a triadic relationship in which a "professional (the consultant), who has specialized expertise, meets with one or more other professionals to improve the professionals' work with current or potential clients" (Neukrug, 2012, p. 258). Consultation can be formal or informal, ongoing, or a one-time event. In some settings, consultation is a built-in part of the counseling role. For instance, in a medical setting, counselors are part of a treatment team that usually consists of psychiatrists, nurses, case managers, and any other service providers related to the client's treatment. In outpatient settings, counselors often need to consult with family members, teachers, medical doctors, or probation officers to offer professional guidance, to exchange treatment-related information, to coordinate client care, and to ensure that the client's treatment needs are being met. It is imperative, however, that counselors remember the ethical standard of confidentiality and ensure that no contact is made without the client's written consent.

Psychoeducation. One of the tools CMH counselors have for helping clients work toward change is psychoeducation. **Psychoeducation** involves teaching clients about concepts or topics that would help them better navigate the challenges they are facing. Counselors may provide psychoeducation related to a client's recent diagnosis (e.g., What is depression? What are the symptoms? How might it affect my family? What can I expect while adjusting to a new medication?). This empowers clients to be partners in their own health care process (Granello & Young, 2012).

Crisis Intervention. Some CMH counselors work in settings that are specifically focused on **crisis intervention**, such as hospitals, rape crisis centers, domestic violence shelters, or suicide hotlines. All counselors, however, must be prepared to respond to client crises that may arise in the course of general counseling services. Clients in crisis include those who are responding to a recent traumatic event, such as the death of a loved one, a car accident, the diagnosis of a serious illness, any kind of loss, violent experiences, natural disasters, or major life transitions. What represents crisis for one client may not have the same effect on another. Regardless, counselors must be prepared to provide support, guidance, education, and counseling to help clients manage the immediate and short-term effects of the crisis situation.

Prevention. As noted previously, focus on prevention is a foundational principle of counseling. Some work settings are specifically geared toward prevention efforts. Some community agencies, nonprofit agencies, and college counseling centers employ outreach specialists tasked with developing workshops, groups, and other prevention programs. These programs may be focused on a broad range of issues such as substance abuse, dating violence, eating disorders, relationship health, sexual health, parenting training, and general self-care.

Advocacy. For CMH counselors, "**advocacy** means becoming agents of social change, intervening not just to help individual clients, but to work to change the world in which our clients live" (Granello & Young, 2012, pp. 66–67). Advocacy efforts may be at the individual level, such as helping a client gain access to needed services; on a community level, such as serving on professional boards or councils to have an influence on community programs; or on a public policy level, such as lobbying legislators on behalf of mental health–related laws.

Research and Evaluation. The counseling field is based on the **scientist-practitioner model**, which emphasizes the bidirectional influence of research and practice. Decisions about effective treatment should be based on sound research, and counseling practice can inform the direction of related research. Effective practitioners are responsible consumers of research, meaning that they are committed to integrating existing research into their practice.

Documentation and Paperwork. Paperwork is an essential, although perhaps unpleasant, part of every counselor's job. This may include case notes, treatment plans, billing, and scheduling. Accurate documentation is important for liability purposes. Counselors keep case notes of their interactions with clients in order to document that ethical procedures were followed. This is especially important in situations involving assessment of potential harm to self or others. Paperwork and documentation are discussed fully in Chapter 9.

CMH Counselor Roles

Individual Counselor. One-on-one direct service of counseling is the central role of most counselors. Most CMH counselor positions include a large amount of individual counseling, in which counselors use a broad array of theoretical approaches and therapeutic techniques to address a variety of client concerns, including depression, anxiety, substance abuse, eating disorders, ADHD, grief or loss, self-esteem, stress management, spirituality, identity, and many more.

Group Counselor. Group work is another method of delivering counseling services. Groups take on many forms, including psychoeducation, prevention, support, or therapy, and may take place in a variety of settings (e.g., inpatient, outpatient, residential, wellness centers). Group work allows for support and vicarious learning from other group members who share common concerns.

Couples/Family Counselor. Some CMH counselors seek additional coursework and training to specialize in working with couples and family systems. Presenting concerns may include issues related to parenting, child behaviors, communication, conflict, intimacy, financial struggles, infidelity, family violence, grief or loss, or developmental transitions.

Administrator. Some CMH counselors find themselves in administrative leadership positions in their work setting. The responsibilities of an administrator require an additional skill set and can be a challenging transition for some counselors. These tasks may include recruiting, managing and supervising staff, organizing office responsibilities (e.g., scheduling, billing, documentation), strategic planning, budgeting, facilities management, and working with other administrators or community stakeholders.

Clinical Supervisor. **Clinical supervision** refers to ongoing guidance provided for a developing counselor (supervisee) by a more experienced counselor, with the multiple purposes of fostering the supervisee's professional development, monitoring the supervisee's effectiveness, and ensuring client welfare (Bernard & Goodyear, 2009). This is a very important role in the counseling profession because every counselor trainee is required to have clinical supervision in order to earn a degree and meet licensure requirements. Practicum and internship supervisors provide clinical supervision during graduate training. After graduation, every state requires counselors to accrue a certain number of supervised hours in order to obtain licensure. Some work settings provide varying levels of supervision, including individual and group supervision. Clinical supervision is described in more detail in Chapter 11.

Reflective Practitioner. The process of becoming a counselor is a personal journey as well as a professional one, and all effective counselors consider themselves to be lifelong learners. Being a **reflective practitioner** requires an ongoing commitment to one's own personal growth and wellness in order to be an effective helper. It also means maintaining an awareness of what additional training or development is necessary to meet the changing needs of your clients.

Populations Served

As CMH counselors are carrying out a variety of functions and roles in diverse settings, they also are serving highly diverse populations of people. Although it is not possible to highlight the full range of this diversity, common populations are delineated here.

Seriously Mentally Ill

At any given time, approximately 6% of the U.S. population, or 1 in 17 individuals has a serious mental illness (SMI). SMIs are those disorders that tend to have a profound impact on an individual's ability to function and have the potential to lead to long-term impairment. Mental illness is more far reaching than it might initially appear, however. According to the National Alliance on Mental Illness (NAMI, 2013),

- Approximately 61.5 million Americans have a mental illness and approximately 13.6 million live with an SMI such as schizophrenia, major depression, or bipolar disorder

- Approximately 20% of youth ages 13 to 18 experience a mental illness in a given year

- Approximately 6.7% of American adults (about 14.8 million people) live with major depression

- Approximately 18.1% of American adults (about 42 million people) live with anxiety disorders

- About 9.2 million adults have co-occurring mental health and addiction disorders

- About 26% of homeless adults staying in shelters live with serious mental illness and an estimated 46% live with serious mental illness and/or substance use disorders

- Approximately 20% of state prisoners and 21% of those housed in local jails have a recent history of mental health issues

- About 70% of youth in juvenile justice systems have at least one mental health condition and at least 20% live with a severe mental illness

From these rather sobering statistics, it is clear, then, that the impact of serious mental illness is far-reaching, and CMH counselors often serve individuals with these conditions. An additional and complicating factor for many individuals who suffer from an SMI is addiction.

Addictions

There are a range of **addictive disorders** that account for a large portion of the services provided by CMH counselors. According to the 2011 National Survey on Drug Use and Health, an estimated 20.6 million persons aged 12 or older were classified with a substance use disorder within the prior year, which represents 8% of the population. As you think about these numbers, it is important to remember that this survey considered *only* substance addictions and did not take into account **behavioral addictions** or **process addictions**, such as addictions to gambling, which first appeared in the *DSM-5*. Although not included in the *DSM-5*, behavioral addictions clients often present include shopping, the Internet, sex, and food. Clearly, addictive behaviors fuel the need for CMH counselors.

The scope of addictive issues requires complex treatment networks that often employ CMH counselors. Within the United States, there are over 14,500 specialized drug treatment facilities that provide counseling, behavioral therapy, medication, case management, and other types of services to individuals with substance use disorders. Similar facilities exist for the treatment of behavioral or process addictions.

In addition to the use of specialized treatment facilities, addictive disorders are treated in physicians' offices and mental health clinics by a variety of providers (e.g., counselors, physicians, psychiatrists, psychologists, nurses, and social workers). Treatment is delivered in outpatient, inpatient, and residential settings (National Institute on Drug Abuse, 2012). In 2011, 3.8 million individuals aged 12 or older received treatment for alcohol or illicit drug use. Of these, 2.1 million received support within a self-help group, and 1.5 million received treatment at a rehabilitation facility as an outpatient. Approximately 1 million individuals received outpatient treatment at a mental health center, and another 1 million individuals received inpatient treatment at a rehabilitation facility. Another 871,000 were treated at a hospital as an inpatient, 700,000 at a doctor's office, 574,000 at an emergency room, and 435,000 at a prison or jail. It is clear, then, that there are large numbers of people seeking services for addictive disorders and a larger number of people who need such treatment but have not yet received services (SAMHSA, 2012).

Developmental Problems

Beyond individuals who experience SMIs and addiction, there are numerous individuals who experience stress, adjustment, and relational issues for which CMH counselors provide services. The range of normal developmental issues that clients experience includes the following:

- Adjustment to school or work
- Relationship struggles with friends, romantic partners, family members, or coworkers
- Loss
- Life transitions
- Career decision making
- Coping with life stressors

These are all examples of the range of normal challenges faced by people who may be seen by CMH counselors.

Based on the prevalence of mental health issues, it should be evident that there is and will continue to be a very real need for CMH counselors to work in a variety of settings with clients diverse in age, gender, ethnicity, socioeconomic status, religious/spiritual beliefs, and disability status to address the ubiquitous life struggles. To paraphrase the words of Helen Keller, the world is both full of suffering and the overcoming of it. Supporting clients in the overcoming of their suffering is at the heart of the work of CMH counselors.

CASE STUDY

Samantha is a 25-year-old student working on a master's degree in clinical mental health counseling. She is interning at a public mental health agency that provides counseling services to children, adolescents, and adults with a wide array of counseling and mental health concerns. Her clinical supervisor is a licensed counselor with extensive clinical experience and is a genuinely supportive person. As is common in such agencies, clients are assigned to Samantha for an intake and subsequent clinical services. The agency provides treatment for virtually any mental health concern presented by a client.

Among the very first clients assigned to Samantha was Claude, a 45-year-old married male who is an alcoholic and acknowledges that he has a drinking problem. Claude's wife threatened divorce when she found him intoxicated and behaving in a verbally aggressive manner with their 14-year-old daughter. As a novice counselor, Samantha is intimidated by the case, seriously doubting her capacity to assist Claude with his complex and utterly foreign (to Samantha) psychological problems.

(Continued)

(Continued)

Discussion Questions

1. What additional information would you want to gather in order to assess the ways in which Claude's **cultural and environmental contexts** affect his current experience?

2. How might Samantha use clinical supervision to deliver high-quality care to Claude?

3. How would you conceptualize Claude's situation from a **developmental perspective**, and how would this perspective differ from the medical model?

4. What might be some potential counseling goals that are consistent with a focus on overall **wellness**, and how would you work collaboratively with Claude to establish and prioritize these goals?

5. What treatment processes can Samantha expect her client to move through during the course of counseling? Which of the processes might be implemented by Samantha? Which by other mental health practitioners?

6. What ideas do you have regarding ways of **empowering** Claude to recognize and use his strengths and resources to address his problem with alcohol?

REFERENCES

Albee, G. W., & Ryan-Finn, K. D. (1993). An overview of primary prevention. *Journal of Counseling and Development, 72,* 115–123.

American Counseling Association. (2013). *Types of counseling specialties.* Retrieved from http://www .counseling.org/learn-about-counseling/what-is-counseling/counseling-specialties.

American Counseling Association. (2014). *ACA Code of Ethics.* Alexandria, VA: Author.

American Mental Health Counselors Association. (2013). *Facts about mental health counselors.* Retrieved from http://www.amhca.org/about/facts.aspx.

Bernard, J. M., & Goodyear, R. K. (2009). *Fundamentals of clinical supervision* (4th ed.). Upper Saddle River, NJ: Pearson.

Bowlby, J. (1969). *Attachment.* New York: Basic Books.

Bureau of Labor Statistics. (2013). Occupational outlook handbook. *Mental health counseling and marriage and family therapists pay.* Retrieved from http://www.bls.gov/ooh/community-and-social-service/mental-health-counselors-and-marriage-and-family-therapists.htm#tab-5.

Bureau of Labor Statistics. (2016). *Occupational employment statistics.* Retrieved from http://www.bls .gov/oes/current/oes211014.htm#nat.

Cass, V. C. (1979). Homosexual identity formation: A theoretical model. *Journal of Homosexuality, 4,* 219–235.

Erikson, E. (1963). *Childhood and society* (2nd ed.). New York: Norton.

Fowler, J. W. (1981). *Stages of faith.* New York: Harper/Collins.

Frank, R., & Glied, S. (2006). Changes in mental health financing since 1971: Implications for policy-makers and patients. *Health Affairs, 25,* 601–613.

Gilligan, C. (1982). *In a different voice*. Cambridge, MA: Harvard University Press.

Gladding, S. T., & Newsome, D. W. (2010). *Clinical mental health counseling*. Upper Saddle River, NJ: Pearson.

Granello, D. H., & Young, M. E. (2012). *Counseling today: Foundations of professional identity*. Upper Saddle River, NJ: Pearson.

Granello, P. F. (2000). Integrating wellness work into mental health private practice. *Journal of Psychotherapy in Independent Practice, 1*(1), 3–16.

Granello, P. F., & Witmer, J. M. (2012). Theoretical models for wellness counseling. In P. F. Granello (Ed.), *Wellness counseling* (pp. 29–36). Upper Saddle River, NJ: Pearson.

Greenwood, E. (1962). Attributes of a profession. In S. Nosow & W. H. Form (Eds.), *Man, work and society* (pp. 206–218). New York: Basic Books.

Gross, E. (1958). *Work and society*. New York: Crowell.

Hays, D. G., & McLeod, A. L (2009). The culturally competent counselor. In D. G. Hays & B. T. Erford (Eds.), *Developing multicultural competence: A systems approach* (pp. 1–31). Boston: Pearson.

Helms, J. E. (1995). An update of Helms' white and people of color racial identity. In J. G. Ponterotto, J. M. Casas, & C. M. Alexander (Eds.), *Handbook of multicultural counseling* (pp. 181–198). Thousand Oaks, CA: Sage.

Hershenson, D. B., & Power, P. W. (1987). *Mental health counseling: Theory and practice*. New York: Pergamon Press.

Hershenson, D. B., & Strein, W. (1991). Toward a mentally healthy curriculum for mental health counselor education. *Journal of Mental Health Counseling, 13*, 247–252.

Hettler, B. (1984). Wellness: Encouraging a lifetime pursuit of excellence. *Health Values, 8*(4), 13–17.

Kegan, R. (1982). *The evolving self*. Cambridge, MA: Harvard University Press.

Kohlberg, L. (1981). *The philosophy of moral development*. San Francisco: Harper & Row.

Lent, R. W., Brown, S. D., & Hackett, G. (1994). Toward a unifying social cognitive theory of career and academic interest, choice, and performance. *Journal of Vocational Behavior, 45*, 79–122.

Lewis, J. A., & Lewis, M. D. (1977). *Community counseling: A human services approach*. New York: Wiley.

Loevinger, J. (1976). *Ego development: Conceptions and theories*. San Francisco: Jossey-Bass.

Maslow, A. (1968). *Toward a psychology of being* (2nd ed.). New York: D. van Nostrand.

McCarn, S. R., & Fassinger, R. E. (1996). Re-visioning sexual minority identity formation: A new model of lesbian identity and its implications for counseling and research. *The Counseling Psychologist, 24*, 508–534.

Myers, J. E. (1992). Wellness, prevention, development: The cornerstone of the profession. *Journal of Counseling and Development, 71*, 136–139.

Myers, J. E., & Sweeney, T. J. (2005). The indivisible self: An evidence-based model of wellness. In J. E. Myers & T. J. Sweeney (Eds.), *Counseling for wellness: Theory, research, and practice* (pp. 29–37). Alexandria, VA: American Counseling Association.

Myers, J. E., Sweeney, T. J., & Witmer, J. M. (2000). The wheel of wellness for counseling: A holistic model for treatment planning. *Journal of Counseling and Development, 78*, 251–266.

National Alliance on Mental Illness. (2013). *Mental illness facts and numbers*. Retrieved from http://www.nami.org/factsheets/mentalillness_factsheet.pdf.

National Board for Certified Counselors. (2013). *Understanding NBCC's national certifications*. Retrieved from http://www.nbcc.org/ourcertifications.

National Institute on Drug Abuse. (2012). *Drug addiction treatment in the United States*. Retrieved from http://www.drugabuse.gov/publications/principles-drug-addiction-treatment-research-based-guide-third-edition/drug-addiction-treatment-in-united-states.

Neugarten, B. (1979). Time, age, and the life cycle. *American Journal of Psychiatry, 136*, 887–894.

Neukrug, E. S. (2012). *The world of the counselor: An introduction to the counseling profession* (4th ed.). Belmont, CA: Brooks-Cole.

Parsons, F. (1909). *Choosing a vocation*. Boston: Houghton-Mifflin.

Piaget, J. (1955). *The language and thought of the child*. New York: New American Library.

Remley, T. P., & Herlihy, B. (2010). *Ethical, legal, and professional issues in counseling*. Upper Saddle River, NJ: Prentice Hall.

Rochefort, D. A. (1984). Origins of the "third psychiatric revolution": The Community Mental Health Centers Act of 1963. *Journal of Health Politics, Policy and Law, 9*(1), 1–30.

Rogers, C. (1942). *Counseling and psychotherapy: Newer concepts in practice*. Cambridge, MA: Riverside Press.

Root, M. P. P. (1998). Experiences and processes affecting racial identity development: Preliminary results from the biracial sibling project. *Cultural Diversity and Mental Health, 4*, 237–247.

Schlossberg, N. (1984). *Counseling adults in transition*. New York: Pantheon.

Spruill, D. A., & Fong, M. L. (1990). Defining the domain of mental health counseling: From identity confusion to consensus. *Journal of Mental Health Counseling, 12*, 12–23.

Substance Abuse and Mental Health Services Administration. (2012). *Results from the 2011 national survey on drug use and health: Summary of national findings*. Retrieved from http://www.samhsa .gov/data/NSDUH/2k11Results/NSDUHresults2011.htm#2.2.

Sue, E. W., Arredondo, P., & McDavis, R. J. (1992). Multicultural counseling competencies and standards: A call to the profession. *Journal of Multicultural Counseling and Development, 20*, 64–89.

Super, D. E. (1990). A life-span, life-space approach to career development. In D. Brown, L. Brooks, & Associates (Eds.), *Career choice and development: Applying contemporary theories to practice* (2nd ed., pp. 197–261). San Francisco: Jossey-Bass.

Sweeney, T. J. (2001). Counseling: Historical origins and philosophical roots. In D. C. Locke, J. E. Myers, & E. L. Herr (Eds.), *The handbook of counseling* (pp. 3–26). Thousand Oaks, CA: Sage.

Witmer, J. M., & Sweeney, T. J. (1992). A holistic model for wellness and prevention over the lifespan. *Journal of Counseling and Development, 71*, 140–148.

Young, M. E. (2009). *Learning the art of helping: Building blocks and techniques*. Upper Saddle River, NJ: Pearson.

Zimpfer, D. G. (1992). Psychosocial treatment of life-threatening disease: A wellness model. *Journal of Counseling & Development, 71*, 203–209.

CHAPTER 2

Legal and Ethical Issues

Jamie Crockett

Learning Goals

Upon completion of this chapter, you will be able to do the following:

1. Describe professional conduct and the role of consultation in ethical practice

2. Understand the moral principles underlying ethical clinical mental health (CMH) counseling practice

3. Discuss and access the professional standards for ethical practice in CMH counseling

4. Describe ethical and legal considerations of CMH counseling practice, including the roles of counselor, consultant, and expert witness

5. Apply an ethical decision-making model to CMH counseling ethical dilemmas

WHAT IS PROFESSIONAL CONDUCT?

The primary goal of counselor education is for graduates of counselor training programs to be **competent** counselors who practice both **ethically** and **legally** (Even & Robinson, 2013). **Ethics** are standards of practice that define professional behavior or conduct toward the public, peers, and other professionals (Remley & Herlihy, 2010). Ethical principles and codes guide day-to-day practice as well as situations that require choices about values and courses of action (Glosoff & Kocet, 2006; Van Hoose, 1980). Ethical practice involves abiding by both legal and professional guidelines. In fact, credentialing bodies, including state licensure boards, require demonstration of up-to-date ethical and legal knowledge (Herlihy & Remley, 2001). Clear training standards may decrease sanctions for ethical misconduct, and researchers have found that graduates of CACREP-accredited programs, who receive standard training in legal and ethical issues, receive fewer ethical sanctions than do graduates of non-CACREP programs (Even & Robinson, 2013). It is unclear, however, the extent to which this finding is a function of training, admissions standards, other factors, or some combination of these factors. Still, the wide variety of ethics training from program to program makes it imperative that counselors take self-responsibility in the pursuit of ethical and legal competence, both during graduate studies and beyond. To do this effectively throughout one's career, counselors continue to

- develop self-awareness;
- know and practice within local, state, and federal law;
- know and apply ethical codes, principles, values, and decision-making models;
- know when and with whom to consult about ethical and legal issues;
- know and act within professional competency areas; and
- seek ongoing continuing education.

This education is just the beginning, in that ongoing legal and ethical education should have a prominent role in your professional training over the course of your career.

Counseling ethical codes identify mandatory professional standards and behaviors and also describe ethical beliefs and aspirations of the profession (Kocet, 2006). Still, there are inherent limitations to ethical guidelines (Kitchener, 1984), and by definition, there often is no "right" answer to an ethical dilemma (Forester-Miller & Davis, 1996). Thus, the responsibility of the counselor is not to arrive at the "right" action but rather to engage in professional conduct and, accordingly, implement a professional course of action. Consultation, laws, ethical guidelines, moral principles, and ethical decision-making models afford counselors the resources to follow a systematic process and offer a reasoned professional justification for choices made in determining the best course of action in professional practice (Stadler, 1986). Whereas this chapter offers a brief introduction to these foundational practices, most facets of practice incur ethical and legal issues, many of which are addressed throughout the chapters of this text (e.g., advocacy and social justice in Chapter 3; diagnosis in Chapter 6; and documentation, confidentiality, informed consent, and professional disclosure in Chapter 9). The following sections serve as an introduction to these key aspects of ethical and legal practice, including consultation, moral principles, standards of practice, legal issues, ethical challenges, ethical decision making, multicultural and social justice considerations, case examples, and resources for continued learning.

CONSULT, CONSULT, CONSULT!

Counselors exhibit a range of responses to the ethical and legal expectations of professional practice. Fortunately, counselors do not need to know every possible response to every possible legal and ethical situation. Rather, counselors are expected to know and uphold ethical principles, professional processes, and codes of conduct designed to promote ethical and legal practice. Chief among these processes is the practice of consultation. Unfortunately, counselors often approach ethical and legal issues through conscious or unconscious avoidance. Whereas some counselors are eager to understand ethical and legal approaches, others avoid these considerations due to feeling overwhelmed or uninterested or perhaps because they believe themselves to have naturally good judgment. Counselors should not limit their use of consultation to extreme situations in which they clearly do not know what to do. Instead, counselors are encouraged to consult also in cases where they are simply uncertain of the best course of action, the so-called gray areas. Discernment of the appropriate use of consultation develops gradually through clinical practice under professional supervision. Initially, beginning counselors are encouraged to err on the side of consultation and "overconsult" to develop this discernment.

Consider the following scenario:

Jane recently completed her master's degree in clinical mental health counseling and is a provisionally licensed counselor in her state. Jane began working as a contract counselor in a private practice, and the owner of the private practice, Amanda, agreed to provide clinical and administrative supervision. The office manager, Laura, provided Jane with an orientation and setup at the practice. Jane was provided with a simple starting contract with the practice to provide fee-for-service counseling. Though confused, Jane was pleasantly surprised when the office manager informed her that she could bill the health insurance companies for which her supervisor was approved because she is the owner of the practice and Jane's supervisor. Jane met with the intake specialists to inform them of her scope of practice, treatment approach, and billing requirements so that they could assign clients appropriately. Despite feeling uncertain, Jane told them that she was able to bill the same insurance companies as her supervisor in addition to fee-for-service. As Jane begins client care, she is eager to discuss challenges and concerns she has about client treatment with Amanda and does not want to waste supervision time with billing questions. Thus, Jane directs questions about client fees and billing to Laura, the office manager, even though Laura has no training or experience in ethical and legal counseling practice.

After Jane's second month, Amanda calls Jane into her office and explains that she is baffled. Amanda elaborates that Laura was fired when Amanda learned that she was billing Jane's clients through her name, an approach that is considered insurance fraud by several insurance companies in their state. In addition to releasing Jane from her position, Amanda required Jane to pay back the related fees so that the affected insurance companies could be reimbursed. Because Jane was just getting started in her career, she was living paycheck to paycheck and had no idea where she would come up with this money. Amanda informs Jane that per her legal and ethical obligations, she will report these actions to the impacted insurance companies, the state licensing board, and the ethical boards of the professional organizations to which Jane belongs. She also suggests that Jane contact her liability insurance carrier and retain an attorney because legal actions may be taken. Finally, Amanda expresses feeling personally betrayed. To fulfill her responsibilities in the supervisory relationship, Jane had agreed to keep Amanda thoroughly informed of her practice. As Jane's supervisor and the owner of the practice, Amanda also may experience ethical sanctions and legal repercussions even though she was unaware of Jane's billing practices. Amanda also reminds Jane that client care is significantly impacted because clients will experience the upheaval of being transitioned suddenly to a new provider. Finally, Amanda iterates that it was Jane's ethical and legal responsibility to consult with Amanda as well as to be knowledgeable about the legal parameters of all aspects of her practice.

In Jane's negligence, a result of unintentional disregard for ethical and legal practice, she violated her moral obligations to clients and the profession. Specifically, she acted without fidelity (in respect to her profession) and also breached the principle of nonmaleficence (in respect to her clients). These moral principles are discussed further in the section that follows.

Clearly, consultation (with supervisors, colleagues, and other professionals) is one of the most important tools a counselor has in ensuring ethical and legal practice. As such, CMH counselors' responsibilities for seeking consultation as well as for acting as competent consultants for colleagues are outlined in professional guidelines for standards of practice (i.e., AMHCA, ACA, and NBCC codes of ethics). Like a competent counselor, a competent consultant (formal or informal) has a comprehensive up-to-date knowledge of ethical and legal practice as well as a strongly developed self-awareness of the role of his or her own values and worldview in practice, moral behavior, and ethical decision making (Newman, 1993). Further information on consultation in the context of supervision is discussed in Chapter 11. The following section discusses the moral principles that act as the foundation for ethical and legal CMH counseling practice.

MORAL PRINCIPLES

The role of counselor is accompanied by responsibilities that are distinct from those of "ordinary citizens" (Stadler, 1986, p. 3). By the very nature of the counseling process, clients are commonly in a position of vulnerability, whereas counselors are in a position of power (Remley & Herlihy, 2010). Counselors must ensure that this power is not abused or misused. Counselors have the utmost responsibility to act as **moral** agents and ensure that the counselor's disposition, judgments, and actions are **virtuous**. Accordingly, five moral principles identified by Kitchener (1984) have been recognized as the foundation of ethical practice in counseling (Forester-Miller & Davis, 1996). The five principles outlined by Kitchener (1984) are autonomy, nonmaleficence, fidelity, beneficence, and justice. Though moral principles do not offer an all-encompassing how-to guide for ethical practice, these principles provide counselors with clearly defined values and may offer clarity when questions of best practice arise. By integrating these moral values in their counseling practice, counselors also are able to limit the potentially negative impact of their own personal values and worldview.

The principle of **autonomy** refers to the client's right to independence. Clients have the right to develop their own values, actions, and choices, and counselors must respect this right (Kitchener, 1984). The counselor must refrain from imposing his or her values, opinions, and clinical "expertise" on clients' culture, worldview, choices, actions, and responses. Also, counselors must assess and help clients to evaluate how their values, actions, and choices impact both themselves and others. Still, the client's right to independence is not without limitation. For instance, counselors must assess the following (Forester-Miller & Davis, 1996):

- Do the client's values or actions cause harm to the client or others?

- Is the client's behavior infringing on the rights of others?

- Does the client have the faculties to make competent choices?

Clients' right to autonomy may be limited if they are not able to understand the repercussions of their choices or are unable to make decisions without harming themselves or others. For example, imagine that a counselor at a mental health agency is conducting an intake session with a new client. The client reports that she has been experiencing suicidal thoughts, including possible methods of killing herself, and is afraid to go home for fear of what she might do. The counselor completes a comprehensive safety assessment and determines that the client is at high risk for self-harm. The counselor discusses the client's options for treatment and outlines the process for voluntary psychiatric evaluation at a local hospital. The client begins to experience panic and adamantly refuses to go for psychiatric evaluation due to fear of what it would be like. The counselor processes the client's fears; describes the facility, assessment, and admission process; and informs the client about the process of involuntary evaluation. The client continues to refuse voluntary evaluation while also maintaining that she thinks she might kill herself if she leaves the counselor's office. The counselor consults with her supervisor and they determine that the counselor has given the client comprehensive information about her choices and adequate time to make an autonomous decision, however, the client's safety is in imminent danger and she has exhibited an inability to make a choice that will protect her from harm. The counselor determines that the client is not able to safely act autonomously and completes the procedures for involuntary evaluation.

The principle of **nonmaleficence** has its roots in the medical tenet of "above all do no harm" (Kitchener, 1984). Counselors should neither inflict harm *nor risk* inflicting harm on others during or outside of counseling sessions. In the case of both autonomy and nonmaleficence, defining and assessing what constitutes harm can be a gray area. For instance, in the counseling process, some client discomfort is expected. The degree of client discomfort that is justifiable versus harmful depends on a host of factors. For instance, is the client adequately informed about treatment and thus able to make an informed choice about engaging in treatment? Is there empirical support for the benefits of the treatment being used? Counselor behavior between sessions also can have the potential to cause harm. For example, imagine that several counselors at a mental health agency are completing paperwork in the file room at the end of the day. Just across from the file room is a restroom that is sometimes, though rarely, used by clients when the lobby restroom is in use. Thinking the area to be clear of clients, the door to the file room is left open. One counselor enters the room and immediately starts to process the challenges of his caseload and struggles he is having with the personality of his last client. He speaks in generalities about his experiences and believes he is being conscientious about the client's right to confidentiality. Suddenly, the counselors realize there is someone in the hall bathroom, within hearing distance. The door to the bathroom opens and the counselor's client emerges, looks at his counselor, and leaves briskly. Though the counselor revealed no personal or identifying information about the client, the therapeutic relationship was likely damaged and the client may have felt his trust had been betrayed whether he was aware he was the client being discussed or not. This is also an example of an issue of fidelity.

Fidelity encompasses behavior that is faithful to the counselor-client relationship (Kitchener, 1984). Faithful conduct includes but is not limited to being loyal, honest, respectful, reliable, and trustworthy. For instance, informed consent and professional disclosure (discussed further in Chapter 9) are examples of professional practices that promote fidelity by clearly informing clients of their rights and responsibilities, the counselor's training and approach, the nature and limitations of the counseling process, and details about counselor and/or facility policies on availability, billing, and more. For example, a counselor recently moved to a state in which custodians have a legal right to information regarding clients under the age of 18. She begins working with a 17-year-old male who was required to come to counseling by his parents. The client reports indifference to counseling and states that he does not trust his parents nor any other "authority." The client does not report experiences of abuse or neglect. In an effort to gain the client's trust, she assures him that counselors are not like other authority figures and that what he shares in counseling will remain confidential. After the session, the client's mother calls and requests information from the session. As the mother is speaking, the counselor realizes that she has put herself in a bind and dishonored the principle of fidelity (and potentially nonmaleficence) by violating her client's trust and his rights when she promised him complete confidentiality rather than making sure that he understood the limitations to confidentiality (see Table 2.1). Instead, to uphold ethical practice and the principle of fidelity, the counselor should have done her homework and

Table 2.1   Common Limitations to Confidentiality

Counselors must ensure client confidentiality within legal limits. Though laws vary from state to state, in general a breach of confidentiality may be required when there is

- suspected abuse or neglect of a child or dependent adult,
- a danger to an identifiable person,
- a danger of contagion of a life-threatening disease,
- a court order for disclosure,
- involvement of a Department of Social Services worker or *guardian ad litem,*
- a request from an adult client, or
- a request for information from the parent of a minor child.

consulted with her experienced colleagues and/or supervisor to develop an intentional approach to ethically and legally addressing confidentiality prior to beginning client care.

Beneficence is the moral principle that suggests it is not sufficient for counselors just to "do no harm" but that clients must also benefit from the relationship with the counselor (Kitchener, 1984). In other words, counselors have an ethical responsibility to help through promoting client welfare. As an example of an issue of beneficence, imagine a counselor working with children at a community agency. The counselor is experiencing burnout. He is frustrated with clients who do not seem to be making progress and also is frustrated with clients' caregivers whom he views as uncooperative. He no longer feels engaged with any of his clients and finds himself "going through the motions" at work. He is looking for a new job in order to work with a different population with whom he hopes he will not feel so disengaged. In the meantime, he continues to manage his caseload in order to receive a paycheck and benefits. He has not talked to his supervisor about this sense of being "checked out" with clients for fear of having his caseload cut back and losing full-time benefits. Though it is possible that the counselor is not directly harming his clients, the counselor should examine if his clients are benefiting from their relationship with him. Further, he is violating the principle of beneficence by valuing his own financial needs over the growth and healing of his clients. In addition to these moral considerations, he is avoiding several ethical responsibilities including, but not limited to, seeking supervision or consultation when necessary, addressing personal issues, and effectively engaging in self-care. In other cases, counselors also may fail to practice beneficence when they are overly invested or opinionated. For example, a counselor may impose her or his authority on the client, thinking this is in the client's best interest (beneficence) when, in fact, it imposes upon client autonomy. In fact, imposing clinical expertise can result in an ethical and legal violation described as **undue influence**.

The principle of **justice** addresses fairness and equality (Kitchener, 1984). Treating clients justly includes, but is not limited to, providing unbiased treatment, ensuring access to services, establishing a fair fee schedule, and engaging in client advocacy when appropriate (Kitchener, 1984). Applying the principle of justice does not require a one-size-fits-all approach to counseling. Rather, counselors are able to customize their approach to clients based on a "rationale that explains the necessity and appropriateness" of treating a client or clients differently from others (Forester-Miller & Davis, 1996, p. 2). As an example of an issue of justice, imagine a counselor who sees clients on a fee-for-service basis. She enjoys working with one of her clients in particular. She finds the client easy to listen to and is continually impressed with the client's progress. Together, they decide to hold 75-minute sessions. The counselor continues to charge the client the rate for 50-minute sessions even though the client did not ask for or exhibit financial need for this exception. All of her other clients pay the correct rate for the timing of their sessions as described in her professional disclosure statement. The counselor does not mention this change in treatment plan when discussing the client in peer supervision at the private practice where she works. There are several ethical considerations. First, this is a violation of justice because there is not an ethical rationale for treating this client differently. Further, there likely is some countertransference motivating the counselor's behavior, yet the counselor consciously chooses not to consult with her peers.

PROFESSIONAL STANDARDS FOR ETHICAL PRACTICE

The purpose of ethical guidelines, or ethical codes, in counseling is to protect clients, educate and protect counselors, ensure professional accountability, maximize therapeutic improvements, promote professional stability, and maintain professional autonomy (Calley, 2009; Pedersen, 1997). The code or codes of ethics that counselors adhere to depends on their professional affiliation and licensure. In the case of clinical mental health counselors, the two primary codes of ethics that counselors are typically expected to uphold are those of the American Mental Health Counselors Association (AMHCA) and the American Counseling Association (ACA); however, other codes may also be relevant. For instance, CMH counselors who become national certified counselors (NCCs) will also uphold the ethical standards of the National Board for Certified Counselors (NBCC). In all of these cases, these codes are considered "living" documents (Kocet, 2006). In other words, they change and evolve over time and are periodically revised. To competently fulfill the role of counselor, it is essential that counselors uphold, are aware of, and integrate changes in these ethical standards over the course of their career.

Reflecting the evolution of these guidelines, the current AMHCA Code of Ethics is available on the AMHCA's website (see Select Resources section at the conclusion of this chapter). Table 2.2 offers an overview of the AMHCA Code of Ethics. Similarly, the most recent version of the ACA Code of Ethics is available on the ACA's website (see Select

Table 2.2 Overview of the AMHCA Code of Ethics

The **Preamble** describes the role and values of the AMHCA as the organization representing CMH counselors. The purpose of the Code of Ethics and expectations for CMH counselors upholding it are also described.

I. **Commitment to Clients** addresses guidelines for fulfilling counselor responsibilities and respecting clients' rights in the following areas.
  A. **Counselor-Client Relationship** addresses the topics of (1) primary responsibility, (2) confidentiality, (3) dual/multiple relationships, and (4) exploitive relationships.
  B. **Counseling Process** includes the topics of (1) counseling plans, (2) informed consent, (3) multiple clients, (4) clients served by others, (5) termination and referral, (6) technology-assisted counseling, (7) clients' rights, and (8) end-of-life care for terminally ill clients.
  C. **Counselor Responsibility and Integrity** offers guidelines for (1) competence, (2) nondiscrimination, and (3) conflict of interest.
  D. **Assessment and Diagnosis** covers the topics of (1) selection and administration, (2) interpretation and reporting, (3) competence, and (4) forensic activity.
  E. **Recordkeeping, Fee Arrangements, and Bartering** addresses (1) recordkeeping and (2) fee arrangements, bartering, and gifts.
  F. **Other Roles** presents guidelines about the counselor roles of (1) consultant and (2) advocate.

II. **Commitment to Other Professionals** addresses the professional behavior and communication expected within professional relationships, settings, and conferences. The areas covered include (1) relationships with colleagues and (2) clinical consultation.

III. **Commitment to Students, Supervisees, and Employee Relationships** presents guidelines for promoting the welfare and professional development of students, supervisees, and employees. Topics addressed include (1) informed consent, (2) confidentiality, and (3) evaluation.

IV. **Commitment to the Profession** addresses guidelines for counselors in fostering the integrity of the counseling profession in counseling, teaching, research, and other professional activities. Topics addressed include (1) teaching, (2) research and publications, and (3) service on public or private boards and other organizations.

V. **Commitment to the Public** concerns counselors' responsibilities within their communities and the general public. Specifically, topics addressed are (1) public statements and (2) advertising.

VI. **Resolution of Ethical Problems** describes recommendations for ethical dilemmas and complaints and the AMHCA's policy in response to member state license suspension or revocation.

Resources). Table 2.3 presents an overview of the ACA Code of Ethics. The NBCC Code of Ethics was most recently updated in 2013 and is available on the NBCC website (see Select Resources). In addition, the NBCC provides practitioners with additional guidelines for upholding the NBCC's policies on providing distance services.

Table 2.3   Overview of the 2014 ACA Code of Ethics

The **Preamble** discusses the ACA as an organization, including characteristics and values of members.

The **Purpose** describes the five main purposes of the ACA Code of Ethics and introduces the format, approach, and application of the eight main sections. Ethical decision-making processes are also briefly discussed.

Section A: The Counseling Relationship discusses issues in the counselor-client relationship such as client welfare, counselor self-awareness, commitment to client growth, cultural competence, and societal contributions. This section addresses specific aspects of the relationship such as dual relationships, receiving gifts, and using the Internet to deliver services. Topics addressed include A.1. Welfare of those served by counselors; A.2. Informed consent in the counseling relationship; A.3. Clients served by others; A.4. Avoiding harm and imposing values; A.5. Roles and relationships with clients; A.6. Roles and relationships at individual, group, institutional, and society levels; A.7. Multiple clients; A.8. Group work; A.9. Counselor competence, choice, and referral; A.10. Fees and bartering; A.11. Termination and referral; and A.12. Technology applications.

Section B: Confidentiality, Privileged Communication, and Privacy presents guidelines related to the client's right to privacy, appropriate professional boundaries, culturally competent communication, and limitations to confidentiality. Topics addressed include B.1. Respecting client rights, B.2. Exceptions, B.3. Information shared with others, B.4. Groups and families, B.5. Clients lacking capacity to give informed consent, B.6. Records, B.7. Research and training, and B.8. Consultation.

Section C: Professional Responsibility discusses counselor competence as related to knowledge, training, providing services, and communicating with both the public and other professionals. Topics addressed include C.1. Knowledge of standards, C.2. Professional competence, C.3. Advertising and soliciting clients, C.4. Professional qualifications, C.5. Nondiscrimination, C.6. Public responsibility, and C.7. Responsibility to other professionals.

Section D: Relationships With Other Professionals addresses the quality of communication and working relationships with colleagues in the counseling field as well as other fields. The topics addressed include D.1. Relationships with colleagues, employers, and employees and D.2. Consultation.

Section E: Evaluation, Assessment, and Interpretation contains guidelines for competent use of assessment and diagnosis for the promotion of clients' wellness within their developmental and cultural context. The topics addressed include E.1. General, E.2. Competence to use and interpret assessment instruments, E.3. Informed consent in assessment, E.4. Release of data to qualified professionals, E.5. Diagnosis of mental disorders, E.6. Instrument selection, E.7. Conditions of assessment administration, E.8. Multicultural issues/diversity in assessment, E.9. Scoring and interpretation of assessments, E.10. Assessment security, E.11. Obsolete assessments and outdated results, E.12. Assessment construction, and E.13. Forensic evaluation: evaluation for legal proceedings.

Section F: Supervision, Training, and Teaching includes directives for professional relationships, appropriate boundaries, and theoretical underpinnings and pedagogical basis in supervision and counselor education. The topics addressed include F.1. Counselor supervision and client welfare; F.2. Counselor supervision competence; F.3. Supervisor relationships; F.4. Supervisor responsibilities; F.5. Counseling supervision, evaluation, remediation, and endorsement; F.6. Responsibilities of counselor educators; F.7. Student welfare; F.8. Student responsibilities; F.9. Evaluation and remediation of students; F.10. Roles and relationships between counselor educators and students; and F.11. Multicultural/diversity competence in counselor education and training programs.

Section G: Research and Publication offers guidelines for professional involvement and ethical practices in counseling research. The topics addressed include G.1. Research responsibilities, G.2. Rights of research participants, G.3. Relationships with research participants, G.4. Reporting results, and G.5. Publication.

Section H: Distance Counseling, Social Media, and Technology
The topics addressed include H.1. Knowledge and legal considerations, H.2. Informed consent and security, H.3. Client verification, H.4. Distance counseling relationships, H.5. Records and web maintenance, and H.6. Social media.

Section I: Resolving Ethical Issues addresses issues of legal, ethical, and moral conduct; decision making; and professional development. The topics addressed include H.1. Standards of the law, H.2. Suspected violations, and H.3. Cooperation with ethics committee.

The **Glossary of Terms** defines keywords used throughout the document.

LEGAL CONSIDERATIONS

Counselors are expected to comply with local, state, and federal **law**. Whereas ethics has been described as professional "shoulds" that reflect the best practices, laws are professional "musts" and represent minimum standards for practice (Herlihy & Remley, 2001). Because counseling ethics and the law are developed based on different conceptualizations of how the world works, it may be useful to consider the process of learning and abiding by the law as an acculturation process (Rowley & MacDonald, 2001). This process begins with developing familiarity with and then staying up to date on the laws related to counseling issues. In addition to issues of professional licensure, many legal issues and processes are relevant to CMH counselors including, but not limited to, confidentiality, recordkeeping, parental/guardian rights, minor rights, rights of adult dependents, duty to warn, diagnosis, fees, and billing. It is beyond the scope of this chapter to address all relevant legal issues, but some examples of common legal issues in CMH counseling practice are presented in Table 2.4. In order to stay up to date on legal requirements and considerations, it is recommended that counselors familiarize themselves with relevant local, state, and federal resources. For instance, the *American Psychology-Law Society News* is recommended for up-to-date information and resources on state and federal law that is relevant for mental health professionals (Rowley & MacDonald, 2001).

Another vital step in legally competent practice is to learn to recognize both when a legal situation has arisen and when to access legal guidance (Remley & Herlihy, 2010). To identify the presence of a legal situation, Remley and Herlihy (2010) suggest a simple test in which

Table 2.4 Examples of Common Legal Issues

• Duty to warn	• Expert witness	• Fees and billing
• Voluntary or involuntary psychiatric evaluation	• Disability suit	• Recordkeeping
	• Child welfare and custody	• Informed consent
• Subpoena for records	• Divorce proceedings	• Undue influence
• Subpoena for testimony	• End-of-life issues	• Assessment and testing

counselors ask themselves if any of the following three circumstances have arisen in their professional counseling practice: (a) legal proceedings, (b) involvement of a lawyer, or (c) personal or public concern about counselor professional conduct. If so, a legal issue clearly exists. If not, counselors may ask themselves if a client or supervisor has asked about or discussed any of the three aforementioned circumstances. If so, a legal issue may be present. Still, some situations may arise outside the scope of these questions, and counselors should always use consultation to assess if a legal issue is present. To determine the best course of action for legal issues, it is recommended that counselors consult with mental health and legal professionals. For this purpose, counselors are advised to develop relationships with mental health professionals who are knowledgeable of the law (Rowley & MacDonald, 2001) and legal professionals who are knowledgeable of the mental health profession. When these relationships are in place, counselors have access to the consultants they need as issues arise.

In addition to addressing legal issues in their own practice, CMH counselors sometimes choose to become involved with the legal aspects of mental health through the role of **expert witness**. An expert witness is a person who testifies in local, state, or federal court based on their expertise in a particular area (Weikel, 1986). This expertise is typically based on education, professional experience, research conducted, and publications. A counselor acting as an expert witness must have extensive knowledge of mental health issues, terminology, and trends as well as the particulars of the specific area of expertise. For instance, a counselor acting as an expert in the area of career counseling, a vocational expert, would also need to have a comprehensive understanding of the work world and relevant legal issues (e.g., social security disability) and might testify in court cases regarding an individual's ability to function in the workplace or their lost career trajectory (as in a wrongful death or malpractice suit; Weikel, 1986). Another example of the counselor as expert witness is the treatment specialist. The role of the treatment specialist is to consult and/or testify about a defendant's need for mental health treatment, resources for treatment, and in some cases to make an appropriate referral (Evans, 1983). Though many counselors are wary of courtroom experiences, the role of expert witness can be an opportunity to advocate for social justice and the holistic mental health needs of the public.

LEGAL AND ETHICAL CHALLENGES

Legal problems and ethical dilemmas can be stressful for counselors at all stages of development. Warren and Douglas (2012) identify some of the most common areas of concern as dual relationships, risk management, multicultural competency, gift receiving, termination, informed consent, treatment timing, counselor wellness, and ethical decision-making processes. In the ACA's (2011) ethics committee report, there were 4,943 informal ethical inquiries in which an ACA member consulted with the ACA office of ethics about an ethical concern. Of those inquiries, approximately 32% addressed confidentiality issues; 27% addressed licensure; 19% related to responsibility, such as duty to warn; 5% related to supervision; and 17% addressed various other concerns. Far more stressful than engaging in effective ethical decision-making processes is receiving an ethical complaint, particularly one that results in an ethical sanction or has legal repercussions. Typically, disciplinary or legal actions occur when the counselor acted in a negligent manner due to intentional or unintentional disregard of moral, ethical, and/or legal practice. Still, there is a relatively low incidence of ethical complaints and sanctions in the counseling profession. The most common decisions that lead to ethical complaints, ethical sanctions, and legal problems are related to confidentiality, sexual misconduct, suicide prevention, and inappropriate treatment. In the ACA (2011) report, counselors did not seek ethical consultation on these latter three issues commonly enough for the frequency of these inquiries to be listed explicitly in the report. This may speak to the tendency for counselors to underuse consultation in CMH practice. It is hypothesized that "professional perfectionism" may lead to counselor silence about issues related to ethical decision making and ethical problems (Warren & Douglas, 2012, p. 134). For instance, counselors may misguidedly remain silent rather than seek out consultation and professional discourse because they believe that

- ethical or legal problems will not happen to them,
- they *should* know something they do not know,
- it is unprofessional to have uncertainties and emotions about client care, or
- denial of their needs and concerns.

Also, some counselors may fear that consultation could result in an ethical complaint against them. An example of this misguided silence might be a counselor who feels sexually attracted to a client and fails to address this in supervision due to fear of what a supervisor would think or do. In fact, attraction is a natural experience in many human interactions, and addressing sexual attraction to clients *as soon as it arises* in consultation with colleagues or supervisors should not be considered shameful but rather an ethical imperative (Hamilton & Spruill, 1999). Further areas Warren and Douglas (2012) identified as high risk for ethical complaints include informed consent, client abandonment, unsupported treatment approaches, misdiagnosis, duty to warn, poor boundaries, transference, risk management, scope of practice, and inappropriate responses to client memories. Additionally, imposition of counselor values and worldview can be a source of significant ethical and, in some cases, legal missteps. Value-laden topics that often arise in the counseling process include abortion, unconventional behavior and beliefs (e.g., cult or gang membership), child or dependent adult neglect or abuse, genetic engineering, sexual conduct, sexual identity, spirituality, religion, race issues, education, career, parenting, caretaking, medical treatment, and more broadly cultural norms and gender roles (Remley & Herlihy, 2010).

In order to resolve ethical issues before they become ethical *problems*, counselors must cultivate self-awareness, learn to recognize early indicators, and take action accordingly. First and foremost, counselors must ensure that they are practicing with competence. In addition to understanding and knowledge of ethical and legal practice, counselors can use self-awareness, self-care, and consultation to ensure competence and assess the presence of an ethical concern. Incompetence is thought to be most commonly caused by counselor impairment due to stress, distress, or burnout (for a more comprehensive discussion of counselor burnout and prevention see Chapter 12). In fact, inadequate self-care and personal wellness may be at the root of many ethical and legal transgressions. For instance, lack of social support has been identified as a risk factor for counselor sexual misconduct (Hamilton & Spruill, 1999). Additionally, when counselors feel mixed or dissonant about a clinical or administrative issue, it can be a strong indication that ethical practice may be in jeopardy. For instance, in the scenario offered at the beginning of the chapter, Jane was both confused and pleasantly surprised when told she could bill insurance companies. This type of persistent mixed feeling indicates a need for self-exploration and consultation. Further, when counselors find themselves justifying or avoiding discussing something with peers or supervisors, it is a clear indication that consultation is needed. Though the list is by no means exhaustive, Table 2.5 presents questions counselors can ask themselves to assess the need to address an ethical issue that may have arisen.

Additionally, Table 2.6 outlines the top 10 risk-management strategies presented by Wheeler, Bertram, and Anderson (2008) for promoting ethical and legal practice and minimizing risk of ethical and legal problems.

Table 2.5   Questions for Recognizing Possible Ethical Issues

- Am I attending to my own holistic wellness?
- Do I prioritize self-care?
- Do I have fulfilling relationships in my personal life?
- Do I have time for leisure? Do I engage in activities that I enjoy?
- Am I tailoring treatment to meet the unique goals, needs, worldview, and cultural and developmental context of my clients? Am I up to date with evidence-based practice for my client's presenting concerns? Is the timing of treatment appropriate for my client's needs?
- Is my approach to counseling collaborative? Empowering for clients?
- Do I take the time to make sure that my clients fully understand their rights and responsibilities as well as my own? Do I make sure that my clients review and understand my professional disclosure statement?
- Do I know what my scope of practice is?
- Am I knowledgeable about referral sources and community resources? Do I make appropriate referrals and use adjunct services effectively?
- Do I know how to conduct a comprehensive safety assessment? Do I know what to do if a client is at risk? Am I willing to follow through?
- Do I regularly seek consultation? When I use consultation do I protect my client's privacy?
- Do I understand limitations to confidentiality? Do my clients?
- Do my clients regularly make progress toward their goals?
- Am I actively engaged in ongoing development of self-awareness and multicultural competence? Do I regularly consider my client's cultural context as well as my own?
- Do I consider my client's cultural and developmental context when making a diagnosis? Do my clients fit the criteria for the diagnosis I give?
- Do my clients understand the diagnosis I made? Do they understand the role of diagnosis in mental health treatment? Do my clients understand the limitations to and possible future implications of having a psychiatric diagnosis?
- Do I understand duty to warn and what is expected of me in my state?

- Am I honest in and current with administrative tasks such as documentation and billing?
- Am I up to date with my understanding and knowledge of ethical codes and legal issues?

If you answered **NO** to any of the previous questions, there may be an ethical issue that needs to be addressed. The recommendation—consult, consult, consult!

- Have my clients expressed any concern about ethical practice? Have I wondered about my ethical responsibilities in any area of my practice? Has a peer or supervisor?
- Have any of my clients asked me to do or not do something that I found confusing or uncomfortable? Is there anything that I have done or not done that has led to any of my clients being confused or uncomfortable with me?
- Do any of my clients remind me of someone with whom I have unresolved issues?
- Do I find myself irritated or annoyed by any of my clients?
- Do any of my in-session behaviors lack a therapeutic rationale?
- Do I feel apathetic about the therapeutic progress of any of my clients?
- Do I find myself thinking my clients should or shouldn't do certain things? Do I sometimes tell my clients what they should do? Do I think that I know what they need better than they do?
- Do I find it difficult to be present with any of my clients?
- Do my own needs influence my treatment planning (interventions, timing, termination, etc.)?
- Do I frequently act like an "expert" with my clients?
- Is there any way that I have been dishonest with any of my clients? Peers? Supervisor?
- Am I embarrassed, confused, or unsure about any aspect of my work with clients?
- Is there anything about my work with clients that I wouldn't want others to know?
- Is there anything about my clinical or administrative work that I feel conflicted about?
- Do I treat any of my clients differently than others?
- Would I categorize any of my interactions with clients or people in their lives as flirtatious?
- Are there any areas of my practice that I'm concerned might be beyond my area of competence?
- Do I find myself wishing I could be or wondering what it would be like to be friends or romantically involved with any of my clients?
- Do I often talk about myself to my clients?
- Do I talk about my clients to others (outside of consultation)?
- Am I engaged in any dual relationships? If so, are they unavoidable?
- Am I lonely? Is my personal support system inadequate?
- Am I sexually attracted to any of my clients or any of the people in their lives?
- Am I hesitant, insecure, minimizing, or dismissing during safety assessment for clients who might be at risk for harming themselves or others? Am I uncomfortable asking clients about safety? Do I find myself being apologetic when conducting safety assessment?
- Do I feel unsure about safety procedures, safety assessment, and/or my professional responsibilities regarding client or other harm?
- Is there anything about my practice I would be afraid or unwilling to discuss with a supervisor or colleague?
- Was I annoyed, defensive, or dismissive about any of these questions?

If you answered **YES** to any of the above questions, there may be an ethical issue that needs to be addressed. The recommendation—consult, consult, consult!

Table 2.6 Risk Management Strategies

1. Create an easy-access digital or hard-copy toolkit with ethical and legal information. Keep up to date with copies of ethical codes, laws and statutes, list of resources, relevant literature, list of consultants, etc. Consider creating or using existing checklists for legal procedures (e.g., subpoena, duty to warn, involuntary evaluation) and including them in the toolkit.
2. Consult, consult, consult! And then consult some more (see Chapter 11).
3. Conduct comprehensive written and verbal informed consent (see Chapter 9).
4. Know your workplace policies and procedures.
5. Termination and abandonment. Give sufficient notice and referrals when terminating. Avoid terminating with a client in crisis, but when absolutely necessary, ensure continued care with another provider.
6. Document clinical decision making (see Chapter 9).
7. Manage dual relationships. When dual relationships are unavoidable be intentional with relevant morals, ethical guidelines, and laws.
8. Recognize and work within your scope of practice.
9. Be intentional about boundaries, roles, and responsibilities when you act as a consultant or supervisor to another counselor.
10. Obtain and maintain professional liability insurance.

ETHICAL DECISION MAKING

Though consultation is an important tool in ethical decision making, there are many additional components to effective decision-making processes. In fact, there are many formal models for ethical decision making. There is also ongoing debate about their benefits, drawbacks, cultural bias, superiority, and/or inferiority (see review by Cottone & Claus, 2000). The following is adapted from the seven-step model of the American Counseling Association (Forester-Miller & Davis, 1996) developed from an integrative review of ethical decision-making literature.

Step 1: Identification. The first step is to identify and clarify the problem. Begin by assembling the information you have about the problem. Identify gaps in information and, when possible, gather additional needed information. It is useful to consider and label the information by type (e.g., fact, hypothesis, value, bias, assumption, concern). Once you have organized the available information you can identify the type of problem you have (e.g., administrative, clinical, ethical, legal). What laws are relevant to your problem? What are your ethical and legal obligations? Do you perceive any disparities between your ethical commitments and the law on this topic? You may need to consult in order to identify the type of problem. For instance, do you adequately understand the laws in this area to assess if this is a legal problem? *If the problem involves a legal issue, always consult with legal and mental health professionals prior to proceeding with the decision-making process.*

The following questions may offer further clarity. How is the problem related to

- You? Your action or inaction? Your values or worldview?

- Your client? Your client's action or inaction? Your client's values or worldview?

- Someone in your client's life? That person's action or inaction? That person's values or worldview?

Step 2: Review and Apply Code of Ethics. Once you have identified the problem, review the code or codes of ethics that you are expected to uphold (e.g., ACA and AMHCA). Is there an ethical standard that clearly and specifically indicates the course of action needed to address your problem? If upon reviewing the code of ethics, the appropriate course of action appears to be clearly identified, move on to Step 6. If, as is often the case with a true ethical dilemma, a specific resolution is not yet clear, proceed to Step 3 of the decision-making process.

Step 3: Do Your Homework. Examine the problem in the context of the following areas:

- Which moral principles are relevant to your problem? Does it appear that there is a conflict between relevant principles? If so, which takes priority and why?

- What are your ethical and legal priorities?

- What are the multicultural considerations relevant to this topic?

- What did you learn in your training and continuing education about this topic?

- What is the thinking in the *current* professional literature about this topic?

- Now that you have explored these areas you may consult with
  - Your supervisor
  - Experienced colleagues
  - Your state and/or national professional organizations
  - Your liability insurance carrier
  - A legal professional if there is a legal issue

Step 4: Brainstorm Options. Use your creativity to generate a list of potential options to resolve this problem. Whenever possible, solicit the help of a colleague and/or supervisor in developing this list.

Step 5: Evaluate Your Options. Review your list of options and consider the potential consequences of each option. For each option ask yourself questions such as these:

- How would this action impact the client? Others? Yourself?

- Are there any options that would have undesirable consequences? What options can be eliminated?

- What option or combination of options is the best fit with your moral, ethical, and legal priorities?

Step 6: Test the Course of Action. Once arriving at a possible course of action, there are several areas to consider in testing the appropriateness of an ethical decision. First, Stadler (1986) outlined three areas to question for this purpose: universality, justice, and publicity. To test **universality**, counselors can ask themselves if the course of action would be appropriate for others in a similar situation. Is this course of action universally appropriate? If not, are you inappropriately considering this a special case outside the realm of what would be recommended to others? To test **justice**, the counselor addresses whether he or she would treat other clients this way. If not, why not? Is there an ethical rationale for treating this client differently? To test **publicity**, the counselor can use the following types of questions: Am I willing to tell others about this action? What would other counselors think about this choice? What would happen if my decision were made public? In addition to these tests, it also is essential to test the **cultural** appropriateness of this option. Have you considered your client's culture and worldview? Are there any explicit or implicit cultural biases or assumptions that might be motivating your course of action? Next, evaluate your **process**. Have you completed a systematic evaluation of your issue involving consultation, morals, ethical codes, and laws? Can you articulate a reasoned professional justification for your decision? If your responses to these tests create a further sense of uncertainty, indicate holes in your process, or if new ethical concerns arise, it is recommended that you review the decision-making process from the beginning and seek consultation. If you assess that your course of action passes these tests, it is time to conduct the final test through **consultation** with your supervisor and/or experienced colleague. Once your course of action has passed the tests of universality, justice, publicity, culture, process, and consultation, it is time to move to Step 7.

Step 7: Implementation and Assessment. Implementing appropriate action is sometimes personally challenging. What professional support and personal self-care do you need in order to follow through with your course of action? After? Once you have followed through with your decision, it is recommended that you assess your actions and their impact. Is the issue resolved? Did new issues arise? What follow-up is needed?

MULTICULTURAL AND SOCIAL JUSTICE CONSIDERATIONS

Culture is inextricably woven into every aspect of counseling practice (Pack-Brown, Thomas, & Seymour, 2008). In fact, multicultural and social justice issues have a great impact on the development of ethical guidelines as well as counselors' intentional and unintentional professional conduct. As ethical codes in the field continue to evolve, they have become increasingly more sensitive to the needs of diverse populations. The AMHCA ethical code references cultural considerations in more than 10 areas, and the ACA Code of Ethics addresses cultural considerations more than 45 times in the document. Still, though much progress has been made, it is important to be aware that cultural bias exists in some areas of counseling theory, practice, ethical guidelines, moral principles, ethical decision-making models, laws, and legal processes. Thus, ongoing and intentional cultivation of multicultural competency and advocacy is a crucial component of ethical CMH practice. To meet the needs of increasingly diverse populations seen by CMH counselors, in addition to the ethical guidelines outlined by the AMHCA, ACA, and NBCC, several divisions of the ACA have outlined more in-depth competencies for various aspects of multiculturally competent CMH counseling practice. For instance, the Association for Multicultural Counseling and Development (AMCD) offers guidelines for multicultural competencies; the Association for Spiritual, Ethical, and Religious Values in Counseling (ASERVIC) outlines competencies for addressing spiritual and religious issues in counseling; and the Association for Lesbian, Gay, Bisexual, & Transgender Issues in Counseling (ALGBTIC) put forth competencies for counseling lesbian, gay, bisexual, and transgendered clients. A more comprehensive discussion of multicultural, social justice, and advocacy issues in CMH counseling is presented in Chapter 3 of this book.

CASE STUDIES

The following case studies were drawn from experiences of CMH counselors in practice. Consider the following questions for each of these case studies:

1. What legal issues are relevant in this case?

2. What ethical concerns and guidelines are relevant to this case?

3. What moral principles are relevant to this case?

4. What multicultural considerations might be important in this case?

5. What questions would you like to ask your supervisor or consultant about this case?

6. Apply the ethical decision-making model described in this chapter. What course of action would you take?

Case 1. You receive a request from your client's lawyer for the client's complete case file for a disability benefits suit. Included in the request is a release signed by the client for all of his clinical files, including intake, assessments, and case notes. Though treatment has addressed issues related to his disability (resulting from a workplace injury), the primary focus has been on resolving early childhood trauma. You believe the majority of the requested information is irrelevant to the client's suit and the extent of this release may be harmful. You wonder if the client fully understood the scope of the release of information to which he agreed.

Case 2. You have been seeing a client in individual counseling for several months. She unexpectedly brings her spouse to counseling to disclose that she has been having an affair. Though this action conflicts with the guideline for including others in session that is outlined in your professional disclosure statement, you facilitate the session, refer them for couples counseling, and remind your client of your policy for future reference. One week later you learn that your client's spouse filed for divorce.

(Continued)

(Continued)

You receive a request from the spouse's divorce lawyer for documentation of the session in which your client informed her spouse of her affair.

Case 3. You are a counselor at a mental health agency that provides services for clients with severe economic need. A third party funds the agency such that clients in need are able to receive services without paying anything out of pocket. One of your clients highly valued his experience in counseling and told you he would sometimes forgo meals in order to have money for the bus tickets necessary to transport him to his counseling appointments. During your termination session the client gives you a thank-you card with a five-dollar bill enclosed.

Case 4. You work at an agency where you have the opportunity to co-counsel families with your supervisor. In the termination session with one such family, the family presents you and the co-counselor with gift certificates for massages at a spa where a parent of the family works as the staff massage therapist. You thank them for their gift and gently decline to accept it. You explain your refusal by referring back to your policy and agency policy about gifts as outlined in your professional disclosure statement. To your surprise, the clients are shocked and explain that they had consulted with your co-counselor (i.e., your supervisor), and the massage gift certificate was her suggestion.

Case 5. You are working in a hospital setting providing counseling services for chronically and terminally ill individuals and their families, both inpatient and outpatient. You have been seeing a client regularly for individual sessions over the past 2 years. Recently, at your client's request, you facilitated several family sessions to address your client's wishes and concerns about her medical care, dying process, and funeral services. One of the client's family members contacts you to inform you of your client's death and asks you to speak at the client's funeral.

Case 6. You greet a client in the lobby for your third session and feel a wave of unexpected nervousness. You are surprised to realize you feel relieved that you have a fresh haircut and are wearing one of your most flattering yet professional outfits. During the session, you find yourself wondering what the client thinks of you. It seems like eye contact is slightly more prolonged than with other clients. As the client is preparing to leave, he initiates a hug.

Case 7. You are working in a community agency and facilitating a psychoeducation group as an adjunct service for clients of the various counselors in the agency. The purpose of the group is coping and social skill development for clients with emotion regulation difficulties. During one group session, the members of the group become highly alarmed in response to a baby crying in the adjacent counseling room. You know that some counselors allow their clients to bring their children to their individual sessions due to lack of resources for childcare. You attempt to use this experience as an opportunity for the group members to practice their coping skills. After several minutes, the crying has not subsided. One of the group members announces that it is her moral responsibility to go make sure the baby is not being harmed and she leaves the room.

Case 8. You have been working with a 9-year-old client whose parent brought her for counseling due to behavioral problems at home and at school. Though you explained the importance of parental involvement in treatment prior to beginning treatment, the client's parent has been largely noncompliant. The client's parent refuses to participate in filial sessions and sometimes fails to bring the client to appointments. Though the client was initially slow to warm to you, eventually you build a strong rapport. The client recently reported that she "loves" counseling. The client's parent reports that the client's behavior has begun to improve at school with no changes at home. You reiterate the necessity of parental involvement for further progress in treatment. In the next session, the client is sullen. She refuses to speak for the duration of the session and is occasionally tearful. With only a few minutes left in the session, you invite her parent to join you so that you can further assess what may be happening for the client. The client's parent informs you that the client will not be coming back for further sessions. The client bursts into tears.

Case 9. You have been subpoenaed to court to testify about the mental status of your client in a child custody suit. The client's children are ages 2 and 4. You have not met the children before, nor witnessed your client or her ex-spouse interacting with the children. At one point in your client's treatment, prior to the couple's separation, her spouse attended two sessions to address a conflict about parenting; however, the majority of your work together has focused on treating your client's experience of recurrent major depression. You have received written release of information from your client to testify about your assessment and diagnosis in court. You have not contacted or been contacted by her spouse.

SELECT RESOURCES FOR ETHICAL AND LEGAL CMH COUNSELING PRACTICE

American Counseling Association (ACA): http://www.counseling.org

- The ACA offers free consultation about ethics and professional standards. Contact the ACA Ethics and Professional Standards Department at (800) 347-6647, ext. 314, or e-mail ethics@counseling.org.

- ACA Practitioner's Guide to Ethical Decision Making: http://www.counseling.org/docs/ethics/practitioners_guide.pdf

American Mental Health Counselors Association (AMHCA): http://www.amhca.org

- Members can consult with the AMHCA Ethics Committee about ethical dilemmas in clinical practice.

National Board for Certified Counselors (NBCC): http://www.nbcc.org

For information about laws and legal services, you can consult http://www.findlaw.com as well as your home state's webpage.

REFERENCES

American Counseling Association (2011). *Ethics Committee summary*. Retrieved from http://www .counseling.org/docs/ethics/ecreport11.pdf?sfvrsn = 2.

Calley, N. G. (2009). Promoting a contextual perspective in the application of the ACA Code of Ethics: The ethics into action map. *Journal of Counseling & Development, 87,* 476–483.

Cottone, R. R., & Claus, R. E. (2000). Ethical decision-making models: A review of the literature. *Journal of Counseling & Development, 78,* 275–283.

Evans, J. (1983). The treatment specialist: An emerging role for counselors within the criminal court system. *The Personnel and Guidance Journal, 61*(6), 349–351.

Even, T. A., & Robinson, C. R. (2013). The impact of CACREP accreditation: A multiway frequency analysis of ethics violations and sanctions. *Journal of Counseling & Development, 91,* 26–34.

Forester-Miller, H., & Davis, T. (1996). *A practitioner's guide to ethical decision making.* Retrieved from http://www.counseling.org/docs/ethics/practitioners_guide.pdf.

Glosoff, H. L., & Kocet, M. M. (2006). *Highlights of the 2005 ACA Code of Ethics.* In G. R. Walz, J. Bleuer, & R. K. Yep (Eds.), *VISTAS: Compelling perspectives on counseling* (pp. 5–9). Alexandria, VA: American Counseling Association.

Hamilton, J. C., & Spruill, J. (1999). Identifying and reducing risk factors related to trainee-client sexual misconduct. *Professional Psychology, Research and Practice, 30,* 318–327.

Herlihy, B., & Remley, T. (2001). Legal and ethical challenges in counseling. In D. Locke, J. Myers, & E. Herr (Eds.), *The handbook of counseling* (pp. 69–91). Thousand Oaks, CA: Sage.

Kitchener, K. S. (1984). Intuition, critical evaluation and ethical principles: The foundation for ethical decisions in counseling psychology. *The Counseling Psychologist, 12,* 43–55.

Kocet, M. M. (2006). Ethical challenges in a complex world: Highlights of the 2005 ACA Code of Ethics. *Journal of Counseling & Development, 84,* 228–235.

Newman, J. L. (1993). Ethical issues in consulation. *Journal of Counseling & Development, 72,* 148–156.

Pack-Brown, S. P., Thomas, T. L., & Seymour, J. M. (2008). Infusing professional ethics into a multicultural/social justice perspective. *Journal of Counseling & Development, 86,* 296–302.

Pedersen, P. B. (1997). The cultural context of the American Counseling Association Code of Ethics. *Journal of Counseling & Development, 76,* 23–28.

Remley, T. R., & Herlihy, B. (2010). *Ethical, legal, and professional issues in counseling* (3rd ed.). Upper Saddle River, New Jersey: Pearson.

Rowley, W. J., & MacDonald, D. (2001). Counseling and the law: A cross-cultural perspective. *Journal of Counseling & Development, 79,* 422–429.

Stadler, H. A. (1986). Making hard choices: Clarifying controversial ethical issues. *Counseling and Human Development, 19,* 1–10.

Van Hoose, W. H. (1980). Ethics and counseling. *Counseling and Human Development, 13,* 1–12.

Warren, J., & Douglas, K. I. (2012). Falling from grace: Understanding an ethical sanctioning experience. *Counseling and Values, 57,* 131–146.

Weikel, W. J. (1986). The expanding role of the counselor as a vocational expert witness. *Journal of Counsel, 64,* 523–524.

Wheeler, A. M., Bertram, B., & Anderson, B. S. (2008). *The counselor and the law: A guide to legal and ethical practice.* Alexandria, VA: American Counseling Association.

CHAPTER 3

Advocacy and Social Justice

Catherine Y. Chang, Simone Lambert, and Emily Goodman-Scott

Learning Goals

Upon completion of this chapter, you will be able to do the following:

1. Describe the ecological view of counseling used by clinical mental health (CMH) counselors

2. Articulate the importance of client advocacy and professional advocacy for CMH counselors

3. Describe the effects of discrimination on the mental health of individuals

4. Outline how CMH counselors can function as advocates for their clients

THE CASE OF YOLANDA

Imagine you are a clinical mental health counselor working in a public mental health agency. Your newest client is Yolanda, a single 22-year-old African American mother who has three children (ages 6 years, 2 years, and 11 months). Yolanda lives well below the poverty line and is unemployed. During the intake assessment, you observe and uncover many signs of depression, low self-esteem, a history of substance abuse, dysfunctional relationships with men, generalized anxiety, and trauma. Yolanda, however, relates her chief complaint: "I have been trying to get on Medicaid for months but have been denied two times. If that isn't bad enough, I am about out of food for the kids and my power

(Continued)

(Continued)

bill is late." She begins to cry talking about the financial issues she faces as well as her difficulty in gaining access to public assistance. It is clear that she needs help in navigating the system to get the support she needs. Yolanda's story is very similar to others you have on your caseload. Upon reflection you begin to wonder if there is more you could do to help clients in this situation. Perhaps focusing solely on her counseling issues (depression, self-esteem, substance use, relationships) is not the best approach to helping Yolanda, who has a different, more pressing need. Identifying such a need and formulating a plan to take meaningful action is advocacy. The desire that your client and others should be treated fairly is social justice.

Clients cannot be served without considering the context of all systems in which they live and interact. To best serve clients, CMH counselors often work as part of an interdisciplinary team. Accordingly, before focusing on social justice and advocacy, it is important to understand client systems and how counselors often work collaboratively with other mental health professionals.

ECOLOGICAL VIEW

Although counselors are trained to use a developmental lens for understanding clients, it is an unfortunate truth that many emerge from training with an individualistic and compartmentalized perspective that fails to fully consider the multiple systems that influence the individual. It is important, then, that in addition to viewing clients' behaviors from a developmental perspective, counselors also explore environmental influences, including family, social networks, and community systems (Gerig, 2007). This multidimensional framework, the **ecological view**, is based on the work of Bronfenbrenner (2005). According to the ecological view, human development and behaviors are influenced by the interaction of individuals and environmental variables (Doerries & Foster, 2001; Greenleaf & Williams, 2009). Thus, "the ecological model of development proposes that behavior can only be understood in context" (Stormshak & Dishion, 2002, p. 197).

Most notably, Bronfenbrenner (2005) refined ecological theory to describe the interaction of individuals within four distinct levels of their environment: the microsystem, mesosystem, exosystem, and macrosystem. Bronfenbrenner (1989) described the **microsystem** as "a pattern of activities, roles, and interpersonal relationships experienced by developing persons in a given face-to-face setting with particular physical and material features, and containing other persons with distinctive characteristics of temperament, personality, and systems of belief" (p. 227). These daily interactive relationships take place at home, school, and work, whereby the individual is influenced by these people and vice versa (Gerig, 2007).

The **mesosystem** is defined as "the linkages and processes taking place between two or more settings containing the developing person (e.g., the relations between home and school, school and workplace, etc.)" (Bronfenbrenner, 1989, p. 227). The mesosystem is a "system of microsystems" (e.g., friends, coworkers, school personnel, and family) that interact concurrently with the individual on an ongoing basis (Gerig, 2007, p. 50). Bronfenbrenner (1989) defined the **exosystem** as interactions between two settings, with one of those settings not including the individual directly. Examples of exosystems are a schoolwide system, religious institutions, government, and community (Gerig, 2007). The **macrosystem** includes the other three levels within a specific culture or subculture (Bronfenbrenner, 1989); these could include components such as an economic system, society, and language (Gerig, 2007). In his later revisions of the ecological model, Bronfenbrenner (2005) included a fifth system, **chronosystem**, which characterized the evolution of the other four levels over a time period that may encapsulate life events. By using the ecological view within case conceptualizations, a CMH counselor sees a client's presenting concerns as more complex and contextual, requiring a treatment plan that includes change at the individual and systemic level (Gerig, 2007). In fact, many client issues stem externally from contextual variables at the exosystem or macrosystem level, resulting in the need for **advocacy** and social justice efforts on the part of the counselor (Greenleaf & Williams, 2009).

Stormshak and Dishion (2002) described a three-tiered ecologically based mental health model for serving children and families and state that clients need to be examined in the context of these levels or systems. The first and most internal level, *relationship processes*, includes the individual's interactions with adults, family, and peers; the *behavior settings* level is composed of the settings impacting the client, such as work, home, neighborhoods, school, activities, and organizations. Finally, the most external level, *community contexts*, lists community factors impacting the individual, such as the mass media; available resources; population density; economic and political climate; cultural majority and minority status; and societal rituals, norms, and perspectives. Thus, clinical mental health counselors should be aware of the myriad contextual factors that influence their clients and their clients' presenting issues.

In fact, the multilevel approach to community-based interventions incorporates the ecological perspective through the inclusion of partnerships with various stakeholders within the community and the role that local culture has on such interventions (Trickett, 2009).

CASE STUDY DISCUSSION

Consider the case of Yolanda presented at the outset of this chapter. With the limited information provided, try to identify aspects of her microsystem, mesosystem, exosystem, macrosystem, and chronosystem. Consider how each of these may be impacting her presenting mental health issues.

Furthermore, when community-level interventions are implemented using an ecological view, interprofessional collaborations and community partnerships can coordinate efforts, services, and resources to address larger public health issues and social problems that impact multiple levels (Trickett, 2009; Trickett et al., 2011). These larger issues have included disease prevention (e.g., HIV/AIDS), health promotion (e.g., engaging in physical activity, eating fruits and vegetables, eliminating cigarette smoking), and social issues (e.g., teen pregnancy) (Richard, Gauvin, & Raine, 2011; Trickett, 2009; Trickett et al., 2011). Additional costly areas where multilevel community-based interventions could be applicable include diabetes and substance abuse prevention.

Lewis, Lewis, Daniels, and D'Andrea (2003) described the *community counseling model* as based in an ecological view that incorporates assessments, therapeutic treatment, program development/evaluation, and research. Lewis et al. (2003) further delineated strategies within the community counseling model to include both focused strategies that are more client centered and broad-based strategies that focus on community or societal issues. Their examples of focused strategies were counseling within the context of multiple levels, outreach services to distressed or marginalized clients, advocacy, and community collaboration. Complementing this, their broad-based intervention strategies included prevention and development as well as macro-level advocacy of a sociopolitical nature (Lewis, Lewis, Daniels, and D'Andrea, 2011). Additionally, Gerig (2007) suggested that a comprehensive mental health counseling model should include the dimensions of mental health/wellness, mental illness/dysfunction, and an ecological context. Because human behavior and development are so intertwined with ecological context, clinical mental health counselors need to employ strategies and interventions that promote the well-being of both their clients and their clients' communities (Gerig, 2007; Lewis et al., 2011).

Additionally, counselors must be **culturally aware and proficient** when working with clients and their service providers and community members. Members of different cultures may value and prefer varied degrees of collaboration, consultation, and involvement from others. For example, clients who value collectivism, or the interdependence of group members, may prefer for their counseling treatment to incorporate other service providers, family, and community members. Clients who value an individualistic perspective may prefer less collaboration and consultation. However, counselors should strive to understand the individual client along with his or her cultural and ecological reality. This perspective prepares the CMH counselor to take on the role of advocate.

UNDERSTANDING ADVOCACY AND SOCIAL JUSTICE

Do you believe that everyone deserves to be treated equitably? Do you believe that people are treated differently because of their race, gender, religion, and sexual identity? Do you believe mental health professionals must be aware of the disparities that exist in society? Do you believe that mental health counselors have a responsibility to address systemic intolerance and social inequities?

Advocacy and social justice are fundamental to the practice of counseling (Chang, Crethar, & Ratts, 2010; Chang & Gnilka, 2010). **Advocacy** refers to the "promotion of the well-being of individuals and groups, and the counseling profession within systems and organizations. Advocacy seeks to remove barriers and obstacles that inhibit access, growth, and development" (ACA, 2005, p. 20). **Social justice** involves "promoting access and equality to ensure full participation in the life of a society, particularly for those who have been systematically excluded" (Lee, 2012, p. 110). Social justice is based on the belief in a just world, a world that respects and protects human rights, and a world with fair treatment and equitable distribution of societal resources (Bell, 1997; Chang & Gnilka, 2010; Lee, 2012; Rawls, 1971). **Social justice counseling** refers to counseling where the mental health counselor recognizes that oppression, privilege, and discrimination have an impact on the mental health of clients, and therefore, a goal of social justice counseling is to establish equal distribution of power and societal resources through advocacy efforts (Chang & Gnilka, 2010). Due to rising concerns related to economic and societal issues, some have argued that social justice counseling should be considered the "fifth force" following psychodynamic, behavioral, humanistic, and multicultural counseling forces (Ratts, 2009).

The importance of addressing advocacy and social justice issues in counseling is reflected in the 2014 *ACA Code of Ethics* and most recently in the revised 2016 Council for Accreditation of Counseling and Related Educational Programs (CACREP) national accreditation standards. According to Standard A.7.a of the *ACA Code of Ethics*, "When appropriate, counselors advocate at individual, group, institutional, and societal levels to examine potential barriers and obstacles that inhibit access and/or the growth and development of clients" (ACA, 2014, p. 5). Additionally, Standard E.5.c directs professional counselors to "recognize historical and social prejudices in the misdiagnosis and pathologizing of certain individuals and groups and strive to become aware of and address such biases in themselves and others" (ACA, 2014, p. 11).

The 2016 CACREP Standards require advocacy knowledge and skills for counselor training first present in the 2009 Standards. In fact, within the 2016 Standards specific to clinical mental health counseling, it is stated explicitly that students must be able to demonstrate "strategies to advocate for persons with mental health issues" (CACREP, 2016, p. 23), which clearly points to the importance of addressing diversity and advocacy issues in the training of mental health counselors.

Additionally, core curriculum standards also highlight the importance of addressing advocacy issues within counselor training. For example, students should be able to demonstrate "strategies for identifying and eliminating barriers, prejudices, and processes of intentional and unintentional oppression and discrimination" (Standard II.F.2.h, CACREP, 2016, p. 9).

Clearly, advocacy and social justice issues are important aspects of the training of professional counselors as evidenced by the code of ethics and the accreditation standards for counselor training. As such, in the following pages we explore the importance of multicultural counseling competence as a precursor to the growth of social justice issues in counseling and the effects of racism and discrimination on the development of professional counselors as well as its impact on their clients. Following this discussion, advocacy as a two-pronged concept that includes both client and professional advocacy (Chang, Barrio Minton, Dixon, Myers, & Sweeney, 2012; Chang, Hays, & Milliken, 2009; Myers, Sweeney, & White, 2002) is described as a way to address the effects of racism and discrimination. Finally, global perspectives on counseling are considered to provide a context for the concepts described in the chapter. The following case study is used throughout the remainder of the chapter to facilitate dialogue.

CASE STUDY

Ann is a counselor in training in a master's program in clinical mental health counseling. She self-identifies as a white, heterosexual, able-bodied female. Currently, she is interning at a community mental health agency. This agency provides a variety of services from individual counseling, psycho-educational groups, and therapy groups to clients diagnosed with a wide range of mental health issues. The agency primarily serves clients with African American heritage and Hispanic heritage and individuals with lower economic statuses. Although the clientele is ethnically and racially diverse, the staff CMH counselors all self-identify as white. Ann has observed that there are several mental health counselors at the agency who always seem to refer out their Hispanic clients.

Over the course of the semester, Ann has seen individual clients and co-leads a psychoeducational group for women with substance abuse issues. This group is co-led by a male staff member, Joe. Joe has no formal educational background in counseling. He is a longtime staff member of the agency who has been in recovery for over 20 years. Ann feels uneasy around Joe and is uncomfortable with derogatory comments he has made about other racial/ethnic groups and women. He tries to tell Ann what she should be doing in group, not as a supervisor but as someone "who knows something about counseling." One day during a psychoeducational group that happens to include only women survivors of sexual abuse, Joe begins talking about ways that women can protect themselves from being sexually assaulted. He makes comments that Ann finds offensive and inaccurate. As Ann scans the group, she notices that the women appear uneasy and begin staring at the floor, avoiding eye contact with her and one another. Ann, although extremely anxious herself, takes this opportunity to challenge Joe and to provide facts related to sexual assault. Following the group, she seeks out her site supervisor and updates the supervisor about the group seeking supervision as well as consultation. Later that day, Joe finds Ann and tells her that she should not take things so seriously. Ann informs Joe about her professional responsibility. She also shares this information with her university supervisor during individual and group supervision. (Case study adapted from Chang, 2012.)

MULTICULTURAL COMPETENCE AND CULTURALLY RESPONSIVE CMH COUNSELING

With the growing diversity within the United States demographics and the increasing attention to the important role that cultural background has on mental health, multiculturalism has been described as the fourth force in counseling (Pedersen, 1991, 1999). As it relates to counseling, multiculturalism can be viewed as a perspective of valuing cultural diversity and recognizing the impact of one's cultural background on one's own mental health and, thus, on the counseling process. Multiculturalism has influenced mental health counselors' awareness and understanding of themselves as cultural beings, changed how mental health counselors conceptualize their clients and client concerns, and impacted mental health counselors' perspective on the counseling process and the counseling relationship. From a multicultural perspective, understanding one's culture is central to understanding human behavior; therefore, a mental health counselor cannot assess, evaluate, diagnose, or interpret a client's behaviors, or facilitate change, without considering the cultural context of the client and oneself (D'Andrea & Heckman, 2008; Hays & McLeod, 2010).

In response to the recognition of the importance of multiculturalism on the counseling profession, Sue, Arredondo, and McDavis (1992) proposed a set of **multicultural counseling competencies** and standards that provide professional counselors with a foundation for culturally responsive practice. These standards include 31 professional competencies across three dimensions of beliefs and attitudes, knowledge, and skills and across three characteristics that include "(a) counselor awareness of own assumptions, values, and biases; (b) understanding the worldview of the culturally different client; and (c) developing appropriate intervention strategies and techniques" (p. 481). The following is a summary of the multicultural counseling competencies (see Sue et al., 1992, for the full competencies).

I. Counselor Awareness of Own Cultural Values and Biases

    A. Attitudes and Beliefs—counselors are aware of their own cultural heritage and its impact on the counseling process.

    B. Knowledge—counselors have knowledge of their own racial and cultural heritage as well as knowledge of the impact of oppression, racism, discrimination, and stereotyping and how these affect them both personally and professionally.

    C. Skills—counselors actively seek out educational and consultative training to improve their cultural competence and strive for a nonracist identity.

II. Counselor Awareness of Client's Worldview

    A. Attitudes and Beliefs—counselors are aware of both their negative and positive emotional reactions toward racial and ethnic groups and the potential impact of these on the counseling relationship.

    B. Knowledge—counselors have specific knowledge regarding the cultural background, the sociopolitical influences, within-group variation, and identity development of their client population.

    C. Skills—counselors seek out relevant research and immersion experiences so that they can gain an understanding of the relevant mental health issues affecting various racial and ethnic groups.

III. Culturally Appropriate Intervention Strategies

    A. Attitudes and Beliefs—counselors respect culture-specific beliefs and values, bilingualism, and indigenous practices.

    B. Knowledge—counselors have knowledge of the limitation of the counseling practice as it relates to working with ethnic minorities, including limitations due to institutional barriers, assessment biases, and discriminatory practices.

C. Skills—counselors recognize that helping skills vary by culture and are open to using a variety of helping and communication styles, as well as seeking consultation from traditional healers to best meet the needs of their diverse clients.

Arredondo and her colleagues (1996) operationalized these standards, which allowed counselor training programs to adopt and include cultural competence as a component of training. Additionally, Arredondo et al. (1996) expanded the scope of multicultural counseling competence to include other diverse identities such as religion, sexual identity, and ability or disability, including the importance of considering historical, political, sociocultural, and economic contexts in understanding one's clients and oneself.

Since the early 1990s, there has been a notable increase in the number of empirical and conceptual publications focused on multicultural counseling competence. Jones, Smith, and Shelton (2009) categorized the multicultural competence research into two main categories. The first category includes researchers who explored counselor multicultural competence response and behavior. The second category includes scale-specific research.

Researchers investigating multicultural competency have explored the multicultural competence of school counselors and school counselor trainees (see Constantine, 2002; Holcomb-McCoy, 2001), play therapists (see Penn & Post, 2012; Ritter & Chang, 2002), marriage and family therapists (see Constantine, Juby, & Liang, 2001), substance abuse counselors (see Lassiter & Chang, 2006), and counselors and counselor trainees in general (see Chao, 2012; Fuertes, Bartolomeo, & Nichols, 2001; Hipolito-Delgado, Cook, Avrus, & Bonham, 2011;

CASE STUDY DISCUSSION

During the beginning of Ann's internship experience, her university supervisor, Lisa, encourages her to reflect on her cultural background and heritage and how her background may impact her relationships with her clients and her supervisors. Ann is also asked to consider the cultural background of her clients and her supervisors. During Ann's first individual supervision session, Lisa discusses the importance of addressing racial and cultural issues during counseling and supervision. Lisa openly discusses her own cultural background and how that impacts her supervision and then encourages Ann to reflect on her cultural background.

Lisa presents the following questions for Ann to contemplate. How are Ann and Lisa similar and distinct as cultural beings? How does Ann describe herself culturally? What are Ann's values and beliefs, and how might they influence her relationship with clients? How might her values and beliefs influence her understanding and implementation of the counseling process? What cultural biases might Ann hold toward her clients? Her supervisors? What cultural biases might her clients and supervisors have toward Ann? What cultural values might enhance or impede her relationship with her clients and supervisors? As you begin your own internship experience, you are encouraged to revisit these questions with serious self-reflection.

Manese, Wu, & Nepomuceno, 2001). Researchers have investigated various factors that relate to multicultural counseling competence and have found that multicultural counseling competence increased with educational level, multicultural education/training, cultural immersion projects, higher levels of racial identity development, religious identity, and sexist ideology. By contrast, researchers have learned that multicultural counseling competence decreased with higher levels of racism and unawareness of racial privilege and racial issues (Balkin, Schlosser, & Levitt, 2009; Chao, 2012; Constantine, 2002; Fuertes et al., 2001; Hipolito-Delgado et al., 2011; Lassiter & Chang, 2006; Manese et al., 2001; Penn & Post, 2012; Ritter & Chang, 2002).

Multicultural competency has been and continues to be an important topic within the counseling literature. An extension of the multicultural competency movement is the growing recognition of the important role that social injustices such as racism, discrimination, privilege, and oppression have on the development of mental health counselors and on the lives of their clients.

SOCIAL INJUSTICE AND MENTAL HEALTH

As CMH counselors become more **multiculturally competent**, they also grow more conscious of the varieties of structural oppression and discrimination that many clients face. Social injustice refers to the unequal distribution of both privilege and burden, and the punishment given for failure to follow societal norms. The importance of considering social injustice in counseling becomes apparent when one considers the relationship between social injustice and mental health. The U.S. Surgeon General's report "Mental Health: Culture, Race, and Ethnicity: A Supplement to Mental Health" (USDHHS, 2001) illustrated the potential consequences of social injustice and predictors of mental illness for racial and ethnic minority groups. This report called on mental health professionals to examine how negative societal conditions and oppression impact members of marginalized groups. Additionally, this report highlighted how various minority statuses (e.g., being an Asian American female) can intersect and create additional adverse stressors. Members of marginalized groups are exposed to greater levels of oppression and stressors, which can threaten their well-being (Greene, 2005). Greater exposure to stress can leave a person more susceptible to depression, suicide, substance abuse, violence, anxiety, and both chronic and acute stress (Ancis, 2004; USDHHS, 2001).

Social injustice includes all of the -isms (e.g., racism, sexism, classism) and discrimination; poverty; child exploitation; racial profiling; educational achievement gaps; and violence against racial, ethnic, and sexual minorities (Chang & Gnilka, 2010; Hays, Chang, & Chaney, 2008). All these social injustices deserve time and consideration. For the sake of brevity, however, this chapter focuses on the broader concepts of privilege and oppression, constructs that underlie all forms of discrimination and the -isms and, therefore, become a central focus for mental health counselors who wish to engage in counseling from a social justice perspective. Additionally, two of the most pervasive -isms faced by mental health counselors and counselor trainees, racism and sexism, are discussed (Hays, Dean, & Chang, 2007).

PRIVILEGE AND OPPRESSION

Privilege and oppression are complex and multifaceted. Privilege involves having power, access, advantage, and a majority status. Conversely, oppression is characterized by domination and subordination, where the dominant individual or group imposes their power on a subordinate group. Being oppressed is related to lack of power, lack of access, lack of advantages, and having minority status and therefore can be viewed as inversely related to privilege (Hays, Chang, & Dean, 2004).

Privilege

Lee and Diaz (2009) conceptualized privilege along three dimensions. First, privilege is unearned. Oftentimes, individuals have privilege based on innate characteristics (e.g., skin color, gender). Second, privileged individuals are generally unaware of their privileged status and the benefits afforded them because of it. Finally, individuals with privilege are in positions of social dominance and experience cultural, social, and economic advantages. White, male, Christian, heterosexual, and able-bodied individuals represent privileged groups in the United States (Chang & Gnilka, 2010; Hays et al., 2007; Lee, 2012).

Privilege cannot be fully understood without discussing power. Power involves the ability to control people and limit access to resources (e.g., education, information, resources). Power is inherent in the counseling relationship regardless of one's theoretical approach due to the fact that clients come to counseling, whether voluntarily or involuntarily, needing some kind of assistance. Mental health counselors must remain aware of the inherent power they hold over clients and possess the skill to use that influence to empower clients to be active partners in the counseling process (Lee & Diaz, 2009). If not addressed, issues of power and privilege within the counseling relationship can damage a client's identity, disrupt the therapeutic process, and lead to misinterpretation of client behavior (Hays et al., 2007; Manuppelli, 2000). Awareness and knowledge of privilege and its impact on the counseling relationship has been linked to increased multicultural counseling competence (Ancis & Szymanski, 2001; Hays et al., 2004, 2007). Recognizing the importance of power in counseling, Lee and Diaz (2009) warn that abuse of the counselor's inherent power has the potential to be the greatest ethical violation. Mental health counselors who are unaware of the inherent power they have over clients are at risk of being culturally insensitive, which may contribute to clients feeling disenfranchised and marginalized. One example of counselors' abuse of power includes counselors who are unresponsive to clients' diverse cultural backgrounds and therefore may conceptualize cultural differences as deficiencies or pathology (Lee & Diaz, 2009).

Oppression

Often, oppression is discussed in relation to privilege. Oppression involves an abuse of power where one individual or group exercises power to dominate another group. Oppression serves to impose undesirable labels, experiences, and conditions on the oppressed group by virtue of their cultural group membership (Ancis & Chang, 2008). Hanna, Talley, and Guindon (2000) described two modalities of oppression (oppression by force and oppression by deprivation) across three types (primary, secondary, and tertiary).

Oppression by force is "the act of imposing on another or others an object, label, role, experience, or set of living conditions that is unwanted, needlessly painful, and detracts from physical or psychological well-being" (Hanna et al., 2000, p. 431). These include sexual assault, hate crimes, and negative media images. Oppression by deprivation involves any action that deprives an individual or group materials or experiences that hinder physical and psychological well-being. Child and elder neglect and depriving an individual of a job promotion due to minority status are examples of oppression by deprivation. Primary oppression involves overt actions, which can include both oppression by force and oppression by deprivation. In secondary oppression, one does not actively engage in the oppressive behavior but benefits from it. In other words, although one does not instigate the oppressive act, neither does he or she object to others who do. Tertiary oppression, also termed internalized racism, occurs when members of the minority group accept dominant messages in an effort to gain approval from the dominant group.

Oppression results in additional stressors for members of an oppressed group and can impact both the physical and psychological well-being of the oppressed individual. Like privilege, oppression can negatively affect the counseling process. It is not unusual for mental health professionals to misdiagnose individuals from oppressed groups because majority norms are used as the standard to which all clients are compared. Additionally, mental health counselors may misinterpret trauma-like symptoms for pathology when these symptoms are reactions to oppressive conditions (Ancis & Chang, 2008). For example, continuous exposure to oppressive conditions can lead to devalued self-worth, self-hatred, feelings of inferiority, isolation, powerlessness, and a range of psychiatric concerns including depression, anxiety, substance abuse, and eating disorders (Ancis, 2004; Ancis & Chang, 2008). Mental health counselors must be aware of oppression in their lives and in the lives of their clients. Awareness and knowledge of oppression and how it functions helps counselors to better understand and conceptualize clients. Such awareness also allows one to better process with clients how oppression influences their self-perception, their behaviors, and their treatment outcome.

Interestingly, one can be a member of both a privileged and an oppressed group simultaneously and experience oppression at various levels by virtue of differing group memberships (e.g., race, sex, gender, sexual identity, class, religious/spiritual affiliation, age, physical and emotional abilities). In this sense, everyone is a potential victim and perpetrator of oppression. Educators and researchers have suggested several strategies for addressing privilege and oppression both in training and in practice. These strategies include increased awareness of yourself as a cultural being, increased knowledge of clients' cultural heritage, fostering empathy, expanding dialogue of invisible minority statuses, and infusing non-Western therapies into instruction (Ancis & Chang, 2008; Chang & Gnilka, 2010; Hays et al., 2004, 2007; Lee & Diaz, 2009).

The inequities that result from systems of privilege and oppression are found in the workplace, the educational system, housing, the media, and legal system. The forces of privilege and oppression make discrimination in the areas of race, ethnicity, gender, religious and spiritual affiliation, ability status, class, and sexual identity a daily reality for members of marginalized groups and for society broadly (Ancis & Chang, 2008). The next section discusses racism and sexism, two forms of discrimination frequently encountered by clients.

RACISM AND SEXISM

Racism and sexism are two examples of -isms, which are prejudices based solely on demographic variables. **Racism** is typically defined as a belief that one's race is superior to another, leading to racial discrimination and abusive behaviors toward members of the "lesser" race. **Sexism** is typically defined as a belief that one sex is superior to another, which leads to sexually discriminatory and abusive behaviors toward members of the other sex. Both racism and sexism have important implications for mental health counselors, clients, and the counseling relationship.

Racism

Some facts about racism and racial discrimination:

- Nearly 90% of hate crimes are perceived to be racially or ethnically motivated (Langton & Planty, 2011).

- Nearly 70% of Hispanic victims of hate crimes are victimized by white offenders (Langton & Planty, 2011).

- Black drivers are more likely to be arrested and ticketed than white drivers during a traffic stop (Eith & Durose, 2011).

- White drivers are more likely to receive a verbal warning from police compared to Hispanic and black drivers (Eith & Durose, 2011).

- Black drivers are three times more likely than white drivers and two times more likely than Hispanic drivers to be searched during a traffic stop (Eith & Durose, 2011).

- White men with a criminal record are more likely to be called back for a job interview compared to black men with no criminal record (Pager, 2003).

- Higher percentages of black and Hispanic students compared to white students report being the target of hate-related words at school (Robers, Zhang, Truman, & Snyder, 2012).

- A higher percentage of Hispanic students compared to white students report having seen hate-related graffiti (Robers et al., 2012).

- In 2008, the homicide victimization rate for blacks was 6 times higher than the rate for whites (Cooper & Smith, 2011).

Varying types of racism include covert, overt, intentional, and unintentional racism (Hall, 2009; Hays & Grimmett, 2010). Covert or unintentional racism can be both conscious and unconscious and therefore may not be immediately discernable. Examples include mental health counselors who consistently refer clients from a specific cultural background and mental health counselors who do not consider the cultural context of their clients when making treatment decisions. By contrast, overt or intentional racism is a willful and visible act against an individual from another race. Examples include making racial slurs or engaging in physical violence against others races.

Jones (2000) developed a framework for understanding racism as it occurs along three levels: institutionalized, personally mediated, and internalized. Institutionalized racism refers to the differential access to goods, services, resources, and opportunities afforded to racial groups. Often, institutionalized racism is a part of societal norms and is sometimes legalized. Access to quality education, gainful employment, quality mental health services, and unearned privileges are examples of the manifestation of institutionalized racism. Personally mediated racism is prejudice held against others that leads to discrimination and can be either intentional or unintentional (i.e., includes acts of commission as well as acts of omission). Examples include providing poor service to individuals from a specific racial group, avoiding a particular racial group, and hate crimes. Internalized racism refers to members of stigmatized races accepting negative messages about their abilities and worth. Embracing "whiteness," self-devaluation, and rejecting your ancestral heritage are examples of internalized racism.

Racism of any type has a profound and lasting impact on individuals who experience it. Mental health counselors must be willing to openly discuss and confront racism with their clients and colleagues who display racist attitudes and beliefs, and clients and colleagues who have been victimized by racist behaviors. Racism affects both whites and members of minority races. For members of a minority race, racism is pervasive and inescapable because it has become normative and entrenched in social structures (i.e., laws, customs, traditions) (Jones, 2000). The cost of racism for whites includes feelings of shame and guilt, anger and denial, irrational fear of other races, and limited exposure to different races (Spanierman, Poteat, Beer, & Armstrong, 2006), which can negatively impact their racial identity development (Hays & Grimmett, 2010).

As great as the cost of racism is for whites, the costs of racism for members of minority racial groups is far greater. The effect of racism on the mental health of individuals from minority races is extensive and well documented. Perceptions of racism and discrimination are negatively associated with both mental and physical health (Pieterse, Todd, Neville, & Carter, 2012; USDHHS, 2001). Individuals who perceive themselves as a victim of racist actions are less physically and mentally healthy. Additionally, membership in a minority race is associated with higher levels of poverty and stress (USDHHS, 2001). Based on a meta-analysis of 66 studies, Pieterse and colleagues (2012) concluded that exposure to racism has a negative impact on the mental health of black Americans, more specifically, "the greater the exposure to and appraised stressfulness of racist events, the greater the likelihood of

CASE STUDY DISCUSSION

Ann has experienced both covert and overt racism during her internship experience. Identify examples of racism that Ann has experienced herself or has witnessed at her internship site. How might Ann address these instances?

reporting mental distress" (p. 6). Pieterse et al. (2012) also provided evidence that racist experiences could be considered within the context of psychological trauma. Black Americans who experienced more racist events reported higher levels of stress, depression, and anxiety that may partially explain the higher rates of hypertension that occur among African Americans. Although racial minorities often are exposed to greater levels of racism, discrimination, and poverty and, therefore, are more susceptible to depression, suicide, substance abuse, violence, anxiety, and chronic and acute stress, they generally have more limited access to medical and mental health services (USDHHS, 2001).

Sexism

Some facts about sexism and sexual discrimination:

- A higher percentage of females compared to males report being the target of rumors at school (Robers et al., 2012).

- There exists a substantial gender gap in wages. Women working full-time earn only 77 cents for every dollar earned by men. This disparity in wages is across occupations, educational levels, and public and private sectors (Maloney, 2010).

- Women tend to be concentrated in midlevel management jobs and tend to be perceived as incapable of managing high-level management positions (Alksnis, Desmarais, & Curtis, 2008).

- The rate for intimate partner victimization for females was 4.3 per 1,000 females compared to 0.8 per 1,000 males in 2008, and about 99% of intimate partner violence against females is committed by male offenders (Catalano, Snyder, & Rand, 2009).

Sexism, like racism, includes institutional and societal barriers. Additionally, sexism includes relational systems of inequality. Gender stereotypes, sexist language, demeaning behaviors, sexually objectifying commentary, the wage gap, and the glass ceiling have been identified as examples of sexism (i.e., sexual discrimination) (Berg, 2006; Chang & Gnilka, 2010). Glick and Fiske (2001) defined two types of sexism: hostile and benevolent sexism. Hostile sexism includes the belief that men are superior to women and, therefore, are more deserving of higher status and power. Hostile sexism leads to power and dominance over women and unfavorable stereotypes of women (Becker & Wright, 2011). In contrast, benevolent sexism represents a chivalrous expression of male dominance and includes three subareas: protective paternalism (women need to be protected), complementary gender differentiation (women are the better sex), and heterosexual intimacy (women fulfill men's romantic needs). Benevolent sexism undermines women and provides justification for gender inequality. In addition, benevolent sexism increases the perception that there are advantages to being a woman, thereby decreasing women's commitment to engage in collective actions to improve their lower status (Becker & Wright, 2011). In contrast, Becker and Wright (2011) found that exposure to hostile sexism decreased women's perception that gender systems are just, reduced the perception of personal advantages of being female, increased negative emotions, and fueled women's desire to engage in collective activities to resist gender inequality.

Daily occurrences of sexual discrimination are thought to contribute to the psychiatric symptoms, psychological distress, and poor mental health sometimes observed in women (Berg, 2006; Borrell et al., 2011; Landrine & Klonoff, 1997). Furthermore, sexism legitimizes and worsens gender inequality (Brandt, 2011). In fact, Landrine and Klonoff (1997) reported that everyday sexism was more predictive of psychiatric symptoms than generic stress. Berg (2006) found that sexism had an effect on patterns of post-traumatic stress disorder (PTSD) symptomatology in women and determined that experiences of everyday sexism contributed to increases in PTSD symptoms. Additionally, Berg (2006) stated that the chronic and cumulative effects of sexist interactions leave women vulnerable to retraumatization.

Of note, women from advantaged social classes with higher levels of education have reported greater perceived sexism (Borrell et al., 2011). Among women who are also members of other marginalized groups, their marginalized group status may bear greater salience for them. For example, an African American female's experience of racism may be the more prominent issue in her life.

Consistent with the multicultural counseling competencies outlined earlier (see Sue et al., 1992), mental health counselors must be aware of their own racist and sexist attitudes and actions and/or experiences as victims of racism and sexism, and how these experiences influence their identity, worldview, and counseling practices. Mental health counselors must possess general knowledge of the impact racism and sexism have on clients. And finally, mental health counselors must develop the skills to confront racism and sexism wherever it is encountered.

Based on the ongoing challenges and struggles with an increased awareness of the systematic intolerance and social injustices in the nation and world (Lee, 2012), scholars argue that social justice counseling should become the "fifth" force in counseling (Ratts, 2009; Ratts, D'Andrea, & Arredondo, 2004). Social justice counseling is the "next evolutionary step in the discipline of multicultural counseling—advancing from understanding the experiences of oppressed or marginalized groups toward social action, with the goal of helping to achieve social equity for these groups" (Lee, 2012, pp. 110–111). In the next section, social justice counseling and advocacy are defined and advocacy is explored as fundamental to the work of clinical mental health counselors.

CASE STUDY DISCUSSION

As a woman, Ann has experienced sexism throughout her life and now experiences it at her internship site. How would you classify Ann's experience of sexism using the categories discussed in the previous section (i.e., hostile and benevolent)? As her supervisor, why would you want Ann to be aware of sexism in her personal and professional life? How might these experiences impact her counseling? How would you help Ann understand the impact of being a female working with male co-counselors in group and other therapeutic settings?

ADVOCACY AND SOCIAL JUSTICE COUNSELING

Advocacy is any "action taken on behalf of clients or the counseling profession to support appropriate policies and standards for the profession; promote individual human worth, dignity, and potential; and oppose or work to change policies and procedures, systemic barriers, long-standing traditions, and preconceived notions that stifle human development" (CACREP, 2009, p. 59). Therefore, any action taken on behalf of a client could be considered client advocacy. Similarly, any action taken on behalf of the counseling profession could be considered professional advocacy.

Social justice refers to a belief in a just world, a world that respects and protects human rights (Chang & Gnilka, 2010; Lee, 2007, 2012). In a study conducted by Hays and her colleagues (2008), a majority of counselor trainees and professional counselors defined social justice as equitable treatment, nondiscrimination, and equitable distribution of advantages and disadvantages. Within the mental health context of social justice, all clients have the right to optimal health and wellness, as well as the right to equitable treatment and fair allocation of societal resources. Advocacy-oriented clinical mental health counselors who engage in social justice counseling take into consideration the impact of racism, discrimination, oppression, privilege, and stereotyping on the mental health of their clients with the goal of ensuring that all individuals have an opportunity to resources such as health care and employment and to achieve optimal mental health (Chang & Gnilka, 2010; Chang et al., 2010; Ratts, 2009).

The American Counseling Association's (ACA) Advocacy Competencies (Lewis, Arnold, House, & Toporek, 2002) and the ACA Governing Council's adoption of these competencies in 2003 undergird the importance of advocacy within the counseling profession. Consistent with other scholars (see Chang et al., 2012; Chang, Hays, & Milliken, 2009; Myers et al., 2002), the ACA Advocacy Competencies include standards that promote both client and professional advocacy. The ACA Advocacy Competencies consist of 43 abilities and skills across two interconnected dimensions: extent of client's involvement (i.e., acting with and acting on behalf of a client) and level of intervention (i.e., client/student, school/community, and/or public arena). These dimensions come together to form six domains: (1) client/student empowerment, (2) client/student advocacy, (3) community collaboration, (4) systems advocacy, (5) public image, and (6) social/political advocacy. These advocacy competencies provide mental health counselors and counselor educators a framework for identifying the skills needed to become effective advocates as well as ascertaining the necessary level at which clients can be supported.

Client Advocacy

Clinical mental health counselors are called on to "advocate with" and "advocate on behalf of" clients. At times it is appropriate for mental health counselors to advocate *with* their clients, and at other times it may be most appropriate to advocate *on behalf of* their clients. Regardless, it is essential to remain mindful of the fact that the needs of clients should drive all advocacy actions (Toporek, Lewis, & Ratts, 2010).

An important aspect of client advocacy is empowerment. **Empowerment** is a process that allows one to become aware of the personal (i.e., oneself as cultural being) and societal issues (i.e., power dynamics, privilege and oppression issues, racism, and sexism) that affect one's life. Additionally, identification of resources needed to challenge these personal, interpersonal, and institutional factors is needed. When empowerment is most effective, changes to both the internal and external conditions that perpetuate social injustice are made (Morrow & Hawxhurst, 1998). Mental health counselors are charged with empowering clients to "understand the nature of privilege and power relations in regard to gender, race, class, ethnicity or sexual orientation in order to achieve empowerment at the personal and interpersonal levels" (Morrow & Hawxhurst, 1998, p. 45). However, empowerment can occur on at least three levels: the personal, the community/organizational, and/or the sociopolitical levels (Hipolito-Delgado & Lee, 2007).

Hipolito-Delgado and Lee (2007) applied the concepts of empowerment theory to school counseling practice. However, their model is easily adapted for mental health counselors engaged in client advocacy. According to these researchers, personal empowerment involves actions that liberate oppressed communities through awareness of critical consciousness, positive identity, and taking social action, a perspective that easily fits within the scope of clinical mental health practice.

Critical consciousness is the awareness of oppression and its impact on the individual, community, and society. As clients develop critical consciousness they are better able to perceive the world and to reject negative messages about their cultural group (Hipolito-Delgado & Lee, 2007). Mental health counselors can facilitate the development of critical consciousness by openly discussing issues of privilege and oppression in the counseling sessions. They can help their clients identify the social, political, and economic factors that affect their issues and concerns.

Positive identity relates to appreciating one's cultural group not in comparison to the dominant group but on its own merit. Positive identity leads to actions that improve the sociopolitical circumstances of the marginalized group (Hipolito-Delgado & Lee, 2007). Mental health counselors can aid clients from marginalized groups in developing a positive identity by encouraging them to explore their cultural heritage. Clinical mental health counselors can encourage their clients to explore their cultural heritage by simply asking them in session questions such as these: "Of what cultural groups are you a member?" "What values do you have, and how have these values informed your life?" "How has membership in your various cultural groups contributed to your well-being?"

Once individuals have developed critical consciousness and a positive identity, they can be encouraged toward social action. Social action requires people to look beyond themselves and to affect change at the community level. This can be accomplished by encouraging clients to join community groups, social advocacy groups, and political rallies (Hipolito-Delgado & Lee, 2007).

Promoting critical consciousness, positive identity, and social action in clients is an example of "advocacy with" clients. In these instances, the mental health counselor is working alongside clients to foster self-awareness and self-advocacy. There are also occasions when it is more appropriate to "advocate on behalf of" clients from marginalized groups. Clients sometimes lack the resources or the access to directly advocate for themselves; therefore, one may need to advocate for them, with their permission. Examples of "advocacy on behalf of" clients include negotiating educational services for a client or helping a client navigate and negotiate access to community services (Lewis et al., 2002).

CASE STUDY DISCUSSION

Ann decides that client advocacy is important to her, and she wants to apply empowerment theory to her counseling. As a part of this process, she begins encouraging her clients to discuss what it is like to be a member of a marginalized group and how this group membership impacts their lives (critical consciousness). She talks about how oppression can affect one's mental health. She encourages them to explore their cultural background. Together, Ann and her clients discuss what they are proud of and what strengths they draw from being a member of their cultural group (positive identity). Finally, Ann is working with her clients to identify ways for them to become involved within the community (social action).

When working with clients from oppressed and marginalized groups, it is an ethical responsibility to engage in client advocacy (see *ACA Code of Ethics* A.7.a.). Mental health counselors must work alongside their clients to foster awareness, knowledge, and skills (see multicultural counseling competencies) so that clients can achieve optimal health and well-being and promote social advocacy. An important and related concept to client advocacy is professional advocacy, which is discussed in the following section.

Professional Advocacy

Professional advocacy, the act of supporting activities that advance the counseling profession, is essential to the work of mental health professionals. Mental health counselors who engage in professional advocacy have the knowledge and skills to influence others to support the counseling profession. Mental health counselors engage in professional advocacy activities because it is often through these efforts that they are afforded the opportunity to provide services to clients and the community. Furthermore, mental health counselors become more effective advocates for clients when other mental health professionals, legislators, and policymakers recognize the profession (Chang, 2012; Chang et al., 2009; Myers et al., 2002; Sweeney, 2012).

The existing research on professional advocacy is quite limited, which is troubling and speaks to the need for additional investigations into the impact of advocacy on the profession. A literature review revealed only two research studies (see Eriksen, 1999; Myers & Sweeney, 2004) that investigated professional advocacy efforts in the counseling profession. Eriksen (1999) used participant observations and interviews with key informants to explore how counselors advocate for the profession. Based on her results, the author identified professional identity (a clear sense of one's role as a counselor) as an essential aspect of the advocacy process. She also delineated six steps for promoting professional advocacy: (1) problem identification (what issue am I going to advocate for?), (2) resource assessment (what resources both internal and external do I have?), (3) strategic planning (involve a small group to help brainstorm both short-term and long-term goals), (4) training advocates (prepare others to assist in your efforts), (5) implementation of the plan (take action and evaluate its effectiveness), and (6) celebration (recognize accomplishments).

Myers and Sweeney (2004) surveyed 71 counseling leaders concerning their advocacy efforts, resources, obstacles, and needs. Participants in this study indicated that whereas a variety of professional advocacy initiatives had been implemented, there was a need for additional resources, interprofessional collaboration, and greater agreement on the importance of professional advocacy for the future of counseling. Study participants identified the public image of counseling and counselors among the most pressing needs. Participants did not believe the public had a clear understanding of counselors or the services provided. This study clearly speaks to the importance of professional advocacy to promote the counseling professional so that counselors may better serve clients. One area within professional advocacy that deserves special attention is mental health policy and legislation, which can help address the concern of public image identified by the participants in the Myers and Sweeney (2004) study.

Although much has been accomplished over the past 30 years to promote the counseling profession, there is still more that needs to be done. To advance the counseling profession, the 20/20: A Vision for the Future of Counseling project was developed with the goal of identifying the most pressing needs of counseling and working collaboratively toward developing solutions to the identified problems. This initiative was cosponsored by the ACA, the American Association of State Counseling Boards (AASCB), and ACA divisions and regions, along with the National Board for Certified Counselors (NBCC), CACREP, the Council on Rehabilitation Education (CORE), the Commission on Rehabilitation Counselor Certification (CRCC), Chi Sigma Iota (CSI), and the National Rehabilitation Counseling Association (NRCA) (Kaplan & Gladding, 2011).

Delegates identified the following guiding principles to strengthen the counseling profession (Kaplan & Gladding, 2011):

1. Sharing a common professional identity is critical for professional counselors.

2. Presenting counseling as a unified profession is beneficial.

3. Working together to improve the public perception and recognition of counseling and to advocate for professional issues strengthens the profession.

4. Licensure portability (i.e., the ability to transfer one's license from one state to another) will benefit professional counselors and strengthen the counseling profession.

5. Expanding and promoting the counseling research base is essential to the efficacy of professional counselors.

6. Focusing on students and prospective students ensures the ongoing health of the counseling profession.

7. Promoting client welfare and client advocacy is a primary focus of the counseling profession.

Delegates agreed on a unified definition of counseling: "Counseling is a professional relationship that empowers diverse individuals, families, and groups to accomplish mental health, wellness, education, and career goals" (Kaplan, Tarvydas, & Gladding, 2014, p. 1). This definition was endorsed by 29 of the 31 participating organizations. The work of this group is significant and an indication that the profession has "finally spoken with one voice and committed themselves to a common vision for the profession. . . . This commitment will help to solidify the identity of professional counseling for the general public and legislators" (Kaplan & Gladding, 2011, p. 371). A better understanding of the counseling profession increases the likelihood of passing legislation that serves the interests of the counseling profession and more importantly serves the interests of clients.

Mental Health Policy and Legislation

Mental health policy and legislation are important to mental health counselors because these policies and laws dictate the scope of practice, determine licensure standards, affect reimbursement, control the ability to work in TRICARE and Veterans Administration (VA) health care systems, and direct VA counselor requirements (ACA, 2008) and, therefore, have a direct and indirect impact on the well-being of clients. Social/political advocacy is one of the six domains of the advocacy competencies (see Lewis et al., 2002). Mental health counselors are called to be social change agents in systems that affect their clients. Recognizing that some of the concerns affecting clients and the profession must be addressed in the larger arena encourages CMH counselors to engage in social/political advocacy. This includes collaborating with allies to lobby legislators and other policymakers (Lewis et al., 2002). Myers and Sweeney (2004) identified mental health policy and legislation as a growth area for professional advocacy, indicating there is an ongoing need for counselors to be directly involved in shaping legislation that impacts the field.

Notable results of professional advocacy efforts have led to all states now credentialing professional counselors (Sweeney, 2012), the U.S. Department of Veterans Affairs (VA) recognition of licensed professional mental health counselor (LPMHC) positions within VA health care facilities, and the Patient Protection and Affordable Care Act that prohibits insurance companies from discriminating against mental health professionals by licensure.

Staying current with legislative changes relevant to mental health counselors can be a daunting task. Within the ACA, there is an Office of Public Policy and Legislation whose mission is to work on federal policy issues in order to advance the counseling profession and to better serve clients. This office works to keep the ACA membership appraised of current federal policy issues and, most importantly, provides training on how to communicate with Congress and influence legislation. There are important considerations when approaching legislators: (a) target legislators who have not yet made up their minds; (b) send messages when they can have the greatest impact (i.e., prior to when the bill is coming up for a vote so that your legislator has time to consider the bill); (c) send a personalized message that explains how a bill affects you; (d) combine advocacy strategies (e.g., send letters to your legislator and send out calls to your colleagues to do the same); and (e) send thank-you messages to legislators who support your issues (ACA, 2008). When communicating with members of Congress it is important to follow a few basic rules: (a) only contact the representative and senators from your state; (b) be brief—no longer than one page for letters and two to four short paragraphs for e-mails; (c) focus on one issue per communication; (d) ask for something specific; (e) keep copies of correspondence for future reference; and (f) follow up (ACA, 2011).

The ACA Office of Public Policy and Legislation warns that advocacy is slow and requires follow-through on advocacy efforts again and again and again. Advocacy does not end once the initial call is made or letter or e-mail is sent. Rather, the end point is the receipt of a concrete, specific response to a request. Furthermore, effective advocacy requires the masses. The more messages a legislator receives the more likely she or he is to take action. Therefore, one request may not convince a legislator to act, but a single request adjoined with the additional requests could indeed make the difference (ACA, 2008).

CASE STUDY DISCUSSION

As a part of her internship, Ann is required to investigate the current federal and state legislation that impacts the counseling profession. A first step is for Ann to visit the Public Policy area of the ACA website (http://counseling.org/PublicPolicy). Here she can see legislative updates, discover current issues, and find resources on how to communicate with Congress. Additionally, she can find contact information for her elected officials.

GLOBAL PERSPECTIVES ON COUNSELING

Given that the core of social justice counseling is a belief that all individuals have a right to optimal health and wellness, it is not surprising to see a growing interest in a global perspective on counseling. Additionally, this global perspective on counseling can be seen as an implementation of multicultural counseling at the macrosystem level (Sells et al., 2007). Unlike the micro level of multicultural counseling integration in which mental health counselors adjust their established mode of treatment based on a cultural understanding of their clients, the macro level of multicultural counseling integration considers the values of the other culture's philosophical understanding of helping and its influence on the structure of counseling (Sells et al., 2007). Hohenshil (2010) credits globalization of communication technology, transportation systems, and business with the global growth of counseling: "The growth of counseling around the world is one of the major and most exciting emerging trends in the counseling profession" (p. 3).

Because of its professional associations, credentialing, number of trained counselors, and number of counseling training programs, it can be argued that the United States has the most advanced counseling system (Hohenshil, 2010), and therefore, CMH counselors are well positioned to provide assistance and consultation to other countries in developing their counseling programs that best meet their mental health needs. In assisting other countries, it is important to be mindful that "one size does not fit all" and each country must develop a program that meets its unique needs and cultural context. Global awareness of counseling is growing and ever-changing. Several writers have described the counseling movement within countries such as Zimbabwe (Richards, Zivave, Govere, Mphande, & Dupwa, 2012), China (Lim, Lim, Michael, Cai, & Schock, 2010), Lebanon (Ayyash-Abdo, Alamuddin, & Mukallid, 2010), Botswana (Stockton, Nitza, & Bhusumane, 2010), Malaysia (See & Ng, 2010), Romania (Szilagyi & Paredes, 2010), Italy (Remley, Bacchini, & Krieg, 2010), Mexico (Portal, Suck, & Hinkle, 2010), Denmark (Dixon & Hansen, 2010), and Honduras (Sells et al., 2007). With a greater understanding of the counseling context in other countries, CMH counselors can develop a worldwide perspective and expand their understanding and knowledge of how cultural context influences behavior.

CONCLUSION

Advocacy for one's clients and for the counseling profession is fundamental to the practice of CMH counseling. Given the relationship between mental health and social injustice (i.e., discrimination and oppression), counselors must become social change agents and confront the social and economic forces that influence the well-being of their clients. In order to provide the best services for their clients and the community, counselors must be willing to challenge the greater social arena through advocacy at the client, community, and public levels.

CMH counselors can become social change agents by working toward self-awareness, awareness of clients' sociocultural background, and development of culturally relevant intervention strategies (see multicultural counseling competencies; Sue et al., 1992). Additionally, CMH counselors will want to develop advocacy skills that promote both client and professional advocacy. The ACA Advocacy Competencies (Lewis et al., 2002) contain 43 competencies that span multiple levels of advocacy across six domains. Mental health counselors will want to be knowledgeable about these competencies and develop strategies for implementing them in their training and practice.

CMH counselors were at the forefront of the fourth wave of counseling, multiculturalism, which helped promote the importance of addressing cultural issues within the counseling relationship and advanced the area of multicultural counseling. Now, counselors are positioned to advance the fifth wave, social justice counseling, and promote equitable treatment and fair allocation of societal resources to all people. CMH counselors have a great opportunity to substantially impact the mental health of all people around the world.

REFERENCES

Alksnis, C., Desmarais, S., & Curtis, J. (2008). Workforce segregation and the gender wage gap: Is "women's" work valued as highly as "men's"? *Journal of Applied Social Psychology, 38,* 1416–1441.

American Counseling Association. (2005). *ACA Code of Ethics.* Alexandria, VA: Author.

American Counseling Association. (2008). *Communicating with Congress: Lessons from recent research.* Retrieved from http://www.counseling.org/PublicPolicy/TP/ResourcesAndReportsMembers/CT2.aspx?ewq = gY-7jc.

American Counseling Association. (2011). *Effective advocacy with members of Congress.* Retrieved from http://counseling.org/PublicPolicy/PDF/Effective_Advocacy-2011.pdf.

American Counseling Association. (2014). *ACA Code of Ethics.* Alexandria, VA: Author.

Ancis, J. R. (2004). (Ed.). *Culturally responsive interventions: Innovative approaches to working with diverse populations.* New York: Brunner-Routledge.

Ancis, J. R., & Chang, C. Y. (2008). Cross-cultural counseling: Oppression. In F. T. L. Leong (Ed.), *Encyclopedia of counseling* (Vol. 3, pp. 1245–1247). Thousand Oaks, CA: Sage.

Ancis, J. R., & Szymanski, D. M. (2001). Awareness of white privilege among white counseling trainees. *The Counseling Psychologist, 29,* 548–569.

Arredondo, P., Toporek, R., Brown, S., Jones, J., Locke, D. C., Sanchez, J., et al. (1996). Operationalization of the multicultural counseling competencies. *Journal of Multicultural Counseling and Development, 24,* 42–78. doi:10.1002/j.2161–1912.1996.tb00288.x

Ayyash-Abdo, H., Alamuddin, R., & Mukallid, S. (2010). School counseling in Lebanon: Past, present, and future. *Journal of Counseling & Development, 88*(1), 13–17.

Balkin, R. S., Schollser, L. A., & Levitt, D. H. (2009). Religious identity and cultural diversity: Exploring the relationships between religious identity, sexism, homophobia and multicultural competence. *Journal of Counseling & Development, 87,* 420–427.

Becker, J. C., & Wright, S. C. (2011). Yet another dark side of chivalry: Benevolent sexism undermines and hostile sexism motivates collective action for social change. *Journal of Personality and Social Psychology, 101,* 62–77. doi:10.1037/a0022615

Bell, L. A. (1997). Theoretical foundations for social justice education. In M. Adams, L. A. Bell, & P. Griffin (Eds.). *Teaching for diversity and social justice: A sourcebook* (pp. 3–15). New York: Routledge.

Berg, S. (2006). Everyday sexism and post-traumatic stress disorder in women. *Violence against Women, 12*(10), 970–988. doi:10.1177/1077801206293082

Borrell, C., Artazcoz, L., Gil-González, D., Pérez, K., Pérez, G., Vives-Cases, C., et al. (2011). Determinants of perceived sexism and their role on the association of sexism with mental health. *Women and Health, 51,* 583–603. doi:10.1080/03630242.2011.608416

Brandt, M. J. (2011). Sexism and gender inequality across 57 societies. *Psychological Science, 22*(11), 1413–1418. doi:10.1177/0956797611420445

Bronfenbrenner, U. (1989). Ecological systems theory. In R. Vasta (Ed.), *Six theories of child development: Revised formulations and current issues* (Vol. 6). Greenwich, CT: JAI Press.

Bronfenbrenner, U. (2005). *Making human beings human: Bioecological perspectives on human development.* Thousand Oaks, CA: Sage.

Catalano, S., Snyder, H., & Rand, M. (2009). *Female victims of violence.* Washington, DC: U.S. Department of Justice.

Chang, C. Y. (2012). Professional advocacy: A professional responsibility. In C. Y. Chang, C. A. Barrio Minton, A. Dixon, J. E. Myers, & T. J. Sweeney (Eds.), *Professional counseling excellence through leadership and advocacy* (pp. 95–107). New York: Routledge.

Chang, C. Y., Barrio Minton, C. A., Dixon, A., Myers, J. E., & Sweeney, T. J. (Eds.). (2012). *Professional counseling excellence through leadership and advocacy.* New York: Routledge.

Chang, C. Y., Crethar, H. C., & Ratts, M. J. (2010). Social justice: A national imperative for counselor education and supervision. *Counselor Education and Supervision, 50,* 82–87.

Chang, C. Y., & Gnilka, P. (2010). Social advocacy: The fifth force in counseling. In D. G. Hays & B. T. Erford (Eds.), *Developing multicultural counseling competency: A systems approach* (pp. 53–71). Columbus, OH: Pearson Merrill Prentice Hall.

Chang, C. Y., Hays, D. G., & Milliken, T. F. (2009). Addressing social justice issues in supervision: A call for client and professional advocacy. *The Clinical Supervisor, 28,* 20–35. doi:10.1080/07325220902855144

Chao, R. C. L. (2012). Racial/ethnic identity, gender role attitudes, and multicultural counseling competence: The role of multicultural counseling training. *Journal of Counseling & Development, 90,* 35–44. doi:10.1111/j.1556-6676.2012.00006.x

Constantine, M. G. (2002). Racism attitudes, white racial identity attitudes, and multicultural counseling competence in school counselor trainees. *Counselor Education and Supervision, 41,* 162–174.

Constantine, M. G., Juby, H. L., & Liang, J. J. C. (2001). Examining multicultural counseling competence and race-related attitudes among white marital and family therapists. *Journal of Marital and Family Therapy, 27,* 353–362.

Cooper, A., & Smith, E. L. (2011). *Homicide trends in the United States, 1980–2008.* Washington, DC: U.S. Department of Justice.

Council for Accreditation of Counseling and Related Educational Programs. (2009). *2009 CACREP Standards.* Alexandria, VA: Author.

Council for Accreditation of Counseling and Related Educational Programs. (2016). *The 2016 Standards.* Retrieved from http://www.cacrep.org/wp-content/uploads/2012/10/2016-CACREP-Standards.pdf.

D'Andrea, M., & Heckman, E. F. (2008). A 40-year review of multicultural counseling outcome research: Outlining a future research agenda for the multicultural counseling movement. *Journal of Counseling & Development, 86,* 356–363.

Dixon, A. L., & Hansen, N. H. (2010). Fortid, nutid, fremtid (past, present, future): Professional counseling in Denmark. *Journal of Counseling & Development, 88,* 38–42.

Doerries, D. B., & Foster, V. A. (2001). Family counselors as school consultants: Where are the solutions? *The Family Journal, 9,* 391–397.

Eith, C., & Durose, M. R. (2011). *Contacts between police and the public, 2008.* Washington, DC: U.S. Department of Justice.

Eriksen, K. (1999). Counselor advocacy: A qualitative analysis of leaders' perceptions, organizational activities, and advocacy documents. *Journal of Mental Health Counseling, 21,* 33–49.

Fuertes, J. N., Bartolomeo, M., & Nichols, C. M. (2001). Future research directions in the study of counselor multicultural competencies. *Journal of Multicultural Counseling and Development, 29,* 3–12.

Gerig, M. S. (2007). *Foundations for mental health and community counseling.* Upper Saddle River, NJ: Pearson Education.

Glick, P., & Fiske, S. T. (2001). An ambivalent alliance: Hostile and benevolent sexism as complementary justifications for gender inequality. *American Psychologist, 56,* 109–118. doi:10.1037/0003-066X.56.2.109

Greene, B. (2005). Psychology, diversity, and social justice: Beyond heterosexism and across the cultural divide. *Counseling Psychological Quarterly, 18,* 295–306.

Greenleaf, A. T., & Williams, J. M. (2009). Supporting social justice advocacy: A paradigm shift towards an ecological perspective. *Journal for Social Action in Counseling and Psychology, 2,* 1–14.

Hall, S. F. (2009). Racism. In American Counseling Association (Ed.), *The ACA encyclopedia of counseling* (pp. 440–441). Alexandria, VA: American Counseling Association.

Hanna, F. J., Talley, W. B., & Guindon, M. H. (2000). The power of perception: Toward a model of cultural oppression and liberation. *Journal of Counseling & Development, 78,* 430–441.

Hays, D. G., Chang, C. Y., & Chaney, M. P. (2008, March). *Becoming social advocates: Counselor trainees' social justice knowledge, attitudes, and behaviors.* Paper presented at the American Counseling Association World Conference, Honolulu, HI.

Hays, D. G., Chang, C. Y., & Dean, J. K. (2004). White counselors' conceptualization of privilege and oppression: Implications for counselor training. *Counselor Education and Supervision, 43,* 242–257.

Hays, D. G., Dean, J. K., & Chang, C. Y. (2007). Addressing privilege and oppression in counselor training and practice: A qualitative analysis. *Journal of Counseling & Development, 85,* 317–324.

Hays, D. G., & Grimmett, M. (2010). Racism and white privilege. In D. G. Hays and B. T. Erford (Eds.), *Developing multicultural counseling competence: A systems approach* (pp. 72–93). Upper Saddle River, NJ: Pearson Education.

Hays, D. G., & McLeod, A. L. (2010). The culturally competent counselor. In D. G. Hays & B. T. Erford (Eds.), *Developing multicultural counseling competence: A systems approach* (pp. 1–31). Upper Saddle River, NJ: Pearson Education.

Hipolito-Delgado, C. P., Cook, J. M., Avrus, E. M., & Bonham, E. J. (2011). Developing counseling students' multicultural competence through the multicultural action project. *Counselor Education and Supervision, 50,* 402–421. doi:10.1002/j.1556-6978.2011.tb01924.x

Hipolito-Delgado, C. P., & Lee, C. C. (2007). Empowerment theory for the professional school counselor: A manifesto for what really matters. *Professional School Counseling, 10,* 327–332.

Hohenshil, T. H. (2010). International counseling introduction. *Journal of Counseling & Development, 88,* 3.

Holcomb-McCoy, C. (2001). Exploring the self-perceived multicultural counseling competence of elementary school counselors. *Professional School Counseling, 4,* 195–201.

Jones, C. P. (2000). Levels of racism: A theoretical framework and a gardener's tale. *American Journal of Public Health, 90,* 1212–1215.

Jones, S. B., Smith, A., & Shelton, K. (2009). Cultural competence. In American Counseling Association (Ed.), *The ACA encyclopedia of counseling* (pp.136–137). Alexandria, VA: American Counseling Association.

Kaplan, D. M., & Gladding, S. T. (2011). A vision for the future of counseling: The 20/20 principles for unifying and strengthening the profession. *Journal of Counseling & Development, 89,* 367–372.

Kaplan, D. M., Tarvydas, V. M., & Gladding, S. T. (2014). 20/20: A vision for the future of counseling: The new consensus definition of counseling. *Journal of Counseling & Development, 92,* 1.

Landrine, H., & Klonoff, E. A. (1997). *Discrimination against women: Prevalences, consequences, remedies.* Thousand Oaks, CA: Sage.

Langton, L., & Planty, M. (2011). *Hate crimes, 2003–2009.* Washington, DC: U.S. Department of Justice.

Lassiter, P., & Chang, C. Y. (2006). Perceived multicultural competency of certified substance abuse counselors. *Journal of Addictions and Offender Counseling, 26,* 73–83.

Lee, C. C. (2007). *Counseling for social justice* (2nd ed.) Alexandria, VA: American Counseling Association.

Lee, C. C. (2012). Social justice as a fifth force in counseling. In C. Y. Chang, C. A. Barrio Minton, A. Dixon, J. E. Myers, & T. J. Sweeney (Eds.), *Professional counseling excellence through leadership and advocacy* (pp. 109–120). New York: Routledge.

Lee, C. C., & Diaz, J. M. (2009). The cross-cultural zone in counseling. In C. C. Lee, D. A. Burnhill, A. L. Butler, C. P. Hipolito-Delgado, M. Humphry, O. Muñoz, et al. (Eds.), *Elements of culture in counseling* (pp. 95–104). Columbus, OH: Pearson.

Lewis, J. A., Arnold, M. S., House, R., & Toporek, R. (2002). *Advocacy competencies.* Retrieved from http://www.counseling.org/Resources/Competencies/Advocacy_Competencies.pdf.

Lewis, J. A., Lewis, M. D., Daniels, J. A., & D'Andrea, M. J. (2003). *Community counseling: Empowerment strategies for a diverse society* (3rd ed.). Pacific Grove, CA: Brooks/Cole.

Lewis, J. A., Lewis, M. D., Daniels, J. A., & D'Andrea, M. J. (2011). *Community counseling: A multicultural-social justice perspective* (4th ed.). Belmont, CA: Brooks/Cole.

Lim, S. L., Lim, B. K. H., Michael, R., Cai, R., & Schock, C. K. (2010). The trajectory of counseling in China: Past, present, and future trends. *Journal of Counseling & Development, 88*(1), 4–8.

Maloney, C. B. (2010). *Invest in women, invest in America: A comprehensive review of women in the U.S. economy.* Washington, DC: A report by the majority staff of the Joint Economic Committee.

Manese, J. E., Wu, J. T., & Nepomuceno, C. A. (2001). The effect of training on multicultural counseling competencies: An exploratory study over a ten-year period. *Journal of Multicultural Counseling and Development, 30,* 316–322.

Manuppelli, L. (2000). *Exploring the therapist's understanding of white privilege: A phenomenological analysis of focus group discussions with culturally diverse therapists.* Unpublished doctoral dissertation, St. Mary's University, San Antonio, TX.

Morrow, S. L., & Hawxhurst, D. M. (1998). Feminist therapy: Integrating political analysis in counseling and psychotherapy. *Women & Therapy, 21,* 37–50.

Myers, J. E., & Sweeney, T. J. (2004). Advocacy for the counseling profession: Results of a national survey. *Journal of Counseling & Development, 82,* 466–471.

Myers, J. E., Sweeney, T. J., & White, V. E. (2002). Advocacy for counseling and counselors: A professional imperative. *Journal of Counseling & Development, 80,* 394–402.

Pager, D. (2003). The mark of a criminal record. *American Journal of Sociology, 108*(5), 937–975.

Pedersen, P. B. (1991). Multiculturalism as a generic approach to counseling. *Journal of Counseling & Development, 70,* 6–12.

Pedersen, P. B. (Ed.). (1999). *Multiculturalism as a fourth force.* Philadelphia: Taylor & Frances.

Penn, S. L., & Post, P. B. (2012). Investigating various dimensions of play therapists' self-reported multicultural counseling competence. *International Journal of Play Therapy, 21*(1), 14–29. doi:10.1037/a0026894

Pieterse, A. L., Todd, N. R., Neville, H. A., & Carter, R. T. (2012). Perceived racism and mental health among black American adults: A meta-analytic review. *Journal of Counseling Psychology, 59,* 1–9. doi:10.1037/a0026208

Portal, E. L., Suck, A. T., & Hinkle, J. S. (2010). Counseling in Mexico: History, current identity, and future trends. *Journal of Counseling & Development, 88*(1), 33–37.

Ratts, M. J. (2009). Social justice counseling—Toward the development of a fifth force among counseling paradigms. *Journal of Humanistic Education, Counseling, and Development, 48,* 160–172.

Ratts, M. J., D'Andrea, M., & Arredondo, P. (2004). Social justice counseling: 'Fifth force' in field. *Counseling Today, 47,* 28–30.

Rawls, J. A. (1971). *A theory of justice.* Cambridge, MA: Harvard University Press.

Remley, T. P., Bacchini, E., & Krieg, P. (2010). Counseling in Italy. *Journal of Counseling & Development, 88,* 28–32.

Richard, L., Gauvin, L., & Raine, K. (2011). Ecological models revisited: Their uses and evolution in health promotion over two decades. *Annual Review of Public Health, 32,* 307–326. doi:10.1146/annurev-publhealth-031210-101141

Richards, K. A. M., Zivave, A. T., Govere, S. M., Mphande, J., & Dupwa, B. (2012). Counseling in Zimbabwe: History, current status, and future trends. *Journal of Counseling & Development, 90,* 102–106.

Ritter, K. B., & Chang, C. Y. (2002). Play therapists' self-perceived multicultural competence and adequacy of training. *International Journal of Play Therapy, 11,* 103–116.

Robers, S., Zhang, J., Truman, J., & Snyder, T. (2012). *Indicators of school crime and safety: 2011.* Washington, DC: U.S. Department of Justice.

See, C. M., & Ng, K. M. (2010). Counseling in Malaysia: History, current status, and future trends. *Journal of Counseling & Development, 88,* 18–22.

Sells, J. N., Giordano, F. G., Bokar, L., Klein, J., Sierra, G. P., & Thume, B. (2007). The effect of Honduran counseling practices on the North American counseling profession: The power of poverty. *Journal of Counseling & Development, 85,* 431–439.

Spanierman, L. B., Poteat, V. P., Beer, A. M., & Armstrong, P. I. (2006). Psychosocial costs of racism to whites: Identifying profiles with cluster analysis. *Journal of Counseling Psychology, 53,* 434–441.

Stockton, R., Nitza, A., & Bhusumane, D. B. (2010). The development of professional counseling in Botswana. *Journal of Counseling & Development, 88*(1), 9–12.

Stormshak, E. A., & Dishion, T. J. (2002). An ecological approach to child and family clinical and counseling psychology. *Clinical Child and Family Psychology Review, 5,* 197–215.

Sue, D. W., Arredondo, P., & McDavis, R. J. (1992). Multicultural counseling competencies and standards: A call to the profession. *Journal of Counseling & Development, 70,* 477–486.

Sweeney, T. J. (2012). Professional advocacy: Being allowed to do good. In C. Y. Chang, C. A. Barrio Minton, A. Dixon, J. E. Myers, & T. J. Sweeney (Eds.), *Professional counseling excellence through leadership and advocacy* (pp. 81–93). New York: Routledge.

Szilagyi, A., & Paredes, D. M. (2010). Professional counseling in Romania: An introduction. *Journal of Counseling & Development, 88*(1), 23–27.

Toporek, R. L., Lewis, J. A., & Ratts, M. J. (2010). The ACA Advocacy Competencies: An overview. In M. J. Ratts, R. L. Toporek, & J. A. Lewis (Eds.), *ACA Advocacy Competencies: A social justice framework for counselors* (pp. 11–20). Alexandria, VA: American Counseling Association.

Trickett, E. J. (2009). Multilevel community-based culturally situated interventions and community impact: An ecological perspective. *American Journal of Community Psychology, 43,* 257–266. doi:10.1007/s10464–009–9227-y

Trickett, E. J., Beehler, S., Deutsch, C., Green, L. W., Hawe, P., McLeroy, K., et al. (2011). Advancing the science of community-level interventions. *American Journal of Public Health, 101,* 1410–1419. doi:10.2105/AJPH.2010.300113

U.S. Department of Health and Human Services. (2001). *Mental health: Culture, race and ethnicity. A supplement to mental health: A report of the Surgeon General.* Rockville, MD: Author.

Continuum of Care

Amy Banner

Upon completion of this chapter, you will be able to do the following:

1. Understand the modalities through which counseling services are provided across the clinical mental health (CMH) counseling continuum of care

2. Articulate the history of the CMH counseling continuum of care

3. Describe the ethical and developmental aspects of the CMH counseling continuum of care

4. Explain the services, settings, and roles of counselors across the CMH counseling continuum of care

5. Understand the professional issues affecting the CMH counseling continuum of care

CONTINUUM OF CARE: ONE SIZE DOES NOT FIT ALL

You have chosen to become a clinical mental health counselor, at least in part, because you want to be helpful to others. Often, however, beginning professionals may not realize the many options available across the CMH counseling continuum of care. As Gerig (2007) stated, "The nature of the profession continues to be one of mental health care's best-kept secrets" (p. 109). This statement is especially true for counseling students, who commonly are asked by friends and family, "Now, what is it that counselors do, exactly?" and "Where can you find a job with that degree?" Often, students themselves struggle to answer these questions and are uncertain about which client population or service setting fits best for them. It is important for students to have an understanding of the different modalities, services, and settings of CMH counseling so that they are aware of the services available to their clients and can make informed internship and career choices. The goal of this chapter, then, is to orient students to the CMH counseling continuum of care in such a way that highlights the broad variety of services available to clients and career options available to students.

MODALITIES OF THE CMH COUNSELING CONTINUUM OF CARE

To fully understand the CMH counseling continuum of care, it is important to be familiar with the modalities through which counseling services are provided across the continuum of care. These modalities are individual, couple, family, and group counseling. Additionally, client advocacy may be considered a modality, but that topic will not be addressed here because it was discussed fully in Chapter 3. Ideally, the client's needs and the type of services being provided determine the modality used. For example, a recently divorced mother of young children grieving her marriage and struggling to discipline her children may benefit most from a combination of modalities, such as individual counseling to address her grief and an educational support group for single parents. In contrast, the family of a gay teenager struggling to understand and support their son may need services delivered through the modality of family counseling in order to reach their goals. Additionally, both they and their counselor may wish to engage in advocacy work toward societal change that would benefit their son. Modalities may be used independently or in combination, depending on clients' presenting problem and goals, and each modality serves an important role in the continuum of care.

Individual Counseling

Typically, when one thinks of counseling, the individual modality comes to mind (Gerig, 2007). Individual counseling can be described as a professional relationship designed to empower an individual to accomplish mental health, wellness, education, and career goals (American Counseling Association, 2010). This modality is appropriate for children, adolescents, and adults and may be used to address any number of presenting problems. Ideally, the client's counseling goals and the length of time required to attain these goals determines the duration of counseling. If a client is paying for counseling sessions by billing an insurance company, it is typical for managed care policies to initially allow for a limited number of sessions, with the possibility of additional sessions being approved. If further sessions are needed, clients may choose to pay out of pocket, or, in some cases, the counselor may choose to offer pro bono or income-based fee-for-service sessions (Glosoff, 1998).

Regardless of the duration of individual counseling, the process should include initial, working, and termination stages (Gladding & Newsome, 2010). Throughout each of these stages, counselors must be aware of clients' current level of readiness for change (precontemplation, contemplation, preparation, action, maintenance) so that interventions can be appropriately tailored (Prochaska & DiClemente, 1984). In other words, it is important for counselors to meet clients where they are to best facilitate growth.

In addition to tailoring interventions to clients' level of readiness for change, counselors must ensure that their clinical approaches are grounded in theory or empirical evidence (American Counseling Association, 2014). Whether counselors use one theory, choose their theoretical approach based on each client's needs, or integrate several approaches, theory serves as a guide. Theory and research facilitate case conceptualization, explain the etiology of clients' problems, and provide a rationale for how clients can heal. Because all of the major counseling theories have been proven effective, some counselors choose to draw on the common factors of healing in their work with clients (Hauser & Hays, 2010).

The common factors approach was first proposed in 1936 by Rosenzweig, who believed that all therapeutic approaches were equally effective and shared common elements of healing. Since then, many researchers have reported results that support Rosenzweig's theory (Hauser & Hays, 2010). At least 89 distinct common factors have been identified and include warmth, acceptance, empathic understanding, exploration of emotional issues, catharsis, insight, and acquisition of new behaviors (Hauser & Hays, 2010). These common factors inform the therapeutic process.

Regardless of the approach used, counselors work to create safe, confiding, therapeutic relationships through the individual counseling modality. Perhaps this is made easier because the counselor's sole focus is on one person, a benefit of this modality, in contrast to multiple people seen in couple, family, or group counseling (Gerig, 2007). Alternatively, a potential limitation of the individual counseling modality is isolation from the client's social contexts and culture. If this is a concern for a particular client, counselors may want to consider using a theoretical approach that encourages the involvement of those important to the client at strategic points of the counseling process. For example, the theory behind narrative therapy posits that clients' growth and change can be solidified and validated when clients include important others as audience members toward the end of their counseling process (Payne, 2003). Approaches such as this have the additional benefit of acknowledging the importance of relational influence in clients' lives, an acknowledgement often lacking in today's individualistic society. When clients' presenting problems are social in nature, counselors may choose to use a group or family counseling modality, both of which allow for the counseling process to occur within a social setting.

Group Counseling

The Association for Specialists in Group Work (ASGW), a division of the ACA, defines group work as

> a broad professional practice involving the application of knowledge and skill in group facilitation to assist an interdependent collection of people to reach their mutual goals which may be intrapersonal, interpersonal, or work-related. The goals of the group may include the accomplishment of tasks related to work, education, personal development, personal and interpersonal problem solving, or remediation of mental and emotional disorders. (ASGW, 2000, pp. 329–330)

As may be evident from this definition, group counseling is an appropriate modality for clients with a wide range of goals. Indeed, there are several types of group modalities. The ASGW (2000) describes four types of groups: task and work groups, psychoeducation groups, counseling groups, and psychotherapy groups.

Each of these group types apply the principles of human development and functioning using cognitive, affective, behavioral, or systemic interventions in a group setting (ASGW, 2000). The four group types differ in goals addressed and clients served. Task and work groups "promote efficient and effective accomplishment of group tasks among people who are gathered to accomplish group task goals" (ASGW, 2000, p. 330). Psychoeducation groups, also known as teaching groups, "promote personal and interpersonal growth and development and the prevention of future difficulties among people who may be at risk for the development of personal or interpersonal problems or who seek enhancement of personal qualities and abilities" (ASGW, 2000, p. 330). The recently divorced mother struggling to discipline her children who was mentioned earlier in this chapter might benefit from a psychoeducation group designed to provide education, training, and support for single parents. Counseling groups, or process groups, "address personal and interpersonal problems of living and promote personal and interpersonal growth and development among people who may be experiencing transitory maladjustment, who are at risk for the development of personal or interpersonal problems, or who seek enhancement of personal qualities and abilities" (ASGW, 2000, p. 331). Counseling groups may be appropriate for a broad range of clients and presenting problems. One example of a group that fits this description is a grief counseling group. Typically, members of grief counseling groups are individuals who have experienced a significant and painful loss and who desire a place to experience and process their loss and grief with people who have similar experiences. Finally, psychotherapy groups "address personal and interpersonal problems of living, remediate perceptual and cognitive distortions or repetitive patterns of dysfunctional behavior, and promote personal and interpersonal growth and development among people who may be experiencing severe and/or chronic maladjustment" (ASGW, 2000, p. 331). Groups designed for clients struggling to recover from addiction fit this description. Often, psychotherapy groups are distinguished from counseling groups based on the severity of presenting issues of group members, but this distinction is often blurred in practice.

Regardless of type, group logistics are important to group success. Group counselors must make decisions about the duration and frequency of group meetings, the size of the group, and whether it will be an open or closed group (Yalom & Leszcz, 2005). Open groups add new members over time, and closed groups do not add members once the group has started. In addition, groups tend to progress through predictable developmental stages as described by Tuckman (1965) and Tuckman and Jensen (1977):

- forming-group members stick to "safe" topics and keep interactions formal;
- storming-group members acknowledge and attend to tension, conflict, and roles;
- norming-group cohesion develops and goals are formulated;

- performing-group members take risks, solve problems, and are more responsible for group process resulting in group productivity; and

- adjourning-group members reflect upon their experience and learning and say goodbye to the individuals in the group and the group itself.

Throughout the group process, counselors are careful to modify interventions so that they are appropriate for the group's current stage (Thomas & Pender, 2008).

According to Irvin Yalom, a leader in the application and study of group counseling, therapeutic factors contribute to positive outcomes in the group counseling modality. These therapeutic factors are instillation of hope, universality, imparting information, altruism, the corrective recapitulation of the primary family group, development of socializing techniques, imitative behavior, interpersonal learning, group cohesiveness, catharsis, and existential factors (Yalom & Leszcz, 2005). These therapeutic factors highlight some of the advantages of the group modality of counseling. Clients in groups have social support and vicarious learning opportunities that are not readily available through individual counseling. Further, the intimate interaction with others who are experiencing similar struggles exposes clients to a wide variety of ways of being that may serve to enhance clients' flexibility and openness. For example, a group for parents who have lost children to a terminal illness may allow participants to share their experiences, struggles, and what has helped them cope. Of course, there also are disadvantages of the group counseling modality. The group modality is not suitable for all clients. Clients who are not ready to participate appropriately within a group have the potential to disrupt the group process for others, or they may have a negative experience themselves. In addition, counselors running groups must always remember they cannot guarantee that all group members will keep the group process confidential. So, whereas the counselor may maintain confidentiality, group members may not. For this reason, counselors must inform group members of this reality before the group experience begins and should reiterate the importance of this policy frequently and as needed (Thomas & Pender, 2008).

Couple and Family Counseling

As with the individual and group modalities of counseling, couple and family counseling may be used to enhance clients' well-being and prevent future problems or to intervene where problems already exist. In other words, it is appropriate for those who wish to enhance their romantic and/or familial relationships as well as for those experiencing problems in these relationships. To encourage growth, couple and family counselors may work with clients toward improving communication, conflict resolution, and assertiveness within relationships. At the other end of the continuum, couple and family counselors help clients heal from problems associated with infidelity, work/life balance, parenting, grief, blended families, family violence, or substance abuse, to name a few. The settings in which this modality of counseling occurs are broad, including clinical mental health agencies, government agencies, employee assistance programs, faith communities, independent practice, inpatient settings, and substance abuse treatment centers (International Association of Marriage and Family Counselors, 2012).

When working in the couple and family counseling modality, it is especially important for counselors to take a systemic and developmental perspective. To have a systemic perspective means that counselors recognize that couple and family relationships are affected by the systems in which they exist. Examples of systems that often affect couples and families are those of extended family, social networks, work and school, religious organizations, neighborhoods, broader community, government, culture, language, and economics (Bronfenbrenner, 1989; McGoldrick & Carter, 2003). To have a developmental perspective means that counselors recognize that couples and families are affected by their developmental stages.

McGoldrick and Carter (2003) present an expanded family life cycle that acknowledges complex layers of influences on a family's ability to navigate developmental transitions. They discuss both "vertical" and "horizontal" stressors. Vertical stressors are those family patterns, myths, secrets, and legacies that are transmitted across generations. Horizontal stressors are those events, both predictable and unpredictable, that a family experiences as it moves through time. Families who have high amounts of vertical stress may find it very difficult to successfully transition through the horizontal stressors that naturally occur as the family moves through its life cycle. The stages of the family life cycle are leaving home as single, young adults; joining families through marriage as a new couple; families with young children; families with adolescents; launching children and moving on; and families in later life. Each of these stages involves emotional processes and requires second-order changes for success (Carter & McGoldrick, 2005).

Some families will progress through the life cycle stages more smoothly than others. In addition, one stage may be far more difficult than others for the same family. Unfortunately, progressing through the family life cycle often is more difficult for families who remain less accepted by society. For example, families in poverty or families who have parents of the same sex or of different racial or ethnic backgrounds may experience higher levels of stress and, thus, may find the life cycle stages more challenging, primarily as a function of systemic oppression. To better understand the continuum of care, it is important to understand the historical context within which this emerged.

HISTORY OF THE CMH COUNSELING CONTINUUM OF CARE

Prior to 1963, only a minority of individuals and families could afford the high cost of mental health services. Thus, public psychiatric hospitals were the only option available to those who were poor and experiencing mental health problems (Staton et al., 2007). Because they were "woefully ill-equipped, underfunded, and understaffed, these overcrowded and dehumanizing institutions became little more than human warehouses" (Staton et al., 2007, p. 17). The public and many in the mental health field began to protest these inhumane conditions and demand better mental health services. Due in part to these advocacy efforts, President John F. Kennedy signed the Community Mental Health Centers Act of 1963 (Lewis, Lewis, Daniels, & D'Andrea, 2011). The purpose of this act was twofold, to deinstitutionalize patients of public psychiatric hospitals and to provide mental health services within the communities where clients live and work.

To this end, the Community Mental Health Centers Act mandated that all states create community mental health centers within each catchment area (geographic area of 75,000–200,000 residents) and provided the federal funding to build these centers (Gladding & Newsome, 2010; Lewis et al., 2011). The ultimate goal was that community members' mental health needs would be met fully in the least restrictive manner possible through a full continuum of mental health services provided by community mental health centers nationwide (MacCluskie & Ingersoll, 2010).

In order to accomplish this goal, the continuum of mental health services was implemented and continues today. This continuum of care may be considered as an arc, beginning with the least restrictive services and continuing on to higher levels of assistance as needed. Originally, services included in the clinical mental health counseling continuum were education, prevention, and consultation; outpatient; partial hospitalization/intensive outpatient; inpatient; and emergency and crisis. Today, these services still exist, and the continuum has been expanded to include additional services such as in-home, residential, and aftercare. At its birth, this continuum of care was revolutionary because of its recognition of the importance of prevention and the promotion of enhanced well-being (Staton et al., 2007).

ETHICAL AND DEVELOPMENTAL ASPECTS OF THE CMH COUNSELING CONTINUUM OF CARE

Further, the emphasis on providing services in the least restrictive manner possible across the continuum of care aligns with the moral principles on which the American Counseling Association's Code of Ethics is based (Kitchener, 1984). As discussed in Chapter 2, the principles of autonomy and justice are particularly relevant here. The principle of autonomy requires counselors to allow for and encourage clients' independence and freedom of choice unless this would harm clients or others. The principle of justice requires counselors to treat clients fairly specific to their needs. The clinical mental health counseling continuum of care is intended to honor these principles by providing counselors with a way to meet clients' mental health needs in a just manner while providing the highest level of client autonomy possible. For example, a woman who is losing sleep, feeling irritable, and having difficulty concentrating because of work-related anxiety is most appropriate for outpatient services, whereas a woman who consumes a combination of narcotics and three bottles of wine each night in order to "black out," who is withdrawn from friends and family, who has ceased to feel that she has a purpose, and who is on the verge of losing her job may require inpatient services.

As the previous example illustrates, CMH counselors recognize that different clients often have vastly different needs, that the same client can have different needs at different points in life, and that these needs are directly influenced by developmental and cultural realities and current life circumstances. Accordingly, the continuum of care allows counselors to help clients of all ages, life stages, and abilities with varying degrees of services using individual, group, couple, family, and advocacy as modalities of service provision. Thus, the roles and functions that counselors may fulfill and the services they may provide vary greatly and are determined by the continuum of care setting in which they work.

SERVICES, SETTINGS, AND ROLES ACROSS THE CMH COUNSELING CONTINUUM OF CARE

The services offered and modalities used across different work settings are described in the following sections. This information provides an understanding of each aspect of the continuum of care and an orientation to the typical roles, functions, challenges, and benefits associated with each setting. Because each state chooses the specific way in which it provides the full continuum of care within its communities, services differ from state to state. Further, the settings in which CMH counseling services can be provided are virtually unlimited. Given these two realities, it is beyond the scope of this chapter to describe each and every possible service and setting. The focus, then, is not to be exhaustive but to discuss commonly offered services and modalities and the typical settings in which they are delivered, beginning with the least restrictive level of care and working through the continuum.

Prevention and Education Services

Of all the services across the clinical mental health counseling continuum of care, prevention and education are both the least restrictive and the most cost efficient (Gerig, 2007). These services are proactive and wellness-oriented in that they are designed to promote mental health and to prevent serious problems from occurring (Gladding & Newsome, 2010; Lewis et al., 2011). By helping those in the public and the broader community, counselors who provide prevention and education services have an opportunity to increase public awareness of what CMH counselors have to offer and to decrease the stigma that is too often associated with those who seek counseling (Lewis et al., 2011).

Any program that provides information, training, and/or skills important to overall well-being may be considered a prevention and education service. Often, prevention and education services are provided using the group modality and can include psychoeducational groups, training and skill-building programs, support groups, independent living groups, physical health groups, and community education programs. The settings in which prevention and education services may be offered vary as well. Possible examples include mental health agencies, courthouses, faith community buildings, inpatient settings, local Department of Human Services offices, school buildings, college campuses, hospitals, and town halls.

As an example, consider a psychoeducational group for coparenting designed for those who share children but are not together as a couple. The group might meet for 2 hours in the early evening once a week for 6 weeks and use a combination of printed educational materials, instructional videos, skills training, practice exercises, and group processing to teach participants the communication, coping, discipline, and parenting skills they need to cooperate with each other as parents. Some participants might self-refer to the program whereas others might be legally mandated to attend.

As the previous example indicates, counselors who provide prevention and education services often fulfill other roles and functions as part of their full-time work. One reason for this is that, unfortunately, there are financial challenges to providing prevention and education services. Despite Benjamin Franklin's assertion that "an ounce of prevention is worth a pound of cure," most insurance companies refuse to pay for mental health services unless the client's mental health concerns meet clinical levels of severity. In other words, insurance companies will only pay for those who have a diagnosable mental disorder to receive mental health services (Staton et al., 2007). These reimbursement policies are reactive instead of proactive and illness-oriented in nature; thus, they contrast with the proactive, prevention- and wellness-oriented philosophy of CMH counselors. This is an example of an external reality that has the potential to negatively affect the well-being of clients and of the counseling profession. As such, it provides an opportunity for client and professional advocacy. Until change is brought about by advocacy efforts in this area, funding for prevention and education services must come from grants provided by a variety of private businesses, public organizations, federal agencies, and/or religious organizations (Staton et al., 2007).

Outpatient Services

When clients need more than prevention and education services, or when such services are not available, outpatient counseling services become appropriate. Typically, the goal of outpatient counseling is to improve emotional, psychological, behavioral, and relational health (Gladding & Newsome, 2010). Outpatient services are appropriate for those with a wide range of levels of distress, from those adjusting to a developmental change to those who struggle with persistent emotional, psychological, and behavioral problems (Staton et al., 2007). Further, outpatient client populations may include children, adolescents, adults, couples, and families with presenting problems that are virtually innumerable. Clients may initiate services on their own or may be referred. Often, teachers, school counselors, or the Department of Children's Services refer children and adolescents for outpatient counseling. Adults often are referred by employers, the Department of Children's or Human Services, court systems, or as follow-up services after completion of inpatient, partial hospitalization, or intensive outpatient services.

Counseling modalities used to provide outpatient services include individual, group, couple, family, and advocacy, depending on clients' needs and presenting problems. In addition to counseling services, outpatient services at many mental health agencies include case management and psychotropic medication services for those who need them. Thus, counselors who provide outpatient services should be prepared to collaborate with a broader treatment team consisting of case managers, social workers, psychiatric nurses, and psychiatrists.

Whereas the most usual setting for outpatient services is community mental health agencies, outpatient services are provided in a wide variety of settings. For example, outpatient services may be provided at county courthouses, schools, neighborhood community centers, hospitals, and private practices to name but a few. Many outpatient services, particularly in agency settings, continue to be supplemented by federal funds through grants that are distributed by each state. However, most outpatient services are funded primarily by state and local funds, by reimbursement for services through clients' Medicare or Medicaid, and by self-paying clients.

The outpatient services described thus far may be considered general, or typical, outpatient services. They serve a wide variety of client populations and needs. In order to meet the unique needs of distinct client groups and to address specific presenting problems, many communities use specialized outpatient services. Examples include trauma services for children and adolescents, private practice for individuals and families, diversion programs to provide counseling or rehabilitation services rather than punitive consequences for those convicted of a crime, group counseling for those struggling with substance abuse, psychoeducational groups on stress management, or a wide variety of other possible outpatient services.

In-Home Services

Also known as "home-based" or "mobile" services, in-home services are appropriate when clients need more intervention and support than is provided by traditional weekly outpatient counseling sessions. At times, in-home services are provided to adult clients; typically, however, they are provided to children, adolescents, and their families (Evans et al., 2003). Usually, the children and adolescents referred to in-home services are experiencing significant emotional, psychological, and/or behavioral problems. For example, clients of in-home services report suicidal ideation, depression, verbal aggression, anxiety, and destruction of property (Evans et al., 2003). For these and other reasons, these children and adolescents often are at risk for removal from their homes and placement in inpatient settings, group homes, or foster care.

In order to prevent home disruption and to stabilize these children, adolescents, and their families, counselors who provide in-home services typically work with each family for several hours per week. Often, families receiving in-home services have access to support from their counselor or from an on-call counselor 24 hours a day, 7 days a week. Interventions are designed to teach coping and communication skills, to improve family relationships, to connect families with community resources (Evans et al., 2003), to empower families and their children or adolescents (Gladding & Newsome, 2010), to provide families with appropriate parenting and discipline skills, and to address underlying problems. Typically, services last for 4 to 6 weeks, but some in-home service programs are designed to be long-term. Two primary types of in-home services for children, adolescents, and their families are family preservation programs and multisystemic therapy programs. By nature, in-home services are designed to address the external realities that affect children, adolescents, and their families negatively (Gladding & Newsome, 2010).

Counselors who provide in-home services are able to interact with clients in their natural environments instead of in an office. This provides opportunities for real-life problems to be assessed and addressed in the moment and in the context in which they occur, a significant benefit of in-home work. Counselors are able to become more familiar with their clients' realities and, as a result, may experience enhanced empathy for them. Additionally, the trust that can be built between in-home counselors and their clients may be enhanced. In order to ensure that the relationship between in-home counselors and their clients remains professional and effective, counselors providing these services must pay special attention to professional boundaries. In fact, in-home counselors are presented with a variety of factors that are not present for counselors working in traditional outpatient settings.

There are many benefits and challenges of providing in-home services; ultimately, this type of service serves the important purpose of ensuring that children and adolescents are able to function at a level that allows them to remain in their own homes, schools, and communities. If these services are not successful, children and adolescents may be referred to partial hospitalization or intensive outpatient services or inpatient services, which are also available to adults.

Partial Hospitalization Programs (PHPs) and Intensive Outpatient (IOP) Services

Partial hospitalization and intensive outpatient services are appropriate for clients who need a level of care between outpatient and inpatient services. Often, such clients are able to maintain safety (i.e., are not suicidal or homicidal) and do not require 24-hour mental health services but have a level of impaired functioning that requires more structured services than outpatient services provide.

Sometimes, clients enter into partial and intensive services because outpatient or in-home services are not fully able to meet their mental health needs. At other times, clients are referred to these services as a "step-down" or "aftercare" service following completion of inpatient services. Thus, although these services are discussed before inpatient services in this chapter, they may be appropriate either before or after inpatient care. In addition, individuals who live in residential or group home facilities often receive services in PHPs or IOPs (MacCluskie & Ingersoll, 2001).

At times, these services are referred to as day programs (Staton et al., 2007). Although PHPs and IOPs are considered to be similar, there are minor differences between the two. Both programs provide structured and intensive treatment, but IOPs usually are the less restrictive of the two because they are designed for individuals who are able to function with slightly less structure and assistance. Although there is variance across programs, it is typical, for example, for an IOP client to participate in service for 3–4 hours a day, for 2–3 days each week. In contrast, it is common for a PHP client to receive services for 8 hours per day, 5 days per week, returning home for evenings and weekends.

Both PHPs and IOPs use a variety of modalities for service delivery, including individual and group counseling, psych-education, life- and social-skills training, psychotropic medication, and recreational therapy (Gladding & Newsome, 2010; MacCluskie & Ingersoll, 2001; Station et al., 2007). PHPs and IOPs may be housed within clinical mental health agencies or in other settings such as inpatient psychiatric settings, medical hospital settings, and schools. Often, PHPs and IOPs provide specialized services for specific presenting problems and/or specific populations. For example, IOPs designed to treat substance abuse and dependence employ 12-step work, relapse prevention skills, medication management, and family counseling or psychoeducation (Gladding & Newsome, 2010).

Inpatient Services

Because inpatient services are highly restrictive, they are reserved for clients with mental health problems that qualify as acute and severe (Gerig, 2007). For example, individuals may be appropriate for inpatient services when they are a danger to themselves or others, are experiencing acute delusions or hallucinations, or are having recurrent and persistent panic attacks. Inpatient services are available for adults, adolescents, and children. The goal of inpatient services is to stabilize clients quickly so that they are able to benefit from less restrictive mental health services. To that end, the average duration of inpatient services is less than 8 days (Gladding & Newsome, 2010).

Clients receive a medical, psychiatric, and psychosocial assessment either upon or very soon after admission and are assigned to a bed. Commonly, a team of psychiatrists, psychologists, nurses, and clinical mental health counselors performs the assessments. Once each part of the assessment is complete, a diagnosis is given and a treatment plan formed (Gladding & Newsome, 2010). If appropriate, psychotropic medications may be given to the client. If stable enough, clients may be encouraged to attend group sessions on their first day. Because clients tend to enter into inpatient services in the midst of a mental health crisis, however, they may spend most of their first 12 to 24 hours stabilizing and resting. Also for these reasons, clients are monitored especially closely for the first 24 hours of their stay.

If clients do not participate in interventions during their first day, they will be strongly encouraged to begin doing so immediately on their second day. Typically, inpatient interventions include individual, group, and family counseling; psychoeducation groups; social- and life-skills groups; support groups; and recreation therapy (Corry & Jewell, 2001; Gladding & Newsome, 2010). Because it is difficult to make significant emotional, psychological, and behavioral changes in an average 8-day inpatient stay, and because clients requiring inpatient services are in severe need, psychotropic medications also are relied on as a method of intervention (Gerig, 2007).

Most inpatient programs provide each client with one individual counseling session and two to three group sessions per day. In addition, clients may have opportunities for recreational therapy. Typically, clients and their families are encouraged to participate in a family counseling session at least once before they are discharged. Usually, this takes place toward the end of a client's stay and is a good way to prepare for the transition to less restrictive services, such as PHP, IOP, or outpatient services.

Many types of inpatient services exist. Some are designed to meet the mental health needs of those with a variety of presenting problems and others are more specific. Some examples of specialized inpatient services are those for substance abuse and dependence, dual diagnosis or coexisting disorders, eating disorders, and services for children and adolescents. The setting for inpatient programs varies and may include stand-alone psychiatric hospitals, behavioral health units within a larger medical hospital, and facilities that specialize in a specific type of inpatient service (e.g., a substance dependence or eating disorder treatment center).

Regardless of the setting, there are both benefits and challenges to inpatient counseling. One benefit is that counselors often witness drastic improvement in clients' functioning from entry to discharge. Also, although counselors are not able to work with clients on long-term goals, they have the opportunity to give clients a positive experience with counseling that may increase the client's willingness to follow up with outpatient services. A challenge of inpatient work is that some clients need a longer duration of services than their insurance providers will reimburse. Thus, some clients may exit inpatient services before they are completely ready, resulting in a "revolving-door" phenomenon (Gerig, 2007, p. 225). For this reason, services such as IOPs, residential, and aftercare have become important parts of the mental health continuum of care.

Residential Services

Whereas inpatient services are typically provided to those in crisis and provide a short-term period of stabilization, **residential services** are typically used when a client requires longer-term, ongoing structure in a less restrictive environment. Residential services range from those provided as a "**step-down**" or transition from **inpatient** services, to those designed to house and heal youth, to those providing long-term care to individuals with developmental delays. The amount of intervention and supervision received depends on the population being served. Some residential services provide supervision from staff members 24 hours a day, 7 days a week (e.g., residential services for youth). Others provide supervision from staff members during the day, but not the evenings. Temporary residential services for those recovering from substance dependence are sometimes called **halfway houses**. These programs provide temporary housing, usually in a group environment, for individuals who have completed inpatient treatment and are currently involved in intensive outpatient programs for substance dependence. Once these individuals complete the intensive outpatient program, they are expected to exit the halfway house (Gladding & Newsome, 2010).

As may be evident, individuals who receive residential services often receive mental health services from other parts of the mental health counseling continuum of care as well. For example, adolescents residing in a group home are likely to receive group mental health services from staff members in the group home setting but may be transported to individual counseling sessions at a local mental health agency. Regardless of how and where the services are provided, individuals who require residential services typically receive individual and group counseling, psychiatric or medication management services, case management, and social- and life-skills training and support. Some residential programs provide support and psychoeducation groups for clients' family members as well.

Aftercare

When the mental health continuum of care was first created and implemented, aftercare was not an official part of offered services. Individuals whose mental health needs were high enough to require intensive outpatient, inpatient, and/or residential services often benefit, however, from ongoing support following the completion of these services (Gladding & Newsome, 2010). Typically, aftercare services are used with individuals who are in recovery from substance dependence. For example, a client who struggled with cocaine addiction for 20 years completes inpatient psychiatric services for detoxification, then completes 6 months of residential and intensive outpatient services in a halfway house. This client will likely need aftercare support in order to maintain his sobriety. Often, aftercare includes group support meetings such as AA (Alcoholics Anonymous) or NA (Narcotics Anonymous). In addition, outpatient counseling services are an appropriate form of aftercare. In summary, aftercare services are an important support to those no longer engaged in services elsewhere in the continuum of care. In other instances, though, crisis situations need immediate attention, so crisis and emergency services also are integral within the continuum of care.

Crisis and Emergency Services

Because crisis and emergency services are discussed in detail in Chapter 10 they are described only briefly here, in order to indicate their function in the broader continuum of care. Those who are already receiving other services within the mental health continuum of care may use crisis and emergency intervention services, but community members who are receiving no other services at the time also may use them. The purpose of crisis and emergency mental services is to intervene with those experiencing acute emotional, psychological, and/or behavioral distress and to connect those individuals with appropriate mental health services. If necessary, inpatient services may be arranged.

Crisis and emergency services are available 24 hours a day, 7 days a week and may be provided via telephone crisis lines, walk-in treatment, or agencies specializing in emergency care (Gladding & Newsome, 2010; Staton et al., 2007). The settings for crisis and emergency services are varied and may include hospital emergency rooms, mental health agencies, and inpatient psychiatric hospitals. Counselors who provide these services may do so full-time or as part of other full-time roles and functions (Staton et al., 2007).

PROFESSIONAL ISSUES AFFECTING THE CMH COUNSELING CONTINUUM OF CARE

As may be evident, clinical mental health services truly do form a continuum of care options that vary in modality, intensity, and setting. Because each service requires counselors to fulfill different roles and functions, a wide variety of options exist for CMH counselors (Garner, Valle, & Moore, 2014). Thanks to the recent progress in mental health parity for counselors, the field of possibilities continues to expand. Clinical mental health counseling as a profession provides many opportunities for counseling professionals to make a difference.

Whatever place along the continuum a counselor chooses to work, it is vital to understand the other services and providers in the area. No one counselor can meet all the mental health needs of every client, so counselors should know the limitations of their skills and work settings and build a strong referral network to use as needed.

Of course, challenges remain for the profession. The 1963 Community Mental Health Centers Act provided communities with the funding required to build community centers; however, these grants were intended to be temporary, not to provide for the continued operation of these centers (Staton et al., 2007). As funding for clinical mental health services has shifted from mostly federal to mostly state and local sources, mental health agencies have struggled financially (Gladding & Newsome, 2010). Making matters worse, because some funding continues to come from governmental sources, changes in government policies and budgets can drastically affect the mental health services that states and communities are able to offer (MacCluskie & Ingersoll, 2010). Unfortunately, when government policy and budget changes require reduction in spending, human services funding often is the first to be reduced or eliminated.

As a result, agencies now rely more and more on providing services that are billable (MacCluskie & Ingersoll, 2010). A billable service is one for which the agency providing the service is eligible to receive reimbursement. Usually, reimbursement for mental health services comes from clients' insurance companies or from Medicare and Medicaid. This creates two problems. The first problem is that a third party (usually insurance companies, Medicare, or Medicaid) determines what services clients are able to receive rather than this decision being made by the client and the counselor. The second problem is that agencies' financial health depends on the productivity of their counselors. In most cases, this means that counselors are required, or strongly encouraged, to provide a certain number of billable hours each day or week. Billable services are counseling sessions to those individuals who have received a mental health diagnosis. Tasks that are not billable include prevention and education services, treatment plans, diagnosis, case notes, supervision, and treatment team meetings. Typically, productivity requirements for counselors are reasonable but may add undue stress to counselors and supervisors.

Both of the problems just discussed are important reasons for counselors and counseling students to continue to advocate for the profession. Counselors prefer to focus their energies on their clients' needs and on being the best counselors possible, instead of on the political and economic realities that affect the profession. If counselors do not take the time to advocate for change where needed, however, they are failing to do their best for their clients. Counselors in training should look forward to the many positive aspects they will experience as they work in the clinical mental health continuum of care and where they find room for improvement, take action.

The following case study is included to better illustrate some of the services and modalities that are part of the clinical mental health counseling continuum of care.

CASE STUDY

Catherine Harmon is a 47-year-old heterosexual woman married to her first husband with whom she has two children. Her oldest, Max, is a high school senior and Penny is a sophomore. Catherine and her husband Sebastian both work full-time, she in a marketing firm and he as an accountant. Catherine's work was always high-pressure, but when her firm laid off many of its employees, Catherine's workload and pressure increased. With the high interest rate on their mortgage, no raises or bonuses coming from work, one child accepted to an expensive university, and another child applying to colleges soon, she and Sebastian were struggling financially. Catherine always struggled with anxiety and perfectionism, and for years her nightly routine was to drink a bottle of wine "to unwind." Without it, her thoughts and heart raced, her chest constricted, and she could not sleep. Although she sometimes saw a psychiatrist for anxiolytics (antianxiety medication), she had never considered herself as someone with mental health concerns.

After learning that Max scored in the clinical levels during a depression screening that was part of a prevention initiative sponsored by Max's school counselor, Catherine's anxiety and drinking increased significantly. Max's school counselor recommended that Catherine and Sebastian take Max

(Continued)

(Continued)

to counseling at the local mental health agency. To calm down enough to sleep, Catherine began taking the anxiolytics along with her wine. After a few weeks, Max's outpatient counselor invited Catherine and Sebastian to join in Max's session. Together, Max and his counselor told Catherine and Sebastian that Max is gay and had been keeping this reality a secret out of fear. Catherine was shocked and overwhelmed. She knew she should accept her son no matter what, and she did love him, but all she could think was how embarrassing this would be for her, how much danger Max would be in, and how his life would be nothing like she had hoped. For days, Catherine could not sleep at all no matter how much she drank. Finally, she overdosed on a combination of wine and anxiolytics, and Sebastian could not wake her up the next morning.

Her stomach was pumped in the emergency room of the local hospital, and once medically stable, Catherine was admitted to inpatient psychiatric services located across the street from the hospital. She received medication to ease her detoxification process and barely remembers the first few days of her stay. Once alert, she protested her need for inpatient services and the diagnosis she had been given. Because Catherine's symptoms included those of substance dependence and anxiety, she was diagnosed with both disorders and classified as having a dual diagnosis. Eventually, she saw that it would be best for her to cooperate with her counselors and psychiatrists and began attending individual and group sessions. Although she maintained that inpatient services were not necessary, she had to admit that it felt good to talk about her worries. She was worried about her family, especially Max, and agreed to a family session on the seventh day of her inpatient stay. In the family session, Sebastian was quiet and angry, Penny seemed nervous and uncomfortable, Max expressed feelings of guilt and resentment, and Catherine alternated between explaining, minimizing, and apologizing for her behaviors.

Catherine was released from inpatient care on the day after the family session. She was referred to an intensive outpatient program for clients with dual diagnosis. After arguing with her husband, Catherine agreed to attend the IOP. She knew her drinking had made Sebastian uncomfortable for years, but they rarely spoke of it. Now, however, he was adamant that she follow through with inpatient recommendations for follow-up treatment. Catherine attended the IOP from 5:00 to 9:00 p.m. three days a week, which allowed her to return to work. The program had its own psychiatrists and counselors, so Catherine adjusted to these new people. Her medications were adjusted, as well, and Catherine began to sleep easier. Although Catherine felt that she did not really belong in the program compared to other group members, she participated. She was learning a lot about substance dependence and anxiety, and although she did not believe she truly had a problem, she did want to feel less anxious and believed she should drink less for health reasons. She liked her counselors, and as the IOP progressed, she saw the value of the coping skills she was learning. She worried that this time should have been spent with her family, though, especially with Max.

Meanwhile, Max continued in outpatient individual counseling. He still felt both guilty and angry about his mother's reaction to the news that he was gay. So, sometimes he and his counselor discussed those feelings and the thoughts connected to them. Other times, they discussed Max's thoughts and feelings about himself. Max's counselor saw that Max could benefit from some support and referred him to a group for LGBTQ teens held within the mental health agency. Max enjoyed the group and began to feel better.

At the end of Catherine's 6-week IOP, she was referred to outpatient counseling at the mental health agency where Max saw his counselor. She was sober and had been since her admission to inpatient services, almost 2 months ago. She felt better than she had in a long time but was still worried about her son. She was sleeping without too much struggle and noticed that her medications really helped with her anxiety. She intended to stay sober and hoped she would not need the wine in the evenings anymore. She signed a release of confidentiality so that her counselor could consult with Max's counselor at the agency. The two counselors quickly agreed that family counseling would be helpful to the Harmon family and referred Catherine, Max, Sebastian, and Penny to a family counselor within their agency. Both Catherine and Max continued to receive weekly individual counseling sessions (the Harmon family's insurance policy was a good one), and the entire Harmon family began attending family counseling sessions once every 2 weeks.

Discussion Questions

1. Many counseling students are not aware of the specific mental health services and settings in their communities. In order to gain an understanding of your community's mental health continuum of care, identify where each of the services included in the continuum of care (prevention/education, outpatient, intensive outpatient/partial hospitalization programs, inpatient, aftercare, crisis/emergency) are provided in your community.

2. Now that you have an understanding of the clinical mental health continuum of care, the next time a friend asks you, "What do clinical mental health counselors do, exactly?" what will you say?

3. In what ways does the mental health continuum of care reflect the philosophy of the counseling profession? In what ways does the mental health continuum of care not reflect the philosophy of the counseling profession?

4. What gaps, if any, can you identify in the modalities and services of the clinical mental health counseling continuum of care? What services or modalities would you like to see added to the continuum of care?

5. To which modalities and settings are you most and least drawn? Why?

REFERENCES

American Counseling Association. (2010). *20/20: A vision for the future of counseling.* Alexandria, VA: Author.

American Counseling Association. (2014). *ACA Code of Ethics.* Alexandria, VA: Author.

Association for Specialists in Group Work. (2000). Professional standards for the training of group workers. *Journal for Specialists in Group Work, 25*(4), 327–342.

Bronfenbrenner, U. (1989). Ecological systems theory. *Annals of Child Development, 6,* 187–249.

Carter, B., & McGoldrick, M. (2005). Overview: The expanded family life cycle: Individual, family, and social perspectives. In B. Carter & M. McGoldrick (Eds.), *The expanded family life cycle: Individual, family, and social perspectives* (4th ed.). Boston: Allyn & Bacon.

Corry, R., & Jewell, T. C. (2001). Psychiatric rehabilitation idealized: Multi-setting uses and strategies over the course of severe mental illness. *Journal of Mental Health Counseling, 23*(2), 93–103.

Evans, M. E., Boothroyd, R. A., Armstrong, M. I., Greenbaum, P. E., Brown, E. C., & Kuppinger, A. D. (2003). An experimental study of the effectiveness of intensive in-home crisis services for children and their families: Program outcomes. *Journal of Emotional and Behavioral Disorders, 11*(2), 92–102.

Garner, N. E., Valle, J. P., & Moore, S. A. (2014). Settings and counseling career choices. In B. T. Erford (Ed.), *Orientation to the counseling profession* (2nd ed., pp. 321–355). Boston: Pearson.

Gerig, M. S. (2007). *Foundations for mental health and community counseling: An introduction to the profession.* Upper Saddle River, NJ: Pearson Education.

Gladding, S. T., & Newsome, D. W. (2010). *Clinical mental health counseling in community and agency settings.* Upper Saddle River, NJ: Pearson Education.

Glosoff, H. L. (1998). Managed care: A critical ethical issue for counselors. *Counseling and Human Development, 31,* 1–16.

Hauser, M., & Hays, D. G. (2010). The slaying of a beautiful hypothesis: The efficacy of counseling and the therapeutic process. *Journal of Humanistic Counseling, Education, and Development, 49*(1), 32–44.

International Association of Marriage and Family Counselors. (2012). *Is marriage and family counseling right for me?* Retrieved from http://www.iamfconline.org/public/Is-counseling-right-for-me.cfm.

Kitchener, K. S. (1984). Intuition, critical evaluation and ethical principles: The foundation for ethical decisions in counseling psychology. *Counseling Psychologist, 12*(3), 43–55.

Lewis, J. A., Lewis, M. D., Daniels, J. A., & D'Andrea, M. J. (2011). *Community counseling: A multicultural-social justice perspective* (4th ed.). Belmont, CA: Brooks/Cole.

MacCluskie, K. C., & Ingersoll, R. E. (2010). *Becoming a 21st century agency counselor: Personal and professional explorations.* Independence, KY: Brooks/Cole.

McGoldrick, M., & Carter, B. (2003). The family life cycle. In F. Walsh (Ed.), *Normal family processes* (3rd ed.). New York: Guilford Press.

Payne, M. (2003). *Narrative therapy.* Thousand Oaks, CA: Sage.

Prochasks, J. O., & DiClemente, C. C. (1984). *The transtheoretical approach: Crossing traditional boundaries of treatment.* Homewood, IL: Dow Jones-Irwin.

Rosenzweig, S. (1936). Some implicit common factors in diverse methods of psychotherapy. *American Journal of Orthopsychiatry, 6,* 412–415.

Staton, A. R., Benson, A. J., Briggs, M. K., Cowan, E., Echterling, L. G., Evans, W. F., et al. (2007). *Becoming a community counselor.* Boston: Lahasksa Press.

Thomas, R. V., & Pender, D. A. (2008). Association for specialists in group work: Best practice guidelines 2007 revisions. *Journal for Specialists in Group Work, 33*(2), 111–117.

Tuckman, B. W. (1965). Developmental sequence in small groups. *Psychological Bulletin, 63,* 384–399.

Tuckman, B. W., & Jensen, M. A. (1977). Stages of small group development revisited. *Group and Organizational Studies, 2,* 419–427.

Yalom, I. D., & Leszcz, M. (2005). *The theory and practice of group psychotherapy* (5th ed.). New York: Basic Books.

Processes and Procedures of Clinical Mental Health Counseling

CHAPTER 5

Assessing Client Concerns

Casey Barrio-Minton

Most people who decide they want to be CMH counselors do so with a vision of a powerful helping process that involves hours of in-depth exploration and processing aimed at alleviating distress, optimizing wellness, and helping clients feel empowered to make positive changes in their lives. These processes and goals are at the heart of the counseling profession and, as they should, receive a great deal of attention during counselor preparation programs. On the other hand, relatively little time is spent attending to counseling procedures—like assessment—that may first appear to be a bit less glamorous or life changing. Yet, as you will discover in this chapter, assessment is a critical, fascinating component of all aspects of the counseling process and involves a specific skill set.

Whitson (2009) described assessment as integral to counseling and warned against assuming that assessment is just about information gathering at the beginning of the process. Assessment helps counselors know what is working and what needs changing. It provides a way to start thinking about client functioning, needs, and experience in the change process. It helps counselors understand starting points and know when their efforts are successful. Indeed, Hohenshil (1996) highlighted the role assessment plays in each of six steps in the counseling process: (1) referral, (2) symptom identification, (3) diagnosis, (4) treatment planning, (5) treatment, and (6) follow-up. Note that treatment, so often thought as the heart of what counselors do, doesn't appear until the fifth step of the counseling process! In short, assessment provides both a foundation and road map for understanding the counseling journey.

So, then, just what is assessment? How is assessment different from and similar to areas such as appraisal or testing? The *Standards for Educational and Psychological Testing* defined **assessment** as "a process that integrates test information with information from other sources (e.g., information from the individual's social, educational, employment, or psychological history)" (AERA, APA, & NCME, 1999, p. 3). Similarly, Hohenshil (1996) defined assessment as

the process of collecting information for use in the diagnostic process. Assessment data can be obtained through a variety of formal and informal techniques, including standardized tests, diagnostic interviews, projective personality measures, questionnaires, mental status examinations, checklists, behavioral observation, and reports by significant others (medical, educational, social, legal, etc.). (p. 65)

Both definitions identify assessment as a process through which the counselor and client construct an understanding through information gathered through a variety of methods and sources. Sometimes people distinguish between assessment and **appraisal**, but most experts use the terms interchangeably. It is important to note that assessment includes, but is not limited to, testing. A **test** is "an individual instrument in which the focus is on evaluation" (Whitson, 2009, p. 449).

In the first part of this chapter, foundations are explored, including training and ethical considerations related to assessment. In the later parts of this chapter, a variety of assessment methods and procedures are identified that one is likely to encounter as a CMH counselor: the intake or diagnostic interview, unstandardized questionnaires and checklists, mental status examinations, standardized instruments, qualitative assessments, and collateral reports. At the end of the chapter, special considerations are discussed, including screening for high-risk situations, cultural bias, and next steps for diagnosis and treatment planning.

ASSESSMENT FOUNDATIONS

Assessment has long played an important role in professional counseling. Assessment scholars (Drummond & Jones, 2010; Erford, 2007; Whitson, 2009) provide evidence that testing for aptitude goes back to ancient Greece and China. In the last century, methods for assessing educational, occupational, and personal considerations have developed rapidly, and professional dialogue has turned to understanding how counselors can harness the power of assessment while minimizing negative effects and abuses of power.

Today, the importance of assessment is noted in the Council for Accreditation of Counseling and Related Educational Programs (CACREP) 2016 Standards, where assessment is highlighted as one of eight core curricular areas for master's-level counselors. The Standards require that counselors in all settings participate in coursework that includes attention to historical perspectives, concepts of standardized and nonstandardized testing, statistical concepts needed to understand assessment, social and cultural factors, and ethical considerations related to assessment. Further, the Standards require that CMH counselors demonstrate a variety of knowledge, skills, and practices specific to assessment.

The *American Counseling Association (ACA) Code of Ethics* (2014) also includes extensive attention to assessment in Section E: Evaluation, Assessment, and Interpretation, in which they open by stating, "Counselors use assessment instruments as one component of the counseling process, taking into account the client personal and cultural context" (p. 11). As you will likely learn about in your professional orientation and assessment coursework, assessment has the potential to do good but also to do harm. CMH counselors are responsible for a host of ethical considerations, including using assessment to promote client welfare; operating within bounds of competence when using and interpreting assessment instruments; making sure clients and key stakeholders understand the nature, purposes, and limitations of assessment data; and ensuring that they use assessment in a culturally sensitive manner. Understanding ethical considerations related to assessment is especially important as you learn to become a counselor so that you do not unintentionally overstep the limits of your training in your enthusiasm for learning. For example, reading this chapter will help you to understand some important considerations in assessment; however, reading this chapter will not mean you are ready to administer an assessment or conduct a diagnostic interview.

To learn more about ethical and professional considerations around the use of assessment, please refer to the *ACA Code of Ethics* (2014). The Association for Assessment and Research in Counseling (AARC) is an ACA division dedicated to promoting and supporting appropriate use of assessment, diagnosis, and evaluation in counseling. Their resources webpage (http://www.counseling.org/resources/aca-code-of-ethics.pdf) also provides a number of documents, policy statements, standards related to assessment, and links to other professional associations with a stake in assessment.

PURPOSES AND METHODS OF ASSESSMENT

Most experts agree that there are four major purposes of assessment (Drummond & Jones, 2010; Erford, 2007; Whitson, 2009). First, CMH counselors use assessment to **screen** for concerns that may warrant further attention. Chances are, you have taken part in at least one brief screening for a mental health or medical concern. For example, most colleges and universities offer awareness weeks in which individuals are screened for depression, eating disorders, partner violence, or health concerns. Depending on results of screening assessments, some individuals, families, or groups are encouraged to seek further consultation or services. Second, CMH counselors use assessment to **identify and diagnose** concerns that may be the focus of counseling. Most commonly, assessment leads to an understanding of strengths and opportunities and, in many CMH counseling settings, a diagnosis that helps one qualify for services. Third, assessment is used to guide **treatment planning** because it helps to understand goals and objectives for counseling while gaining a sense of which approaches to counseling might be most effective for a particular client or client system in a particular situation. Finally, assessment is used to **evaluate** client progress and determine whether counseling services are effective. You will learn more about each of these functions in later parts of this textbook. For now, the focus is on understanding assessment procedures you are most likely to encounter as a CMH counselor.

On a practical level, there are countless ways to gather information, and each way has its own strengths and limitations. Imagine that I came to you wanting to improve my relationship with my family. You would probably want to understand more about those relationships so you can better understand *if* you have the skills to help me and, if so, *how* best to go about our counseling. You would probably also want to figure out a way you could get a baseline of where we are starting so that we can know when counseling is successful. Take a moment to brainstorm all the ways you could find out about my relationship with my family. After you have made your list, compare it the following list:

- Use essential counseling skills to get me to talk about my family

- Use a structured or semistructured interview to get me to talk about my family

- Ask me to fill out a questionnaire you created

- Ask me to fill out family functioning questionnaires you purchased from a testing company

- Have me create a picture, timeline, sandtray, or puppet show about my family

- Ask me to keep a journal regarding my family experiences

- Observe me interacting with my family in our home

- Observe me completing a task with my family in your office

- Hook me up to machines and measure my physiological responses to thinking and talking about my family

- Ask my family about our relationships

- Ask my neighbors about our family

- Review family documents, such as pictures, records, and videos

Now, think for a moment about the strengths and limitations to each of these methods. Talking directly about my family may be fast and easy, but the information you will gather is only as accurate as my openness and insight. A family functioning questionnaire might generate useful information so long as it was written at a level I could understand and got at the types of things most important to me. Filling out a questionnaire you created might save us some time in session, but I might not be in a place where I am able or willing to write down some of the things most troubling to me. We could go on, but you probably get the point.

The best assessment protocols use **multiple sources** and **multiple methods**. Of course, we need to balance our desire for comprehensive information with theoretical and practical considerations regarding time, cost, and agency or insurance expectations. Most counseling is time-limited, so CMH counselors must be practical and diligent in creating assessment protocols. Six hours would not be enough time to do all the things we just brainstormed, yet 6 hours might be my annual benefit for counseling services.

Counselors also need to match their assessment procedures to (a) clients' developmental, cultural, and educational status; (b) one's theoretical orientation; and (c) funder demands. For example, children and individuals with intellectual disabilities may not be able to complete some assessment tasks. People for whom English is a second language or who do not have high levels of formal education might not be comfortable with the reading or writing involved with certain assessment tools. By definition, clients who are in crisis might not be able or willing to participate in lengthier assessment given the pressing demands they are experiencing. One's counseling theories also provide guidance regarding what type of information is most important and how to go about collecting that information. For example, the Adlerian counselor might do a semistructured interview regarding early recollections, the solution-focused counselor might interview for exceptions (i.e., times when the symptom does not occur), and the cognitive behavioral counselor might ask clients to complete standardized assessments regarding mood, thought patterns, and other symptoms. All these methods might feel distracting to the person-centered counselor. Finally, agency and insurance expectations factor into the decisions counselors make. Most public and nonprofit organizations will specify assessment procedures, and many will have all clients complete outcome measures as a way of documenting counseling effectiveness to stakeholders, including board members and third-party reimbursement groups.

Despite the number of factors that play into counselors' decisions, it is important to remember that appropriate assessment is a professional responsibility and a hallmark of effective practice. In most cases, assessment options include a unique combination of clinical interviews, unstandardized questionnaires and checklists, direct observations, standardized tests, qualitative assessments, and collateral records and reports.

CLINICAL, INTAKE, AND DIAGNOSTIC INTERVIEWING

Almost all CMH counselors will rely heavily on interviewing throughout the counseling process. As you begin working with clients and client systems, you will find yourself balancing multiple tasks and processes. Most importantly, you will need to begin building rapport and establishing the core conditions upon which counseling will progress. At the same time, you will be responsible for securing informed consent, helping your client understand your roles and responsibilities in the counseling process, gathering the clinical assessment information you need to inform your work together, and instilling hope regarding the potential for change.

You will likely find yourself using a number of **clinical interviewing** strategies as you set out on this process. Sommers-Flanagan and Sommers-Flanagan (2003) identified four "basic requirements for clinical interviewers" (p. 9): technical knowledge, self-awareness, other-awareness, and practice and experience. Later, they provided a humorous look at clinical interviewing when then noted the following:

1. You must know what famous philosophers know: the importance of knowing yourself . . .

2. You must know what good landscapers know: the terrain . . .

3. You must have what successful music teachers have: a good ear . . .

4. You must do what successful athletes do: practice . . .

5. You must know what good office managers know: how to prioritize information . . .

6. You must know what efficient wardrobe managers know: how to mix and match . . .

7. You must know what good car mechanics know: how to troubleshoot . . . (pp. 28–29)

As a CMH counselor, you will have a variety of interviewing tools available to help you conduct the most effective clinical interviews possible.

Types of Interviews

Interviews are classified as structured, semistructured, or unstructured. **Structured interviews** "are a type of diagnostic interview procedure that consists of a standardized list of questions; a standardized sequence of questioning, including follow-up questions; and the systematic rating of client responses" (Jones, 2010, pp. 220–221). Structured interviews may be general or specific in focus. For example, the Diagnostic Interview Schedule (DIS) (Robins, Cottler, Bucholz, & Compton, 1995) includes a series of 19 modules to evaluate 30 DSM disorders and can take in excess of 2 hours to complete. The Children's Interview for Psychiatric Syndromes (ChIPS) (Teare, Fristad, Weller, Weller, & Salmon, 1998) is used to assess 20 different Axis I disorders and other concerns in youth ages 6–18, and it can be administered in 20–50 minutes. Because they are developed and conducted with a degree of rigor, structured interviews maximize reliability by increasing the likelihood that two interviewers gather the same information and arrive at the same conclusion. Depending on the content, structured interviews may be appropriate for use by paraprofessionals. Most often used in research settings, structured interviews' strength is counterbalanced by a lack of flexibility that may make them impractical for use in clinical settings.

Semistructured interviews provide a systematic structure in which the interviewer gathers standardized information; however, the interviewer is allowed to deviate from the protocol by following up on specific items, using reflections, asking clients to expand on responses, and reordering questions (Drummond & Jones, 2010; Erford, 2007). Semistructured interviews provide structure while also allowing for greater attention to relationship and clinical judgment than structured interviews.

The **unstructured interview** involves a process through which the CMH counselor uses his or her clinical judgment to determine which open-ended questions, closed-ended questions, and reflections will best yield the type of assessment information. Jones identified unstructured interviews as the "primary assessment tool for diagnosing mental disorders" (2010, p. 220). Often, CMH counselors will use open-ended questions to elicit general information and follow up with reflections and closed-ended questions to elicit more specific information. Certain topics, however, might be better initiated with closed-ended questions and follow-up prompts for exploration. Strengths of unstructured interviews include flexibility for CMH counselors and clients to determine the focus of the interview while building rapport (Drummond & Jones, 2010). However, accuracy of the interview is directly related to the clinician's diagnostic understanding, skill, and clinical judgment. Sometimes, CMH counselors use unstructured interviews to identify areas for which they would like to gather more assessment information via other forms of interviews, standardized assessments, and qualitative assessments. As you'll learn in the next section, the initial or intake interview is perhaps the most common type of unstructured interview.

Initial or Intake Interview

The **initial or intake interview** allows CMH counselors to build the therapeutic relationship, get to know the client and client systems in a holistic manner, define the problem, identify counseling goals, and determine what type of counseling approach might be most appropriate. You may need to spend some time setting the tone for counseling, letting your client know you hear her, helping your client understand how the intake session will be different from future sessions, and helping her discover a reason to come back. These relational considerations are also important because they influence the quality of information the client chooses to share, especially as you must broach sensitive topics during your initial meeting.

CMH counseling settings vary regarding the amount of time spent with the intake interview, the focus of the interview, and who conducts the interview. Some agencies will require that you complete a lengthy, structured process that ends in a diagnosis. When using the clinical interview for diagnostic purposes, you are conducting a **diagnostic interview** (Jones, 2010). For example, a county mental health agency that can only service individuals who have severe and persistent mental illnesses (SPMI) such as schizophrenia, bipolar disorder, or major depression may spend a great deal of time determining whether a person meets criteria for diagnosis and has sufficient impairment in functioning to warrant specific services. Other CMH counseling settings will have an open-ended intake format that will allow you to use your clinical judgment in structuring the intake; they may or may not require that you arrive at a diagnosis at the end of the interview. For example, a family services agency may be most interested in family and community functioning with a particular focus on the possible presence of intimate partner violence, and a counseling training clinic may serve a wide range of clients who are seeking to enhance holistic wellness. Still other agencies will employ paraprofessionals to conduct intake interviews and write up results for CMH counselors so that a greater proportion of your time is spent in intervention rather than assessment. Although degree of focus varies, intake interviews tend to include coverage of the topics described in Table 5.1 (Erford, 2006; Jones, 2010; Sommers-Flanagan & Sommers-Flanagan, 2003; Whitson, 2009).

Table 5.1 Intake Interview Topics and Examples

Topic	Examples
Identifying information	name, contact information, age, gender, race/ethnicity, relationship status, occupational or student status, referral status
Presenting problem	nature and history of major concerns, attempts at coping, impact on functioning
Current situation and functioning	impact of presenting problem on current situation as well as current life situations, stressors, and supports in each major life area—family, social, educational/occupational, leisure, spiritual
Family history	description of family of origin, major events and experiences in family history including abuse or trauma, current relationship with family
Social/relational history	description of social/relational history, major events and experiences as related to peer and romantic relationships including abuse or trauma, current peer and romantic relationships
Developmental history	developmental events and milestones from infancy to current life stage, known developmental issues or concerns
Educational/occupational background	description of school and work background, major events and experiences related to educational and employment history, current functioning at work and at school
Medical history	past and present medical conditions and health concerns, participation in physical wellness activities, injuries, hospitalizations, medications, screening for medical concerns
Mental health and substance use history	past and present mental health concerns and diagnoses, history of help-seeking for mental health and substance abuse concerns, outcomes of previous treatment, family history of mental health and substance abuse concerns, screening for high-risk concerns
Cultural considerations	role of cultural considerations in presenting problem, coping with concerns, or desired counseling approach; experiences related to privilege and oppression
Counseling goals	hopes and expectations for counseling

The list in Table 5.1 is only a starting place. The amount of attention you spend in any given area will depend on your client, his or her context, and your work setting. For example, family systems counselors will likely spend much more time in family and relational history, whereas those who specialize in work with children and adolescents might be more thorough when conducting the developmental history.

UNSTANDARDIZED QUESTIONNAIRES AND CHECKLISTS

CMH counselors may find themselves using **unstandardized questionnaires and checklists** to assist in the assessment process. As discussed in Chapter 9, many agencies use background forms for clients to provide an account of their history and functioning, thus freeing the CMH counselor to focus the intake interview on those issues that seem most clinically relevant. These forms might be sent to a client prior to a session or made available along with other new-client paperwork via an agency website. A CMH counselor might also find it helpful to construct a checklist or rating form including common concerns and ask clients to complete the checklist as part of the initial paperwork or interview, especially because the checklist might help a client to report experiences or concerns he or she might not otherwise share. Although it might be fun to construct one's own checklist, CMH counselors must use them with caution because one cannot know the degree to which the checklist yields reliable and valid information.

Just as unstructured interviews provide flexibility for the interviewer, unstandardized questionnaires and checklists may be customized to provide the type of information most important to the counseling setting. The quality of the information generated by the questionnaire will be limited by how well it is constructed. Just as intentionality is important in unstructured and semistructured interviewing, it is critical in creating a useful unstandardized questionnaire. Individuals who create unstandardized questionnaires and checklists to use in CMH counseling practice will want to consider a number of factors, including the following:

- What information is most important for me to know? Why do I want to know this? Is a written format the best way to gain this information?

- Should I gather open-ended information or closed-ended information?

- How will I integrate information gathered in the questionnaire or checklist?

- Will my clients be able to understand and respond to my questionnaire? At what reading level is it written? Do I provide enough space and flexibility for a client to complete the form comfortably?

There are a number of resources available for CMH counselors to begin creating questionnaires and checklists. For example, *Forms for the Therapist* (Hedberg, 2010) and *The Clinical Documentation Sourcebook: The Complete Paperwork Resource for Your Mental Health Practice* (Wiger, 2010) provide multiple examples of customizable questionnaires and checklists. For a sample current concerns checklist used with adult clients, please see the appendix at the end of this chapter. The authors of Chapter 9 provide additional discussion regarding documentation and provide examples of common forms used in CMH counseling practice.

MENTAL STATUS EXAMINATIONS

The mental status examination (MSE) is a clinical assessment tool used by CMH counselors in a wide variety of settings. When used properly, the MSE allows CMH counselors to use powers of observation to understand more about a client's functioning and experiences.

Although not scientific, people conduct informal MSEs in everyday life. Have you ever sensed a loved one's anger or sadness just through nonverbal cues? Or gathered through one's behavior, voice, or dress that he or she was under the influence of substances or out of contact with reality? If so, you are already tuned in to important mental status considerations.

Although MSEs were traditionally used in mental health professions such as psychology or psychiatry, CMH counselors now work in settings where they are expected to be fluent in MSE language (Polanski & Hinkle, 2000). Counselors tend to use MSEs as an initial screening tool to "provide a framework for the comprehensive evaluation of mental functioning" (Daniel & Carothers, 2007, p. 49) and identify potential indicators of underlying physical, substance, or severe mental health concerns. In some settings, such as inpatient behavioral health units and hospitals, CMH counselors use MSEs frequently to monitor for changes in status. In most other settings, they note mental status considerations at intake and revisit them when clients experience a change in functioning. For example, I once worked with a counseling client who never used makeup, always dressed very casually, and usually presented herself in a dull, muted manner. One week, she presented to session wearing makeup, a new haircut, crisper clothes, and a brighter hue about her. My MSE observations immediately told me that something was different; within minutes, she accounted to me how she had finally taken action to end a long, unhappy relationship.

Whereas MSEs may be unstructured, semistructured, or structured (Erford, 2007), skilled CMH counselors are able to integrate MSE considerations into the flow of an intake interview in a way that is almost unperceivable to the lay observer. Most writers identify a number of MSE domains (Daniel & Carothers, 2007; Polanski & Hinkle, 2000; Sommers-Flanagan & Sommers-Flanagan, 2003) in which one may observe clients. Table 5.2 includes overarching questions for each domain and a list of questions most commonly associated with each domain.

Table 5.2   MSE Domains and Overarching Questions

Domain	Overarching Questions
Appearance	What is the client's apparent age, gender, sex, and race? What are her distinguishing physical characteristics or features? How might I describe her dress, grooming, cleanliness, and body art?
Behavior or motor activity	What is the client's nonverbal behavior? Is his degree of movement more or less than expected? What is his eye contact like? Do I detect any mannerisms, tremors, or tics?
Attitude toward interviewer	What is the client's attitude toward me? To what degree does she appear attentive, open, and cooperative in the interview?
Mood and affect	How does the client describe his mood? Based on his external expression, what affect does he express? How stable, intense, and appropriate is this experience and expression of emotion?

Domain	Overarching Questions
Speech	At what rate, rhythm, and volume does my client speak? How much does she have to say? Does she seem to be able to express her thoughts through speech? How clearly does she articulate her words?
Thought process and content	To what degree is the client able to form and organize his thought process in a logical manner? Am I able to follow his flow of thought? Does he show any thought processes indicative of a deeper problem? Does the client indicate concerns with suicidal or homicidal ideation, obsessions, delusions, or phobias?
Perceptual disturbances	To what degree does what the client sees, hears, smells, tastes, and feels correspond with reality? Is she experiencing any hallucinations (sensory experiences without stimuli) or illusions (perceptional distortions)?
Orientation and consciousness	Does the client know who he is, where he is, and when it is? Does he understand the current situation? Does he appear to be fully and appropriately conscious?
Memory and intelligence	Does the client appear to have any problems with short- or long-term memory? Given the client's level of formal education, use of language, and level of knowledge, does her intelligence seem below average, average, or above average?
Insight and judgment	To what degree does the client understand his problems? How well can he make sound decisions? Is he able to control impulses and desires appropriately?

When considering a client's mental status, what is not present is often as important as what is present. For that reason, one should document presence and absence of concerns in each of the areas in Table 5.2. In most instances, CMH counselors will use written forms or checklists to document the MSE; however, they might also integrate a narrative description of the MSE in a progress note or report.

When conducting an MSE, CMH counselors will be particularly careful to consider contextual and cultural factors that may be influencing a client's presentation. One's cultural context can influence appearance, verbal and nonverbal behavior, apparent attitude toward the interviewer, thought process and content, and perceptions or reality. CMH counselors should be particularly careful to avoid assuming certain ways of being, thinking, speaking, or perceiving things as abnormal when they might be normal within a client's culture. Similarly, one must consider context when conducting the MSE. Although I might wear my pajamas for a late-night ice cream run, my students would surely be concerned if I showed up to class wearing them!

Mini–Mental State Exam

The mini–mental state exam (MMSE; Folstein, Folstein, & McHugh, 1975) is a semistructured or structured interview that serves as a screening tool for cognitive disorders including dementia and delirium. It is often used in conjunction with the MSE, especially in settings where clients tend to have more substantial levels of impairment or the interviewer might be concerned about the client's cognitive functioning based on the MSE. The MMSE takes less than 10 minutes to administer and includes a series of scored questions that assess a client's orientation and ability to engage in a number of cognitive tasks involving memory, attention and calculation, recognition, language, and complex commands. Individuals who score below a certain cut-point on the MMSE should be referred for further assessment of cognitive function.

USING STANDARDIZED TESTS AND INVENTORIES TO INFORM COUNSELING

CMH counselors across settings also encounter and use **standardized tests and inventories** within the counseling process. Standardized tests are developed using rigorous instrument construction principles that help to ensure the items generate consistent results (are reliable) about the topics they purport to assess (are valid) for the population they are intended to serve. The *ACA Code of Ethics* (2014) specifies a number of ethical standards specific to appropriate development, administration, and interpretation of standardized tests and inventories. The *Responsibilities of Users of Standardized Tests (RUST)* (Association for Assessment in Counseling, 2003) specifies additional considerations regarding use of standardized tests, including qualifications of test users, technical knowledge, test selection, test administration, test scoring, interpreting test results, and communicating test results.

This background is important to being able to decide which tests are appropriate for use with individuals, groups, and families; understand results; and communicate about results effectively. For these reasons (and a few political ones that are beyond the scope of this chapter), test publishers, professional associations, and some state licensing boards restrict use of standardized assessments to users who meet predetermined qualifications (Naugle, 2009). In most cases, CMH counselors who hold a master's degree, have a license to practice counseling in their state, and have appropriate training are able to administer and interpret most standardized tests discussed in this chapter. CMH counselors must be aware of some notable exceptions. For example, Alabama, Alaska, Arkansas, Tennessee, and Texas do not allow counselors to use projective techniques to assess personality, Tennessee does not allow counselors to use tests and assessments to diagnose or identify pathologies, and Nebraska does not allow use of personality testing for diagnosis and treatment planning (Naugle, 2009). Although individual test publishers may vary slightly, the following qualification or level requirements published by Pearson (2012) are fairly standard in the profession: Qualification/Level A tests do not require special qualifications to purchase products, Qualification/Level B tests require membership in a professional association that requires training related to assessment or a master's degree in an appropriate area and formal training in assessment, and Qualification/Level C tests require licensure or certification to practice in the corresponding field or a doctoral degree with formal training in assessment.

Most assessment textbooks include a great deal of attention to standardized tests in three key areas: intelligence and general ability, achievement, and aptitude. Consider the following definitions provided by Whitson (2009):

- **Intelligence test.** Instrument designed to measure the mental capabilities of an individual. These assessments are also referred to as general ability tests.

- **Achievement test.** An assessment in which the person has "achieved" either knowledge, information, or skills through instruction, training, or experience. Achievement tests measure acquired knowledge and do not make any predictions about the future.

- **Aptitude test.** A test that provides a prediction about the individual's future performance or ability to learn based on his or her performance on the test. Aptitude tests often predict either future academic or vocational/career performance.

Although CMH counselors must be familiar with these types of standardized tests and may even administer them, CMH counselors are more likely to look to other **personality assessments** for use in everyday practice. Technically, broad and specific symptom inventories used for clinical assessment and diagnosis as well as personality inventories used to "identify and measure the structure and features of one's personality, or one's characteristic way of thinking, feeling, and behaving" (Drummond & Jones, 2010, p. 249) are all classified as personality assessments. CMH counselors will use personality assessments to identify potential problems for further investigation, gain insight into client modes of functioning, and evaluate change. The following sections provide examples of each of these three types of standardized personality assessments: broad-symptom inventories, specific-symptom inventories, and structured personality inventories.

Broad-Symptom Inventories

Broad-symptom inventories are designed to assess a wide array of symptoms and problems that may apply to a client, family, or group. CMH counselors may use broad-symptom inventories at time of intake to establish a baseline score and identify areas in which counselors may need to spend additional time in interviewing or administering additional assessments. Because standardized symptom inventories have been developed with attention to psychometric properties and norming, many yield results that can help a CMH counselor determine if the client's functioning is in the "normal" (probably not a problem), "borderline" (might be a problem), or "clinical" (almost definitely a problem) range. In many cases, the inventories provide validity scales that help CMH counselors identify when a client might be overreporting, underreporting, or reporting contradictory information. Although CMH counselors should not diagnose based on one inventory alone, they can use results as part of holistic, multimethod assessment protocols.

Some of the more common broad-symptom inventories in use today include the following:

- **Symptom Checklist-90-Revised** (SCL-90-R; Derogatis, 1994). The SCL-90-R takes 12–15 minutes to complete and contains 90 items that are rated on a 5-point scale. Appropriate for individuals ages 13 and over, the SCL-90-R is written at a 6th-grade reading level. Symptom scales include somatization, obsessive-compulsive, interpersonal sensitivity, depression, anxiety, hostility, phobic anxiety, paranoid ideation, and psychoticism.

Global indices include global severity index, positive symptoms distress index, and positive symptom total. The SCL-90-R is a Level B instrument.

- **Outcome Questionnaire 45.2** (OQ-45.2; Lambert et al., 1996). The OQ-45.2 may be administered via paper or software versions, takes 3–5 minutes to complete, and contains 45 items. Appropriate for individuals ages 18 and over, the OQ-45.2 is written at a 5th-grade reading level. The OQ-45.2 yields scores in symptom distress, interpersonal relations, and social roles and contains items to assist with risk assessment for suicide, substance abuse, and workplace violence. The OQ-45.2 is designed for repeated administration and tracking of change over time. OQ Measures also offers several shorter adult and youth outcome measures.

- **Achenbach System of Empirically Based Assessment** (ASEBA; Achenbach, 2012). ASEBA offers a number of assessment measures appropriate for use with preschool-aged children, school-aged children, adolescents, adults, and older adults. The system includes options for self-report, caregiver report, teacher report, and direct observation of behaviors. Some of the more common standardized instruments include the Child Behavior Checklist (CBCL/6–18), which yields a variety of syndrome scales and DSM-oriented scales. The Adult Self Report (ASR) includes multiple adaptive functioning scales, syndrome scales, DSM-oriented scales, and substance use scales. ASEBA includes Level B instruments.

Specific-Symptom Inventories

Specific-symptom inventories are designed to assess concerns related to a specific clinical area of concern. Some settings will ask all clients to complete a standard battery of specific-symptom inventories at intake, especially if the agency provides service for a particular issue or concern (e.g., childhood trauma, youth behavior concerns, family violence, or eating disorders). Most symptom inventories are more focused on pathology and dysfunction than wellness; however, some symptom inventories allow for identification of positive areas of functioning. Table 5.3 includes examples of a variety of specific-symptom inventories.

Table 5.3 Examples of Specific-Symptom Inventories

Name	Purpose	Details	Results
Beck Depression Inventory-II (BDI-II) (Beck, Steer, & Brown, 1996)	Screen for depression in adults	• 21 items on 4-point scale • 5–10 minutes • Level B	Minimal, mild, moderate, or severe levels of depression
Children's Depression Inventory 2 (CDI 2) (Kovacs, 2010)	Multirater assessment for signs of depression in youth ages 7–17	• 28 items • 15–20 minutes • Level B	Emotional problems, functional problems, negative mood/physical symptoms, negative self-esteem, interpersonal problems, ineffectiveness

Name	Purpose	Details	Results
Substance Abuse Subtle Screening Inventory-3 (SASSI-3) (Miller & Lazowski, 1999)	Screening for probability of substance disorders in adolescents and adults	• 67 true-false items • 26 self-report items • 15 minutes • Level A	Face valid alcohol, face valid other drugs, obvious attributes, subtle attributes, defensiveness, supplemental addiction measure, family vs. control measure, correctional
Eating Disorder Inventory-3 (EDI-3) (Garner, 2004)	Screening for eating disorders in females ages 13–53	• 91 items • 20 minutes • Level B • Also offers symptom checklist and referral forms	Eating disorder risk composite, ineffectiveness composite, interpersonal problems composite, affective problems composite, overcontrol composite, global psychological maladjustment composite
Trauma Symptom Checklist for Children (TSCC) (Briere, 1996)	Evaluation of post-traumatic stress and impacts in youth ages 8–16	• 54 items on 4-point scale • 15–20 minutes • Level B	Anxiety, depression, anger, post-traumatic stress, dissociation, and sexual concerns
Marital Satisfaction Inventory, Revised (MSI-R) (Snyder, 1997)	Assess nature and extent of conflict for couples ages 16–92	• 150 true-false items (129 if no children) • 20–25 minutes • Level B	Affective communication, role orientation, problem-solving communication, aggression, family history of distress, time together, dissatisfaction with children, disagreement about finances, conflict over child rearing, sexual dissatisfaction, global distress
Parenting Stress Index, 3rd edition (PSI) (Abidin, 1995)	Assess parent-child problem area in parents (ages 18–60) of children ages 1 month–12 years	• 120 items • 20–30 minutes • Level B	Total stress, child characteristics (distractibility/hyperactivity, adaptability, reinforces parent, demandingness, mood, and acceptability), parent characteristics (competence, isolation, attachment, health, role restriction, depression, and spouse), optional life stress score

Structured Personality Inventories

The assessments discussed previously are largely developed to assess **states**, that is, experiences or behaviors that are situation dependent and change over time. The personality inventories covered in this section, however, are designed to cover enduring **traits** or characteristics. According to Erford (2006), trait personality has four major characteristics: it is within the individual, it is adaptive, it is stable over time, and it is consistent from one situation to another. CMH counselors may wish to use standardized personality inventories to better understand patterns in client functioning and information processing. In turn, they might use the information to foster insight and match counseling approach to clients' ways of being. Some of the more common personality inventories used by CMH counselors today are highlighted in Table 5.4.

Table 5.4 Examples of Personality Inventories

Name	Purpose	Details	Results
Minnesota Multiphasic Personality Inventory (MMPI-2) (Butcher et al., 2001)	Identify social and personal maladjustment in adults ages 18 and older	• 567 true-false items • 60–90 minutes • Level C	Extensive reports including 9 validity scales, 5 superlative self-presentation scales, 10 clinical scales, 9 restructured clinical scales, 15 content scales, 27 content component scales, 20 supplementary scales, and 31 clinical subscales
Revised NEO Personality Inventory (NEO-PI-3) (Costa & McCrae, 2010)	Assess domains of personality grounded in the five factor model for adolescents and adults ages 12 and older	• 240 personality items • 40 minutes • Level B	Neuroticism, extraversion, openness to experience, agreeableness, conscientiousness
Myers-Briggs Type Indicator (MBTI) (Myers, McCaulley, Quenk, & Hammer (1998)	Assess major domains of psychological type grounded in Jungian theory in adolescents and adults ages 14 and older	• 93 forced-choice items • 15–25 minutes • Level B	Extraversion/introversion, sensing/intuition, thinking/feeling, judging/perceiving
Sixteen Personality Factor Questionnaire (5th ed.) (16PF5) (Cattell, Cattell, & Cattell, 1993)	Assess normal personality in individuals 16 and older	• 185 multiple-choice items + 26 multiple-choice couples items • 30–50 minutes • Level Q	16 dimensions of personality (warmth, reasoning, emotional stability, dominance, liveliness, rule-consciousness, social boldness, sensitivity, vigilance, abstractedness, privateness, apprehension, openness to change, self-reliance, perfectionism, tension) and 5 global factors (extraversion, anxiety, tough-mindedness, independence, self-control)

PROJECTIVE TECHNIQUES

Projective techniques provide yet another way to assess an individual's, a family's, or a group's personality and experiences. **Projective techniques** are

> a form of personality assessment that provides the client with a relatively ambiguous stimulus, thus encouraging a nonstructured response. The assumption underlying these techniques is that the individual will project his or her personality into the response. The interpretation of projective techniques is subjective and requires extensive training in the technique. (Whitson, 2009, p. 447)

Although CMH counselors are less likely to use formal projective techniques, it is helpful to be familiar with the more common projective tests. Lindzey (1959) provided a number of ways in which to classify projective techniques, including the mode of response requested by clients and examples of techniques; many of these approaches are still in use today! **Associative** techniques provide individuals with stimuli to which they respond immediately. The Rorschach inkblot test is perhaps the most well-known projective technique; associative techniques also include word association tasks. **Constructive** techniques involve providing clients with stimuli, such as pictures, and asking them to create stories about the stimuli. The Thematic Apperception Test (TAT) is a well-known constructive technique. **Completion** techniques involve providing the client with incomplete stimuli, such as sentence stems, and asking them to complete the items. **Choice or ordering techniques** include those that allow individuals to arrange or rank-order stimuli. CMH counselors are likely most interested in **expression** techniques in which clients are asked to create a drawing or scene. Common techniques include the house-tree-person, kinetic family drawing, and draw-a-person tests. In each case, the projective technique has a number of guidelines to assist in interpretation and understanding. For example, expression techniques might be interpreted based on size and placement of items, degree of detail provided, and type of lines and shading used when drawing. Although they may appear simple and fun, projective tests require a great deal of training to administer and interpret and are not always included within the scope of counselor licensure laws. Like other assessment procedures, projective personality assessments should not be used without proper training and supervision.

QUALITATIVE ASSESSMENT

In addition to calling on interviews, mental status examinations, and a variety of standardized assessment tools, CMH counselors may employ a plethora of qualitative assessment procedures. Often creative in nature, qualitative assessment procedures serve as both assessment and intervention. Goldman (1992) provided an overview of a number of qualitative assessment methods for counselors, noting that qualitative assessment methods are particularly useful in counseling because they allow for greater flexibility, do not require statistical sophistication, lend to client self-awareness, are more integrative and holistic, and are easily used with groups as well as individuals. Goldman highlighted several qualitative assessments, including lifelines, card sorts, and games. Qualitative assessments play an especially important role in family assessment because they are interactive and empowering, provide opportunity for context and depth, and are flexible across settings, populations, and theoretical foundations (Deacon & Piercy, 2001). A few of the more popular qualitative assessment methods you are likely to encounter in your training and role as a CMH counselor include the following:

- **Lifelines** or **timelines** in which a client is called on to depict key events or experiences using a timeline. Timelines may be general or focused. For example, Lucey and Staton (2003) proposed a solutions timeline for family counseling, whereas Curry (2009) provided guidelines for using spiritual timelines in counseling.

- **Genograms** in which clients construct a multigenerational family history and use symbols and graphics to create a visual depiction of a wide variety of issues (McGoldrick, Gerson, & Petry, 2008). Most often used to explore family functioning and relationships in a visual manner, genograms can be tailored to include attention to specific elements such as gender, culture, and spirituality (Butler, 2008). Genograms are often used to help counseling students develop self-awareness in a variety of areas related to multicultural and family counseling. Although genograms are emotionally intense, counselor education students who used them developed a healthier sense of self, understood their families and family dynamics in a new way, and reported developing as counselors (Lim, 2008).

- **Sandtray** experiences in which an individual is provided with a sandtray, a wide selection of miniature figures (e.g., people, animals, natural elements, objects), and a nondirective (e.g., "create your world") or directive (e.g., "show me what is happening at school") prompt. Although sandtray is an intervention, it yields very powerful assessment information about the client and his or her family and community context. Appropriate for use with children, adolescents, and adults and across a variety of theoretical orientations (Homeyer & Sweeney, 2010), some counselor educators are beginning to incorporate sandtray techniques in counselor preparation and supervision (Markos, Coker, & Jones, 2007).

Because they can be incredibly powerful in eliciting subconscious material and strong emotions, qualitative assessments must be used with appropriate supervision and preparation.

COLLATERAL SOURCES

The previous sections focused mostly on collecting information directly from clients or, when working with young children, from clients and their caretakers. As noted in the introduction, the most effective assessments will incorporate multiple methods and multiple sources. **Collateral sources**, or third parties, may be able to provide insights and observations that are helpful to the counseling process. This information might support client reports, add an additional layer or depth of understanding, or shed light when a client might be less than accurate in self-reporting. Of course, the CMH counselor is responsible for securing permissions to make contact with collateral sources and conducting the contacts in ways that protect client privacy.

Drummond and Jones (2010) classified potential sources of collateral information into three major areas: (1) **personal sources** such as partners, family members, roommates, coworkers, and neighbors; (2) **professional sources** such as mental health professionals, teachers and school professionals, medical professionals, social services workers, guardian ad litems, and probation/parole officers; and (3) **records** related to mental health, school, medical, social services, court, military, and criminal history.

The types of collateral information you use will depend on your setting and population. When working with minors, CMH counselors will likely wish to gather collateral information from as many parents and guardians as feasible as well as the child's teachers. If a client is under the care of another mental health professional, it is a counselor's professional responsibility to ensure that he or she is not providing duplicate services; such assurances can only come via direct contact. If the client had previous mental health services, a records review might be especially helpful in understanding the context of the current concern and identifying the counseling approaches that did (and did not) work the last time. Finally, CMH counselors in crisis settings might look to previous mental health, legal, and medical records to understand current concerns. For example, a CMH counselor who is working in an emergency room when police arrive with someone with a greatly altered mental status might find a wealth of information regarding mental health and substance abuse history by reviewing records from previous visits.

In situations where a client has a long history of involvement with mental health systems or is engaged with a number of professional sources, CMH counselors may have the opportunity to take part in interdisciplinary teams as part of the assessment and treatment process. For example, a client in therapeutic foster care may be participating in services with a host of providers: a counselor at a youth services agency, therapeutic foster parents, a guardian ad litem, a social services caseworker, a county mental health caseworker, a psychiatrist, a school counselor, or a juvenile probation officer. Imagine the richness of assessment information that would emerge from meetings wherein this diverse group of professional and personal collateral sources came together to share insights and brainstorm solutions.

SCREENING FOR HIGH-RISK SITUATIONS

Throughout their assessment duties, CMH counselors must be alert to a number of high-risk situations that may indicate the need for more immediate, intensive, or specialized response. Upon screening, CMH counselors must document the nature of screening and results as part of the formal client record (see Chapter 11). High-risk situations overviewed here include general medical conditions, suicide risk, violence risk, intimate partner violence and abuse, and substance concerns.

General Medical Conditions

CMH counselors must stay alert to the reality that a number of medical or substance-related issues might first appear as mental health concerns; medical concerns may also make mental health concerns worse. In short, CMH counselors should be sure clients see a medical professional for first episodes of major disorders, fast or intense onset of concerns, initial concerns emerging at or after midlife, concerns that arise around the same time as an illness or medication use, absent or minimal stressors, rapid changes in mental status, hallucinations (other than auditory), changes in motor functioning, changes in perception, changes in cognitive functioning, and history or signs of medical concerns (Pollak, Levy, & Breitholtz, 1999). This is especially important given that nearly all of these concerns could indicate a medical emergency.

Note that many of the more dramatic signs noted by Pollak et al. (1999) should be clear during the mental status examination, and gathering good history regarding medical status during intake will help illuminate potential medical concerns. CMH counselors should be aware that many common medical disorders are frequently misdiagnosed as mental disorders (APA, 2000). Interested readers may see Pollak et al. (1999) for a list of questions they might use to screen clients for medical concerns. When in doubt, CMH counselors should recommend clients visit physicians to ensure symptoms are not medically caused. For example, I once worked with a college student who reported struggling with low mood, self-esteem, and poor body image, especially since gaining 20 pounds and losing a significant relationship. Although she worked hard in our sessions and had no history of concerns, she seemed to make little progress, leading me to recommend she visit student health services for a checkup. The resulting diagnosis, hypothyroidism, explained nearly all her symptoms; the simple treatment had her feeling back to herself within weeks.

Suicide Risk

Perhaps the most nerve-wracking situation for new CMH counselors is the prospect of working with a client who is having thoughts of suicide. Unfortunately, suicide is a leading cause of death in the United States (Centers for Disease Control, 2010), and individuals are exponentially more likely to think about suicide than to die by suicide. When we consider this along with the reality that most people seek counseling services when they are at a crisis or turning point, it becomes critical that CMH counselors assess for suicide risk at the first session and again throughout the counseling process as necessary. In my experience, clients share thoughts of suicide in different ways. For that reason, I prefer a trifold approach to screening for suicide: use a standardized symptom inventory that includes screening questions regarding suicide risk, include a question related to suicide in the background paperwork, and always ask the client directly during the intake interview.

Granello (2010a) provided 12 core principles of suicide risk assessment CMH counselors may use to guide their thinking around suicide risk assessments. Her principles are as follows: suicide risk assessment: (1) of each person is unique; (2) is complex and challenging; (3) is an ongoing process; (4) errs on the side of caution; (5) is collaborative; (6) relies on clinical judgment; (7) takes all threats, warning signs, and risk factors seriously; (8) asks the tough questions; (9) is treatment; (10) tries to uncover the underlying message; (11) is done in a cultural content; and (12) is documented.

Although there are a number of standardized instruments, semistructured interviews, and structured interviews one might find useful for suicide risk assessment, the most common method of assessment is the clinical interview. The clinical interview begins with ascertaining whether a client is having thoughts of suicide via a clear and direct prompt (e.g., "You have shared tremendous pain and frustration with me today. I wonder, are you having thoughts of suicide?"). Once a counselor has identified that **suicidal ideation**, or thoughts of suicide, is present, attention must turn to understanding the nature of the suicide risk so that a counselor can help a client take steps to stay safe. Key elements of the suicide risk assessment include the following:

- Precipitating events

- Nature of the suicidal ideation (frequency, intensity, specificity)

- Presence and nature of a suicide plan (specificity of plan, access to means, action taken toward plan, intent to carry through with plan)

- Reasons for dying

- Reasons for living, supports, and suicide deterrents

- Presence and nature of suicide warning signs or red flags as identified by the American Association of Suicidology using the mnemonic IS PATH WARM: ideation, substance abuse, purposelessness, anxiety, trapped, hopelessness, withdrawal, anger, recklessness, and mood changes (Rudd et al., 2006)

- Specific client history and context of risk and protective factors including stressors, personal history, family history, and mental health history

The suicide risk assessment must be tailored to the client and population. Once the risk assessment is conducted, CMH counselors create suicide management plans that ensure access to appropriate levels of treatment and resources clients need to stay safe. Management plans will vary depending on the degree of risk the client is believed to have (e.g., minimal, mild, moderate, severe, or extreme) and the degree to which the client has supports who can help ensure his or her safety. To learn more about suicide risk assessment and intervention, you may wish to refer to Barrio (2007); Granello (2010b); Jobes (2006); Lee and Bartlett (2005); Rudd, Mandrusiak, and Joiner (2006); and Shea (2002).

Violence Risk

Although CMH counselors in most settings tend to see more clients with suicidal ideation than those with thoughts of hurting others, they are still responsible for screening for violence risk. Haggård-Grann (2007) provided evidence that calls into question the degree to which CMH counselors are accurate in predicting violence risk when using unstructured clinical assessments and provided several structured means for assessing violence risk. Becoming familiar with these resources is particularly important for counselors who work with youth, offender populations, and individuals who have previous histories of aggression toward others.

Intimate Partner Violence and Abuse

Unfortunately, physical abuse, sexual abuse, and intimate partner violence (IPV) are all too common in our world. Throughout counseling, CMH counselors are wise to incorporate screening assessments in hopes of detecting child or adult clients who are at risk in their living situations. The CDC (Basile, Hertz, & Back, 2007) provided a review of multiple assessment tools for use in clinical settings. The review includes coverage of the scale, characteristics, administration method, reliability, validity, and sensitivity and also provides a number of examples that could easily be integrated into an intake interview or client background form. For example, the Woman Abuse Screening Tool (WAST)–Short (Brown, Lent, Schmidt, & Sas, 2000) has just two questions, "In general, how would you describe your relationship . . . a lot of tension? some tension? no tension?" and "Do you and your partner work out arguments with . . . great difficulty, some difficulty, no difficulty?" Individuals who indicate the more severe option on either question, or indicate at least the middle option on both, should be assessed more closely for IPV.

All children and adolescents should also be screened for abuse and neglect. The first step in screening for these issues is recognizing associated signs and symptoms. The Child Welfare Information Gateway (2007) provides a fact sheet with checklists regarding child and parental signs of physical abuse, sexual abuse, emotional maltreatment, and neglect. The Futures Without Violence (2003) organization also offers a free 30-minute DVD, *Screen to End Abuse*, demonstrating ways to screen for family violence within medical settings. In addition, CMH counselors might use intake prompts such as the following: "Tell me about a typical day at home," "How safe do you feel at home?" "What are some of the rules at home? What happens when you break the rules?" or "Has anyone ever touched you in a way you did not like?" Once CMH counselors are alert to potential indicators of abuse or neglect, they may use that information as a reason for additional discussion during the interview and use information gleaned to report suspected abuse or neglect for investigation. CMH counselors must be aware that it is not their job to investigate child abuse; attempting to do so without appropriate training may jeopardize the integrity of subsequent investigations.

Substance Concerns

Substance use disorders are among the most common mental health disorders, with approximately 15% of the general population experiencing a substance use disorder in their lifetime (Kessler et al., 2005). Unfortunately, CMH counselors without substance abuse backgrounds and those who do not work in substance abuse settings are likely to miss signs and symptoms. Again, CMH counselors may use a combination of standardized instruments, intake interviews, and background forms to identify substance concerns. Indeed, most of the broad-symptom inventories mentioned previously include attention to substance use; a number of more specialized tools, such as the SASSI-III (Miller & Lazowski, 1999), Alcohol Use Disorders Identification Test (Babor, Higgins-Biddle, Saunders, & Monteiro, 2001), and the National Institutes of Health (2009) NIDA Quick Screen and NIDA-modified ASSIST are also available for screening purposes. Of course, CMH counselors will need to use an understanding of assessment concepts to determine which tools are most appropriate for use.

CULTURAL BIAS IN ASSESSMENT

As the world becomes more diverse, CMH counselors must remain aware of and guard against cultural bias in assessment. The *ACA Code of Ethics* (2014) includes numerous references to multicultural considerations related to assessment, including Standards A.2.c, E.5.b, and E.8, which read:

> **A.2.c. Developmental and Cultural Sensitivity.** Counselors communicate information in ways that are both developmentally and culturally appropriate. Counselors use clear and understandable language when discussing issues related to informed consent. When clients have difficulty understanding the language that counselors use, counselors provide necessary services (e.g., arranging for a qualified interpreter or translator) to ensure comprehension by clients. In collaboration with clients, counselors consider cultural implications of informed consent procedures and, where possible, counselors adjust their practices accordingly.

> **E.5.b. Cultural Sensitivity.** Counselors recognize that culture affects the manner in which clients' problems are defined and experienced. Clients' socioeconomic and cultural experiences are considered when diagnosing mental disorders.

> **E.8. Multicultural Issues/Diversity in Assessment.** Counselors select and use with caution assessment techniques normed on populations other than that of the client. Counselors recognize the effects of age, color, culture, disability, ethnic group, gender, race, language preference, religion, spirituality, sexual orientation, and socioeconomic status on test administration and interpretation, and they place test results in proper perspective with other relevant factors.

Finally, the Association for Assessment in Counseling and Education (2012) compiled the *Standards for Multicultural Assessment* to guide counselors in culturally sensitive assessment.

Cultural bias is an issue across assessment methods because assessment procedures do not always account for differences among diverse groups, worldview, acculturation and language, socioeconomic status, and client factors (Erford, 2007). Standardized instruments are said to have **bias** when experiences other than those that are being assessed factor into results (Whitson, 2009). This may take place in the form of content bias (when test material is more familiar to certain groups), internal structure bias (when scores are more reliable for some groups than others), and predictive bias (when tests are more or less accurate at predicting performance for different groups).

Attending to cultural bias in clinical assessment is important because mental health professionals have a long, unfortunate history of imposing dominant social views on others, pathologizing diverse individuals, and overdiagnosing or underdiagnosing on the basis of culture (Eriksen & Kress, 2005; Zalaquett, Fuerth, Stein, Ivey, & Ivey, 2008). A good deal of diagnostic assessment bias and misdiagnosis is related to a combination of information processing errors that include things like stereotyping, self-confirmatory bias, and self-fulfilling prophecy (McLaughlin, 2002). Hays, Prosek, and McLeod (2010) explored the role of culture in clinical decision making by having CMH counselors formulate diagnoses for hypothetical clients. The researchers found that a disproportionate number of racial/ethnic minority clients were diagnosed with bipolar disorder, and women were disproportionality diagnosed with major depressive disorder, alcohol abuse/dependence, and personality disorders. Counselors also tended to minimize culture as influencing their decisions even when cases included cultural variables for consideration; this was especially true when client and counselors were mismatched in terms of characteristics. Finally, awareness of oppression was associated with client prognosis. Cultural bias need not be limited to race/ethnicity and gender. Simply knowing a hypothetical client's birth order influenced clinicians' perceptions of him, assumptions regarding characteristic and family experiences, and overall prognosis for counseling (Stewart, 2004). After completing formal coursework in assessment, diagnosis, and multicultural counseling, you will begin developing the sensitivities needed to customize assessment procedures in a culturally sensitive manner.

USING ASSESSMENT TO INFORM COUNSELING

This chapter has focused on a multitude of ways in which CMH counselors use assessment to gather information about client functioning, needs, and strengths from beginning to end of the counseling process. Although assessment is therapeutic in its own right, the true power of assessment is in the context of informing case conceptualization, diagnosis, treatment planning, and evaluation. As counselors develop a solid information base, they are better able to use theoretical tools to conceptualize client needs and the counseling process. This information will inform the degree to which counselors believe the client's functioning is optimal, normal, and pathological and will flow directly into diagnostic efforts (see Chapter 6). In turn, counselors will be best able to identify treatment implications for their clients (see Chapter 7), including determining appropriate levels of care (see Chapter 4) and deciding when to refer for possible medication management (see Chapter 8).

CASE STUDY

In the following pages, you will have the opportunity to get to know Mahdi Taylor, a composite client created by Drs. Daniel and Maria Paredes. In Chapter 7 Dr. Paredes and Dr. Paredes will provide a treatment plan for Mahdi. In this way, you will have an opportunity to see just how closely assessment, diagnosis, and treatment planning are connected.

Overview

Mahdi Taylor was referred to his Employee Assistance Program (EAP) by the human resources department at his place of employment. Given the brief nature of services provided by the EAP, the EAP counselor asked Mahdi to complete a background information form; current concerns checklist (see appendix); and the Adult Self-Report (ASR), a standardized general-symptom inventory that is part of the Achenbach System of Empirically Based Assessment (Achenbach, 2012), prior to taking part in the unstructured intake interview.

On the Current Concerns Questionnaire and Checklist, Mahdi wrote that he was seeking counseling because he was "missing work due to family responsibilities," and he checked items related to feeling anxious, parent-child relationship, and stress/time/life management. Overall, Mr. Taylor's responses to the ASR indicated that he was within the "normal" range for men his age in all but three areas; his responses to the Job Adaptive Functioning, Somatic Complaints, and Attention Problems scales flagged in the "borderline clinical" range. With the exception of two items related to concentration and focus and one item related to alcohol use, he did not endorse any critical items. The following includes a summary of Mr. Taylor's unstructured intake interview.

Intake Report

Identifying Information. Mahdi Taylor, a 23-year-old African American male was referred for short-term counseling services via his Employee Assistance Program (EAP) due to a high degree of absenteeism at work. Mr. Taylor is single, has no children, and lives alone. He works full-time as an engineer at a small consulting firm.

Presenting Problem. Mr. Taylor was referred to his EAP due to an increasing degree of absenteeism over the last 3 months. The client reported that he has been in "crisis mode" since his mother was diagnosed with stage 4 cancer earlier this year. Mr. Taylor attributed his absenteeism to taking his mother to medical appointments at a local cancer clinic, researching treatment options, and caring for her after treatments. He noted that his philosophy of life is that just about any problem can be solved with the right understanding of the problem and the correct application of remedial action, thus fueling his desire to "just keep it moving." Although Mr. Taylor admitted to difficulty sleeping, weight loss, and feeling "on edge" more days than not the last 2 months, he denied other emotional or behavioral concerns, noting he "hasn't the luxury of being vulnerable right now."

Mental Status Examination. Mr. Taylor presented for the interview well-groomed and wearing business-casual attire. He had no unusual physical characteristics, appeared his age, and appeared to be of average height and weight. Although he appeared reluctant to participate in portions of the interview related to his functioning and coping, Mr. Taylor was calm and cooperative, making appropriate eye contact throughout the interview. The client's speech was soft but clearly articulated, and his motor behavior was within normal limits. Mr. Taylor showed few signs of emotion, even when discussing his mother's condition and his resulting "crisis mode"; he reported his mood as "fine." The client denied suicidal and homicidal ideation; his thinking was logical and coherent, demonstrating no disturbance in memory, orientation, thought content, process, or perception. Although he demonstrated excellent judgment and impulse control and his level of educational and occupational

(Continued)

(Continued)

attainment indicate he is likely of above-average intelligence, Mr. Taylor struggled to demonstrate insight into the impact of the current situation on his personal and professional well-being.

Current Situation and Functioning. As will be discussed, Mr. Taylor reported that, as the oldest of two children in a single-parent family, he serves as primary caregiver to his mother. Although he reported living alone in an apartment, Mr. Taylor has been spending a great deal of time at his mother's home. He described a typical day as waking up by 6:00 a.m., driving to his mother's home to ensure she takes her medications as prescribed, taking his mother to radiation or chemotherapy appointments, and returning her to her home around 12:00 p.m. He noted that he makes decisions about whether to stay with her or go to work based on her day-to-day energy level and treatment side effects. He reported returning to his mother's home most evenings, spending several hours researching treatment options via the Internet, and returning home at approximately 10:00 or 11:00 p.m. each evening. On weekends, Mr. Taylor reports a similar schedule with the exception of taking his mother to church or preparing the home for visitors from church on weeks she is too ill to attend service.

Mr. Taylor reported working for a small engineering firm for approximately 2 years since graduation, expressing gratitude that his employer was willing to work with him on absences due to his mother's condition as long as he followed EAP recommendations. He noted with pride that he did not miss one day of work in the first 18 months on the job. Mr. Taylor denied current financial concerns, noting that his salary was sufficient to cover his cost of living, student loans, and entertainment. However, the client expressed worry about the uncertainty of his job and the likelihood that he would need to assist with his mother's health care or living expenses while ensuring his younger sister had enough money to cover tuition and living expenses to finish her degree.

Mr. Taylor reported that, prior to his mother's illness, he went to the gym 5 days per week, attended church service with his mother at least once a week, and saw friends from college an average of 2 nights per week. He described maintaining these activities as impractical, noting that he has not been to the gym since his mother's diagnosis, does not have time for social events, and does not wish to introduce "negativity" by talking about his concerns with friends of extended family members. Similarly, he reports withholding details regarding his mother's diagnosis and prognosis from his sister so that she is not "distracted" from her studies.

Relevant History. Given the nature of the presenting concern and time-limited nature of EAP services, the following brief histories were collected.

Family History. Mr. Taylor, the oldest of two children, was raised outside Charlotte, North Carolina. He reports that his mother served 25 years as an administrative assistant in the local school district, and his sister, age 20, is a college student studying abroad in Brazil. He noted no memory of his father and expressed admiration for his mother's ability to provide a stable and loving home despite a lack of financial and familial support. Although he noted that his mother was not afraid to give a "whooping" when it was deserved, he denied experiencing emotional, physical, or sexual abuse as a child.

Social/Relational History. Mr. Taylor described himself as a "normal" child who had several steady friends throughout childhood and adolescence and got along well at school with the exception of a few minor pranks and incidents that resulted in disciplinary action at home or school. He reported engaging in organized athletics throughout middle and high school and beginning to date around age 15. He describes having the "normal" college experience and, despite a lack of contact the last 2 months, keeping in contact with friends since graduation. Mr. Taylor reported that he previously engaged in three serious romantic relationships but noted that he is "not in the place" for a romantic relationship now.

Educational/Occupational History. Mr. Taylor graduated from high school with honors at age 17, attended a 4-year college on scholarship, and graduated with a bachelor's degree in engineering at age 21. He reports working part-time since age 16, holding a work-study position throughout college, and working full-time for the last 2 years. As described, his current situation has led to difficulty at work and the current referral.

Developmental History. Mr. Taylor reported reaching developmental milestones as expected throughout life and denied knowledge of developmental concerns at birth, in childhood, or in adolescence. His reports of family, social/relational, and educational/occupational histories support these reports.

Medical History. Mr. Taylor denies any history of hospitalization or treatment for medical or health concerns. Aside from taking over-the-counter medication for seasonal allergies, Mr. Taylor denies taking any medication.

Mental Health and Substance Abuse History. Mr. Taylor denied any past or present mental health or substance abuse concerns or diagnoses, noting that this is the first time he is seeking treatment. Prior to his mother's illness, Mr. Taylor noted that he used alcohol socially, perhaps consuming two to three beers on a weekend when out with friends. He admitted to drinking more heavily while in college, attributed his use to "normal college stuff," and denied any consequences of use during that time. Mr. Taylor admitted that he will occasionally "have a few" drinks when he returns home from caring for his mother; he noted drinking as many as six beers on "bad days." The client denies drinking daily, driving under the influence, or missing work as a consequence of his alcohol use, noting that he only misses work when he needs to be with his mother. The client denied use of illicit or prescription drugs.

Cultural Considerations. As a young African American male living in the South and raised in a single-parent family, Mr. Taylor acknowledged that he is accustomed to "facing and rising above adversity." He attributes much of his success to strength demonstrated by his mother, sense of personal responsibility fostered within his faith community and the historically black university he attended, and personal resolve. Indeed, these strengths and supports have served him well in terms of his personal attainment and will be critical to the success of the counseling process. At the same time, he appears to be approaching his mother's illness with a belief that proper action and control on his part will

(Continued)

(Continued)

ensure her recovery. This belief, coupled with his young age, high degree of responsibility, and decreased coping via exercise and social outlets, has led to impairment in functioning, signs of growing anxiety, and coping through alcohol use.

Counseling Goals. Mr. Taylor admits that he is attending counseling primarily to satisfy his employer. He reports little interest in processing his experiences, coming to terms with his mother's illness, or learning coping skills. Rather, he reports a primary goal for counseling to be learning about different oncology providers and ensuring that he does all he can to "be the son [his] mother deserves."

Questions for Discussion

1. What similarities and differences do you see among concerns noted on Mr. Taylor's ASR results, items endorsed on the Current Concerns Checklist, and self-reports during the unstructured intake interview? What "new" information does the ASR provide?

2. As a CMH counselor, what additional types of assessment information would be helpful for guiding your counseling process with Mr. Taylor?

3. What are the benefits and drawbacks of requesting that Mr. Taylor
   a. participate in a structured diagnostic interview,
   b. complete additional standardized assessments, and/or
   c. participate in qualitative assessment procedures?

4. How can you use the initial assessment results reported in this case study to better understand Mr. Taylor's strengths, supports, stressors, and counseling preferences? How will the report inform your proposed approach to counseling?

REFERENCES

Abidin, R. R. (1995). *Parenting stress index* (3rd ed.). Odessa, FL: Psychological Assessment Resources.

Achenbach, T. (2012). *Achenbach system of empirically based assessment.* Retrieved from www .aseba.org.

American Counseling Association. (2014). *Code of Ethics.* Alexandria, VA: Author.

American Educational Research Association, American Psychological Association, and National Council on Measurement in Evaluation. (1999). *Standards for educational and psychological testing.* Washington, DC: Author.

American Psychiatric Association. (2000). *Diagnostic and statistical manual of mental disorders* (4th ed.). Alexandria, VA: Author.

Association for Assessment in Counseling. (2003). *Responsibilities of users of standardized tests* (3rd ed.). Retrieved from www.theaaceonline.com/rust.

Association for Assessment in Counseling & Education. (2012). *Standards for multicultural assessment.* Retrieved from www.theaaceonline.com/resources.

Babor, T. F., Higgins-Biddle, J. C., Saunders, J. B., & Monteiro, M. G. (2001). *The alcohol use disorders identification test: Guidelines for use in primary care* (2nd ed.). Retrieved from World Health Organization, whqlibdoc.who.int/hq/2001/who_msd_msb_01.6a.pdf.

Barrio, C. A. (2007). Assessing children for suicide risk: Guidelines for developmentally appropriate interviewing. *Journal of Mental Health Counseling, 29,* 50–66.

Basile, K. C., Hertz, M. F., & Back, S. E. (2007). *Intimate partner violence and sexual violence victimization assessment instruments for use in healthcare settings: Version 1.* Atlanta, GA: Centers for Disease Control and Prevention, National Center for Injury Prevention and Control.

Beck, A. T., Steer, R. A., & Brown, G. K. (1996). *Manual for the Beck Depression Inventory-II.* San Antonio, TX: Psychological Corporation.

Briere, J. (1996). *Trauma symptom checklist for children: Professional manual.* Lutz, FL: Psychological Assessment Resources.

Brown, J. B., Lent, B., Schmidt, G., & Sas, G. (2000). Application of the woman abuse screening tool (WAST) and WAST-short in the family practice setting. *Journal of Family Practice, 49,* 896–903.

Butcher, J. N., Graham, J. R., Ben-Porath, Y S., Tellegen, Y. S., Dahlstrom, W. G., & Kaemmer, B. (2001). *MMPI-2: Minnesota Multiphasic Personality Inventory-2: Manual for administration and scoring* (Rev. ed.). Minneapolis: University of Minnesota Press.

Butler, J. F. (2008). The family diagram and genogram: Comparisons and contrasts. *American Journal of Family Therapy, 36,* 169–180. doi:10.1080/01926180701291055

Cattell, R. B., Cattell, M. D., & Cattell, H. E. P. (1993). *Sixteen Personality Factor Questionnaire* (5th ed.). Champaign, IL: Institute for Personality and Ability Testing.

Centers for Disease Control. (2010, Summer). *Suicide facts at a glance.* Retrieved from www.cdc.gov/violencepresenvetion/pdf/suicide_datasheet-a.pdf.

Child Welfare Information Gateway. (2007). *Recognizing child abuse and neglect: Signs and symptoms.* Retrieved from http://www.childwelfare.gov/pubPDFs/signs.cfm.

Costa Jr., P. T., & McCrae, R. R. (2010). *NEO inventories professional manual: NEO-PI-3, NEO-FFI-3, NEO PI-R.* Lutz, FL: Psychological Assessment Resources.

Council for Accreditation of Counseling and Related Educational Programs. (2016). *2016 Standards.* Retrieved from www.cacrep.org.

Curry, J. R. (2009). Examining client spiritual history and the construction of meaning: The use of spiritual timelines in counseling. *Journal of Creativity in Mental Health, 4,* 113–123. doi:10.1080/15401380902945178

Daniel, M., & Carothers, T. (2007). Mental status examination. In M. Hersen & J. C. Thomas (Eds.), *Handbook of clinical interviewing with adults* (pp. 49–63). Los Angeles: Sage.

Deacon, S. A., & Piercy, F. P. (2001). Qualitative methods in family evaluation: Creative assessment techniques. *American Journal of Family Therapy, 29,* 355–373.

Derogatis, L. R. (1994). *SCL-90-R: Administration, scoring, and procedures manual-II* (2nd ed.). Towson, MD: Clinical Psychometric Research.

Drummond, R. J., & Jones, K. D. (2010). *Assessment procedures for counselors and helping professionals* (7th ed.). Boston: Pearson.

Erford, B. T. (2006). *Counselor's guide to clinical, personality, and behavioral assessment.* Boston: Lahaska.

Erford, B. T. (2007). *Assessment for counselors.* Boston: Lahaska.

Eriksen, K., & Kress, V. E. (2005). *Beyond the DSM story: Ethical quandaries, challenges, and best practices.* Thousand Oaks, CA: Sage.

Folstein, M. F., Folstein, S. E., & McHugh, P. R. (1975). "Mini-Mental State": A practical method for grading the cognitive state of patients for the clinician. *Journal of Psychiatric Research, 12,* 189–198.

Futures Without Violence. (Producer). (2003). *Screen to end abuse* [DVD]. Available from http://www.futureswithoutviolence.org/screen-to-end-abuse/

Garner, D. M. (2004). *Eating Disorder Inventory-3.* Lutz, FL: Psychological Assessment Resources.

Goldman, L. (1992). Qualitative assessment: An approach for counselors. *Journal of Counseling & Development, 70,* 616–621. doi:10.1002/j.1556–6676.1992.tb01671.x

Granello, D. H. (2010a). The process of suicide risk assessment: Twelve core principles. *Journal of Counseling & Development, 88,* 363–370. doi:10.1002/j.1556–6678.2010.tb00034.x

Granello, D. H. (2010b). A suicide crisis intervention model with 25 practical strategies for implementation. *Journal of Mental Health Counseling, 32,* 218–235.

Haggård-Grann, U. (2007). Assessing violence risk: A review and clinical recommendations. *Journal of Counseling & Development, 85,* 294–301. doi:10.1002/j.1556–6678.2007.tb00477.x

Hays, D. G., Prosek, E. A., & McLeod, A. L. (2010). A mixed-methodological analysis of the role of culture in the clinical decision-making process. *Journal of Counseling & Development, 88,* 114–121. doi:10.1002/j.1556–6678.2010.tb00158.x

Hedberg, A. G. (2010). *Forms for the therapist.* San Diego, CA: Academic Press.

Hohenshil, T. H. (1996). Editorial: Role of assessment and diagnosis in counseling. *Journal of Counseling & Development, 75,* 64–67. doi:10.1002/j.1556–6676.1996.tb02316.x

Homeyer, L. E., & Sweeney, D. S. (2010). *Sandtray therapy: A practical manual* (2nd ed.). New York: Routledge.

Jobes, D. A. (2006). *Managing suicidal risk: A collaborative approach.* New York: Guilford Press.

Jones, K. D. (2010). The unstructured clinical interview. *Journal of Counseling & Development, 88,* 220–226. doi:10.1002/j.1556–6678.2010.tb00013.x

Kessler, R. C., Berglund, P., Demler, O., Jin, R., Merikangas, K. R., & Walters, E. E. (2005). Lifetime prevalence and age-of-onset distributions of DSM-IV disorders in the national comorbidity survey replication. *Archives of General Psychiatry, 62,* 593–602.

Kovacs, M. (2010). *Children's Depression Inventory 2 (CDI 2) manual.* Toronto: Multi-Health Systems.

Lambert, M. J., Hansen, N. B., Umpress, V., Lunnen, K., Okiishi, J., Burlingame, G. M., et al. (1996). *Administration and scoring manual for the OQ-45.2.* Stevenson, MD: American Credentialing Services.

Lee, J. B., & Bartlett, M. L. (2005). Suicide prevention: Critical elements for managing suicidal clients and counselor liability without the use of a no suicide contract. *Death Studies, 29,* 847–865. doi:10.1080/07481180500236776

Lim, S. (2008). Transformative aspects of genogram work: Perceptions and experiences of graduate students in a counseling training program. *Family Journal, 16,* 35–42. doi:10.1177/1066480707309321

Lindzey, G. (1959). On the classification of projective techniques. *Psychological Bulletin, 56*(2), 158–168. doi:10.1037/h0043871

Lucey, C. F., & Staton, A. R. (2003). Constructing a solutions timeline: Creating possibilities in counseling. *Family Journal, 11,* 409–412. doi:10.1177/1066480703254803

Markos, P. A., Coker, J. K., & Jones, W. P. (2007). Play in supervision: Exploring the sandtray with beginning practicum students. *Journal of Creativity in Mental Health, 2,* 3–15. doi:10.1300/J456v02n03-02

McGoldrick, M., Gerson, R, & Petry, S. (2008). *Genograms: Assessment and intervention* (3rd ed.). New York: W.W. Norton.

McLaughlin, J. E. (2002). Reducing diagnostic bias. *Journal of Mental Health Counseling, 24,* 256–269.

Miller, F. G., & Lazowski, L. E. (1999). *The SASSI-3 manual.* Springville, IN: SASSI Institute.

Myers, I. B., McCaulley, M. H., Quenk, N. L., & Hammer, A. L. (1998). *MBTI manual: A guide to the development and use of the Myers-Briggs Type Indicator instrument* (3rd ed.). Palo Alto, CA: Consulting Psychologists Press.

National Institutes of Health, National Institute on Drug Abuse. (2009). *Screening for drug use in general medical settings: Resource guide* (NIH Publication No. 09–7384). Retrieved from http://www.drugabuse.gov/publications/resource-guide.

Naugle, K. A. (2009). Counseling and testing: What counselors need to know about state laws on assessment and testing. *Measurement and Evaluation in Counseling and Development, 42,* 31–45. doi:10.1177/0748175609333561

Pearson Education. (2012). *Qualification levels.* Retrieved from www.pearsonassessments.com.

Polanski, P. J., & Hinkle, J. S. (2000). The mental status examination: Its use by professional counselors. *Journal of Counseling & Development, 78,* 357–364. doi:10.1002/j.1556-6676.2000.tb01918.x

Pollak, J., Levy, S., & Breitholtz, T. (1999). Screening for medical and neurodevelopmental disorders for the professional counselor. *Journal of Counseling & Development, 77,* 350–358. doi:10.1002/j.1556-6676.1999.tb02459.x

Robins, L. N., Cottler, L., Bucholz, K., & Compton, W. (1995). *Diagnostic Interview Schedule, Version IV.* St. Louis, MO: Washington School of Medicine.

Rudd, M. D., Berman, A. L., Joiner Jr., T. E., Nock, M. K., Silverman, M. M., Morton, M., et al. (2006). Warning signs for suicide: Theory, research, and clinical applications. *Suicide & Life-Threatening Behavior, 36,* 255–262.

Rudd, M. D., Mandrusiak, M., & Joiner Jr., T. E. (2006). The case against no-suicide contracts: The commitment to treatment statement as a practice alternative. *Journal of Clinical Psychology, 62,* 254–251. doi:10.1521/suli.2006.36.3.255

Shea, C. S. (2002). *The practical art of suicide assessment: A guide for mental health and substance abuse counselors.* New York: Wiley.

Snyder, D. K. (1997). *Marital Satisfaction Inventory-Revised (MSI-R) manual.* Los Angeles: Western Psychological Services.

Sommers-Flanagan, J., & Sommers-Flanagan, R. (2003). *Clinical interviewing* (3rd ed.). Hoboken, NJ: John Wiley & Sons.

Stewart, A. E. (2004). Can knowledge of client birth order bias clinical judgment? *Journal of Counseling & Development, 82,* 167–176. doi:10.1002/j.1556-6678.2004.tb00298.x

Teare, M., Fristad, M. A., Weller, E. B., Weller, R. A., & Salmon, P. (1998). Study I: Development and criterion validity of the Children's Interview for Psychiatric Syndromes (ChIPS). *Journal of Child and Adolescent Psychopharmacology, 8,* 205–211.

Whitson, S. C. (2009). *Principles and applications of assessment in counseling* (3rd ed.). Belmont, CA: Brooks/Cole.

Wiger, D. E. (2010). *The clinical documentation sourcebook: The complete paperwork resource for your mental health practice.* Hoboken, NJ: John Wiley & Sons.

Zalaquett, C. P., Fuerth, K. M., Stein, C., Ivey, A. E., & Ivey, M. B. (2008). Reframing the DSM-IV-TR from a multicultural/social justice perspective. *Journal of Counseling & Development, 86,* 364–371. doi:10.1002/j.1556-6678.2008.tb00521.x

Current Concerns Questionnaire and Checklist (Adult)

Why are you seeking counseling today?

Below is a list of some reasons people seek counseling. Please mark your concerns below. Then, circle the item that you see as the most important issue.

Mood-Related Concerns

❑ Feeling sadness or depression NOT related to grief

❑ Feeling sadness or depression related to grief

❑ Feeling angry or irritable

❑ Feeling anxious (nervous, fearful, worried, panicky)

❑ Feeling guilty or shameful

❑ Having suicidal thoughts or urges

❑ Making a suicide attempt

Relationship Concerns

❑ Family or stepfamily relationship

❑ Significant other/spouse relationship

❑ Parent-child relationship

❑ Nonfamily relationship

Addictive Behavior

❑ Alcohol

❑ Illegal/prescription drugs

❑ Gambling

❑ Other (explain: _____)

Other Life Concerns

❑ Personal growth (no specific problem)

❑ Adjustment to life changes

❑ Career decisions or dissatisfaction

❑ Stress/time/life management

❏ Health concerns

❏ Self-image/self-esteem

❏ Learning/academic difficulties

❏ Religious or spiritual concerns

❏ Sexual identity concern

❏ Other life concern
(explain: _____)

Other Behavioral Concerns

❏ Eating problem (overeating or refusal to eat)

❏ Sleeping problem

❏ Problem with drugs or alcohol

❏ Harming self without wanting to die

❏ Illegal behaviors

❏ Speech problem

❏ Concerns about sexual functioning

❏ Unusual behaviors
(explain: _____)

❏ Unusual experiences
(explain: _____)

Problems Related to Trauma or Abuse

❏ Current or past physical abuse

❏ Current or past emotional abuse

❏ Current or past sexual abuse

❏ Current or past neglect

❏ History of abandonment

❏ History of family domestic violence

❏ Other traumatic experience

Couple Concerns (complete if couple)

❏ Enrichment/growth (no specific problem)

❏ Premarital/preunion counseling

❏ Communication

❏ Concerns with family relationships or parenting

❏ Financial concerns

❏ Sexual concerns

❏ Concerns regarding abuse/violence

❏ Seeking divorce

Remember to circle the most significant issue

When did you first become concerned about this issue?

How have you attempted to deal with this issue?

Have you sought other treatment related to any of the concerns above? If yes, please explain:

CHAPTER 6

Diagnosis

Gary Gintner

Epidemiological studies over the past 20 years have shown that mental disorders are not only common but also are on the rise (Kessler, 2011; Keyes, 2007). In any one year, roughly one in five individuals will have some mental disorder (Kessler et al., 1994; U.S. Public Health Service, 1999). Complicating the problem is the finding that disorders like depression, bipolar disorder, and anxiety disorders are appearing at earlier ages (Keyes, 2007; Keyes & Lopez, 2002). According to the World Health Organization (WHO, 2004a), these prevalence rates are evident worldwide and lead to significant disability burden as indexed by premature death and years of living with a disabling condition. In the United States, only the costs associated with heart disease and physical disabilities exceed the costs associated with mental disorders (Keyes, 2007). These types of statistics highlight the critical role of diagnosis in identifying these conditions in a timely manner so that effective treatments can be rendered.

Simply put, diagnosis is the process of determining whether an individual has some maladaptive condition or mental disorder as manifested by a particular set of signs and symptoms (Maxmen, Ward, & Kilgus, 2009). Symptoms are reports of personal experience (e.g., feeling sad or hopeless), whereas signs are observed behaviors (e.g., crying or talking rapidly). A diagnostic classification system lays out the rules and the criteria for making a diagnosis using a particular constellation of these signs and symptoms. The two major classification systems currently in use are the *Diagnostic and Statistical Manual of Mental Disorders*, 5th edition (*DSM-5*; American Psychiatric Association [APA], 2013a) and the *International Classification of Disease*, 10th edition (*ICD*; WHO, 1992). The primary focus of this chapter is on the *DSM-5* because it is the dominant system used in the United States.

A diagnosis serves three major clinical purposes. First, a diagnosis is a way of defining a mental health problem so that mental health professionals, researchers, and other stakeholders have a common language for describing clinical entities such as depression, phobias, and substance dependence (First & Tasman, 2004; Hohenshil, 1996). Second, a diagnosis provides valuable information for making treatment decisions. For example, if a client has bipolar disorder, then mood stabilizers like lithium are the primary indicated treatment (First & Tasman, 2004). Third, a diagnosis helps to predict the likely course of a disorder (First, 2010). Research has shown that disorders vary from those that are more chronic and recurrent (e.g., schizophrenia, bipolar disorder, personality disorders) to those that are more acute and time-limited (e.g., acute stress disorder, adjustment disorder; First & Tasman, 2004). This prognostic information helps clinicians make decisions about the duration of treatment and the need for maintenance therapies to prevent recurrence (APA, 2010). Considering these benefits, diagnosis is deemed an essential clinical function in the delivery of mental health services (First, 2010; First & Tasman, 2004; Gintner & Mears, 2009; Gladding & Newsome, 2004).

A diagnosis, however, can also have associated risks that counselors need to take into account. The very process of naming something can lead to labeling the person (e.g., borderline or alcoholic) rather than designating the disorder. It is important to remember that a diagnosis describes a disorder a person *has*, not who a person *is* (APA, 2000, 2013a). A second problem is that many diagnoses, such as schizophrenia, are associated with stigma and the perception that those with the disorder are "crazy" or potentially dangerous. These negative stereotypes can impact help seeking, personal perception, and social acceptance (Ben-Zeev, Young, & Corrigan, 2010). A third problem is that DSM diagnostic codes, like diagnostic codes for medical disorders, can follow individuals throughout their lives, affecting their ability to obtain health insurance, secure employment in certain professions, and to even find housing (Ben-Zeev et al., 2010; Remley & Herlihy, 2007). These types of issues highlight the need for counselors to be aware of their own attitudes and to advocate for social changes that address these stereotypes and biases. This is addressed more fully in Chapter 3 of this volume.

The purpose of this chapter is to provide an overview of the diagnostic process. First, the concept of psychopathology is discussed relative to how "abnormality" is defined. Next, factors that contribute to the development of psychopathology are examined using the biopsychosocial model. Drawing upon this information, the diagnostic process itself is discussed using the *DSM-5*. Four guidelines for making an accurate diagnosis are then outlined and illustrated using a case study. A theme throughout is the role of diagnosis in defining the problem and informing treatment planning.

PSYCHOPATHOLOGY AND ETIOLOGY

The diagnostic process rests upon a fundamental understanding of **psychopathology** and factors that contribute to its **etiology**. Psychopathology is the manifestation of a disorder in terms of distress, maladaptive behaviors, and impairment. Etiology, on the other hand, refers to the causal factors that contribute to the development of a disorder or abnormal condition (Maxmen et al., 2009). The following sections discuss the relationship between psychopathology and mental health, the dimensions of psychopathology, and etiological issues using the biopsychosocial model.

Mental Health and Mental Illness

Counselors have had an uneasy relationship with the concept of "pathology" or "illness" because of the profession's positive developmental tradition and focus on wellness (Ivey & Ivey, 1999; Remley & Herlihy, 2007). According to this tradition, psychological problems are seen as "problems in living" that stem from normal developmental challenges (Remley & Herlihy, 2007). By overcoming these developmental obstacles, individuals can enhance their personal growth and state of positive mental health.

A significant challenge to this perspective, however, arose in the early 1990s with the emergence of managed care. Suddenly, a formal mental disorder diagnosis had to be documented in order to access mental health benefits. As a mental health professional, if you could not diagnose, you had a hard time finding employment. Throughout the country, there was a scramble to revise state licensing laws to authorize diagnosis in the scope of practice of mental health counselors. These types of pressures led many to rethink the traditional stance of the counseling profession and to call for efforts to integrate the pathology and wellness perspectives (Gintner & Mears, 2009; Hinkle, 1999; Hohenshil, 1996; Seligman, 2002).

The rise of positive psychology in the late 1990s would ironically provide the necessary bridge. From this perspective, mental health is more than the absence of symptoms or impairment (Haidt, 2006; Seligman, 2002). Rather, it also includes life-enhancing qualities such as well-being, life satisfaction, capacity for intimacy, and use of talents (Seligman, 2002; Seligman, Rashid, & Parks, 2006). Subsequent research bore out this distinction by showing that measures of positive mental health were only modestly correlated to indexes of pathology (Keyes, 2005, 2007). In other words, improving positive aspects of mental health does not necessarily result in corresponding reductions in symptomatology. Conversely, reducing symptoms does not necessarily improve indexes of positive mental health. This led to the development of what Keyes (2007) calls the **complete model of mental health**, which posits that mental health professionals need to not only promote positive development but also take steps to reduce symptoms and other factors that contribute to impairment or disability. Thus, assessing and treating pathology cannot be neglected because it is a critical part of promoting overall mental health.

Dimensions of Psychopathology

How is psychopathology determined? It entails some judgment of an individual's behavior relative to what is considered "normal" or adaptive for the cultural circumstances.

Psychopathology is usually considered an **abnormality** that causes harm to the individual or to others (Sue, Sue, & Sue, 2003). Three general dimensions are drawn on to make this determination: subjective distress, impaired role functioning, and norm violations (Maxmen et al., 2009).

Subjective Distress. We all have had periods of feeling depressed, panicky, anxious, or overly stressed. But when it becomes too intense or too prolonged, it can be considered abnormal and harmful (Sue et al., 2003). This dimension is especially applicable to internalizing disorders that are characterized by excessive anxiety, worry, rumination, and physiological arousal. Common internalizing disorders include depression and anxiety disorders (Gintner, 2008).

But *too much* subjective distress is not always a good index of psychopathology. Under some conditions, significant emotional distress is a normal and expected reaction to extreme life events (APA, 2013a). In fact, the *DSM-5* has a precautionary note that significant losses like the death of loved ones, financial ruin, and natural disasters can result in normal and expected symptoms that may resemble symptoms of a major depressive episode (APA, 2013a). On the other hand, *too little* subjective distress can be indicative of a maladaptive response. Consider the individual with an alcohol problem who denies any adverse consequences or the bully who experiences very little distress about hurting others. Thus, subjective distress can be a useful indicator, but the situational context counts in judging the extent of adaptation or pathology.

Impaired Role Functioning. A second index of psychopathology is difficulty performing expected life roles in areas such as work, school, family, and social relationships. In contrast to subjective distress that looks at how someone *feels*, role functioning assesses the adequacy of what a person *does*. For example, individuals with agoraphobia may not be able to work or socialize because they may be unable to leave the house. The child with conduct disorder who bullies others may be friendless, failing at school, and nonengaged with family members.

Although impaired role functioning is generally considered a good index of problem severity (APA, 2013a; First & Tasman, 2004), it too has limitations. For example, depression and anxiety problems can be quite distressing without having noticeable ramifications on social, work, or school functioning. Also, some impairments in role functioning are normal or expected perturbations to a significant life stressor or a developmental challenge. For example, adolescence is considered a period in which significant conflict with parents is considered normative (Wagner, 2008).

Norm Violations. Deviance from socially acceptable behavior is another way to judge psychopathology. Examples range from psychotic symptoms like delusions of grandeur ("I'm becoming God") to eccentric behaviors like collecting pieces of garbage to accent personal attire. Other examples include externalizing disorders that entail antisocial behavior (e.g., conduct disorder and antisocial personality disorder) or socially unacceptable sexual practices (e.g., pedophilia). Everyday language illustrates this view of deviant as disturbed when people say things like, "He must be really sick to do something like that."

Like the other indices discussed so far, deviance also needs to be judged cautiously. It is particularly subject to prevailing norms and cultural standards. The history of the mental health field provides numerous instances. For example, in the 1940s, women who aspired to professional careers were considered unconsciously conflicted about their female role by many in the mental health community, then dominated by psychoanalytic thinking (Deutsch, 1945). Homosexuality was listed as a disorder in the *DSM* until 1973 when it was removed by a vote of the American Psychiatric Association establishment. In the current thin-conscious culture, those who are overweight often are stigmatized with aspersions that they are psychologically unhealthy.

Each of these indices of pathology fits some situations but not others. None of them can accurately reflect the extent of psychopathology without reference to contextual factors like culture, developmental phase, and situational characteristics. These considerations are important to keep in mind in using the *DSM* and determining whether particular symptoms should count toward the diagnosis.

Etiological Factors and the Biopsychosocial Model

Etiological models of psychopathology try to explain underlying causes and factors that maintain a mental disorder. Early models attempted to provide universal explanations of psychopathology. Psychoanalysis, for example, postulates that most mental disorders are the result of unconscious conflicts that can be traced back to early childhood traumas and fixations (Prochaska & Norcross, 2010). Traditional behavioral models contend that standard learning principles can be used to explain how mental disorders develop and are maintained over time (Spiegler & Guevremont, 2010). Cognitive models emphasize the role of faulty information processing and dysfunctional underlying cognitive schemas (Beck, 1976). The medical model assumes that all disorders have an identifiable genetic, biochemical, or disease causal agent. Family system models reject the idea that mental disorders simply reside in the individual and see the dysfunctional family system as the more appropriate level of analysis (Prochaska & Norcross, 2010; Wicks-Nelson & Israel, 2000). More recently, multicultural models have emphasized the roles of culture, class, gender, sexual orientation, and other societal factors in defining abnormality and how it manifests itself (Sue et al. 2003). Today, we know that each of these models only provides a partial explanation or piece in the psychopathology puzzle. Whereas we do not know the precise cause of most mental disorders, research has shown that multiple factors are usually operative (First & Tasman, 2004; Roth & Fonagy, 2005; Sue et al., 2003).

The **biopsychosocial model** originally emerged out of dissatisfaction with the medical model and the lack of adequate alternatives (Engels, 1977). It assumes that health and illness are determined by the interaction of biological, psychological, and sociocultural factors. It also considers the role of developmental factors in determining how health and adaptation unfold and when windows of vulnerability occur. From this perspective these factors are dynamic, influencing each other throughout the course of a disorder's life. This section provides an overview of each component of the biopsychosocial model and discusses how each may operate as a predispositional, precipitating, or maintenance factor in the development of a mental disorder (see Table 6.1).

Table 6.1 Biopsychosocial Domains: Predisposing, Precipitating, and Maintaining Factors for Mental Disorders

Domain	Predisposing	Precipitating	Maintaining
Biological	Genetics Illness Biochemical abnormalities	Acute illness (infection) Acute exacerbation of chronic illness Maturation Toxins, substances, or medications	Continued exposure to toxins, substances, or medications Underlying biochemical problems or physiological adaptations Physiological adaptation to stress
Psychological	Attachment Defensive style Cognitive style Coping skills	Developmental crisis Conflict Perceived threat Inadequate coping skill Dysfunctional thinking	Attachment style Defensive style Cognitive style Coping repertoire
Sociocultural	History of losses or traumas Cultural and societal issues Family issues Social network Poverty Discrimination	Stressful life event Changes in the social network Family developmental crisis	Lack of social support Additional stressors Societal or cultural expectations and inequalities Stigma and marginalization

Biological Factors

This set of factors looks at how physiological malfunctioning, especially in the brain, contributes to the etiology of mental disorders. Contemporary views identify four general mechanisms through which physiological impairment can impact the appearance and persistence of mental disorders: diseases, toxins and substances, genetics, and neurotransmitter aberrations. First, physical diseases like cancer, Parkinson's disease, and infectious disease can damage the brain through direct effects (e.g., tumors in the case of cancer) or indirect systemic changes (e.g., cardiovascular disease) that ultimately affect the brain. For example, obsessive compulsive symptoms can be caused in children by the body's autoimmune response to a streptococcal infection, a new class of disorders called pediatric autoimmune neuropsychiatric disorders associated with streptococcal infections (PANDAS; Department of Health and Human Services [DHHS], 1999; Erk, 2008).

Toxins and substances are another class of causal agents (Choate & Gintner, 2011; Stevens & Smith, 2013). For example, lead exposure can cause hyperactive behavior (First & Tasman, 2004). Similarly, heavy alcohol consumption can precipitate depression, psychosis, and anxiety problems (APA, 2013a).

Genetics are a third major class. Heritability refers to how much genetics contributes to the variation of a disease or trait (DHHS, 1999). A number of mental disorders have a significant genetic contribution, including depressive disorders, bipolar disorders, schizophrenia spectrum disorders, anxiety disorders, attention deficit hyperactivity disorder (ADHD), severe alcohol use disorder, and certain personality disorders (e.g., antisocial personality disorder; APA, 2013a; First & Tasman, 2004; Sue et al., 2003). For example, in the case of bipolar disorder, one of the most heritable disorders, genetics explains about 50% of the variance in this disorder (DHHS, 1999; First & Tasman, 2004). Data suggest that multiple genes interact in complex ways to affect the development of the brain, other organ systems, personality dispositions (e.g., introversion, sensation seeking), and the timing of developmental changes. In terms of the latter, for example, girls who enter puberty early, a factor with a strong genetic contribution, are at increased risk for depression, adjustment problems, and eating disorders (Choate, 2009; Wagner, 2008).

Finally, biochemical abnormalities in the brain are another potential biological contributor to mental health problems. Neurotransmitters, the chemical messengers between neurons, have gotten the most attention (see Chapters 10 and 17). They are responsible for regulating the activation or inhibition of brain activity. When this regulating function becomes impaired somehow, for example, by too much or too little neurotransmitter activity, the resulting brain changes can contribute to the development of particular mental disorders. Neurotransmitter anomalies are associated with a number of mental disorders, including schizophrenia, major depression, bipolar disorder, ADHD, and certain anxiety disorders (First & Tasman, 2004; Sue et al., 2003).

Biological factors do not simply operate as predispositional factors. They too can be affected by other factors in the biopsychosocial model. For example, early trauma can precipitate alterations in neurotransmitter activity and other brain functions that alter sensitivity to environmental stressors (First & Tasman, 2004; Maxmen et al., 2009). These biological changes can operate as maintenance factors, modifying the brain's set point to react to stress.

Psychological Factors

Thoughts, emotions, and behavior comprise the major aspects of the psychological domain. Psychodynamic theories have focused on emotional development and the role of early trauma and fixation in shaping personality and coping style (Prochaska & Norcross, 2010). Early trauma, deprivation, and overgratification can adversely affect personality development, resulting in immature ways of coping and relating to others. Defense mechanisms that individuals characteristically use are believed to reflect the level of maturity in personality development. For example, children and adolescents tend to use less sophisticated defenses such as denial, projection, and fantasy, which reflect a lower level of reality awareness and psychological maturity. On the other hand, healthy adults rely more on higher-level defenses such as humor and sublimation, which are indicative of better problem solving and reality testing (Ginter & Glauser, 2008; Perry & Bond, 2012). In line with this theory, there is some evidence that individuals with personality disorders and other psychological disorders use more primitive defenses that predispose them to more impaired functioning (APA, 2013a; First & Tasman, 2004; Perry & Bond, 2012). Also, there is evidence that even healthy individuals can regress and begin using lower-level defenses temporarily when coping with an extreme stressor (Gintner, 2001a). For example, it is not unusual to see marked denial in survivors in the weeks following a sudden violent death of a loved one (Gintner, 2001a). Thus, assessing defenses and the conditions under which they appear can be diagnostically significant.

Attachment theory (Bowlby, 1980; Horowitz, Rosenberg, & Bartholomew, 1993) has provided a more systematic and empirically supported account of how early life experiences with caregivers can affect current relationships and emotional health. Attachment refers to the parent-child bond that begins in the infant's first year of life. The nature of this relationship has been shown to influence how children see themselves and relate to others (Erk, 2008; Horowitz et al., 1993). Four attachment styles have been identified (Horowitz et al., 1993). Individuals who are **securely attached** tend to have a positive view of themselves, are comfortable with both autonomy and intimacy in relationships, and report high levels of life satisfaction. Those with a **preoccupied attachment style** report more personal insecurity, have difficulty with separation and autonomy, and are at greater risk for developing internalizing disorders like anxiety disorders and eating disorders. Individuals with a **dismissing style** tend to avoid close relationships, are more self-reliant, and are more likely to develop externalizing disorders such as conduct disorder. **Fearful-avoidant** individuals tend to be loners who have difficulty accepting themselves and others and are more likely to develop more serious psychopathology. Diagnostically, attachment can be an important marker of health or an indicator of potential risk for a variety of disorders.

How individuals think and process information is another psychological factor to consider. Cognitive theories assume that the way people think will affect how they feel and act. Information processing theories look at how individuals take in and use information from the environment (Erk, 2008). For example, children with anxiety disorders may overly attend to threat information. Likewise, children with early onset conduct disorder tend to attribute malintent to the actions of others and then respond in ways that escalate conflict (Gintner, 2000). Other cognitive theories like that of Beck (1976) have looked at dysfunctional thinking and cognitive distortions such as overgeneralization, all-or-nothing thinking, and emotional reasoning. Cognitive factors have been implicated in a number of disorders, including anxiety disorders, depression, eating disorders, and personality disorders (Roth & Fonagy, 2005).

Behavior is a final area to consider in the psychological domain. Learning theories and social learning theory (Bandura, 1977; Prochaska & Norcross, 2010) have elucidated how classical and operant conditioning as well as observational learning contribute to the development of psychopathology. Classical conditioning deals with the acquisition of *involuntary* responses like fear, anxiety, and physiological reactivity, common in disorders such as phobias and post-traumatic stress disorder (PTSD; Spiegler & Guevremont, 2010). Operant conditioning pertains to *voluntary* behaviors that are controlled by expected consequences (e.g., reinforcement or punishments). To illustrate these two conditioning principles, consider a child who witnesses a school shooting. Classical conditioning may explain why particular events (e.g., the school, broadcasts about the incident) trigger anxiety and discomfort. But operant conditioning principles (e.g., negative reinforcement) account for the development of avoidance behaviors such as school refusal that often complicate recovery.

Sociocultural Factors

Biological and psychological factors can only be understood in relation to their environmental contexts such as family, community, culture, and important life events. A discussion of each of these is beyond the scope of this chapter, but several examples illustrate how sociocultural factors can operate as predispositional, precipitating, or maintenance factors.

A number of environmental factors have been associated with vulnerability to the development of mental disorders. A major risk factor is chronic exposure to life adversities such as poverty, discrimination, community crime, and family related dysfunction such as abuse and neglect (WHO, 2004a). A basic developmental principle is that the younger the person, the stronger the impact of these types of adversities (Ginter & Glauser, 2008). For example, marital discord has been associated with later depression and conduct problems in the children (WHO, 2004b). Of these vulnerability factors, poverty has been studied quite extensively, consistently showing increased risk for a range of mental disorders, including depression and schizophrenia (First & Tasman, 2004). Particular cultural and societal factors can also be formative factors. For example, eating disorders are clustered in societies around the globe that espouse a thinness ideal (APA, 2013a; WHO, 2004a). These types of environmental factors can affect biological systems as discussed earlier as well as psychological factors such as attachment.

Precipitating factors frequently entail some sort of acute life event, family developmental transition, or social network change. For example, depression is more likely to follow loss events such as death of a loved one, end of a relationship, and incurring a physical disability (Goldberg & Goodyear, 2005). On the other hand, danger or threat events (e.g., sexual assault, a life-threatening accident) are more likely to be antecedents for anxiety disorders. Peer affiliation can also be an important precipitant, especially at developmentally vulnerable periods. For example, deviant peer affiliation is a major risk factor for adolescent onset delinquency and conduct disorder (Gintner, 2000). Finally, triggering events can include family life cycle transitions such as birth of the first child and the last child leaving home (Wicks-Nelson & Israel, 2000).

Sociocultural factors also can create conditions that sustain a disorder. Lack of social support, for example, has been shown to contribute to the persistence of disorders such as depression, PTSD, bipolar disorder, and childhood behavioral disorders (First & Tasman, 2004; Gintner, 2001a, 2001b). Precipitating stressful events also can set the stage for subsequent stressful events that prolong or worsen the initial response. For example, following Hurricane Katrina, stressors like relocation and loss of community complicated recovery (Mills, Edmondson, & Park, 2007).

As a way of illustrating the biopsychosocial model, consider the development of PTSD. Researchers have shown that whereas about half the population will experience a serious traumatic event, only about 10% to 15% will develop PTSD (First & Tasman, 2004; Gintner, 2001a). Those who do are more likely to have predispositional factors such as a family history of depression or anxiety disorders, previous traumas, and a more anxious personality style. Whereas these types of characteristics may put individuals on a more vulnerable pathway, subsequent factors such as the family and peer network can either heighten risk or serve as protective factors associated with resiliency. In terms of precipitating factors, the nature of the traumatic event (e.g., degree of imminent danger or threat) interacts with the characteristics of the victim (e.g., cognitive style, emotional reaction, coping style, and sociocultural background) to predict the extent of any maladaptive response. Maintaining factors like social support, community, additional stressors, and contact with the criminal justice system all have been shown to influence whether symptoms are short-lived or become full-blown (First & Tasman, 2004; Gintner, 2001a).

An understanding of psychopathology and etiology helps to answer the question, Why is *this* person, with *this* life history, having *these* problems, now? The answer to this question helps to gauge whether the client's problem is a normative response to life circumstances or something more serious that can be indicative of a mental disorder. Thus, the concepts of psychopathology and etiology are fundamental building blocks in the diagnostic workup. With this in mind, the more formal aspects of diagnosis are discussed next.

DIAGNOSTIC ISSUES WITH THE *DSM*

If the assessment process could be likened to a funnel, then diagnosis occurs toward the end of this process, drawing on information from the intake, mental status exam, and psychometric instruments (see Chapter 5). The clinician integrates and tries to interpret this information through the lens of a particular diagnostic system to generate a diagnosis (Hohenshil, 1996). The *DSM* is a descriptive classification system based on common presenting signs and symptoms. For example, social anxiety disorder (social phobia) is characterized by marked anxiety and fear in social situations in which the individual may feel judged or scrutinized by others (APA, 2013a). In this section, a historical perspective on the *DSM* is discussed first, because it highlights how critical features of the current *DSM* emerged. Next, the *DSM-5* is reviewed in more detail describing its innovations, organization, and diagnostic process.

DSM: A Look Backward

The specificity and scope of the *DSM* have evolved considerably over time. *DSM-I* (APA, 1952) was originally developed out of dissatisfaction with the *ICD*'s coverage of mental disorders. Both *DSM-I* (1952) and its later revision, *DSM-II* (1968), were simplistic by current standards, merely providing the name of a disorder based on a brief narrative description. These early manuals had three major shortcomings. First, the content of the manual was largely determined by the clinical consensus of a small group of experts. Second, the narratives for each disorder were so general that agreement between clinicians was very low. Third, the diagnosis only included a diagnostic label with no capability of noting special features or other important domains of functioning.

DSM-III (1980) introduced two major innovations to address these problems: (a) explicit criteria for each disorder (e.g., requiring 5 out of 7 symptoms listed) and (b) a multiaxial system that facilitated a more biopsychosocial evaluation. The specificity of criteria both enhanced reliability of diagnosis and increased research. The multiaxial system encouraged clinicians to consider the client's problem in the context of interacting systems like personality factors, health issues, stressors, and life functioning. A revised edition

(APA, 1987) corrected some inconsistencies in criteria sets and began infusing more research findings into the manual. These developments took the *DSM* from relative obscurity to central prominence in mental health practice and clinical research.

The major innovation of *DSM-IV* (APA, 1984) was requiring research evidence for any substantive change. This introduced a more conservative approach to adding new disorders and clearer criteria that were better discriminators for the disorder. Another important innovation was the addition of a section on specific culture, age, and gender variations for each disorder. Finally, the multiaxial system was further refined and streamlined so that the five axes provided the following information:

Axis I: Psychiatric disorders and other codes except for those listed on Axis II

Axis II: Personality disorders as well as mental retardation and related codes

Axis III: General medical conditions

Axis IV: Social and environmental problems

Axis V: Global assessment of functioning (GAF)

Because of the extended span of time anticipated between *DSM-IV* and *DSM-5*, *DSM-IV-TR* (text revision; APA, 2000) was published to update the narrative text information in the manual. However, no substantial changes to the criteria sets were made.

DSM-5

The New Look

DSM-5 is a major paradigm shift in the manual that reflects the burgeoning research on psychopathology over the past 20 years. Three fundamental changes characterize the new look of *DSM-5*. First, the multiaxial system of the previous *DSMs* has been jettisoned in favor of a single axis system on which all mental disorders, medical disorders, and other conditions that may be the focus of clinical attention are coded. There were several reasons for this change. The primary impetus was to have more consistency and harmony with the single-axis system of the *ICD* (WHO, 1992). Secondarily, research questioned the validity of the distinction between Axis I and II disorders. On more practical grounds, some insurance benefit plans used the multiaxial system to discriminate against covering particular psychiatric disorders, especially those coded on Axis II (Frances, First, & Pincus, 1995). Despite the merits of these considerations, *DSM-5* loses the descriptive richness of the multiaxial system that provided a more multidimensional and biopsychosocial picture of the person.

A second fundamental change is the new organization of chapters. Previous manuals relied on convention and expert opinion for grouping disorders. The *DSM-5* chapter organization draws on scientific evidence that better reflects how disorders actually cluster together. For example, formerly in a larger chapter of anxiety disorders (APA, 2000), trauma- and stressor-related disorders groups together disorders that are maladaptive reactions to significant external events (APA, 2013a). Another aspect of this reorganization is the infusion of a life span perspective to each chapter (Pine et al., 2011). In previous iterations of the *DSM*, many of the child and adolescent disorders were listed together in a single chapter. *DSM-5* departs from this practice and redistributes these disorders in relevant chapters with related symptomatology. Each chapter is organized more developmentally with disorders of infancy, childhood, and adolescence listed first, followed by disorders that usually appear later in life. The text portion of each chapter also has been expanded to highlight how the particular disorders are related to one another and how symptoms may unfold across the life span.

A third major change is the introduction of spectrum disorders. Research showed that the *DSM* categorical system to classify disorders actually resulted in a great deal of overlap between disorders and coding of more than one disorder (Goldberg, Simms, Gater, & Kruger, 2011; Jones, 2012; Widiger, 2005). Furthermore, clinicians used the "not otherwise specified" (NOS) category about a third of the time because the presentation did not fit available categories. An alternative approach that has gained increasing empirical support is the notion that disorders occur on a spectrum or continuum (Widiger, 2005). Like with blood pressure, certain cut-points could be used to determine severity and the level of psychopathology. For example, research showed that a number of the pervasive developmental disorders like autism and Asperger's (APA, 2000) actually overlapped a great deal and shared many common symptoms (APA, 2013a). The *DSM-5* merges these types of disorders into autism spectrum disorder, providing a severity rating to indicate where the individual is on a continuum of impairment. Whereas *DSM-5* has some formerly identified spectrum disorders, this dimensional approach is more evident in the severity rating added to many of the disorders. Thus, *DSM-5* takes a hybrid approach that retains categories but adds dimensional ratings within many of the diagnostic criteria sets.

What Is a Mental Disorder in *DSM-5*?

At the heart of any classification system is the definition of what it is trying to classify. A clear definition delineates what constitutes a true case (i.e., validity) and hopefully promotes consistency in doing so (i.e., reliability). An important aspect of this definition is the demarcation boundary between psychopathology and normal behavior. If this boundary line is set too conservatively, some who may need help will be excluded, but if it is set too liberally, individuals with transient and expected problems will be pathologized and subjected to unnecessary treatment.

The *DSM-5* attempts to address these issues by defining a mental disorder in terms of both qualities that have to be present (inclusion criteria) and qualities that should be absent (exclusion criteria). In terms of inclusion criteria, a mental disorder is considered a *syndrome* or pattern of symptoms that causes significant *disturbance* that is apparent in an individual's behaviors, emotions, or cognitions (APA, 2013a). This disturbance is clinically significant as manifested by significant distress (e.g., disturbing thoughts, upset throughout the day, agitated behavior) or noteworthy impairment in functioning (e.g., low grades, errors at work, or alienation from peers). Importantly, the *DSM-5* suggests that the disturbance is a reflection of an underlying *dysfunction* in psychological, biological, or developmental processes that impact an individual's mental functioning (APA, 2013a; Stein et al., 2010).

The exclusion criteria list conditions that would not be sufficient to be indicative of a mental disorder. These include expected or culturally sanctioned responses to life events (e.g., bereavement following the death of a loved one), conflicts with society (e.g., delinquent gang behavior), and social deviance (e.g., sexual behavior, religious practices). These conditions provide the contextual check in judging dysfunction. As can be seen, the definition integrates the three dimensions of psychopathology discussed earlier with the components of the biopsychosocial model.

Major Categories of Disorders

DSM-5 organizes the various mental disorders and other conditions that require clinical attention into the following major sections:

- Neurodevelopmental disorders (e.g., autism spectrum disorder, ADHD, and specific learning disorder)

- Schizophrenia spectrum and other psychotic disorders (e.g., schizophrenia, schizoaffective disorder, delusional disorder)

- Bipolar and related disorders (e.g., bipolar I and bipolar II disorders)

- Depressive disorders (e.g., disruptive mood dysregulation disorder, major depressive disorder, persistent depressive disorder)

- Anxiety disorders (e.g., agoraphobia, panic disorder, social anxiety disorder)

- Obsessive-compulsive and related disorders (e.g., obsessive-compulsive disorder, hoarding disorder)

- Trauma- and stressor-related disorders (e.g., post-traumatic stress disorder, acute stress disorder, adjustment disorder)

- Dissociative disorders (e.g., dissociative amnesia, dissociative identity disorder)

- Somatic symptom and related disorders (e.g., conversion disorder)

- Feeding and eating disorders (e.g., anorexia nervosa, bulimia nervosa, avoidant/restrictive food intake disorder)

- Elimination disorders (e.g., encopresis, enuresis)

- Sleep-wake disorders (e.g., insomnia disorder)

- Sexual dysfunctions (e.g., male erectile disorder, female orgasmic disorder)

- Gender dysphoria

- Disruptive, impulse control, and conduct disorders (e.g., oppositional defiant disorder, conduct disorder, intermittent explosive disorder)

- Substance-related and addictive disorders (e.g., alcohol use disorder, gambling disorder)

- Neurocognitive disorders (e.g., major neurocognitive disorder, mild neurocognitive disorder)

- Personality disorders (e.g., borderline, narcissistic, antisocial, obsessive-compulsive, avoidant, and schizotypal personality disorders)

- Paraphilic disorders (e.g., exhibitionistic disorder, pedophilic disorder)

- Other conditions that may be the focus of clinical attention (e.g., Z codes for relational problems, occupational problems)

An initial diagnostic question is whether the client's complaint falls into any of these broad diagnostic areas (Andreasen & Black, 2001; Shaw, 1991). This may be more challenging than it first appears because clients often present with more than one disorder, a situation referred to as comorbidity. In this situation, counselors should code conditions that meet diagnostic criteria, listing the disorder that is the focus of treatment first. For example, an individual in an acute manic episode who also has a history of borderline personality disorder would be diagnosed as follows:*

F31.13 Bipolar I disorder, current episode manic, severe severity

F60.3 Borderline personality disorder

In this instance, the diagnosis indicates that the bipolar disorder is the principle focus of treatment. Note how the diagnostic system helps to communicate treatment considerations in a clear and easy-to-understand manner.

Next, the diagnostic process itself is examined in more detail. Guidelines for thinking through the complexities of making a differential diagnosis are discussed and illustrated using the *DSM-5.*

DIAGNOSTIC PROCESS: FOUR GUIDING PRINCIPLES

What do we know about good diagnosticians? The findings are unsettling in one respect and encouraging in another. Surprisingly, factors like level of education (e.g., master's vs. doctoral) and years of experience are not strong predictors of diagnostic accuracy (Falvey, 2001; Spengler et al., 2009; Witteman, Weiss, & Metzmackeher, 2012). For example, whereas confidence in a diagnosis is directly related to one's years of clinical experience, accuracy is not (Smith & Dumont, 2002; Spengler et al., 2009; Witteman et al., 2012). Part of the problem here is that experienced clinicians may use personal prototypes of what a disorder looks like instead of relying on the diagnostic criteria (Smith & Dumont, 2002; Widiger, 2005). Inaccuracy can be further compounded by confirmatory bias, which is the tendency to seek out information that supports the diagnosis and to disregard information that is inconsistent (Garb & Grove, 2005; Smith & Agate, 2004; Smith & Dumont, 2002). Thus, good diagnostic judgment is more than simply having the knowledge and experience.

---

* *DSM-5* (APA, 2013a) code numbers are derived from the official United States version of the *ICD.* Two code numbers are listed for a particular disorder, one bolded and the other in parentheses. For example, post-traumatic stress disorder lists **309.81** (F43.10). The bolded code refers to the *ICD-9* code numbers used prior to October 1, 2014. After that date the official system in the United States shifted to *ICD-10*, which uses the codes noted parenthetically. It is important to note that the narrative diagnosis remains the same.

Diagnostic expertise seems to draw on a set of critical thinking *skills* that enable the counselor to process complex clinical information in an unbiased and self-correcting manner (Sarason & Sarason, 2005; Witteman et al., 2012). Like the scientific method itself, it is a hypothesis testing approach in which a broad set of possibilities are considered and then winnowed down based on available evidence (Smith & Agate, 2004). Critical elements in this process are considering alternatives in a systematic manner, avoiding premature closure, and reflecting on the adequacy of clinical decisions (Smith & Agate, 2004; Smith & Dumont, 1997; Witteman et al., 2012). Researchers suggest that these thinking skills can be learned with specific training and practice (Falvey, 2001; Smith & Agate, 2004; Witteman et al., 2012). Drawing on this literature, this section discusses four principles to guide differential diagnosis and the diagnostic decision-making process (First & Tasman, 2004; Maxmen et al., 2009; Morris, 2007; Smith & Agate, 2004; Witteman et al., 2012).

Principle 1: Check the Adequacy of Your Information

Your diagnosis is only as good as the information on which it is based. The quality of the information can be affected by informant characteristics, situational and temporal factors, and method of assessment. In terms of informants, mandated clients and those who deny or minimize the problem (e.g., drug use) may not provide reliable responses to diagnostic questions. Likewise, developmental factors limit the capacity of children to self-report internal states and life circumstances (Wagner, 2008). Some mental disorders may cause impairments in the ability to accurately recall (e.g., dementias) or report information (e.g., psychosis). In these situations, it is critical to obtain collateral information from other informants such as the parent, teacher, employer, or partner.

Situational and temporal factors are another consideration when weighing diagnostic information. Whereas it is always a good idea to collect a good social history, it is important to keep in mind that memory effects and current mood color these recollections. For example, individuals will report a more unfavorable accounting of their early history when they are depressed than when they are in a positive mood (Morris, 2007). Care should also be taken when evaluating clients in a crisis state. The acuity of the situation can exaggerate symptomatology and the client's report of life circumstances. Although the crisis likely needs immediate attention, the diagnosis should be deferred. A good rule of thumb with regard to crisis situations is to wait 1–2 weeks after the crisis to more clearly evaluate which symptoms diminish or disappear and which may require further clinical attention.

Finally, a basic finding in the area of psychological assessment is that multiple methods of assessment tend to yield a richer and more valid picture of the client than a single method (Meyer et al., 2001; Segal & Coolidge, 2007). As such, the diagnostic evaluation should ideally include nonquantitative methods like the diagnostic interview as well as quantitative methods such as structured interviews or symptoms rating scales. Quantitative assessment methods afford increased reliability, validity, and a more quantifiable measure. For example, symptom inventories like the Beck Depression Inventory II (Beck, Steer, & Brown, 1996) provide an index measure as well as a comparative baseline for later assessment. A number of structured interviews for assessing *DSM* disorders are available (see Segal & Coolidge, 2007, for a review), but the Structured Clinical Interview for DSM-IV

Axis I Disorders (SCID-I; First, Spitzer, Gibbon, & Williams, 1997) is the most widely used. In addition, the American Psychiatric Association has posted a number of assessment measures that are free to download online (APA, 2013b).

In summary, multiple informants and multiple assessment methods are preferable to simply interviewing the client. These multiple lenses on the problem enhance the adequacy of the information that will be drawn on to make diagnostic decisions (Maxmen et al., 2009).

Principle 2: Use Diagnostic Hierarchies for Differential Diagnosis

Differential diagnosis is the process of considering possible diagnostic candidates, especially among those with similar symptoms (First & Tasman, 2004). This can be a daunting task, however, considering the range of possibilities. The *DSM-5* (APA, 2013a) uses the principle of diagnostic hierarchies to systematically consider possible causes for the presenting symptoms. Physical disorders and substance use are considered first, followed by mental disorders in a descending order of severity. Symptoms that can be attributable to a more severe disorder preempt the diagnosis of a less severe disorder with similar symptoms. For example, if an individual develops major depressive disorder following retirement, you would not also diagnose adjustment disorder with depressed mood. Three diagnostic questions can aid differential diagnosis using this hierarchy.

Could the symptoms be due to a medical disorder, a medication, or a substance? The first question is whether the symptoms are due to the physical effects of a medical disorder or exogenous substance that client is taking. Clues that a medical condition is etiologically significant include symptoms covarying with the onset, worsening, and improvement of the medical disorder. Another differentiating feature is that medically related symptoms often do not have the full complement of presenting symptoms and age of onset that characterize the particular mental disorder. For example, a daughter referred her 79-year-old father after he began accusing her of poisoning him with an invisible substance. A paranoid delusion like this does not usually first appear this late in life if it is due to a psychotic disorder like schizophrenia (APA, 2000). In this case, a brain scan showed that he recently had a small stroke that triggered the psychotic symptoms.

Medications also should be considered as a possible cause for the presenting symptoms. Many prescribed and over-the-counter medications and supplements can produce side effects on their own or as a result of interactions with other medications (First & Tasman, 2004; Sinacola & Peters-Strickland, 2012). These side effects can include symptoms like depression, fatigue, anxiety, sleep problems, delusions or hallucinations, and sexual dysfunction (Morris, 2007). For example, a cardiologist referred a client for depression 2 months after a heart attack. The client reported low energy, depressed mood, and decreased interest in life activities. However, self-worth and optimism about the future were still intact, atypical in an individual with severe depression. The medical records indicated that these symptoms emerged shortly after the client began taking a high-blood-pressure medication known to cause depression-like symptoms. The counselor consulted with the cardiologist who agreed to change the medication. Within a week, the client's mood improved significantly.

Substance use and withdrawal also can cause a variety of psychiatric symptoms. There are two major ways that the symptoms can be related to a substance problem. First, the symptoms may be the direct result of the substance's effect on the central nervous system (APA, 2013a). Substances like alcohol, benzodiazepines, stimulants, and opiates can cause substance-induced symptoms like depression, anxiety, psychosis, and sleep problems. If these symptoms occur as a result of intoxication or withdrawal from the substance, they can be coded as a substance-induced disorder (APA, 2013a). For example, an individual who develops paranoid delusions during a cocaine binge would be diagnosed with cocaine-induced psychotic disorder.

A second possibility is that the substance problems and psychiatric symptoms represent two independent disorders, a substance use disorder (e.g., alcohol use disorder) and another mental disorder (e.g., major depressive disorder). This type of comorbidity is referred to as *dual diagnosis* (First & Tasman, 2004; Morris, 2007). Epidemiological data suggest that about 50% of individuals with a substance problem also have another mental disorder, most commonly an anxiety or mood disorder (Stevens & Smith, 2013). Conversely, about 20%–30% of those with an anxiety or mood disorder also will have a co-occurring substance use disorder (First & Tasman, 2004).

Diagnostically, however, how can you tell if the symptoms are substance induced or part of an independent mental disorder? Three indicators can help to answer this question. First, if the symptoms are substance induced they should occur during periods of intoxication or withdrawal and then clear within a month after cessation of that substance (APA, 2013a). For example, a male client's panic attacks started the day after he quit drinking but subsided within 2 weeks. If the symptoms had persisted beyond a month after cessation, however, then the symptoms would have likely been attributable to another mental disorder (e.g., panic disorder). A second indicator is whether the symptoms were present earlier in the client's life during periods of no substance use. For example, if the client had a major depressive episode 2 years prior to initiating opiate use, then the current mood problem is likely to be an independent disorder that co-occurs with the opiate problem. A third indicator is an atypical presentation of symptoms. For example, older individuals who abuse a benzodiazepine (e.g., Xanax) may develop substance-induced depressive symptoms such as fatigue and concentration problems without significant depressed mood or crying spells.

These types of diagnostic considerations highlight the importance of asking about the client's medical conditions, medications, and substance use. Most disorders in the *DSM* have an exclusion criterion, "not attributable to the physiological effects of a substance or medical condition," to remind the diagnostician to assess for substance use, medical conditions, and medications that might cause similar symptoms (APA, 2013a). A good rule of thumb is to ask clients to see their primary care physician if they have not done so in the past year. Also, it is important to know how to check the client's medications for potential side-effect problems. Fortunately, there are a number of good references available like the *Physicians' Desk Reference* (2012) and online resources (e.g., medicinenet.com, PDR.net).

Could the symptoms be due to a major mental disorder? The second question in diagnostic hierarchies is whether the symptoms could be due to a major mental disorder such as a psychotic disorder or a mood disorder. These types of major disorders not only have their specific defining features but also have a number of associated symptoms that can look like less severe disorders. For example, schizophrenia often has chronic depressive symptoms as an associated feature. In this case, the diagnostic hierarchy principle would dictate that only the diagnosis of schizophrenia would be made. These major mental disorders also are arranged hierarchically among themselves. For example, schizophrenia is at the top of the psychotic disorder hierarchy, after substance-induced and medical conditions are ruled out. In terms of the disorder profile, schizophrenia usually appears in late adolescence or early adulthood. The active phase of the disorder is characterized by *positive symptoms* such as delusions, hallucinations, disorganized speech, and disorganized behavior as well as *negative symptoms* like flat affect, social withdrawal, and lack of motivation (avolition). An important cautionary note here is to be sure that these unusual beliefs or experiences are not culturally sanctioned or normative for the client's background.

Mood disorders are the next class of disorders to consider, ordered in severity from bipolar disorder to unipolar forms of depression. Considering this sequence, a counselor should always ask about a history of manic, hypomanic, or mixed-mood episodes whenever assessing some kind of mood problem. On the other hand, those with only depressive episodes should first be considered for major depressive disorder if there are numerous depressive symptoms, especially if they have occurred over weeks to months. More low-grade and chronic depressive symptoms that occur over 2 years or longer are characteristic of persistent depressive disorder (dysthymia). When the depressive symptoms are a clinically significant response to a stressful event but do not meet criteria for a more significant mental disorder, adjustment disorder with depressed mood should be considered.

Which disorders fit with the distinctive symptoms? Having ruled out physical causes and major mental disorders, the third question attempts to narrow the possibilities to likely candidates based on the distinctive symptoms present (Andreasen & Black, 2001; Maxmen et al., 2009). What general category best fits the prominent symptoms? For example, anxiety, panic, and/or behavioral avoidance are cardinal features of anxiety disorders (APA, 2013a). Acting out, overactivity, and oppositional behavior characterize disruptive behavior disorders like ADHD, ODD, and conduct disorder. Somatic symptom disorder has as a defining feature preoccupation or concerns about having physical or medical problems that cannot be accounted for by a medical disorder. The presence of personality traits that impair work, social, or school functioning may indicate the presence of a personality disorder.

Once the general category is located, then the disorders within that category can be reviewed. For example, a client presented with a fear of going into stores during the day. Two diagnostic possibilities are agoraphobia and social anxiety disorder. In further assessing the fear, the client reported that "if I see people in the store, I have the thought that they think I look stupid." This preoccupation with a negative social evaluation is a cardinal feature of a social anxiety disorder, rather than something agoraphobic, which is often associated with the fear of experiencing panic.

There are two places in the *DSM-5* to find information about making close diagnostic distinctions. Many of the criteria sets will have an exclusion phrase of "not better explained by" (APA, 2013a) to indicate disorders that can present similarly. In addition, each disorder will have a differential diagnosis section in the narrative portion that describes common disorders to rule out.

Principle 3: Resolve Diagnostic Uncertainty by Examining the Usual Suspects

If the diagnosis remains unclear at this point, there are four "usual suspects" that can often account for the uncertainty. These include inadequate information, individual differences in symptom presentation, comorbidity, and subthreshold symptoms.

Inadequate Information. The first possibility is inadequate information (Maxmen et al., 2009; Morris, 2007). In considering the various diagnostic alternatives, for example, there may be information gaps that cloud the diagnostic picture. To address this problem, it may require taking a more detailed history, contacting additional informants, or administering relevant assessment instruments. For example, a client with anxiety problems also presented with a number of unaccounted work-related issues (e.g., tardiness and unplanned absences). A more detailed history revealed that these problems were likely due to an alcohol problem that he was reluctant to disclose up to that point. Diagnostically, the term "provisional" can be used after a diagnosis if there is the presumption that criteria will probably be met once more information is obtained.

Client Characteristics. Culture, age, and gender factors have been shown to affect how disorders manifest themselves, which may be different than the prototypical presentation. For example, depression often is overlooked in children and adolescents because it frequently presents with irritability or crankiness instead of the classic depressed mood typical in adults. Similarly, ADHD in girls can be missed because girls tend to have more inattention symptoms that are less overtly disruptive than the impulsivity and hyperactivity typical in boys (First & Tasman, 2004). *DSM-5* describes age-related differences in presentation for each disorder in the section titled Development and Course. Gender issues are discussed in a new section, Gender-Related Diagnostic Issues.

Cultural factors cannot only impact how symptoms present but also how pathology is defined. *DSM-5* addresses these multicultural factors in two major ways. First, each disorder has a special section on culture-related diagnostic issues, which has been expanded from previous iterations of the *DSM*, reflecting the burgeoning research in the area over the past decade. For example, those from Latino and Mediterranean cultures tend to express depression more in terms of "nerves" and headaches than sadness or guilt (APA, 2013a). Second, *DSM-IV-TR*'s (APA, 2000) cultural formulation outline has been further refined and supplemented with a formal interview schedule, the cultural formulation interview (CFI; APA, 2013a). The CFI is a set of open-ended questions that ask clients about four major cultural concerns: the client's cultural identity, the cultural explanation and expression of symptoms, culturally relevant stressors and supports, and the impact of cultural differences on the client-counselor relationship. Consulting the literature, seeking specialty training, and obtaining consultation and supervision can further enhance multicultural competencies in assessing and diagnosing diverse groups (Li, Jenkins, & Sundsmo, 2007; Remley & Herlihy, 2007; Sue et al., 2003).

Comorbidity. If there are symptoms not accounted for by the initial diagnosis, it could be due to the presence of another mental disorder. Comorbidity is important to recognize because it can impact prognosis and treatment outcome significantly (First & Tasman, 2004). For example, adolescents with conduct disorder and depression have about three times the suicide risk as adolescents with just depression (Gintner, 2000). Diagnostically, there are two useful steps in considering possible comorbid disorders. First, consult the *DSM*'s differential diagnosis section for your primary disorder that lists common comorbid disorders. If this does not solve the problem, review the symptoms that are unaccounted for and try to consider possible alternatives using diagnostic hierarchies.

Subthreshold Symptoms. A final contributor to diagnostic uncertainty is subthreshold symptoms that do not meet criteria for any of the conventional disorders but are nonetheless clinically significant. *DSM-5* replaces the former NOS category of *DSM-IV-TR* (APA, 2000) with two options, other specified disorder and unspecified disorder. The other-specified option allows the clinician to note narratively the reason why a disorder is significant but does not meet the specific criteria for any disorder in that chapter. For example, if a client has four severe depressive symptoms that do not meet criteria for a major depressive episode, the clinician could code, other specified depressive disorder, four serious depressive symptoms. The unspecified disorder option can be used if the clinician chooses not to specify the reason, which may occur, for example, in emergency room situations. In determining whether an other-specified or unspecified disorder is an option, first try to locate which chapter is most consistent with the subthreshold symptoms. Then review the other-specified section in that chapter to see how the presentation fits with the examples provided.

Principle 4: Your Diagnosis Is a Hypothesis That May Need Correcting

The last principle reminds the counselor to hold on to any diagnostic formulation tentatively, ready to revise it in the face of disconfirming evidence. The key point here is to periodically reassess the adequacy of the diagnostic formulation. Smith and Dumont (1997) suggest the following questions in this regard:

- What evidence does not fit my diagnostic formulation?

- What other information do I need to get a more complete picture of the client?

- How has my diagnostic formulation held up over time?

There is some evidence that clinicians who are more cautious and willing to rework their diagnosis are more accurate than those who arrive at a diagnosis quickly and report high levels of confidence (Smith & Agate, 2004; Smith & Dumont, 2002; Spengler et al., 2009).

These four principles can be thought of like a set of healthy habits. As such, their positive effects are best realized when done routinely, even if a formal diagnosis is not required. The following case study illustrates how these principles can be incorporated into the diagnostic process and the formulation of a *DSM-5* diagnosis.

CASE STUDY

Background

Miriam is a 55-year-old widowed white female who sought treatment at a community mental health center. She reports that she has been "unbelievably depressed" since she was fired from her job about 2 months ago. Her former employer told her that she was let go because she made too many mistakes and seemed to have trouble using the company's data system, even after 3 months on the job. This is particularly troubling for her because this is the third job that she has lost in the past year.

In discussing her depression, Miriam admits that she becomes very sad and cries uncontrollably. She has trouble sleeping, often waking up very early and being unable to go back to sleep. This is particularly disturbing to her because "mornings are the worst." For the rest of day, she often feels tired and sluggish. Things that used to be enjoyable to her like participating in a Bible reading group and visiting with friends no longer seem interesting to her. Most days are spent staying in her apartment watching TV or lying in bed. She denies any suicidal ideation but admits that "life is just going through the motions." One friend was so worried about her that she convinced Miriam to seek treatment.

Miriam was raised in New Orleans, the youngest of three children. She was an average student in most respects but excelled in classes that required more creative or artistic work. Throughout high school, she described herself as "real social" but always concerned about what other people thought of her. Her first bout of depression occurred after the breakup of her first serious romantic relationship. She went on to study interior design in college and then was hired by a local design firm where she worked for close to 20 years. She was married at age 25 and settled in an older neighborhood in the city.

In 2005, Hurricane Katrina struck New Orleans, destroying many of the area homes and businesses. The couple was forced to move to Houston to find work and a new place to live. Miriam described the transition as quite difficult because "it was so spread out and I knew no one." In 2007 her husband died of a sudden heart attack. The next few years were described as "very hard" because she felt all alone in this new city with no real job prospects. She began to feel more and more depressed until she made a suicide attempt by taking an overdose of her husband's old pain medication. After about a year, she started to feel better and made a concerted effort to find employment. She reinitiated several friendships and began to be more active in her church. She was able to find an office job that paid relatively well that involved data entry. Things were finally improving and she was feeling like her old self again.

Then she received a poor performance evaluation that cited her difficulty picking up the company's new computer system. In describing this time, she simply explained that "I felt lost. I had a

(Continued)

(Continued)

hard time remembering all the programs and what they wanted me to do." She then received a layoff notice that cited the company's need to "downsize." Afterward, she began to feel her depression return. She was able to find another office job a few months later but was terminated because she made too many errors in processing customer claims. Her depression intensified even more and she started to isolate herself at home. A concerned friend helped her find her most recent job, which was at a national data processing firm.

Despite these difficulties, Miriam has a number of positive mental health indicators that she tends to overlook. She is socially outgoing and is able to maintain a good sense of humor even when she feels depressed. She has a good network of friends that only became stronger after her husband's death. Her spirituality plays a very central role in her life and is a source of inspiration and hope. She has been active with her church and often does volunteer work in the community that she finds very fulfilling.

Medically, she is in good health except for a history of high blood pressure. She takes a diuretic that does a good job of keeping her pressure within normal limits. She went through menopause in her early 50s during which time she was briefly on estrogen replacement therapy. After her husband's death, her family physician prescribed an antidepressant that she took for about a year. At about the same time, she also was prescribed Zolpidem (Ambien) for sleep problems, which she continues to use nightly. She has an occasional glass of wine when she goes out with friends but does not drink otherwise or use any other substances.

Ultimately, she wishes she could just find that old life and spirit that she once had in New Orleans. That seemed like another lifetime now. She is very concerned that her work problems indicate that "there is something wrong with my brain." She does have a family history of Alzheimer's disease. At her lowest points she wonders, *Will I ever be happy again?*

Diagnostic Workup

Miriam presents with a number of depressive symptoms as well as possible cognitive problems. Both distress her a great deal and appear to contribute to impairments in social (isolating) and work functioning. The biopsychosocial model helps the counselor consider potential causal factors and ways that they can interact with one another. With this in mind, the case presents a number of diagnostic questions:

- Does she have clinically significant depression, or are her depressive symptoms normal reactions to the death of her husband and the transition after Hurricane Katrina?

- Depression can cause slowed thoughts, poor concentration, distractibility, and reduced capacity to process information (APA, 2013a; Gintner, 1995). Are the cognitive problems simply associated symptoms?

- Ambien use and menopause can cause impairments in mood and cognitive processing (APA, 2013a). What role do these physical factors play?

- Could the cognitive problems be an independent problem resulting from an undiagnosed neurological problem like early onset Alzheimer's disease?

- On the other hand, are her cognitive problems simply a reflection of a poor match between the type of work and her interests and skill set?

These are all legitimate considerations and have important implications for the course of treatment.

Drawing on Principle 1, the assessment incorporated quantitative and nonquantitative methods as well as information from collateral sources. The assessment included a detailed social history; a mental status exam; administration of the BDI-II; and self-monitoring of her daily mood, thinking, and activities. Two sources of collateral information were critical to obtain in this case: a medical evaluation to rule out medical or neurological problems and information from the employers. Because it was not realistic to contact her former supervisors, Miriam was asked to bring in her termination letters, which might provide additional information that she was not able to self-report. Findings from these assessment points will be used in the discussion of each of the subsequent principles.

Diagnostic hierarchies helped to systematically consider the range of diagnostic possibilities. The first step was to consider medical problems and Ambien use as potential contributing factors. The medical evaluation indicated that she was in good health for her age and that there were no complications related to menopause. As a precautionary step, the primary care physician had Miriam see a neurologist who reported that there was no evidence of any significant cognitive abnormalities or signs of neurological impairment. The consensus was that her depression was the likely contributor to her cognitive problems associated with her work difficulties. Her Ambien use only exacerbated these symptoms. The recommendation was to discontinue her Ambien and to place her on an antidepressant that also might help her sleep.

The intake, social history, and mental status exam were consistent with these findings. Her history indicated that her work-related problems began after the depression intensified. Later, she began taking Ambien, which coincided with her reports of feeling "foggy" at work. Her termination letters indicated that she would have "good and bad days" on the job. Another mentioned that she did well when she seemed particularly interested in an assignment. All these lines of evidence seemed to support depression as the primary contributing factor, although Ambien likely aggravated these problems.

The second consideration in diagnostic hierarchies is whether a serious mental disorder is present. She does have prominent mood problems so the next step would be to rule out bipolar disorder, which is at the top of the mood hierarchy. In this regard, she denied any history of elevated mood, and there was no family history of bipolar disorder. However, her grandmother was hospitalized for depression on several occasions. Next, major depressive disorder was considered. She does meet diagnostic criteria with five or more symptoms of depression that show a pattern of intensifying,

(Continued)

(Continued)

improving for, and then returning. Her BDI-II score of 42 indicated severe depression that was characterized by negative thinking, concentration problems, fatigue, loss of interest, crying spells, hopelessness, and sleep problems. Her daily self-monitoring confirmed many of these symptoms and indicated that her mood was usually about a 2 on a 10-point scale (with 10 = good mood). The severity and duration of her symptoms would rule out other possibilities lower in the hierarchy like an adjustment disorder with depressed mood or normal bereavement. In terms of the latter, the death of her husband occurred close to 6 years ago and does not seem to be related to the current episode of depression.

Having identified the relevant major category, the next question is to determine the particular diagnostic category related to major depression. Miriam shows a recurrent pattern, with her first depressive episode dating back to high school. The number and types of symptoms also are relevant in coding specific features of her major depression. Her current episode would be considered severe because of the functional impairment and the number of symptoms. The type of symptoms (very depressed mood, loss of interest, depression worse in the morning and early morning awakening) are consistent with major depression with melancholic features (APA, 2013a). All of these feature components are important to consider because they can inform which treatments are likely to be most effective (APA, 2010; First & Tasman, 2004).

Principle 3 reminds the clinician to consider the role of missing information, client characteristics, possible comorbid conditions, and subthreshold symptoms. In this case, missing information and possible comorbidity need to be considered. Miriam has had depression throughout her life. Were these only major depressive episodes, or was there also a pattern of chronic underlying depressive disorder like persistent depressive disorder (dysthymia)? The history revealed that there was never of period of 2 years or longer with dysthymic-like symptoms. Rather, her pattern indicated episodes of significant depression that would persist for months and then clear from months to years. As a result, the clinical picture seemed to indicate a pattern of recurrent episodes of major depression. In addition, because employment problems would be an important target of the treatment plan, a Z code could also be added to the diagnosis. The working diagnosis at this point was the following:

F33.2 Major depressive disorder, recurrent, severe with melancholic features

Z56.9 Other problems related to employment

The last diagnostic principle reminds the counselor to periodically reevaluate the adequacy of the diagnosis. How did this diagnostic formulation hold up over time? Within 2 weeks of discontinuing her Ambien use, Miriam reported feeling "sharper" mentally, especially in the morning. She did not have any withdrawal-like problems, primarily because she never increased her use from a minimum dose. All of these findings ruled out any potential dependence or abuse issue. Furthermore, whereas her mood improved somewhat in that time, it did not appear that the Ambien was a significant cause of her depressive symptoms.

The subsequent sessions clarified how a number of etiological factors contributed to her significant depression. Her positive family history for depression is an important predisposing factor that is associated with developing more serious forms of depression and depression with melancholic features (First & Tasman, 2004). In terms of psychological factors, her history indicated a preoccupied attachment style that sensitized her to separation issues and approval seeking from others. It also seemed to contribute to a general cognitive style in which she would personalize and blame herself when things went wrong in her life. Hurricane Katrina was also an important predisposing factor because of all the losses she experienced in terms of community, friendships, career, and the dreams she had for her life. It also seems to have triggered the onset of her dysthymic symptoms. All these factors put her at greater vulnerability to developing more serious depression.

The death of her husband was a critical triggering event for the major depressive episode that followed. Whereas most people will have an uncomplicated bereavement process, about one in five will go on to develop major depression in the months and years following the loss (APA, 2010). For Miriam, her thinking style and tendency to cope by isolating were critical maintaining factors. The subsequent job losses further undercut her tenuous self-esteem and made her wonder if she was becoming cognitively impaired and perhaps developing dementia. Developmentally, this series of losses occurred at a time when adults usually are experiencing increased security and satisfaction in their intimate relationships and a sense of confidence in their career achievements (Super, 1990). Fortunately, her personal strengths (e.g., outgoing style, friendships, and spirituality) helped to keep her afloat emotionally and provided a source of support and hope.

The diagnostic workup played a critical role in treatment planning. Practice guidelines recommend a combination of medication and psychotherapy for major depression that is in the severe range and has complicating features like melancholia (APA, 2010). In terms of psychotherapy options, cognitive-behavioral therapy and interpersonal therapy have the best evidence for effectiveness for marked depression (APA, 2010). A cognitive-behavioral approach was selected because of the prominent role of negative thinking and behavioral isolation. The counselor periodically consulted with her primary-care doctor who was prescribing her antidepressants. Employment issues also were critical to address. She was relieved to learn that her work problems were really "normal' or expected reactions to an unfamiliar work area in combination with the Ambien use and her depression. An interest assessment provided a number of career possibilities that resonated with her artistic and social interests. She followed up by pursuing a training course in precious stones and jewelry design. She found a job with a family owned jewelry store that provided opportunities to create her own designs. By the time she actually began working, her depression had improved significantly. For the first time in years she felt like she was moving forward again and may have found a new home in Houston.

It is important to recognize the role of diagnosis in the overall counseling endeavor. Drawing on the complete model of mental health (Keyes, 2007), a diagnosis helps to define problem aspects of functioning that will need to be addressed in concert with efforts to build on strengths and talents. From this perspective, the diagnostic enterprise is an important aspect of helping clients flourish.

(Continued)

(Continued)

Miriam's case illustrates this well. In many respects she saw her diagnosis as liberating. The obstacles ahead of her were now identifiable and potentially resolvable, opening the possibility of a more satisfying life.

Discussion Questions

1. A diagnosis can be an invaluable source of information for making important treatment decisions, but it can also result in harm if it is not accurate. What are the harms to the individual and to society for each of the following situations:

   a. Overdiagnosing conditions that are not mental disorders
   b. Underdiagnosing conditions that actually meet criteria for a mental disorder
   c. Misdiagnosing a condition as one disorder (e.g., major depressive disorder) when it is really another (e.g., bipolar I disorder)

2. How would you conceptualize Miriam's condition using the three dimensions of psychopathology?

3. Using the biopsychosocial model, discuss Miriam's biological, psychological, and sociocultural contributing factors. Which are predisposing, precipitating, and/or maintaining factors?

4. Using another case study, discuss how the four diagnostic principles can be used to consider diagnostic alternatives and to decide on a *DSM-5* diagnosis.

REFERENCES

American Psychiatric Association. (1952). *Diagnostic and statistical manual of mental disorders.* Washington, DC: American Psychiatric Association.

American Psychiatric Association. (1968). *Diagnostic and statistical manual of mental disorders* (2nd ed.). Washington, DC: American Psychiatric Association.

American Psychiatric Association. (1980). *Diagnostic and statistical manual of mental disorders* (3rd ed.). Washington, DC: American Psychiatric Association.

American Psychiatric Association. (1987). *Diagnostic and statistical manual of mental disorders* (3rd ed., rev.). Washington, DC: American Psychiatric Association.

American Psychiatric Association. (1994). *Diagnostic and statistical manual of mental disorders* (4th ed.). Washington, DC: American Psychiatric Association.

American Psychiatric Association. (2000). *Diagnostic and statistical manual of mental disorders* (4th ed., text rev.). Washington, DC: American Psychiatric Association.

American Psychiatric Association. (2010). Practice guidelines for the treatment of major depressive disorder, third edition. [Supplement]. *American Journal of Psychiatry, 167*(10). doi:10.1176/appi .books.9780890423387.654001

American Psychiatric Association. (2013a). *Diagnostic and statistical manual of mental disorders* (5th ed.). Washington, DC: American Psychiatric Association.

American Psychiatric Association. (2013b). *Online assessment measures*. Retrieved from http://www
.psychiatry.org/practice/dsm/dsm5/online-assessment-measures.

Andreasen, N. C., & Black, D. W. (2001). *Introductory textbook of psychiatry*. Washington, DC:
American Psychiatric Association.

Bandura, A. (1977). *Social learning theory*. Upper Saddle River, NJ: Merrill Prentice Hall.

Beck, A. T. (1976). *Cognitive therapy of emotional disorders*. New York: International Universities
Press/Meriden.

Beck, A. T., Steer, R. A., & Brown, G. K. (1996). *Beck Depression Inventory-II*. San Antonio, TX: Harcourt
Brace.

Ben-Zeev, D., Young, M. A., & Corrigan, P. W. (2010). DSM-V and the stigma of mental illness. *Journal
of Mental Health, 19,* 318–327. doi:10.3109/09638237.2010.492484

Bowlby, J. (1980). *Sadness and loss*. New York: Basic Books.

Choate, L. H. (2009). *Girls' and women's wellness: Contemporary counseling issues and interventions*.
Alexandria, VA: American Counseling Association.

Choate, L. H., & Gintner, G. G. (2011). Prenatal depression: Best practices for diagnosis and treatment. *Journal of Counseling and Development, 84,* 373–382. doi:10.1002/j.1556-6678.2011
.tb00102.x

Department of Health and Human Services. (1999). *Mental health: A report of the Surgeon General*.
Rockville, MD: National Institute of Mental Health.

Deutsch, H. (1945). *The psychology of women: A psychoanalytic interpretation*. New York: Grune &
Stratton.

Engels, G. L. (1977). The need for a new medical model: A challenge for biomedicine. *Science, 196,*
129–136. doi:10.1126/science.847460

Erk, R. R. (2008). Understanding the development of psychopathology in children and adolescents. In
R. R. Erk (Ed.), *Counseling treatments for children and adolescents with DSM-IV-TR mental
disorders* (pp. 39–90). Upper Saddle River, NJ: Prentice Hall.

Falvey, J. E. (2001). Clinical judgment in case conceptualization and treatment planning across mental
health disciplines. *Journal of Counseling & Development, 79,* 292–303. doi:10.1002/j.1556-6676
.2001.tb01974.x

First, M. B. (2010). Clinical utility in the revision of the "Diagnostic and Statistical Manual of Mental
Disorders" (DSM). *Professional Psychology: Research and Practice, 41*(6), 465–473. doi:10.1037/
a0021511

First, M. B., Spitzer, R. L., Gibbon, M., & Williams, J. B. (1997). *Structured Clinical Interview for DSM-IV
Axis I Disorders (SCID-I)—Clinical version*. Washington, DC: American Psychiatric Association.

First, M. B., & Tasman, A. (2004). *DSM-IV-TR mental disorders: Diagnosis, etiology & treatment*.
Washington, DC: American Psychiatric Association.

Frances, A., First, M. B., & Pincus, H. A. (1995). *DSM-IV guidebook*. Washington, DC: American Psychiatric Association.

Garb, H. N., & Grove, W. M. (2005). On the merits of clinical judgment. *American Psychologist, 60,*
658–659. doi:10.1037/0003-066X.60.6.658

Ginter, E. J., & Glauser, A. S. (2008). Assessment and diagnosis: The developmental perspective and its
application. In R. R. Erk (Ed.), *Counseling treatments for children and adolescents with DSM-IV-TR
mental disorders* (pp. 2–38). Upper Saddle River, NJ: Prentice Hall.

Gintner, G. G. (1995). Differential diagnosis in older adults: Dementia, depression, and delirium.
Journal of Counseling & Development, 73, 346–351. doi:10.1002/j.1556-6676.1995.tb01762.x

Gintner, G. G. (2000). Conduct disorder and chronic violent offending: Issues in diagnosis and treatment selection. In D. S. Sandhu & C. B. Aspy (Eds.), *Violence in American schools: A practical guide
for counselors* (pp. 335–351). Alexandria, VA: American Counseling Association.

Gintner, G. G. (2001a). Sudden violent loss: Clinical guidelines for screening and treating survivors. In D. S. Sandhu (Ed.), *Faces of violence: Psychological correlates, concepts, and intervention strategies* (pp. 355–376). Huntington, NY: Nova Science.

Gintner, G. G. (2001b). Diagnosis and treatment of adults with depressive disorders. In E. Reynolds Welfel & R. E. Ingersol (Eds.), *The mental health desk reference* (pp. 112–118). New York: Wiley.

Gintner, G. G. (2008). Treatment planning guidelines for children and adolescents. In R. R. Erk (Ed.), *Counseling treatments for children and adolescents with DSM-IV-TR mental disorders* (pp. 344–380). Upper Saddle River, NJ: Prentice Hall.

Gintner, G. G., & Mears, G. S. (2009). Mental health counseling. In W. G. Emener, M. A. Richard, & J. J. Bosworth (Eds.), *A guidebook to human service professions: Helping college students explore opportunities in the human services field* (pp. 154–165). Springfield, IL: Charles C. Thomas.

Gladding, S. T., & Newsome, D. W. (2004). *Community and agency counseling*. Columbus, OH: Pearson.

Goldberg, D., & Goodyear, I. (2005). *The origins and course of common mental disorders*. New York: Routledge.

Goldberg, D., Simms, L. J., Gater, R., & Krueger, R. G. (2011). Integration of dimensional spectra for depression and anxiety into categorical diagnoses for general medical practice. In D. A. Regier, W. W. Narrow, E. A. Kuhl, & D. J. Kupfer (Eds.), *The conceptual evolution of DSM-5* (pp. 19–35). Arlington, VA: American Psychiatric Association.

Haidt, J. (2006). *The happiness hypothesis*. New York: Basic Books.

Hinkle, J. S. (1999). A voice from the trenches: A reaction to Ivey and Ivey. *Journal of Counseling & Development, 77*, 474–483. doi:10.1002/j.1556–6676.1999.tb02475.x

Hohenshil, T. H. (1996). Role of assessment and diagnosis in counseling. *Journal of Counseling & Development, 75*, 64–67. doi:10.1002/j.1556–6676.1996.tb02316.x

Horowitz, L. W., Rosenberg, S. E., & Bartholomew, K. (1993). Interpersonal problems, attachment style, and outcome to brief dynamic psychotherapy. *Journal of Consulting and Clinical Psychology, 61*, 549–560. doi:10.1037/0022–006X.61.4.549

Ivey, A. E., & Ivey, M. B. (1999). Toward a development diagnostic and statistical manual: The vitality of a contextual framework. *Journal of Counseling & Development, 77*, 484–490. doi:10.1002/j.1556–6676.1999.tb02476.x

Jones, K. D. (2012). Dimensional and cross-cutting assessment in "DSM-5." *Journal of Counseling & Development, 90*, 481–487. doi:10.1002/j.1556–6676.2012.00059.x

Kessler, R. C. (2011). The National Comorbidity Survey (NCS) and its extensions. In M. T. Tsuang, M. Tohen, & P. B. Jones (Eds.), *Textbook of psychiatric epidemiology* (pp. 221–241). West Sussex, UK: Wiley.

Kessler, R. C., McGonagle, K. A., Zhao, S., Nelson, C. B, Hughes, M., Eshleman, S., et al. (1994). Lifetime and 12-month prevalence of DSM-III-R psychiatric disorders in the United States. Results from the National Comorbidity Survey. *Archives of General Psychiatry, 51*, 8–19. doi:10.1001/archpsyc.1994.03950010008002

Keyes, C. L. (2005). Mental illness and/or mental health? Investigating axioms of the complete model of health. *Journal of Consulting and Clinical Psychology, 73*, 539–548. doi:10.1037/0022–006X.73.3.539

Keyes, C. L. (2007). Promoting and protecting mental health as flourishing: A complementary strategy for improving national mental health. *American Psychologist, 62*(2), 95–108. doi:10.1037/0003–066X.62.2.95

Keyes, C. L., & Lopez, S. J. (2002). Toward a science of mental health: Positive directions in diagnosis and treatment. In C. R. Snyder & J. Lopez (Eds.), *Handbook of positive psychology* (pp. 45–59). New York: Oxford University Press.

Li, S. T., Jenkins, S., & Sundsmo, A. (2007). Impact of race and ethnicity. In M. Hersen, S. M. Turner, & D. C. Beidel (Eds.), *Adult psychopathology and diagnosis* (pp. 101–121). Hoboken, NJ: Wiley.

Maxmen, J. S., Ward, N. G., & Kilgus, M. (2009). *Essential psychopathology and its treatment* (3rd ed.). New York: W. W. Norton & Company.

Meyer, G. J., Finn, S. E., Eyde, L. D., Kay, G. G., Moreland, K. L., Dies, R. R., et al. (2001). Psychological testing and psychological assessment: A review of evidence and issues. *American Psychologist, 56,* 128–165. doi:10.1037/0003-066X.56.2.128

Mills, M. A., Edmondson, D., & Park, C. L. (2007). Trauma and stress response among Hurricane Katrina evacuees. *Journal of Public Health, 97,* Supplement 1, S116.

Morris, J. (2007). *Diagnosis made easier.* New York: Guilford Press.

Perry, J. C., & Bond, M. (2012). Change in defense mechanisms during long-term psychodynamic therapy and five-year outcome. *American Journal of Psychiatry, 169,* 916–925. doi:10.11.76/appi.2012 11091403

Physicians' desk reference. (66th ed.). (2012). Montvale, NJ: Thomson PDR.

Pine, D. S., Costello, E. J., Dahl, R., James, R., Leckman, J. F., Leifenluft, E., et al. (2011). Increasing the developmental focus in "DSM-5." In D. A. Regier, W. E. Narrow, E. A. Kuhl, & D. J. Kupfer (Eds.), *The conceptual evolution of DSM-5* (pp. 305–321). Washington, DC: American Psychiatric Association.

Prochaska, J., & Norcross, J. (2010). *Systems of psychotherapy: A transtheoretical approach* (7th ed.). Belmont, CA: Brooks/Cole.

Remley, T. P., & Herlihy, B. (2007). *Ethical, legal, and professional issues in counseling.* Upper Saddle River, NJ: Prentice Hall.

Roth, A., & Fonagy, P. (2005). *What works for whom* (2nd ed.). New York: Guilford Press.

Sarason, I. G., & Sarason, B. R. (2005). *Abnormal psychology: The problem of maladaptive behavior.* Upper Saddle River, NJ: Prentice Hall.

Segal, D. L., & Coolidge, F. L. (2007). Structured and semistructured interviews for differential diagnosis: Issues and applications. In M. Hersen, S. M. Turner, & D. C. Beidel (Eds.), *Adult psychopathology and diagnosis* (pp. 79–100). Hoboken, NJ: Wiley.

Seligman, M. E. (2002). *Authentic happiness: Using the new positive psychology to realize your full potential for lasting fulfillment.* New York: Free Press.

Seligman, M. E., Rashid, T., & Parks, A. C. (2006). Positive psychotherapy. *American Psychologist, 61,* 774–778. doi:10.1037/0003-066X.61.8.774

Shaw, S. (1991). Practical use of "DSM-III-R." In M. Hersen & S. M. Turner (Eds.), *Adult psychopathology and diagnosis* (pp. 23–43). New York: Wiley.

Sinacola, R. S., & Peters-Strickland, T. S. (2012). *Basic psychopharmacology for counselors and psychotherapists.* Boston: Pearson.

Smith, J. D., & Agate, J. (2004). Solutions to overconfidence: Evaluation of an instructional module for counselor trainees. *Counselor Education & Supervision, 44,* 31–44. doi:10.1002/j.1556-6978.2004.tb01858.x

Smith, J. D., & Dumont, F. (1997). Eliminating overconfidence in psychodiagnosis: Strategies for training and practice. *Clinical Psychology: Science and Practice, 4,* 335–345. doi:10.1111/j.1468-2850.1997.tb00125.x

Smith, J. D., & Dumont, F. (2002). Confidence in psychodiagnosis: What makes us so sure? *Clinical Psychology and Psychotherapy, 9,* 292–298. doi:10.1002/cpp.336

Spengler, P. M., White, M. J., Egisdottir, S., Maugherman, A. S., Anderson, L. A., Cook, R. S., et al. (2009). The meta-analysis of clinical judgment project: Effects of experience on judgment accuracy. *The Counseling Psychologist, 37,* 350–399. doi:10.1177/0011000006295149

Spiegler, M. D., & Guevremont, D. C. (2010). *Contemporary behavior therapy* (5th ed.). Belmont: CA: Wadsworth.

Stein, D. J., Phillips, K. A., Bolton, D., Fulford, K. W. M., Sadler, J. Z., & Kendler, K. S. (2010). What is a mental/psychiatric disorder? From "DSM-IV" to "DSM-V." *Psychological Medicine, 40*(11), 1–7. doi:10.1017 /S0033291709992261

Stevens, P., & Smith, R. L. (2013). *Substance abuse counseling: Theory and practice* (5th ed.). Boston: Pearson.

Sue, D., Sue, D. W., & Sue, S. (2003). *Understanding abnormal behavior* (7th ed.). Boston: Houghton Mifflin.

Super, D. E. (1990). A life-span, life-space approach to career development. In D. Brown, L. Brooks, & Associates (Eds.), *Career choice and development: Applying contemporary issues to practice* (2nd ed., pp. 197–261). San Francisco: Jossey-Bass.

U.S. Public Health Service. (1999). *Mental health: A report of the Surgeon General.* Rockville, MD: U.S. Department of Health and Human Services, Substance Abuse and Mental Health Services Administration, Center for Mental Health Services, National Institutes of Health, National Institute of Mental Health.

Wagner, W. G. (2008). *Counseling, psychology, and children.* Upper Saddle River, NJ: Pearson/Prentice Hall.

Wicks-Nelson, R., & Israel, A. C. (2000). *Behavior disorders in childhood.* Upper Saddle River, NJ: Prentice Hall.

Widiger, T. A. (2005). Classification and diagnosis: Historical development and contemporary issues. In J. E. Maddux (Ed.), *Psychopathology: Foundations for contemporary understanding* (pp. 63–83). Mahwah, NJ: Lawrence Erbaum.

Witteman, C. M., Weiss, D. J., & Metzmackeher, M. (2012). Assessing diagnostic expertise of counselors using the Cochran-Weiss-Shanteau (CWS) Index. *Journal of Counseling & Development, 90,* 30–34. doi:10.1111/j.1556–6676.2012.00005.x

World Health Organization. (1992). *International classification of disease* (10th ed.). Atlanta, GA: Centers for Disease Control and Prevention.

World Health Organization. (2004a). *Prevention of mental disorders: Effective interventions and policy options* (Summary report). Geneva: World Health Organization.

World Health Organization. (2004b). *Promoting mental health: Concepts, emerging evidence, practice* (Summary report). Geneva: World Health Organization.

CHAPTER 7

Treatment Planning

Daniel M. Paredes and Maria A. Brunelli Paredes

Learning Goals

Upon completion of this chapter, you will be able to do the following:

1. Define treatment planning as part of the counseling process

2. Understand the relationship between assessment, diagnosis, and treatment planning

3. Develop goals and objectives in treatment planning

4. Describe how counselor cultural identity, theoretical orientation, and other personal characteristics impact appropriate treatment plan development

Treatment planning, whereby the goals and objectives of counseling are agreed on by the client and counselor, and the intentionality that follows from the initial assessment phase are important components of what makes counseling a professional activity. Often, the process of counseling is derisively boiled down to "just listening to people." However, one could argue that such a simplification is akin to starting to sail around the world without first considering the route one might take, weather conditions at differing points on the globe, or what provisions would be necessary. Could you simply get into your boat, pick a direction, and go? Yes. Would it be wise? No. Instead, much like planning for a sea voyage, there must be a foundation of purposeful choices with an ability to flexibly respond to unplanned circumstances. In this chapter, we discuss the process for determining client needs and appropriate services, the use of community resources in treatment planning, and special circumstances in treatment planning. Case studies are provided throughout the chapter, many with sample treatment plans (albeit simplified!).

DETERMINING CLIENT NEEDS AND APPROPRIATE SERVICES

Case of Tara

Tara, a 5th-grade teacher, is a 25-year-old Puerto Rican woman who has presented in your office. She lets you know at the outset that she was reluctant to come, but came to counseling on a coworker's recommendation and because she has exhausted all other options. She states that she believes she is depressed, "like the commercials on TV." She states that she feels like she is always tired, is finding it more and more difficult to get to her second job, has lost motivation to do the one thing that she used to like doing with her limited free time (exercising), is sleeping a lot more than she thinks she should, is often irritable, and is feeling bad about herself. She states that on the weekends when her husband is away for work, she just wants to lie in bed and watch movies. During the course of your intake, she shares that she has seen her gynecologist for regular exams but has not been seen by a general practitioner since she had the flu in college—about 4 years ago. She reported that the last experience confirmed her belief that doctors generally don't know what they are doing.

Based on her presenting concerns, you decide that additional information is needed before a treatment plan can be initiated. You provide Tara information about the mind-body connection and how other issues, such as hypothyroidism, can look like depression. You explain how certain medical conditions can make one think and feel that they are depressed. You agree to set up a follow-up appointment 3 weeks out so that she has time to meet with a general practitioner before your next meeting.

Ten days later, Tara calls to cancel her appointment because she has indeed been diagnosed with hypothyroidism. She shares that she would like to wait and see how the medication that she has been prescribed works before engaging in counseling. The decision to develop only an informal treatment plan that focused on referral to a physician for a general checkup rather than a formal treatment plan for a mood disorder clearly met the client's need. This case illustrates how the counselor was effective in his or her choice to gather additional assessment information prior to formulating a treatment plan.

Treatment planning, like assessment, is an ongoing process that requires a delicate balance between respecting a client's inherent knowledge of his or her presenting concerns while also leveraging the expertise of a clinical mental health counselor (Falvey, 2001; Feltham & Dryden, 1993; Seligman, 2004; VandenBos, 2006). In the case of Tara, the clinical mental health counselor used professional skills to create an inviting space for an already reluctant client to share her feelings of depression. At the same time, the counselor was able to resist the temptation to prematurely conceptualize the client as one suffering from a mood disorder and consequently focus counseling on a faulty premise. In this case, developing a treatment plan to address Tara's depressive symptoms would have been responding to Tara's needs on a superficial level. Instead, the counselor introduced information that Tara did not possess regarding the relationship between physiological processes and psychological health and, therefore, introduced other possible attributions for the cause of "depression." In this example, the counselor did not dismiss Tara's perception of depression but instead used the initial session as an opportunity to develop trust, collect assessment information, and identify what needs should be addressed prior to the development of a detailed counseling treatment plan. In fact, although a formal treatment plan with goals, objectives, and interventions was not developed, the referral to a medical provider for a more accurate assessment was in and of itself therapeutic. If nothing else, it certainly constituted best practice, determining client needs (e.g., ruling out a medical disorder) through a comprehensive assessment prior to formulating a treatment process.

The process of determining client needs and appropriate referral requires a thorough assessment process. Assessment, however, is not in and of itself a final course of action. Rather, the purpose of assessment is to facilitate counselor **case conceptualization,** an integration of client features (i.e., what Seligman [2004] identified as cognitive attributes, behaviors, personality and affect, interpersonal relationships and context, physical/biological attributes, and the social and multicultural environment), the theoretical framework from which the counselor prefers to operate (e.g., psychodynamic, solution-focused, intergenerational family systems), and the demands of the work setting (Brew & Kottler, 2007; Osborn, Dean, & Petruzzi, 2004; Seligman, 1993, 2004). The conceptualization that develops from the assessment process then influences the development of the treatment plan.

FROM CONCEPTUALIZATION TO TREATMENT PLANNING

A treatment plan is the framework that outlines for client and counselor the aims of counseling. The plan should present as the logical extension of the assessment, conceptualization, and diagnosis phases of counseling (Feltham & Dryden, 1993; Gladding, 2006; Osborn et al., 2004). However, a number of variables can influence the formulation of an accurate **case conceptualization,** that is, "the client's and/or counselor's view of the client's problem, what it comprises, from whence it may derive, and what may be the best means of attempting to resolve it" (Feltham & Dryden, 1993, p. 34). Assessment techniques and data, which are used to formulate a case conceptualization and treatment plan, are influenced by the counselor's personal style, the counselor's theoretical orientation, and the constraints of the treatment setting (Brew & Kottler, 2007).

Personal Style

Personal style refers to a clinical mental health counselor's preference for an informal or formal approach to counseling. As an illustration of personal style, consider that beginning counselors often prefer a formal, interview-like intake (Seligman, 1993), which matches the developmentally appropriate concern related to the mechanics of counseling (i.e., am I doing this intake correctly?). By contrast, more advanced practitioners who have developed a high degree of comfort with the mechanics of counseling (i.e., providing informed consent, discussing confidentiality, and conducting an intake session) may assume a relatively relaxed style. Similarly, how intake paperwork is presented can be influenced by a clinical mental health counselor's personal style. A counselor who is more flexible about first how paperwork is presented might be more sensitive to the needs of a client experiencing acute distress. Such a counselor would know a client in acute distress should not be handed stacks of forms and clinical inventories to complete without first being provided support when it is evident that the client's distress makes completion of extensive intake forms extremely difficult.

A possible complement to a counselor's personal style is his or her use of formal assessment techniques. Presenting a standardized pencil-and-paper assessment without a clear understanding of why it is being administered and an adequate explanation to the client of its utility can skew the assessment data that are collected, making conceptualization and planning difficult or inaccurate (AMHCA, 2010).

Another component of a counselor's personal style that influences the conceptualization and planning process is his or her adeptness at working cross-culturally. Cross-cultural competence influences the selection and interpretation of assessment data. Therefore, counselors should be mindful of the cultural implications of their preferred way of conceptualizing clients and their presenting concerns. For example, it might be inappropriate for a clinical mental health counselor who prefers formal assessment data to ask an English language learner to complete a Minnesota Multiphasic Personality Inventory (MMPI-2) as an initial assessment. Such a long assessment could be intimidating for clients who have a low comfort level with written English, could create anxiety for a client who sees little connection between the assessment and his or her presenting concern, and could ultimately render useless data.

Finally, counselor beliefs about the nature of counseling itself should be considered in developing a conceptualization and treatment plan. Sometimes, counselors assume that all clients are ready to take significant steps to address presenting concerns. However, client anxieties about participating in counseling, as well as client motivation for change, influence the quality of information provided at intake (McLoughlin & Geller, 2010). A client with low motivation for change who is mandated to attend counseling may provide socially desirable answers in an effort to "get it over with."

In some treatment settings, counselors experience pressure to practice using brief counseling strategies and therefore to develop treatment plans as soon as possible. However, a comprehensive conceptualization often cannot naturally be collected in a single 50- or 90-minute session. In such cases, the counselor might initially develop a set of provisional hypotheses that are examined over time as more concrete information becomes available. The evolution of one's conceptualization may then require an update of the initial treatment plan.

Counselor Theoretical Framework

The counselor's theoretical framework has a clear influence on client conceptualization and treatment planning. Theoretical orientation impacts the questions asked about problem etiology and, by extension, what feedback is provided to the client in the process of coconstructing a treatment plan. In other words, theoretical orientation affects case conceptualization and preferred interventions, which in turn affect the treatment plan. Although a full discussion of how specific theoretical orientations affect treatment planning is beyond the scope of this chapter, the relationship is briefly discussed in general terms in this section. Many textbooks used in teaching counseling theories include sections on the strengths and limitations of the various orientations with respect to problem etiology, as well as direct discussion of the application of theories with a multicultural perspective.

From some theoretical perspectives (for example, solution-focused brief therapy, rational emotive behavior therapy), an emphasis is placed on the present. Few questions about historical antecedents to the presenting concern might be posed. As such, a treatment plan developed by a counselor with a present-oriented theoretical outlook would include interventions to address the here-and-now manifestation of client distress—antecedents and the generalization process are left to the client to address at a later time. Typically, such counselors would structure counseling as a process to address the thoughts, behaviors, and perhaps affective states that characterize the presenting concern.

Conversely, counselors who place a greater emphasis on the circumstances that precipitated the onset of symptoms, such as Adlerian or Jungian counselors, would develop a treatment plan where the emphasis of counseling is recognizing and addressing the factors that predisposed the client to the current distress. For example, when conducting couple counseling, such a counselor might approach the family of origin and childhood frameworks that influence the client's view of his or her role in romantic relationships, as well as the expectations placed on a romantic partner.

The objectives presented to the client for inclusion in the treatment plan are a direct result of how the counselor facilitates the client describing his or her problems and, therefore, how they may be resolved. The conceptualization, planning process, and plan therefore are influenced directly by how a counselor introduces the therapy process to the client. It should be noted however, that third-party payers are increasingly influencing which orientations are used to provide counseling (SAMHSA, 2010).

Expectations of the Counselor's Work Setting

Client conceptualization and treatment planning are influenced by the expectations of the setting as well as the circumstances under which he or she is being seen. Third-party payers (insurance companies and Medicaid administrators) often demand the adoption of counseling strategies focused on short-term symptom relief. Additionally, third-party payers shape the process counselors use to conduct assessment and develop treatment plans by requiring the completion of specific treatment planning paperwork. In a practical sense, the emphasis on facilitating immediate symptom relief can create pressure to develop a treatment plan prematurely. An example of the tension between the demands of payers and client needs arises when a client presents ready to "unload," to share his or her concerns, but must be redirected to complete extensive assessment forms and treatment planning documents before counseling can commence. Some counseling agencies respond to documentation demands by adopting assessment protocols that counselors must complete with all clients with the knowledge that the information collected is to meet the expectations of various third-party payers rather than client needs. Counselors can help assuage client concerns by explaining the process and noting that if additional sessions are even to be an option, the assessment must be completed. In such circumstances, mental health counselors may advocate systemically to ensure that the content of standardized assessment protocols is clinically relevant to treatment planning for a majority of clients. Furthermore, providing clients with adequate information about the importance of thorough assessment so that quality services can be provided is essential.

Work settings influence treatment planning as a result of how equipped a particular agency is to meet identified needs. Some agencies have policies in place that set limits on the number of sessions a client may receive, whereas others may have caseloads so large that the availability of appointment times is effectively limited. Agencies who serve a large number of clients with third-party payers may find that client access to services is limited by the payer. For example, an adolescent whose care is publicly funded (i.e., Medicaid is the third-party payer) may only attend counseling if precertification is granted (approval from Medicaid managers) based on an approved treatment plan and documentation of adequate progress toward plan completion. Another example of how the work setting influences the treatment plan, one that is often misunderstood by the lay public, is the role that psychiatric hospitals have in providing treatment. The role of psychiatric hospitals in the current landscape is primarily crisis stabilization, that is, providing treatment to the point that the client is no longer a danger to self or others. The parameters for hospitalization as a result of alcohol or drug intoxication, or active psychosis, vary in application and from case to case. Treatment plans in inpatient settings are therefore focused on a specific goal (crisis stabilization) and ideally prepare the client for the work of addressing the concerns that precipitated the crisis through outpatient or intensive outpatient counseling.

DEVELOPING AND IMPLEMENTING TREATMENT PLANS

Although differing language may be used, treatment plans are characterized by the creation of goals, objectives, and interventions. A graphic representation of the relationship between goals, objectives, and interventions is provided in Figure 7.1. In this example, the client is suffering from a fear of public speaking. Therefore, the treatment goal is to help the client overcome this anxiety with anxiety management techniques (an objective) by the teaching of relaxation techniques (an intervention). Regardless of the specific clinical issues, all treatment plans constitute an agreement between the client and counselor about the purposes of the counseling relationship. This agreement has the ethical purpose of assuring that services for which the client (or a third-party payer) is paying are efficient and efficacious. In a basic sense, the treatment plan provides an index for both the client and the counselor to determine if the client is getting what he or she is paying for (Jongsma & Peterson, 2003; Seligman, 1993). Yet a treatment plan is unlike other professional contracts, which are often static in nature. In practice, a treatment plan often evolves as the client and counselor clarify the desired counseling outcome. Furthermore, treatment plans, even for seemingly enthusiastic clients, are limited by a client's motivation for change (McLoughlin & Geller, 2010). Regardless of what wishes the counselor might hold for the client, progress is only possible with the client's buy-in and willingness to do the hard work of counseling both in and out of session.

The various components of a treatment plan have predictable relationships to one another. Though the terms *goals* and *objectives* are sometimes (incorrectly) used interchangeably, there is a difference. Objectives define strategies or implementation steps to attain the goals, are usually specific and measurable, and may have a defined completion date. Generally, there are more objectives than goals, and there may be more interventions than objectives. Both a generic model and an example model for a client who has expressed anxieties related to public speaking are provided in Figure 7.1. Largely depending on agency policy and client characteristics, additional parameters such as expected completion dates, assignment of tasks (i.e., who is responsible for tasks identified in the intervention section of the plan), or a listing of existing strengths to address the objectives might be included in a treatment plan.

Treatment Goals

Mears (2010) identified counseling goals as broad statements that speak to desired counseling outcomes. Sometimes when clients present for counseling, they are able to articulate that they are in distress and that their level of distress needs to be lowered (their goal). For some clients, however, assessment serves as an intervention when it is used to help clients clarify the nature of their distress and their desired experience of relief. Regardless of one's theoretical orientation, solution-focused and behavioral philosophies of working toward what the client wants (rather than what he or she wants less of) can be especially helpful in developing treatment plans. Such language helps establish at the outset when counseling will be complete—at least for now. The case of Joseph and Sofia provides an example of how the treatment planning process can assist clients (in this case a couple) clarify desired outcomes while reframing the goal as more of a good thing, rather than less of a bad one.

Case of Joseph and Sophia

Joseph, a 33-year-old Polish American male, and Sophia, a 32-year-old Asian American (Korean ancestry) female have presented for couple counseling. They have dated for 3 years and have sought counseling because they are concerned about being able to "work through their issues" before getting married. In the assessment phase, the counselor met with both partners together, each separately, and then together again to identify their rationale for initiating counseling, as well as their strengths as a couple. Joseph and Sophia were asked to complete assessment instruments such as the Dyadic Adjustment Scale (Spanier, 1989) to expedite the assessment process. One concern that arose in the assessment phase, now being presented to the couple in the treatment planning process, was differences in the ratings of frequency of verbal disagreements. Sophia reported that she believed they fight "all the time," whereas Joseph did not. Sophia stated that she believes fighting less should be a treatment goal for counseling. Rather than simply adding the goal as stated, the counselor responds by helping the couple clarify what characterizes their fighting, helping the couple clarify their expectations for disagreements within romantic relationships, and eventually helping them restate the goal as becoming more effective at communicating during times of disagreement.

Treatment Objectives

Treatment objectives should follow from the broad directions outlined in the goals statements. Like goals statements, objectives should be developed collaboratively to increase the likelihood of their being met. The counselor's role is to assure that objectives are appropriate to the related goal, are stated in a way that is specific, and are measureable.

Counselors might assist in the treatment planning process by providing clients information about objectives sometimes used to attain the previously identified goals. Beginning
counselors should not misconstrue coconstruction or working collaboratively to mean that
their role should be a passive one. In fact, clients often lack knowledge about how to begin
identifying objectives. Therefore, counselors can respond by presenting a menu of options

Figure 7.1   Counseling Treatment Plan

Client(s): Joseph & Sophie _____

Date of Intake: _____   Initial Plan ❏   Revised Plan ❏   Revision Date: _____

Goal(s)	Objective(s)	Intervention(s)	Expected completion date
Improve communi-cation skills during disagreements	Use "I" statements to express displeasure	Partners will learn to use "I" statements in session	Session 4
		Partners will complete worksheets on assertive communication skills	Session 2
	Focus on events in the present when having a disagreement	Partners will practice present-oriented problem solving in session	Session 2
	Share disagreements with each other rather than other family members	Partners will agree to communi-cate directly with each other rather than triangulating family members	Session 3
		Partners will establish a time during each day to provide feedback to the other partner	Session 3

*Parties involved in the development of this treatment plan will sign below to indicate that the plan
describes what is understood as the purpose of this counseling relationship. All parties understand that this is a flexible document open to revision, as appropriate.*

Client Signature(s): _____

Counselor Signature & Credentials: _____

based on past clinical experience, consultation with colleagues, and familiarity with the literature while still empowering clients to make their own choices. Besides providing examples of possible objectives, counselors can encourage clients to use action-oriented verbs in writing objectives (e.g., *abstain, access, attend, complete, construct, develop, engage, identify, maintain, participate, practice, read, share, use, write*). The use of action verbs instills in clients a sense of movement and direction or of encouragement—things often lacking when a client presents for counseling. Furthermore, counselors can help translate objectives identified and endorsed by the client into more clinical terms that can be understood by other professionals.

The collaborative strategy with action-oriented verbs is important because treatment plans are likely to be reviewed by other professionals. Situations where a treatment plan might be reviewed include evaluation by a quality assurance specialist at an insurance company, peers at an agency as part of an internal audit, or by another counselor reviewing what has been done if the client is being transferred.

Treatment objectives should be stated as a way to operationalize the goal to which they are related. To assure client buy-in, counselors should create open dialogue with a client to assure the goals are viewed as reasonable, attainable, and measureable. At the same time, objectives should be somewhat challenging for the client. It is common for multiple objectives to underlie a specific goal; in fact, one might include two or three objectives of increasing difficulty associated with each goal. Yet, because the counseling process can be emotionally and physically difficult, it is wise for counselors to plan for periods of client discouragement. Establishing objectives of increasing difficulty allows the counselor to challenge client pessimism by reorienting him or her to past clinical successes, thereby reorienting the client to a more accurate sense of self-efficacy. The action-oriented nature of objectives makes the intervention section of a treatment plan somewhat easier to draft; quite simply, interventions should describe the steps to be taken both in and out of session to meet stated objectives.

Treatment Interventions

Once clinical objectives have been defined, interventions that will be used to meet the objectives follow. As with objectives, the client may need the counselor to provide suggestions based on the counselor's past clinical experience or other professional resources. Interventions should also be action oriented with verbs that make clear what the specific tasks to be completed in counseling are. With specific, task-oriented statements, the counseling process is less likely to become unfocused and inefficient. When the counselor or client notes that there is some deviation from the plan or that progress is lacking, the process can be reoriented to the foci specified in the treatment plan (McLoughlin & Geller, 2010; Seligman, 1993). Alternatively, a discussion regarding the need to revise the treatment plan may need to occur.

When coconstructing interventions with a client, the counselor must strike a balance between allowing the client the space to make his or her own decisions about readiness to participate in specific interventions and confidently guiding the client toward deeper or more challenging clinical work (Linhorst, Hamilton, Young, & Eckert, 2002; Mills, 2011). Counselors can use discussions around interventions to introduce the concept of accountability. In this instance, accountability refers to the client's self-accountability. A conversation about self-accountability helps orient the client toward interventions that are a bit uncomfortable—after all, how can change be expected without some discomfort? Often, clients need their counselor to have an honest dialogue about the beliefs that underlie preference for certain interventions. Clients sometimes gravitate toward specific interventions because of erroneous beliefs about other possible interventions (for example, "I can't see a psychiatrist for medication because that would mean I'm *really* messed up."). Clients also may underestimate their ability to complete interventions (for example, "I couldn't do that, that's too hard."). If the idea of making objectives difficult enough to make noticeable progress had been discussed early in the counseling relationship, then some cheerleading and pointing out of strengths may help the client feel empowered when difficulties arise. Additionally, the counselor can intentionally use the intervention selection part of treatment planning to build in a graduation in level of difficulty (i.e., establish interventions of increasing difficulty). Increasing difficulty in interventions assures an appropriate level of challenge throughout the counseling relationship while also helping to establish greater client self-efficacy.

Not unlike the relationship between goals and objectives, frequently a single objective will have multiple interventions designed to address it. In the case of Joseph and Sophia, it would be reasonable to have interventions associated with "fighting fair," using "I" statements during arguments, keeping arguments present focused (versus bringing up concerns from the past), and keeping disagreements between the couple so as not to triangulate other family members or friends.

Additional Treatment Plan Components

The core elements of a treatment plan include goals, objectives, and interventions. Other aspects may be included depending on the requirements of mental health agencies, practical requirements set by the client's realities (e.g., court involvement), or by third-party payers. Examples of such components include target dates (when objectives will be met), completion dates (actual date objective was met), who is responsible for completing specific tasks, and what assets or strengths are available to the client so that he or she may successfully meet the objectives (Osborn et al., 2004). Whereas the need for target dates, completion dates, and strengths may seem straightforward, the need to indicate who is responsible for certain tasks may be ambiguous. When working with children, adolescents, families, or couples, it can be useful to identify for all stakeholders the nature of their role in the treatment plan.

Coconstruction of Treatment Plans

Throughout the earlier discussion of treatment plan components, the term *coconstruction* was used. **Coconstruction** is the process by which a counselor and client collaborate to develop goals, objectives, interventions, and any other components of the plan. Consistent with the ethical underpinnings of the counseling profession, coconstruction is the behavioral manifestation of a belief that clients have the right to autonomously determine the course of counseling (ACA, 2014; AMHCA, 2010). Coconstruction or collaborative treatment planning is consistent with the belief that clients inherently have the ability to operate on their presenting concerns. The process of coconstructing a treatment plan can be more challenging when the stakeholders involved include individuals other than those who will be participating in the counseling process, however (e.g., a child's guardian or a court official who is responsible for monitoring completion of mandated anger management counseling). The coconstruction process is characterized by frequently checking in with the client about the alignment of the treatment plan with his or her desired counseling outcomes and the perceived feasibility of objectives being met. Whereas counselors should encourage clients to articulate their own objectives, counselors must be actively engaged in the process. At times, clients possess accurate knowledge of how to resolve their presenting concern but simply need support and encouragement to do so. At other times, however, clients have few sound ideas about how to operate on the presenting concern (e.g., "I wouldn't get into so many fights if they just left me alone"). After assessing the degree to which the client needs help formulating objectives and interventions, the counselor might offer suggestions while allowing the client to choose from among those suggestions (Linhorst et al., 2004; Puterbaugh, 2006). It is important for the counselor to trust the clinical intuition that he or she has developed over time; is the client avoiding some suggestions for reasons he or she is not sharing (Falvey, 2001)? Clinical mental health (CMH) counselors should encourage clients to view the counseling office as a place where genuineness is imperative so that sensitive issues (even client reluctance about being in counseling) can be explored. Some suggestions for questions the counselor might ask himself or herself in the process of developing a treatment plan are presented in Table 7.1. Client objective and intervention choices might also be limited by inaccurate information or by other barriers consistent with the symptoms that led the client to seek out counseling (e.g., difficulties concentrating). One interesting aspect of the questioning consistent with the treatment planning process is that even just having that space for a client to give words to his or her experience can be therapeutic. Figure 7.2 demonstrates how counseling goals are translated into treatment objectives and ultimately guide the formulation of clinical interventions.

Table 7.1   Checklist for Counselor Self-Reflection During Treatment Plan Coconstruction

- Do the client's stated concerns seem to be the "real" issue?
  - If not, is now the time to confront the client's defenses?
- Is nonverbal communication consistent with stated concerns?
  - If not, what is the client feeling right now?
- Do the possible causes for distress identified at intake provide a sufficient starting point for counseling?
- Are the client's concerns within my scope of expertise?
  - If not, where should I refer the client?
  - Do the client's concerns and/or acuity warrant referral for psychotropic medication?
- What strengths or assets have been leveraged in the past to address the issue?
  - Does the client need additional support to recognize assets before other objectives are approached?

Figure 7.2 Relationship Between Goals, Objectives, and Interventions

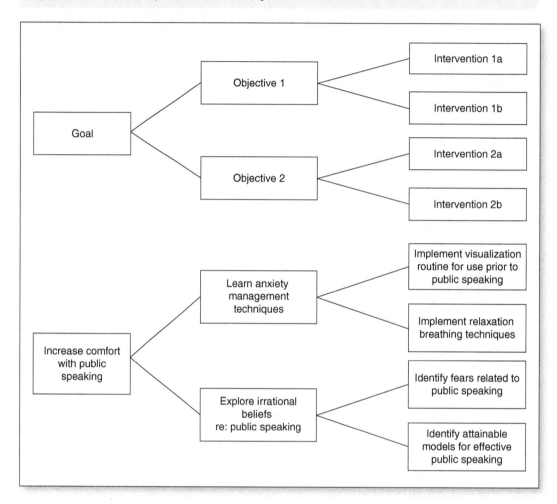

REFERRAL, KEEPING A RESOURCE LIST, AND APPLICATION

Interventions listed on a treatment plan might refer to community resources when a client has a need beyond the scope of professional counseling or, perhaps, beyond the counselor's competence. In trying to be helpful, counselors sometimes focus on a client's mental health concerns when presenting concerns are more readily addressed by noncounseling providers (as in the case of Tara at the beginning of the chapter). Another example might be a disaster relief care worker who wants to focus on processing emotional reactions when the client being served is most concerned with how to find the loved ones from whom he or she was separated during the disaster. In this example, the client obviously wants help locating survivor lists from shelters, but the process-focused counselor is inappropriately preoccupied with his or her notion of how support should be provided—clearly not effective practice. With respect to providing services for which a counselor is not competent, the need for referral is clear. Accrediting and credentialing bodies provide a clear requirement for learning units on the codes of ethics (for example, ACA, 2014; AMHCA, 2010) that directly proscribe counselors from providing services beyond their training.

Keeping a Resource List

Ethical practice requires that CMH counselors respect the limits of their competence and know when to refer. The challenge many clinical mental health counselors face is knowing where to refer clients. Though the clinical mental health counseling standards in the CACREP Standards (CACREP, 2016) specify that students receive training in how to compile a resource list, we have found that the more time we spend in practice, the more we find it necessary to find new or different kinds of referral resources. Also, it should be pointed out that although practice guidelines provide a reason for keeping resource lists, having the flexibility to step out of the talk therapy process and into the case management role is consistent with the profession's view that advocacy for clients is an important role, one consistent with the social justice underpinning of the counseling profession. A sample list of community resources that might be kept in one's contact list is provided in Table 7.2.

Table 7.2   Sample Community Resources

• Local support groups
  ○ 12-step groups (e.g., Alcoholics Anonymous)
  ○ Psychiatric peer support groups (e.g., a mood disorders group hosted by Mental Health America)
  ○ Professional-led support groups (e.g., VetCenter support groups, hospital-based groups for families with a cancer patient)
• Online support
  ○ Forums/support groups for specific populations (e.g., military veterans, GLBT)
  ○ Relaxation video/music clips
  ○ Informational sites (e.g., SAMHSA information on clinical trials)
• Physical health care services
  ○ General practitioners
  ○ Nutritionists
  ○ Physical trainers
  ○ Alternative medicine providers
• Legal services
  ○ Legal Aid
	• Career-related support
	  ○ State employment agencies
	  ○ Goodwill career centers
	  ○ Job clubs
	  ○ Speaking/interview groups (e.g., Toastmasters)
	• Psychiatric emergency centers
	  ○ Psychiatric hospitals
	  ○ County mental health centers
	• Issue-specific service providers
	  ○ Domestic violence women's shelters
	  ○ Alcohol and other drug detoxification/rehabilitation centers
	  ○ Runaway youth centers
	• Housing and home service assistance
	  ○ Government agencies
	  ○ Faith-based relief agencies
	  ○ School homeless student service coordinators
	  ○ Homeless shelters
	  ○ Halfway houses
	  ○ Credit counseling agencies

Some of these resources seemingly have little to do with counseling but are relevant to help clients work on needs that might have to be addressed before the psychological needs to which counseling is best suited can be approached. Broadly speaking, resource lists should include other professionals who are specialists for particular mental health concerns, professionals from other disciplines, support groups, government agencies (e.g., departments of social services, workforce development agencies), and service organizations (e.g., food banks, job centers).

Determining the utility of available resources is a process that requires an investment of time and a decision to be mindful of the feedback received from other users. Many counseling centers include staff development as a regular part of the monthly office calendar. Whereas staff development may mean attendance to area workshops and networking with others in attendance, a more efficient way for multiple staff members to learn about a community resource is to invite representatives from area resources to provide in-service training. The in-service presenter can be asked to present information about the services available at his or her facility but also to discuss what the intake process entails, information that could be used to prepare clients who might access the resource. Those in private practice and others who might not have in-service meetings might adopt a similar strategy during group consultation with other private practitioners.

Application

At times, use of community resources in the treatment planning process requires addressing client anxieties about accessing the resource or client concerns about the resource. As in the case of Tara presented earlier in the chapter, clients sometimes hold beliefs about a resource that discourage the use of an available and potentially helpful resource. Tara had the belief that if she engaged in regular counseling appointments, she would cross a threshold toward "craziness." Furthermore, she was unaware of the impact her physical health could have on her mental health. As such, when developing a treatment plan that will include a resource outside of the counseling relationship, it is important to assess what the appropriate level of challenge is for that particular client. In other words, the treatment plan needs to reflect whether the appropriate therapeutic challenge is for the client to explore resources (i.e., appropriate sources of support versus unhelpful websites) or for the client to commit to using the resource. In either case, the client may need the counselor's help to coconstruct a reasonable target for the use of the resource so that progress can subsequently be documented. An example of a situation where the client's presentation dictates how outside resources might be used is provided in the case of Emily.

Case of Emily

Emily is a 23-year-old African American graduate student who is majoring in clinical mental health counseling. Emily has shared that she moved into town specifically because she wanted to attend the program in which she has enrolled, even though she knew she might be the only African American in her department. She shares that the adjustment process has been difficult and that she feels somewhat isolated. She reports that her feelings of loneliness aren't related to outright hostility; if anything, she feels that her department, her classmates, and the school have generally been welcoming. She and her roommate "get along just fine." She shares that it seems like a lot of "little things" are adding up and have her feeling different. She shares examples of little things like going to the store and discovering there aren't hair products for hair like hers. She states that she feels like the entire classroom starts to watch her whenever the subject of minorities is brought up in one of her classes. She reports that she would like to date but is having a difficult time finding interesting candidates. Over the course of the session she conveys a groundedness with who she is and her goals in life.

In developing a treatment plan, you and she identify some of the resources that made her undergraduate experience feel less isolating (and less distant from home). These resources include the friendships from her sorority, her connection with the advisor at the campus multicultural center, a job that was mindless and had nothing to do with school, and finding a church that she felt was a lot like her home church. Your treatment plan includes objectives and interventions that describe her accessing university offices and student groups, accessing community resources, and building relationships with her advisor to share some of her concerns.

Counselors referring clients to other professional providers might take into consideration the level of communication that is appropriate among providers. If it is appropriate to communicate with the other provider, a written release of information should be obtained from the client. Depending on the type of provider, it may be helpful to offer the provider an opportunity to discuss the referral prior to the client's first appointment, as well as an opportunity for periodic follow-up. Kertez (2011) recommended that when referring to primary-care physicians, counselors work with the physician's office staff to secure the necessary releases of information from that office and to schedule a brief phone conversation to discuss the referral. A checklist for consultation with referral providers is provided in Table 7.3.

Table 7.3   Checklist for Consulting With Another Provider During a Referral

1. Discuss the reason for the referral with the client; secure commitment.
2. Obtain release of information from the client.
3. If the referral provider is already providing services to the client and needs a different release of information form, have it completed.
4. Offer to discuss the reason for referral with the other provider prior to their first meeting with the client; schedule time for a brief conversation with the other provider.
5. Be succinct when discussing the case with the other provider (be aware that providers who are not mental health specialists may not understand counseling-related jargon or complicated conceptualizations).
6. Discuss the need for follow-up consultation. If needed, schedule a date and time to follow up.

Termination Versus Maintenance

Though it may seem counterintuitive to be focused on termination during an initial session or during the treatment planning process, in order to have a clear direction for counseling, termination must always be in mind. In fact, one might argue that the main goal for any client *is* the termination of counseling. Introducing termination at the outset signifies that the client mentality is one where the client will achieve counseling goals and have lower needs for professional support. There are numerous reasons why counseling may come to an end. These include planned endings (e.g., therapy goals met, graduation from college, fixed number of sessions met) and unplanned endings (e.g., client or counselor moves, counselor becomes ill, referral is warranted, client stops attending sessions). In some cases, clients may fully intend to return to counseling but for some reason end up not finding their way back, perhaps because of lack of readiness for continued work or perhaps because they no longer need the counselor's support. Whether termination is planned or unplanned, it is important for counselors to remember that termination is not a onetime event; rather, it is an evolving process with important implications for the overall experience of clients.

Figure 7.3 provides an example of a treatment plan that a CMH counselor might use in clinical practice.

Making a determination as to a client's readiness for termination should not occur hastily because the process of terminating the counseling relationships may mirror earlier endings or losses in the client's life, ones that may have been unexpected, undesired, or generally negative experiences. Bearing this in mind during the treatment planning phase, the counselor may even include positive termination of counseling as a treatment goal. This is important not only to avoid recapitulating a client's former hurts but also to increase the likelihood that the client will pursue counseling in the future if needed. In fact, for some clients, a central purpose of counseling may be to prepare them for future therapeutic work, perhaps with a different counselor.

In some cases, particularly when treatment goals are especially clear, specific, and achievable, it may be easier to determine the timing of termination. For example, if a client's presenting concern is panic attacks and the therapist and client coconstruct a goal of reducing the frequency of panic attacks, termination may make sense once the client is no longer or seldom experiencing panic attacks. As is often the case, however, treatment goals may not be so clear-cut. Often, clients may initially present to counseling with Issue A (panic attacks), but in order to work on Issue A, Issues B (previous trauma experience), C (generalized anxiety), and D (self-confidence) must also be addressed. Likewise, as Issues B, C, and D are sufficiently addressed, Issues E (assertiveness) and F (relationships with men) may emerge.

Though it is important to work toward completion of set goals, it is equally important for both client and counselor to recognize that not all issues may be fully resolved at the conclusion of counseling. In fact, it can be beneficial for clients to build comfort with the presence of unfinished business, paralleling the inevitability of unexpected obstacles and the imperfect nature of life in general. This form of distress tolerance is an important skill not only for clients but for CMH counselors as well. That is, counselors should be comfortable with the idea that clients may not meet all goals in an ideal or anticipated way. Counselors can periodically check in with themselves about their own expectations, needs, and wants in the therapy relationship and how these might impact their clients positively or negatively. The following questions may be helpful for counselors to explore with themselves, a colleague, or a supervisor:

Figure 7.3 Counseling Treatment Plan

Client(s): Emily _____

Date of Intake: _____   Initial Plan ❑   Revised Plan ❑   Revision Date: _____

Goal(s)	Objective(s)	Intervention(s)	Strengths
Improve adjustment to life during graduate school	Make connections with her school's support systems	Client will register with Office of Multicultural Affairs	Past success using campus resources
		Client will join Black Graduate Student Association	Outgoing personality
		Client will contact advisor for the university's chapter of her sorority	High ego strength Sorority induction
	Access a local faith community	Client will attend services at two different churches a month until she finds one that "feels right"	Openness to new experiences
	Address feeling like the "spokesperson" for all minorities in her classes	Client will discuss her experience with her advisor	Good relationships with faculty
		Client will state (using humor) that she can't speak for all minorities the next time it comes up	Good sense of humor

Parties involved in the development of this treatment plan will sign below to indicate that the plan describes what is understood as the purpose of this counseling relationship. All parties understand that this is a flexible document open to revision, as appropriate.

Client Signature(s): _____

Counselor Signature & Credentials: _____

- What are my expectations for this client?
  - Are these expectations realistic?
  - Are these expectations aligned with my client's goals?
- Are we moving at a pace that is appropriate for the client?

- How is my role helping move the client forward?
  - Hindering the client from moving forward?

- Am I holding on to this client because *I* am not ready for the relationship to end?

- Are my client's presenting concerns within my scope of expertise?

- Would this client fare better with another counselor?
  - With another treatment modality or form of support?

At times, it may be appropriate to continue working on emerging issues as they arise, whereas at other times it may be in the client's best interest to take a break from counseling or take a break from doing heavy insight-oriented work. Much like a runner training for a long race needs to include step-back days (i.e., walking, light jogging) or rest days, clients need step-back sessions or time away from counseling. After a session or two of intense work focused on a traumatic experience, a counselor may intentionally steer the focus of a subsequent session to less charged subjects to provide the client an opportunity to process the insights gained and replenish his or her emotional energy stores. Counselors should attend to cues from clients that signal "breaks" are needed (e.g., rescheduling or missing sessions, avoiding discussion of the presenting concern, affect that is more guarded or incongruent). Time away from counseling can serve as a way for insights gained to be integrated, can allow clients to practice accessing coping strategies, and can provide the space for the use of skills learned in counseling. Also, insights gained between sessions may inform later work. For example, a client may realize during a "break" from counseling that certain coping strategies are working but need to be tweaked slightly. When counseling is resumed, the client and counselor can focus on modifying the coping strategies to better fit the client's needs.

Whether the CMH counselor and client decide that a temporary break or more permanent ending is warranted, the counselor should prepare the client for the ending of the counseling relationship with the understanding that the client may not return. When possible, clients should be aware of the date for their final session with ample time to fully process both the ending of counseling and any reactions that surround the ending. As indicated earlier, counselors should prepare their clients for the termination of counseling from the very first session, even though a specific date or session number probably cannot be specified. Questions the counselor can pose as discussion points throughout the course of counseling, but particularly leading up to final sessions, include the following:

- Are you comfortable with your current progress regarding (the presenting concern)?

- Have we (sufficiently) met the goals you had when you began counseling?

- What kind of support will you need after this?
  - Who can serve as supports?

- What potential roadblocks to maintaining your progress do you anticipate?

- What needs to be in place for you to continue making gains?

- What more did we need to do in therapy that we have not yet done?

Answers to these questions help to evaluate progress made and may inform changes or additions needed to the treatment plan and to the focus of remaining sessions. Indeed, these are examples of ongoing informal assessment. Likewise, this process of evaluating progress can lead into two other important components of ending counseling: gathering tools gained during counseling and celebrating accomplishments.

It can be important for clients to feel they are leaving counseling with tools they can continue to access. This could be concrete items like handouts or workbook recommendations, cognitive or behavioral skills, recommendations regarding self-care activities, general knowledge about identifying future triggers or roadblocks, or receipt of reassurance and validation of self. Thus, sessions leading up to the final session may focus on reviewing, practicing, and fine-tuning skills and coping strategies learned. Included in this can be time reserved for reflection on accomplishments made as well as time for client and counselor to reflect on what they are taking away from the experience.

Counselor: "Joseph, I really appreciated your willingness to explore some tough issues in our sessions. You demonstrated a great deal of courage and commitment to your own self-care."

This ritual of reflecting on the relationship and stating appreciation can be useful both in individual and group settings as a way of bolstering gains made in sessions and reinforcing the meaningfulness of the therapeutic relationship. In a group setting, the counselor might lead group members in taking turns stating things they appreciate about what other group members brought to the overall group experience. Often, group members comment that they had not realized their individual impact on the group, occasioning validation that they offered something impactful to others.

Finally, it may be helpful for counselors to explore their own conception of termination and how this conception is communicated to clients. Various terms used to describe the conclusion of counseling include *termination*, *ending*, *transition*, and *beginning*. We like the term used by a former supervisor of one of the authors (MBP), *launching*, which communicates less finality while suggesting both a beginning and a continuation, together with hope and confidence that the new leg of the client's journey will be a positive one. Additionally, this way of viewing the end of counseling is conducive to counselor wellness and prevention of burnout.

TREATMENT PLANNING AND SPECIAL POPULATIONS

Select client groups require an approach to treatment planning that is distinct from the approach used with most adult clients. Specifically, when creating a treatment plan for children and adolescents, clients who otherwise are members of a vulnerable population, or clients who have been mandated to participate in counseling, one must take into account outside stakeholders (Linhorst et al., 2002; McLoughlin & Geller, 2010; Mills, 2011). The ACA (2014) Code of Ethics describes these groups as "unable to give voluntary consent" (p. 4). The degree of involvement of outside stakeholders will vary on a case-by-case basis; as such, only broad guidelines are presented here.

Treatment Planning With Children and Adolescents

Ethically and legally, a minor's guardian has the right to the privileged information from his or her child's counseling. In working with children, guardians are an integral part of the treatment planning process because guardians have some idea of the desired outcome. In fact, the challenge faced by counselors in treatment planning with children is helping guardians acknowledge that the plan should focus not only on the child but also on the behaviors of adults in the child's life. In other words, the very adult who referred the child may expect the counselor to "fix" the child without expecting to be involved in the treatment process. Obtaining parental buy-in is critical to developing a plan that features attainable objectives and realistic interventions. Because guardians play a decisive role in a child's continuation in counseling, the establishment of clear expectations in the planning phase reduces the risk of premature termination. It is important that children are involved in the planning process in a way appropriate to their development and that their assent is obtained such that counseling is viewed as a participatory process rather than something that is happening to them.

Counselors working with adolescents must negotiate more difficult circumstances with respect to the involvement of other stakeholders—particularly guardians. Often, adolescents have concerns about how much of the information divulged in counseling will be shared with guardians. In part, these concerns are an outgrowth of developmentally appropriate needs for autonomy. Among this age group, however, autonomy is only partial—guardians still play a deciding role in whether their adolescent will participate in counseling. Other stakeholders (e.g., school officials, medical providers) also can contribute to counseling success or failure (Cauce et al., 1994). Therefore, it is important to recognize that whereas it is impossible to make progress toward treatment goals without child and adolescent assent, the consent for treatment must ultimately come from guardians. In these instances, the clinical mental health counselor is challenged with negotiating the concerns and desired outcomes identified by both the client and the guardian. The concerns and desired outcomes identified by both parties are ideally one and the same, but often this is not the case. Therefore, it is imperative that during the initial meeting the counselor establishes with both the client and guardians the limits to confidentiality. Generally, it would be a mistake to agree to pass on all information from counseling to the guardian because the client then has a disincentive to be forthright. Providing a summary of the goals to be addressed, some periodic general updates on progress toward the goals for the guardian, and clearly defined boundaries with respect to risky behaviors in the treatment plan is often helpful. Periodic check-in meetings with guardians also provide an opportunity to gather outside information needed to evaluate client progress.

Treatment Planning With Mandated Clients

Clients are mandated to participate in counseling for a variety of reasons. Depending on the nature of the referral for mandated counseling, a clinical mental health counselor may have to share information with the referral source about attendance, the treatment plan, and progress toward the goals established in the plan. In some instances, the goals themselves may be determined to a large extent by the referring person or office. Clients in these circumstances may have a clear understanding of what the counseling goals are "supposed" to be, but when there is uncertainty, it is wise to obtain a release of information and to make phone calls along with the client to find out. In instances where there are no clearly mandated goals (i.e., the client is required to attend counseling, but there are no concrete parameters pertaining to goals), client buy-in to identify how mandated sessions could be used productively is critical. Therefore, the treatment planning process with mandated clients could be a combination of compliance with the requirements set by the referral source and an opportunity to address concerns identified during intake. Reframing the treatment planning process as an opportunity to take control over a situation where the client feels a lack of control often helps to assure buy-in as well as active participation.

Treatment planning, which establishes the purpose for continued meetings with clients, be they mandated or voluntary, is a skill that gets easier over time. Though every time a counselor is presented with a new case, he or she is challenged to fit the plan to that specific person, the CMH counselor's familiarity with appropriate interventions and referral resources makes the process more fluid. The challenge for those who plan to remain in the field over time is to remain focused and creative to avoid the use of staid treatment plan templates. In this regard, continuing education and supervision are vital.

CASE STUDY

A colleague at the local University Counseling Center referred Kristi, a 21-year-old Caucasian (Irish ancestry) female, to you. At the intake session, Kristi states that she is graduating and has an interest in continuing the counseling that she initiated approximately 3 months ago. After several months of counseling, she is able to succinctly state that her presenting concern is an inability to trust people. She further clarifies that she is able to trust people (her previous counselor had helped her recognize that there are indeed people that she fully trusts) but is having difficulties allowing herself to be emotionally available to her boyfriend or allowing her mother to strengthen their currently distant relationship.

Kristi goes on to explain that she had been sexually assaulted by a cousin's friend when she was 14 years old and had contracted a sexually transmitted infection (STI). Upon receiving treatment by a physician for the STI symptoms, Kristi disclosed to her mother that she had been assaulted, but her mother kept her from going to the authorities or otherwise addressing the assault for fear that others would think she was promiscuous. Kristi never spoke about the assault again until she met with her counselor at the university. She acknowledged that in the present she has unresolved feelings of anger toward her mom for not responding in a more supportive manner, difficulties trusting men because she feels like she should have known not to trust her cousin's friend, problems in her romantic relationship because of her trust concerns, and flashbacks during sex with her partner.

Other aspects of your assessment lead you to understand that she reports no physical complaints, has secured employment for after graduation, will be staying in her current apartment after

(Continued)

(Continued)

graduation, and has a support network she trusts with information other than her rape. She has never taken psychotropic medication, drinks two to three alcoholic beverages approximately once per week, and denies other drug use. She reports no known family history of mental illness. She denies having participated in support groups or advocacy groups for victims of sexual assault.

Based on the information provided,

1. What additional information would you collect during the intake session to develop a treatment plan with Kristi?

2. What counseling goals might be established with Kristi?

3. What one or two objectives might be established to operationalize the goals identified in Question 1?

4. Identify one intervention for each of the objectives you have identified.

REFERENCES

American Counseling Association. (2014). *Code of Ethics*. Alexandria, VA: Author.

American Mental Health Counselors Association. (2010). *Code of Ethics* (Rev. ed.). Alexandria, VA: Author.

Brew, L., & Kottler, J. A. (2007). *Applied helping skills: Transforming lives*. Thousand Oaks, CA: Sage.

CACREP. (2016). *2016 CACREP Standards*. Alexandria, VA: Author.

Cauce, A. M., Morgan, C. J., Wagner, J., Moore, E., Sy, J., Wurzbacher, K., et al. (1994). Effectiveness of intensive case management for homeless adolescents: Results of a 3-month follow-up. *Journal of Emotional & Behavioral Disorders, 2*, 219–227.

Falvey, J. E. (2001). Clinical judgment in case conceptualization and treatment planning across mental health disciplines. *Journal of Counseling & Development, 79*, 292–303.

Feltham, C., & Dryden, W. (1993). Treatment plan. In C. Feltham & W. Dryden (Eds.), *Dictionary of counselling* (p. 199). London: Whurr.

Gladding, S. T. (2006). Treatment plan. In S. T. Gladding (Ed.), *The counseling dictionary: Concise definitions of frequently used terms* (2nd ed., p. 145). Upper Saddle River, NJ: Merrill Prentice Hall.

Jongsma, A. E., Jr., & Peterson, M. L. (2003). *The complete adult psychotherapy treatment planner* (3rd ed.). Hoboken, NJ: Wiley.

Kertez, J. (2011, October). *Simplified psychotropics*. Workshop presented at the annual meeting of the Licensed Professional Counselors Association of North Carolina, Greensboro, North Carolina.

Linhorst, D. M., Hamilton, F., Young, E., & Eckert, A. (2002). Opportunities and barriers to empowering people with severe mental illness through participation in treatment planning. *Social Work, 47*, 425–434.

McLoughlin, K. A., & Geller, J. L. (2010). Interdisciplinary treatment planning in inpatient settings: From myth to model. *Psychiatric Quarterly, 81*, 263–277.

Mears, G. (2010). Assessment, case conceptualization, diagnosis, and treatment. In B. E. Erford (Ed.), *Orientation to the counseling profession: Advocacy, ethics and essential professional foundations* (pp. 269–297). Upper Saddle River, NJ: Pearson.

Mills, I. (2011). Understanding parent decision making for treatment of ADHD. *School Social Work Journal, 36,* 41–60.

Osborn, C. J., Dean, E. P., & Petruzzi, M. L. (2004). Use of simulated multidisciplinary treatment teams and client actors to teach case conceptualization and treatment planning skills. *Counselor Education and Supervision, 44,* 121–134.

Puterbaugh, D. T. (2006). Communication counseling as part of a treatment plan for depression. *Journal of Counseling & Development, 84,* 373–380.

SAMHSA. (2010). *Results from the 2010 National Survey on Drug Use and Health: Summary of national findings.* Retrieved from http://archive.samhsa.gov/data/NSDUH/2k10nsduh/2k10results.htm.

Seligman, L. (1993). Teaching treatment planning. *Counselor Education and Supervision, 32,* 287–297.

Seligman, L. (2004). *Diagnosis and treatment planning in counseling* (3rd ed.). New York: Springer.

Spanier, G. B. (1989). *Dyadic Adjustment Scale manual.* North Tonawanda, NY: Multi-Health Systems.

VandenBos, G. R. (2006). Treatment plan. In G. R. VandenBos (Ed.), *APA dictionary of psychology* (p. 956). Washington, DC: American Psychological Association.

CHAPTER 8

Psychiatry and Psychopharmacology

Todd Lewis and John Culbreth

Learning Goals

Upon completion of this chapter, you will be able to do the following:

1. Articulate the major classes of psychotropic medications

2. Understand how psychotropic medications affect the brain

3. Understand how psychotropic medications can enhance client well-being

4. Understand common side effects to psychotropic medications

5. Understand the importance of collaboration with psychiatrists and other medical personnel

6. Articulate the importance of an advocate for clients related to medication

7. Understand important legal and ethical issues involving psychotropic medications

A 38-year-old male client came in for counseling after suffering a disabling back injury in his construction business. The injury occurred 3 years earlier, and the client had been in a legal battle with his insurance provider about coverage for his medical expenses. He reported a long history of depression symptoms and met the necessary criteria for major depressive disorder. The client identified numerous major changes and struggles in his life, including constant back pain, ineffective corrective surgeries, loss of his career and ability to provide for his family, inability to participate in everyday family activities with his wife

189

and two children, mounting debt due to medical expenses, and the ongoing stress of a lawsuit that was repeatedly delayed by the defendant's attorneys. In the initial interview, the client reported being on several pain medications in the past that made him very lethargic and incoherent, resulting in his opposition to any further medications. During the first three sessions the client appeared extremely tense and on edge and was barely able to maintain daily functioning. He also continued to express no interest in adding to his medication regimen.

The fourth session provided a turning point for the client. After spending the first few sessions establishing a positive relationship, the counselor reintroduced the topic of psychotropic medications, specifically antidepressants. The client stated that he did not want to live a life where he was dependent on medicine to be artificially happy. The counselor then spent a good part of the session explaining the neurobiology of antidepressant medication, helping the client to understand just how these medications interact with the primary chemicals in the brain, while reminding the client several times that the decision was ultimately up to him (i.e., valuing client autonomy). The counselor also explained that the use of medication was not a permanent solution, but that it would give the client assistance in managing the depressive symptoms during which he could develop more effective coping strategies that were not dependent on medication. Toward the end of this conversation, the client stated that no one had ever provided this level of explanation about these medications to him before. He agreed to make an appointment with his referring family physician for a medication evaluation. Within a few weeks of beginning Lexapro, the client began to notice significant changes in his mood. He was better able to work in his counseling sessions on his life transition issues and daily stressors.

Psychotropic drugs (i.e., medications that affect brain function) appear to be a mainstay in the treatment of mental health problems. With 1 in 5 Americans experiencing a mental health disorder within the course of a year (King & Anderson, 2004), consider the astonishing fact that there are more than 200 million psychotropic drug prescriptions written annually in the United States (Breggin, 2008). The prevalence of psychotropic drugs across the life span suggests that clinical mental health (CMH) counselors will see medication use daily in their practice (King & Anderson, 2004). As the previous case indicates, counselors are in a unique position to offer information about medications to their clients. And yet counselors consistently enter the field with a limited view of medication usage in treatment. Some counselors are very opposed to medications, believing that clients should be able to address their issues with only talk therapy, whereas other counselors are not familiar with psychotropic medications and, therefore, do not discuss the options available with their clients. Further, some counselors may believe that psychotropic medications are a panacea for all problems, thus referring all clients for medication evaluations. Regardless of whether you are supportive of psychotropic medication use, it is clear that its use has become an integral part of mental health care worldwide.

Despite the widespread use of psychotropic medications, the counseling profession's flagship journal, *The Journal of Counseling & Development*, has had only two articles since 1985 address this issue and its implications for counselors. Ponterotto (1985) argued that psychopharmacology had become widespread enough in the 1980s to suggest that all mental health professionals need to become at least familiar with the main psychotropic medications. This argument is even more relevant today. Mental health counselors work with psychotropic medications in a number of ways, including the following:

- Working with clients who are on medications that impact their treatment

- Providing psychiatric referrals for clients for medication evaluation

- Educating clients on typical effects and drawbacks of medication

- Helping clients understand and manage side effects

In some instances, when clients lack the skills or abilities to advocate for themselves, counselors also have to advocate for clients with medical professionals who prescribe the medications. Communication and rapport are enhanced when counselors can discuss drug effects, side effects, and compliance issues with psychiatrists (Ponterotto, 1985). Unfortunately, counselors have historically had limited knowledge of psychotropic medication in the treatment and management of mental health problems.

King and Anderson (2004) suggested that clinical mental health programs do not provide enough training in psychopharmacology. However, this trend may be changing. The 2016 Standards of the Council for Accreditation of Counseling and Related Educational Programs (CACREP) include provisions for CMH counselors to have knowledge related to psychopharmacology. Specifically, section 2.H under the 2016 Standards states that CMH counselors should know "classifications, indications, and contraindications of commonly prescribed psychopharmacological medications for appropriate medical referral and consultation" (CACREP, 2016, p. 22).

The intentional inclusion of psychopharmacology knowledge into the accreditation standards suggests that the counseling profession recognizes this as an important component of counselor training. CACREP's endorsement of the need for counselors to have knowledge of psychopharmacology has increased training emphasis on psychopharmacology either through inclusion of already established courses (e.g., diagnosis and treatment planning) or the formation of independent courses on the topic.

CMH counselors do not need to be experts in brain science, physiology, or the exact effects of psychiatric medications to be effective clinicians. CMH counselors should have a *basic* understanding of the human brain and how psychotropic drugs impact the brain (and body), as well as drug categories, side effects, and withdrawal symptoms. Having this basic knowledge can help counselors in a number of ways:

1. Providing clients with referral options if medication seems appropriate or if they are open to trying medication.

2. Aiding in treatment planning. Will medication be a part of the client's care? How will the medication help the client?

3. Helping clients understand the dangers of combining medication with other medications or substances (e.g., alcohol).

4. Helping clients prepare for and manage negative side effects.

5. Assisting clients in setting realistic expectations about medications, such as providing an overview of typical effects and the time it may take for some medications to work.

6. Supporting clients when they are frustrated with a lack of results from medication or severe side effects.

7. Giving clients a basic overview of how psychiatric drugs impact the brain and neurotransmitters.

8. Showing clients that you have an interest (Brooks & McHenry, 2010).

CMH counselors are in a position to advocate for the best care of their clients and explore, discuss, and cocreate effective treatment plans. Perhaps the greatest challenge for CMH counselors is to use knowledge of the brain, medications, and medication effects in a way that empowers their clients.

Knowledge of psychopharmacology issues is an important component of successful counseling. Being able to communicate a range of treatment options for clients is critical for appropriate informed consent. In addition, common counselor tasks, such as making medication referrals, understanding side effects, and communicating with medical doctors suggest that knowledge of psychopharmacology is imperative. In our clinical experience, a collaborative, respectful relationship with psychiatrists not only helps the client but also helps the mental health agency run more effectively and smoothly.

This chapter provides readers with a broad overview of psychopharmacology and how it is integrated within a comprehensive treatment plan. We begin with a basic overview of brain physiology (see Chapter 14 for a more in-depth discussion of the brain), a rationale for using medications to treat mental disorders, and strengths and limitations of the medical model approach to manage mental health problems. We then outline the classes, effects, and side effects of the most commonly prescribed medications. Because psychopharmacology can be a complicated topic with a myriad of possible drugs, only the major classes of psychotropic medications are discussed. Strategies for working with psychiatrists and physicians, along with legal and ethical considerations, are discussed. The chapter concludes with a case study demonstrating how a counselor might integrate knowledge of psychopharmacology into her or his counseling practice

BRAIN PHYSIOLOGY, NEUROTRANSMITTERS, AND MEDICATION: A BASIC OVERVIEW

Psychiatric drugs impact the central nervous system and brain in highly complex ways. The brain is equipped with thousands of nerve receptor sites where medications produce multiple effects, although psychotropic drugs are usually targeted toward one or more brain systems. The brain operates promoting an intricate balance of excitatory and inhibitory influences (Kuhn, Swartzwelder, & Wilson, 2008). The average human brain is made of billions of cells, many of which are called *neurons*. Neurons have been found to fire at an extraordinarily fast pace, with messages crossing the brain almost instantaneously. The average neuron makes thousands of connections with other neurons, showing an intricate interplay of communication and connection (Hanson, 2011).

A typical neuron possesses dendrites, a cell body, axon, and terminal buttons. Dendrites are thin structures that emanate from the cell body, often extending and branching out to receive messages from other neurons. The cell body extends from the dendrites and then gives rise to one, and only one, axon. The axon is a long, tubelike extension arising from the cell body. The axon may branch numerous times at its termination, giving rise to terminal buttons where neurotransmitters are released. With a few notable exceptions, nerve signals are sent from the axon of one neuron to a dendrite of another.

Neurons communicate with each other through neurotransmitters, or chemical substances that are released from a nerve impulse (Cutler, 2004). When an electrical impulse travels through the axon to the terminal buttons, neurotransmitters are fired into the synaptic region (or synapse), the small area between releasing and receiving neurons. The neurotransmitter then attaches to the receiving neuron, culminating in an excitatory or inhibitory response (Cutler, 2004). Often, the receiving neuron does not absorb all of the neurotransmitter, leaving excess in the synapse. Through a process called *reuptake*, the excess neurotransmitter is reabsorbed back into the original releasing neuron (Kuhn et al., 2008). Psychotropic medications have their most beneficial effect by influencing these processes of neuronal communication. The basic structure of a neuron, as well as the process of neurotransmission at the level of the synapse, is illustrated in Figures 8.1a and 8.1b.

According to Brooks and McHenry (2010), there are over 200 variations of neurotransmitters in the brain. Neurotransmitters are implicated in our mood states, how much we sleep, our anxiety levels, and how much pleasure we derive from life. Too much or too little of these neurotransmitters and we feel out of balance, overstimulated, or so tired that it is hard to get going during the day. Certain mental health disorders, such as major depressive disorder, bipolar disorder, or generalized anxiety disorder are thought to be associated with problems in neurotransmission (Cutler, 2004). Deficiencies or irregularities can occur when releasing neurons do not emit enough neurotransmitters or receiving neurons do not respond to the chemical messengers. The neurotransmitter system is a delicate process and can be disrupted by a range of

Figure 8.1a Basic Structure of a Neuron

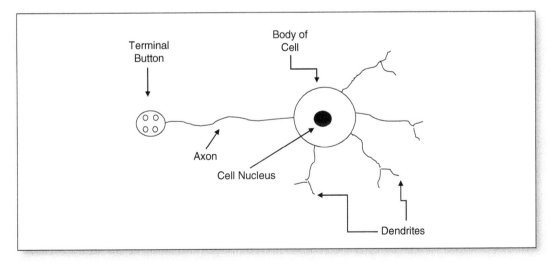

Source: Adapted from Wegmann, 2011

Figure 8.1b   Process of Neurotransmission at the Synapse Level

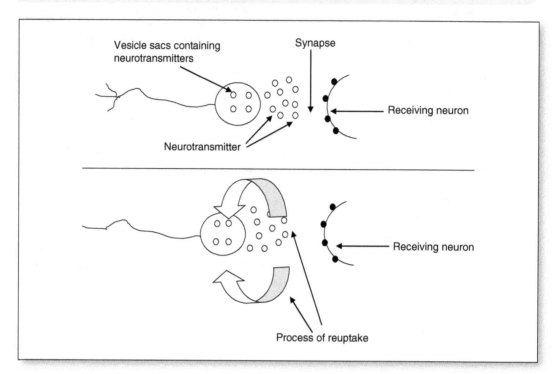

Source: Adapted from Wegmann, 2011

life stressors and/or negative lifestyle habits. It is believed that psychotropic drugs generally act by either increasing or decreasing the activity level of selected neurotransmitter systems (Cutler, 2004) and help to restore balance among selected neurotransmitters, although the nature of this chemical balancing process is not known (Carlat, 2010). The following is a list of the most common neurotransmitters implicated when taking psychotropic medication.

1. *Serotonin.* Serotonin regulates sleep, mood, pain, sexual behavior, and appetite (Brown, 2010). One class of medications, called *selective serotonin reuptake inhibitors* (SSRIs; discussed later), is specifically designed to increase the amount of serotonin in the synaptic region.

2. *Gamma-Aminobutyric Acid* (GABA). Decreased levels of GABA in the brain correspond to increased anxiety. GABA, then, is important in the experience of relaxation (Wegmann, 2011). Benzodiazepines, mild tranquilizing drugs, exert their relaxing effects by influencing the GABA system in the brain (Hyman, 2009).

3. *Catecholamines.* Catecholamines function as both hormones and neurotransmitters in the brain and body, with norepinephrine and dopamine being the most common. Dopamine influences emotional behavior and cognition, regulates motor activity and endocrine activity, and promotes motivation and feelings of pleasure

(Wegmann, 2011). Dopamine is thought to play a large role in psychotic disorders. Norepinephrine stimulates the fight or flight response (i.e., sympathetic nervous system; Brown, 2010) and is considered adrenaline for the brain (Wegmann, 2011). Irregularities in norepinephrine production can lead to anxiety problems.

Mechanisms of Action

The effect that psychotropic drugs have on the brain and nervous system is complex. Simply picking up a textbook on the neurobiology of psychotropic medication is intimidating. We do not believe that mental health counselors need to master this complex information. However, a basic understanding of the different mechanisms of action that psychotropic drugs promote in the brain is important. Plotnik (1996) outlined four key mechanisms of action.

1. *Drugs cause some neurons to release excess neurotransmitters.* CNS stimulant drugs increase the release of norepinephrine and dopamine (Plotnik, 1996). Ritalin and Dexedrine, typically prescribed to treat ADHD, are two examples.

2. *Drug effects mimic the actions of neurotransmitters.* Agonist drugs mimic neurotransmitters by binding to the receptor sites in the same manner as neurotransmitters do, producing the same or a similar effect. For example, benzodiazepines, prescribed to treat anxiety, are psychotropic drugs that mimic the action of GABA.

3. *Drugs block the reabsorption of neurotransmitters.* The reuptake process is designed to sweep surplus neurotransmitters out of the synaptic region and back into the releasing neuron. Some psychotropic medications preclude or slow down reuptake, resulting in excess neurotransmitters in the synaptic region. Selective serotonin reuptake inhibitors (SSRIs), such as Paxil and Zoloft, are examples of drugs that block reuptake of serotonin.

4. *Drugs block the reception of neurotransmitters.* Neurotransmitters have their effect by connecting to, and communicating with, receiving neurons. Certain drugs block the reception of neurotransmitters, precluding communication between neurons. For example, several of the antipsychotic medications block dopamine receptors in the brain.

These mechanisms of action illustrate basic methods for how drugs exert their influence in the brain. The *specific actions* (which may fall under one of the four basic mechanisms of action just mentioned) that drugs have in the brain and body, however, may number in the thousands, and the effects of one drug and dose in one person may be different from the effects in another person (Kuhn et al., 2008). Nonetheless, we have found that the four mechanisms of action serve as a useful guide when exploring the effects and influences of psychotropic medications with clients.

Why Use Medication in the Treatment of Mental Disorders?

Ponterotto (1985) was one of the first to argue in the counseling literature that mental health counselors need to have at least some familiarity with psychopharmacology, citing that improved research techniques and technologies have enhanced medication efficaciousness.

More recently, King and Anderson (2004) noted that a psychotropic medication in conjunction with psychotherapy is the standard of care across many mental health conditions. They also supported Ponterotto's belief that counselors need to be knowledgeable around issues of psychopharmacology and medications lest they negatively impact their relationship with clients.

Indeed, psychotropic medications are here to stay. The scientific evidence strongly supports the effectiveness of medications to treat mental health disorders (for an excellent review of the most up-to-date clinical trial research, visit the National Institutes of Mental Health website at www.nimh.gov). Although a review of the extant literature on the effectiveness of psychotropic medication is beyond the scope of this chapter, clinical research trials seem to confirm that medications, if used properly, are effective. We have witnessed firsthand how the proper use of medication has helped numerous clients live more satisfying lives. And medication use in combination with counseling appears to be more effective than either alone for a number of mental health conditions (King & Anderson, 2004). One obvious way that medications may enhance counseling interventions is that they serve to reduce symptoms and promote greater stability. When client symptoms are stabilized, clients may be more willing to participate in counseling and gain benefit from trying nonmedication-based strategies. For example, consider a client who is experiencing frequent panic attacks that seem to appear without precipitant. His heightened arousal state would make it very difficult for him to focus in counseling and try relaxation strategies that, whereas effective, take time to work. Psychotropic medication helps reduce the anxiety so that he can benefit from counseling.

It is important to note that psychotropic medications do not "cure" people of their mental health problems but help alleviate associated symptoms. To understand the rationale for why psychotropic medications are used to treat mental health conditions, it is important to know the underlying philosophy that drives modern mental health care, the medical model. According to the medical model, problems in living such as depression, anxiety, and psychosis result primarily from imbalances in the brain. Let's take a closer look at the major assumptions of the medical model.

Medical Model

Proponents of the medical model suggest that mental health problems are disease states that progressively worsen. Mental health problems result from a chemical imbalance in the brain and can be managed but not cured, similar to other chronic health conditions such as diabetes. If a mental health problem is indeed a disease of the brain, then corresponding treatment should primarily focus on the biological origins and manifestations of the condition. The medical model serves as the foundation of many addiction and mental health treatment programs in the United States.

Proponents of the medical model are not without their critics. The medical model is the major assumption used to support psychotropic medication use (Murray, 2006). In essence, psychiatric disorders are believed to have a specific biological etiology, and medications are then used to "correct" whatever is wrong within the brain (Kendler, 2005). According to Murray (2006), the driving forces behind a strict medical model interpretation of mental illness are psychopharmacologists and physiological psychiatrists who believe that mental health issues boil down to problems in cell communication between two or more neurons. Unfortunately, backed by a scientific community that is biased toward biological explanations of mental health problems, psychotropic medications are sometimes marketed aggressively and, in some cases, overprescribed (Murray, 2006). In addition, Murray (2006) noted the manifold problems with research on psychotropic medications, often supported by pharmaceutical companies, in which results are biased or misleading. Indeed, the mental health counselor needs to be a vigilant consumer of this research in order to get a comprehensive, balanced view.

Are Mental Disorders Really Caused by a Chemical Imbalance?

The short answer to this question is that it is possible but unknown for certain. The chemical imbalance theory holds that mental disorders develop due to a neurotransmitter deficiency or a chemical imbalance among one or more neurotransmitters. This theory was primarily derived by reasoning backward based on the effects psychotropic drugs had on neurotransmitters and, consequently, symptoms (Carlat, 2010). For example, antidepressants appear to improve some forms of depression by increasing the level of serotonin in selective synapses in the brain. Based on this observation, it was concluded that a serotonin shortage is the cause of depression (and perhaps other mental health problems; Carlat, 2010). The intuitive nature of the argument is appealing; however, there is no *unequivocal* scientific evidence that these "deficiency" or "imbalance" theories are implicated in depression or other mental health problems (Carlat, 2010).

Glasser (2003) and Carlat (2010) noted that part of the problem is how extremely difficult it is to measure levels of neurotransmitters in the brain. Doctors cannot simply draw fluid from a functioning brain to measure neurotransmitter levels (Carlat, 2010). Indirect measurements exist but are imperfect. Even pulverizing neurons postmortem and measuring levels of neurotransmitters has not confirmed deficiency or imbalance theories (Carlat, 2010). Critics of the medical model (Breggin, 1991, 2008; Carlat, 2010; Glasser, 2003), including some psychiatrists, have pointed out that psychiatry is one of the only medical professions in which doctors do not examine the organ they are trained to heal before dispensing medication. That is, the mechanisms of what is causing a disturbance are not entirely known, in that there is no good way to assess this other than client or collateral self-report. When clients visit a psychiatrist's office, they are usually not subjected to rigorous diagnostic tests or machines that take pictures of their brain (as you might see done with the heart, for example, in a cardiologist's office). Not only are there no tests to measure what neurotransmitters are deficient, neither can medical professionals determine how much they are deficient, or in what combination they are deficient. Indeed, because of this uncertainty, psychiatrists may try several medications before a therapeutic response is found, a fact that often surprises many CMH counselors.

Controversy in Using Medication in the Treatment of Mental Disorders

As the previous discussion suggests, controversy surrounds the use of psychotropic medications for the treatment of mental disorders. Indeed, even within the ranks of psychiatry, a growing minority of psychiatrists has begun to speak out against the indiscriminant use of medications (Carlat, 2010), noted the fact that no firm genetic basis for mental disorders has been found (Glasser, 2003; Kendler, 2005), and, especially among clinical psychiatrists, voiced appreciation for the role of environmental and contextual factors on the onset of mental health problems (Murray, 2006). Research into the exact neurochemical mechanisms of mental disorders continues, and in time we may be able to know exactly what is happening within a client's brain and tailor specific medications unique for that client, but we are a ways from that point (Wegmann, 2011).

Increasingly, clients have become more sophisticated consumers of mental health services. In our combined clinical experiences, clients often express concern about going on a medication. They share with us concerns about side effects, what a pill can really do to help them, and how long they must stay on medication to experience benefit. These concerns are important to validate in the counselor's office and, once again, speak to the importance of counselors having a basic understanding of medications, including their effects and drawbacks. Clients should be well informed before attempting any treatment strategy.

The Mental Health Counselor's Dilemma

So, given the pros and cons of the medical model perspective, what is a clinical mental health counselor to do? First, it might be important to state the dilemma that many mental health counselors face when working at a facility or within a treatment paradigm that strongly supports the use of psychotropic medication. We believe that our dilemma is this: How do we integrate our developmental, strength-based, nonmedical philosophy of helping with the medical model establishment's belief that mental health problems are the result of imbalances within the brain?

Although there is no easy answer, we support many of Bentley and Walsh's (2000) suggestions of roles for nonphysician helping professionals, which include being a consultant/collaborator with psychiatrists, advocating for the best treatment possible, monitoring positive and negative effects of medication, and educating clients about medication usage. We also would add that counselors should strive to help clients come to their own decisions about medication rather than deciding for them. Mental health counselors would do well to stress clients' personal responsibility for their own care, thereby promoting client autonomy, while also working to ensure that clients clearly understand the consequences of not following through with a medication regimen.

Mental health counselors should not be dissuaded from supporting medication usage among their clients. Indeed, both scientific and clinical evidence suggests that psychotropic medication can be effective in alleviating suffering, especially if combined with psychotherapy or counseling. As the medical model continues to expand within the counseling profession and impacts its future work, however, we support Murray's (2006) contention that counselors need to be vigilant consumers of psychopharmacology information and rigorously examine the uses, effects, and consequences of psychotropic medications. Indeed, given the expected rise of psychotropic medications to address mental health issues (King & Anderson, 2004), there is no doubt that mental health counselors will need to incorporate psychopharmacology into their treatment plans. We believe that a positive stance for mental health counselors is to support and encourage clients to consider medication when it seems like a viable treatment option and to keep apprised of recent developments as new medications emerge. We also support the idea that "counselors cannot provide comprehensive treatment planning, ensure client well-being, and minimize professional liability without proper training in psychopharmacology" (King & Anderson, 2004, p. 329). Knowledge of psychotropic medications and their effects is imperative in the professional world of the mental health counselor.

CLASSES OF PSYCHOTROPIC MEDICATIONS, THEIR EFFECTS, AND SIDE EFFECTS

The number of psychotropic medications currently being used in the mental health field is too high to discuss specifically within the context of this chapter. Further, how these medications are grouped for discussion varies greatly, depending on the focus of the writer, with categories based on (a) treatments for certain mental health diagnoses, (b) the action of the medication on the body, or (c) the chemical classification of the medication. For this discussion of psychotropic medications, we provide information about the classes of medication based on four general diagnostic areas: antidepressant, antianxiety, antipsychotic, and bipolar medications. Following this is a brief description of how the medication (and any subcategories of the medication class) works for clients, as well as general side effects. For a more comprehensive list of specific medications and uses, please review Preston, O'Neal, and Talaga (2010) and Kelsey, Newport, and Nemeroff (2006).

Antidepressant Medications

Unfortunately, the class of medications known as antidepressants suffers from having been given a name that does not accurately reflect what it does. Many people consider antidepressant medication to be a happy pill that results in euphoria, similar to that experienced with alcohol or other recreational drugs. In reality, one should consider antidepressants more like a brain chemistry stabilizer/enhancer. All three of the major subclasses of antidepressants (tricyclics, reuptake inhibitors, and monoamine oxidase inhibitors [MAOIs]) are believed to create a better balance of the three main brain chemicals: dopamine, serotonin, and norepinephrine (Preston et al., 2010).

Current research indicates that a greater presence in the brain of these three primary neurotransmitters—serotonin, norepinephrine, and dopamine—results in improved mood and functioning for individuals struggling with depression. Clients experiencing depression typically have reduced levels of one, two, or all three of these chemicals in their brain or, more specifically, the synaptic space between neurons. The antidepressant medications work to increase the levels of these neurotransmitters, thus improving mood and reducing the negative effects of depression. The primary differences among the three groups of medications are in the side effects that they create.

Tricyclic antidepressants were the primary choice for treatment of depression for many years, but the side effects of these medications are significant. Some examples of these side effects include dry mouth, blurred vision, constipation, profuse sweating, orthostatic hypotension (dizziness when standing caused by sudden decrease in blood pressure), sedation, weight gain, sexual dysfunction, cessation of intestinal movement, intestinal rupture, urine retention leading to bladder rupture, elevated heart rate, anxiety, and cardiac arrhythmia. Due to the strength of the tricyclic medications, or their toxicity level, small overdoses can lead to death (Preston et al., 2010), which is problematic given that some clients with depression may also have thoughts of suicide.

MAO inhibitors work to reduce the amount of monoamine oxidase in the brain. The purpose of monoamine oxidase is to chemically break down "the big three" neurotransmitters of serotonin, norepinephrine, and dopamine. Thus, a reduction of MAO in the system allows for greater amounts of "the big three" to be present in the brain. Whereas there are several milder side effects associated with the MAOIs, such as agitation, insomnia, sedation, and edema (swelling from fluid buildup), the primary concern is centered around the medication causing hypertension reactions, or significant and fast elevations in blood pressure. Some form of hypertensive reaction occurs in approximately 7% of clients who use MAOIs (Preston et al., 2010). In addition, MAOIs must be constantly monitored because of serious, potentially fatal, interactions with certain foods and other medications.

The primary medications used for depression and related mood disorders today are reuptake inhibitors. As with the other two groups, reuptake inhibitors work to increase levels of "the big three" in the brain, thus reducing symptoms of depression and other related mood disorders. The way that these medications work is quite simple. Some reviewing of information is necessary to illustrate the processes involved.

The neurons in the brain communicate with each other as part of normal functioning. They do this through chemical messaging, using various combinations of neurotransmitters, including the big three, gamma aminobutyric acid (GABA), and endorphins. These chemicals are introduced into the synapse, from the axon of the nerve cell. The dendrites of the adjacent nerve cell receive the chemical message and repeat the message to the next nerve cell in line to continue the message on its pathway. Once the communication between cells has occurred, there is a residual amount of the neurotransmitters left in the synapse. The axon that sent the neurotransmitters into the synapse is then responsible for absorbing the chemicals that were not used. This is the reuptake portion of the process. In clients experiencing mood disorders, the amount of free floating neurotransmitters in the synapses is reduced. Inhibiting the reuptake of these transmitters allows for more serotonin, norepinephrine, or dopamine to remain in the synaptic space, thus improving the individual's mood. To accomplish this, the chemicals in the reuptake inhibitors essentially "plug" the receptor holes in the axon that would ordinarily be used to absorb the leftover neurotransmitters, not allowing the axon to collect the chemicals.

In general, one of the reasons that reuptake inhibitors have become preferred over tricyclics in the treatment of depression has been the reduced severity of side effects combined with comparable levels of effectiveness. Typical side effects of reuptake inhibitors may include dry mouth, sedation, anxiety, sweating, gastrointestinal upset, insomnia, weight gain, headaches, and sexual dysfunction. Clients who experience distressing levels of side effects should consider an alternative medication to determine if the side effect can be lessened while maintaining benefits of the medication. An additional course of action would be to consider other medications that can be added to reduce the side effects of the reuptake inhibitor (Freeth, 2004; Preston et al., 2010). In some instances, however, more severe side effects can be experienced, such as increased blood pressure, shortness of breath, skin rashes, seizures, and gastrointestinal bleeding. These side effects, of course, require immediate medical attention. The clinician should be prepared to discuss these possibilities with clients and to help them understand what side effects should be dealt with immediately.

One of the primary considerations when using reuptake inhibitors is that all clients who experience depression do so with a variety of different characteristics. In addition to depression, some clients may experience heightened anxiety or panic attacks, whereas others may experience lethargy or obsessive-compulsive features. As a result, it is important for counselors to be familiar with the medications, their side effects, and their secondary benefits. Many of these medications have a secondary benefit for other areas of mood disturbance, such as anxiety or obsessive-compulsive features. These secondary treatment areas allow psychiatrists to tailor the medication for specific client needs.

There are many reuptake inhibitors available for clients. Collectively, these medications often are referred to as serotonin and norepinephrine reuptake inhibitors (SNRIs). And whereas most of the reuptake inhibitors work to manage levels of both serotonin and norepinephrine, there are some medications that target only one of these neurotransmitters. For example, Celexa, Prozac, and Lexapro are selective serotonin reuptake inhibitors (SSRIs) that block the reuptake of serotonin, whereas Strattera and Norpramin are norepinephrine reuptake inhibitors (NRIs) that block the reuptake of norepinephrine. Various other medications, such as Cymbalta, Paxil, and Effexor, block both serotonin and norepinephrine, but in different amounts (Preston et al., 2010). Therefore, it is critical that the counselor understand what additional benefits a drug may have that also can be used to help other symptoms that a client may be experiencing. Table 8.1 provides a brief overview of the most common antidepressants, including the advantages and disadvantages of each, secondary benefits, and common side effects.

Table 8.1 Drug Name, Advantages, and Disadvantages of Common Antidepressant Drugs

Drug Brand Name (Generic Name)	Advantages	Disadvantages or Side Effects
Celexa (Citalopram)	Minimal interaction with other drugs; minimal sedation/weight gain	May cause initial anxiety
Cymbalta (Duloxetine)	Good for severe depression	May cause nausea/sedation
Effexor (Venlafaxine)	Good for severe depression, social anxiety, GAD, and possibly chronic pain	May cause hypertension; increased gastrointestinal side effects
Lexapro (Escitalopram)	Minimal interaction with other medications; minimal weight gain/sedation	May cause initial anxiety
MAO inhibitors	Good for treatment resistant depressions	Dangerous drug-drug and drug-food interactions make these a last resort
Paxil (Paroxetine)	Good antianxiety benefit	Prone to discontinuation symptoms, weight gain; may interfere with other meds; contraindicated in pregnancy
Prozac (Fluoxetine)	Energizing effect; long half-life	Initial anxiety but tends to fade in 1 to 2 weeks; may interact with other medications

(Continued)

Table 8.1 (Continued)

Drug Brand Name (Generic Name)	Advantages	Disadvantages or Side Effects
Remeron (Mirtazapine)	Good for severe depression and insomnia; causes less sexual dysfunction	Significant weight gain and sedation
Serzone (Nefazodone)	Added benefit of reducing anxiety; fewer sexual side effects	Sedating; prone to medication interactions; rare reports of liver damage
Strattera (Atomoxetine)	Good for cognitive-based depression; minimal sexual side effects	May cause sedation or anxiety
Wellbutrin (Bupropion)	Energizing effect; few sexual side effects; less weight gain	May increase anxiety and insomnia; can cause seizures, especially at doses over 400 mg/day
Zoloft (Sertraline)	Neither too sedating, nor too prone to cause anxiety	More prone to gastrointestinal side effects

Source: Adapted from Preston et al. (2010)

Antianxiety Medications

There are numerous types of antianxiety medications available for clients who suffer from this class of disorders. Most of these medications are in the benzodiazepine category, such as Valium, Klonopin, Ativan, and Restoril. Recently, a new group of benzodiazepine derivatives has been developed that minimize some of the detrimental effects of traditional benzodiazepines. These new medications include ProSom, Ambien, and Lunesta. These derivatives offer a faster onset with a reduced half-life, thus they do not build up or accumulate in the system as much as the other benzodiazepines (Preston et al., 2010).

Buspirone is an antianxiety medication different from benzodiazepines that is unique in how it works in the body. The action of buspirone is not completely understood, although it appears to work with the serotonin receptors. Advantages of this medication are that it does not build a tolerance, which can lead to dependence, and it does not have negative interaction effects with typical CNS depressants. Other groups of medications that have antianxiety qualities include antihistamines, beta blockers, Clonidine, and Tiagabine. All of these medications have a variety of other uses as sedatives, hypnotics, anesthetics, treatment of epilepsy, and in the management of withdrawal symptoms associated with various addictions (Freeth, 2004; Preston et al. 2010).

Two significant issues that must be followed by counselors are benzodiazepine addiction and withdrawal. These medications have a long history of abuse and dependence. This is mainly due to the sedative effect produced and the tolerance levels that are created over time. Whereas certainly these medications are safer than those used for anxiety treatment in the past (i.e., barbiturates), clients can still develop problems with overuse or incorrect use of these medications. Further, once clients decide to go off these medications, they must work with their physician or psychiatrist to slowly reduce usage levels in a controlled manner. Completely stopping the use of benzodiazepines can create a dangerous withdrawal situation for clients. In addition to a reoccurrence of the anxiety, removing the medication from the system abruptly can cause insomnia, nightmares, restlessness, disruption of sleep patterns, seizures, high fever, psychosis, and even death (Preston et al., 2010).

During the titration process, it is important for counselors to closely monitor the symptoms reported by clients. Some of these symptoms mimic the original anxiety symptoms that began the treatment process, and it may be difficult for the client to discern which is a withdrawal symptom and which is an original symptom of the anxiety. Typically, the withdrawal symptoms will resolve themselves within approximately 2 weeks after completion of the titration process. Any remaining symptoms should be considered due to the original diagnosis. If this is the case, then the counselor should consider whether stopping the medication at this point was appropriate. If stopping the medicine was initiated by the client, then this experience can provide the client with information about the status of his or her treatment process, and that there is more work to be done on the underlying issue, and that resuming use of the medication might be in the client's best interest (Preston et al., 2010).

Antipsychotic Medications

This class of medication has been used to treat psychotic disorders since the early 1950s. Since that time, there have been significant refinements made that have greatly improved both the effectiveness of the medication and the negative side effect profiles. In the early phases of use, the actions of these medications were unknown. It is now known that, in general, these medications work to block dopamine receptors in the brain. The medications that produced greater dopamine blockades were considered more potent in the treatment of psychotic symptoms. As the use of these treatments progressed, significant side effects were found in clients. Many of the side effects are neurological in nature, which occasioned the other name, neuroleptics, that is used for this classification of medications. As the science of treating psychosis developed, a second generation of antipsychotic medications was created. Second-generation antipsychotics focused more on serotonin blocking with some level of dopamine blocking. Side effects for these medications are significantly less than those of the first-generation medications (Preston et al., 2010).

When considering the use of antipsychotics, regardless of which generation, the most important issue is to create a balance between the beneficial effects for the psychotic symptoms and the negative side effects of the medication. This is particularly true given the strong nature and neurological aspects of many of the side effects (Preston et al., 2010). Controlled experimentation with supervision by a medical professional can help clients in fine-tuning this process.

Early onset side effects related to the first-generation antipsychotic medications include those that mirror Parkinson's disease (e.g., shuffling gait, resting tremor, and slowed movements), sustained muscle spasms in the neck and shoulder areas, and significant feelings of restlessness, also known as akathisia. It is important to note that akathisia can be mistaken for psychotic agitation, so it is very difficult to differentiate between the psychotic features of an illness and the side effects of medication. Often, akathisia is the cause of clients being noncompliant in taking their medications and may also increase the risk for suicidal ideation and behavior. Another group of side effects are related to the parasympathetic nervous system. The result is exhibited in the client's mucous membranes. A client may experience dry mouth, blurred vision, slowing of the gastrointestinal system, difficulty urinating, and sexual dysfunction. Orthostatic hypertension, or sudden elevation of blood pressure when standing up, is another significant side effect with these medications. Finally, after extended periods of use, clients may begin to develop some form of tardive dyskinesia, or involuntary body movements (Preston et al., 2010).

Side effects associated with the second-generation antipsychotic medications are similar to the first generation, but typically less pronounced. Clients can usually tolerate these medications better, and very few clients experience tardive dyskinesia. These medications can produce a level of sedation, however, that may need to be addressed. In addition, weight gain has been noted as a significant side effect that should be monitored. The most troubling side effect associated with this group of medications is agranulocytosis, a blood disorder that results in a significant drop in white blood cells, thus resulting in a client being more susceptible to bacterial infections, on rare occasions leading to death. Therefore, it is vitally important that clients who are taking a second-generation antipsychotic be monitored with regular blood work to ensure adequate white blood cell counts (Freeth, 2004; Preston et al., 2010).

Overall, given the strong and sometimes uncomfortable nature of these side effects, clients who are struggling with psychotic disorders should be carefully monitored for medication compliance. There are numerous medications that can be used to reduce the side effects from antipsychotic medications. Careful work with a psychiatrist or family physician is needed to help manage all of the physical issues that may develop when using these medications. If medication noncompliance is a persistent issue with clients, then extended release, injectable forms of the medication may be used (Freeth, 2004; Preston et al., 2010).

Bipolar Medications

The primary treatment for most bipolar disorders has been with lithium, a naturally occurring salt, which was discovered to positively affect mood in the early 1800s. In the 1950s, lithium was scientifically determined to help patients with mania, both in the acute phase and in the prevention of future episodes. And yet, in spite of the successes that have been achieved with lithium therapies, it is still not known exactly how this medication works in the body (Kelsey et al., 2006).

Lithium works well for treating bipolar mania and for treating depressed clients who do not respond to traditional antidepressants. Clients who meet the criteria for depression may instead have a form of unipolar depression, which many times will respond to lithium treatment. Where lithium does not work as well are with clients who have mixed episodes of mood (experiencing both manic and depressive symptoms within one week) and clients who have rapid mood cycling (experiencing at least 4 mood episodes within 12 months. These forms of bipolar disorder may respond more effectively to anticonvulsants (e.g., Tegretol, Depakote, and Lamictal) or some of the second-generation antipsychotics (e.g., Abilify, Zyprexa, and Risperdal). Interestingly, as with lithium, the exact mechanism of action for the anticonvulsants on bipolar disorders is still unknown (Kelsey et al., 2006; Preston et al., 2010).

When considering side effects of these medications, it is critical, if not life threatening, to closely monitor clients who are taking lithium. The window of difference between the therapeutic effectiveness levels and levels of toxicity are very small. Mild side effect symptoms from lithium include increases in thirst (and increased urination caused by increased fluid intake), nausea, vomiting, gastrointestinal distress, small hand tremors, and muscle weakness. Muscle twitching, persistent or worsening nausea, vomiting or diarrhea, and confusion are considered moderate symptoms. Severe symptoms include decreases in urination, seizures, coma, and death. Also, lithium is known to adversely affect thyroid hormones and thyroid function, which can lead to hypothyroidism. Because lithium is only removed from the body through the kidneys, it is important to monitor kidney function. If kidney function is compromised, then a client can experience a significant buildup of lithium in the system, leading to toxic levels. Many of these side effects can be managed through the use of additional medications or the adjustment of the lithium dosage. The single most important way for side effects and toxicity reactions to be managed, however, is through consistent blood serum monitoring (Kelsey et al., 2006; Preston et al., 2010).

Side effects of the anticonvulsants include gastrointestinal distress, vomiting, dizziness, tremors, sedation, and weight gain. Tegretol has been known to decrease the white blood cell count of clients, thus making them more susceptible to infection. Many of the anticonvulsants also produce a dermatological side effect in the form of a rash or hives. In rare cases, Lamictal has been known to cause Stevens-Johnson syndrome, a life-threatening dermatological condition. A very challenging psychological issue that arises in the treatment of bipolar disorder is the loss of euphoria that clients experience as they are cycling up toward mania. The earlier stages of mania, sometimes referred to as hypomania, are often quite exhilarating for clients, leaving them full of energy, creativity, and excitement. They experience boundless energy, enthusiasm, and joy in life. Remembering these times may result in the client discontinuing his or her medication in an effort to regain these feelings. Many clients have described this experience in ways similar to being high on certain drugs, along with a significant craving to experience those feelings again. It is very important for counselors to help clients understand how this craving is like an addiction. Whereas there is a euphoric period, there will also be the back end of the experience, the uncontrollable manic phase that often leads to personal and family distress, dysfunction, and, in many cases, hospitalization. Clients need to learn that as they progress through treatment, similar to addicted clients, the craving for the hypomanic stage will lessen over time (Preston et al., 2010).

Given the nature of the side effects associated with these medications, it is important that counselors provide their clients with detailed education about medication treatment options. Some clients may be reluctant to try these medications for fear of the side effects. Considering the side effect possibilities, this caution is certainly warranted. However, it is also important to note that successful medication management, combined with good therapy, can result in significant improvements in the lives of clients with bipolar disorder.

WORKING EFFECTIVELY WITH PSYCHIATRISTS

Referring back to the male client discussed at the beginning of this chapter, it is important to remain involved and aware of clients' experiences with their medication. The client progressed very well over the course of the next year. At that point, the client saw a different physician, a psychiatrist, for a more specialized evaluation. At that time he was prescribed a different antidepressant medication. Over the course of the next 3 to 4 weeks, the client noticed a distinct change in his mood that was not positive. He reported a return of several of his depressive symptoms and was concerned that he was regressing. The counselor discussed how the client felt about the medication change, validating the client's frustration with the doctor changing something that was already working. With the support of the counselor, the client then developed a plan to address his concerns with the psychiatrist and request that he return to Lexapro, because it had been working so well. The client was successful in his self-advocacy at his next medication evaluation appointment, easily shifting back over to Lexapro once the psychiatrist listened to his concerns.

It is important for mental health counselors to stress to clients that even though they are not medical doctors, they can help them sort out some of the information, confusion, and concerns clients may hold regarding their medication. Indeed, mental health counselors, especially those in outpatient settings, will usually have much more contact with clients than they will have with their prescribing physicians. Many clients will have simple or straightforward questions about their medications but cannot see their doctor for several weeks. Any questions that fall outside the realm of expertise (e.g., giving advice about dosage) of the counselor's duties should be referred to an appropriate medical specialist.

Working effectively with psychiatrists involves promoting a collaborative relationship in which communication is open and flexible. Most practicing clinical psychiatrists understand the limitations of medication and are open to counseling as an additional form of care. The ideal scenario is where both psychiatrists and mental health counselors are knowledgeable and open to all forms of treatment. Thus, counselors are discouraged from keeping medication treatment options hidden from clients because this greatly increases the risk of counselor liability (King & Anderson, 2004).

An ethical dilemma can sometimes arise when working with clients who take medication: treatment splitting (King & Anderson, 2004). Treatment splitting is when a mental health counselor and psychiatrist interfere with the other treatment modality. For example, a counselor may not support the use of medication and share this with his or her client, undermining the psychiatrist's role. Conversely, a psychiatrist may be hesitant to engage in a collaborative relationship with a mental health counselor who does not support the use of medication (King & Anderson, 2004). As one can see, with treatment splitting, the client is caught in the middle, and her or his care may be compromised as a result. We recommend that both counselors and psychiatrists (or prescribing physicians) cultivate respect and understanding when working together. Even when views of treatment are discordant, communication can go a long way in helping to clarify treatment problems and issues. The most important aspect to remember, however, is that the client should receive the most effective care possible and that he or she must be fully informed as to what treatment options exist, the benefits, and the common side effects.

Making Medication Referrals

Staying current on psychopharmacological issues can help mental health counselors make appropriate referrals to psychiatrists for a medication evaluation. In general, clients who present with personality disorders, adjustment problems, and mild forms of depression and anxiety probably do not need to be placed on medication, although certainly that option exists. For clients who present with more severe forms of mental health problems, such as major depressive disorder, bipolar disorder, psychotic disorders, and severe substance-related disorders, medication often is indicated as a viable treatment option. If a formal diagnostic assessment (and other objective assessments, such as the Minnesota Multiphasic Personality Inventory; MMPI-2) reveals a serious mental health issue, counselors should discuss referral to a psychiatrist or other medical specialist (preferably one who has a background in psychotropic medication). Clients are sometimes reluctant to meet with a psychiatrist, and in these instances, counselors can explain that they are under no obligation to take medication if they do not want to; however, visiting with a psychiatrist may provide them with information and quell any fears they have regarding medication use. For clients who present with less severe issues, counselors may wish to mention medication as a treatment option and provide instructions for how to make an appointment.

A basic referral for a psychiatric evaluation depends on the agency and its policy. In agencies with a psychiatric staff in house, referrals can be as simple as filling in the client's name on the agency schedule. In other settings, a referral may include providing the client with the name and phone number of an area psychiatrist who specializes in the medication management of the presenting problem. For clients who present with more severe problems, counselors may wish to help the client make the referral by calling the psychiatrist's office and setting up the appointment. Whatever method is used, the counselor should document what referral was made and why and follow up with the client and address any potential barriers if possible.

Medication Compliance

On occasion, clients will not follow a doctor's orders. Medication noncompliance can unfortunately be a common issue, especially when the side effect profiles of certain psychotropic medications are extensive. Clients may have legitimate reasons for not following through on their medication. In these situations, counselors should encourage clients to seek medical assistance and see if there is another medication that might work better or produce fewer side effects. Irrational fears or misinformation also can be addressed. Counselors should never encourage clients to stop medication abruptly, which is not only dangerous but also unethical. If clients are considering going off a medication, counselors need to encourage that they do so under the guidance of a medical specialist. As a rule of thumb, counselors should state during informed consent that they work collaboratively with any medical specialist who might be involved in the treatment plan. In other words, communication between counselor and psychiatrist (or any medical specialist) should be open, including discussions or concerns about medication compliance.

Assessing and Managing Side Effects

One of the most disconcerting aspects of many psychotropic medications is the profile of side effects. Who has not listened to the nightly news and, during a commercial, learned of the next best medication for depression, only to be told about a litany of side effects, some so severe one must wonder if the benefits outweigh the risks. Keeping psychiatrists abreast of disturbing side effects that clients experience is an important role for counselors to assume. It is good practice to inquire with clients every session about how their medication is going and if they are experiencing any problems. Clients may very well experience troubling side effects but be unable to see their psychiatrist for several weeks. In these instances, counselors are encouraged to make contact with the prescribing physician (with client consent) to determine if anything can be done, such as agreeing to see the client earlier or providing recommendations on dosage revision until the subsequent appointment. In collaboration with their psychiatrist or prescribing physician, clients can learn to better manage or reduce side effects. For example, understanding that side effects tend to diminish with time, microdosing (i.e., starting out with a very small dose and gradually increasing), and being persistent in finding the right medication can help clients navigate some of the difficulties with side effects (Fast, 2013). It is important for the client to work closely with her or his physician and counselor to lessen these effects.

In other cases, counselors may be able to help clients manage side effects via self-help strategies. For example, it is well known that Lexapro (antidepressant) can produce anxiety when first taken. Helping the client to manage anxiety through deep breathing, relaxation training, and meditation can help the client work through the anxiety, increasing the client's compliance with the medication.

WORKING EFFECTIVELY WITH CLIENTS AND MEDICATION

Talking to Clients About Medication

It is important that clients understand at least the basics of their medications and how the medicine works in the body. This allows clients to feel more a part of their treatment process and lets them take some level of control in discussing various treatment options. Given the significant number of medications available today, clients do not have to accept the side effects of a particular drug because there are no other options. They can weigh their options based on many factors: side effects, cost, benefits, length of effectiveness, and convenience of administration.

Some clients come to counseling adamantly opposed to the use of medications in their treatment. Often this is due to misunderstanding the purpose of medication, how it works, and how it will be used in their case. A reasonable explanation of these factors can help clients feel better about a psychotropic medication. Also, there are some clients who believe that they should be able to manage their problems without taking pills. In response to this, we have told clients that when they are experiencing emotional difficulties, it is like being at the bottom of an 8-foot hole. The options that they can see to get out of the hole are very limited. Using appropriate medications for a period of time can provide clients with a stool, if you will, that lets them see above the rim of the hole and consider what resources they have available to them to help pull themselves from this hole. Once they are solidly out of the hole, they can begin to discuss and consider when they will reduce or stop taking their medications.

Helping clients understand how antidepressants generally work within the brain is an excellent way to address concerns about medications. Many physicians merely prescribe a medication for patients without any kind of explanation as to what it does, how it works, or what the side effects may be. We have been surprised at how many clients have come in for counseling already taking an antidepressant medication and yet have no understanding of neurotransmitters in the brain. Explaining the concept of reuptake inhibitors and the role of serotonin, norepinephrine, and dopamine in the brain helps clients understand that these medications are not "happy pills" but rather brain chemistry stabilization medication that will allow the brain to function more effectively.

Medication Advocacy

Some physicians may not provide much explanation about a medication to a client. Counselors are in a position to fill those gaps of information as part of the counseling process. Additionally, counselors can provide time to discuss client fears and concerns about medication, as well as regular check-ins about side effects and medication effectiveness. There are still some individuals who do not question the authority of a physician, assuming that the physician knows everything there is to know about a client and a condition. Counseling and education about medications can help clients learn how to talk proactively with their physicians and make sure that a medication is working the best that it can, with the least amount of side effects. Some of these clients may need to use counseling sessions to practice how they will speak with the physician, what they will say, and how they will advocate for themselves.

Counselors also will likely know more about the mental health issues of the client and thus be able to suggest specific medications that may also provide necessary secondary benefits for clients. For example, Paxil has an antianxiety secondary benefit, whereas Strattera may actually increase anxiety levels. Knowing this and informing the client can help reduce the amount of time necessary to find a medication that is a good fit for a specific client and his or her spectrum of symptoms. To accomplish this, counselors should consider developing a formal letter of introduction to physicians that presents the clinical diagnosis that has been developed, discusses the work being done with a client, and relays the desired outcomes. In addition, this letter can be used to make medication recommendations, providing the rationale for the request and support for the specific medication (Beulow, Hebert, & Beulow, 2000; King & Demille, 2012).

An interesting area of medication advocacy for clients is related to subclinical diagnoses (Ratay & Johnson, 1997). Counselors may see clients who do not meet the required number of diagnostic criteria areas related to a specific diagnosis. For example, in order to diagnose a client with a specific condition, five out of the eight diagnostic criteria must be met. However, some clients may meet only four of the diagnostic criteria, and yet they still report a level of distress related to the mental condition. In these instances, clients may still benefit from medication. It seems unreasonable to rule out a diagnosis and a treatment option simply based on being one diagnostic criteria short of the diagnosis. Having four areas of distress instead of five can still negatively impact the everyday life of a client. Ratay and Johnson (1997) suggested that these clients may benefit from the use of psychotropic medications, though possibly at a slightly lower dosage level. In their work, counselors are in a position to understand their clients greatly, which in turn allows counselors to advocate for pharmacological treatment with clients' family physicians. This is especially true if a psychiatrist is not available for the client or if the client's family physician is very conservative in the use of psychotropic medications (see Ratay & Johnson, 1997, for a more in-depth discussion of how this works with a variety of mental health diagnoses).

LEGAL AND ETHICAL ISSUES WITH PSYCHOPHARMACOLOGY

Whenever the topic of psychopharmacology is raised, an initial concern expressed by most professionals is that this is the domain of physicians, and it is an ethical violation for non-physicians to have these conversations with clients. According to the *ACA Code of Ethics* (2005), however, counselors are expected to "promote the welfare of clients" (p. 4). Understanding all aspects of a client's treatment, including psychopharmacology, seems to be a necessary part of promoting client welfare. There is case law precedence established that allows professionals other than physicians to discuss medications with clients. Merely talking with clients about medication options and treatment considerations does not constitute practicing medicine without a license (Ingersoll, 2000). Counselors can and should learn about psychotropic medications, including regular continuing education on medication updates, in an effort to help clients in their overall treatment. If medication issues arise, then counselors can provide clients with good, up-to-date information that is tailored specifically for them and then provide guidance on how clients can consult with their physicians to begin psychopharmacological treatment.

CASE STUDY

The following case study is designed to illustrate how counselors might integrate knowledge and information about psychopharmacology into their practice with clients. In this case, the counselor demonstrates several ideas and tips from this chapter, especially in correcting misinformation on the use of psychotropic medications.

William, a 54-year-old retired veteran, was diagnosed with generalized anxiety disorder and major depressive disorder. After the initial diagnostic intake interview, the counselor outlined the psychotherapy options related to these disorders, as well as the possible use of medication. To address initial concerns of medication use, the counselor explained the advantages of medication, such as reduced worry, rumination, and feelings of worthlessness or hopelessness, as well as possible side effects of taking medication for any psychological problem. The counselor emphasized that all specific side effects cannot be known at this time because each person uniquely responds to medication; however, consultation with the staff psychiatrist can clear up any questions or confusion. William was reluctant to try psychotropic medications at first, and it was discovered that this reluctance was based on the belief that he would need to be on drugs for the rest of his life. The counselor corrected this misperception by assuring William that often individuals take medication as a way to achieve greater balance and stability in their life and that many discontinue medication once they learn additional life skills to help their symptoms. The counselor noted that William and his psychiatrist can work collaboratively to construct a reasonable medication plan and also that he would consult with the psychiatrist as a way to keep the lines of communication open (William agreed to sign a consent form to allow for this communication). William agreed to give medication a try because he was tired of feeling anxious and depressed all the time.

During the next counseling session, the counselor asked William if he had followed through with visiting the staff psychiatrist. William was pleased that he was able to meet with her 3 days following the last counseling session. William was prescribed Zoloft (an SSRI) at 50 mg per day and a small dosage (5 mg per day) of Valium (a long-duration benzodiazepine) to provide additional help with his levels of anxiety. After 2 weeks on his new medication, William stated that his anxiety and worry were better but that he still felt depressed and became discouraged that his medication was not working as well for these symptoms. In addition, he began to notice side effects that were uncomfortable such as nausea and bouts of insomnia. He reported that his next appointment with his psychiatrist was in 2 weeks and that he would reluctantly try to continue the medication until that time to give it "one more chance" to work.

During the sixth session, William noted significant reductions in his experience of anxiety and began touting the effectiveness of Valium. He also admitted that he likes to have "a couple of beers" at night to help him unwind. The counselor, aware of the dangers of combining any substance (especially benzodiazepines) with alcohol, saw an appropriate occasion to play the role of information provider. The counselor offered information about the combination of alcohol and benzodiazepines, both central nervous system depressants. The counselor mentioned that two concerns arise when these drugs are combined: potentiation and cross-tolerance. Potentiation refers to one drug (alcohol) increasing the action of another (Valium) and vice versa. If William continued to drink and take Valium, he may reach dangerous levels of depression, both physically and psychologically. And because alcohol and Valium are in the same class of drugs, William might find that developing a tolerance to one transfers to the other (cross-tolerance). For example, if William develops a tolerance to alcohol, there is a good chance this tolerance also may occur with Valium (and, hence, Valium would have less of an effect). The counselor also explained the possibility that taking Valium and alcohol together might interfere with the effectiveness of Zoloft and thus contribute to William's continuing depressive symptoms.

(Continued)

(Continued)

The counselor functioned as information provider in addressing William's discouragement with Zoloft. In addition to pointing out potential problems with combining alcohol and Valium, the counselor validated William's experience with Zoloft and suggested that, especially with SSRIs, it can sometimes take several weeks to notice the full benefits. In addition, the dosage level may not be adequate to address William's symptoms. The counselor encouraged patience and suggested that William discuss any concerns he has with his psychiatrist before making a firm decision regarding Zoloft.

William was not aware of the information that the counselor provided. He was open to stopping his alcohol use while he was still on psychotropic medication. In addition, he was aware that any concerns about alcohol combined with medication could be addressed further with his psychiatrist or physician. Finally, William felt more confident about Zoloft, knowing that it takes time to work for some people and he can discuss increasing his dosage with his doctor.

This case study illustrates several concepts discussed in this chapter. At first, William was reluctant to try medication. The counselor provided information on the most effective treatments for his conditions and suggested that medication may help with symptom management. Benefits and side effects and risks were discussed. The counselor also vowed to be in contact with his psychiatrist, promoting a collaborative relationship. When William shared that he was using alcohol, the counselor took the opportunity to educate William by providing information in a nonthreatening manner. Finally, when William was discouraged by the lack of noticeable effect from Zoloft, the counselor encouraged him to be patient, provided information, and suggested that he raise his concerns with a medical specialist.

REFERENCES

American Counseling Association. (2005). *ACA Code of Ethics*. Alexandria, VA: Author.

Bentley, K. J., & Walsh, J. (2000). *The social worker and psychotropic medication: Toward effective collaboration with mental health clients, families, and providers* (2nd ed.). Pacific Grove, CA: Brooks/Cole.

Beulow, G., Hebert, S., & Beulow, S. (2000). *Psychotherapists resource on psychiatric medications: Issues of treatment and referral* (2nd ed.). New York: Cengage Brooks/Cole.

Breggin, P. R. (1991). *Toxic psychiatry*. New York: St. Martin's Press.

Breggin, P. R. (2008). *Medication madness: A psychiatrist exposes the dangers of mood-altering medications*. New York: St. Martin's Press.

Brooks, F., & McHenry, B. (2010). *A contemporary approach to substance abuse and addiction counseling: A counselor's guide to application and understanding*. Alexandria, VA: American Counseling Association.

Brown, S. (2010). *Brain based treatment strategies for children and adolescents*. Eau Claire, WI: PESI Seminars.

CACREP. (2016). *2016 CACREP Standards*. Alexandria, VA: Author.

Carlat, D. J. (2010). *Unhinged: The trouble with psychiatry—A doctor's revelations about a profession in crisis*. New York: Simon & Schuster.

Cutler, L. (2004). *Psychotropic medications and neurotransmitters.* Retrieved from http://www.wisc-online .com/objects/ViewObject.aspx?ID = NUR3503.

Fast, J. A. (2013). *Bipolar disorder medications and side effects: The first and most important things to know.* Retrieved from http://www.bipolarhappens.com/bipolar-medication-side-effects.

Freeth, R. (2004). Psychopharmacology for counsellors and psychotherapists: Part 2. *Healthcare Counselling & Psychotherapy Journal, 4*(2), 30–32.

Glasser, W. (2003). *Warning: Psychiatry can be hazardous to your mental health.* New York: Quill.

Hanson, R. (2011). *Buddha's brain: The practical neuroscience of happiness, love, and wisdom.* Eau Claire, WI: PESI Seminars.

Hyman, M. (2009). *The ultramind solution.* New York: Scribner.

Ingersoll, R. (2000). Teaching a psychopharmacology course to counselors: Justification, structure, and methods. *Counselor Education & Supervision, 40*(1), 58.

Kelsey, J. E., Newport, J., & Nemeroff, C. B. (2006). *Principles of psychopharmacology for mental health professionals.* Hoboken, NJ: Wiley.

Kendler, K. S. (2005). Toward a philosophical structure for psychiatry. *American Journal of Psychiatry,162,* 433–440.

King, J. H., & Anderson, S. M. (2004). Therapeutic implications of pharmacology: Current trends and ethical issues. *Journal of Counseling & Development, 82,* 329–336.

King, J. H., & Demille, S. M. (2012, March). *Navigating the complex world of psychopharmacology to promote client-prescriber-counselor alliances.* Paper presented at the American Counseling Association World Conference, San Francisco.

Kuhn, C., Swartzwelder, S., & Wilson, W. (2008). *Buzzed: The straight facts about the most used and abused drugs from alcohol to ecstasy* (3rd ed.). New York: W. W. Norton.

Murray, T. L. (2006). The other side of pharmacology: A review of the literature. *Journal of Mental Health Counseling, 28,* 309–337.

Plotnik, R. (1996). *Introduction to psychology* (4th ed.). Belmont, CA: Cengage Learning.

Ponterotto, J. G. (1985). A counselor's guide to pharmacology. *Journal of Counseling & Development, 64,* 109–115.

Preston, J. D., O'Neal, J. H., & Talaga, M. C. (2010). *Handbook of clinical psychopharmacology for therapists* (6th ed.). Oakland, CA: New Harbinger.

Ratay, J. J., & Johnson, C. (1997). *Shadow syndromes: The mild forms of major mental disorders that sabotage us.* New York: Bantam Books.

Wegmann, J. (2011). *Psychopharmacology: What you need to know about psychiatric medications.* Eau Claire, WI: PESI Seminars.

CHAPTER 9

Managed Care, Billing, and Documentation

Laura Welfare, Paige Greason, and Keith Mobley

As you read in Chapter 1, CMH counselors work in a variety of settings and serve a variety of clients. As such, CMH counselors are health professionals who provide behavioral health services that may be covered by client health insurance. Like in medical care, a specific process must be followed to receive reimbursement, and only some conditions and services qualify. In this chapter, we describe the process by which CMH counselors can bill for their services from private health insurance, government health insurance, and self-pay clients, including becoming an approved provider, securing authorization for services, and filing for payments. The important role that documentation plays in the reimbursement process also is discussed. Although it may seem daunting, the ability to navigate managed care, client billing, and documentation is necessary for practicing clinical mental health counselors. Working with insurance companies makes it possible for people to access counseling who could not otherwise afford it, and it expands the counselor's potential client base.

MANAGED CARE

Managed care is a term applied to the system of organizations that administer health care services for public and private health insurance companies. Managed care administrators review requests for authorization of treatment based on client needs and deliver payments to approved providers when authorized services are rendered. Many managed care organizations have a specialized unit to administer behavioral health care, which includes mental health and substance abuse assessment and treatment.

Managed care is regulated by federal and state laws regarding health care, so managed care organizations revise their operations to comply with new and changing law. A thorough description of the history of managed care is available elsewhere (Kongstvedt, 2008). This chapter highlights three laws that have had a direct influence on clinical mental health counseling and billing: the Health Insurance Portability and Accountability Act of 1996 (HIPAA; United States Department of Health and Human Services, 1996), the Mental Health Parity and Addiction Equity Act of 2008 (Substance Abuse and Mental Health Services Administration, 2008), and the Affordable Care Act of 2010 (United States Department of Health and Human Services, 2010).

MANAGED CARE LAWS AND LEGISLATION

Health Insurance Portability and Accountability Act (HIPAA)

Whereas ethical standards and state laws make the privacy and security of counseling records always of key importance in relation to clinical documentation, the Health Insurance Portability and Accountability Act (HIPAA) of 1996 set privacy and security rules for medical records from a legal perspective in ways that have major implications for mental health practice. In fact, HIPAA has required some of the most important and pervasive changes in the practice of clinical mental health in the last two decades. In spite of the fact that HIPAA guidelines have existed since 1996, many current practitioners remain confused about these federal requirements, including what they mean and how they apply to their practice. In fact, many may still not be compliant with the standards (Appari, Anthony, & Johnson, 2009), and recent changes to the enforcement of HIPAA via the Health Information Technology for Economic and Clinical Health Act of 2009 (HITECH) have increased the stakes for CMH counselors and added to the confusion. Despite what you may have heard or experienced, HIPAA is a manageable and reasonable law when you consider that confidentiality is essential to health care practices—could counselors do their jobs if clients didn't trust them with their personal and private information? Furthermore, when the law is broken down into its components, it is more logical and commonsensical than many are led to believe.

HIPAA was established to protect the privacy of individually identifiable health information and the use of that information (Leyva & Leyva, n.d. a). It clarifies to whom the act applies directly (known as *covered entities*) and under what arrangements the business of health care can be conducted with non–health care services that are essential for doing business (known as *business associates*). This act established the HIPAA Privacy and Security Rules, which set national standards for the health information it is intended to protect, known as *protected health information* (PHI). HIPAA outlines administrative and technical requirements for policies and procedures regarding data, data users, and client authorizations. HIPAA also describes the enforcement and penalties for noncompliance.

Covered Entities and Business Associates

HIPAA makes clear that professional counselors, by name, are included within its definition of health care. However, the deciding factor that determines if a particular CMH counselor is a covered entity according to HIPAA depends on whether that provider "transmits any health information in electronic form" (Leyva & Leyva, n.d. b) for any of the nine transactions covered by HIPAA: (1) injury reports, (2) health care claims, (3) health care payments, (4) coordination of benefits, (5) enrollment, (6) eligibility, (7) claim status inquiries, (8) certification, or (9) authorizations with third parties. In other words, three main criteria constitute practitioners who must abide by HIPAA: (1) they must provide health care, as does a CMH counselor; (2) they must transmit health information electronically; and (3) their transmissions must be specific transactions related to business. Therefore, it is not merely the identity of the practitioner that constitutes a covered entity but also the type of information used and the mode of transmission, as well as other behavioral practices and equipment used for billing and communications. Once a CMH counselor meets the definition of a covered entity, then *any* transaction, whether in writing, verbal, or electronic, is required to meet the requirements of HIPAA. HIPAA applies to the vast majority of those who practice CMH counseling, therefore it is important to understand the three distinct areas of requirements: (1) the Privacy Rule, (2) the Security Rule, and (3) enforcement.

HIPAA Privacy Rule

The HIPAA Privacy Rule is related to safeguarding protected health information (PHI) that is individually identifiable to a recipient of care. This includes information that is transmitted or maintained electronically, including demographics, physical or mental health information from the client's history, the provision of services or payments, and other info that can be used to identify a client. The Privacy Rule is unique in that it begins by broadly prohibiting all uses or disclosures of PHI but then grants limited exceptions, mostly regarding treatment and payment issues. This rule requires that covered entities provide notification to all health care recipients of how PHI may be disclosed, their rights, and the covered entities' responsibilities, as well as their recourse in the event of questions or concerns of violations. Basically, clients must have the opportunity to authorize or object to all elements of the disclosure of PHI required for doing business in that practice. HIPAA requirements limit the amount and type of information an insurance company may request for billing purposes, so clients have the authority to decide to share more than the minimum needed for claims. This rule is behind the almost ubiquitous disclosures on electronic forms of communication that are provided to anyone seeking health care in any setting. You may have seen a similar example to the standard clause that the HIPAA Privacy Rule requires on faxes and e-mails:

> This fax/e-mail and any files transmitted with it are confidential and intended solely for the use of the individual or entity to whom they are addressed. Nothing in this fax/e-mail is intended to constitute a waiver of a privilege or the confidentiality of this message. Any dissemination, copying, or use of this information by anyone other than the designated and intended recipient(s) is prohibited. If you have received this fax /e-mail in error, please notify me immediately by reply and delete and destroy this message and information immediately.

Of particular relevance to CMH counselors is a specific exception for *psychotherapy notes*, which are for "documenting or analyzing the contents of conversation during a private counseling session or a group, joint, or family counseling session and that are separated from the rest of the individual's medical record" (Leyva & Leyva, n.d. c). Under this exception, these notes require a specific authorization request and are not covered by a general records request, giving a higher standard of protection to both the client and the CMH counselor. However, these psychotherapy notes may be used for treatment purposes (such as treatment teams or care coordination), training during supervision, and defensive legal action without special authorization. When a client does sign an authorization to release records, the Privacy Rule requires the minimal disclosure of the records that is deemed necessary for the intended purpose (consistent with *ACA Code of Ethics* Standard B.2.d) but excludes the psychotherapy notes and even limits clients' access to them without the specialized authorization. Finally, the Privacy Rule requires all covered entities to designate a *privacy official* who is responsible for developing and maintaining policies and procedures in writing and coordinating training for all staff who have access to PHI. Without this privacy official, there would be no consistent application of or training in HIPAA practices in a given setting, undermining the accountability the law seeks to establish. Clearly, there is a great deal of overlap in the HIPAA Privacy Rule and the ACA and AMHCA Code of Ethics (see Chapter 2) that assist CMH counselors in meeting the Privacy Rule, but there are many special considerations when PHI is in electronic format. This is covered more thoroughly in the Security Rule.

HIPAA Security Rule

The Security Rule relates to the confidentiality and integrity of electronic personal health information (EPHI) that is handled by a covered entity from administrative, physical, and technical aspects. The Security Rule is embedded within the Privacy Rule and is oriented more toward the *process* of securing health care information (Hixson & Hunt-Unruh, 2008), although the process requirements also include issues of setting and storage. The physical safeguards under HIPAA relate to access and hardware for EPHI. Policies to secure workstations with EPHI, dispose of data and hardware containing data, and reuse data media require CMH counselors to apply the ethical standard of confidentiality to the access and maintenance of electronic records within federal guidelines. The technical safeguards under the Security Rule require CMH counseling practices to assign unique user identification, have automatic log-off and encryption software, and provide ways to monitor activity and protect against alteration of EPHI.

The administrative safeguards under the Security Rule require a risk analysis of all EPHI data, security measures codified in policy, a sanctions policy, and a method to monitor all data system activity. These safeguards also require an EPHI security officer to be delegated and to develop and implement measures to back up, restore, or use data when systems fail or in the event of an emergency. Finally, the security officer must develop and implement procedures for identifying, responding to, and reporting breaches of EPHI. The title of *security officer* underscores the critical nature of HIPAA and serves as a reminder that there are consequences for noncompliance, especially due to unauthorized breaches of confidential information.

HIPAA Enforcement

Although HIPAA rules are commonplace and have set an industry standard that would be unorthodox to disregard, mistakes do happen and often have far-reaching effects. In 2011, for example, over 19,000,000 patient records were affected by 395 reported breaches, and 60% of those breaches involved theft or malicious intent. Although almost 90% of those breaches were from the 20 largest incidents, it is unknown how those breaches affect mental health practices. What is clear is that the onus is on clinicians for implementing thorough HIPAA procedures. As of the passing of HITECH in 2009, the Office of Civil Rights within the Department of Health and Human Services is exclusively responsible for enforcing HIPAA violations. The only recourse a client has for perceived or actual HIPAA violations is to file a complaint with this office; courts have consistently held that patients do not have a right of private action under HIPAA. Historically, the Office of Civil Rights is believed to have favored the covered entities over complainants (Gray, 2007); the office has rarely imposed fines or penalties without first allowing the provider an opportunity to demonstrate compliance. However, a CMH counselor's exposure to liability remains critical, given precedents of fines up to $50,000 for a single breach and up to $1.5 million for multiple offenses. These violations fall into three categories, based on the degree of diligence of the provider to avoid a breach of confidentiality: (1) was not known and could not have been known through due diligence, (2) was due to reasonable cause and not willful neglect, and (3) was due to willful neglect. In cases where diligence is evidenced, a corrective action plan has been accepted to avoid a fine (Gray, 2007), but HITECH mandates notification of breaches to the individuals affected and also to print or broadcast media if they discover inaccurate contact info for more than 10 patients or if the breach involves more than 500 patients.

The Privacy Rule of HIPAA requires that CMH counselors, health insurance companies, and managed care organizations keep client health information confidential unless consent is provided for it to be shared. For health insurance to pay for counseling services, information about the client's condition (e.g., diagnosis, risk factors, and treatment history) must be shared with the managed care organization. Clients must consent to this release of information. CMH counselors include information about payment options in their professional disclosure statements and intake process. If clients wish to have insurance pay for part of the charges (as opposed to paying out of pocket or receiving services through another funding source), they must consent to this release of information. HIPPA and the ACA Code of Ethics (ACA, 2014) also assure clients the right to receive a copy of their health records and to know specifically what information counselors release to others. In the case of a minor or legally incompetent client, information is accessible to the parent or guardian. Therefore, it is important that counselors discuss with their clients the information that will be released for billing purposes. An addendum to the 1996 HIPPA Act in 2004 required all health care providers who bill independently for services to register for a National Provider Identifier (United States Department of Health and Human Services, 2004). CMH counselors record their National Provider Identifier on billing documentation. Registering for a National Provider Identifier requires identifying demographic information and state license information, but it is separate from the process of becoming a managed care approved provider. It allows tracking of a provider's work across multiple insurance companies and managed care organizations. More information about becoming an approved provider is included shortly. In sum, HIPPA put into law good practices regarding confidential client information and increased provider accountability by introducing a method for tracking providers more efficiently.

MENTAL HEALTH PARITY AND ADDICTION EQUITY ACT

The **Mental Health Parity and Addiction Equity Act** of 2008 requires that most health insurance plans cover behavioral health services in the same way they cover medical health services. For example, if a client is charged a $30 copay when he or she sees a medical specialist such as a dermatologist, the client cannot be charged more than a $30 copay when he or she sees a behavioral health specialist such as a licensed professional counselor. Before this law passed in 2008, many health insurance plans charged subscribers more for behavioral health services than they did for medical services. A few health insurance plans do not cover behavioral health services at all, and others are too small to be subject to this law. The act does apply, however, to more than 100 million people covered by private and public insurance. Passage of this act resulted from extensive advocacy efforts on behalf of behavioral health providers and clients and represents acknowledgement that mental and medical health are integrated and therefore both fit within the scope of health insurance.

Affordable Care Act

The **Affordable Care Act** was approved in 2010 and includes some changes that were implemented immediately with additional changes to be implemented over time. The Affordable Care Act expands the reach of federal mental health parity requirements and creates a mandated benefit for the coverage of mental health and substance abuse disorder services in certain types of insurance plans. The law expanded Medicaid criteria to increase the number of people who qualify, added support for Medicare enrollees, required states to provide insurance options to individuals who have preexisting conditions and become uninsured, and extended coverage for young adults on parent health insurance policies. In short, these changes mean more people qualify for health insurance. Also, the law supports preventative care, screening, and early intervention for behavioral health issues by prohibiting most insurance companies from charging the client a copay when he or she receives behavioral health screening services. Specifically, primary-care providers are encouraged to screen for alcohol abuse, depression, obesity, tobacco use, autism, behavioral problems, and interpersonal violence during medical care services. The client is not charged any out-of-pocket costs for such screening, and the provider receives additional reimbursement for providing the extra services. Although this does not apply to services provided by CMH counselors, it does suggest that more clients may be identified and referred for treatment and that medical professionals are being encouraged to more actively address behavioral health needs in their patients.

These three laws shaped the way insurance companies and managed care organizations administer client benefits. Knowledge of these laws and the other potential changes under review by state and federal legislatures is important for clinical mental health counselors. Often, clients are unaware of or confused about their rights and benefits so counselors are important educators and advocates for them as they learn how to best get their needs met within the system.

Managed Care: Becoming an Approved Provider

The first step for CMH counselors who wish to work with client health insurance is to become an **approved provider**. Each public or private insurance company determines its own criteria for becoming an approved provider of professional behavioral health services. This is sometimes referred to as joining the panel of core providers. The managed care organization reviews applications to become approved providers per the insurance company criteria. The typical application process for CMH counselors is outlined next.

Typical Credentialing Process

Each insurance company has its own criteria for credentialing providers, and the criteria must be made available to potential providers and to clients who are members of the insurance plan. Typically, CMH counselors must have graduated from an approved master's degree program, be licensed to practice independently by their state of residence ("licensed professional counselor" in most states; "licensed clinical professional counselor" or "licensed mental health counselor" in others), carry malpractice insurance, and have no legal and ethical infractions. Most plans also have requirements of the counseling practice, such as an emergency response capability, which may or may not be provided by the individual counselor (e.g., clients can access emergency services within 6 hours). A few insurance companies will approve prelicensed counselors to provide services (e.g., Medicaid in some states) if they are receiving adequate supervision, but most require a license to practice independently and receive fee-for-service reimbursement. Some insurance companies do not accept applications to become a provider on their panels unless there is a shortage of existing providers in a geographic area for a specific need (e.g., limited number of counselors who serve clients with eating disorders). The application process usually takes 3 to 6 months, and many managed care organizations charge administrative fees for processing applications.

The credentialing process can be time-consuming and arduous, but some recent changes have improved efficiency. Because insurance companies set their own criteria for approval, CMH counselors may have to prepare multiple applications if they wish to bill multiple companies. The Council for Affordable Quality Healthcare is a nonprofit organization that maintains a universal provider database. CMH counselors can submit their credentialing information to the database, and over 600 health insurance plans, hospitals, and health care organizations use the database to streamline the provider application process. At the time of this writing, several of the biggest behavioral health managed care organizations use the database (e.g., Magellan, United Behavioral Health, CIGNA Behavioral Health), but others do not (e.g., ValueOptions).

When the credentialing information is submitted, either through the universal provider database or individually, the insurance company's managed care group will review the applicant's qualifications and consider approving her or him as an independent provider of relevant behavioral health services. When approved provider status is awarded, it is for specific services (e.g., intake, individual counseling, family counseling, group counseling). Most managed care organizations use the service names and code numbers defined by Medicare for consistency. Those code numbers are called **current procedural terminology** or **CPT codes**, and the names may not match the language used by CMH counselors. For example, CPT Code 90837 is for "Psychotherapy, 60 minutes with patient and/or family member," and CPT code 90853 is for "Group psychotherapy, other than multiple-family group" (Centers for Medicare and Medicaid Services, 2016). CMH counselors practicing individually are typically approved to provide assessment and individual, family, and group counseling services. Approval for treatment team services such as intensive outpatient treatment, residential treatment, or inpatient treatment requires a more extensive facility-level review. After initial provider approval, continuing education and performance reviews are required at varying intervals as determined by the insurance company.

As noted, insurance companies usually do not approve unlicensed CMH counselors as independent providers. That does not mean, however, that prelicensed or provisionally licensed counselors cannot provide services to clients—rather, these counselors often provide treatment team-based services that are billed as a unit. For example, home-based, inpatient, intensive outpatient, crisis intervention services, and assertive community treatment do not require every member of the treatment team to be licensed. The service is billed as a unit, and prelicensed counselors can provide part of the treatment without being independently billable. The prelicensed counselor's services are supervised or directed by approved providers per the managed care company's requirements. In addition, some insurance companies (e.g., Medicaid in some states) will approve prelicensed counselors to function as independent providers.

Managed Care: Securing Authorization for Services

When a CMH counselor becomes an approved provider, he or she agrees to follow the rules for determining client eligibility and authorization for services. Failure to follow the rules results in refusal of payment. Managed care organizations have varying rules for which services require preauthorization, what client characteristics must be present to qualify, and how frequently they review client eligibility, but some rules are fairly consistent. Eligibility criteria must be made available to providers and clients who subscribe to the insurance.

CMH counselors work most effectively when they are familiar with the criteria and can gather necessary information efficiently (Anderson, 2000). CMH counselors working in outpatient settings use information gathered in the intake to document the need for outpatient treatment to the client's managed care company. The primary information required for authorization is the client diagnosis, and most managed care organizations will accept the *Diagnostic and Statistical Manual of Mental Disorders* (DSM-5; American Psychiatric Association, 2013) or *International Classification of Diseases* diagnoses (ICD-10; World Health Organization, 2004). For example, Anthem Behavioral Health's (2013) criteria for approval of outpatient substance abuse treatment requires that the client have

- a DSM or ICD substance abuse and/or dependence diagnosis, including excessive, maladaptive use for at least one month;

- motivation as evidenced by expression of a desire to work toward recovery; and

- a social system that is supportive of recovery.

Different levels of care have different criteria for eligibility. For comparison, acute inpatient psychiatric hospitalization is a higher level of care than outpatient counseling and requires a *DSM* or *ICD* Axis diagnosis and one of the following (Anthem, 2013):

- Imminent suicidal risk or danger to others

- Acute psychotic symptoms

- Grave inability to care for self

- Uncontrollable destructive behavior

Some CMH counselors find the eligibility criteria restrictive because there are clients who can benefit from counseling but do not meet criteria for a *DSM* diagnosis, and some CMH counselors have concerns about the ramifications of diagnosing clients at all (e.g., Braun & Cox, 2005; Cooper & Gottlieb, 2000; Daniels, 2001; Mead, Hohenshil, & Singh, 1997; Wilcoxon, Magnuson, & Norem, 2008).

If preauthorization is required for the service, the counselor must submit the required paperwork that documents the client's need and secure approval before providing any services. Services provided prior to approval will not be covered. If preauthorization is not required, the counselor can begin providing services immediately. The counselor still must ensure, however, that the client meets the criteria and maintain appropriate treatment planning documentation and case notes or payment will be denied when the claim for payment is filed.

Continued review of individual cases occurs for all levels of care. For ongoing services beyond the initially authorized amount to be approved (e.g., 8 outpatient sessions or

4 inpatient days), the counselor must document that the client is making progress, needs continued service at this level of care, and can continue to benefit. If the client is not making progress, the counselor must document that the treatment plan has been modified to increase effectiveness of the service. Most plans have annual limits for the number of services that will be covered and an added level of scrutiny for claims that are deemed to be potentially excessive. Often, managed care administrators are licensed behavioral health professionals who are trained to evaluate the information provided by the client's counselor to ensure it fits with the insurance company's criteria. If the managed care administrator does not agree with the counselor's recommendation for client services, a second review can be requested. Knowledge of the insurance company criteria and managed care protocols is essential in preventing the administrative hassle of multiple requests and denied claims (Anderson, 2000).

Managed Care: Getting Paid

When CMH counselors become approved providers, they also agree to the managed care program's terms for payment. Managed care organizations usually negotiate discounts from the provider's full fee. For example, if the CMH counselor's session fee is $100, the managed care organization may agree to pay $70. If the counselor wishes to be an approved provider on that panel, he or she must agree to accept $70 for the session. Part of that $70 likely comes from the client, because most plans have a client copay that is due the day of service (Medicaid is a common exception). For example, if the client's copay is $25, he or she would pay that on the day of service, and the counselor would file the managed care claim to receive the remaining $45 ($70 − $25 = $45). The counselor is not permitted to require the client to pay the additional $30 that would have been charged for the full session fee. Also, the counselor is not permitted to waive the copay and accept a reduced payment for the session. Acceptance of the approved provider status requires adherence to all aspects of the billing and payment arrangements. Payment amounts vary widely and, anecdotally, can be a source of frustration for many providers. Counselors can advocate for increased rates and in some instances may be successful. Clients receive a statement that delineates all services received and what the provider was paid for each service.

Processing claims and billing documentation can be time-consuming and frustrating. Many managed care companies have developed online submission systems to streamline the process. Approved providers typically have a system in place through which they file claims, track payments, and collect client copays. Some counselors do so independently, and others have administrative support staff who manage these aspects of the practice (Phelps, Eisman, & Kohout, 1998). Regardless of the system, attention to detail is essential. Claims with mistakes in code numbers, mismatched identifying information, or even typographical errors will be denied, and repeated submission adds to the administrative burden.

Counselors who choose not to pursue approved provider status may still be approved on an individual basis to provide reimbursable services. Clients can ask their managed care group to approve the counselor as an ad hoc provider. In those cases, the client may pay the session fee upfront and manage the billing documentation himself or herself, with the counselor completing forms or providing information as requested by the client.

INSURANCE: PRIVATE AND PUBLIC PAYERS

Private Insurance

The largest American health insurance companies at the time of this writing were UnitedHealthcare, Anthem (formerly WellPoint and a conglomerate of Blue Cross and Blue Shield), Kaiser, Aetna, and Humana. All of these companies approve licensed CMH counselors to provide behavioral health services for their private health insurance plans. As described earlier, specific criteria for approved providers, client eligibility, and claims vary and are available on insurance company websites or printed materials. CMH counselors who wish to become approved providers often choose a few insurance companies from the major employers in their local area. Doing so means that counselors can expect the effort required to become an approved provider and learning to navigate the system efficiently will be worthwhile because many people in the area have that insurance. Insurance companies provide a registry of approved providers so customers can search and locate the type of professionals they need. Often, counselors do not continue to pursue approval status with additional insurance companies once their practice becomes adequately filled.

Government-Sponsored Insurance

The federal government sponsors three programs that provide health insurance coverage to three specific populations—the elderly or disabled, low-income individuals and families, and military personnel and their families. These programs include **Medicare**, **Medicaid**, and **TRICARE**, respectively. In addition, under certain circumstances per the Affordable Care Act, the government provides subsidies to individuals who meet specific criteria to help them pay for private insurance. President Lyndon Johnson signed the Medicare and Medicaid programs into law in 1965 as amendments to the Social Security Act (Centers for Medicare & Medicaid Services, n.d. a). TRICARE replaced the Civilian Health and Medical Program of the Uniformed Services (CHAMPUS) program in 1993 (United States Department of Defense, n.d.). All three of these government-sponsored health insurance programs serve distinct populations and are administered differently. The differences between the three programs and implications for counselors are outlined next.

Medicare

Medicare is a federal health insurance program signed into law as Title XVIII of the Social Security Act for people age 65 and older, people under 65 with certain disabilities, and people with end-stage renal disease (Centers for Medicare and Medicaid Services, n.d. b; Health Assistance Partnership, 2010; Health Care Financing Administration, 1995). Medicare was established so that beneficiaries would share in the cost along with the federal government through mandatory payroll deduction, premium payments, and deductibles. The overall administration of the Medicare program is managed by various agencies of the federal government within the Department of Health and Human Services (DHHS), including the Centers for Medicare and Medicaid Services (previously known as the Health Care Financing Administration) and the Social Security Administration. Independent administrative contractors process enrollment applications and serve as a contact point for providers. Each state has one or more contractors. Lists of contractors are available on the Centers for Medicare and Medicaid Services (CMS) website (www.cms.gov). State agencies assist in the identification, inspection, and certification of providers and provider facilities in consultation with federal agencies, but states are not involved in program administration. Therefore, Medicare programs are generally the same state to state.

Medicare is divided into four parts—Part A, Part B, Part C, and Part D. Part A is hospital insurance (Centers for Medicare and Medicaid Services, n.d. d). Most people do not have to pay a premium for Part A because it was paid through their Social Security payroll deductions. For Part B, which is the program that covers doctors' services and outpatient care (including mental health services), most people pay a monthly premium. Part C is an optional program that operates like a health maintenance organization or preferred provider organization. It provides all of the insured's hospital, outpatient, and prescription drug coverage and is offered by private companies approved by Medicare. Those choosing Part C do pay an additional monthly premium in addition to their Part B premium. Part D is Medicare prescription drug coverage. As of 2006, prescription drug coverage is available to everyone with Medicare. Those who choose to participate pay an additional premium that is based on the drugs used, the plan chosen, whether the pharmacy is within network, whether drugs are on the plan's formulary, and whether the individual receives extra help (a program offered through Medicare) to cover costs.

As of this writing, services provided by counselors or marriage and family therapists are not covered by Medicare (American Counseling Association, 2013). Legislation is pending in Congress to change the law (GovTrack.us, n.d.; NBCC, 2012). The Seniors Mental Health Access Improvement Act of 2015 is aimed at amending the Medicare Act to provide coverage for services provided by mental health counselors and marriage and family therapists under Part B. The bill was previously proposed in 2007 and reintroduced in 2011 and 2013. As of this writing, it never became law.

For other mental health providers (e.g., social workers, psychologists) who are able to bill Medicare, the credentialing process involves the submission of an application and an evaluation of the provider's capacity to administer specific services. Administrative contractors process enrollment applications (Centers for Medicare and Medicaid Services, n.d. c). The CMS established an Internet-based enrollment process called Provider Enrollment, Chain, and Ownership System (PECOS). This system allows potential providers to enroll, make changes to Medicare enrollment, track their application, view their enrollment information, and reactivate or withdraw from the Medicare program. However, supplemental materials such as the certification statement must be mailed to the Medicare contractor reviewing applications within 7 days of the electronic submission. For those submitting a paper application, the form is CMS 855I—Medicare Enrollment Application for Physicians and Non-Physician Practitioners and is available on the CMS website. These forms may be revised periodically so it is important to submit the most current version. A National Provider Identifier is needed to complete the application and can be obtained through the National Plan and Provider Enumeration System, as mentioned earlier. Also, background checks are performed to ensure the legitimacy of education, licenses, and certifications.

Once a mental health provider is approved, he or she becomes part of the Medicare network, and he or she receives an identification number that is used when submitting claims. Approved providers agree to accept fees set by Medicare, which may be less than what the provider typically charges for the same service. Depending on their coverage, clients may or may not be responsible for a copay. Bills are submitted directly to Medicare, and providers must agree to receive payments through electronic funds transfer.

Medicare covers a variety of mental health services, including individual psychotherapy, family medical psychotherapy (i.e., meeting with family members in order to help in treatment of identified client), group psychotherapy, and hypnotherapy, among others (NHIC, 2010). Medicare covers biofeedback only for muscle reeducation or muscle abnormalities when more "conventional" treatments have not been successful. Medicare does not cover biofeedback for psychosomatic illness or ordinary muscle tension, nor does it cover marriage counseling. As of 2014, Medicare pays 80% of the approved amount and clients pay 20%. For example, if the approved amount for individual psychotherapy is $66.50, Medicare will pay $53.20 and the client will be responsible for $13.20. Clinical mental health counselors who want to be Medicare providers should contact the administrative contractor.

Medicaid

The Medicaid program is a federal/state health insurance program signed into law as Title XIX of the Social Security Act to provide medical coverage to individuals and families with low incomes who meet certain eligibility requirements (Centers for Medicare and Medicaid Services, n.d. a). It is the nation's largest program providing health-related services to needy individuals and families (American Academy of Family Physicians, 2005). Medicaid was initially linked to welfare, but as of 1996, the two programs are no longer connected. In addition to Medicaid, the Children's Health Insurance Program (formerly the State Children's Health Insurance Program) was enacted in 1997 to provide matching federal funds to states to cover children and eligible parents who fall in the gap between qualifying for Medicaid and being able to afford private insurance (National Conference of State Legislatures, n.d.).

Federal and state governments jointly fund Medicaid. Federal funding per state is determined by comparing the state's per capita income to the national average. The federal government establishes broad guidelines for the program and provides oversight through the Centers for Medicare and Medicaid Services (CMS), a branch of the U.S. Department of Health and Human Services. However, individual states administer their own programs. This includes determining eligibility standards, scope and duration of services covered, and fee rates. Therefore, there is considerable variability in Medicaid programs from state to state. Because of these differences, a low income alone does not necessarily qualify an individual for Medicaid.

Under the Affordable Care Act, each state may choose to expand Medicaid coverage to all individuals with income up to 133% of the poverty level (Centers for Medicare and Medicaid Services, n.d. a).

This variability in state programs means that counselors need to understand the specific program requirements for reimbursement for counseling services in their state. Some states reimburse counselors directly, some reimburse counselors through approved service providers, and others do not reimburse counselors at all. In states that do reimburse counselors directly, the process for becoming an authorized provider is extensive.

The enrollment process for individuals typically includes credentialing (review of provider credentials to provide services), licensure verification (investigation of provider's professional background), and possibly a criminal background check. As with other insurance plans, a National Provider Identifier is required. States may require providers to be recredentialed every few years. This process is typically streamlined and may include criminal background checks and a review of credentials and qualifications to ensure that providers continue to meet state guidelines. Many states have an online enrollment process and claims process.

Medicaid providers must adhere to strict documentation and billing requirements in order to be reimbursed for services. Making false claims or failure to comply with billing and recordkeeping requirements may result in withholding of payment, penalties, termination as a provider from the program, or other enforcement actions. Agents of the state may visit provider facilities to certify compliance. Such visits may be unannounced and must be allowed, so it is important that counselors providing Medicaid services maintain complete and accurate records in accordance with the state's recordkeeping requirements.

TRICARE

TRICARE is a health care program for uniformed service members and retirees, as well as their families and survivors. Most services are provided in military treatment facilities, but this network is supplemented with a network of civilian providers and facilities. TRICARE is available worldwide and is managed in six regions—North, South, West, Eurasia-Africa, Latin America and Canada, and Pacific. Each region is managed by its own managed care support contractor (MCSC), which also establishes the provider network in each region.

Depending on which TRICARE plan a client is participating in and the region, authorization by a TRICARE health provider may be required prior to service (TRICARE, 2011). Generally, active-duty service members are required to obtain a prior authorization for mental health services from their military treatment facility, when available. All other TRICARE beneficiaries can self-refer for most mental health services to a TRICARE mental health provider and receive eight outpatient behavioral health services per year. Authorization is required for additional sessions. Beneficiaries can receive two sessions of outpatient psychotherapy (i.e., individual therapy, family/conjoint therapy, group therapy, and information-gathering sessions) per week. Services that require prior authorization include substance abuse treatment, inpatient treatment, partial hospitalization, psychoanalysis, and electroconvulsive therapy. Behavioral health services that are covered include (a) anger management, (b) eating disorder treatment, (c) hospitalization, (d) partial hospitalization, (e) intensive outpatient programs, (f) psychological testing when considered medically necessary for treatment, (g) outpatient behavioral health, (h) residential treatment, (i) sexual abuse treatment, and (j) substance use treatment. Marriage counseling is not a covered benefit under TRICARE. Family therapy is considered outpatient psychotherapy, however, when determined necessary for the treatment of a diagnosed mental health disorder. All behavioral health services must be deemed necessary to treat a mental health disorder.

TRICARE also covers "telemental health" services, which are behavioral health services available through a secure audio/video webcam when it is difficult to schedule with a particular provider. Clients, however, cannot access the program through their home.

They must go to the office of a provider that offers approved telemental health access. From there, they can connect with another offsite provider. Web-based video counseling that clients can access from their homes is also available under the TRICARE Assistance Program.

TRICARE authorizes two types of providers: network providers and nonnetwork providers. Both types must be certified by the MCSC in their region. Network providers contractually agree to provide services at a negotiated rate and file claims for beneficiaries. Nonnetwork providers do not sign a contract with the MCSC. There are two types of nonnetwork providers: participating providers and nonparticipating providers, and nonnetwork providers can choose to be either one on a claim-by-claim basis. Participating providers agree to file claims for beneficiaries, accept payment directly from TRICARE, and accept the fee structure set by TRICARE. Nonparticipating providers can set their own fee structure and do not file beneficiary claims. TRICARE's maximum allowable fee is tied to Medicare's allowable fee.

To enroll as a provider, a National Provider Identifier is needed. Each region has different forms and processes for enrolling. The provider section of the TRICARE website (http://www.tricare.mil/providers) is the portal to information on regions and enrollment processes.

For many years, counseling organizations have advocated for counselors to be able to provide services independently under TRICARE (NBCC, 2012). In December 2011, the Department of Defense released an interim rule that established a new provider category of CMH counselor (United States Department of Defense, 2011). This certification allows licensed counselors who meet certain training, education, experience, certification, and licensure requirements to provide services independently. Prior to this rule, licensed counselors were required to be supervised by a physician, and clients of licensed counselors were required to obtain physician authorization prior to services. As of January 1, 2017, CMH counselors seeking provider status with TRICARE must meet the following criteria:

- Possession of a state license for independent practice in mental health counseling from the state in which the counselor is practicing

- Possession of a master's degree or higher from a mental health counseling training program accredited by the Council for Accreditation of Counseling and Related Educational Programs (CACREP)

- A passing score on the National Clinical Mental Health Counseling Examination or its successor

- A minimum of 2 years' post–master's degree supervised mental health counseling practice that includes a minimum of 3,000 hours of supervised clinical practice and 100 hours of face-to-face supervision with a licensed mental health counselor

Criteria for certification are based on a study by the Institute of Medicine (IOM) of the National Academies of Science. That report concluded that despite increasing standardization over the years, significant variability still exists in training programs for counselors, thus the requirement that CMH counselors possess a degree from a CACREP-accredited training program.

Self-Pay and Other Means

If clients do not have health insurance or choose to pay out of pocket for counseling, the administrative burden of managing client billing is substantially less. Some CMH counselors limit their practices to self-pay clients only and set a session fee that all clients must pay the day of service. If counselors wish to expand their services to clients who cannot afford the full fee, they use a sliding scale based on income or financial resources of the client. Some organizations have grant funds that can be used to pay all or part of the counselor's session fee, and others retain counselors who provide services for a flat salary that is not directly tied to the client's payment for services.

MAINTAINING RECORDS

Counselors maintain records. These are simple yet far-reaching words establishing the expectation for CMH counselors to document their work within the ethical codes of both the American Counseling Association (A.1.b, B.6; ACA, 2014) and the American Mental Health Counselors Association, (E.1; AMHCA, 2015). Each of these codes requires ethical counselors to address issues of thoroughness, protection, storage, disposal, contingency plans, and even how to correct errors. However, the documentation of counselors' work isn't as simple as it may seem, and that may be due to the fact that it can elicit less than positive reactions from practitioners. The fact that paperwork may take an hour (or more) away from billable service to complete and that it can be tedious or complex often leads one to question why such thorough and detailed documentation is necessary.

In fact, if you were to survey a room filled with CMH counselors on the topic of documentation, chances are that several things will gain consensus quickly. First, completing paperwork probably isn't the favorite activity of CMH counselors. Actually, it may be among the least favorite. In fairness, it is easy to see how that conclusion is reached based on the hours of paperwork sometimes required in contemporary mental health practice, often when energy is dwindling after an intake or at the end of a long day. Second, CMH counselor training in completing the necessary documentation is diffuse. Usually, it happens experientially while in the role of counselor. This on-the-job training approach has its merits, but frankly more intentional preparation in advance of receiving corrective feedback in the field is sorely needed. Third, CMH counselors by nature tend to gain more satisfaction from interpersonal encounters rather than working alone at a desk or computer. CMH counselors may believe that paperwork tends to distract them from the "real" work of counseling with clients and that it contributes little to the overall betterment of their clients, or even takes something away. This disconnect between the completion of documentation from the counseling process is perhaps the most problematic barrier to acquiring the requisite documentation skills. A helpful reframe could be that it is likely not the paperwork itself that is the bane of counseling existence but rather the *perception* of it. In other words, with more intentional training and reflection, a thorough understanding of the utility of paperwork and a positive (or at least more balanced) connotation of clinical documentation can be achieved. The final conclusion that CMH counselors would likely reach is that paperwork justifies their existence. "If it's not documented, it didn't happen" is a maxim that leads counselors to a very different way of considering their realities, a way that contradicts many other ways they may receive validation, feedback, and meaning from their work. Ultimately, documentation helps counselors to ensure the continuity and ongoing improvement of services they provide their clients and to protect their integrity as providers in the broad arena of mental health care.

Documentation is defined as any written, digital, audio, visual, or artistic recording of the work within the counseling relationship between counselor and client. Although the information in this chapter is not exhaustive and may not make the paperwork as rewarding as the counseling work itself, the intent is to help CMH counselors view documentation as a necessary tool for sound counseling practice. Specifically, this chapter provides an overview of the importance of paperwork, connects paperwork with the critical federal and ethical guidelines for CMH counselor practice, describes the functions for various types of paperwork relevant to CMH counselors, and reviews common complexities and challenges related to documentation in the practice of CMH counseling.

Importance of Paperwork

In all of the wonderful ways that the world and society have evolved in the modern era, the changes also have resulted in more informed consumers, shrewder and savvier criminals, a sometimes litigious health care environment, and an overall attitude of caution and skepticism—all of which have led almost all professions to greater accountability and higher standards of practice. This accountability is not inherently negative, however, considering the vulnerable populations CMH counselors serve and the enormous instances of fraud that have been committed by a few unethical service providers. The era of accountability has emphasized that counselors provide evidence of their service provision and protect consumers.

At a minimum, documentation can provide proof that counselors are meeting the standard of care for counseling and are fulfilling their ethical and legal obligations. Beyond this, however, documentation may also play a role in both establishing and improving counseling practices, ultimately to the benefit of clients. Additionally, documentation also is a way to review progress toward goals and plan for future sessions, ensure continuity of care, and provide a manner for the counselor to examine the counseling process more objectively. If CMH counselors frame their relationship with documentation to serve these functions, the utility of paperwork can be observed with the full variety of forms, whether administrative or clinical, as described in later sections.

Administrative and Clinical Documentation Practices

Administrative documentation is related to the management or responsibility for the operation of a business and provides structure and clarity of expectations. Training in CMH counseling puts much focus on therapeutic relationships, where counselors apply structure to sessions to pace or adjust their work with clients in an effort to assist them with learning new skills to manage their behavior, cognitions, or emotions. In contrast, when considering the business aspects, counselors tend to minimize the importance of structure, perceive it as separate from therapeutic work, and may even associate administrative practices with bureaucracy or needless busywork. All aspects of the relationship provide an opportunity to be therapeutic, however, including administrative paperwork practices. CMH counseling is a nuanced profession dealing with the complex issues of human behavior and relationships. Transference and countertransference happen and unforeseen events occur, allowing the risk for clients to interpret these in ways counselors did not intend. It is important for counselors to reframe their approach to administrative procedures as providing the needed structure to the practice of clinical mental health, managing understanding or expectations of the outcomes, aiding in clarifying respective roles with clients, and a method of documenting counselors' work. These are among the first therapeutic tasks in the field, usually beginning at first contact, which may even be prior to meeting face to face. In other words, administrative practices go beyond the tasks at hand and overlap considerably with counselors' therapeutic use of self.

Administrative and intake procedures are intended to not only communicate aspects of the business and ethical or legal responsibilities but are critical to formulating realistic perceptions of the relationship and building trust. Many authors have characterized relationship variables that lead to greater trust, greater disclosure, and greater opportunities for the corrective experiences for clients, which can be summarized in three broad categories: expertness, interpersonal attractiveness, and trustworthiness (Cormier, Cormier, & Cormier, 1997; Sullivan, Martin, & Handelsman, 1993; Zamostny, Corrigan, & Eggert, 1981). Expertness includes one's education, reputation, fluency, status, competence, and responsiveness. Interpersonal attractiveness can be represented as likability, similarity, friendliness, structuring, and moderate amounts of self-disclosure (in contrast to what clients perceive as too much or too little). Trustworthiness relates to how a professional provides role clarification, honesty, sincerity, and openness. These characteristics have been associated with positive outcomes among CMH counseling clients, and administrative and intake procedures are the formative opportunity to build these trajectories and document fulfillment of this standard of practice. In speaking confidently and clearly, seeking mutual understanding with clients, and revealing aspects of themselves and the relationship they intend to establish, they effectively set the stage for therapeutic rapport. The criticality of administrative and intake procedures may become even more obvious when considering that clients who present at CMH counseling settings often have impairment with thought processes and mood regulation and may need clear, concise, logical introductions.

Awareness of the ability of administrative documentation to catalyze rapport between CMH counselors and their clients can inform the development and discussion around administrative and intake paperwork and procedures. Administrative procedures are not only important from the legal or ethical aspect of practicing CMH counseling but constitute a standard of care, hold potential to sow the seeds of therapeutic relationships, and prompt critical discussion that may frame the client's experience.

Administrative paperwork is best characterized as the needed disclosure forms and authorizations that serve to inform clients of the respective responsibilities of the client and the clinic and/or CMH counselor. Often, clients have many questions or simply lack awareness of what they may soon consider important, and this is counselors' first opportunity to clarify the arrangements. In fact, they not only want to provide clarifying information but also document that they have done so. Common questions that clients have may include "How much will this cost, and what will my insurance pay?" "Who will know what I talk about in counseling?" "Do parents have a right to their child's record?" and "What makes you qualified to work with me?" The remainder of this section discusses the various aspects of administrative paperwork that relate to CMH counseling practices, including professional disclosure, client rights and responsibilities, consent to treatment, and consent to release confidential information.

Professional Disclosure

True autonomy as an ethical concept is not possible without the thorough and accurate information necessary to make informed decisions (Beauchamps & Childress, 1984). Professional disclosure is a key aspect of gaining autonomous, informed consent from clients; is essential to administrating a CMH counseling practice; and should always be provided prior to request for formal consent to treatment. Typically, this information is covered in a contractual format at or immediately prior to the first meeting and must include the following, as stated in the ACA (2014) Code of Ethics:

> the purposes, goals, techniques, procedures, limitations, potential risks, and benefits of services; the counselor's qualifications, credentials, relevant experience, and approach to counseling; continuation of services upon the incapacitation or death of the counselor; the role of technology; and other pertinent information. Counselors take steps to ensure that clients understand the implications of diagnosis and the intended use of tests and reports. Additionally, counselors inform clients about fees and billing arrangements, including procedures for nonpayment of fees. Clients have the right to confidentiality and to be provided with an explanation of its limits (including how supervisors and/or treatment or interdisciplinary team professionals are involved), to obtain clear information about their records, to participate in the ongoing counseling plans, and to refuse any services or modality changes and to be advised of the consequences of such refusal. (p. 4)

In addition to these elements outlined in the Code of Ethics, various writers have recommended inclusion of theoretical orientation (Corey, Corey, & Callanan, 2007); alternatives to counseling, such as self-help programs, books, or related therapies (Bray, Shepherd, & Hays, 1985); whether the sessions will be recorded and/or supervised (Corey et al., 2007); and the methods of handling complaints, including contact information of relevant licensing or professional organizations (Welfel, 2006).

The act of providing and documenting thorough professional disclosure and obtaining informed consent is perhaps the most proactive and strongest defense against a complaint filed by a client (provided, of course, counselors live up to their parts of the agreement). In essence, an informed consent is the contract that stipulates the parameters and expectations of the relationship, and any breach of these is grounds for a lawsuit (Remley & Herlihy, 2010) or puts the therapeutic relationship at extreme risk. Although professional disclosure/informed consent is considered a discrete event that happens at the first encounter, it bears reminding that it also is an ongoing process in the practice of CMH counseling, especially as it is applied to the unique circumstances throughout counseling, when diverse clients require alterations in communication to ensure developmental and cultural understanding (Pope & Vasquez, 2007) or when addressing the limitation of the counseling process or the parameters of confidentiality as they arise.

Often, professional disclosure is embedded as a requirement within state licensure laws, but a signed statement of professional disclosure dated on the first contact should be included in every client record. The format or style applied to this essential information depends on agency policies, the practice setting, and even the personality of the practitioner. However, CMH counselors are advised to put the information in a more formalized structure in their practices, complete with headings or bulleted ideas, so that it can be as clear and concise as possible, without distractions (such as graphics or humor) or complex presentation that might require focused attention or a high reading level.

It is worth noting that administrative documentation does not apply exclusively to clients. Clinicians have relevant documents that apply to their training and their contracts with third-party payers. CMH counselors should make an effort to clearly display their counseling degrees, licenses, and certifications. Additionally, CMH counselors should maintain documentation that supports these credentials, such as relevant graduate transcripts, copies of degrees or certificates conferred, relevant licenses, continuing education, and other relevant training. A professional disclosure statement is only as good as the supporting documentation, so it is encouraged that counselors maintain their own equivalent of a personnel file for administrative ease. For independent or group practitioners, insurance contracts should be maintained in an organized manner so that counselors can refer easily to the terms, expectations, and potential renewal expectations. The way counselors practice clinically (e.g., service definitions, session limits, quality assurance) may be established in these agreements and should be maintained, even though it is not the central aspect of daily paperwork.

Disclosure statements are intended to inform clients but not to replace oral presentation and discussion, so counselors should consider a format that serves to catalyze or prompt discussions about themselves and the nature of the counseling relationship and practice at the first encounter. In addition to disclosing about oneself as a CMH counselor, a review of the client's rights and responsibilities may be helpful from an administrative and ethical perspective.

Client Rights and Responsibilities

Whether in a client bill of rights or combined into a single document with other required information, certain information must be framed from the client rights perspective according to industry standards of practice, ethical codes, HIPAA, and the principles of contract law (Remley & Herlihy, 2010; Wiger, 2009). Clients are consumers of mental health services and have rights beyond just informed consent and notification of confidentiality. In addition to their right to decide whether to enter into a counseling relationship, client rights may include the ability to refuse to discuss a topic, access to their records, being treated with dignity and respect, nondiscriminatory practices, and, ultimately, being able to complain about their treatment. Responsibilities of the client may include providing accurate information, their level of participation, attendance at appointments, payment for sessions, respect toward the staff, and adherence to other policies established by a practice. Organizing these aspects into a single document, usually divided into two sections, can ease the discussion and facilitate understanding and agreement.

Ultimately, counselors can proceed with the counseling relationship only after they receive express consent from the client, and it is advisable to have a signed consent for treatment dated on the first session in every client's file.

Consent for Treatment

The professional disclosure procedures just described are intended to inform clients so they can provide their consent to treatment. Evidence of professional disclosure at the onset of a counseling relationship is suitable according to contract law, even without a written consent. Although often practiced concomitantly or even merged within a professional disclosure and/or rights and responsibility statement, the consent statement must be addressed discretely according to some accreditation agencies, such as the Joint Commission for the Accreditation of Healthcare Organizations (JCAHO), and must include a statement that the client acknowledges reading and understanding his or her rights, the circumstances to arrange payment, and the limits of confidentiality. In cases of counseling minor children, parents are the only ones who can enter into a contract, and for family counseling, all parties who participate must provide consent. Because this is considered a legal document, it is in the counselor's best interest to ensure an attorney reviews and approves the consent form.

Release of Information

A consent for the release of confidential information form (aka "a release") may be required to discuss specific kinds of information with specific individuals or organizations in the interest of sharing information; reporting treatment progress; and planning, coordinating, or administering counseling plans. Clients frequently want to share information with family members who are not directly involved with treatment, other care providers (such as psychiatrists, former CMH counselors, physicians, or case managers), or legal representatives such as attorneys or probation officers. Essential information to be included in a release of information is the following:

- Client's name, address, telephone number, and social security or identification number

- A specifically identified person or entity to whom the release is directed

- The purpose of releasing the information

- A description or list of the records or information to be shared; a reference to "any and all records" may also be an option

- The format of the information (oral, written, or electronic)

- Any restrictions on the time period the authorization will be in effect

- All language required by HIPAA's Privacy Rule

- An itemization of any records that *should not* be produced

- The time period during which the consent is in effect, typically 1 year unless otherwise noted

- Dated signature of the client and a witness

Not every client will request a release of information, but when a client requests that information be shared, it is still a critical opportunity to apply confidentiality. Along the continuum of absolute confidentiality to no confidentiality, the extreme stances (disclose or not disclose) provide the clearest course of action. It is the middle area of when certain information may be shared for a distinct purpose that is often subtle and requires prudence and judgment, an area CMH counselors contend with on a regular basis. A signed release does not always equate to free disclosure. Especially when a client permits in writing disclosure of information to another, counselors must use discernment in achieving the goals of the disclosure while maintaining the foundation of confidentiality. Clearly documenting the kinds of information to be shared, the manner in which to share them, and the goal to be achieved will assist in balancing disclosure with privacy. It is this type of subtle balance that counselors must achieve via their actions but also capture in the clinical documentation created on an ongoing basis.

CLINICAL DOCUMENTATION PRACTICES

Both administrative and clinical practices relate to ethical and legal aspects of CMH counseling; however, administrative documentation can be considered related to managing the *process* of counseling, whereas clinical documentation practices are more focused on the *content*. Consider this: Counseling begins by CMH counselors using their special knowledge to make observations and take inventories that lead to assessments and conceptualizations of clients. Next, they apply this knowledge to help clients understand a problem (or strength) differently and then identify and implement a plan of action. However, the new reality for a CMH counselor is that "if there isn't documentation, it didn't happen"; therefore, these steps must be thoroughly documented to be valid. Typically, this documentation takes the form of three categories: intake assessment forms, screening and outcome assessments, and clinical case notes.

Intake Assessment Forms

Clinical assessment information from any initial client meeting is available to CMH counselors from multiple sources, such as a diagnostic interview, a mental status examination, and psychological testing (Wiger, 2009), as well as historic or collateral reports from other providers and family members. Because diagnosis and assessment are covered elsewhere in this text (Chapters 5 and 6), this section focuses on perhaps the most common type of assessment documented at an initial meeting, the self-report intake.

A self-report intake form is distinct from administrative documentation because it is based on client content instead of the process of counseling. It is important to view the collection of intake information as an assessment of background and status information that will be the context for the counseling process. In fact, the amount and type of information collected and analyzed will impact the entire counseling process (Meyer & Melchert, 2011), spanning from diagnosis to discharge, and is therefore of critical importance. An example of an intake form can be found in the appendix of this chapter.

Typically, demographic information is included on the front page of an intake form for easy reference and is often called a face sheet. The Joint Commission on the Accreditation of Healthcare Organizations (JCAHO; 2003) suggests the following information be collected on intake forms: name, home address, home telephone number, date of birth, sex, race or ethnic origin, next of kin and contact information, education, marital status, type and place of employment, date of initial contact or intake, and legal status (minor, immigrant, incompetent) including relevant documents. If the client is a minor, other information about parental relationships and custodial arrangements may be needed. Other practical information may include the client's statement of the initial problem, the best times to contact the client (and whether it is okay to leave a voice message), and the referral source. Similar information may be required of other accrediting agencies, such as the Commission on Accreditation of Rehabilitation Facilities (CARF).

In addition to this demographic information, intake data may be best conceptualized from a biopsychosocial framework. The biopsychosocial model is generally considered a comprehensive and systematic framework for collecting intake information in a mental health care setting and is considered essential to mental health assessment by almost all standards of practice guidelines and accrediting or licensing bodies (Meyer & Melchert, 2011), although a variety of styles and formats can be employed to collect this information. "Bio" represents the biological aspects of the client's history and status and may include issues related to physical health status, physiological symptoms, medications, medical conditions, family history, and developmental history. "Psycho" refers to psychological functioning, and categories include emotional experiences and stability, intellectual functioning, behavioral motivations, and previous and current psychological status and treatment. "Social" refers to the interactional or relational domain and includes living circumstances, relational quality, and familial/social support. The biopsychosocial intake is intended to be global in nature to assist the CMH counselor in initializing client conceptualization but also provide the prompts necessary for follow-up and further assessment.

A final consideration for intake assessment forms is any client background documentation, such as discharge summaries from previous treatment episodes, psychological assessments or reports, medical and legal documentation as it relates to client functioning, and school or work reports. It is typically obtained by a written release of information request form signed by the client, although at times may be provided by the client.

A thorough intake also involves a separate source of data to help confirm or refine clinical impressions, and screening tools used systematically beginning at intake can be a helpful way to assess and monitor progress.

Screening and Outcome Measures

Given the reality of the need to demonstrate clinical competence with diligence, measurements of client status and counseling outcomes are needed. Most CMH counseling training programs have adopted the scientist-practitioner model, which promotes the generation and application of data to the practice of counseling. Coupled with the increased pressure from managed care organizations to justify services and to implement evidence-based practices, CMH counselors must use effective screening and outcome measures in their practice.

A review of specific screening assessment tools, especially considering the numerous choices that may suit a particular setting, is beyond the scope of this chapter, but the integration of appropriate instrumentation and objective data into the documentation of the counseling relationship is critical. Common screening tools include symptom/problem checklists (e.g., SCL-90, BSI), mental health screenings (e.g., BDI, BAI, GWBS), substance abuse screenings (e.g., DAST, AUDIT, or SASSI-3), and adaptive functioning assessments (e.g., ABAS, Vineland). The use of these tools at intake and discharge can provide two data points to evaluate client progress and provide feedback to the clinician in the interest of practice improvement, but these data can be collected more frequently or systematically to provide more refined feedback on client progress.

Whereas client-specific data are important for documenting outcomes, another type of data that has gained popularity applies to client experiences with the relationship and counseling process. An example of this client-directed, outcome-informed (CDOI) practice was developed by Duncan et al. (2003) and appears to be a promising approach to improving client retention and perceptions of improvement. The protocol involves the administration of an Outcome Rating Scale (Miller, Duncan, Brown, Sparks, & Claud, 2003), a 1- to 2-minute survey on the main areas in a client's life (individual, interpersonal, social, and overall well-being), which can help the counselor give focus to the most salient issues of a client at that time. Furthermore, this assessment can be graphed over time, allowing the counselor and client to note specific areas of progress or areas that may need a new approach. Similarly, the protocol requires the administration of a different four-domain instrument, the Session Rating Scale, at the end of each session that empowers the client voice and provides the clinician immediate feedback on the areas of relationship, goals and topic, approach and method, and overall (satisfaction of the session). The intent of this measure is to either reinforce effective practices and content of the sessions or to inform a new approach to the relationship itself and provide supporting documentation accordingly. Research has shown that this system can greatly enhance desired outcomes, but more importantly, it is an efficient way to document both client progress and counselor intervention. Although this method is an option for CMH counselors, it should only be used to enhance the process of counseling and supplement the most prevalent manner of documenting sessions, the clinical case note.

Clinical Case Notes

The documentation of the interactions between a CMH counselor and a client during a counseling session occurs in many formats according to discipline, theoretical orientation, and agency practice. For example, *process notes* are a popular psychodynamic format that includes personal thoughts and reflections on the unconscious dynamics of a client in therapy. Many professionals have either reduced or eliminated the use of process notes, however, due to their problematic nature in legal proceedings and the greater transparency embraced by modern ethical codes and laws (Baird, 2007; Fox & Gutheil, 2000). By contrast, *progress* or *case notes* focus more on externally observable events (rather than the psyche of the client and CMH counselor) and are part of a problem-oriented medical record (POMR) system (i.e., focused on deficits, assessment, and treatment plan), which has become the standard in the modern health care practice.

In fact, case notes have become so essential in contemporary practice that they consume a great deal of the counselor's time. Standard practice requires a counselor to document each therapeutic encounter in a consistent format within 24 hours of the session occurring. Again, notes serve to protect clients as a means of accountability, document the counselor's fulfillment of ethical and legal obligations, and often justify the counselor's ability to continue working with the client. Furthermore, case notes provide counselors an opportunity to reflect on the events of a session more objectively, organize perceptions in a meaningful way, and project future tasks along the course of counseling with a client. Case note writing itself is not a billable service but is considered an extension of a face-to-face meeting and an expectation by agencies, insurers, and the profession itself. Considering the frequency with which counselors must write notes, the expectation that these notes are brief yet comprehensive, and the importance these notes can hold from financial, legal, and ethical standpoints, it can be helpful to know that the skills needed to write these can be learned and can improve with time and effort.

Writing Skills for Case Notes

One of the first skills to strengthen as a developing CMH counselor is mind-set. As emphasized throughout this chapter, counselors must see both the value and function of writing case notes. However, CMH counselors must also guide their thinking with some fundamental questions: Do the case notes relate to the client goals, the interventions I have selected, and the process of counseling? How can I document my actions to a third-party payer? How can I describe that I am meeting an established standard of care on the client's presenting issues? Connecting the intervention to the plan and using terms within the service definition when possible are essential in case notes.

The other critical skill in documenting sessions is related to writing itself. Because the format, subject, style, and purpose of clinical case notes are unique, they require a unique kind of writing to which you may not be accustomed. However, some basic reminders of writing style can be helpful. Both Baird (2007) and Mitchell (Mitchell & ACA, 2007) offer some helpful reminders on style summarized in the Table 9.1.

Remember, the content of a case note *is* your work and constitutes one of the standards of care that you provide. Case notes are the primary evidence that you provided competent services and abide by ethical and legal codes; they endure where memories fade. For some, it is their only impression of the counselor's professionalism. However, there are many stylistic choices and formats from which to choose.

Writing Formats

Supervisor preference and agency policy vary greatly when it comes to the format of case notes in the practice of CMH counseling. Two common and useful formats are SOAP notes and DART notes. Even when these are not the identified format and a narrative writing style is used, these acronyms define the areas for documentation. The important

Table 9.1 Writing Skills for Clinical Case Notes

Whenever Possible . . .	Rationale	Examples
Use definite, specific, and concrete language	General, vague, and abstract statements are open to interpretation or disputation.	"The client was uncomfortable" could mean he didn't like your office chair. "The client shifted in his chair, avoided eye contact, and expressed discomfort in discussing his sister" is much more specific.
Omit needless words	Case notes should be a concise yet impactful record of events. Economy of words conveys the essential information and minimizes time and resources.	"The client does not have any brothers or sisters" can easily be replaced with "No siblings." "During the interview, the client said that she had never before been seen in therapy by any therapist" (18 words) can be summarized as "The client indicated no previous experience in therapy" (8 words).
Choose words carefully	Be aware of subtleties in language, be both precise and accurate, and consider the "test of publicity."	Consider this example: "Mr. Smith denies any drug use." Do I infer that he uses drugs but is in denial? How might he (or his attorney or insurance company) interpret this if he reviewed his record? An alternative might be "Mr. Smith said he does not use any drugs."
Achieve clarity	Avoid ambiguous terms or abbreviations that are not standardized.	The vague term "coping skills" can be specifically stated as "thought stopping" or "relaxation techniques." "SA" could represent sexual abuse or substance abuse.
Be organized	Sentence organization and syntax often determine meaning.	"The therapist told the client about his problems" may be more accurate if written "The therapist described the developmental tasks related to the issue and provided education on how to achieve the tasks effectively."
Write linearly	Follow a logical sequence of events, connecting action and reaction to the client's goals.	Write as it happened, but only as it relates to the overall treatment plan or session goals.
Document behavior	Use verbs when possible (e.g., *recommended, assisted, discussed, evaluated, reviewed*). Qualify statements with supporting behaviors, such as "as evidenced or indicated by."	"The session felt comfortable by the end but felt tense at first" is subjective and not action oriented. An alternative might be "The client expressed frustration to the clinician when the nonverbal gesture of pulling legs to her chest was addressed. After additional probing questions, the client connected her discomfort with the topic of distress management and was able to review.
Don't eradicate mistakes	Alterations must be traceable, lest they be construed as hiding something incriminating. To alter a record, draw a single line, write "error" with initials and date, and write legibly the correction. You may add to a record but never take away.	The client requested that his wife participate in the next session. ERROR 2/14/12 AKM. The client stated that his wife asked to participate in the next session, but he did not feel ready.

Whenever Possible . . .	Rationale	Examples
Know your audience	The client may review your notes, another therapist could take over, the client may request notes sent to a physician or school, or a judge may require their release.	Consider the test of publicity: Would you be willing to have these notes reviewed by colleagues or family members of the client or read in a courtroom?

objectives of case notes, regardless of format, are to include (a) the specialized observation and assessment skills the clinician brings to the session, (b) the clinician's interventions with the client, (c) the response of the client to the interventions, and (d) the next logical and informed steps to fulfill the treatment plan.

SOAP is an acronym for subjective, objective, assessment, and plan and is a part of problem-oriented medical records developed by L. L. Weed (see Cameron & Turtle-Song, 2002). This method was developed in the medical setting to standardize entries in the patient file but has been adopted by many mental health agencies. In this format, *subjective* refers to the client's subjective concern and report (e.g., "Client complained of frequent arguments and increased irritability over the past 3 days," "Client reported improvement in managing mood this week"). *Objective* is external data that are factual and concrete, which in CMH counseling is limited to two sources: observation and written materials. In medical settings, objective data are more easily attained and quantified (e.g., blood test results, temperature, blood pressure), but in CMH counseling it may include mannerisms, affect, and appearance, whereas written materials may include assessment instruments or client materials (e.g., journals, letters, homework). *Assessment* involves the diagnosis and clinical impressions of the CMH counselor. Although there is often resistance in the counseling discipline to render a diagnosis, it is important to highlight that diagnosis is congruent with contemporary clinical practice (Ginter & Glauser, 2001) and often needs to be addressed for accreditation standards (JCAHO, 2003) and in order to be reimbursed by managed care entities. Clinical impressions may be diagnoses to "rule in or rule out" or hunches or conceptualizations related to presenting concerns. Last, the *plan* includes both action steps and prognosis. Items such as next appointment, the topic or intervention to be addressed, and the anticipated gains or rationale for the interventions would be included here. Although a common and useful format, some (e.g., Baird, 2007) have noted that SOAP is rigid and not always pertinent to CMH counseling practice, as compared to the medical settings that prompted the development of the format. For example, it is especially difficult in CMH counseling to sort out what is objective and what is subjective, and the meaning of events may be lost.

As an alternative, Baird (2007) developed the DART format specifically for mental health practice, where DART is an acronym for description, assessment, response, and treatment. In this system, the *description* contains the Ws—who, when, where, what—both in the byline of the note (e.g., 12/2/09, 10 a.m., individual session with CX) and in a description of the observations by the counselor and the topics or goals discussed (*what*). *Assessment* can be considered the *why* to the client's presentation or report, based on the counselor's hypothesis or conceptualization. It is an analysis of any observations (e.g., the client is normally quiet and reserved but was animated and energetic today) or an interpretation of an issue or goal (e.g., the client appeared to lack awareness of her anxiety or high energy). This section may also include the overall conceptualization of the client according to the counselor's theoretical orientation (e.g., the client appears to be experiencing anxiety and grief due to unfinished business [Gestalt], or the client may have irrational beliefs and self-destructive thoughts that result in the experience of anxiety [REBT]). In other words, the most important task is to give thought to what is observed or learned about the client and relate it to the overall understanding, goals, and interventions with the client. In *response*, both the interventions the counselor provided (e.g., confronted client with change in demeanor, facilitated an empty chair exercise) and efficacy or client response (e.g., the client stated she gained awareness of her change in behavior and was able to identify, label, and express her anxiety) are written. Last, *treatment* includes action steps for future sessions. It could be a simple note stating "scheduled additional session to review thought emotion record" or more elaborate, such as "next session we will explore family issues related to styles of emotional expression. Client will bring a written description of each family member and we will complete family diagrams." This will help practitioners become intentional and have continuity across sessions.

Case notes are used to document in sufficient detail the daily activities that CMH counselors conduct and will likely become routine, given their important function and the frequency with which they are written. However, there are often exceptional cases for case notes and some complexities of case notes and other paperwork that all CMH counselors must consider.

Complexities of Clinical Documentation

There are many complexities of clinical documentation that require special consideration. Risk management or self-protection related to high-risk or acute cases is an important aspect of documentation to continually address (Wheeler & Bertram, 2008), as well as the special protections for documentation among federally funded programs and the handling and storage of clinical documentation.

High-risk counseling scenarios that warrant additional attention beyond routine completion of case notes are not limited to physical safety issues, such as threats of harm to self or others. From a risk protection perspective, high-risk issues include relationship issues with clients related to transference or countertransference, impulsive or irate clients, or gaining competence in a new practice area or with a new set of techniques. There are also myriad areas of content addressed in counseling that have inherent risk, such as abortion, substance abuse of a minor client, sexual activities, illegal activity of a client, custody issues, or infidelity. Wheeler and Bertram (2008) recommend the following perspective for cases in which actions must be carefully documented:

- *Clarify the at-risk situation*—document what the client did or said to indicate high-risk activity

- *Assessment*—document the severity of the threat

- *Options*—list options that demonstrate that you considered a range of alternatives

- *Rule out*—describe how you ruled out options as inappropriate in order to clarify your clinical decision making

- *Consultation and/or supervision*—receiving a second opinion can demonstrate your diligence in evaluating the most suitable course of action

- *Action taken*—making decisions must lead to the implementation of an action plan

- *Follow up*—what you did in order to seek resolution of the risk

The handling, storage, and destruction of clinical documentation within client records are influenced by many regulations and standards, including HIPAA, an accrediting body such as JCAHO or CARF, and ethical codes (e.g., ACA, 2014; AMHCA, 2015). Policies and procedures for storage, access, and destruction must be considered by a practicing CMH counselor or agency. Physical storage must include ample space that is readily accessible to the practitioner but secured from others, typically within the office. However, storage or centralized locations may be needed for terminated clients or large agencies. Regardless of agency structure, it is critical that records are kept locked with a records manager or security officer to ensure they are handled responsibly, returned to their secured location, have limited access, and are destroyed systematically according to the laws in the state of practice.

An important distinction to be made is that a practice or independent practitioner might own the paper and ink within a client file, but clients themselves own the content. Not only do clients have access to the information, but their ownership of the contents requires that counselors share the information as directed. As previously stated, CMH counselors must ensure that they have written permission to transfer a file or information and know what is included and excluded from sharing. An exclusion for documentation not generated by the specific CMH counselor or agency must always be made for transferring or sharing information with a third party (Remley & Herlihy, 2010).

Both the ACA and AMHCA Codes of Ethics require that records be secured and have access limited to those who need it. Whereas HIPAA mandates that records are retained for 6 years, the statute of limitations for civil lawsuits varies from state to state. CMH counselors must establish a policy to ensure that adequate storage exists and a procedure for destroying documentation thoroughly and systematically is in place.

Strategies for Conducting Paperwork

Another complexity of clinical documentation is *how* and *when*. There is a high standard for diligence, timeliness, and thoroughness when it comes to CMH counseling, and when added with the other demands and pressures of counselors' work role, it is sometimes difficult to prioritize or complete paperwork. The following are some suggestions that beginning CMH counselors may find helpful:

Establish good habits. The formative period of graduate school is the best time to learn new habits (and to break old ones, if needed).

Find your preferred method. Some clinicians save 30 minutes for each intake and use the 10 minutes between sessions effectively. Others may save an hour a day or schedule an early end to scheduled clients to complete paperwork.

Assemble your tools. Essential resources for keeping clinical documentation are the current edition of the *DSM*, a dictionary, and a thesaurus. Some clinicians keep a running list of essential verbs that describe their interventions.

Seek feedback. Request feedback from supervisors and coworkers regularly on the accuracy and thoroughness of your case notes.

Think about case notes during sessions. There is a fine line between documenting adequately the relationship and dialogue between client and counselor and preserving the privacy and dignity of the client. Often, counselors have to attend to more than one aspect during a session, such as the events or reactions of a client in contrast to their own experience or impressions. What are the essential events that need to be documented or detailed, and what is important but can be left out? This kind of discernment can only be achieved and refined with practice and intention.

Self-monitor. Act as a reviewer and audit your own work. Part of practice improvement is ongoing analysis of one's own skills and needs. Is the information complete? Clear? Essential? What is conveyed about one's status as a professional by reviewing his or her documentation?

CONCLUSION

The information in this chapter is not intended to be an exhaustive resource for all managed care, billing, and documentation issues. However, the topics covered are consistent with current and prevalent standards established by the JCAHO and HIPAA and common clinical practice and can serve as an important resource. Even though there may be times when you are overwhelmed with navigating the rules around insurance payments and the required documentation of your work, remember to keep calm, reorganize, and reframe the regulations as an important component of the process that shows how counselors thrive in their work with clients. Becoming an approved provider on insurance company panels expands the potential client base for private practitioners. Navigating the credentialing and billing process is daunting at first but becomes a routine administrative aspect of managing a counseling practice. Furthermore, it allows CMH counselors to deliver affordable services to clients who would otherwise go untreated. Maintaining adequate records of one's work is necessary both for the welfare of clients and the protection of the counselor.

CASE STUDY 1: NAVIGATING INSURANCE COVERAGE

Allison is a 25-year-old community college student studying nursing and working full time as a nursing assistant at a local assisted living center. She has experienced depression for as long as she can remember but has never been to counseling. She has Anthem health insurance through her employer but has not been going to the doctor regularly. She has had trouble sleeping for several months. At the suggestion of a coworker, she schedules an appointment for a standard annual physical with a primary-care physician in hopes of getting a prescription for medication to help her sleep. In addition to the medical evaluation, the family doctor screens her for depression and realizes she could benefit from counseling services. He spends a few minutes exploring Allison's depression, discusses benefits and risks of medications that treat depression and insomnia, and shares with her the benefits of counseling. Allison declines prescription medication at this time and agrees to try counseling. The standard annual physical and depression screening are part of the Affordable Care Act's expansion of free wellness care so she does not pay anything out of pocket for these services.

The physician recommends Allison look up counselors who are approved providers for her Anthem health insurance and gives her several names of counselors to whom he has referred patients in the past. Allison arrives for an intake with her new counselor the following week. Allison's counselor explains that her services might be covered by Anthem if Allison's needs fit certain criteria. She completes the intake and determines that Allison fits the criteria for 300.4 persistent depressive disorder as described in the *DSM-5*. She reviews Anthem's eligibility criteria for outpatient psychiatric treatment and confirms that Allison's diagnosis, combined with her motivation for treatment and likelihood of benefitting, qualify her for services. The counselor explains the diagnosis and other eligibility criteria to Allison and secures her consent to bill Anthem. On Allison's policy, no preauthorization is required for outpatient counseling services, and up to eight sessions can be provided with no review. If additional sessions are needed, the counselor will file a request for continued services at that time. The counselor's session fee is $75, but the agreement with Anthem is that she will accept $62 per session. Allison's copay is $20, and Anthem reimburses the remaining $42 after each claim is filed. Allison and her counselor work well together and after seven sessions make plans to terminate for the time being. The counselor invites Allison to return anytime.

Several months later, Allison contacts the counselor again and reports that recent events have caused an increase in her depression. A relationship breakup, her mother's remarriage, and failure of several classes in nursing school have left Allison feeling lost and hopeless about the future. She has ideas of committing suicide by overdosing on Tylenol and admits she is holding the bottle in one hand as she talks with the counselor over the phone. Allison agrees to walk to the apartment next door where her friend lives while the counselor is on the phone and the friend agrees to take her to the local hospital emergency room. Allison agrees to tell the emergency room behavioral health clinician how she is feeling and ask for voluntary admission to the inpatient unit. The counselor tells Allison she will contact her health insurance to make arrangements for them to pay for the hospitalization. The counselor contacts Anthem's preauthorization service and gives information about Allison's current condition. At this time, Allison meets criteria for 296.23 major depressive disorder, single episode, severe without psychotic features. She is an imminent risk to herself and needs 24-hour-a-day care. Anthem concurs with the counselor that Allison's symptoms meet admission criteria for inpatient treatment and awaits final arrangements from the hospital staff. Ultimately, Anthem approves 4 days

(Continued)

(Continued)

of inpatient treatment; Allison improves with medication and counseling on the unit and is discharged home with a plan to resume outpatient care with the counselor and medication management with the psychiatrist she met on the inpatient unit. Allison's copay for inpatient treatment was $250. The hospital has a negotiated package reimbursement rate for standard inpatient psychiatric hospitalization that includes services provided by nurses and counselors on the unit. Counselors on the inpatient unit are paid a flat salary by the hospital and do not bill independently for their services. After hospital discharge, Allison will continue to pay the $20 copay at each outpatient counseling session and each medication management session, and the counselor will continue to be paid $42 per session by Anthem. The counselor can request additional sessions as needed for Allison's care.

Discussion Questions

1. What would Allison's total out-of-pocket charges be for 16 outpatient counseling sessions? What was her out-of-pocket charge for the inpatient hospitalization? Now consider the total amount Anthem would pay for the remainder of the charges (use $1,500 per day as the estimate for inpatient hospitalization).

2. What are the behavioral health benefits for your health insurance?

   a. What would your outpatient counseling copay be?
   b. What would your inpatient hospitalization copay be?
   c. Identify three local clinical mental health counselors who are approved providers for your insurance plan.

3. If you do not currently have health insurance, explore your options for getting coverage. Is there a policy available through your employer or school? Do you qualify to be added to a parent's policy under the extended age program of the Affordable Care Act? What would it cost you to purchase an individual policy if you are not covered elsewhere?

4. Explore if there are organizations in your local area that provide pro bono counseling services to clients who have no insurance and no ability to pay.

5. What are the advantages and limitations of having service eligibility tied to *DSM* diagnoses?

CASE STUDY 2: WRITING EFFECTIVE CASE NOTES

Following is a clinical case note for a fictitious client. Review the note and then consider the questions that follow.

Description. Met with client for 1 hour. The goal of the session was to follow up with client on efforts to identify and dispute cognitive distortions related to anxiety.

Assessment. Client was punctual for the meeting; alert; and oriented to person, place, time, and situation. Client continues to suffer from anxiety that results from the dysfunctional thoughts he creates in his head. Client may have clinical levels of depression too.

Response. He reported that he was resistant to feedback on making the intervention work, as evidenced by his self-doubt and skepticism. However, I assisted the client in identifying samples of distorted thoughts that contribute to his anxiety and brainstormed ways to dispute them. Encouraged client to practice on his own this week and obtained his commitment to attempt once per day.

Treatment plan. Continue to meet with client weekly to provide the same intervention. Review benefits and techniques for relaxation with client next session.

Discussion Questions

1. What elements of a well-written case note are missing from this example?

   ANSWER: There is no risk assessment related to client safety, no sample thought replacement statements practiced in-session with the client, the symptoms of assessment of "clinical depression" needs substantiation—what specifically did the client report about his anxiety?

2. What language is included in the note that should be removed or modified?

   ANSWER: "Results from the dysfunctional thoughts he creates in his head" is biased; instead, the language should be neutral and objective. "Provide the same intervention" is vague; what specifically did the counselor do? "Cognitive behavioral interventions related to anxious thoughts" would be much clearer.

3. What are the strengths and weaknesses in the case note?

   ANSWER: Strengths include the use of action verbs "identifying" and "brainstormed." Weaknesses include that no comments were included in the case note about the counseling process or the therapeutic relationship.

REFERENCES

American Academy of Family Physicians. (2005). *Medicaid: Overview and policy issues.* Retrieved from http://www.aafp.org/dam/AAFP/documents/advocacy/coverage/medicaid/ES-Medicaid OverviewandPolicyIssues-121305.pdf

American Counseling Association. (2013, March). *Medicare coverage of licensed professional counselors.* Retrieved from http://www.counseling.org/government-affairs/public-policy/public-policy-news-view/position-papers/2013/03/19/medicare-coverage-of-licensed-professional-counselors-bill-introduced-in-113th-congress

American Counseling Association. (2014). *ACA Code of Ethics.* Alexandria, VA: Author.

American Mental Health Counselors Association. (2015). *AMHCA Code of Ethics.* Alexandria, VA: Author.

American Psychiatric Association. (2013). *Diagnostic and statistical manual of mental disorders* (5th ed.). Washington, DC: American Psychiatric Press.

Anderson, C. E. (2000). Dealing constructively with managed care: Suggestions from an insider. *Journal of Mental Health Counseling, 22*(4), 343.

Anthem. (2013). *Behavioral health medical necessity criteria.* Retrieved from http://www.anthem.com/provider/noapplication/f5/s1/t0/pw_e186989.pdf?refer = ahpprovider&state = in.

Appari, A., Anthony, D., & Johnson, E. (2009). *HIPAA compliance: An examination of institutional and market forces.* The 8th Workshop on Economics of Information Systems, University College, London, June 24–25.

Baird, B. (2007). *Internship, practicum, and field placement handbook: A guide for the helping professions.* Charlottesville, VA: Pearson/Prentice Hall.

Beauchamps, T. L., & Childress, J. F. (1984). *Principles of biomedical ethics* (4th ed.). Oxford, UK: Oxford University Press.

Braun, S. A., & Cox, J. A. (2005). Managed mental health care: Intentional misdiagnosis of mental disorders. *Journal of Counseling & Development, 83,* 425–433.

Bray, J. H., Shepherd, J. N., & Hays, J. R. (1985). Legal and ethical issues in informed consent to psychotherapy. *American Journal of Family Therapy, 13,* 50–60.

Cameron, S., & Turtle-Song, I. (2002). Learning to write case notes using the SOAP format. *Journal of Counseling & Development, 80,* 286–292.

Centers for Medicare and Medicaid Services. (2016). *HCPCS—General information.* Retrieved from https://www.cms.gov/MedHCPCSGenInfo.

Centers for Medicare and Medicaid Services. (n.d. a). *Affordable Care Act.* Retrieved from http://www.medicaid.gov/AffordableCareAct/Affordable-Care-Act.html.

Centers for Medicare and Medicaid Services. (n.d. b). *History.* Retrieved from http://www.cms.gov/About-CMS/Agency-Information/History/index.html?redirect = /history.

Centers for Medicare and Medicaid Services. (n.d. c). *Medicare provider-supplier enrollment.* Retrieved from http://www.cms.gov/Medicare/Provider-Enrollment-and-Certification/MedicareProvider-SupEnroll/index.html?redirect = /medicareprovidersupenroll.

Centers for Medicare and Medicaid Services. (n.d. d). *Your Medicare coverage choices.* Retrieved from http://www.medicare.gov.

Cooper, C. C., & Gottlieb, M. C. (2000). Ethical issues with managed care: Challenges facing counseling psychology. *The Counseling Psychologist, 28,* 179–236.

Corey, G., Corey, M., & Callanan, P. (2007). *Issues and ethics in the helping professions* (7th ed.). Pacific Grove, CA: Brooks/Cole.

Cormier, B., Cormier, L. S., & Cormier, W. H. (1997). *Interviewing strategies for helpers: Fundamental skills and cognitive behavioral interventions.* Pacific Grove, CA: Brooks/Cole.

Daniels, J. A. (2001). Managed care, ethics, and counseling. *Journal of Counseling & Development, 79*(1), 119–123.

Duncan, B. L., Miller, S. D., Sparks, J. A., Claud, D. A., Reynolds, L. R., Brown, J., et al. (2003). The session rating scale: Preliminary psychometric properties of a "working" alliance measure. *Journal of Brief Therapy, 3*(1), 3–12.

Fox, R., & Gutheil, I. A. (2000). Process recording: A means for conceptualizing and evaluating practice. *Journal of Teaching in Social Work, 20,* 39–57.

Ginter, E. J., & Glauser, A. (2001). Effective use of the "DSM" from a developmental/wellness perspective. In E. R. Welfel & R. E. Ingersoll (Eds.), *The mental health desk reference* (pp. 69–77). New York: Wiley.

GovTrack.us (n.d.). *S.604: Senior mental health access improvement act.* Retrieved from http://www.govtrack.us/congress/bill.xpd?bill = s112-604.

Gray, K. (2007). The privacy rule: Are we being deceived? *DePaul Journal of Health Care Law, 11,* 89–118.

Health Assistance Partnership. (2010). *Overview of the Medicare program.* Retrieved from http://www.hapnetwork.org/original-medicare/ship-resource-guide/overview.pdf.

Health Care Financing Administration. (1995, June 24). *Overview of Medicare Program*. Retrieved from http://www.netreach.net/ ~ wmanning/medicare.htm.

Hixson, R., & Hunt-Unruh, D. (2008). Demystifying HIPAA. *Annals of the American Psychotherapy Association, 11*(3), 10–14.

Joint Commission on Accreditation of Healthcare Organizations. (2003). *Accreditation manual for mental health, chemical dependency, and mental retardation developmental disabilities services*. Oakbrook Terrace, IL: Joint Commission on Accreditation of Healthcare Organizations.

Kongstvedt, P. R. (2008). *Managed care: What it is and how it works* (3rd ed.). Sudbury, MA: Jones & Bartlett.

Leyva, C., & Leyva, D. (n.d. a). *HIPAA survival guide*. Retrieved from http://hipaasurvivalguide.com/hitech-act-text.php.

Leyva, C., & Leyva, D. (n.d. b). *General administrative requirements, 45 C. F. R. pt. 160*. Retrieved from http://www.hipaasurvivalguide.com/hipaa-regulations/part-160.php.

Leyva, C., & Leyva, D. (n.d. c). *Security and privacy, 45 C. F. R. pt. 164*. Retrieved from http://www.hipaasurvivalguide.com/hipaa-regulations/part-164.php.

Mead, M. A., Hohenshil, T H., & Singh, K. (1997). How the DSM system is used by clinical counselors: A national study. *Journal of Mental Health Counseling, 19*, 383–401.

Meyer, L., & Melchert, T. P. (2011). Examining the content of mental health intake assessments from a biopsychosocial perspective. *Journal of Psychotherapy Integration, 21*(1), 70–89.

Miller, S. D., Duncan, B. L, Brown, J., Sparks, J. A., & Claud, D. A. (2003). The outcome rating scale: A preliminary study of the reliability, validity, and feasibility of a brief visual analog measure. *Journal of Brief Therapy, 2*(2), 91–100.

Mitchell, B., & American Counseling Association. (2007). *Documentation in counseling records: An overview of ethical, legal, and clinical issues*. Alexandria, VA: American Counseling Association.

National Conference of State Legislatures. (n.d.). *Children's health insurance program overview*. Retrieved from http://www.ncsl.org/issues-research/health/childrens-health-insurance-program-overview.aspx.

NBCC. (2012, Winter). *Medicare provider coverage of licensed counselors*. Retrieved from http://www.nbcc.org/About/AdvocacyUpdates.

NHIC. (2010, July). *Medicare services billing guide*. Retrieved from http://www.medicarenhic.com/providers/pubs/Mental%20Health%20Services%20Guide.pdf.

Phelps, R., Eisman, E. J., & Kohout, J. (1998). Psychological practice and managed care: Results of the CAPP practitioner survey. *Professional Psychology: Research and Practice, 29*, 31–36.

Pope, K. S., & Vasquez, M. J. T. (2007). *Ethics in psychotherapy and counseling: A practical guide* (3rd ed.). San Francisco: Jossey-Bass.

Remley, T. P., & Herlihy, B. (2010). *Ethical, legal, and professional issues in counseling* (3rd ed.). Upper Saddle River, NJ: Prentice Hall.

Substance Abuse and Mental Health Services Administration. (2008). *Mental Health Parity and Addiction Equity Act*. Retrieved from http://www.samhsa.gov/healthreform/parity.

Sullivan, T., Martin, W. L., & Handelsman, M. M. (1993). Practical benefits of an informed-consent procedure: An empirical investigation. *Professional Psychology: Research and Practice, 24*(2), 160–163.

TRICARE. (2011, April). *TRICARE behavioral health care services*. Retrieved from http://www.tricare.mil/tricaresmartfiles/Prod_807/TRICARE_BHC_Brochure_2012_LoRes.pdf.

United States Department of Defense. (2011, December 27). *TRICARE certified mental health counselors*. Federal Register, 76, 80741-80744. Retrieved from http://www.regulations.gov/#!documentDetail; D = DOD-2011-HA-0134-0001.

United States Department of Defense. (n.d.). *Military health system overview*. http://www.health.mil/About_MHS/History.aspx.

United States Department of Health and Human Services. (1996). *The Health Insurance Portability and Accountability Act of 1996: Privacy and security rules.* Retrieved from http://www.hhs.gov/ocr/privacy.

United States Department of Health and Human Services. (2010). *The Affordable Care Act.* Retrieved from http://www.healthcare.gov/law/index.html.

Welfel, E. R. (2006). *Ethics in counseling and psychotherapy: Standards, research, and emerging issues* (3rd ed.). Pacific Grove, CA: Brooks/Cole.

Wheeler, A. M., & Bertram, B. (2008). *The counselor and the law* (5th ed.). Alexandria, VA: American Counseling Association.

Wiger, D. E. (2009). *The clinical documentation sourcebook: The complete paperwork resource for your mental health practice.* Hoboken, NJ: Wiley.

Wilcoxon, S. A., Magnuson, S., & Norem, K. (2008). Institutional values of managed mental health care: Efficiency or oppression? *Journal of Multicultural Counseling and Development, 36*(3), 143–154.

World Health Organization. (2004). *International statistical classification of diseases and health related problems.* Geneva: Author.

Zamostny, K. P., Corrigan, J. D., & Eggert, M. A. (1981). Replication and extension of social influence processes in counseling: A field study. *Journal of Counseling Psychology, 28*(6), 481–489.

Personal History and Intake Form

Date:

1. CONTACT INFORMATION

Full name _____
          Last   First   Middle

Date of birth _____   Age _____

Gender _____   Race/Ethnicity _____

Address _____

City/State/Zip _____

How did you hear about us? _____

Emergency Contact _____
             Name   Relationship   Phone#

If client is a minor, who has legal custody? _____

Telephone Information:

			OK to call?	❑ Yes	❑ No
HOME	(	)	OK to call?	❑ Yes	❑ No
			OK to leave msg?	❑ w/person	❑ on voicemail
WORK	(	)	OK to call?	❑ Yes	❑ No
			OK to leave msg?	❑ w/person	❑ on voicemail
MOBILE	(	)	OK to call?	❑ Yes	❑ No
			OK to leave msg?	❑ w/person	❑ on voicemail

2. PRESENTING ISSUES AND GOALS

3. HEALTH AND WELLNESS

Do you have any physical complaints?   ❏ Yes   ❏ No

      Explain: _____

Are you currently under a physician's care?   ❏ Yes   ❏ No

      Explain: _____

When was your last physical examination? _____

      Results: ❏ *Good Health*   ❏ *Acute Problem*   ❏ *Chronic Problem*

      Explain: _____

Any women's health concerns? _____

Prescription medications: _____

Prescribing Physician _____ Phone # _____

Name of Drug	Purpose	Dosage	Frequency
_____	_____	_____	_____
_____	_____	_____	_____
_____	_____	_____	_____

Overall physical condition   ❏ *Excellent*   ❏ *Good*   ❏ *Fair*   ❏ *Poor*

Diet/nutrition   ❏ *Excellent*   ❏ *Good*   ❏ *Fair*   ❏ *Poor*

Work efficiency   ❏ *Excellent*   ❏ *Good*   ❏ *Fair*   ❏ *Poor*

Sleep ❏ *Regular* ❏ *Adequate* ❏ *Peaceful* ❏ *Irregular* ❏ *Inadequate* ❏ *Disrupted*

Is religion/spirituality important to you?   ❏ Yes   ❏ No

      Religious/spiritual "preference": _____

      Rate your satisfaction with your religion/spirituality   ❏ *Excellent* ❏ *Good* ❏ *Fair* ❏ *Poor*

4. PRESENTING CONCERNS (CURRENT SITUATION, HISTORY OF THE PROBLEM, AREAS OF LIFE AFFECTED):

5. CURRENT HOUSEHOLD INFORMATION

Please check the one response that <u>best</u> describes your current relationship status:

❏ Single (How long? _____)

❏ Dating (How long? _____)

❑ Significant other (How long? _____)

❑ Partnered (How long? _____)

❑ Married (How long? _____ # of marriages _____)

❑ Recent breakup (When? _____)

❑ Spouse/partner deceased (When? _____)

❑ Separated (When? _____)

❑ Divorced (When? _____)

❑ Other

CURRENT HOME LIFE

Children and adults currently living with you (e.g., parent, roommate, daughter, nephew, partner)

Name	Age	Gender	Any significant traits or problems?
_____	_____	_____	_____
_____	_____	_____	_____

Other important <u>current</u> relationships (e.g., parent, son, partner, grandchild, niece, grandparent, coparent)

Name	Age	Gender	Any significant traits or problems?
_____	_____	_____	_____
_____	_____	_____	_____

6. FAMILY HISTORY

Describe your family of origin _____

Current family members who provide you support _____

Current family members whom you do not find supportive or with whom you have frequent conflict _____

7. TRAUMA HISTORY

Do you have any history of traumatic experience (including physical, emotional, and/or sexual abuse; family trauma; crime victimization; rape or sexual assault; disasters)?

Explain _____

What resources do you draw on to cope with trauma experiences?

Are you a veteran? If so, please explain _____

8. CURRENT WORK/FINANCES

If not currently employed, state "NONE." If a student, state "STUDENT." _____

Please indicate the <u>total</u> number of hours of paid employment.

Hrs. worked per week: _____ Your annual income: $ _____

Current Job: Job title _____

Employer _____

Hrs. worked per week _____ Wage: $ _____ hr./wk./mo. _____

How long at this position? _____ Are you satisfied with this job? _____

9. EDUCATIONAL HISTORY

Highest grade completed _____

College (completion year and major) _____

10. MENTAL HEALTH HISTORY

Have you ever seen another mental health professional? ❑ Yes ❑ No

When   Who (Name)   Type of Professional   Reason

_____   _____   _____   _____

Have you ever been hospitalized for mental/emotional problems or substance abuse? ❑ Yes ❑ No

When   Where   Reason

_____   _____   _____

Have you ever attempted suicide? ❑ Yes   ❑ No

Explain _____

Have you had any thoughts of harming yourself or others? ❑ Yes   ❑ No

Explain _____

Do you have a history of violent behavior? ❑ Yes   ❑ No

Explain_____

Other pertinent information (mental status) or footnotes (include section number) _____

_____

Client signature _____   Date _____

Intake counselor signature _____   Date _____

Crisis Management and Disaster Relief

Amber L. Pope and Allison Marsh Pow

Learning Goals

Upon completion of this chapter you should be able to do the following:

1. Define crisis, emergency, and disaster

2. Identify normative and serious psychological reactions following a crisis or disaster

3. Understand the range of services provided by crisis and disaster mental health counselors

4. Apply evidence-based response strategies to crisis and disaster counseling case scenarios

"The world breaks every one and afterward many are strong at the broken places." In *A Farewell to Arms*, Ernest Hemingway makes this astute observation about the vulnerability and strength inherent in being human. Crisis is an inescapable part of life. Some crises are temporary and pass by day's or week's end; others feel larger and more impactful. Crises may alter the fabric of a person's life, challenging one's sense of being, reality, and routine while requiring adaptation to an altered way of life. In this way, some crises leave permanent scars.

Counselors are trained as facilitators of change. They specialize in life transitions, whether they emanate from within the self or are externally imposed by forces beyond human control. Counselors are taught about the importance of meeting clients where they are. In moments of pain, joy, devastating sadness, or hopeful anticipation, counselors are fellow travelers, as Irvin Yalom describes, along the many paths their clients traverse

(Yalom, 2002). How, then, can counselors help clients navigate those paths when their lives take an abrupt turn in times of crisis—when something so impactful happens in a client's life that his or her usual way of being, of coping, of moving forward is suddenly incapacitated? How does a counselor not only meet clients there but help them to find strength where they feel broken?

The idea of working with clients in crisis often raises anxiety in beginning and veteran counselors alike. A crisis can be sudden, unexpected, overwhelming, and paralyzing for the individuals in its midst, as well as for those charged with helping them. A goal of this chapter is to demystify the "unknown" aspects of working with clients in crisis by providing a structured framework by which to conceptualize, assess, and best support these individuals. Readers are provided with specific information to prepare them for encountering and working effectively with clients experiencing either a personal or community crisis, as well as useful tools and intervention strategies to keep clients on track, even in the most overwhelming circumstances.

DIFFERENTIATING CRISIS MANAGEMENT AND DISASTER RELIEF

According to Greenstone and Leviton (2011), "A **crisis** occurs when unusual stress temporarily renders an individual unable to direct life effectively" (p. 1). A crisis can result from a single event or multiple events occurring simultaneously or over time (Greenstone & Leviton, 2011). The Chinese character for "crisis" is widely referenced in the literature on crisis management and disaster relief because it symbolically portrays the paradox of crisis as both a threat and a potential growth experience (see Figure 10.1). The symbol is actually a combination of two characters representing the words *danger* and *opportunity* (Wiger & Harowski, 2003). It encompasses the idea that change, even when sudden and impactful, is not inherently traumatic or defeating. It can also bring great opportunity for positive growth (Callahan, 2009; Hoff, 2001; Wiger & Harowski, 2003).

Two types of crisis are discussed in this chapter. First, we explore what it means to experience an **individual crisis**, as well as effective approaches to working with clients in

Figure 10.1 *Chinese Character for Crisis*

CRISIS

危

A time of danger

机

A time of opportunity

different stages of individual crisis. Second, we turn to **disaster**, a type of crisis brought about when large-scale traumatic events affect entire communities for months to years following the impact. Readers will discover throughout this chapter that crises, whether emanating from a localized event or a large-scale disaster, impact individuals in similar ways across groups. Thus, crisis management and disaster mental health work have significant overlap. The primary difference in the two is that disasters often disrupt and damage available community resources, further affecting individuals' abilities to cope. Whereas clients experiencing individual crisis can draw on the support of normal societal functions and resources, those involved in disasters are at risk for experiencing extended trauma as their communities struggle to regroup and rebuild.

CRISIS MANAGEMENT

What Is a Crisis?

Imagine a veteran sailor, adept at navigating even rough waters and confident in skills that have been tried and tested countless times. One day, a tumultuous storm descends on the sailor's boat, creating massive waves so powerful that no level of sailing mastery could possibly withstand the impact. The sailor tries every tactic to save the boat before grasping desperately for a life vest as the storm overcomes the tiny vessel and he is swept out to sea. Although dramatized, the vividness and intensity of the images this story evokes represent the chaos that many individuals experience in moments of individual crisis.

An **individual crisis** occurs when a person's interpretation of an event creates distress so profound that the person's usual coping mechanisms prove ineffective (Golan, 1978; Hoff, 2001; Roberts, 2000). As opposed to disaster, individual crisis is localized, affecting one or a small number of individuals. *Crisis* has become the accepted professional term for what was once referred to as a "breakdown," although the latter may more accurately describe the subjective experience (Allen, 1999). A crisis response is, in essence, the breakdown of normal coping mechanisms. This can lead to **functional impairment**, rendering a person emotionally incapacitated and unable to move forward from the crisis event (Allen, 1999; Golan, 1978). As Greenstone and Leviton (2011) noted, a person experiencing individual crisis may face "extreme feelings of grief, hostility, helplessness, hopelessness, and alienation from self, family, and society" (p. 1) as his or her normal coping mechanisms fail to provide relief or resolution to the crisis at hand.

It is important to note that most people adapt to developmental changes without incident, and most normative stressors do not lead to a crisis reaction (Callahan, 2009). A stressful event can disrupt that equilibrium temporarily, but most potential crisis clients are already trying to regain their sense of stability before counselors ever enter the situation. In general, individuals in crisis will draw on whatever resources are available in an effort to restabilize. Therefore, from the very beginning of crisis intervention, the counselor and client have the same ultimate goal of reestablishing stability and functioning in that client's life (Greenstone & Leviton, 2011).

Crisis Counseling

Crisis counseling evolved as a unique specialty during World War II out of a need for psychologists and psychiatrists to treat soldiers experiencing severe "battle fatigue" (later referred to as post-traumatic stress disorder [PTSD] during the Vietnam War; American Psychiatric Association, 2013; Dattilio & Freeman, 2007). These professionals found that the most immediate interventions were also the most effective and therefore began treating distressed soldiers directly on the front line. The original goal of crisis management during World War II was much the same as it is today—to return individuals to baseline functioning as quickly as possible so they could return to active duty (Dattilio & Freeman, 2007). Formal recognition of crisis intervention as a clinical specialty did not occur until 1989, when first acknowledged by the American Psychological Association (APA; Hillman, 2002). Although the American Counseling Association (ACA) does not currently recognize a separate division for crisis counselors, the topic has been a focus of interest in the ACA's publications since 1970 (Tucker, Megenity, & Vigil, 1970).

The study of individual crisis management has advanced significantly since the 1970s. The Council for Accreditation of Counseling and Related Educational Programs (CACREP) now recommends that counselors have comprehensive knowledge about the "effects of crisis, disasters, and trauma on diverse individuals across the lifespan" (CACREP, 2016, p. 11) and be versed in "crisis intervention, trauma-informed, and community-based strategies, such as Psychological First Aid" (CACREP, 2016, p. 12). According to Hillman (2002), nearly 40% of men and 70% of women in the United States will experience at least one traumatic event in their lifetimes. Many people do not seek counseling until they find themselves in crisis, highlighting the importance of confidence and competence in crisis intervention. The presence of effective and timely intervention can make the difference between the exacerbation of trauma symptoms and **posttraumatic growth**, or positive changes in spirituality, appreciation of life, improved relationships, and finding new possibilities and meaning in life (Boyraz, Horne, & Sayger, 2010).

Nationwide budget cuts to community mental health services over recent years have coincided with heightened demand, resulting in a paucity of resources available to most agencies (National Alliance on Mental Illness, 2011). According to the National Alliance on Mental Illness (NAMI) 2011 Report, over $1.6 billion, roughly 8% of the preexisting budget, was cut from state mental health agency budgets between 2009 and 2011 (Gold, 2011). In an effort to maximize the value of existing funds, more emphasis is now being placed on crisis prevention and intervention services, a growing niche in the counseling field. Therefore, skills and knowledge in crisis management are not only essential but also quite marketable.

Range of Individual Crises

Normative and Traumatic Stress

A common misperception is that a psychological crisis must involve events that are sudden and catastrophic. In fact, crisis can evolve from the trials and tribulations of daily life and may even be considered normative (Dattilio & Freeman, 2007; Wiger & Harowski, 2003).

A crisis does not result from the situation itself. Rather, it is the individual's perception of and response to a given situation based on the person's unique cognitive, behavioral, and affective predispositions that turn a stressful event into an individual crisis (Allen, 1999; Callahan, 2009; Hoff, 2001; Roberts, 2000; Wiger & Harowski, 2003). Callahan (2009) distinguishes between two types of stress: **normative stress**, resulting from developmentally predictable events such as job loss, the illness of a family member, or a relationship breakup, and **traumatic stress** from events that involve a potential threat of death, serious injury, or harm to one's physical well-being or that of a close relation (APA, 2013). Often reactions to normative versus traumatic stress look remarkably similar and may include emotional disequilibrium and symptoms of anxiety and/or depression. Both have the potential to induce crisis in an individual. However, traumatic stress is more likely to precipitate the psychiatric disorder known as acute stress disorder (ASD), the precursor to PTSD (APA, 2013; Callahan, 2009). Responses to normative stress are more likely to be diagnosed as depressive, substance abuse, or adjustment disorders (APA, 2013; Callahan, 2009).

Types of Life Stressors

Individual crises can evolve from a multitude of normative and traumatic stressors. There are five primary categories within which most common types of stressors fall (adapted from Greenstone & Leviton, 2011):

1. Significant life changes
   - Employment (loss of job, underemployment, change in work responsibilities)
   - Relationship (separation, divorce, other significant change in status of close relationship)
   - Family composition (gaining or losing a family member through birth, adoption, parental remarriage or separation/divorce, relocation, parents or adult children moving in)
   - Abortion, miscarriage, or out-of-wedlock pregnancy
   - Living conditions (loss of home, considerable change to living arrangements)
   - Entering/exiting school
   - Military deployment
   - Retirement

2. Threats to health and physical well-being (self or significant relation)
   - Accidents (with or without physical injury)
   - Physical illness
   - Acute episodes of mental disorder
   - Acute influence of chemical substances
   - Sexual difficulties
   - Death of significant relation
   - Episodes of abuse (physical, sexual, mental, emotional)

3. Financial crisis
   - Foreclosure on a mortgage or loan
   - Sudden loss of or dramatic change in income

4. Legal crisis
   ○ Arrest
   ○ Court appearance
   ○ Episodes of delinquency in childhood

5. Disaster (to be discussed later in the chapter)

Mental Health Emergency

When any type of individual crisis, regardless of the nature of the stressor, becomes so overwhelming that the individual requires immediate intervention in order to avoid potential physical harm, the crisis then becomes a **mental health emergency** (Callahan, 2009). Clients who are experiencing a mental health emergency may report thoughts of harming themselves or others or may be temporarily unable to care for themselves (i.e., experience psychosis or severe symptoms of depression or anxiety that render them out of touch with reality). Emergencies may include suicidal gestures or attempts, violent behavior (may be related to acute mania or psychosis), or interpersonal victimization (i.e., rape or assault; Callahan, 2009).

Responding to a mental health emergency requires some additional skills, including triage and assessment, quick decision making, consultation, and often referral to other professionals who can help a counselor create and maintain a physically and emotionally safe space for the client. These professionals may include other mental health practitioners, law enforcement, and medical personnel. Individuals who have sustained physical injury prior to intervention should always be medically evaluated before being assessed by a crisis counselor. During some mental health emergencies, it may be in the best interest of a client's safety to refer for temporary hospitalization in order to stabilize the client's mental, emotional, and physical state until he or she feels better able to manage the stressors at hand.

Presentation of Clients in Crisis

The breakdown of coping mechanisms during times of individual crisis can lead to a loss of perceived control over self and environment as well as feelings of isolation and helplessness (Kaniasty, 2006; van der Kolk, 1987). The experience of such extreme disequilibrium can lead to a variety of individual reactions, including behaviors that are beyond the scope of the individual's normal functioning. It is important to recognize that client reactions to crisis are usually an attempt to communicate feelings of intense emotional pain and to reestablish a sense of normalcy.

Acute responses to crisis often involve some common symptoms and characteristics. These can include confusion, anxiety, shock, disbelief, anger, depression, and low self-esteem. "The person in crisis may appear to be incoherent, disorganized, agitated, and volatile or calm, subdued, withdrawn, and apathetic" (Roberts, 2000, p. 7). The **diagnostic triad** of **intrusion** (intrusive and uncontrollable thoughts and images related to a traumatic event), **numbing** (avoidance of thoughts and feelings related to a traumatic event), and **hyperarousal** symptoms (heightened vigilance, reactivity, and anxiety) are hallmarks of a PTSD presentation and may signal the onset of acute stress disorder (van der Kolk, 2006). Although individuals in crisis may act in ways that are far different from their normal behavior, counselors must be careful not to attribute such behavior too readily to an emotional or mental illness (Hoff, 2001). A crisis response is not, in and of itself, a diagnosis or mental health disorder. Although preexisting disorders may contribute to the crisis response, and should be taken into account when assessing the situation, counselors intervening in crisis situations should approach the crisis as an acute stress reaction rather than a mental illness (Hoff, 2001).

Principles of Crisis Management

Timely intervention is imperative in any crisis situation in order to minimize potential for exacerbation of the crisis and to maximize opportunities for growth (Allen, 1999). In the following sections, we offer some basic guidelines for approaching, assessing, and managing clients experiencing individual crisis. Although these guidelines apply during any level of individual crisis, emphasis is placed on achieving and maintaining client safety in the midst of a mental health emergency.

Caplan's Stages of Crisis Development

Gerald Caplan, one of the first researchers to comprehensively study crisis management, and a cofounder of the country's first community crisis center, proposed **four stages of crisis development** that are widely cited in the literature (Allen, 1999; Hillman, 2002; Roberts, 2000):

1. A *rise in tension* brought on by a precipitating event or unresolved issue

2. *Escalating tension and disruption* as the individual attempts unsuccessfully to resolve the stress-inducing situation

3. Achievement of *critical mass*—the point at which the tension becomes so intense that existing resources are exhausted and the individual attempts to seek help from others such as friends, family, or professionals

4. *Crisis resolution or exacerbation*—the immediate crisis is either resolved using new coping skills or left unresolved, which may lead to worsening of clinical symptoms and potential development of ASD and PTSD

J. S. Tyhurst referred to three overlapping phases that take place during a crisis response: impact, recoil, and posttraumatic recovery (Roberts, 2000). These phases succinctly embody Caplan's concept of crisis development. Caplan believed that the speed of initial intervention was of the utmost importance. He asserted that intervention during Stages 2 or 3 of his crisis development model maximizes the potential for healthy client outcomes (Allen, 1999).

Individual Crisis Intervention

Crisis intervention is a time-limited and targeted process in which a clinical mental health (CMH) counselor enters into the client's life situation in order to (a) create a structured and stable environment that reduces the potential for further physical or emotional harm;

(b) assess and prioritize areas of greatest need; and (c) mobilize available resources (Greenstone & Leviton, 2011; Hoff, 2001; Roberts, 2000). Intervention during an individual crisis should be as immediate as possible and tailored to the specific needs of the client. Interventions may take place in many different settings, including counseling centers, hospital emergency departments, a client's home, or a location in the community.

The settings in which CMH counselors may encounter client crisis will depend in part on that counselor's specific role within an organization. Some agencies employ crisis counselors whose sole job it is to intervene in crisis situations. These counselors may be stationed at the agency itself or may be on call to area hospitals and community locations. Other CMH counselors are not designated as crisis counselors but will need to be prepared to intervene with routine clients who may present in crisis.

Emotional First Aid

Researchers have used the term **emotional first aid** to describe the unique approach to individual crisis intervention that distinguishes it from most forms of traditional counseling (Greenstone & Leviton, 2011; Wiger & Harowski, 2003). The premise of emotional first aid is that just as people need emergency treatment in order to stop physical bleeding, they also need first aid to control emotional bleeding in a crisis situation (Greenstone & Leviton, 2011). This highlights a very important distinction in the practice of crisis management: *Crisis intervention is not therapy* (Greenstone & Leviton, 2011; Hoff, 2001; Wiger & Harowski, 2003). Whereas traditional counseling often involves multiple sessions over a period of time with a focus on changing an individual's underlying cognitive, emotional, and behavioral patterns, crisis intervention is about triage, critical decision making, and damage control (Greenstone & Leviton, 2011; Hoff, 2001).

Greenstone and Leviton (2011) wrote that "psychotherapy and crisis intervention must never be confused. To do so could deny what victims need at a critical time in their lives" (p. 2). Clients in crisis are not mentally or emotionally prepared to explore and evaluate deeper life patterns. In fact, clients who are currently experiencing a crisis are more vulnerable to stressors that, under other circumstances, would be quite manageable, but in the throes of a coping system failure might overwhelm or further traumatize these individuals (Hoff, 2001). Although CMH counselors who are more accustomed to traditional counseling may struggle to remain solution-focused and brief during crisis intervention, it is of the upmost importance to do so (Wiger & Harowski, 2003). Just as emergency medicine is to medical practice, crisis intervention is to counseling (Greenstone & Leviton, 2011). The initial intervention is meant to provide emotional first aid with the least collateral damage possible, and follow-up is meant to manage recovery and to maintain gains.

Crisis Management Planning

In order to create and maintain the sense of structure, control, and organization essential to an effective crisis intervention, a specific plan to address individual crises must be established (Greenstone & Leviton, 2011). It is wise to first check with agency administration and determine if an established protocol for crisis intervention is in place. A CMH counselor can then build a plan around this protocol to ensure that it meets clients' needs and agency procedures. It can be helpful to write down the basic steps of a crisis intervention plan and to keep them in an accessible place. Subsequently, when a client crisis occurs, the counselor will not have to rely on memory to know the steps to take. Crisis situations can evolve at any time, in any place. Knowing what to expect is the key to reducing counselor anxiety while simultaneously meeting client needs.

A Model of Crisis Intervention

Multiple models in the literature provide guidelines for crisis intervention. Most encompass the same basic objectives: stabilization, assessment, and disposition (using available resources to formulate a longer-term plan). Greenstone and Leviton (2011) offer a particularly comprehensive yet succinct model with six steps.

Step 1: Immediacy. Immediacy alludes to Caplan's priority of timely intervention. Greenstone and Leviton (2011) note that intervention begins the moment the CMH counselor first encounters the client in crisis. Top priorities on first encounter include relieving anxiety, preventing further disorientation, and ensuring the safety of the client and others involved (Greenstone & Leviton, 2011). This may involve relocating a client to a safer setting, requesting medical intervention (in the event of injury), asking family members or others involved to clear the area (if the presence of others is creating additional anxiety for the client), and ensuring that the client's surroundings are as calm and stable as possible. It is important to also consider one's own safety when beginning an intervention. If a CMH counselor is responding to a client at home or in the community, and there is reason to believe that the situation may be unsafe, request a law enforcement escort or ask that an emergency response team be called to transport the client to an area hospital or other nearby setting that is more secure.

Step 2: Take Control. Often, the loss of self-efficacy in a crisis situation leaves clients feeling overwhelmed and helpless. An important role for a CMH counselor during crisis intervention is to take control of the situation on the client's behalf, until he or she can regain a sense of mastery (Greenstone & Leviton; Kaniasty, 2006). **Mastery** is a "belief in one's ability to control and manage life challenges" (Kaniasty, 2006, p. 133) and is an important contributor to posttraumatic growth. Therefore, creating control within the client's immediate environment not only helps to reduce anxiety but also models strategies for achieving mastery that the client can use moving forward.

In order to take control, Greenstone and Leviton (2011) recommend that a CMH counselor (a) be clear about what to control (the environment, not the client); (b) enter the crisis scene cautiously, using mindfulness skills to attend to any safety issues and to ground oneself in the space; (c) appear stable, supportive, and confident; (d) be clear and direct and orient oneself so as to attract the client's attention; (e) do not promise things that may not happen (i.e., telling the client that the counselor will "fix" the situation or that "everything will be all right"); and (f) guide the client using verbal and nonverbal communication, *only* using physical restraint if trained to do so (and only as a last resort). Although crisis intervention differs significantly from routine therapy, it is still important to use the core conditions of genuineness, acceptance, and empathic understanding as a framework for any therapeutic interaction. If control and structure are imposed too harshly, or are used only as a technique and are not genuine, the client will not respond favorably and may be further traumatized.

Step 3: Comprehensive Psychological Assessment. After a client has been medically stabilized and is in a safe and secure location, a comprehensive psychosocial assessment is the next step to effective crisis intervention. Remember that crisis is not the event itself but the individual's perception of the event. Therefore, the primary goal of the assessment is to gather as much pertinent information as possible while developing an understanding of the client's unique perspective and way of thinking about the situation (Greenstone & Leviton, 2011). This will facilitate the making of sound decisions that truly meet the client's individual needs and will build trust through communication of empathy and unconditional positive regard.

A vital part of any crisis assessment is evaluation of safety concerns. The crisis experience can feel isolating and hopeless and can in turn lead to a mental health emergency for some clients. **The SAD PERSONS Scale**, created by Patterson, Dohn, Bird, and Patterson (1983), is a brief, semistructured, and comprehensive assessment of safety concerns, with strong reliability and validity measures and a history of successful integration in counselor training programs (Juhnke, 1994; Juhnke & Hovestadt, 1995). SAD PERSONS is an acronym representing 10 safety risk factors that are assessed by the counselor and then scored based on a simple yes-or-no determination. The 10 risk factors are sex, age, depression, previous suicide attempt, ethanol (or other chemical substance) abuse, rational thinking loss, social supports lacking, organized plan (to harm self or others), no significant other, and sickness (chronic disease). These are detailed in Table 10.1, which also contains scoring guidelines. The SAD PERSONS Scale is particularly useful because it assesses several different areas of a client's life that may contribute to safety risk, and because it is easy to remember using a simple mnemonic. Juhnke (1996) also developed an adapted version of the SAD PERSONS Scale for use with children.

Other important areas of assessment include (a) the immediate circumstances of the crisis development, including triggering event; (b) the current status of family and other close relationships, noting sources of support and potential conflict; (c) medical history; (d) employment history (noting recent changes or lack of employment); (e) mental health and substance abuse history, including past diagnoses, treatment episodes, hospitalizations, current treatment providers, current psychotropic medications, and recent use of any chemical substances; and (f) strengths and coping skills that have or have not worked in the past. A good crisis intervention is quick, accurate, and comprehensive enough to provide an overall conceptualization of the client's current life state without going into a lengthy history. The assessment should be focused on the present crisis and events within the preceding 48 hours (Greenstone & Leviton, 2011).

Step 4: Disposition. After conducting a thorough assessment, determining a disposition is the next step of crisis intervention. A disposition is simply a decision about how best to handle the crisis, based on the counselor's appraisal of the client's prioritized needs. Deciding on the most appropriate disposition requires creative exploration of the available

Table 10.1   SAD PERSONS Scale

Risk Factors	Description	Scoring
SAD PERSONS	**Risk factor criteria**	**Add the following # of points if criteria met**
S = Sex	Male	1
A = Age	<19 or >45	1
D = Depression or hopelessness	Admits to feeling depressed or endorses multiple symptoms of clinical depression	2
P = Previous attempts or psychiatric care	History of attempting to harm self/others or significant periods of inpatient or outpatient care	1
E = Ethanol or drug abuse	Chronic or recent frequent abuse of alcohol or drugs	1
R = Rational thinking loss	Loss of touch with reality; inability to reason clearly	2
S = Social supports lacking	No close family, friends, job, or active community involvement	1
O = Organized plan	Thought-out plan to harm self/others	2
N = No significant other	Separated, divorced, widowed, recent significant breakup	1
S = Sickness	Chronic illness or disease	2
	TOTAL SCORE (Out of 14 possible)	
RECOMMENDED SCORE INTERPRETATION		
Total Points	**Proposed Clinical Action**	
0 to 2	Send home with follow-up	
3 to 5	Close follow-up; consider hospitalization	
6 to 7	Strongly consider hospitalization, depending on confidence in follow-up arrangements	
8 to 14	Inpatient treatment recommended	

Source: Adapted from Patterson, Dohn, Bird, & Patterson (1983)

resources and options, as well as collaborative consultation with supervisors and other professionals involved in the intervention (i.e., physicians, nurses, other service providers familiar with the client; Greenstone & Leviton, 2011).

A CMH counselor should avoid making determinations about disposition independently. Although there are times when circumstances do not allow for extensive consultation, eliciting the thoughts and opinions of other professionals who are unbiased will help a counselor feel comfortable regarding decisions and ensure that the most appropriate actions are taken. Disposition determination may involve making decisions about referral for inpatient versus outpatient follow-up care. Under some circumstances, an involuntary referral to an inpatient facility is appropriate. In making decisions about disposition, one should consider the outcome of the safety assessment, the expressed concerns of client collaterals (supportive family, friends, and other service providers), the wishes of the client, and what makes the most sense from the counselor's perspective. One should weigh all available input and be confident in a professional assessment of the situation. It is important to keep in mind that the disposition should be based on *the counselor's* professional appraisal of the client's needs, which may differ from what the client or client's family requests. When in doubt, it is always best to err on the side of caution and to opt for the recommendation that will best protect the client's safety and the safety of others.

Step 5: Referrals. Once a disposition is determined, the counselor should facilitate appropriate referrals. It is helpful to create a list of local referral sources in the area to have on hand for crisis intervention situations. Ask other professionals about referral options and get to know the available resources in the community so that referrals can be tailored to the client's specific needs. Referral lists should be updated regularly to make certain that contact information is current. One should also learn about fees and payment options at referral facilities in order to inform clients up front. Offering a detailed explanation of how the client should make contact with the facility and what he or she should expect will improve the chances of follow-through. If possible, CMH counselors should help the client call and make an appointment with the referral facility immediately following the assessment. Having a plan in place, and providing the client with a written copy of that plan, can significantly reduce the anxiety of a crisis situation. Ideally, significant others are involved as well, and the client is asked to sign a release of information so that friends or family members may be informed about the plan. Collaterals can help make sure the client gets to the referral facility for his or her appointments.

Step 6: Follow Up. Follow up with crisis clients to verify that contact with referral agencies has been made. The time frame for follow-up will depend on the recommendations and severity of the client crisis. If the crisis involved an emergency, and the client was not referred for hospitalization, follow-up should occur within 24–48 hours of the crisis intervention. If, however, the crisis did not involve an emergency, follow-up within the week may suffice. If the individual has not made contact with referral sources, the counselor will want to inquire about potential obstacles (Greenstone & Leviton, 2011). It is not uncommon for individuals to minimize the need for continued support and services after an acute crisis has passed. However, appropriate follow-up treatment is essential to maximizing the potential for growth after crisis, preventing worsening of clinical symptoms, and building effective coping skills to guard against future crises.

Crisis Resolution

The ultimate goal of any crisis intervention is **crisis resolution**, a return to equilibrium and reestablishment of effective, functioning coping mechanisms (Hoff, 2011; Roberts, 2000).

Although the intervention itself is usually quite brief, ideally occurring within the first 24 to 72 hours (Wiger & Harowski, 2003), more extensive crisis management may be necessary following the initial intervention in order to provide additional professional support, guidance, and structure as the client works to reach crisis resolution. Crisis management may take place on an outpatient or an inpatient/residential basis, depending on what the immediate safety and stabilization needs were upon assessment. Longer-term crisis management can last anywhere from one to 12 weeks following the crisis onset and frequently draws on resources within the client's family, peer group, and community as a means of establishing reliable support networks to reinforce new coping skills (Roberts, 2000).

Ethical Considerations

Any discussion of crisis planning should include a reflection on related ethical guidelines. In the role of professional assessor and decision maker, a CMH counselor intervening with an individual in crisis holds a unique position of power (Hillman, 2002). If abused, that power could easily influence a client and his or her family to make decisions about care that are neither safe nor in the client's best interest (ACA, 2014; see A.4). Thus, adhering to ethical guidelines for professional practice outlined by the American Counseling Association and other related organizations is vital to effective and professional crisis intervention. Current ACA ethical guidelines regarding consent, disclosure, and consultation are particularly salient.

Even in the midst of individual crisis, it is best practice to request consent from a client before delivering professional services or transmitting protected health information (ACA, 2014). However, some circumstances may arise in which a client is unable to give consent or in which the physical health and well-being of the client or others is threatened. Under such circumstances, consent and confidentiality may be waived *if* doing so will protect the client and/or others from "serious and foreseeable harm" (ACA, 2014; B.2.a). If and when information about a client is disclosed to another source, the ACA calls for counselors to limit the information shared to only that which is necessary to the client's care (ACA, 2014; B.2.a).

EMERGENCY AND DISASTER RELIEF

The imagery of a sailor was evoked earlier to provide a metaphor of the inundation and terror individuals can experience during a crisis. Now imagine the storm that swept away the sailor's boat has formed into a tsunami moving toward the towns situated along the shoreline. As the massive wave heads toward shore, people stare in horror and helplessness as their lives, loved ones, and property are threatened. A very real form of disaster, the image of a tsunami wave demonstrates the difference in the magnitude of impact between an individual crisis and a disaster. In contrast to an individual crisis, a disaster constitutes a traumatic event on a larger scale that affects a wider area and population of people, often leaving a permanent mark on the environment or community (Myers & Wee, 2005). A **community emergency** is a type of individual crisis that may impact multiple individuals at once and require additional community resources in response to the crisis, but typically local personnel can manage the incident. Examples of community emergencies include automobile accidents, house or apartment fires, or crimes that affect only a small part of the community. A disaster, on the other hand, is both an individual crisis and a community emergency that (a) tends to occur quickly with an acute onset, (b) has a collective impact on multiple individuals, (c) significantly disrupts day-to-day life and biopsychosocial resources, (d) affects everyone who witnesses it, and (e) involves multiple traumatic events and a spectrum of losses (Halpern & Tramontin, 2007).

The focus on disaster mental health (DMH) training has become a recent trend in the counseling profession. Starting in the 1980s, mental health practitioners realized that personal crises could be better understood by studying the psychological effects after a disaster, because the reactions of large numbers of people could be studied in the aftermath (Halpern & Tramontin, 2007). Moreover, knowledge about normative stress reactions, risk and protective factors, and social responses can guide small- and large-scale crisis preparedness and response. In the past century, the rise in technology has led to an increase in the frequency of disasters due to inventions such as modern transportation and man-made weaponry, leading to larger-scale human-caused disasters and terrorism. Additionally, the intensity of natural disasters has been magnified as larger numbers of people cluster together in cities with large infrastructure (Halpern & Tramontin, 2007). Thus, the need for DMH services is more relevant than ever.

Just as there are different types of individual crises, disasters can occur in multiple forms. Most DMH experts agree that there are three types of disasters (Myers & Wee, 2005).

- **Natural disasters**. Natural disasters are those that are beyond human control and are often described as "acts of God." Many natural disasters, however, are predictable, and wide-scale damages can be avoided through warnings and preparation. Natural disasters include weather phenomena such as floods, hurricanes, tornadoes, droughts, landslides, wildfires, earthquakes, heat waves, and blizzards, as well as disease epidemics.

- **Technological or human-caused disasters**. Natural and technological or human-caused disasters are not discrete categories in that natural disasters can lead to technological ones, or vice versa. Technological or human-caused disasters are those that occur due to human disregard, error, or at times, intentionality. Large transportation accidents, residential or urban fires, toxic pollution, structural collapse, and nuclear accidents are all elements of technological or human-caused disasters. Whereas natural disasters are seen as inevitable, technological or human-caused disasters tend to be perceived as more preventable, leading to feelings of intense anger, betrayal, confusion, and distrust among survivors.

- **Terrorism**. Terrorism, although a technological or human-caused disaster, is often defined as a specific type of disaster because terrorism is an act of "*commission* as opposed to *omission*" (Myers & Wee, 2005, p. 10). From the Latin word *terrere*, terrorism means "to frighten," and indeed the goal of terrorism is to psychologically attack an entire group of people by evoking fear, horror, and distress through a targeted act (Dass-Brailsford, 2007). Because terrorism is an intentional act of malevolence toward a specific group of people, it tends to produce more severe symptomology in survivors than the other two types of disasters (Norris et al., 2002).

DMH experts have identified five major phases of a disaster: (1) predisaster, (2) heroic or rescue, (3) honeymoon, (4) disillusionment, and (5) recovery (Myers & Wee, 2005). The **predisaster** phase includes the stages of threat, warning, and impact. The **threat** stage encompasses the time before a potential disaster occurs, and the **warning** stage begins when a disaster is imminent. Although the threat stage occurs in all types of disasters, the warning stage typically happens in just natural disasters, because it is almost impossible to predict when technological disasters and terrorism will occur. The lack of a warning stage is in part why the psychological impact is greater for technological disasters and terrorism because individuals have little control over their situations once the impact occurs. The **impact** stage is the period of time during which the disaster takes place. During the impact stage, people may experience fear, physical symptoms of stress (i.e., the fight-or-flight response), time distortion, confusion, and disbelief. Most people will take action to preserve the physical well-being of themselves and their loved ones.

During the **heroic or rescue** phase, survivors move from disbelief and fear into action to help save lives and property of others in the community. Typical responses during this stage include shock, horror, euphoria, high energy, confusion and disbelief, and difficulties in problem solving and priority setting. The heroic phase also includes a period of taking inventory, in which people try to orient themselves to the aftermath, assess the scope and extent of the damage, and seek information about the condition of loved ones and property. After the heroic period, the **honeymoon** phase can start within several days after the disaster and last up to 3 months. Often, the affected community is inundated with financial, material, and human resources from large-scale relief efforts from the government or community organizations. During this phase, media attention helps bring additional support to the community in the form of donations and relief workers. The community comes together with a spirit of survival, optimism, hope, and the sense that the worst is over.

After the initial outpouring of support for the affected population and sense of community cohesion of the honeymoon phase, the **disillusionment** phase sets in during the days to weeks after impact. Survivors begin to realize the limitations that will prevent them from rebuilding their selves, homes, and community, such as complicated regulations, bureaucratic red tape, drawn-out procedures of the government and insurance companies, and scarce resources. Often, survivors experience fatigue, fear, anxiety, and depression as they encounter barrier after barrier in returning to normalcy. Individuals shift from a focus on community cohesion to rebuilding their own personal lives. During the **recovery** phase, which can last for years after a disaster, survivors work toward establishing predisaster functioning. Individuals work to heal physically, mentally, emotionally, spiritually, and financially. Communities work to rebuild infrastructure and foster social connections across individuals. There will be delays and setbacks, and anniversaries of the disaster may trigger unpleasant memories and distress. As time passes, most survivors are able to come to a point where they can reflect on their experience during the disaster, acknowledge how far they have come, appreciate those who helped them heal, and look forward to a stable future. Some individuals and communities may experience longer-lasting effects and never fully reach their predisaster functioning or stability following the disaster.

During the course of a disaster, counselors are an integral part of disaster response procedures to help reduce the psychological stress that survivors experience. Thus, counselors should be aware of the unique needs related to counseling survivors of a disaster. The U.S. Department of Health and Human Services (U.S. DHHS, 2003) identified guidelines for DMH counseling following emergencies and disasters, which are applicable to survivors across all cultural contexts and locations (Bemak & Chung, 2011). The key concepts for DMH counseling are as follows (U.S. DHHS, 2003):

- All individuals who witness a disaster are affected by it.
- Most individuals are resilient and will adequately function during a disaster, although their effectiveness may be diminished.
- Distress and grief are normal reactions following a disaster.
- Most of the emotional reactions of survivors stem from the disruption of everyday life due to the disaster.
- Most people do not think they need mental health support and will not seek out mental health services following a disaster.
- DMH counseling is more practical than psychological in nature.
- DMH counselors must uniquely tailor their interventions to the cultural context of the community in which they are working.
- DMH counselors must set aside traditional counseling methods, avoid mental health labels, and actively reach out to survivors.
- Social support systems are crucial to survivors' recovery.

These nine key concepts are explored in more depth throughout the chapter.

IMPACT OF CRISES AND DISASTERS

Erikson (1976) identified two types of disaster trauma, individual and collective trauma. **Individual trauma** refers to the distress and grief that individual survivors experience as a result of the trauma. **Collective** or **community trauma** occurs after a disaster when the social ties of survivors with each other and their daily activities are severed or disrupted. Social institutions, such as schools, health clinics, churches, and government, may be damaged or destroyed in the aftermath of a disaster. People may need to relocate to temporary housing away from their social support networks. Day-to-day tasks, such as washing clothes or obtaining prescriptions, may become complicated. Workers may lose their jobs if businesses fail, or find it difficult to commute to or concentrate at work in the aftermath of a disaster. Stress and fatigue can lead to familial conflict. As noted in the key concepts of DMH counseling, this collective trauma in the days, months, and years following a disaster can impact survivors' emotional response. Thus, an essential part of immediate, intermediate, and long-term DMH interventions is to address collective trauma to support individual healing (Myers & Wee, 2005).

Factors Influencing Mental Health After an Emergency or Disaster

Trauma experts have identified characteristics that influence the psychological impact of an emergency or disaster, which include characteristics of the event itself, community preparedness and response, and individual experiences and traits (Halpern & Tramontin, 2007; Myers & Wee, 2005; Warheit, 1986). Risk factors that influence individuals' mental health following an emergency or disaster are listed in Table 10.2.

Table 10.2 Risk Factors for Psychological Impairment Following Emergencies and Disasters

---

EVENT-RELATED RISK FACTORS

- Scope of impact
  - Refers to the number of people and structures affected
- Speed of onset
- Intensity
  - The violence level of the disaster
  - Terror and horror
- Duration of impact: Length of time that people are affected by the disaster

COMMUNITY RISK FACTORS

- Social preparedness
  - Predictability of involvement in crisis
  - Unfamiliarity with the crisis
- Sociocultural changes
  - Activities of daily living
  - Social support networks
  - Community structures left intact
- Rapidity of involvement in recovery efforts by population in crisis
  - Leadership
  - Relief resources

INDIVIDUAL RISK FACTORS

- Predisaster functioning
  - Predisaster emotional state and ability to manage stress
  - Predisaster psychological symptoms
  - Personality traits
- Perception that one can cope
- Centrality to event
  - Primary victims: Those directly experiencing impact of disaster
  - Secondary victims: Those who witnessed disaster but did not experience actual impact
- Threat
  - Separation from family
  - Fear and panic during disaster
  - Injury to self or family member
  - Property damage

Groups at Risk

Although some populations may be more at risk for experiencing severe psychological symptoms after an emergency or disaster, counselors should note that everyone who witnesses a disaster is affected by it (Myers & Wee, 2005). First responders and counselors are susceptible to **vicarious**, or secondary, **traumatization**, which occurs due to the stress of working at length with trauma survivors. Further, media coverage alerts the public to an emergency or disaster and brings relief efforts, yet extensive viewing of media coverage also can create vicarious trauma. Just as any crisis temporarily interrupts an individual's ability to cope and function normally, vicarious trauma can deeply impact an individual's functioning on both professional and personal levels (Trippany, Kress, & Wilcoxon, 2011). Thus, in an era where humans are bombarded by information through the media, the efforts of DMH counselors need to extend to the community at large and not just the area affected by the disaster (Myers & Wee, 2005).

For counselors responding to those who experience an emergency or disaster directly, researchers have identified populations at risk for distress and severe mental health issues. Groups that are more at risk for psychological impairment after a traumatic event include children and adolescents, middle-aged adults, parents, and females, particularly married women and mothers. Effects by gender and age might vary based on the sociocultural and economic context of the area where the disaster occurs (Norris et al., 2002). Individuals with preexisting psychological symptoms and serious physical health problems or disabilities tend to experience more distress. Moreover, individuals with family instability, economically disadvantaged populations, and those who live in developing countries are at risk for moderate to severe distress following a disaster. Finally, survivors who experienced threat to themselves, loved ones, or property as well as those with firsthand exposure to severe life threats or visual horrors of the disaster fare worse psychologically in the aftermath of a disaster (Halpern & Tramontin, 2007; Norris, Friedman, & Watson, 2002; Norris et al., 2002).

Groups that show more resilience following a disaster are those with higher education levels and incomes, males, the elderly (65 years and older), and those with extensive social support networks. Belief in one's ability to cope, regardless of coping mechanisms used (except for avoidance and blaming), is related to better psychological functioning after a disaster (Norris et al., 2002).

Most individuals exposed to traumatic stress will not develop persistent mental health problems. Of 60,000 disaster victims studied between 1981 and 2001, 39% showed severe to very severe psychological impairment following the disaster (Norris, Friedman, & Watson, 2002). Most people, however, will experience stress reactions that are transient right after a disaster, lasting up to 2–3 months (Katz, 2010) and occasionally may experience similar reactions even years later (Ruzek et al., 2007). Typical reactions to a disaster are summarized in Table 10.3 (Dass-Brailsford, 2007; Halpern & Tramontin, 2007; Myers & Wee, 2005).

Although most survivors do not develop severe psychological impairment after an emergency or disaster, some survivors may experience great distress and require clinical intervention, particularly after acts of terrorism (Norris, Friedman, & Watson, 2002; Norris et al., 2002). CMH counselors need to be able to recognize signs than an individual may need follow-up care or medical treatment in addition to immediate DMH interventions. Signs of mental and emotional distress include serious disorientation (to self, others, place, time),

Table 10.3 Typical Reactions to Emergency and Disasters

EMOTIONAL REACTIONS

- Shock and disbelief
- Grief
- Denial or emotional numbness
- Anxiety, fear, or panic
- Impatience, irritability, or edginess
- Anger, resentment, or hostility
- Sadness, tearfulness, or depression
- Apathy or detachment
- Guilt and shame
- Feeling helpless and vulnerable
- Moodiness and emotionality

BEHAVIORAL REACTIONS

- Changes in eating patterns
- Hypervigilance
- Social withdrawal and isolation
- Increased conflict with others
- Need to surround self with family
- Difficulty communicating
- Hyperactivity
- Avoidance of reminders of the event
- Increased use of substances
- Changes in sex drive

EXISTENTIAL REACTIONS

- Crisis of faith
- Renewal/strengthening of faith
- Disruption to sense of self
- Difficulty making meaning

PHYSICAL REACTIONS

- Increased heart rate and blood pressure
- Short and shallow breathing
- Indigestion, nausea, diarrhea, constipation
- Headaches
- Exaggerated startle response
- Faintness or dizziness

(Continued)

Table 10.3 (Continued)

- Exhaustion and fatigue
- Sleep disruption
- Muscle tension or body pain
- Sweating, chills, or other changes in body temperature
- Lowered immune system response

COGNITIVE REACTIONS

- Worry
- Rumination or preoccupation
- Confusion
- Difficulty concentrating
- Loss of ability to problem-solve or prioritize tasks
- Memory impairment
- Slowness in thinking
- Forgetfulness
- Difficulty comprehending
- Idealization of or overidentification with the dead

diminished alertness and confusion, extreme feelings of panic or flashbacks, blunted affect, apathy, withdrawal and isolation from social support networks, extreme anger and impulsivity, suicidal or homicidal ideation, and episodes of dissociation (Ruzek et al., 2007). Symptoms that are intense enough to interfere with a person's basic functioning (e.g., drinking, eating, sleeping, finding safety) or moderate symptoms that last more than several months warrant more attention than immediate DMH care (Katz, 2010). Counselors should assess for intensity and duration of symptoms and take steps to ensure a person's safety if necessary. Common psychological disorders after exposure to disaster include PTSD, major depressive disorder (MDD), generalized anxiety disorder (GAD), panic disorder, and death anxiety phobias (Norris et al., 2002).

EMERGENCY AND DISASTER RESPONSE

Despite the distress that emergency and disaster survivors experience, many are reluctant to seek out mental health services (U.S. DHHS, 2003), in part due to the continuing stigma attached to issues of mental health (Myers & Wee, 2005). A normal stress reaction after a disaster, particularly human-caused disasters, is distrust and wariness. Thus, survivors may naturally be reluctant to share intimate thoughts and feelings with a complete stranger. In order to reach those experiencing distress after a disaster, counselors need to actively enter community sites and initiate discussions with survivors. DMH experts recommend that counselors avoid using labels that refer to mental health services, such as "counselors," or words that indicate psychopathology. Rather, it is recommended that DMH counselors refer to themselves as "support staff" or "human services workers" and describe their services as "assistance" or "stress support" (Bemak & Chung, 2011; Myers & Wee, 2005). Moreover, counselors need to be flexible in the ways they make connections and build rapport with survivors (Bemak & Chung, 2011). Rather than just sitting and talking about mental health issues as in traditional counseling, DMH counselors work in creative ways to initially connect with survivors by chatting about topics unrelated to the disaster, involving themselves in physical relief efforts, or joining in activities of social groups (e.g., throwing a football around or listening to music).

Individual mental and emotional healing is complicated by the disruptions to day-to-day life associated with collective trauma. Thus, DMH work tends to be more practical than psychological in nature (U.S. DHHS, 2003). People need social support and practical resources to return to normalcy after a disaster (Ruzek et al., 2007), rather than traditional clinical diagnosis and treatment. Moreover, pressuring survivors to talk about their trauma experience is *not* helpful and even potentially damaging (NIMH, 2002; Watson, 2004). Thus, counselors should not push survivors to "tell their stories," but instead focus on the immediate needs of the individual or group while creating an opening for the sharing of the traumatic experience if the survivor is ready. Three intervention approaches that have been implemented in the aftermath of disasters, psychological first aid (PFA), critical incident stress management (CISM), and disaster cross-cultural counseling (DCCC), were developed to address the practical life and coping issues that first responders and survivors of disasters may experience.

Immediate Interventions

When entering an emergency or disaster area, counselors need to coordinate with on-site agencies and organizations to set up the logistics and establish credibility of mental health services (Bemak & Chung, 2011). Counselors can connect with local and state departments of mental health or emergency services agencies. At a national level, both the American Red Cross (ARC) and Federal Emergency Management Agency (FEMA) have programs that coordinate with DMH counseling teams to employ mental health services at the site of a disaster.

Psychological First Aid

PFA was developed though the National Child Traumatic Stress Network (NCTSN) and the National Center for PTSD by a team of researchers and consultants based on previous research with postdisaster interventions that identified five intervention areas to address immediately following a disaster: (1) promoting psychological sense of safety, (2) introducing calming techniques, (3) encouraging self- and community efficacy, (4) advance social connectedness, and (5) instilling hope (Hobfoll et al., 2007). Although easily confused with the individual crisis intervention concept of emotional first aid, PFA is a specific intervention developed for disaster relief situations. PFA is aimed at solving short- and long-term practical issues (e.g., housing, food, medical care, financial aid), reducing distress, and supporting short- and long-term adaptive coping skills and can be delivered anywhere survivors are found (Vernberg et al., 2008). Moreover, PFA interventions are designed to be multiculturally appropriate for people of all ages, developmental levels, and backgrounds (Vernberg et al., 2008) and acknowledge the importance of the family and other social systems (Ruzek et al., 2007). The core actions and goals of PFA are outlined in Table 10.4. The full *Psychological First Aid Field Operations Guide* (Brymer et al., 2006) is available online at www.ncptsd.va.gov and www.nctsn.org.

Although the concept of psychological first aid has been used in DMH services for years, the systemized PFA approach has only occurred in the past decade, and thus the research examining PFA's effectiveness is virtually nonexistent. PFA, however, was developed on an empirical review of the literature to identify core intervention areas (Vernberg et al., 2008), and Halpern and Tramontin (2007) suggest that significant components of therapeutic relationships that lead to successful outcomes, such as empathy, goal consensus, and collaboration, are incorporated into PFA. At this time, PFA is a DMH approach that adapts

Table 10.4   Core Actions and Goals of Psychological First Aid

1. Contact and Engagement

   Goal: Respond to contacts initiated by affected persons or initiate contacts in a nonintrusive, compassionate, and helpful manner.

2. Safety and Comfort

   Goal: Enhance immediate and ongoing safety and provide physical and emotional comfort.

3. Stabilization (if necessary)

   Goal: To calm and orient emotionally overwhelmed or distraught survivors.

4. Information Gathering: Current Needs and Concerns

   Goal: Identify immediate needs and concerns, gather additional information, and tailor PFA interventions.

5. Practical Assistance

   Goal: To offer practical help to the survivor in addressing immediate needs and concerns.

6. Connection with Social Supports

   Goal: To reduce distress by helping structure opportunities for brief or ongoing contacts with primary support persons or other sources of support, including family members, friends, and community helping resources.

7. Information on Coping Support

   Goal: To provide the individual with information (including education about stress reactions and coping) that may help him or her deal with the event and its aftermath.

8. Linkage with Collaborative Services

   Goal: To link survivors with needed services and inform them about available services that may be needed in the future.

Source: Reprinted from Ruzek et al. (2007) with permission from the American Mental Health Counselors Association.

the core helping skills used in traditional therapy to enhance survivors' adjustment after a trauma based on specific, empirically grounded intervention areas, creating a practical and flexible approach for survivors of all backgrounds.

Disaster Cross-Cultural Counseling

Bemak and Chung (2011) created disaster cross-cultural counseling (DCCC), a targeted group counseling intervention based on the nine key concepts of DMH services (U.S. DHHS, 2003) reviewed earlier in the chapter. The DCCC model focuses on culturally competent counseling that is applicable internationally and that can reach marginalized populations following a disaster. The goals of the DCCC model are to promote psychological safety and stability; integrate predisaster and postdisaster coping skills; clarify short- and long-term future directions; and foster a sense of hope, meaning, purpose, and mastery with survivors. Group supervision is incorporated into the DCCC model to promote accountability among mental health professionals, lessen the impact of the disaster on DMH workers, and to help group workers join with survivors to advocate for resources and services (Bemak & Chung, 2011). Because DCCC is a new approach to DMH, there currently are no published studies on its effectiveness. Similar to PFA except in a group setting, DCCC offers a framework for culturally sensitive, feasible, adaptable, and empowering interventions for survivors following a disaster.

Critical Incident Stress Management

Critical incident stress management (CISM), sometimes referred to as the Mitchell model, was developed in the 1980s and is designed for use with emergency workers and first responders. CISM is a multicomponent program that includes interventions of precrisis education and training, ongoing one-on-one psychological support and stress education, on-scene support interventions for disasters such as demobilization or crisis management briefings, small-group defusings, family and organizational support, critical incident stress debriefing (CISD; sometimes termed psychological debriefing), and follow-up and referral services for continued care (Myers & Wee, 2005). Because CISM was one of the first crisis intervention models designed to reach large numbers of people at once, CISM, particularly CISD, was quickly adapted to be used with community members, in addition to first responders, in the aftermath of a disaster. The goals of CISM are to provide support and primary prevention to lessen the impact of the disaster for first responders and members of a community after a traumatic experience (Mitchell, 2003).

There has been significant debate among DMH experts about the usefulness of CISM, particularly CISD. In terms of long-term psychological impairment, such as PTSD, depression, and anxiety symptoms, some researchers have suggested that participating in CISD right after a disaster did not affect, or sometimes negatively affected, survivors of a trauma (NIMH, 2002). The main concern with CISD is that immediate postdisaster interventions that focus on emotional processing may interfere with protective coping skills like psychological distancing and may lead to increased symptoms of trauma (Ruzek et al., 2007). Despite these critiques, CISM, including the use of CISD, remains a prominent approach in the DMH field, used by organizations such as the International Critical Incident Stress Foundation.

Proponents for the use of CISD within the context of CISM argue that CISD was never intended for use with primary victims (i.e., those directly experiencing the impact of a disaster), in an individual context, or outside of the context of the CISM multimodal approach to disaster responses (Mitchell, 2003; Myers & Wee, 2005). Multiple studies with first responders found that CISD participants found the debriefing to be subjectively helpful immediately afterward, whether or not CISD decreased long-term psychological symptoms. Finally, some researchers have found that participants in CISM show a decrease in symptoms of distress and improved work functioning in the weeks and months following the intervention (Myers & Wee, 2005).

Although the use of CISD remains a hotly debated topic within the DMH field, the take-home points for CMH counselors who choose to use CISM are that (a) CISM is intended for homogeneous groups of first responders, staff workers, or other community members who may have experienced vicarious traumatization; (b) CISM needs to be implemented as a holistic approach—CISD should not be implemented as a stand-alone intervention; (c) CISD is intended to be a group intervention, not an individual one; (d) participation in CISD should never be compulsory but voluntary; (e) CISD should not be used with those who will be exposed to chronic stressors or trauma; and (f) CISM requires that counselors be trained in the program modules before implementation (Mitchell, 2003).

Intermediate and Long-Term Interventions

Although DMH tends to be focused on short-term early interventions, some survivors will need additional mental health treatment to address issues beyond that of transient distress. Brief cognitive behavioral therapy (CBT) is suggested to reduce symptoms of distress associated with PTSD and anxiety when secondary stressors have subsided, approximately 2 weeks to several months posttrauma. Researchers have found brief CBT, particularly the interventions of exposure therapy and cognitive restructuring, to positively affect psychological functioning months to years later with individual survivors of personal trauma (e.g., industrial accidents, motor vehicle accidents, and nonsexual assault; Ruzek et al., 2007; Watson, 2004). Supportive or trauma-focused group therapy also may be appropriate interventions to help survivors relieve PTSD, depression, or grief. Family therapy can be used as an adjunct to individual therapy to support survivors dealing with severe trauma symptoms. It also may be warranted to help resolve familial conflict or aid family members in dealing with loss (Halpern & Tramontin, 2007).

DISASTER MENTAL HEALTH TRAINING

Because DMH efforts differ significantly from traditional therapy, CMH counselors who want to provide DMH services need to seek additional training in order to effectively respond to survivors. Counselors can receive training and become part of disaster response teams through the American Red Cross. For more information on DMH training, contact your local Red Cross agency. Additionally, the National Organization of Victims Assistance (www.trynova.org) and Green Cross Academy of Traumatology (www.greencross.org) offer

DMH training and response networks. Counselors can be trained in PFA online through the NCTSN and the National Center for PTSD, and CISM training is offered through the International Critical Incident Stress Foundation (www.icisf.org) and the Salvation Army (www.salvationarmyusa.org).

There are practical considerations that counselors need to take into account when deciding to respond to emergencies or disasters. Counselors need to have conversations with their family, employer, friends, and colleagues before becoming part of a response team because DMH work requires leaving your family and job for a period of time, and with little advance notice, to respond to a crisis. Moreover, the support from loved ones and colleagues is essential to self-care. During DMH work, the chaotic environment following a disaster may lead to ethical dilemmas such as maintaining confidentiality, dual relationships, unavoidable professional boundary crossings, and difficulty in obtaining informed consent (Halpern & Tramontin, 2007). Counselors can ensure professional and ethical practice when responding to an emergency by following the ACA Code of Ethics; adhering to the policies of volunteer organizations or agencies; and consulting with response team coordinators, supervisors, and fellow DMH workers. Finally, counselors planning to engage in DMH services need to check with their employers about the extension of liability and worker's compensation coverage when responding to an emergency or inquire about coverage when signing up to respond through a nongovernmental or governmental agency (Kantor, 2010).

IMPACT OF CRISIS COUNSELING AND DISASTER RELIEF WORK ON CMH COUNSELORS

Following the recommendations outlined for client conceptualization, intervention, crisis management, and crisis planning will help prepare CMH counselors for handling client crises effectively. Working closely with clients in crisis, however, can have a profound impact on a counselor's well-being. Earlier in this chapter, we noted that exposure to clients in crisis can create a crisis for the counselor as well; even the most practiced crisis counselors are susceptible to burnout, vicarious trauma, and compassion fatigue. The effects of burnout and compassion fatigue, as well as self-care strategies, are outlined extensively in Chapter 12 on wellness, self-care, and burnout prevention. In terms of working with clients in crisis, having a personal crisis intervention plan in place can lower anxiety and boost counselor mastery in handling such situations with professionalism and confidence (McAdams & Keener, 2008). Moreover, Trippany et al. (2011) recommend that counselors who work frequently with crisis management take some specific measures to guard against the development of vicarious trauma: (a) limit the number of crisis interventions and trauma clients you work with in a given week, (b) engage in peer supervision groups, (c) seek specific training in crisis work in order to maintain your skills, and (d) spend time focusing on personal self-care. Knowing how and when to engage in your own self-care is integral to any counseling practice and especially relevant in this context.

Similar to crisis counselors, counselors responding to emergencies and disasters will face psychological stress because everyone who witnesses a disaster and its aftermath is impacted.

Practicing self-care can decrease counselors' risk for vicarious traumatization, burn-out, compassion fatigue, and other symptoms of distress. Steps for managing stress during DMH operations include sticking to assigned shifts, taking breaks, taking time off from DMH work if needed, eating and drinking well, exercising, seeking support from colleagues and family, breathing deeply, and continuing to engage in everyday stress relief activities on site (American Red Cross, 2012). Upon returning home from the disaster site, counsel-ors should consider taking a few extra days off from their everyday jobs to decompress and seek out a loved one, colleague, or professional to process the experience (Halpern & Tramontin, 2007).

CASE STUDY 1: CRISIS MANAGEMENT

Erik is a 15-year-old African American boy whose stepmother has brought him to the hospital emer-gency department. She claims that he has been refusing to go to school and has stayed locked in his room for the past 3 days. His stepmother reports that Erik has seemed depressed for months and that she and Erik's father have tried on several occasions to talk to him but that Erik continually refuses. She mentions that Erik and his father do not get along very well and that they "get into it" a lot. She states that earlier today while Erik was in the kitchen getting a soda, she noticed that he was bleed-ing and had a long, deep cut running down the length of his forearm. Upon realizing that she had seen the cut, he appeared angry and retreated to his room. Erik's stepmother had to call his father home from work in order to get him out and bring him to the hospital. The emergency physician has already evaluated Erik and treated his cut, which required six stitches. He has called you in to conduct a crisis assessment and intervention, advising that Erik has no known history of mental health or substance abuse treatment.

Discussion

1. What first steps would you take in approaching Erik and his family, based on Greenstone and Leviton's model of individual crisis intervention?

2. What additional information would you want to know as part of your assessment?

3. Let's assume you used the SAD PERSONS Scale to assess Erik's immediate safety needs, and he scored a 5, indicating moderate risk. What follow-up questions might you have for Erik, his family, or other collaterals in order to formulate an appropriate disposition? What dispositions would you consider?

4. Would you consult with anyone outside of Erik's family in formulating your disposition? If so, whom?

5. What follow-up might be indicated based on your chosen disposition?

CASE STUDY 2: DISASTER MENTAL HEALTH

Approximately a week after a devastating earthquake strikes southern California, you respond as part of a DMH team trained in psychological first aid. Thousands of people were injured as major infrastructures collapsed. As you walk through a temporary housing area, you encounter Camila, a Latino woman in her early 50s who is standing alone in a corridor among the houses. You notice that Camila appears extremely anxious and is trembling, sweating, and breathing shallowly.

Discussion

1. According to PFA, what are the first steps you would take in helping Camila?

2. What types of stabilization interventions may be appropriate for Camila?

3. What other information would you need to determine whether Camila's reaction is normative stress or serious psychological impairment?

4. How would you go about providing Camila with multiculturally appropriate care?

5. Would other DMH counseling strategies besides PFA be appropriate to use with Camila? Discuss the pros and cons of these counseling strategies.

REFERENCES

Allen, K. (1999). What are crisis services? In D. Tomlinson & K. Allen (Eds.), *Crisis services and hospital crises: Mental health at a turning point* (pp. 1–12). Brookfield, VT: Ashgate.

American Counseling Association. (2014). *ACA Code of Ethics*. Alexandria, VA: Author.

American Psychiatric Association. (2013). *Diagnostic and statistical manual of mental disorders* (5th ed.). Washington, DC: Author.

American Red Cross. (2012). *Disaster mental health handbook: Disaster services*. Retrieved from http://www.cdms.uci.edu/pdf/disaster-mental-health-handbook-oct-2012.pdf.

Bemak, F., & Chung, R. C. (2011). Post-disaster social justice group work and group supervision. *Journal for Specialists in Group Work, 36*, 3–21.

Boyraz, G., Horne, S. G., & Sayger, T. V. (2010). Finding positive meaning after loss: The mediating role of reflection for bereaved individuals. *Journal of Loss and Trauma, 15*, 242–258.

Brymer, M., Layne, C., Jacobs, A., Pynoos, R., Ruzek, J., Steinberg, A., et al. (2006). *Psychological first aid field operations guide* (2nd ed.). Los Angeles: National Child Traumatic Stress Network and National Center for PTSD.

Callahan, J. (2009). Emergency intervention and crisis intervention. In P. M. Kleespies (Ed.), *Behavioral emergencies: An evidence-based resource for evaluating and managing risk of suicide, violence, and victimization* (pp. 13–32). Washington, DC: American Psychological Association.

Council for Accreditation of Counseling and Related Educational Programs. (2016). *The 2016 Standards*. Retrieved from http://www.cacrep.org.

Dass-Brailsford, P. (2007). *A practical approach to trauma: Empowering interventions.* Thousand Oaks, CA: Sage.

Dattilio, F. M., & Freeman, A. (2009). Introduction. In F. M. Dattilio & A. Freeman (Eds.), *Cognitive-behavioral strategies in crisis intervention* (3rd ed., pp. 1–22). New York: Guilford Press.

Erikson, K. T. (1976). *Everything in its path: Destruction of community in the Buffalo Creek flood.* New York: Simon & Schuster.

Golan, N. (1978). *Treatment in crisis situations.* New York: Free Press.

Gold, J. (2011). *States' mental health budgets fall in recession.* Retrieved from http://www.kaiserhealthnews.org.

Greenstone, J. L., & Leviton, S. C. (2011). *Elements of crisis intervention.* Belmont, CA: Brooks-Cole.

Halpern, J., & Tramontin, M. (2007). *Disaster mental health: Theory and practice.* Belmont, CA: Thomson Higher Education.

Hillman, J. L. (2002). *Crisis intervention and trauma: New approaches to evidence-based practice.* New York: Kluwer Academic/Plenum.

Hobfoll, S., Watson, P., Bell, C., Bryant, R., Brymer, M., Friedman, M. J., et al. (2007). Five essential elements of immediate and mid-term mass trauma intervention: Empirical evidence. *Psychiatry, 70,* 283–315.

Hoff, L. A. (2001). *People in crisis: Clinical and public health perspectives* (5th ed.). San Francisco: Jossey-Bass.

Juhnke, G. A. (1994). SAD PERSONS scale review. *Measurement and Evaluation in Counseling and Development, 27*(1), 325–327.

Juhnke, G. A. (1996). The adapted-SAD PERSONS: A suicide assessment scale designed for use with children. *Elementary School Guidance and Counseling, 30*(4), 252–258.

Juhnke, G. A., & Hovestadt, A. J. (1995). Using the SAD PERSONS scale to promote supervisee suicide assessment knowledge. *The Clinical Supervisor, 13*(2), 31–40.

Kaniasty, K. (2006). Sense of mastery as a moderator of longer-term effects of disaster impact on psychological distress. In J. Strelau & T. Klonowicz (Eds.), *People under extreme stress* (pp. 131–147). New York: Nova Science.

Kantor, E. (2010). Liability issues. In F. J. Stoddard, C. L. Katz, & J. P. Merlino (Eds.), *Hidden impact: What you need to know for the next disaster: A practical mental health guide for clinicians* (pp. 195–205). Sudbury, MA: Jones & Bartlett.

Katz, C. L. (2010). Assessment: A spectrum from normal to psychopathology. In F. J. Stoddard, C. L. Katz, & J. P. Merlino (Eds.), *Hidden impact: What you need to know for the next disaster: A practical mental health guide for clinicians* (pp. 45–52). Sudbury, MA: Jones & Bartlett.

McAdams, C. R., & Keener, H. J. (2008). Preparation, action, recovery: A conceptual framework for counselor preparation and response in client crisis. *Journal of Counseling & Development, 86*(4), 388–398.

Mitchell, J. T. (2003). *Crisis intervention and CISM: A research summary.* Retrieved from http://www.cism.cap.gov.

Myers, D., & Wee, D. F. (2005). *Disaster mental health services.* New York: Routledge.

National Alliance on Mental Illness. (2011). *State mental health connections: The continuing crisis.* Retrieved from http://www.nami.org/budgetcuts.

National Institute of Mental Health. (2002). *Mental health and mass violence: Evidence-based early psychological intervention for victims/survivors of mass violence. A workshop to reach consensus on best practices* (NIH Publication No. 02–5138). Washington, DC: Government Printing Office.

Norris, F. H., Friedman, M. J., & Watson, P. J. (2002). 60,000 disaster victims speak: Part II. Summary and implications for disaster mental health research. *Psychiatry, 65,* 240–260.

Norris, F. H., Friedman, M. J., Watson, P. J., Byrne, C. M., Diaz, E., & Kaniasty, K. (2002). 60,000 disaster victims speak: Part I. An empirical review of the empirical literature, 1981–2001. *Psychiatry, 65,* 207–239.

Patterson, W. M., Dohn, H. H., Bird, J., & Patterson, G. A. (1983). Evaluation of suicidal patients: The SAD PERSONS scale. *Journal of Consultation Liaison Psychiatry, 24*(4), 343–349.

Roberts, A. R. (2000). An overview of crisis theory and crisis intervention. In A. R. Roberts (Ed.), *Crisis intervention handbook: Assessment, treatment, and research* (2nd ed., pp. 1–30). New York: Oxford University Press.

Ruzek, J. I., Brymer, M. J., Jacobs, A. K., Layne, C. M., Vernberg, E. M., & Watson, P. J. (2007). Psychological first aid. *Journal of Mental Health Counseling, 29,* 17–49.

Trippany, R. L., Kress, V. E. W., & Wilcoxon, S. A. (2011). Preventing vicarious trauma: What counselors should know when working with trauma survivors. *Journal of Counseling & Development, 82*(1), 31–37.

Tucker, B. J., Megenity, D., & Vigil, L. (1970). Anatomy of a campus crisis center. *The Personnel and Guidance Journal, 48*(5), 343–348.

U.S. Department of Health and Human Services. (2003). *Developing cultural competence in disaster mental health programs: Guiding principles and recommendations.* DHHS Pub. No. (SMA) 3828. Rockville, MD: Center for Mental Health Services and Substance Abuse and Mental Health Service Administration.

van der Kolk, B. A. (1987). *Psychological trauma.* Washington, DC: American Psychiatric Press.

van der Kolk, B. A. (2006). The body keeps the score: Brief autobiography of Bessel van der Kolk. In C. R. Figley (Ed.), *Mapping trauma and its wake* (pp. 211–226). New York: Routledge.

Vernberg, E., Steinberg, A., Jacobs, A., Brymer, M., Watson, P., Osofsky, J., et al. (2008). Innovations in disaster mental health: Psychological first aid. *Professional Psychology: Research and Practice, 39,* 381–388.

Warheit, G. J. (1986). A propositional paradigm for estimating the impact of disasters on mental health. In B. J. Sowder & M. Lystad (Eds.), *Disasters and mental health: Contemporary perspectives and innovations in services to disaster victims.* Washington DC: American Psychiatric Press.

Watson, P. (2004). Behavioral health interventions following mass violence. *Traumatic Stresspoints, 12,* 4–5.

Wiger, D. E., & Harowski, K. J. (2003). *Essentials of crisis counseling and intervention.* Hoboken, NJ: Wiley.

Yalom, I. (2002). *The gift of therapy: An open letter to a new generation of therapists and their patients.* New York: Harper Collins.

Maximizing Your Effectiveness as a Clinical Mental Health Counselor

SECTION III

Maximizing Your Effectiveness as a Clinical Mental Health Counselor

The Importance of Clinical Supervision to Effective Practice

DiAnne Borders

I took my first tennis lessons during my 20s. I had been playing tennis for some time and was good enough to be competitive against similarly amateur friends. I wanted to take lessons to enhance my skills and enjoyment of the game. Not surprisingly, my tennis teacher focused on the basics, such as how to hold the racket, appropriate trajectory of forehand and backhand strokes, foot movement, placement of the ball, and all the small movements that made up a good serve. We practiced these individually, over and over. It was some time before the lessons included extensive volleying of the ball back and forth over the net. When I played with my friends during this time, I was distracted by my self-consciousness, evaluating what I was doing: Am I holding the racket correctly? Did I turn my body at the correct angle? Can I toss the ball up at the right height to fully extend my swing for this serve? Should I go for a backhand return of this ball? Am I ever going to get this right? How can I remember everything? Will this ever feel smooth? I felt awkward and unsure about just about every aspect of my game.

The hardest part was unlearning the wrong things I had been doing for years, changing bad habits that I didn't know were bad habits before my lessons. I distinctly remember my teacher's deep sigh during one lesson, and then she said, "Sometimes I wish you had never played before."

My experience with tennis lessons comes to my mind often when I am supervising new counseling students. Many of them enrolled in a counseling program because friends had told them what a good helper they were, and helping others brought them much satisfaction. In their helping skills classes and prepracticum experiences, however, they were challenged to *unlearn* "bad habits" of helping, such as giving advice, problem solving, and trying to make friends feel better. In their skills courses, they have practiced, over and over, the individual skills of reflecting content, reflecting feelings, and asking open-ended questions, as well as an open body stance. They have experienced confusion, felt awkward and not very effective, and perhaps even questioned their decision to pursue a counseling degree.

They arrive at practicum or internship with these questions and doubts about their ability to work with "real" clients. They have a relatively good grasp of the basic skills, as performed individually in practice sessions. Now they are going to play a real game. Their challenge now is to put all those basic pieces together within a session in a way that helps the client. Here comes the ball (a client statement). Do I use a forehand stroke (reflection of content) or a backhand stroke (reflection of feeling)? Do I rush the net (use immediacy) or stay back (ask an open-ended question)? How do I know what is the *right* thing to do?

Welcome to clinical supervision!

MODELS OF CLINICAL SUPERVISION

Developmental Models

Developmental models (Blocher, 1983; Loganbill, Hardy, & Delworth, 1982; Stoltenberg, 1982; Stoltenberg & McNeill, 2009) help explain the experiences of new counselors. These models include stages of counselor development, starting with the first day in a counseling program to the master counselor who has been practicing 20 or more years. Similar to other developmental theories (e.g., Erikson, Piaget), the stages are **sequential** and **hierarchical**, suggesting that, as uncomfortable as some stages are, it is necessary for counseling students to experience the whole process to achieve their goal of becoming an effective counselor.

In early developmental stages, counseling students are very concerned with doing the "right" thing and typically believe there is *one* right thing to do. They look to their supervisors to tell them what that right thing is and can be frustrated by the lack of one right answer.

Beginning counselors listen intently to the client's story, work hard to remember all the details of the story, and worry when they can't remember everything. All the details of the story seem equally important, so the counselor tries to make sense of the details. Cognitively, beginning counselors are creating **schemas** or categories to help them understand clients and their issues. At this point, their categories tend to be rather basic due to their lack of experience, so there will be overgeneralizations. For example, new counselors may categorize clients broadly by the presenting issue or a particular client characteristic, such as "woman going through a divorce" or "low self-esteem" or "college freshman." They do not yet have the experience to see, nevertheless attend to, the variations and nuances within those broad categories. In addition, they tend to assume the client's story is *the* true and accurate story. To consider other perspectives seems overwhelming, perhaps even disrespectful. After all, is not the client the focus? To consider what information the client is *not* providing usually is outside their awareness.

Beginners tend to stay in their heads during sessions, trying to figure out what to say next. They also focus on how to help clients change their current circumstances, the sooner the better! The intention here is laudable but often leads new counselors to focus on problem solving too soon, before fully exploring relevant factors, such as unspoken feelings (e.g., anger beneath sadness), family context, and cultural values. They are surprised and confused when clients "resist" changing what they said they wanted to change. New counselors may then begin to question whether they are effective in working with clients. Indeed, after a few weeks I often hear, "This is a lot more complicated than I realized," and, sometimes, "I'm not sure I want to do this work"—especially the challenges of dealing with clients' intense feelings and pain and the often slow rate of progress and change.

Beginning counselors have heard that "their stuff" may get in the way of their counseling work but are not yet sure how their stuff will come up in sessions and fear if this happens it will signify that they are not appropriate for the counseling profession. They may have had discussions in their courses around "hot button" issues (e.g., abortion) and cultural factors (e.g., race/ethnicity, gender, sexual orientation) but likely have not bumped into their more individual beliefs, personality traits, and family messages that may emerge during their counseling work. They may be particularly unaware of how their *positive* leanings may get in the way. For example, a "protect the weak" value can lead to rescuing clients; an optimistic outlook can lead to rushing past a client's barriers to change; a "we don't whine in our family" message can lead to frustration with listening to a client's "complaints."

These, then, are some of the many concerns and questions new counselors bring to supervision. In fact, they often appear in supervision with long lists of questions about a client and session. Their focus at this stage is the counseling skills they are trying to apply. They want their supervisors to tell, teach, and model. They appreciate role-plays and practicing alternative responses while reviewing tapes of counseling sessions. These are all appropriate supervisory interventions for beginning counselors.

Usually, around the midpoint of the practicum semester, counseling students begin to feel some confidence, believing at least that they can make it through a session and that they have at least some potential to be effective, although some doubts about their work and their fit for the work remain. Their focus on self (What should I do?) shifts more to a focus on the client (What does this client need today? What is the client trying to tell me?). They have seen the power of the use of basic skills, as clients explored their fears and hesitations around change. As a result, these counselors have seen enough "exceptions" to their categories that they are creating more and more subcategories in their schemas for understanding clients (e.g., not all divorced women have the same stories, challenges, strengths, and options). In supervision, they are ready to start applying counseling theories to help them understand their clients, choose appropriate interventions, and identify relevant desired outcomes that are in line with their theoretical case conceptualizations. Increasingly, they are bringing their own voices into the counseling session.

According to developmental models, counselors' growth will continue into internship, where they will face new challenges with new clientele at the site as well as new professional experiences with site policies and procedures. Early on, they may feel they are regressing, as their anxiety or nervousness about their new setting and new clinical issues may shake their confidence, but they typically recover within a few weeks through their work with their supervisors. Their focus, having shifted earlier from self to client, now is reoriented to the counseling relationship, including the mutual influences in this and other relationships in the client's life. Their conceptualizations about their clients and counseling work will become more and more complex, they will become more comfortable with the ambiguity of clinical work, and they may begin to see and even appreciate paradoxes. They may struggle even more with ethical issues, given their more complex understanding of all the dynamics involved. They will become more accepting of a variety of worldviews and value systems. They will be able to reflect on their work more objectively and deeply. They will be able to state their strengths and growing edges, will be quite aware of assumptions and values that may trip them up, and will know which clients and clinical issues tend to "trigger" their issues. They will approach supervision as more of a consultative relationship, because they are better able to know what is not going well and where they need help and thus collaborate with their supervisors around gaining insights and determining how to proceed.

A caveat to the assumed developmental growth in these models is needed. Just as in general developmental theories (e.g., Piaget, Erikson, Mahler), growth can be stunted in several ways, such as the lack of a stimulating environment. It is likely that the work with clients and supervisors will provide a rich environment that encourages counselors' growth; at some points, all the new experiences may feel like too much stimulation!

Another potential barrier to development is the counselor's anxiety, even fear, about taking the risks necessary for growth. Clearly it is normal for beginning counselors to feel anxiety about their new role and responsibilities as well as receiving feedback from supervisors and peers. Learning to manage that anxiety, however, is critical. Counselors can consider how they generally experience anxiety in their lives (e.g., why types of situations make them anxious) as well as how they have pushed through to complete the feared action.

Counselors may find existing coping strategies will be helpful for managing their anxiety during counseling and supervision sessions, or they may ask their supervisors to help them brainstorm ideas. Some potential strategies include identifying and challenging one's thoughts (e.g., "I'm not doing this perfectly and my supervisor will see that" to "I'm just learning and will do this better next time"); scheduling a few minutes for quiet, calming, mindful focusing before each session; and creating notecards of "cheat sheets" listing topics that need to be covered in the session or steps in a counseling intervention planned for the session.

Developmental models suggest supervisors are primarily in a teacher role and primarily focused on counseling skills when working with beginning counselors. Bernard's (1979) discrimination model expands on the roles and focus areas of the supervisor.

Discrimination Model

Bernard's discrimination model has withstood the test of time; it seems as relevant today as it did when it was first published in 1979 (see also Bernard, 1997). This model is especially instructive around the appropriate content and goals of clinical supervision. The original model named three areas to be covered in supervision.

First, supervision includes a focus on counseling performance skills and behaviors, or what the counselor *does* during counseling sessions (Borders & Brown, 2005). Counseling skills include basic helping skills, such as reflection of feeling and open-ended questions, as well as more advanced skills, such as confrontation, immediacy, and interpretation. Also included are theory-based techniques and interventions, such as directing a gestalt two-chair experiment, disputing irrational beliefs, and asking solution-focused scaling questions.

Second, supervision includes a focus on cognitive counseling skills, or how the counselor *thinks* about a client, a session, and counseling in general. Bernard (1979) called this "conceptualization skills," which includes pulling together all the information a counselor has about a client to understand the etiology of the presenting problem and what factors may be influencing how the problematic thoughts, feelings, and behaviors are manifested. The client's coping style, sources of support, cultural contexts, and relationships with family and friends are other factors that may need to be considered. Often, this type of case conceptualization is the basis for discussion during group supervision.

Bernard's definition can be expanded, however, to include other counselor cognitions (Borders & Brown, 2005). In particular, counselors' cognitions *during* counseling sessions can be important to identify and discuss during supervision. Counselors are constantly making decisions about what to say or do next during a session, and doing this well is a critical cognitive skill. So, during supervision, counselors might be asked to identify the information they used to make a decision at some point in the session (e.g., invite the client to experience a two-chair experiment) and then encouraged to reflect on the information they failed to consider (e.g., nonverbal and verbal signals that the client is not ready for this intervention). Supervisors also may help the counselor recognize what aspects of the client's story they emphasized or gave priority (e.g., financial challenges affecting the client's marriage rather than the client's depression).

Third, supervision includes a focus on personalization (Bernard, 1979), or counselor self-awareness, how counselors *feel* about a client, their work, and themselves (Borders & Brown, 2005). Counselors' reactions to clients often provide insightful information—about the client (e.g., what type of response or reaction clients engender in others) and about the counselor (e.g., what personal values clients activate through their stories and actions). Counselors sometimes think growing in their self-awareness means discovering what their "deep issues" are, and this certainly can happen. More often, self-awareness insights are less dramatic. Counselors rediscover messages from their own early development that are affecting their counseling. Common messages include "we don't talk about negative emotions" or "we don't get angry" in our family. Counselors with those messages, then, would experience discomfort when a client talks about negative emotions or expresses anger, even as they are aware that this is exactly what the client needs to do. As counselors become aware of such messages during supervision, they also may remember how disempowering those messages felt, which may be a helpful motivation to get past the discomfort, or even fear, of discussing "forbidden" topics.

Similarly, counselors may discover their values are influencing their counseling work. Even positive values may be problematic when the client does not seem to share those values. For example, most counselors have a strong value around education; when an undergraduate client shares that she is just trying to get by and a grade of C will be fine, the counselor may react negatively. If the value can be identified during supervision, the counselor also may be guided to consider how the life circumstance of the client may be affecting her approach to her course; a single mother who is working full time and going to school full time may value the college degree for the job advancement it will allow her to achieve, and thus her ability to better provide for her family. It may be that the client would love to have the opportunity to experience her college education in ways similar to the counselor's valuing but is unable to give the time and energy that the counselor can give to her degree. Counselors may have identified other values through coursework, such as a multicultural counseling course, and may want to reflect on those values when they have positive or negative reactions to clients. Finally, counselors' awareness of their stress levels and ability to cope with demands in their lives is important. Counseling is demanding work that taxes all professionals at various points of time and can be especially challenging for new counselors who are experiencing those demands for the first time.

Lanning (1986) identified a fourth focal point for the discrimination model, that of professional behaviors. This area includes a range of behaviors, including "on the job" behaviors such as being on time to sessions, completing case notes on time, following protocols for scheduling or cancelling sessions, and dressing appropriately (in ways that do not distract the client). Other important professional behaviors involve adhering to ethical codes and acting in accord with legal mandates, including an agency's protocols for dealing with ethical and legal situations. Finally, this focus includes counselors' behaviors during supervision, such as being prepared for supervision (e.g., thorough evaluation of tapes of counseling sessions submitted for review), being receptive to supervisors' and peers' feedback, and providing constructive feedback for peers.

Bernard (1979) also identified three supervisor roles for addressing the counselor focus areas, creating a matrix of roles and focus areas (see Borders & Brown, 2005, p. 7). *Teachers* provide information and construct learning experiences (e.g., role-play) during supervision. In this role, for example, supervisors help counselors practice skills, ask questions to broaden counselor's case conceptualizations, describe how the counselor's reactions to a client give insights into that client, and explain how an ethical standard may apply to the client. *Counselors* apply their counseling skills during supervision to help the counselor achieve new insights. In this role, for example, they model facilitative skills, reframe counselors' negative conceptualizations so the counselor can have more empathy for a client (e.g., resistance as self-protection), and explore counselors' feelings about a peer's feedback. Importantly, supervisors operating from the counselor role do not act as counselors for their supervisees. When, together, the supervisor and counselor identify issues interfering with the counselor's work, the supervisor focuses on helping the counselor manage those issues and keep them out of the counseling room. If it appears that the counselor could benefit from additional work around the issue, the supervisor can encourage the counselor to seek her or his own counseling.

Consultants are more collaborative and rely more on the counselor to set the agenda for supervision. In this role, for example, they may brainstorm with the counselor potential interventions that would be appropriate with the client, ask questions that help the counselor determine how family dynamics are restricting the client's choices, explore potential countertransference with a client, and evaluate whether breaking confidentiality is necessary.

The discrimination model suggests supervisors can, should, and do operate from all three roles, but it is not prescriptive about which role is preferred when. Developmental models provide some guidance because they indicate beginning counselors likely will be best served by supervisors who primarily employ the teacher role, perhaps also relying on the counselor role to help new counselors manage their anxieties, questions about their fit for the counseling profession, and their reactions to clients.

Whatever the supervisor role, counselors should expect all four focus areas of skills, cognitions, self-awareness, and professional behaviors to be addressed during supervision. In fact, they may find that the evaluation form for their practicum or internship experiences references all four areas. It might be helpful, then, for counselors to use the four areas to write goals for their practicum and internship experience (discussed shortly).

Peer Models

The models presented thus far are appropriate primarily for individual supervision. Counseling students, however, also will be involved in group supervision with their peers and may have the opportunity to participate in triadic supervision, a relatively new supervision modality that involves one supervisor working with two supervisees simultaneously. Group supervision is required by the Council for Accreditation of Counseling and Related Educational Programs (CACREP, 2016); triadic is allowed by CACREP as a substitute for individual supervision. Beginning counselors often benefit from being in supervision with a peer, especially hearing that others have the same concerns, questions, fears, challenges, and doubts that they do.

For both group and triadic supervision, an additional underlying goal is helping supervisees learn to give each other constructive feedback, which can be challenging, intimidating, and even frightening for beginning counselors. Authors of triadic and group models, then, often propose some structure that teaches supervisees what to look for in their peers' work and how to deliver their observations and suggestions. Several examples of each modality are described next. Supervisees likely will experience some variation on these as part of their practicum and internship supervision.

Group Supervision Models

Wilbur and associates (Wilbur & Roberts-Wilbur, 1994; Wilbur, Roberts-Wilbur, Morris, Betz, & Hart, 1991) described one structured model. Their goals for the model include increasing group members' ability to give and receive feedback as well as reduce conflict and resistance to feedback. Their model follows these seven steps: (1) the presenting supervisee provides background information about a case, plays a portion of a session with the client, and then states a request for assistance (e.g., "I would like suggestions about where to go next with this client"); (2) other group members ask questions for clarification in a round-robin format; (3) the supervisor helps to identify the specific focus of the presenter's request (e.g., skills, self-awareness); (4) group members give feedback about how they would handle the identified issue in round-robin format (e.g., "If I were in your situation I would . . .") while the presenter remains silent (but might take notes); (5) the group takes a short break to allow the presenter to reflect on the group's feedback and prepare for the next phase; (6) the presenter reports which statements were helpful and which were not while the group members remain silent; (7) the supervisor leads a discussion of the process and/or group dynamics (optional). Wilbur and associates reported that students using their model experienced both personal growth and skill development.

Borders (1991; see also Borders & Brown, 2005; Lassiter, Napolitano, Culbreth, & Ng, 2008) outlined several goals for her structured peer group model, including making sure that all members are involved and give focused, objective feedback; encouraging supervisee self-monitoring and self-growth; enhancing awareness of group dynamics; and promoting cognitive complexity. First, the presenting supervisee states a request for feedback, which the supervisor may help to clarify (e.g., the broad request of "What could I do differently?" becomes "How can I help the client move toward a clearer understanding of her troubling relationship with her father and what she wants to do about it?"). Based on the presenter's request, the supervisor assigns *roles* or *perspectives* that group members assume while viewing a portion of the taped counseling session. Potential roles include the client, counselor, and significant person in the client's life relevant to the case (e.g., spouse, parent, teacher). Potential perspectives include focused observation of a particular skill (typically a skill identified by the presenter as problematic), applying a counseling theory to the case, attending to diverse perspectives within the counseling relationship, and creating a metaphor that describes the session or counselor-client relationship. After group members learn the model, the presenter (rather than the supervisor) may assign roles or members may request roles they think will facilitate their own learning (e.g., watching for the use of immediacy and/or opportunities to use immediacy when increasing the use of that skill is the supervisee's goal).

After watching the taped session, group members give their feedback from their roles and perspectives. Those speaking from a role are encouraged to use first-person language (e.g., "As the client, I wondered if you knew how scary it is for me to disclose these feelings to you"; "As the counselor, I am feeling a lot of pressure to 'fix' this client"; "As the client's husband, when she talks about what changes she wants in our relationship, I hear that it's all my fault, but I don't think that's true!"). Those speaking from a skills perspective highlight effective use of the skill, how it could be improved, and missed opportunities to use the skill (e.g., "You reflected the feeling, which was great, and then immediately asked a question before the client could respond"). Those speaking from a theoretical orientation provide a more academic perspective that may enhance case conceptualization and treatment planning (e.g., "It sounds like the client has some irrational beliefs about how her relationship with her father *should* be"). Those providing a metaphor may create a unique metaphor or use a common metaphor for the session and/or counseling relationship, such as a dance (e.g., "What's the pace of the dance/session? Are client and counselor doing the same dance? Who is leading the dance, or are both trying to lead?"; "I see you inviting her to dance, but when you hold out your hand she jumps away. You follow and again hold out your hand, and away she jumps again. You two are all over that room"). Those focusing on cultural dynamics offer their observations (e.g., "When she is talking about how upset she is that the white doctor discounted her symptoms, I wondered what it is like for her to tell this to a white counselor"). After each group member shares these observations and reflections, all discuss the feedback. Finally, the supervisor or presenter summarizes the feedback, new insights, and plans for next sessions, and the presenter indicates whether his or her needs were met.

The supervisor has several important roles during this process. As a *moderator*, the supervisor keeps the group on task and watches the time allocated to each counselor. As a *process observer*, the supervisor facilitates exploration of the feedback. For example, a group member may state, "As the client, I am not sure talking about this will help." The supervisor may ask the "client," "What did you want from the counselor just then?" and then ask the presenting counselor, "Were you aware the client felt this way?" Should the presenting counselor say yes, the supervisor might ask, "What did you want to say or do with that awareness?" and "What kept you from saying that?" In the process observer role, the supervisor also comments on group dynamics and process (e.g., "The group is pushing you to push her, and that seems difficult for you to hear"). Over time, as the group learns the model and develops trust among themselves, supervisees may begin to take on some of the supervisor's roles. In addition, counselors may begin to use the roles and perspectives during their counseling sessions, such as asking themselves, *What does the client want from me right now?*

Several researchers have investigated Borders's (1991) model. School counselors in Crutchfield and Borders's (1997) study rated specific, concrete feedback about counseling skills and techniques as the most helpful aspect of the model. Counseling students in Christensen and Kline's (2001) study said they gained more self-awareness than they had in other types of groups, reported peer feedback was key to their engagement in the model, and said the structure helped them learn how to give and receive feedback. Participants also indicated that the structured process helped them feel more interdependent and intimate within the group.

Triadic Supervision

Triadic supervision varies in terms of whether one or both supervisees present a case each week. Lawson, Hein, and Getz (2009) described a rotating or single-focused model. Each week, one supervisee presents a case and portions of the taped counseling session. The other supervisee takes roles or perspectives based on Borders (1991) and follows the directions for feedback from Wilbur & Roberts-Wilbur (1994) ("If I were the counselor, I would . . ."). The supervisor also may use other "action techniques," such as role-play. Lawson et al. (2009) emphasized the importance of a good peer match (e.g., similar skill levels and developmental needs) in triadic supervision.

Spice and Spice (1976) described a triadic method in which the members rotate roles of supervisor, commentator, and facilitator. In this approach, the presenter describes a case and plays a portion of a taped session, which the commentator has viewed before the session. The commentator shares observations and encourages dialogue about the points he or she thinks are most important. The facilitator focuses on the present, here-and-now dialogue, seeking to deepen the dialogue, much like Borders's (1991) process observer.

Stinchfield, Hill, and Kleist (2007, 2010) adapted a reflecting team approach from the marriage and family supervision literature. In their **reflecting process approach**, the supervisee presents tape of a session and discusses it with the supervisor while the peer is in an observer-reflector role. Then the supervisor and the peer discuss the session while the presenter listens silently in the reflective role. Finally, the supervisor processes the reflective role with the presenter while the peer observes. Stinchfield et al.'s students reported that the reflective role gave them the freedom to just listen, kept them from getting defensive, and helped them gain multiple perspectives. They said the observer role enhanced their conceptual and feedback skills.

Clearly, a key aspect of peer models is the quality of peer feedback. Beginning counselors may be reluctant to provide constructive feedback, sometimes falling into a "I'll be nice to you and you be nice to me" game, and/or they may not know what type of feedback they should give. Guidelines for giving feedback in triadic, especially, seem helpful. Recently in the counseling program at my institution, we have experimented with a different approach in triadic that our beginning counselors have found helpful in learning to give constructive feedback. Each peer selects a counseling session and completes a review form and then the peers exchange these and watch the peer's entire counseling session before the triadic supervision. We provide some specific questions for the session review, and counselors' responses to those questions are shared and discussed in session with the peer, facilitated by the supervisor. Review questions we have found helpful are listed here.

Peer Review Guidelines

As you listen to the counseling session, take on the *role of the client*. In giving peer review feedback, answer the following questions. Please write or speak in the first person (i.e., as the client).

What did you want from the counselor?

How did you feel during the session?

How was the counselor helpful?

No session is perfect, so what was one thing you wished for during the session that you didn't get?

What is your hope for the next session?

Now, thinking as the *peer counselor*, please respond to these questions:

What were the counselor's strengths during this session?

What metaphor seems to represent this session, the counselor-client relationship, and/or the client? Explain your metaphor.

Now, from your own perspective, respond to this question:

Name at least one thing you learned from hearing and observing this session.

How might you apply what you learned in your own counseling sessions?

In summary, developmental models help normalize the concerns new counselors bring to supervision, the discrimination model helps explain what they can expect in supervision, and group and triadic models describe some approaches supervisors may use to structure supervision that involve peer feedback. As needed, supervisors might use additional approaches, such as live observation and live supervision, which typically are used when the beginning counselor is working with particularly challenging clients and may need more immediate assistance.

Regardless of the model, structure, or approach used by the supervisor, however, supervisees have many opportunities to shape the supervision process so that it best meets their needs. In the following sections, actions that supervisees (especially beginning counselors) can take to maximize their supervision experience are described.

MAXIMIZING YOUR SUPERVISION EXPERIENCE

Practice Self-Assessment and Create Learning Goals

Conducting an honest self-assessment is an important skill for counselors, one that will be valuable throughout one's career. Self-assessments are the basis for identifying learning goals and evaluating progress toward those goals. Beginning counselors should practice self-assessments on an ongoing basis and typically have formal opportunities to do so at the beginning, middle, and end of a semester.

Learning goals are based on accurate and honest self-assessments of skills and other aspects of one's counseling work. Learning goals give the counselor and the supervisor a mutual focus for their work together in supervision. Beginning counselors, however, often have difficulty writing concrete goals because they are still learning the vocabulary of counseling and, even more, are still learning about their strengths and growing edges, and some may struggle, in particular, to "expose" their weaknesses through the goal-setting process.

The discrimination model provides a useful framework for creating learning goals that are specific and comprehensive. A list of concrete examples for each of the four focus areas is provided in Table 11.1, the evaluation form for a practicum course for first-year master's students in the Department of Counseling and Educational Development at The University of North Carolina at Greensboro. Counselors can use this form as an initial self-assessment; clearly those with lower ratings, or rated *not applicable* because counselors have not yet used them, would be a logical starting point for determining learning goals. Counselors should create at least one goal in each of the focus areas of counseling skills, case conceptualization skills, self-awareness, and professional behaviors/supervision behaviors. If the form also is used for midterm and final evaluations, counselors have a clear record of their progress toward their goals of increasing or improving the skills and behaviors they listed as their goals.

Table 11.1 Evaluation Form for Beginning Counselors' Practicum

Evaluation Form

Counseling Practicum

Practicum student/counselor _____   Semester _____

Assigned supervisor _____

Midterm evaluation _____ (date)   Final evaluation _____ (date)

Person completing this form _____

Evaluate each skill area using a scale of 1 (lowest) to 5 (highest). Use NA if not applicable.

Counseling Skills						
Demonstrates effective facilitative (basic helping) skills	1	2	3	4	5	NA
Creates a safe environment for client, rapport building	1	2	3	4	5	NA
Demonstrates effective and collaborative goal setting with clients	1	2	3	4	5	NA
Effectively handles informed consent	1	2	3	4	5	NA
Accurate and meaningful reflections of content	1	2	3	4	5	NA
Accurate and meaningful reflections of feeling	1	2	3	4	5	NA

Counseling Skills						
Ability to understand the uniqueness and meaning of client's story	1	2	3	4	5	NA
Demonstrates congruence in session	1	2	3	4	5	NA
Appropriate use of silence	1	2	3	4	5	NA
Appropriate use of self-disclosure	1	2	3	4	5	NA
Appropriate use of immediacy	1	2	3	4	5	NA
Appropriate use of open- and close-ended questions	1	2	3	4	5	NA
Understand and respond appropriately to nonverbal communication	1	2	3	4	5	NA
Ability to conduct intake sessions	1	2	3	4	5	NA
Ability to conduct first sessions	1	2	3	4	5	NA
Ability to conduct closure sessions	1	2	3	4	5	NA
Ability to accurately respond to a variety of client emotions	1	2	3	4	5	NA
Ability to keep the focus of the session on the client	1	2	3	4	5	NA
Ability to deal with client resistance	1	2	3	4	5	NA
Appropriate pacing and management of time in sessions	1	2	3	4	5	NA
Use of a variety of appropriate and intentional counseling approaches/strategies/interventions (e.g., cognitive, affective, behavioral)	1	2	3	4	5	NA
Ability	1	2	3	4	5	NA
Rationale	1	2	3	4	5	NA
Uses assessment instruments/results appropriately	1	2	3	4	5	NA
Ability to conduct crisis assessments/intervention	1	2	3	4	5	NA
Demonstrates growth/change in skills	1	2	3	4	5	NA
Comments:						

Case Conceptualization Skills						
Ability to create comprehensive, holistic assessment of client	1	2	3	4	5	NA
Considers background/demographic/cultural (worldview) information	1	2	3	4	5	NA
Considers environmental factors (e.g., stressors and resources)	1	2	3	4	5	NA
Considers cognitive, affect, behavioral, and interpersonal aspects of client	1	2	3	4	5	NA
Identifies patterns and themes	1	2	3	4	5	NA
Uses conceptualization as basis for planning sessions, choosing culturally sensitive interventions, collaboratively setting goals, and evaluating clients progress	1	2	3	4	5	NA

(Continued)

Table 11.1   (Continued)

Case Conceptualization Skills						
Comments:						
Self-Awareness						
Demonstrates willingness to explore self	1	2	3	4	5	NA
Uses reactions to clients appropriately and therapeutically	1	2	3	4	5	NA
Avoids imposing beliefs and/or values on clients	1	2	3	4	5	NA
Demonstrates sensitivity to cultural/multicultural dynamics	1	2	3	4	5	NA
Ability to understand personal culture and its effect on clients, sessions, and personal development as a counselor	1	2	3	4	5	NA
Ability to understand personal worldview and its effect on clients, sessions, and personal development as a counselor	1	2	3	4	5	NA
Able to manage transference and countertransference	1	2	3	4	5	NA
Demonstrates emotional stability	1	2	3	4	5	NA
Demonstrates ability to use awareness to seek additional supervision and assistance as needed	1	2	3	4	5	NA
Comments:						
Professional Behaviors						
Follows ethical and legal guidelines (e.g., confidentiality) and moral principles in all aspects of practicum	1	2	3	4	5	NA
Recognition of boundaries of personal competencies and limitations, and takes responsibility for seeking supervision and consultation regarding these	1	2	3	4	5	NA

Professional Behaviors						
Completes practicum paperwork in a timely manner	1	2	3	4	5	NA
Completes practicum paperwork accurately and completely	1	2	3	4	5	NA
Dresses appropriately	1	2	3	4	5	NA
Is on time for client sessions	1	2	3	4	5	NA
Observes clinic procedures and policies	1	2	3	4	5	NA
Is respectful of clinic staff members	1	2	3	4	5	NA
Appropriately seeks consultation outside of regularly scheduled supervision	1	2	3	4	5	NA

Comments:

Supervision Behaviors						
Ability to complete self-evaluation that includes strengths and areas for improvement	1	2	3	4	5	NA
Is receptive to feedback from supervisor	1	2	3	4	5	NA
Is receptive to appropriate feedback from peers	1	2	3	4	5	NA
Provides constructive feedback and suggestions to peers	1	2	3	4	5	NA
Is prepared for individual/triadic supervision sessions	1	2	3	4	5	NA
Is prepared for group supervision sessions	1	2	3	4	5	NA
Seeks out supervision outside of designated times, as appropriate	1	2	3	4	5	NA

Comments:

Student signature _____   Supervisor signature _____   Date _____

Note: Counselors complete this form as a self-assessment before midterm and final evaluation sessions. Supervisors complete the form for midterm and final evaluation sessions, during which the two ratings can be compared and discussed. At final evaluation, student counselors must achieve at least an average rating of 3 within each section, except for the starred items, which must have a rating of at least 4 for each. The form was created by Drs. L. DiAnne Borders, A. Keith Mobley, Kelly L. Wester, Derrick A. Paladino, and José A. Villalba, Department of Counseling and Educational Development, The University of North Carolina at Greensboro.

An added bonus in using an evaluation form as the basis for creating goals, and for monitoring one's progress toward those goals, is that counselors and supervisors have a common agreement (and common language) about the desired outcomes and expectations of supervision. The supervisor knows what is important to the counselor and can give specific attention to those goals during supervision sessions, such as identifying moments in a counseling session that are relevant to the goal and replaying those moments in session for skill practice, role-play, and other learning activities. Beginning counselors also should be aware that supervisors have the responsibility of adding additional learning goals, based on their knowledge of the counseling site and clients, review of the counselors' work, and understanding of the evaluation criteria. They add these goals to expand the counselor's effectiveness and protect client welfare.

Prepare for Supervision

Supervision is not a "by the seat of your pants" activity for either the supervisor or the supervisee. Counselors benefit more from supervision when they have reviewed their tapes and communicated specific requests for help to their supervisor beforehand. New counselors, however, may be challenged in knowing what to ask for in supervision. A concrete approach can be helpful. Some of the items from the evaluation form (see Table 11.1) have been used to create a session review form for beginning counselors (see Table 11.2). Completing that form allows counselors to evaluate their work (and the consistency of their work and use of the skills) and identify areas to be addressed in supervision.

Table 11.2   Session Review Form for Beginning Counselors

CL _____   CO _____   SUP _____   SES # _____   DATE _____

Practicum Session Review Form

Category	Evaluation	Comments (minimum of one comment per section)
Session Management		
1. Prepared for client prior to session	1 2 3 4 5 NA	
2. Created a safe clinical environment	1 2 3 4 5 NA	
3. Conducted comprehensive informed consent	1 2 3 4 5 NA	
4. Conducted comprehensive intake session	1 2 3 4 5 NA	
5. Appropriate pacing and management of time during sessions (transition through phases of session)	1 2 3 4 5 NA	
6. Appraised client when session was almost over	1 2 3 4 5 NA	
7. Conducted ending phase of session and discussed time between sessions	1 2 3 4 5 NA	

Category	Evaluation	Comments (minimum of one comment per section)
Counseling Skills and Abilities		
8. Overall demonstrated effective facilitative (basic helping) skills	1 2 3 4 5 NA	
9. Ability to establish relationship and build rapport	1 2 3 4 5 NA	
10. Ability to accurately respond to variety of client emotions	1 2 3 4 5 NA	
11. Accurate and meaningful reflections of feeling	1 2 3 4 5 NA	
12. Accurate and meaningful reflections of content	1 2 3 4 5 NA	
13. Understanding the uniqueness and meaning of the client's story	1 2 3 4 5 NA	
14. Timing—responding at the optimal moment	1 2 3 4 5 NA	
15. Demonstrated congruence in session	1 2 3 4 5 NA	
16. Appropriate use of silence	1 2 3 4 5 NA	
17. Appropriate use of self-disclosure	1 2 3 4 5 NA	
18. Appropriate use of immediacy	1 2 3 4 5 NA	
19. Appropriate use of open- and close-ended questions	1 2 3 4 5 NA	
20. Understanding and response to nonverbal communication	1 2 3 4 5 NA	
21. Ability to keep the focus of the session on the client	1 2 3 4 5 NA	
22. Ability to deal with client resistance	1 2 3 4 5 NA	
23. Demonstrated developmentally appropriate multicultural competence	1 2 3 4 5 NA	
Case Conceptualization, Goals, and Interventions		
24. Considered cognitive, affect, behavioral, and interpersonal aspects of client issue	1 2 3 4 5 NA	
25. Ability to create ongoing holistic assessment of the client with consideration to background/demographic/ cultural (worldview) information	1 2 3 4 5 NA	
26. Used conceptualization as basis for planning session, choosing culturally sensitive interventions, collaboratively setting goals, and evaluating client progress	1 2 3 4 5 NA	
27. Considered environmental factors (e.g., stressors and resources)	1 2 3 4 5 NA	
28. Identified patterns and themes	1 2 3 4 5 NA	
29. Demonstrated effective collaborative goal setting with clients	1 2 3 4 5 NA	
30. Facilitated movement toward goals	1 2 3 4 5 NA	

(Continued)

Table 11.2 (Continued)

Category	Evaluation	Comments (minimum of one comment per section)
Case Conceptualization, Goals, and Interventions		
31. Used and matched a variety of appropriate and intentional counseling approaches/strategies/interventions	1 2 3 4 5 NA	
32. Conducted comprehensive crisis assessments/intervention as appropriate	1 2 3 4 5 NA	
33. Competent analysis and resolution of ethical issues/dilemmas	1 2 3 4 5 NA	

Note: For CL enter client's initials; for CO enter counselor's initials; for SUP enter supervisor's initials; for SES # enter which counseling session is being rated; for DATE enter the date of the counseling session that is being rated. Counselors complete this form, including the ratings and the comments, for each counseling session they submit to their supervisor for review and discussion in supervision. Supervisors may or may not complete the form as they review the session, for comparison. This form was created by Drs. Kelly L. Wester and A. Keith Mobley, Department of Counseling and Educational Development, The University of North Carolina at Greensboro.

Take Risks

Now is the time for new counselors to push themselves—try new skills and interventions, explore their own values, take on a challenging client. During practicum and internship, new counselors have a lot of support from their supervisors and peers. Sometimes I have made a course requirement that practicum counselors must make three mistakes. Although this requirement is tongue in cheek, the point is that counselors are not growing if they are not taking risks, which likely will result in a less than stellar performance the first try. When counselors present such "growing moments" in supervision, it is more likely that a future example will be a "shining moment."

Practice Self-Reflection

Self-assessment is the first step in a reflection process, which is the heart of what happens in supervision, and accurate, in-depth self-reflection is a characteristic of counselors at higher developmental levels (Skovolt & Rønnestad, 1992). Reflection (see Schön, 1983) refers to stepping back from a counseling session (or even a supervision session) to analyze objectively and critically what happened. Reflection requires self-awareness, slowing down, taking a broader perspective that includes comparisons to previous sessions and counseling work with this client and other clients, and recalling previous feedback and how it might be relevant to the current work. Such reflections culminate in decisions about future directions in the work with a client or in the counselor's general approach to counseling work.

Beginning counselors can start practicing self-reflection by asking questions such as the following:

- What new information did I hear from the client today? How does that new information add to my picture or conceptualization of this client?

- What further information do I need to better understand this client?

- In general, how did I feel after the session?

- What was the highlight of the session for me? What seemed to be the highlight of the session for the client?

- Where in the session did I feel unsure, confused, or stuck? When was I surprised during the session?

- What risks did I take in the session? What risks did I want to take? What kept me from taking those risks?

- What was the dance of counselor and client in that session? What other metaphors come to mind around this client or this session?

- How would the client describe this session to a trusted friend? Would the client say he or she got what he or she needed? Wanted?

- How would the client describe me and my counseling to that trusted friend?

The beginning counselor can bring their thoughts in response to these questions to supervision sessions for further reflection and discussion with the supervisor.

Consider Power and Authority; Evaluation and Feedback

Supervision is an evaluative process. It is hierarchical in that the supervisor has power and authority over the supervisee. Supervisors work to diminish the anxiety associated with this dynamic in supervision, but it is neither helpful nor honest to pretend that supervisors will not be evaluating the supervisee at the end of the semester. Thus, beginning counselors would benefit from reflecting on their previous experiences in similar power-related relationships, including with parents, teachers, employers, and others. Counselors should consider their typical response to power and authority even when it is handled well by the more powerful person. Counselors' history with persons in authority and evaluative situations certainly will influence how they view their supervisors (expert? mentor? tyrant? Likely to be fair or unfair?) and their response to supervisors' feedback. Some supervisees, for example, debate every feedback statement they receive. Others, for whatever reason, will not tell a supervisor when they disagree with feedback. Additional behaviors related to power fall between these extremes but can diminish the supervisory experience. Such dynamics may be addressed explicitly in supervision.

Some supervisors ask counselors in an initial session about their experience with feedback, including the counselor's thoughts about how he or she best hears feedback and typical responses to challenging feedback. Supervisors might even ask questions such as the following: "How will I know when you are unhappy with feedback? Most of us are sensitive to some types of feedback; which types of feedback are hardest for you to hear?" "Describe a time that feedback was well received by you. Describe a time that feedback was *not* well received by you." What can follow is a discussion about how the counselor's experiences with feedback may influence the feedback process in supervision, including how the counselor can be aware of his or her responses, share them with the supervisor at the moment, and learn to manage them so that they do not interfere with the counselor's learning.

Counselors should remember that the purpose of supervisory feedback is to maximize their growth as counseling professionals. That is the intent of constructive feedback. So, in those difficult moments, which will occur, the beginning counselor might remind himself or herself, *I really want to help this client, and I don't want the supervisor* not *to tell me something that I can do or change that would keep me from helping my client.* Thus, it is vital that beginning counselors do the work they need to do so that they can be truly open and receptive to supervisors' feedback. Without supervisory feedback, there is no growth.

Practice Peer Feedback in Triadic and Group Supervision

Beginning counselors likely have had positive and not-so-positive experiences in peer groups, especially those that involve peer feedback. It may be helpful to review those experiences along the same lines of the counselor's review of experiences with power and authority and feedback and evaluation. Discussion of these experiences, including fears and concerns, could be helpful in early triadic and group supervision sessions, with the purpose of being aware and helping each other, not for the purpose of what kind of feedback not to give each other. What is easy for you to share and disclose to peers? What is hard for you to share and disclose to peers?

Supervisors typically share some guidelines for feedback in triadic and group supervision sessions. Generally, peer feedback should be stated tentatively, because this is the peer's best guess or hypothesis regarding the client, the counselor's intention, or the needed intervention. Peer feedback also should be both supportive and constructive. Supervisors may use one of the structured approaches described earlier or other methods to help peers achieve a balance in their feedback. In addition, a guide for reviewing a peer's taped counseling session and preparing to provide feedback is offered in the Peer Review Guidelines box earlier in this chapter.

Bring Difficult Topics to Supervision

There are some topics that all counselors may hesitate to bring to supervision but really need to be addressed with a supervisor. Beginning counselors need specific encouragement to attend to and bring these issues to supervision.

One topic is client resistance. Most beginning counselors experience client resistance, and often that resistance is a message more about the counselor than the client. This does not mean that the counselor is doing something wrong per se. More likely, it means that the counselor has not yet explored the client's story, emotions, and fears adequately and so the client's message is *You don't know the whole story yet* or *Slow down; I have more to tell you*. It may be that the counselor has moved into problem solving too soon, and so the client message is *You haven't prepared me to do that yet* or *You don't know some other critical parts of this story that make it difficult for me to do what you suggest*. It may be that the counselor is imposing a value or expectation on the client but is unaware of this; the client message may be *That may be true for you, or that may work for you, but my situation is different, so please look at this from my point of view*. Client resistance also may be an expression of the fear of change; the client's message may be *You have not yet discovered my fear of what I will lose if I make that change*.

A second topic is cultural influences. In short, assume there always are cultural influences at play. No two white males have had the same life experiences, and neither have two African American females, but it is normal and easy to make assumptions. So, regardless of similarities and differences, beginning counselors should look for and discuss with their supervisors what potential cultural influences may be present; this conversation should be ongoing. Cultural influences within the supervisory relationship also need to be addressed openly (Borders & Brown, 2005).

A third topic is when the counselor is attracted to a client. In short, counselors should be aware that this likely will happen at some point, if not points, in their career, given that they are human. Feelings of attraction and acting on those feelings of attraction are two different things. Pretending the feelings are not there only gives them more power. Counselors should bring these feelings to their supervisors, who can help explore what they mean and what actions are needed (e.g., physical attraction may mean referring the client; discovering that the client has a trait the counselor admires may be manageable once this is in the counselor's awareness; realizing that the client reminds the counselor of someone special in his or her life may put the feelings into perspective).

On the flip side, counselors should not be fearful of sharing negative feelings about clients with their supervisors. Again, a range of possible insights and actions are possible. A female counselor who is going through a divorce likely does not need to work with a male client who reminds her of her husband, so referral is the answer. A counselor's feelings of irritation or frustration likely provide insightful information about both the client (e.g., Do others in her life respond to her this way? What is the "positive intent" or message in the client's behavior that leads to the counselor's feelings?) and the counselor (e.g., "This is a value that I have to manage better in sessions with this client").

Poor Supervision

Unfortunately, not all supervisors have received adequate training or supervision of their supervision. In addition, sometimes there is a problematic mismatch between a supervisor and a supervisee based on personality traits, counseling background, or other factors. Some counselors have reservations about being supervised by a doctoral student who is in supervision training. Sometimes, because they are in training, doctoral students provide more time and attention to their work with counselors than a busy faculty member can. Beginning counselors should understand that there is no perfect supervisor-supervisee match. Nevertheless, there are some reasonable expectations for their experience.

Supervisors should provide their supervisees with a professional disclosure statement that describes their experience as both a counselor and a supervisor. The content and format of such a statement parallels a counselor's professional disclosure statement but also includes expectations and responsibilities of the supervisor and the counselor for preparing for supervision sessions. The statement also should clarify the supervisor's role (e.g., university vs. site supervisors). Other expectations and responsibilities may be outlined in a syllabus for the practicum or internship experience. Additionally, supervisors should make clear how the counselor will be evaluated; ideally, the evaluation form and criteria are shared in early sessions, in that this practice helps alleviate some of the stress and anxiety around evaluation, especially for beginning counselors.

Beginning counselors also can expect supervisors to be on time and prepared for their supervision sessions, show interest in the supervisee's development and success, work to establish a safe and trusting supervisory relationship and environment, tell the supervisee immediately when there is a concern about the supervisee's ability to complete the practicum or internship experience successfully, and be open to feedback themselves as supervisors. Additionally, when needed, a supervisor should provide a contract that states explicitly what must be done and by when for successful completion of the practicum or internship.

If the supervision process is not going well, counselors first should talk to the supervisor about their concerns to determine if the problematic issue can be resolved. If this is not successful, the counselor next should talk to the supervisor's supervisor, who should be named in the supervisor's professional disclosure statement. Other options include meeting with one's academic advisor or another counseling faculty member.

CONCLUSION

Most of the supervisors I know really enjoy working with beginning counselors. They experience a lot of satisfaction from supervising new counselors because they get to be a part of big growth spurts, share aha moments, and celebrate successes (large and small). They feel pride in watching growth in their supervisees' confidence and counselor identity. It is likely, then, that new counselors will work with supervisors who are greatly invested in their growth and development.

Beginning counselors can expect their first experiences with supervision to be intense, exhausting, exhilarating, confusing, clarifying, rewarding, and ever so impactful. Be open to all that the experience has to offer.

Grab that tennis racket and *swing!*

CASE STUDIY

Carol is a 24-year-old Caucasian master's student enrolled in a practicum course. Her practicum experience is located in the counseling program's on-site clinic; her clients are undergraduate volunteers. She asked her supervisor, Dr. Green, to watch a third session with her client, a female college sophomore who has spent much of the sessions talking about her relationship with her boyfriend and her indecision about whether to move with him to another city next summer. In previous supervision sessions, Carol and Dr. Green have practiced using more reflections of feeling, which has allowed the client to become more aware of her uncertainty and ambiguity around the relationship and the move. During the third session, Carol asked the client to create a list of pros and cons for staying in the relationship and making the move. Carol reports that there were many fewer pros than cons, but the client seemed no clearer about what she would do. Carol wrote on her tape review form that she wanted to discuss the client's resistance to counseling.

Dr. Green:	Tell me more about the client's resistance.
Carol:	Well, she just keeps going back and forth, just contradicting herself. And when I suggested that she talk to her boyfriend about some of her concerns, she got all protective of him and how he needs her.
Dr. Green:	You sound frustrated with her.
Carol:	Yes, I guess I am frustrated with her. It is so very clear what she needs to do, but she just won't make the right decision, or any decision.
Dr. Green:	What is the "right" decision?
Carol:	Oh, she needs to drop this guy. He's a deadbeat. He's getting in the way of her career plans. She has *got* to be more assertive with him.
Dr. Green:	OK, so clearly *you* would drop this guy.
Carol:	You're right about that! But when we talk about her concerns, she ends up defending him.
Dr. Green:	Let's look at that part of the tape where you said she defended him. Let's watch nonverbals, yours and hers.
Carol:	OK.
(Watch tape)	
Dr. Green:	What did you notice?
Carol:	She looks sort of defeated.

(Continued)

(Continued)

Dr. Green:	And what about your nonverbals?
Carol:	Hmm, well, I can see that I'm getting frustrated.
Dr. Green:	I wonder if she can see and feel your frustration also. Maybe that's why she defends him?
Carol:	I'm not following.
Dr. Green:	Have you ever been in a conversation where you knew that the other person wanted you to do something you didn't want to do, or you weren't sure you wanted to do that? They didn't say it in words, but you knew what they wanted you to do.
Carol:	Sure.
Dr. Green:	And how did that feel to you?
Carol:	Like they weren't on my side. Like they really didn't understand what I was saying. OK, so she might be feeling the same way.
Dr. Green:	And what does that suggest to you?
Carol:	That I need to stop pushing her to make a decision. But that's what she said she wanted to do, to decide what to do about the relationship.
Dr. Green:	I hear your concern for her, that you don't want a man to get in the way of her goals and career plans. If you were in that situation, you would be strong enough to move forward on your own.
Carol:	Of course.
Dr. Green:	Perhaps she's not as strong as you. Perhaps she believes she needs him in some ways, for some reasons that we haven't discovered yet.
Carol:	Like some irrational thoughts about having to be in a relationship?
Dr. Green:	Perhaps. So that would be one way to try to help her, and you, understand why she is hanging on to the relationship. I'm also remembering your intake session with her, what she said about her family. Do you remember?
Carol:	She's not in contact with her father, and she and her mother just don't get along.
Dr. Green:	What does that suggest to you about her relationship with her boyfriend?
Carol:	Hmm, that she has no other support in her life.
Dr. Green:	Which might explain why she holds on to him?
Carol:	Yeah. No wonder she pushes me back. I've got to let go of *my* expectations for her, what *I* want her to do.
Dr. Green:	Great insight. So, what seems a good way to proceed here?

Discussion Questions

1. What focus areas from the discrimination model did the supervisor give attention to during this portion of the supervision session?

2. What supervisor role or roles, as described in the discrimination model, did the supervisor take during this portion of the supervision session?

3. What characteristics of the beginning counselor, as outlined in developmental models of counselor development, are represented in Carol's work?

4. How would you describe the supervisory relationship between Carol and Dr. Green? What actions does it appear that *Carol* has taken to maximize her supervision experience?

5. If you had watched Carol's counseling session, how might you have provided her with similar feedback? What approach suggested in one or more of the peer models described in the chapter might have been helpful for you in providing Carol with your feedback?

6. What do you think will happen next in this supervision session between Carol and Dr. Green?

REFERENCES

Bernard, J. M. (1979). Supervisory training: A discrimination model. *Counselor Education and Supervision, 19,* 60–68.

Bernard, J. M. (1997). The discrimination model. In C. E. Watkins, Jr. (Ed.), *Handbook of psychotherapy supervision* (pp. 310–327). New York: Wiley.

Borders, L. D. (1991). A systematic approach to peer group supervision. *Journal of Counseling & Development, 69,* 248–252.

Borders, L. D., & Brown, L. L. (2005). *The new handbook of counseling supervision.* Mahwah, NJ: Lawrence Erlbaum/Lahaska.

Blocher, D. H. (1983). Toward a cognitive developmental approach to counseling supervision. *The Counseling Psychologist, 11*(1), 27–34.

Christensen, T. M., & Kline, W. B. (2001). The qualitative exploration of process-sensitive peer group supervision. *Journal for Specialists in Group Work, 26,* 81–99.

Council for Accreditation of Counseling and Related Educational Programs. (2016). *2016 Standards.* Alexandria, VA: Author.

Crutchfield, L. B., & Borders, L. D. (1997). Impact of two clinical peer supervision models on practicing school counselors. *Journal of Counseling & Development, 75,* 219–230.

Lanning, W. (1986). Development of the Supervisory Emphasis Rating Form. *Counselor Education and Supervision, 25,* 191–196, 207–209.

Lassiter, P. S., Napolitano, L., Culbreth, J. R., & Ng, K-M. (2008). Developing multicultural competence using the structured peer group supervision model. *Counselor Education and Supervision, 47,* 164–178.

Lawson, G., Hein, S. F., & Getz, H. (2009). A model focusing triadic supervision in counselor preparation programs. *Counselor Education and Supervision, 48,* 257–270.

Loganbill, C., Hardy, E., & Delworth, U. (1982). Supervision: A conceptual model. *The Counseling Psychologist, 10*(1), 3–42.

Schön, D. A. (1983). *The reflective practitioner: How professionals think in action.* New York: Basic Books.

Skovolt, T. M., & Rønnestad, M. H. (1992). Themes in therapist and counselor development. *Journal of Counseling & Development, 70,* 505–515.

Spice, C. G., Jr., & Spice, W. H. (1976). A triadic method of supervision in the training of counselors and counseling supervisors. *Counselor Education and Supervision, 15,* 251–280.

Stinchfield, T. A., Hill, N. R., & Kleist, D. M. (2007). The reflective model of triadic supervision: Defining an emerging modality. *Counselor Education and Supervision, 46,* 172–183.

Stinchfield, T. A., Hill, N. R., & Kleist, D. M. (2010). Counselor trainees' experiences in triadic supervision: A qualitative exploration of transcendent themes. *International Journal of Advanced Counselling, 32,* 225–239.

Stoltenberg, C. D. (1981). Approaching supervision from a developmental perspective: The counselor complexity model. *Journal of Counseling Psychology, 28,* 59–65.

Stoltenberg, C. D., & McNeill, B. W. (2009). *IDM supervision: An integrative developmental model for supervising counselors and therapists* (3rd ed.). New York: Routledge.

Wilbur, M. P., & Roberts-Wilbur, J. (1994). Structured group supervision (SGS): A pilot study. *Counselor Education and Supervision, 33,* 262–279.

Wilbur, M. P., Roberts-Wilbur, J., Morris, J. R., Betz, R. L., & Hart, G. M. (1991). Structured group supervision: Theory into practice. *Journal for Specialists in Group Work, 16,* 91–100.

CHAPTER 12

Wellness, Self-Care, and Burnout Prevention

Gerard Lawson and Jennifer M. Cook

Learning Goals

Upon completion of this chapter you will be able to do the following:

1. Identify the high-touch hazards of clinical mental health (CMH) counseling

2. Understand burnout and strategies for preventing burnout

3. Analyze the impacts of vicarious trauma and compassion fatigue

4. Formulate a personal plan for career-sustaining behaviors

5. Apply what you learned to a case study

CMH counselors are highly trained professionals who, when licensed, are endorsed by the state in which they practice as someone who can provide high-quality mental health care. There are many rewarding and challenging personal and professional outcomes as a result of this training and work. By virtue of their role, CMH counselors come into regular and intimate contact with individuals who are in great emotional pain, experiencing difficulty in their relationships, or struggling with extreme life challenges. Yet CMH counselors take on the task of helping them. Many practitioners recognize that clinical work places them at greater risk for their own psychological, emotional, spiritual, and relationship challenges. Still others believe that their in-depth mental health training makes them immune to these personal challenges. In fact, this is a myth that should be challenged early and often. Although research into counselor wellness has suggested that counselors are overall fairly well as a group (Lawson & Myers, 2011), the reality is that there are a number of factors that can positively or negatively impact counselor wellness. When counselors' wellness is impacted negatively, they are just as vulnerable as anyone else (if not more so) to emotional and psychological problems. Therefore, a long career in the clinical mental health profession requires keen awareness to the unique challenges of the profession and vigilance to maintain one's own wellness.

The American Counseling Association Code of Ethics (2014) charges counselors with monitoring their own wellness: "Counselors are alert to the signs of impairment from their own physical, mental, or emotional problems" (p. 9, C.2.g). In addition, counselors are directed to "engage in self-care activities to maintain and promote their emotional, physical, mental, and spiritual well-being to best meet their professional responsibilities" (p. 9). These excerpts from the Code of Ethics outline the two ends of the counselor wellness spectrum, impairment and well-being, and although most counselors live their day-to-day lives somewhere between the extremes, there is instruction for the practice to be found there. The risk of impairment becomes tangible for counselors with the axioms *Hurt people hurt people* and *Well counselors produce well clients* (Witmer & Young, 1996). This chapter outlines the risks inherent to work as a CMH counselor and strategies one may employ to stay balanced and well professionally.

CMH COUNSELING RISKS AND CHALLENGES

CMH counseling takes place in the context of a unique relationship. The relationship is a professional one and, at the same time, intimate, with high stakes for both parties involved. Skovholt and Trotter-Mathison (2011) described counseling as one of the "high-touch" professions, meaning that counselors (along with teachers, nurses, and social workers, among others) work especially closely with those whom they serve. CMH counselors know intimate details of their clients' history; physical, mental, and emotional struggles; intimate relationships; and traumatic experiences. CMH counselors meet regularly with these clients and listen to stories of suffering, while trying to help them to overcome the challenges they face. CMH counselors invest heavily in assisting clients to improve their situation, but success is sometimes elusive, even for highly skilled, well-trained clinicians. One of the unique challenges of sustaining a career as a CMH counselor over time is that the very skills and characteristics that make CMH counselors effective also make them vulnerable to burnout, compassion fatigue, and vicarious traumatization. Resiliency is a helpful framework to understand the difficulties CMH counselors face and in turn, how counselors can be more professionally hardy and buoyant even in the midst of challenges. Fundamentally, resiliency refers to a dynamic process of positive adaptation, or the ability to maintain or regain mental health, despite experiencing adversity (Taylor, Wald, & Asmundson, 2006).

High-Touch Hazards

In order to be resilient, it is important to understand the features of clinical mental health work that can pose challenges. Skovholt and Trotter-Mathison (2011) identified several positive characteristics inherent to work in high-touch professions, like counseling, and how, at the same time, these characteristics can become potentially hazardous. Skovholt and Trotter-Mathison (2011) describe 20 **high-touch hazards**, but some of these hazards are specifically relevant to CMH counselors and, therefore, are worth highlighting here. Again, in order for CMH counselors to be resilient, it is necessary for them to acknowledge and embrace the possible pitfalls of the work they do.

Empathy, Sensitivity, and Caring.   At the beginning of the counseling process the CMH counselor establishes a relationship that by design is built on **constant empathy**, **interpersonal sensitivity**, and **one-way caring**. This is the first hazard. Counselors are trained to meet the needs of their clients without reciprocity. It would be inappropriate and unethical for counselors' needs for caring and interpersonal connection to be met through their contact with clients. In fact, a hallmark of a helping relationship that has violated an ethical boundary is when counselors' personal needs are met through clients. An additional challenge of this high-touch hazard is that counselors are quite skilled at being in relationships that require one-way caring and constant empathy, so much so that there is the potential that not only their therapeutic relationships but all of their relationships can become one-way caring relationships. Therefore, counselors must be attentive to maintaining balance both in the workplace, where sensitivity and one-way relationships are appropriate, and in their personal lives, by sustaining awareness of, and attending to, their relationship needs. In personal relationships, counselors should seek out and nurture reciprocal and mutually beneficial relationships and minimize those relationships that drain them.

Emotional Stress.   Another high-touch hazard is **living in an ocean of emotional stress**. Most counselors in training recognize that clients are often under great emotional stress during their first clinical experiences. Counselors meet clients fully in their pain and remain calm themselves, even as clients' emotions may be labile. Thankfully, there are also moments when counselors are privileged to share the joy and successes of their clients! Nevertheless, the balance is shifted heavily toward clients who struggle. Skovholt's (2001) powerful image of an ocean of emotional stress is not lost on anyone who has ever been to an ocean. One can imagine a counselor engaged in intense clinical dialogue, encountering wave after wave of clients suffering throughout the course of a day. Sitting across from a client who is clearly in pain, CMH counselors feel the push and pull of client emotions. If you extend the metaphor further, there are potential riptides in the work that counselors do—issues just below the surface that if unnoticed, can take one's feet right out from under him or her. Subsequently, counselors must meet clients in their pain and yet not take on this pain.

Professional Loss and Elusive Success.   Two closely related and relevant high-touch hazards for CMH counselors are **ambiguous professional loss** and **elusive measures of success and normative failure**. From the first time a CMH counselor meets with a client, she or he works to establish a meaningful and productive relationship. Often, these relationships extend over time, producing meaningful results for clients: symptom relief, behavioral change, relationship transformation, or improvement to overall quality of life. Unfortunately, however, this is not always the case. Many times, clients simply stop coming to counseling. In fact, approximately 20% of clients in outpatient settings drop out of treatment prematurely, and of those, 70% do so after just one or two sessions (Olfson et al., 2009). It could be that their insurance benefits are limited, they may have experienced some relief, or they may be uncomfortable with what they disclosed during a session, but it also could be true that the counselor failed to meet their expectations for counseling. Although the process of termination is designed to bring clients closure, it serves a similar purpose for counselors as well. When the counseling relationship ends prematurely, counselors may be left wondering if a client is okay, if they somehow contributed to the client's choice to prematurely terminate, or if they should have done or said something differently. These wonderings are the result of an ambiguous professional loss that occurs when the professional counseling relationship ends before treatment goals are achieved. It is difficult for beginning counselors to make accurate attributions regarding premature termination, so consultation with supervisors may be needed.

Even when clients continue in counseling, their problems are often highly complex, which can make it difficult to assess whether treatment has been successful. Another unfortunate reality is that not every client experiences marked clinical improvements. Subsequently, counselors who genuinely wish to help their clients can experience strong feelings of dissatisfaction, sadness, or grief when ambiguous loss occurs; when they have difficulty assessing therapeutic success; or when they realize that some are not benefitting from their counseling services.

Cognitive Deprivation. Whereas a high-touch hazard can occur when counselors' work results in failure, ironically it can also occur when their work results in success. Skovholt (2001) described **cognitive deprivation** as a potential high-touch hazard that manifests as the result of overly specialized work (e.g., working with only one population or presenting issue) or as a result of becoming very good at work with a specific population. Imagine a CMH counselor who works in an outpatient setting and discovers that she has a real affinity for working with adolescent females with anger issues. The result is that her colleagues begin to refer such clients to this counselor because of her demonstrated skill. Counselors like to hear that they are good at what they do and that colleagues recognize and value their contributions. Additionally, counselors often have difficulty saying no (a separate hazard in and of itself). Subsequently, this counselor's caseload may consist entirely of clients who are adolescent females with anger issues. This specialization becomes more problematic when a counselor, who experiences deprivation, begins to see her clients as problems rather than people. This can be heard creeping into counselors' language when they refer to their client as "another angry teenager." Such counselor communication shorthand may reflect a loss of perspective into the rich individuality of clients and a tendency to quickly pathologize clients' lives and experiences.

Legal and Ethical Anxiety. CMH counselors encounter legal and ethical anxiety as the result of the complex and ambiguous nature of their work. Skovholt (2001) described **legal and ethical fears** as a potential high-touch hazard and a very real, daily concern for

CMH counselors. Often, clients seek counseling because they are unhappy in their life, and unfortunately, solving those problems is neither simple nor quick. By their very nature, clients' complex problems present challenges that often lack straightforward solutions. Often, conflict arises between client wants and counselors' ethical responsibilities, and this can place counselors in the position of making choices clients may find objectionable (e.g., reporting suspected abuse or neglect to social services). Further, the unfortunate reality is that we live in a litigious society in which counselors who have done no wrong can be sued and forced to endure the stress, expense, and inconvenience of defending themselves. As a result, CMH counselors can feel pressure to practice exactly "right" in an effort to avoid litigation.

Physical and Emotional Trauma.   A final high-touch hazard especially relevant to CMH counselors is the counselor's own **physical and emotional trauma** (Skovholt, 2001). Most, if not all, CMH counselors have had their own life challenges. Bringing the individual self into the therapeutic relationship is a requisite for effective treatment, yet it makes counselors vulnerable. When counselors make themselves vulnerable, simply observing clients' struggles can trigger one's past trauma or perpetuate countertransference. Counselors typically learn about transference and countertransference conceptually but only develop sensitivity to its practical manifestations with experience over time and through clinical and peer supervision. This is yet another example of how the person of the counselor enters into the counseling relationship. It is not possible to separate one's personal life and history from one's work as a helper. Whereas this means that counselors can effect change, similarly, clients' issues can also affect counselors deeply. When this occurs, it can manifest in numerous ways, and among the most common are burnout, compassion fatigue, and vicarious traumatization.

BURNOUT

The term **burnout** has become common in today's vernacular. Most people have an intuitive sense of what burnout entails. Individuals who work at a restaurant or in a retail shop may complain of burnout when they work long hours and feel tired, drained, and frustrated by their work. Yet there are specific, less common aspects of burnout to which CMH counselors are susceptible. Freudenberg and Richelson (1980) offered one definition of burnout that brings the concept into clearer focus: "A state of fatigue or frustration brought about by devotion to a cause, way of life, or relationship that failed to produce the expected reward" (p. 13). This definition reveals that, although waitstaff may feel frustrated and tired, unless they are working in support of a devotion to a cause or way of life, their experience is not truly burnout. Often, counselors are devoted to the work that they do, and they understand the importance of that work. With burnout, the emotional stakes are higher, and CMH counselors often work in very high-stakes positions.

A commonly accepted definition of burnout, provided by Maslach, Schaufeli, and Leiter (2001), describes a syndrome distinguished by emotional exhaustion, depersonalization or cynicism, and a lack of personal accomplishment. Most counselors in training can imagine a state of emotional exhaustion that results from investing oneself in another. Although counselors have some influence on another person's change process, they ultimately have little control over people's decisions, which primes the counselor for emotional exhaustion. As a result, a counselor may desperately hope for a client to stop abusing drugs, to leave an abusive relationship, or to follow through with treatment, and it takes an emotional toll when they do not. Furthermore, when counselors struggle with their limited power of influence, they may begin to lose sight of the client altogether. Occasionally, a counselor may refer to a session with a "borderline," accompanied by an eye roll or a heavy sigh. The counselor's intended shorthand for a taxing session with a client who has borderline personality disorder can also represent the depersonalization that comes with burnout. When clients are viewed as problems, a salient signal of burnout is present.

A final characteristic of burnout syndrome is diminished feelings of personal accomplishment. Counselors experiencing burnout have become unable to see efforts as contributing to client healing. Often, counselors internalize feelings of diminished self-efficacy by feeling defeated, or externalize these feelings by blaming clients, community, workplace, or society more broadly. This characteristic is congruent with the high-touch hazard of **elusive measures of success and normative failure**. CMH counselors who feel as if their work is not contributing in a positive way are particularly susceptible to burnout.

What Burnout Looks Like

Although there are some common features of burnout, how burnout manifests for an individual counselor can vary. Lee, Cho, Kissinger, and Ogle (2010) defined three types of counselor burnout based on scores across five domains of interest: **exhaustion, perceived incompetence, negative work environment, devaluing clients**, and **deterioration in personal life**. There are three counselor types associated with burnout: the well-adjusted counselor, the disengaged counselor, and the persevering counselor.

Well-adjusted counselors are those who have moderately low scores across all five domains. The disengaged counselor scores in the moderate range on the exhaustion, negative work environment, and deterioration in personal life subscales but higher on the incompetence scale and exceptionally high on the devaluing clients subscale. These counselors continue to show up to work but have disconnected from their clients significantly and no longer see the value of the work they do. The final group of counselors are the persevering counselors. These individuals scored highest on exhaustion, negative work environment, and deterioration in personal life but scored low to moderate on incompetence and devaluing clients. Despite experiencing serious personal impacts, these individuals value their work and continue to feel dedicated to their clients. With both the disengaging or persevering strategy, it is unclear if these individuals were aware of their burnout, but it seems likely that the strain accompanying burnout was recognizable.

Maslach (2003) explored the consequences of burnout. Whereas the author was careful to avoid implying a causal relationship, individuals who experienced burnout also were likely to experience physical exhaustion, insomnia, headaches, ulcers, lingering illnesses, muscle tension, and neck and back pain. In addition to somatic symptoms, burnout creates psychological and emotional strains such as feelings of guilt, anger, isolation, bitterness, and depression and a decline in feelings of accomplishment and self-esteem. Ultimately, it is the client who is most impacted by a distressed counselor. A counselor who possesses low motivation, decreased empathy, reduced sensitivity to client feelings, a tendency toward dehumanization of clients, poor presession preparation, and chronic lateness, and simply ceases to care, is clearly at serious risk for harming clients.

Counselors should be concerned about burnout both personally and among their colleagues. The personal consequences of burnout are profound, and often colleagues are the first to notice (Maslach, 2003). **Signs of burnout** include struggling to manage alone, showing self-sacrifice, struggling to achieve unattainable goals, showing signs of "falling apart," and distancing and isolation (Ericson-Lidman & Strandberg, 2007). Even when such dramatic symptoms are present, intervening with a burned-out colleague is challenging. Imagine a colleague who may be experiencing the onset of burnout as evidenced by his distancing and increased isolation. How does one intervene? To reach out by expressing concern, suggesting he cut back or take a vacation, may be interpreted as judgment or an impediment to his capability to do his job (e.g., a vacation means more work will pile up). Although after it occurs, burnout can be arrested and treated successfully, it is clear that prevention is both easier and more efficient than reversing the effects of the condition.

Burnout Prevention

There are six broad factors considered essential to the prevention of burnout: a sustainable workload; feelings of choice; recognition and reward; a sense of community; fairness, respect, and justice; and meaningful valued work (Maslach & Leiter, 1997). A sustainable workload is perhaps the most elusive of the list. A sustainable workload may hold a different meaning to the counselor providing services than to an administrator focused on clients on a waiting list and the financial bottom line. This fact does not imply that administrators are calloused to the needs of CMH counselors but rather that they are responding to different demands. It is worth noting that an important strategy for preventing burnout is *feelings* of choice, as opposed to actual choice. Counselors recognize that there are many demands and many more needs in the agencies and communities in which they work. Helpful is the perception that one has some say in the size and composition of one's caseload and the approach to one's work.

Similarly, counselors need to find meaningful value in their work in order to feel accomplished and avoid burnout. Counselors' work needs to be consistent with their values and in line with their motivations for entering the field. In order to avoid burnout, counselors need to feel recognized and rewarded for services they provide. Occasional recognition or reward comes directly from clients, but these measures of success are elusive and ambiguous loss is inevitable. When a client does express appreciation, or shares a significant life accomplishment, counselors should take notice. I (GL) occasionally got graduation or wedding announcements from clients I worked with years ago. They sent them to the agency where I worked, which forwarded them to me. Those reminders that my work paid off for someone in a way that he or she believed was meaningful helped to sustain me in the midst of other day-to-day stressors. More often, however, CMH counselors rely on clinical supervisors, colleagues, and peers to provide them with feedback that recognizes efforts made, and to reward those efforts. Finally, counselors need fairness, respect, and justice in the workplace, meaning settings free of harassment, respect for individual differences, and valuing the contributions that each team member makes. Healthy work environments support the important work counselors do, thereby minimizing the frustration and challenges that lead to burnout.

VICARIOUS TRAUMATIZATION

All counselors listen to the life narratives clients present. Client stories are rarely simple, picturesque accounts of happy families, carefree days, and the gentle winding curves of life. Most frequently, client stories are fraught with distrust, abuse, betrayal, and life-altering events that result in clients' understanding their lives through feelings of terror, shame, and brokenness. And sometimes, as counselors bear witness to the traumatic events in clients' lives, it can be nearly as difficult for counselors to *hear* these stories as it is for clients to tell them.

McCann and Pearlman (1990) coined the term **vicarious traumatization** to encapsulate the cognitive and emotional responses counselors have to the explicit and lurid trauma accounts of their clients. Not only do counselors have cognitive and emotional responses, they may also experience visceral sensations of shock, horror, or disgust resulting from what they have heard. The experience of vicarious traumatization can cause counselors to question their views of the nature of good and evil and the human capacity to harm others, which indelibly shifts their understanding of the world (Pearlman & Saakvitne, 1995).

Trippany, White Kress, and Wilcoxon (2004) noted that people increasingly are exposed to traumatic events that range from natural disasters to sexual abuse and from school shootings to war. Subsequently, the populations counselors serve will contain larger percentages of clients affected by trauma. Thus, counselors are more prone to vicarious trauma than ever before.

Symptoms and Signs of Vicarious Trauma

Unlike burnout, which develops over time and can occur in any profession, vicarious trauma affects only professionals who work with trauma. Furthermore, it can strike in a short period of time, perhaps in a single counseling session, from exposure to a specific client situation (Trippany et al., 2004). Because vicarious trauma is not the cumulative result of working with a variety of clients over time, the symptomatology is different than burnout. When counselors experience burnout, they feel tired, apathetic, and disconnected and many times cannot put their finger on one specific event that caused their feelings and impacted their functioning. In cases of vicarious traumatization, however, the time when one learned of a specific client trauma can be pinpointed and described in explicit detail.

Often, CMH counselors who experience vicarious traumatization experience symptoms similar to their clients who have post-traumatic stress disorder (PTSD; Figley, 2004). In fact, vicarious traumatization also has been called secondary traumatic stress because of the similarities between the client's experience of the trauma and the counselor's vicarious experience of the trauma. The *DSM-5* criteria for PTSD require that an individual experience or be exposed to a traumatizing event and experience symptoms that fall into four broad categories: intrusion symptoms (e.g., intrusive thoughts or dreams), avoidance symptoms (e.g., avoiding stimuli that may remind the individual of the trauma), arousal/reactivity symptoms (e.g., sleep disturbances, angry outbursts), and negative mood and cognitions (Miller et al., 2012). In addition, the symptoms must cause clinically significant distress or impairment in important areas of functioning. This last point is of particular significance because it points to *impairment* in both professional and personal functioning. Counselors experiencing vicarious trauma are seriously impaired, so vicarious trauma must be taken seriously.

In addition to symptoms related to PTSD, vicarious traumatization may cause symptoms similar to those associated with burnout such as "physical symptoms, emotional symptoms, behavioral symptoms, work-related issues, and interpersonal problems" (Trippany et al., 2004, p. 32). McCann and Pearlman (1995) reported that sufferers also might experience short- and long-term memory loss and changes in thinking patterns and ways of understanding the world.

Pearlman and Mac Ian's (1995) empirical study of vicarious traumatization among counselors who specialize in trauma work revealed that practitioners with a personal history of trauma and counselors with more than 2 years' experience as a trauma counselor were more susceptible to vicarious traumatization. Tabor (2011) suggested that ongoing stress combined with high-demand service needs contributes to one's susceptibility to vicarious trauma so, ultimately, all helping professionals are at risk. It is the *content* of a client's story, combined with how his story interacts with the counselor's history and vulnerabilities, on myriad levels that creates vicarious traumatization.

Addressing Vicarious Trauma

Vicarious trauma impacts counselors both personally and professionally, and some counselors are more affected than others. But what can be done? One step is to seek supervision or consultation with other professionals. Sommer and Cox (2005) studied counselors who work with trauma and identified four strategies that, when used in the clinical supervision process, proved beneficial. First, participants benefited from talking about the effects of the work and addressing related personal feelings. Second, effective supervisors acknowledged that vicarious trauma is a real occurrence and validated participants' experiences as true and real. Third, participants cited that having a supervisor who provided "multiple perspectives, collaborative guidance, a calming presence, and attention to self-care" (Sommer & Cox, 2005, p. 127) helped them process through their vicarious trauma and to work more effectively. Fourth, participants discussed the importance of working in an accommodating environment where they felt supported. Counselors may choose to bring issues of vicarious trauma to supervision. Part of the benefit of sharing this information with a supervisor is to normalize the counselor's experiences and to gain access to another person's perspective on the issues. For counselors who do not have access to formal clinical supervision, peer supervision can help address some of those issues, but the structure of clinical supervision should include regular attention to the challenges of the work counselors do.

Vicarious trauma is a real phenomenon that can acutely affect counselors who work with clients who have significant trauma histories. Given the extensive trauma clients can be exposed to, it is implausible to assume that because you are not a "trauma counselor" or that because you do not intend to treat folks who have experienced trauma, you will not be impacted. The fact is, you will work with individuals who have experienced trauma, and to some degree, it will affect you. It is important to be prepared to recognize the effects of client trauma and know how to seek help when you feel affected. In sum, you cannot control the information clients share, but you can control the care you provide yourself.

COMPASSION FATIGUE

Compassion fatigue can be conceptualized simply as the cost of caring (Figley, 1997). This means that all helping professionals who take a risk and care about their clients are susceptible to compassion fatigue. Although there may be a small percentage of counselors who care little for their clients, the vast majority of counselors care very deeply. The depth of care exhibited, combined with the breadth of trauma clients experience, make compassion fatigue prevalent and of great concern. In fact, an array of helping professions are considered vulnerable to compassion fatigue because of the roles they fulfill, including social workers, nurses, physicians, law enforcement officers, and religious personnel (Fahy, 2007; Huggard, 2003; Osofsky, Putnam, & Lederman, 2008; Radey & Figley, 2007; Roberts, Flannelly, Weaver, & Figley, 2003).

Compassion Fatigue Described

Figley (1997) defined compassion fatigue as a "state of exhaustion and disfunction [*sic*]—biologically, psychologically, and socially—as a result of prolonged exposure to compassion stress and all that it evokes" (p. 23). Counselors who experience compassion fatigue feel mentally, emotionally, bodily, and functionally depleted due to working, over an extended period of time, with clients who have experienced trauma. To unpack this definition, an understanding of compassion stress and its contribution to compassion fatigue is required.

Compassion Stress

Compassion stress is the tension and anxiety that result from working with victims of trauma (Figley, 1997). Figley's (1997) model of compassion stress includes six components that ultimately lead to *some form* of compassion stress. It is important to emphasize, however, that compassion stress does not always result in compassion fatigue but can also manifest as compassion satisfaction.

Figley's (1997) model encourages one to recognize that counselors have a choice in how they view the work that they do, particularly with clients with a trauma history. Through their empathetic ability, counselors choose how to interpret client trauma, either with empathetic concern (positive) or with emotional contagion (negative). Either of these choices impacts counselor response, and that response can lead to a sense of achievement (positive) or disengagement (negative). Compassion stress results, with the potential for this stress to be positive or negative. On the one hand, counselors may experience a more positive or sustaining approach to working with clients who have experienced trauma.

Alternatively, counselors may experience a less sustaining approach. In other words, counselors who understand that making a connection with their client is a therapeutic activity in and of itself often will see more success and feel buoyed by being able to contribute positively to someone's life. Alternatively, those who overfocus on the depth of challenges or struggles that some traumatized clients experience, and do not feel as if they are making sufficient progress, are likely to struggle with compassion fatigue. Radey and Figley (2007) suggested it is possible to work from a place of achievement, or compassion satisfaction, and mitigate compassion fatigue through self-care and personal resources. Mulligan (2004) proposed interventions such as setting personal intentions, meditating, and journal writing to sustain selfhood and to inhibit compassion fatigue.

For further clarity, consider an example of students and test taking. A certain amount of stress, or motivation, is necessary in order for students to attend classes, take notes, read class texts, and study for an exam. For one student, the stress she feels motivates her, and she chooses to focus on things she can control or influence directly. So she tries to study thoroughly, to do her best, and she does not measure her self-worth based on her test performance. This student rests comfortably with the balanced notion that she studied to the best of her ability and that she will take the exam to the best of her ability. For another student, the stress she feels debilitates her; she focuses on the anxiety of "what ifs" and "musts." As a result, her study time is guided by anxiety. She works hard, puts in more hours studying than anyone else in the class, obsesses about the test day, and assigns a large part of her self-worth to the grade she receives on the test. On test day, both students feel some degree of stress, yet each student channels her stress and responds to her effort on the test in different ways. When the test is over, the first student walks away, feels she has done her best, and feels satisfied with her effort. When the second student finishes her test, she rushes to her notes and looks up answers she had forgotten. She feels mentally and emotionally spent, expects she did not do well, and wonders if the instructor will give the class extra-credit opportunities.

Most people can relate on some level to this scenario. Many students are not on one extreme or the other like the students in the example, but this scenario gives you a keen sense about two divergent attitudes with regard to studying and test taking that is strikingly similar to work with clients who have experienced trauma and how counselors might experience compassion stress. CMH counselors work with clients who have experienced trauma in different ways, and thus, the way compassion stress manifests for each counselor is different.

Contributing Factors to Compassion Fatigue

As described, compassion stress can be one factor that contributes to compassion fatigue. Counselors who become emotionally enmeshed with their clients, who disengage from their own emotional needs, and who do not enact healthy self-care behaviors are at serious risk for feeling the negative effects of compassion fatigue.

Burnout and secondary traumatization, when combined, contribute to compassion fatigue (Gentry, Baranowsky, & Dunning, 2002). Burnout is discussed earlier in this chapter, and secondary traumatization occurs when people are exposed to the trauma of others, often through stories, reports, or narratives (Figley, 1997). Counselors' work is built on clients' self-reports, and it is necessary for counselors to hear clients' stories. When clients have experienced trauma or if they have a post-traumatic stress disorder (PTSD) diagnosis, the details clients share about their experiences·can be jarring, unsettling, and even scary to counselors. At times, counselors report feeling symptoms of trauma similar to their clients' reported experiences (Gentry et al., 2002). Figley (2004) noted how counselors may persistently reexperience the traumatic story of their client, avoid stimuli associated with the trauma, and experience increased arousal—all of which fit the criteria for a PTSD diagnosis. This is a sign of compassion fatigue. And it is especially important to note here that *every* counselor does trauma work because every counselor hears traumatic client reports, not just trauma specialists. In fact, Lawson and Myers (2011) found that 35% of American Counseling Association members' caseloads were survivors of some sort of trauma, such as sexual abuse, intimate partner violence, or victimization. Even if counselors do not specifically identify themselves as trauma specialists, individuals who have endured traumas find their way to them. Counselors certainly can help them and need to remember that *no one* is immune to compassion fatigue!

The amount of time CMH counselors spend working with individuals who have experienced trauma is also a factor. This is to say that compassion fatigue is a phenomenon that develops in individuals *over time* so prolonged exposure is important to consider. CMH counselors should not underestimate, however, the powerful and sometimes destabilizing effect client stories can have on them in a brief period of time, especially when counselors are unfamiliar with trauma work or when counselors have experienced their own trauma. Unprocessed countertransference can quickly lead to compassion fatigue (Figley, 1997).

Identifying Compassion Fatigue

Gentry et al. (2002) provided a helpful summary of key signs of compassion fatigue. Though not exhaustive, this list can be helpful in understanding if one's professional work is having a negative personal impact:

- Increased negative arousal

- Intrusive thoughts or images of another's critical experiences (or caregiver's own historical traumas)

- Difficulty separating work from personal life

- Lowered frustration tolerance; increased outbursts of anger or rage

- Dread of working with certain individuals

- Marked or increasing transference or countertransference issues with certain individuals

- Depression

- Perceptive or "assumptive world" disturbances (i.e., seeing the world in terms of victims and perpetrators coupled with a decrease in subjective sense of safety)

- Ineffective and/or self-destructive self-soothing behaviors

- Hypervigilance

- Decreased feelings of work competence

- Diminished sense of purpose or enjoyment with career

- Reduced ego functioning (time, identity, volition)

- Lowered functioning in nonprofessional situations

- Loss of hope

Stamm and Figley (1996) developed the Compassion Satisfaction and Fatigue Test, and later, Stamm (2009–2011) revised this early instrument and created the Professional Quality of Life: Compassion Satisfaction and Fatigue Version 5 (ProQOL) to aid counselors and other helping professionals to gain understanding about their personal balance of compassion satisfaction, burnout, and secondary trauma. The ProQOL is free and available online for CMH counselors (http://www.proqol.org).

Before moving on to counselor wellness, on the other side of the balance, it is worth noting the numbers regarding burnout and compassion fatigue. In a survey of American Counseling Association members, Lawson (2007) found that 5.2% of members scored above the cut-point for burnout, and 10.8% of respondents scored above the cut-point for compassion fatigue/vicarious traumatization. To put that in context, the ACA has over 50,000 members, so on any given day, about 2,500 ACA members went to work feeling burned out, and about 5,000 went to work feeling that they could not connect to their clients successfully. Interestingly, counselors fared better than some allied professions, and just as well as others, but counselors must recognize that the risks are real, and they end up affecting real counselors and their clients.

COUNSELOR WELLNESS

Although the risks are real, most counselors are able to find balance in their work and stay in it for the long haul. So what can be done to remain well, vital, and engaged in clinical work throughout a career? It begins with (and continues through) an honest assessment of your strengths and your areas for growth. Based on self-assessment, counselors must make choices that allow them to achieve a work-life balance. Meyer and Ponton (2006) observed that resiliency in counselors is not an accident, but "rather it is the cumulative effect of counselors' healthy decision making" (p. 206).

Counselor wellness is not static. One cannot "achieve" wellness one day and then be set for life. Rather, wellness is about striving to see what is working well and what needs to be done differently. Myers, Sweeney, and Witmer (2000) defined wellness as "a way of life oriented toward optimal health and well-being, in which body, mind, and spirit are integrated by the individual to live life more fully within the human and natural community" (p. 252). Counselors spend their days helping others to strive toward optimal health and well-being yet also are challenged to turn that compassion, keen observational skills, and problem-solving ability inward to support their own wellness.

A formal way to assess wellness levels across multiple domains is with the Five Factor Wellness Evaluation of Lifestyle (FFWel), which is based on the indivisible self model of wellness crafted by Myers and Sweeney (2005). This research-validated model conceptualizes wellness as a global characteristic, made up of five domains and 18 subdomains. The five domains include creative self (thinking, emotion, control, work, positive humor), coping self (leisure, stress management, self-worth, realistic beliefs), social self (friendship and love relationships), physical self (exercise and nutrition), and essential self (spirituality, gender identity, cultural identity, and self-care). Counselors, on average, score higher than the norm group on the FFWel (Lawson & Myers, 2011). Nonetheless, individual wellness is affected by wellness activities at work and other arenas of life.

The FFWel is available online for a fee and provides a comprehensive snapshot of overall wellness. There are also free assessment resources available on the American Counseling Association website, compiled by the ACA Taskforce on Counselor Wellness and Impairment (http://www.creating-joy.com/taskforce/tf_wellness_strategies.htm). When using any assessment, remember that honest responses are required to obtain a true picture of one's coping at that moment in time. Based on an honest assessment, one can decide what adjustments need to be made in various areas.

MINDFULNESS

Mindfulness has become a more prominent part of counseling practice over the past three decades (Brown, Marquis, & Guiffrida, 2013). CMH counselors now commonly use mindfulness with clients, and the effectiveness of mindfulness-based interventions has been demonstrated with individuals with addictions (Bowen, Chawla, & Marlatt, 2011), eating disorders (Wolever & Best, 2009), depression (Shapiro & Carlson, 2009; Teasdale & Ma, 2004), and anxiety disorder (Hofmann, Sawyer, Witt, & Oh, 2010; Shapiro & Carlson, 2009), among others. Curiously, counselors do not always practice the same mindfulness strategies that they recommend for their clients. But the benefits to counselors who practice mindfulness are every bit as compelling as the benefits to clients.

Mindfulness Defined

For many people, mindfulness is part of a broader spiritual practice and is commonly associated with meditation as part of Zen Buddhist practice (Shapiro & Carlson, 2009). Additionally, though, mindfulness can be considered and practiced as formal or informal activities that involve deliberate concentration, attention, and acceptance (without judgment) of whatever is being experienced in the present moment (Bishop et al., 2004). Gellar, Greenberg, and Watson (2010) make the connection between this mind-set and the concept of **therapeutic presence**. These authors defined therapeutic presence as "bringing one's whole self into the encounter with clients by being completely in the moment on multiple levels: physically, emotionally, cognitively, and spiritually" (p. 599). Ponton (2012) gives a more practical description of what is involved in being mindful as a counselor: "Show up, shut up, listen up, roll your sleeves up. . . . Mindfulness is showing up in the present moment.

Mindfulness is nonjudgmental acceptance—shutting up. Mindfulness is attentive relating to experience—listening up. Rolling up sleeves—applying both the practice and the fruits of mindfulness to the work we are called to do" (p. 189).

There is a significant body of literature on the benefits of mindfulness to counselors, in addition to the benefits for clients. Students who were trained in mindfulness practice reported fewer fears of being inadequate or incompetent counselors. They enjoyed improved abilities to trust themselves in session, to tolerate the ambiguous material clients often bring, to give up the need to be in control in the sessions, and to be present with their client (Marris, 2009). Other researchers have found that counselors in training who were trained in mindfulness had new and more effective ways of conceptualizing their role as a counselor and their work with clients. They described themselves as being more aware of what was going on in session, more patient with the process, and abler to focus on the important parts of what clients bring (Christopher, Christopher, Dunnagan, & Schure, 2006). Finally, Grepmair et al. (2007) found that when counselors practice mindfulness, their clients benefit from that practice, whether the client practices or not and even if the client is unaware that the counselor practices.

Overall, mindfulness is a powerful strategy for assisting clients and to help CMH counselors. Campbell and Christopher (2012) noted the well-established finding that training counseling students in mindfulness practice as part of their self-care strategies helped to prevent burnout, vicarious traumatization, and compassion fatigue. The benefits of that practice can extend far into counselors' careers. "Mindfulness helps therapists develop their ability to experience and communicate a felt sense of clients' inner experiences [and] be more present to clients' suffering; and helps clients express their body sensations and feelings" (Davis & Hayes, 2011, p. 202). There are myriad resources for counselors who want to learn more about how to incorporate mindfulness into their practice, or their self-care, from formal strategies like the mindfulness-based stress reduction (MBSR) approach developed by Jon Kabat-Zinn (1982) or less formal mindfulness programs available online. The benefits of mindfulness in counseling practice are compelling.

Balance

A wellness assessment can be useful periodically, but day to day, the question is, "Am I working and living in balance?" This term, **balance**, shows up over and over in discussions of life and work. What is balance, and how do we know when it has been achieved? The first balance counselors should be aware of is the work/life balance. It is easy to spend extensive time immersed in work and forget to make time for oneself and other important relationships. Similarly, counselors often interpret the private and confidential nature of their work to mean they cannot talk about any aspects of their vocation with loved ones. Certainly one should not burden partners or children with details of the challenges clients face, nor can counselors discuss information that is potentially identifiable. However, counselors can confide in their partner about a stressful day at work or express concern over a client who is doing poorly and what it is like to be the counselor. Ideally, clinical and peer supervision is the professional outlet for such struggles, but it may also be useful to discuss concerns at home so that family can understand one's professional struggles and provide support in personal, caring ways.

A key to work/life balance is time *away* from work. It is a given that there will always be needs at the workplace, yet some CMH counselors convince themselves that they are the only one who can meet client needs. Such thinking can contribute directly to burnout. Counselors must care for themselves in *at least* equal measure to the care they extend to their clients. This could mean staying home or going to the doctor when they are not feeling well, attending parent-teacher meetings, playing with one's kids, or taking planned vacations to spend quality time with family. Of course, there will be clients to see and work to be done when you return, but you will be better prepared to meet those challenges.

Career-Sustaining Behaviors

Kramen-Kahn and Hansen (1998) recommended a number of career-sustaining behaviors that help one to feel vital and satisfied in his or her work. Further, career-sustaining behaviors help with the prevention of negative career effects and with the maintenance of overall positivity in counseling practice. Lawson (2007), in a study of counselor wellness and impairment, found that not only are career-sustaining behaviors indicative of counselor wellness but that counselors who are considered "highly satisfied" use 14 positive career-sustaining behaviors "to maintain their effectiveness and positive outlook" (p. 32). These behaviors are the following:

- Maintain sense of humor
- Spend time with partner or family
- Maintain balance between professional and personal lives
- Maintain self-awareness
- Maintain sense of control over work responsibilities
- Reflect on positive experiences
- Try to maintain objectivity about clients
- Engage in quiet leisure activities
- Maintain professional identity
- Participate in continuing education
- Spend time with friends
- Turn to spiritual beliefs
- Read literature to keep up to date
- Perceive clients' problems as interesting

It is likely that some career-sustaining behaviors are a part of your personal repertoire of behaviors, helping you to maintain personal and professional balance. However, the goal is to raise awareness about behaviors known to sustain counselors over time, producing a stronger sense of balance in one's life.

In striving for balance and practicing career-sustaining behaviors, a final area to consider is day-to-day wellness maintenance. What practices can be incorporated into one's work life to insulate one from burnout, compassion fatigue, and vicarious traumatization?

Skovholt, Grier, and Hanson (2001) suggested several avenues for professional and personal self-care. First, counselors are encouraged to create and sustain an active, individually designed process for staying engaged in their personal and professional development. Often, this includes cultivating new activities and interests outside of work, as well as continually challenging oneself to learn more about emerging counseling approaches to maintain ongoing professional improvement. Second, Skovholt et al. (2001) recommended creating a professional "greenhouse" at work, which involves engaging with a mentor to learn from his or her successes. Identify someone who has found balance between self-care and other-care and remain open to support from colleagues. This process begins with obtaining good clinical supervision (see Chapter 11). Clinical supervision is designed to help counselors improve clinical skills, but supervision also assists in keeping client issues in proper perspective, identifying counselor overfunctioning, identifying emotional distancing or overinvolvement with client issues, and affording an appropriate format for processing through work-related concerns. In short, clinical supervision, as well as peer supervision, can serve as the antidote to daily stressors for counselors.

In addition to receiving clinical supervision, counselors should strive for meaningful work and variety in their clinical pursuits. Lawson and Myers (2011) found that counselors who work in private practice revealed higher wellness scores than those working in community agency settings. The researchers hypothesized that this was due in part to the greater control private practitioners have over the size and makeup of their caseloads. Similarly, they found that counselors with larger caseloads and a higher proportion of suicidal or self-injurious clients reported lower wellness scores. Even if one cannot control the size or makeup of one's caseload, steps can be taken to maintain variety. Volunteering to do community outreach or serving on committees that make positive contributions to one's agency can be beneficial. Regardless of specific steps taken, it is important to be vigilant in monitoring one's wellness, while recognizing that colleagues and supervisors often have a clearer view of one's overall functioning. By letting supervisors know of one's struggles, they can offer support that can serve to prevent frustration from becoming more serious and disruptive.

Healthy Habits

Healthy habits can be practiced that serve as a solid foundation for a long career as a CMH counselor. Some suggestions include the following:

- Allow yourself time to arrive at work early enough to spend a few minutes to review the coming day and reflect on your expectations about what you will encounter. Being rushed and feeling hurried creates an internal climate that makes it much easier to lose focus on the real work.

- Pay attention to client scheduling. Clustering more challenging clients at the end of the day to postpone a difficult session is unwise. Instead, schedule challenging cases when you are most fresh and are less likely to carry difficult material home. If you find yourself dreading a session with a particular client, discuss this case with your clinical supervisor or peer supervision group.

- Suggest a "no shop talk" rule at lunch. There is good reason not to spend lunchtime engaged in conversation about work stress while nourishing your body. Instead, allow yourself an opportunity to enjoy colleagues' company without work stress intruding.

- Be aware of who you spend your time with. Cynical, negative, or critical colleagues can sap your energy (Skovholt, 2001). Colleagues who are burned out consume great amounts of one's time and energy because they need help to feel better about their work.

- Get centered between clients. We often encourage counselors to do a "system check" between clients, which includes asking (1) How am I feeling right now (physically, mentally, emotionally)? (2) Am I holding any tension or stress in my body? Where? Why? (3) What do I expect to encounter with my client today? (4) How can I best help them meet their goals today? Adjust these prompts to meet your needs. A system check can assist the transition from one client to the next and allow you to be fully present.

- Use an end-of-the-day ritual to close your workday. For example, some counselors are deliberate about the act of locking their file cabinet, as an intentional reminder that the day is closed. Others make a ritual of turning off the lights or watering plants as a reminder that the day has come to a close. Without an overt reminder that work is over, professional thoughts and concerns can more easily intrude into one's personal life.

- Create a ritual related to entering your home life. During an age when pagers, cell phones, and e-mails can follow one anywhere, one must be deliberate about being at home. Change out of work clothes into something more comfortable immediately when you arrive home as a metaphorical "shedding" of the work day and wrapping oneself in the comfort of home.

These suggestions may sound simplistic, but the practice of straightforward strategies allows for the development of more complex tactics as work demands increase. Similarly, basic wellness strategies serve as the foundation for all counseling work. Basic wellness strategies include sleep, exercise, and nutrition. Be sure to get enough rest each night, which generally entails at least 7 hours of sleep and preferably 8 (NHLBI, 2009). Failure to get adequate sleep means more difficulty focusing and remembering information and is linked to difficulty with regulating mood and engaging in relationships. Exercise also is linked to overall wellness. Many researchers suggest at least 20 minutes of exercise, three times per week, yet taking a brisk walk at lunch can be a great way to break up your day and tap into new energy for the afternoon. Balanced nutrition and sufficient hydration are also part of staying well. Eat regular healthy meals and attend to alcohol and caffeine intake. Many individuals rely on caffeine as a substitute for natural energy. If you are physically fatigued, your body is trying to tell you to rest, and you would be wise to listen. Similarly, if you hold religious or spiritual beliefs and feel ungrounded or disconnected, it may be time to attend to your spiritual life with spiritual practices, consultation with religious leaders, or engagement with your religious community.

It can be tempting to avoid dealing with one's wellness needs even when things begin to go poorly. If physically sick, you should take time to go see a doctor and, similarly, if you struggle with work challenges, you should seek help. Sometimes clinical supervision is sufficient to prevent burnout or compassion fatigue, but if work stress has become overwhelming, seek personal counseling. Eighty-three percent of American Counseling Association members surveyed reported that they have been to personal counseling (Lawson, 2007). Further, according to Orlinsky, Botermans, and Ronnestad (2001) 76.9% of mental health clinicians in their study who had received therapy reported that personal therapy had a strong positive influence on their professional development. So, personal counseling may, in fact, make you a better counselor.

Like so many aspects of one's work, staying well personally and professionally is simple but not always easy. Deliberate attention to what is needed to stay in balance and asking for support is key to staying in the clinical mental health field for the long haul. Carl Rogers (1995) once reflected, "I have always been better at caring for and looking after others than I have in caring for myself. But in these later years, I made progress" (p. 80). There are three hopeful notes in that short quotation. First, even giants in the field struggle with wellness. No one is immune to the hazards of the work, and because counselors are valued for how they care for others, balance is elusive. Second, it takes time to see and feel progress, which leads to the third point. You have an advantage over Rogers, in that others have blazed the trail, providing guideposts, so learn from their wisdom.

CASE STUDY

Anthony is a counselor in a local community agency that provides mental health services to families. He recently completed his graduate degree, he has worked at the agency for about 4 months, and he receives clinical supervision toward licensure at his workplace. He enjoys the work he does, and he usually feels good about it. The families on his caseload are challenging, and many are court-referred as a result of child abuse or neglect or other court involvement. Anthony has grown very aware of the fact that his colleagues often joke about the horrific stories they hear about their clients' lives. They describe this as "dark humor," warning that if you don't laugh about it, you will certainly cry. Secretly Anthony is more likely to cry, and he is uncomfortable when colleagues make light of the abuses clients have experienced.

Anthony has two new clients on his caseload: a brother (9 years old) and sister (11 years old) who were recently placed with their aunt and uncle after the discovery that their biological father had

(Continued)

(Continued)

sexually abused both children. Anthony believes that the aunt and uncle are well meaning and sincerely care for the children, but they have limited skills to help the children cope with their trauma. Anthony began by conducting family therapy, and he added individual, nondirective play therapy for both children. In addition, he visits the children at school once a week. When a colleague heard how much time Anthony was spending on this one family, he snickered, "No amount of time is going to make those kids less sexually abused." The comment infuriated Anthony, fueling him to work even harder on the children's behalf.

As the weeks went by, the children shared more of their stories with Anthony, and he regularly finds himself shaken by the graphic details reported. Worse yet, no matter how hard he works, the aunt and uncle complain about disruptive behavior problems at home, and they have begun to wonder aloud about the usefulness of coming to counseling. Anthony regularly talks about the case in clinical supervision, and he often presents a more optimistic picture than he actually feels. He does not share with his supervisor how he loses sleep wondering if he serves the children well enough and how he frequently doubts whether he possesses the necessary skills. Over time, Anthony becomes less engaged, eliminating the school visits and the play therapy, until he feels he is going through the motions. If he is honest with himself, Anthony is afraid he cannot help these children, and it is simply difficult to witness their struggles up close.

Discussion Questions

1. What risks or hazards are present in Anthony's work and workplace?

2. What conditions is Anthony experiencing as a result of his work with the children (e.g., burnout, compassion fatigue, vicarious traumatization)?

3. What wellness concerns can you identify in his colleagues (e.g., burnout, compassion fatigue, vicarious traumatization)?

4. What steps might Anthony take to maintain a better work/life balance?

5. If you were offering support to Anthony, what would you suggest he do differently over the long term?

REFERENCES

American Counseling Association. (2014). *ACA Code of Ethics*. Alexandria, VA: Author.

Bishop, S. R., Lau, M., Shapiro, S., Carlson, L., Anderson, N. D., Carmody, J., et al. (2004). Mindfulness: A proposed operational definition. *Clinical Psychology: Science and Practice, 11,* 230–241. doi:10.1093/clipsy.bph077

Bowen, S., Chawla, N., & Marlatt, G. A. (2011). *Mindfulness-based relapse prevention for addictive behaviors: A clinician's guide.* New York: Guilford Press.

Brown, A., Marquis, A., & Guiffrida, D. (2013). Mindfulness-based interventions in counseling. *Journal of Counseling & Development, 91*(1), 96–104. doi:10.1002/j.1556-6676.2013.00077.x

Campbell, J., & Christopher, J. (2012). Teaching mindfulness to create effective counselors. *Journal of Mental Health Counseling, 34*(3), 213–226.

Christopher, J., Christopher, S., Dunnagan, T., & Schure, M. (2006). Teaching self-care through mindfulness practices: The application of yoga, meditation, and qigong to counselor training. *Journal of Humanistic Psychology, 46,* 494–509.

Davis, D. M., & Hayes, J. A. (2011). What are the benefits of mindfulness? A practice review of psychotherapy-related research. *Psychotherapy, 48,* 198–208. doi:10.1037/a0022062

Ericson-Lidman, E., & Strandberg, G. (2007). Burnout: Co-workers' perceptions of signs preceding workmates' burnout. *Journal of Advanced Nursing, 60*(2), 199–208.

Fahy, A. (2007). The unbearable fatigue of compassion: Notes from a substance abuse counselor who dreams of working at Starbuck's. *Clinical Social Work Journal, 35*(3), 199–205. doi:10.1007/s10615-007-0094-4

Figley, C. R. (1997). Burnout as systemic traumatic stress: A model for helping traumatized family members. In C. R. Figley (Ed.), *Burnout in families: The systemic costs of caring* (pp. 15–28). New York: CRC Press.

Figley, C. R. (2004). *Compassion fatigue educator course workbook.* Tallahassee, FL: Green Cross Foundation.

Freudenberg, H. J., & Richelson, G. (1980). *Burnout: The high cost of high achievement.* New York: Anchor Press.

Geller, S. M., Greenberg, L. S., & Watson, J. G. (2010). Therapist and client perceptions of therapeutic presence: The development of a measure. *Psychotherapy Research, 20,* 599–610. doi:10.1080/10503307.2010.495957

Gentry, J. E., Baranowsky, A. B., & Dunning, K. (2002). ARP: The accelerated recovery program (ARP) for compassion fatigue. In C. R. Figley (Ed.), *Treating compassion fatigue* (pp. 123–138). New York: Brunner-Routledge.

Grepmair, L., Mitterlehner, F., Loew, T., Bachler, E., Rother, W., & Nickel, M. (2007). Promoting mindfulness in psychotherapists in training influences the treatment results of their patients: A randomized, double-blind, controlled study. *Psychotherapy and Psychosomatics, 76,* 332–338.

Hofmann, S. G., Sawyer, A. T., Witt, A. A., & Oh, D. (2010). The effect of mindfulness-based therapy on anxiety and depression: A meta-analytic review. *Journal of Consulting and Clinical Psychology, 78,* 169–183.

Huggard, P. (2003). Compassion fatigue: How much can I give? *Medical Education, 37*(2), 163–164. doi:10.1046/j.1365-2923.2003.01414.x

Kabat-Zinn, J. (1982). An outpatient program in behavioral medicine for chronic pain patients based on the practice of mindfulness meditation: Theoretical considerations and preliminary results. *General Hospital Psychiatry, 4,* 33–47.

Kramen-Kahn, B., & Hansen, N. D. (1998). Rafting the rapids: Occupational hazards, rewards, and coping strategies of psychotherapists. *Professional Psychology: Research and Practice, 29*(2), 130–134.

Lawson, G. (2007). Counselor wellness and impairment: A national survey. *Journal of Humanistic Counseling, Education, and Development, 46*(1), 20–34.

Lawson, G., & Myers, J. E. (2011). Wellness, professional quality of life, and career sustaining behaviors: What keeps us well? *Journal of Counseling & Development, 89*(2), 163–171.

Lee, S., Cho, S., Kissinger, D., & Ogle, N. (2010). A typology of burnout in professional counselors. *Journal of Counseling & Development, 88,* 131–138.

Maris, J. A. (2009). The impact of a mind/body medicine class on counselor training: A personal journey. *Journal of Humanistic Psychology, 49,* 229–235.

Maslach, C. (2003). *Burnout: The cost of caring.* Cambridge, MA: Malor Books.

Maslach, C., & Leiter, M. P. (1997). *The truth about burnout.* San Francisco: Jossey Bass.

Maslach, C., Schaufeli, W. B., & Leiter, M. P. (2001). Job burnout. *Annual Review of Psychology, 52,* 397–422.

McCann, I. L., & Pearlman, L. A. (1990). Vicarious traumatization: A framework for understanding the psychological effects of working with victims. *Journal of Traumatic Stress, 3*(2), 131–149. doi:10.1007/BF00975140

Meyer, D., & Ponton, R. (2006). The healthy tree: A metaphorical perspective of counselor well-being. *Journal of Mental Health Counseling, 28*(3), 189–202.

Miller, M. W., Wolf, E. J., Reardon, A., Greene, A., Ofrat, S., McInerney, S. (2012). Personality and the latent structure of PTSD comorbidity. *Journal of Anxiety Disorders, 26,* 599–607.

Mulligan, L. (2004). Overcoming compassion fatigue. *The Kansas Nurse, 79*(7), 1–2.

Myers, J. E., & Sweeney, T. J. (2005). The indivisible self: An evidence based model of wellness. In J. E. Myers & T. J. Sweeney (Eds.), *Counseling for wellness: Theory, research, and practice* (pp. 29–38). Alexandria, VA: American Counseling Association.

Myers, J. E., Sweeney, T. J., & Witmer, J. M. (2000). The Wheel of Wellness counseling for wellness: A holistic model for treatment planning. *Journal of Counseling & Development, 78*(3), 251–266.

National Heart, Lung, and Blood Institute. (2009). *Healthy sleep at a glance.* Retrieved from http://www .nhlbi.nih.gov/health/public/sleep/healthy_sleep_atglance.pdf.

Olfson, M., Mojtabai, R., Sampson, N. A., Hwang, I., Druss, B., Wang, P. S., et al. (2009). Dropout from outpatient mental health care in the United States. *Psychiatric Services, 60*(7), 898–907.

Orlinsky, D. E., Botermans, J-F., & Ronnestad, M. H. (2001). Towards an empirically grounded model of psychotherapy training: Four thousand therapists rate influences on their development. *Australian Psychologist, 36*(2), 139–148.

Osofsky, J. D., Putnam, F. W., & Lederman, C. S. (2008). How to maintain emotional health when working with trauma. *Juvenile and Family Court Journal, 59*(4), 91–102.

Pearlman, L. A., & Mac Ian, P. S. (1995). Vicarious traumatization: An empirical study of the effects of trauma work on trauma therapists. *Professional Psychology: Research and Practice, 26*(6), 558–565.

Pearlman, L. A., & Saakvitne, K. W. (1995). Treating therapists with vicarious traumatization and secondary traumatic stress disorders. In C. R. Figley (Ed.), *Compassion fatigue: Coping with secondary traumatic stress disorders in those who treat the traumatized* (pp. 150–177). New York: Brunner/Mazel.

Ponton, R. F. (2012). Mindfulness and mastery in counseling: Introduction. *Journal of Mental Health Counseling, 34*(3), 189–196.

Radey, M., & Figley, C. R. (2007). The social psychology of compassion. *Clinical Social Work Journal, 35*(3), 207–214. doi:10.1007/s10615–007–0087–3

Roberts, S. B., Flannelly, K. J., Weaver, A. J., & Figley, C. R. (2003). Compassion fatigue among chaplains, clergy, and other respondents after September 11th. *The Journal of Nervous and Mental Disease, 191*(11), 756–758. doi:10.1097/01.nmd.0000095129.50042.30

Rogers, C. R. (1995). *A way of being.* Boston: Houghton Mifflin.

Shapiro, S. L., & Carlson, L. E. (2009). *The art and science of mindfulness: Integrating mindfulness into psychology and the helping professions.* Washington, DC: American Psychological Association.

Skovholt, T. M. (2001). *The resilient practitioner.* Boston: Allyn & Bacon.

Skovholt, T. M., Grier, T. L., & Hanson, M. R. (2001). Career counseling for longevity: Self-care and burnout prevention strategies for counselor resilience. *Journal of Career Development, 27*(3), 167–176.

Skovholt, T. M., & Trotter-Mathison, M. (2011). *The resilient practitioner: Burnout prevention and self-care strategies for counselors, therapists, teachers, and health professionals* (2nd ed.). New York: Routledge/Taylor.

Sommer, C. A., & Cox, J. A. (2005). Elements of supervision in sexual violence counselors' narratives: A qualitative analysis. *Counselor Education and Supervision, 45,* 119–134.

Stamm, H. B. (2009–2011). *The ProQOL5.* Retrieved from http://proqol.org/ProQol_Test.html.

Stamm, B. H., & Figley, C. R. (1996). *Compassion Satisfaction and Fatigue Test.* Retrieved from https://ncwwi.org/files/Incentives__Work_Conditions/Compassion-Satisfaction-Fatigue-Self-Test.pdf.

Tabor, P. D. (2011). Vicarious traumatization: Concept analysis. *Journal of Forensic Nursing, 7*(4), 203–308. doi:10.1111/j.1939-3938.2011.01115.x

Taylor, S., Wald, J., & Asmundson, G. J. G. (2006). Factors associated with occupational impairment in people seeking treatment for posttraumatic stress disorder. *Canadian Journal of Community Mental Health, 25,* 289–301.

Teasdale, J. D., & Ma, S. H. (2004). Mindfulness-based cognitive therapy for depression: Replication and exploration of differential relapse prevention effects. *Journal of Consulting and Clinical Psychology, 72,* 31–40.

Trippany, R. L., White Kress, V. E., & Wilcoxon, S. A. (2004). Preventing vicarious trauma: What counselors should know when working with trauma survivors. *Journal of Counseling & Development, 82*(1), 31–37.

Witmer, J. M., & Young, M. E. (1996). Preventing counselor impairment: A wellness approach. *The Journal of Humanistic Education and Development, 34*(3), 141–155.

Wolever, R. Q., & Best, J. L. (2009). Mindfulness-based approaches to eating disorders. In F. Didonna (Ed.), *Clinical handbook of mindfulness* (pp. 259–287). New York: Springer.

Using Research to Improve Clinical Practice

Kelly L. Wester and Tamarine Foreman

Learning Goals

Upon completion of this chapter, you will be able to do the following:

1. Describe the nature and goals of empirical research

2. Understand the steps of the research process

3. Explain the role of the clinical mental health (CMH) counselor as scientist-practitioner

4. Apply approaches to research (e.g., single subject, case study, and program evaluation) to the work of CMH counselors

$\mathbf{A}$s you sit in your office having a stare-down with Amanda, the 17-year-old client you have been counseling, you wonder to yourself, *Is this the most effective way to work with this client? Is there something else I should be doing instead of having staring matches? Is there another way to try to get her to talk or to share what is going on? I don't feel like I am helping.* All counselors have had these thoughts at some point in their career.

The question is how do you answer these difficult questions and figure out how to work with different clients and different presenting concerns? The very nature of clinical practice allows for a great deal of discretion (Gambrill, 2005). You get to make decisions on questions to ask, assessments to use, length of counseling sessions, diagnoses you provide, structure of treatment, interventions you select, and the goals you pursue with clients. With all of this freedom and variance in direction, what can you use to drive your decisions? The answer: research. Whether it is research conducted by you in your own practice with clients or using what has already been conducted and published by others, research provides direction for your work.

RESEARCH DEFINED AND DESCRIBED

Research is a frightening word for some, an area of study from which many counselors shy away. However, research is simply systematically collecting and looking at information to answer the questions one already has (Hadley & Mitchell, 1995). Everyone has questions—about clients, clinical work, effective treatments, and impact of supervision. There are five ways or sources of information one can use to answer these questions: tenacity, authority, intuition, experience, and scientific method (Heppner, Wampold, & Kivlighan, 2008). Some ways of knowing are grounded in empirical research whereas others are not.

Before moving further into the discussion of research and counseling practice, it is important to first define *empirical research*. Merriam-Webster defines *empirical* as originating in or based on observations; capable of being verified or disproved by observation or experiment. In more general terms, empirical means data. Thus, empirical research involves questions answered in a systematic way through the collection of data. Data can be qualitative or quantitative. It can be collected through observation or watching people, interviews and asking questions, archival or existing information, or the use of questionnaires, assessments, or surveys. Throughout the rest of this chapter, the term *research* refers to that of empirical research, or questions that have been answered through the systematic collection of some form of data.

WAYS OF KNOWING

The first way of knowing is **tenacity**. Tenacity is defined as perseverance or holding fast. Thus, whatever you believe to be true must be true because you have always known it to be true. The second way of knowing is **authority**, which is to believe something because someone in authority (e.g., faculty, supervisor, president, workshop presenter) says it. Thus, the assumption is that those in authority speak the truth. An example of these two forms of knowing is that we have known for many decades that there are nine planets that orbit the sun. We were taught this by an authority figure throughout our early school years and have believed it to be true; thus, it has always been true. In the past few years, however, scientists (authority) have rescinded this tenacious knowledge and have questioned whether Pluto is truly a planet. This questioning has arisen from new information or knowledge that has changed the definition of a planet. So who is correct . . . the previous authorities who identified nine planets, the current authorities who indicate we have eight planets, or your previous existing knowledge?

A third way of knowing is through **intuition**. Intuition is defined as a perception of the truth; a keen insight; or an immediate cognition or feeling about a situation, person, or object. This knowledge does not come from a specific person or source; thus, it is not originating from tenacity or authority but is more about an internal reaction. A fourth way of knowing is through **experience**, thus what one has learned across time in similar or different experiences. For example, you know what to expect in graduate school based on your earlier experiences in high school and undergraduate courses.

Finally, a fifth way of knowing is through **research**, or the use of the scientific method. Research uses empirical tests to establish verifiable, tested facts. The scientific method provides knowledge through a systematic process to gain information. Specifically, one must select a topic or a problem to examine, look for explanations to the problem, state a hypothesis or what one believes about the problem, and then test the belief or hypothesis by collecting information or data to support or reject it. Interestingly enough, this is what counselors do daily in their practice with clients (see Figure 13.1).

Each way of knowing could drive the decisions you make with your clients; however, there are problems inherent in the first four ways of knowing. For instance, simply because we believe something (i.e., tenacity) does not make it true. As stated earlier, we have long "known" that nine planets existed (knowledge through tenacity); however, simply because we have believed that for most, if not all, of our lives, does not mean that the information currently is correct. Based on new information and knowledge collected through research, Pluto is no longer considered a planet. However, knowledge provided by an authority

Figure 13.1 Scientific Method Connected to Clinical Practice

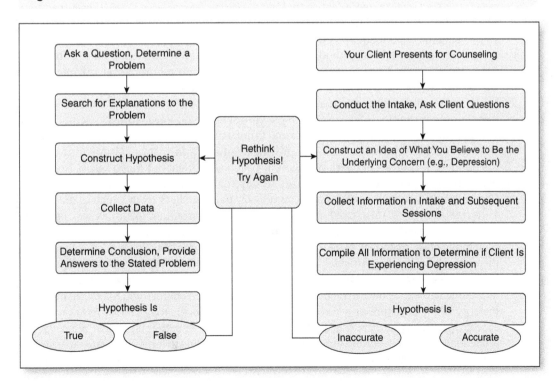

figure still needs to be assessed for accuracy and not blindly accepted as true. Therefore, in this case, merely because a scientist (or group of scientists) provided a new definition of a planet does not mean this should alter your perspective. Instead, it should cause you to critically think through the new information, in comparison to previous information and other research findings, thereby searching for support for what authority is saying.

Intuition, or the idea that truth equates simply with what makes sense, is not how decisions should be made with clients. This is like saying that because we "feel good" about a particular client using over-the-counter cold medicine to lower depression, this makes this decision accurate. The fourth way of knowing, one's experience with the world, does hold credence; however, this should not be the only way one makes decisions. For example, my experience informs me that carrots are orange, because that is the only color carrot that I have purchased and eaten in my life. Walking through the grocery store, however, you may see purple and yellow carrots. My previous experience with carrots might cause me to believe that purple and yellow do not equate to a carrot; thus, these objects must not be carrots. Instead, I should use this experience to create more knowledge and then look for support for the existence of purple and yellow carrots.

Tenacity, authority, experience, and intuition are ways of knowing that are based in human error (Sexton, Whiston, Bleuer, & Walz, 1997). Human decision, when based on these four ways of knowing, is biased in one's judgments and memories. Using intuition and tenacity, one may select and implement interventions based on one's personal styles or beliefs, which may not be accurate or appropriate for the client (Gambrill, 2005). In regard to using one's experiences in making decisions, Sexton et al. (1997) discussed how one's memory is flawed and reconstructed to fill in the gaps in knowledge. He indicated that when using the experiential way of knowing when working with clients, counselors use the comparison method. This method bases one's decisions solely on memory (i.e., comparing the client sitting in front of you with previous clients). He reported that this method is flawed in many ways, cautioning that using the comparison method with clients is limited by the extent of one's experiences. For example, if Amanda, presented at the beginning of this chapter, is the first 17-year-old female with whom you have worked, the number of clients you can compare her to is zero. Comparing her to the resistant 29-year-old you worked with last week might not provide adequate information. Or Amanda may be the hundredth adolescent client with whom you have worked but might be the first client who has been adopted, or who refuses to talk, or whose second language is English. Consequently, you may not have an accurate comparison client from which to draw.

Sexton et al. (1997) also cautioned against the comparison method (or experiential way of knowing) based on the fact that memory is reconstructed. Take a moment . . . try to remember class from last week. In that class many things may have taken place. First, there may have been a particular topic that was discussed, a chapter or two that you read before class, PowerPoint slides that were presented, and peers that may have asked questions. There may have even been a classroom activity. Whereas you may remember the majority of the structure or events that took place, the details may be lost. What were the specific questions that were asked from your peers? What were the slide titles? What was the sequential order of events and topics discussed? In attempting to remember, one reconstructs what took place and fills in the voids in one's memory with details, some or most of which may be incorrect even though you *believe* them to have existed (Sexton et al., 1997).

In class, you might take a moment to jot down everything from last week, in order with details, and then compare it to a classmate's notes. You may find that not all of the details are the same but that you and your peer wholeheartedly believe your experiences to be correct. This experience is based on your memory, reconstruction of your memory, and your experience in the classroom.

As stated so clearly by Heppner et al. (2008), "To be credible, reliable, and effective, a profession must be built on dependable facts or truths rather than on tenacity, degrees from authority figures, or subjective opinions. . . . [Instead our decisions] must be based on knowledge outside of personal beliefs and biases" (p. 5). Accordingly, we must base our decisions in empirical knowledge, otherwise known as the scientific method or research. Our beliefs, gut feelings, and experience should not be discarded completely, however, because they provide useful information. Ideally, empirical research should provide the grounding or basis for our knowledge; then we should use our beliefs, hunches, and experiences to make meaning of the findings in the research. This blending speaks to the evidence-based practice model.

EVIDENCE-BASED PRACTICE

Evidence-based practice, which arises out of the medical model for evidence-based medicine, has been discussed as far back as the 19th century (Sackett, Rosenberg, Gray, Haynes, & Richardson, 1996). One of the most common or frequently used definitions of evidence-based medicine is provided by David Sackett (Sackett et al., 1996), who denoted that evidence-based medicine is "the conscientious, explicit, and judicious use of current best evidence in making decisions about the care of individual patients. The practice of evidence based medicine means integrating individual clinical expertise with the best available external clinical evidence from systematic research" (p. 71). Whereas Sackett spoke specifically of medicine, this definition and idea can be used in the field of counseling when discussing evidence-based practice. Evidence-based practice is the use of current research evidence about a treatment, intervention, clinical process, or diagnosis/symptom and pairing that with your clinical expertise, skill, and judgment. In addition to empirical research evidence, and clinical expertise, another aspect of evidence-based practice not frequently discussed is client values and preferences (Gambrill, 2005). The combination of these three factors of clinical work is considered evidence-based practice (EBP; see Figure 13.2).

Consider this example of evidence-based practice. During an intake with Sam, a 45-year-old male, you find that he has been unable to sleep, has lost his ability to enjoy life and participate in tasks that have previously provided him pleasure, is unable to focus at work, and has lost his appetite. Throughout the intake, you focus mostly on these symptoms and gain more information from him. Once you feel like you have gathered enough information you diagnose Sam with major depressive disorder and set the treatment goal of decreasing depression and increasing functioning in his life. According to recent literature on major depressive disorder, some evidence-based treatments include antidepressant medication, electroconvulsive therapy, light therapy, and cognitive-behavioral therapy (e.g., Kennedy, Lam, Cohen, & Ravindran, 2001; Manber et al., 2008). Selecting one or many of these treatments might bring positive outcomes for Sam (i.e., decreasing his depressive symptoms and increasing enjoyment

Figure 13.2   Evidence-Based Practice (EBP)

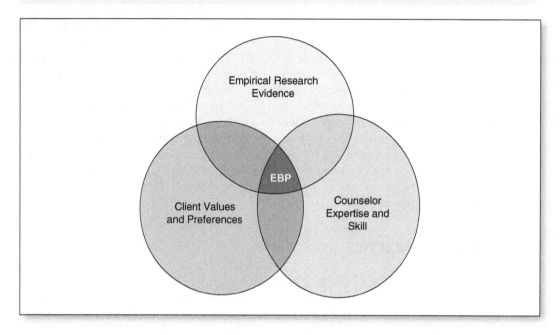

and life functioning). However, the diagnosis of major depressive disorder is based on the counselor's skill and expertise. Simply stated, as the clinician, do you know enough about the diagnostic system to diagnose correctly? Did you ask Sam the right questions? Did you gather enough information to determine the cause or reason for his depressive symptoms? Sometimes clients do not always offer the causes or originating events of their symptoms, or even know them, but it is up to the counselor to use his or her skill and judgment in gaining the correct information in order to apply relevant empirical research to practice.

In asking more questions of Sam in the second session, you find that his depressive symptoms are a result of his partner of 20 years being diagnosed with a terminal illness. This new information would possibly change the course of treatment or change the suggested direction based on research evidence. Research evidence for bereavement, which can have depressive symptoms but not necessarily require a diagnosis of major depressive disorder, reveals a different method of treatment than what was found earlier for major depressive disorder. Specifically for Sam's case, research evidence indicates that receiving preloss help from hospice will minimize the possibility of Sam receiving the actual diagnoses of major depressive disorder postloss; that receiving complicated grief disorder treatment has better treatment effects for decreasing grief symptoms than psychotherapy as usual; and that therapy combined with medication can be helpful (Zhang, El-Jawahri, & Prigerson, 2006). Thus, the need to combine clinical expertise with research evidence is important. If the wrong diagnosis is provided, it doesn't matter what research evidence indicates is effective—it will be the wrong treatment.

The third factor of evidence-based practice is that of client preference, so Sam's values and preferences play a role in what treatment is provided. Whereas the effective treatment of grief and bereavement for Sam is a combination of a 16-week counseling program, hospice, and medication (Zhang et al., 2006), Sam may decide he does not want to take medication and that 16 weeks is too long because it would take him away from his partner who may only have a few months to live. Thus, your role as a counselor is to determine how to amalgam Sam's preferences, with empirical research evidence and your experiences and clinical judgment to provide the best treatment possible for Sam.

SCIENTIST-PRACTITIONER MODEL

The goal of evidence-based practice is to break down the barrier between research and practice (Gambrill, 2005). Another model that attempts to break this barrier down or narrow the gap so that counselors use research in their practice is the **scientist-practitioner model**. The scientist-practitioner model emerged in the 1970s at a conference in Boulder, Colorado. The model highlights the need for a balance between empirical knowledge (i.e., research) and the practice of counseling or therapy (Stoltenberg & Pace, 2007). The idea behind the model is to help both researchers and practitioners understand that research and clinical practice do not happen in isolation; the integration of both is necessary for the counseling profession to continue to grow and be effective (King & Otis, 2004).

To be a scientist-practitioner means to incorporate research into your practice as a counselor. The American Counseling Association (2005) stresses the need to ensure that, as a counselor, you are effective and engaged in practices with your clients that are known to work. Specifically, the *ACA Code of Ethics* (2005) stipulates, "Counselors and their clients work jointly in devising integrated counseling plans that offer reasonable promise of success" (A.1.c), which stresses the combination of client values and preferences, counselor expertise, and research evidence provided in the evidence-based practice model stated earlier. In addition, the 2014 *ACA Code of Ethics* states, "Counselors have a responsibility to the public to engage in counseling practices that are based on rigorous research methodologies," and "counselors continually monitor their effectiveness as professionals and take steps to improve when necessary" (p. 8).

Based on the ACA Code of Ethics, in order to be a scientist-practitioner, ethical counselors need to know how to consume research, how to apply it, and how to evaluate the treatment they are providing. Research consumption is reading existing empirical research that has been conducted and published. Most counselors have been found to consume some format of research, with 70% indicating they read professional literature to remain current on evidence-based practices (Wester, Mobley, & Faulkner, 2006). A **research-informed practice** is one in which the counselor bases decisions on evidence, not on charisma and intuition, and integrates existing knowledge into practice, rather than relying on the comparison method between clients (Karam & Sprenkle, 2010).

Research application is to apply the information one has consumed. Once you have read the existing literature, the next step is to take the knowledge you have gained about diagnosis, treatment planning, and interventions and apply that in your clinical practice with clients. Application may be implementing a new intervention, creating or applying a new treatment protocol, or simply asking a few questions related to a diagnosis or presenting concern you recently learned were relevant. Whereas the majority of counselors were found to consume research, slightly less indicated they applied it in their practice (Stoltenberg & Pace, 2007). Of those who consumed empirical research, only 77% indicated they agreed to apply what they learned (Wester et al., 2006).

Fewer counselors reported collecting their own data or engaging in evaluation of their services (25% to 56%; Wester et al., 2006). Those who did evaluate their services indicated they did so through assessing client change or client reports of satisfaction. Whereas consumption, application, and evaluation may sound simple to some, there are many steps involved in this process. In order to help make it easier to understand, the process has been broken into 8 steps (see Table 13.1). This 8-step process is a combination of how to use research in practice delineated by Williams, Patterson, and Miller (2006) and the evidence-based practice model provided by Schardt and Mayer (2010). Notice how this scientist-practitioner process mimics the scientific method stated earlier.

To fully explain this 8-step scientist-practitioner process, consider the following case study.

Table 13.1 Eight-Step Scientist-Practitioner Process to Consuming, Applying, and Conducting Research in Clinical Practice

Step	Description
1. Assess the client	It all starts with your client, regardless if it is about the presenting concern, diagnosis, client context, or desired treatment.
2. Create a well-formulated question	Determine what it is that you want to know, what questions you are trying to answer.
3. Conduct a search for evidence	Select the appropriate resources to search for existing research.
4. Select and access articles to read	Find articles and research that are available to you.
5. Evaluate and appraise the quality of research	Is what you found valid, reliable, trustworthy? Was a quality study conducted?
6. Synthesize information	Identify the trends and patterns and integrate the information to provide a more holistic finding of what is effective or appropriate.
7. Clinical application	Apply the findings to your client or use the information in practice, if appropriate.
8. Evaluation	Evaluate your performance and/or the effectiveness of the evidence-based treatment in your clinical practice or with your client.

CASE STUDY

Timothy, a 14-year-old male, does not want to come to counseling. Timothy is being required to come to counseling by his mother. She indicates that he has been defiant in school and at home, his grades are dropping, he does not do his chores, and he spends all of his discretionary time in his room by himself or playing video games. She indicates that recently he has been getting in trouble at school and just spent 2 days in in-school suspension. Timothy's mother also indicates that she and Timothy's father are separated and will divorce soon and that she has had previous problems with chemical addictions. When you ask Timothy about his mother's previous addictions and the impending divorce, Timothy responds, "Not gonna talk about it." Timothy's mother also reports that he had cut crosses into his hands this past week, and she was concerned about this behavior. During this intake, Timothy reports to you—to the surprise of his mother—that he has had frequent suicidal ideations but currently has no plan to kill himself. He reports that cutting crosses in his hands was stupid and he was not going to do that again.

Step 1: Assess the Client

The first step in the scientist-practitioner model is a basic step in any clinical work with a client: assessing the client. As Schardt and Mayer (2010) so candidly stated, evidence-based practice "always begins and ends with the [client]." Assessment of the client includes determining the client's presenting concerns and diagnosis, demographics, and strengths and the surrounding familial and/or environmental context. It is this information that will help you determine the intervention or treatment that you will select to counsel the client.

In the case of Timothy, assessment includes gathering the information from his mother about the presenting concerns (i.e., suicidal ideation, cutting behaviors, school difficulties, defiance at school and home) and about his family (i.e., what is his mom's addictive behavior?; when did the divorce occur?; what is the interaction between family members, and how does this interaction differ before and after the divorce?). This assessment might lead you to consider diagnoses such as disruptive disorder NOS (not otherwise specified), oppositional defiant disorder (ODD), or depending on the time the divorce occurred, it may be adjustment disorder or depressive disorder. Another possibility or co-occurrence might be attention deficit disorder (ADD), which may lead to some of the difficulties at school. The information provided in the case study hints at some of these disorders but does not lead you specifically to one. Thus, continued assessment is important.

Step 2: Create a Well-Formulated Question

The next step in the process is to clearly articulate what it is you want to know (Williams et al., 2006). Are you looking for more information on diagnoses, to determine the treatment goals you should set with this client based on the assessment in Step 1, or are you trying to determine the treatment options? Let's say that through further assessment with Timothy and his mother you determine that his diagnoses include oppositional defiant disorder (ODD) and attention deficit disorder (ADD). What you are wondering now is the most effective way of working with Timothy based on these diagnoses. The well-formulated question helps to narrow the search you will conduct of existing empirical research. In this case you are looking for treatment options that have been shown to work and have positive outcomes for adolescent clients with a combination of ODD and ADD.

Step 3: Conduct a Search for Evidence

Whereas consumption, application, and evaluation of research are a foundation for quality, ethical clinical practice, they are easier to discuss than to do. Up to this point you may have met with a client for intake, or even a few sessions, and finally formulated your question—or what it is you want to know. The next step is to search for the existing empirical information. This step has to occur before you can even begin to consume the research.

Different resources exist to conduct searches. While in a training program and enrolled as a student, searching for literature is fairly easy because most colleges and universities have multiple research databases (e.g., PsycINFO, EBSCO, PubMed) and typically provide students with free electronic copies of journal articles. However, once you graduate and are in full-time practice, access to research and articles is not always as easy or free. One location that provides links to other organizations that support and provide free access to evidence-based practice research is the Social Work Policy Institute (http://www .socialworkpolicy.org/research/evidence-based-practice-2.html#resources). Also the state of North Carolina has an online digital collection of knowledge and scholarship produced by faculty and researchers residing in the state (http://libres.uncg.edu/ir), and other states may have similar collections. See Table 13.2 for a few online search engines, or Schardt and Mayer (2010) and Williams and colleagues (2006) for additional resources.

Table 13.2   Mental Health Literature Search Engines

Search Engine	Location	Free/Cost Search Ability	Free/Cost Article Access
PsycINFO	www.apa.org/psycinfo	Free to search for abstracts and articles	Minimal cost (<$25) to print articles
Google Scholar	www.scholar.google.com	Free to search for abstracts and articles	Fee per article dependent on publisher of article
Evidence-Based Mental Health journal	http://ebmh.bmj.com	Free to search for abstracts and articles	Fee per article or for subscription
NC Docks	http://libres.uncg.edu/ir	Free to search for abstracts and articles	Free articles

For the purpose of Timothy, you would want to search for ODD and ADD treatments. Putting these two diagnostic labels into PsycINFO results in over 1,000 articles relevant to this topic. Whereas you may be able to peruse the first few articles to see if they are relevant, that may not be the best use of your time. Instead, think about how to narrow your search to be more specific (if that is appropriate! If you are interested in treatment for these two disorders because a myriad of youth are coming into your practice dually diagnosed, then this broad search might be more appropriate than a narrow one). For Timothy, you can further narrow the search by indicating an age range that includes 14-year-olds. You can further specify in the advanced search option in PsycINFO that you are only interested in empirical studies. This search (ADD, ODD, 14-year-old, empirical study) results in two articles. One article is titled "Effectiveness of a New Social/Cognitive Therapeutic Model for Aggressive Children" (Sahebi & Mirabdollahi, 2004), and the second article is "The Efficacy of Psychoanalysis for Children With Disruptive Disorders" (Fonagy & Target, 1994). Depending on the usefulness of these articles, other searches you may deem relevant in working with Timothy might be working with children of divorced families, suicidal ideation, or cutting behaviors. Interestingly, conducting the same search in Google Scholar turns up different articles, so it behooves you to use multiple search engines.

Step 4: Select and Access Articles to Read

Not all of these search engines provide you access to articles, particularly after you graduate from a university and no longer have free access. Some search engines (e.g., PsycINFO) require you to purchase articles for a nominal fee. For example, PsycINFO will allow you to search for articles for free but requires you to purchase a $12 24-hour pass to download all of the articles you have found. You may have access to other articles based on organizations of which you are a member. For example, members of the American Counseling Association are able to search for and freely access journal articles from the divisions in which they hold membership.

Once you have a pool of articles, you can read through the abstracts to determine which articles may be relevant to your originally stated question in Step 2. Selecting specific articles by using abstracts will limit the cost you might incur by paying for each article, and you may find that some articles are not as relevant as you thought based solely on their title.

What you need to consider is which articles will provide you with information you need to implement treatment or gain new knowledge about a diagnosis or presenting concern. In Timothy's case, the question formulated in Step 2 was What is the most effective way of working with Timothy? In looking at the abstract of the two articles found for Timothy in our PsycINFO search, Sahebi and Mirabdollahi's (2004) study appears to have implemented a treatment for students exhibiting ADD and ODD behaviors. Sahebi and Mirabdollahi (2004) examined 157 adolescents in this treatment and found that this treatment model reduced anxiety and depression, social problems, attention problems, and aggressive conduct. This article sounds very relevant, and you may want to access it for more information. The article by Fonagy and Target (1994) listed earlier included 135 children and adolescents with disruptive disorder diagnoses. The authors examined the outcome of therapy for these youth and found that those diagnosed with ODD had greater improvement than those diagnosed with ADD. This study may provide information for your work with Timothy given that you have dually diagnosed him with both of these disorders.

Step 5: Evaluate and Appraise the Quality of Research

It is essential to learn where to locate research and how to evaluate it (Karam & Sprenkle, 2010; Williams et al., 2006). One challenge with consumption, however, is that articles are not labeled as a "good" study or "bad" study. It is important to note that not everything that is published is high-quality research (Fong & Malone, 1994; Wester, Borders, Boul, & Horton, 2013). Thus, you need to become an informed consumer (Lebow, 2006; Stoltenberg & Pace, 2007), which means that you need to know how to critically read articles and integrate the findings, if appropriate, into your clinical practice. Stoltenberg and Pace (2007) stressed that counselors need to use the scientific method to evaluate the quality and applicability of a study rather than rely on authority (i.e., researchers) to tell them what they should be doing.

Critiquing studies is not always easy; it requires knowledge of the scientific method or research process and basic knowledge of what to look for in the study. Lebow (2006) reflects that consumers need to understand who published the study and where it was published. For example, was the study published in a newsletter or a peer-referred journal? Journals typically have more stringent criteria for publication than a newsletter. In the example of Timothy and the two articles cited earlier, in looking closer you will find that the study conducted by Sahebi and Mirabdollahi (2004) was published in *Journal of Iranian Psychologists*, and both researchers reside in Australia. Whereas the study's methodology may be sound, this information is important because it reflects the likelihood that the sample is not based in the United States. This information has relevance to the applicability to Timothy, who is a 14-year-old in the United States. It does not rule this article out in terms of relevance or the degree to which it can provide you important information but simply is a factor to consider.

Lebow (2006) stressed that counselors also need to evaluate the methodology used, whether the conclusions have been found in other studies, and who the study may be applicable to based on the sample. The American Counseling Association and the Association for Counselor Educators and Supervisors (ACES) funded the National Institute for Counseling Research. In 2012, this institute developed guidelines for qualitative and quantitative research that designates the best practices in counseling research. The guidelines stress that best practices in research stem from the introduction of the article through the discussion; however, a large portion of the criteria for best practices lies within the methodology of a study. In addition, ACES endorsed a list of criteria that highlights the skills, knowledge, and attitudes required for a counseling professional to be considered competent in conducting quality research (Wester & Borders, 2011). As stated by Sink and Mvududu (2010) and Wampold (2006), the degree to which research can effectively inform practice is bound by the quality of the research produced, or limited by the weakest point of the study. This means that the more problems, or the greater the problem, inherent in a study, the less likely it will provide you helpful information to use in your practice with Timothy or any other client.

Whereas there is a great deal in a methodology section to evaluate to determine whether a study was well done, only a few criteria are highlighted here. Other information can be found in other resources or books. For example, for an overview of all quantitative statistical analyses, please see Hancock and Mueller (2010) or Salkind (2000). For information on qualitative research, please see Hays and Singh (2012), and for information on criteria relevant for literature reviews refer to Boote and Beile (2005). Important issues to pay attention to when consuming research include (a) sampling method and relevance of the sample to your client and practice, (b) the reliability of the methodology, (c) the findings of the study, and (d) the validity of the findings.

Sampling Method and Relevance of Sample

It is important first to consider the sampling method and the relevance of the research sample to those with whom you work. When a researcher is attempting to select his or her sample, there are many factors involved, including access to a specific population, the sample size needed to conduct the study (different statistical analyses and design procedures require different sample sizes to adequately answer a research question), and the representativeness of the final sample (the more representative the sample is in demographics and presenting symptoms, the more generalizable it is to the population and potentially to your practice). Therefore, when consuming and evaluating a study for quality and relevance to your practice you would want to ensure that the sampling method was appropriate, the sample size was adequate to find a result, and the final sample was relevant to the researcher's original population as well as to your clientele.

Different research questions lend themselves to different populations, which in turn determines the ease of gaining access to that sample. For example, is a researcher studying 18-year-old female college students and body image or examining the relationship between communication styles with 15-year-olds who engaged in cutting behavior? As you can see, the second population would be harder to access because it is not always clear who cuts and who does not. Easy access and larger population groups (e.g., 18-year-old college females) provide the ability to do more randomized sampling. Random sampling suggests that everyone in the population has the same chance of being selected (Heppner et al., 2008), which in turn increases the ability to generalize the findings to the larger population or to your clinical practice (if your clinical practice is about body image and college females).

Whereas random sampling may be ideal in increasing the ability to generalize the findings to those not in the sample, it may not be feasible. For example, a list of all 14-year-old boys, such as Timothy, who have been diagnosed with ODD and ADD while experiencing suicidal ideation does not exist. Random sampling may be unrealistic for a researcher interested in this sample. Instead, a more practical way of sampling would be to go to counseling agencies and ask for clients who meet these criteria. This would create more of a purposeful method of sampling such as snowball or convenience sampling. Whereas purposeful methods of sampling have less ability to generalize (Heppner et al., 2008), it may be the most realistic way of sampling a specific population to ensure all participants in the study meet your designated criteria (ODD and ADD combined), and you may find that it has greater relevance to your question stated in Step 2 for Timothy.

Therefore, when evaluating a research study, not only do you need to determine the researcher's method used for sampling (i.e., random versus purposeful), but you also need to determine the representativeness of the sample to the population *and*, more specifically, to your client. For example, if a researcher studied body image in college females from the Division of Nutritional Science at Cornell University, the results might differ from those sampled from two or three universities that included all degrees (e.g., nutrition, family studies, business, sociology, psychology). Thus, assessing how representative the sample is to who the population *could* be is important. Second, does the resultant population match your client or practice on important demographic factors? More specifically, if the study included only 18-year-old college females and examined body image, is this who you are working with in clinical practice? Or is your clientele 50-year-old women struggling with body image or 18-year-old women who are not in college? As a counselor, you need to take into consideration the sample demographics of the study (i.e., sex, age, race/ethnicity, and possibly geographical location) and your client demographics to see how they match up. The less they are similar, the lower the likelihood that the results are applicable to your client or clinical practice.

Let's apply this concept to Timothy. As mentioned earlier, the study conducted by Sahebi and Mirabdollahi (2004) represented a specific treatment applied to adolescents referred by their teachers who found the treatment to be effective. Whereas this study provides a specific treatment you might be able to implement, when looking further at the sample, you find that it was a study conducted with youth who reside outside of the United States. The demographics in terms of sex, age, and race seem to apply well to Timothy, and the research participants seem to be having difficulty in school similar to Timothy's situation. However, geographical location of the two (i.e., research participants and Timothy) significantly differs, which brings into question the relevance of this treatment to Timothy simply because the culture in which these youths grew up is different. However, you need to consider that whereas the cultural expectations of behaviors may differ, the usage of the diagnostic criteria of ODD and ADD would not differ. Simply because the geography of Sahebi and Mirabdollahi's (2004) study differs from Timothy's does not rule this study out completely but simply should provide you with caution in applying the treatment blindly to Timothy or other clients. It would require you to consider the treatment and decide if you need to alter it to fit the culture of your geographical location and clients.

To examine Fonagy and Target's (1994) study more closely, their sample was derived from a convenience sample of 763 closed clinical case files, in which 135 youth with a primary diagnosis of a disruptive disorder were selected. Due to the year in which this study was conducted, the *Diagnostic and Statistical Manual (DSM) III-R* was used, which impacts the criteria used to select participants with ODD and ADD. The authors provided most of the youth (67%) intensive (4–5 times a week) psychoanalytic treatment with the remainder of youth receiving nonintensive treatment only 1 to 2 times a week. The sample was mostly male, average age of 9 years old, with some living at home and others living in residential treatment facilities. Thus, this sample is younger than Timothy by 5 years, and the therapeutic contact (i.e., 2–5 times per week) may not be realistic to what you would be able to provide in an outpatient agency. So this study may be less relevant than the study conducted by Sahebi and Mirabdollahi.

Sample Size

Sample size plays a large role in the generalizability of the findings, as well as whether the researcher could find statistical significance (Heppner et al., 2008). Although an in-depth discussion of the impact sample size will have on power, statistical significance, and effect size is beyond the scope of this chapter, it should be known that the larger the sample size, the greater the likelihood of finding significant results (Cohen, 1988). Smaller sample sizes (e.g., 30 or 40) may be too small to find a significant result (e.g., significant change from intake to termination of the therapeutic treatment; significant relationship between divorce and behavioral symptoms) in quantitative studies even when one exists. Therefore, researchers need to consider how large the sample needs to be in order to answer their research question before the study begins (Sink & Mvududu, 2010).

Reliability of the Methodology

Once you have determined if the sample is appropriate for your practice or clientele, the next step is to take a look at the methodology. Specifically, one thing to look for includes the measures or instruments used to collect the information. Does the instrument or assessment measure what it says it should measure? If the study wanted to examine depression but used a measure of general wellness, does this mean that the treatment would impact depression? Not necessarily. Therefore, make sure that what you are interested in, or what the researcher indicated he or she wanted to know in the research question, is actually being measured.

The second aspect of looking at measures is to explore the validity or reliability of the instrument (Carmine & Zeller, 1979). The validity of an instrument determines if the instrument measures what you say it will measure. A quick overview of validity is that the instrument has high correlations with other instruments that measure similar constructs (e.g., Beck Depression Inventory should relate highly to another measure of depression) and does not statistically correlate or correlate negatively with measures that are different (e.g., Beck Depression Inventory would be expected to have a negative correlation with a measure of happiness and life satisfaction). In addition to examining validity of the measure, reliability is important to examine. Reliability of an instrument is the degree to which it consistently measures a construct. Thus, if the same person took a measure of classroom behavioral conduct on Monday, would that person have similar results on Friday if she or he took the same measure again? Both validity and reliability typically range from 0 (no relationship or not consistent) to 1 (perfect relationship). A common benchmark in social science research is that estimates of reliability should be at least 0.70, with higher estimates of reliability preferable.

Another aspect in reliability of methodology is based on the design of the study. For example, for treatment studies, typically researchers have a treatment group (i.e., a group that received a new treatment or intervention) and a control group (i.e., a group that was on a wait list and received no treatment or received treatment as usual). Specifically, treatment reliability is whether the treatment was implemented as indicated in the protocol. For example, Fonagy and Target (1994) indicated that the control group received treatment approximately 2 times per week and the treatment group received treatment 4 to 5 times per week. The question is, Was the treatment implemented in this way, and what was the quality of implementation (e.g., did the counselor stick to the desired treatment protocol and do what he or she was supposed to do, or did some youth only receive the experimental treatment 3 times per week instead of 4 to 5)?

Results

This aspect of evaluation simply answers "What was found?" Were groups significantly different? Was a relationship found between the variables of interest? Was the treatment found to work? Basically, what were the answers to the researcher's questions? As a consumer, you are interested in whether the researcher found statistically significant results and whether these findings impact your practice and clients. Statistical significance is the probability of finding the study's results in the larger population or whether the results were due to chance and would not be found in the population (Schardt & Mayer, 2010). The commonly used value for statistical significance in the behavioral sciences is $p = 0.05$, thus giving a 5% chance that the statistical results are due to chance happenings in the sample.

Another aspect to consider in findings is the applicability to your practice as a counselor. Whereas most researchers do not discuss practical or clinical significance, these are things that you, as a clinician, might want to consider. Practical significance provides information related to the impact the finding has or the strength of the finding (Thompson, 2002). This impact is usually discussed in terms of effect size. The stronger the effect (i.e., the larger the number), the more impact the treatment would have, the greater the change, or the larger the difference. As a counselor, practical significance is important to consider. For example, if you read an article that indicated that the effect of the treatment (i.e., the degree to which the treatment changed disruptive behavior in school from the intake to termination) was $R^2 = 0.02$, this informs you that the treatment only explained 2% of the behavior change in a client similar to Timothy. For a counselor, this does not explain much of the change and in fact leaves approximately 98% of the change in behavior left unexplained. Practically, this treatment may not be worth the investment of the time and money it would take to implement, and Timothy and his mother may not prefer something that was not found to have practical benefits. There are many ways in which effect size or practical significance can be calculated (for an overview, see Cohen, 1988).

The final aspect to consider in the results is the clinical significance (Thompson, 2002). It should be noted that statistical significance (i.e., the degree to which a researcher is willing to allow results to be due to chance) does not indicate clinical significance (Schardt & Mayer, 2010; Thompson, 2002). Clinical significance signifies that an individual, or client, made a substantial change due to the treatment; therefore, it focuses on the magnitude of change (Schardt & Mayer, 2010). To put this into a clinical scenario, based on Timothy's report of suicidal ideation, you may be trying to decide during your assessment what his risk level might be and whether you need to hospitalize him. This decision is related to clinical significance, not to statistical significance. It is the magnitude of the suicidal ideation, plans, and the possibility of behavioral change that will help you make this decision, not whether he statistically differs from someone else's suicidal ideations and behaviors. Most studies will only report statistical significance and not clinical significance. It is important to note that whereas a study may be statistically significant (i.e., reveal that the treatment group was statistically more likely to decrease disruptive behaviors than the control group, and this difference is likely not due to chance), and practically the treatment was moderate, or explains 30 % of the variance in disruptive behavioral change, the treatment may not be clinically significant (i.e., whereas disruptive behavior decreased, it did not alter Timothy's behavior in school or at home; he was still defiant, had bad grades, and got in trouble). Therefore, the treatment, in terms of clinical change, did not substantially change the behavior. Typically in a study, clinical significance—if reported—is based on the relative risk reduction (RRR) or the proportional reduction of risk between the rates of change in the control and treatment group, or will be discussed as the number needed to treat (NNT), which is reported as the number of clients that need to be treated in order for one client to experience a substantial change (Schardt & Mayer, 2010). For more information on clinical significance, see Kraemer et al. (2003).

Validity of the Results

Once you determine the findings, and ascertain that the findings are important enough for you to consider, the next step is determining the validity of the findings. Specifically, what you are trying to determine here is whether there is any other explanation for the findings. Most of the time you can find this information in the limitation section in the discussion; however, not all limitations or alternative explanations for the findings will be known or reported. For example, consider Fonagy and Target (1994) in terms of applying the information to Timothy. Once they had their sample and assigned youth into the treatment and control groups, they found that their control group (treatment 2 times a week) and treatment group (treatment 4 to 5 times a week) were different in terms of family living situation (e.g., single-parent household, residential treatment facility). This creates automatic differences between the control and the treatment group that could have impacted the findings. More specifically, it may be that findings between the treatment and control groups are due more to the demographic differences between the groups than the actual treatment.

Step 6: Synthesize Information

Once you have searched for, accessed, and evaluated articles, the next step is synthesizing the information (Williams et al., 2006). In the case of the search we conducted for Timothy, we only found 2 articles in PsycINFO. Conducting a larger search with different terms (e.g., oppositional defiant with suicidal ideation; attention deficit disorder in youth and family divorce) or using different search engines may bring up additional articles to read and evaluate. Regardless of the number of studies you find, once you have read through the different articles, it is important to integrate what you have read. What are the patterns in the results that exist across the studies? More studies with similar findings increases the confidence in what will work with your clients and what might be appropriate to apply in your work as a counselor. For example, if both studies we found for Timothy implemented solution-focused behavioral therapy, and both studies found this treatment to work (per statistical, practical, and/or clinical significance), it would provide more assurance that solution-focused behavioral therapy might be appropriate to apply to Timothy, particularly because the two samples were so different.

If differences in the research are found, the question becomes what was the cause of the differences? For example, did the researchers of the studies have different outcome measures (i.e., one measured depression whereas another measured communication skill), were the samples different (i.e., one was 9-year-olds whereas another was 15-year-olds; one was females from the inner city, another was males from rural locations), or were different treatments used (i.e., one compared solution-focused therapy to cognitive behavioral therapy; another study compared solution-focused therapy to clients on a wait list receiving no therapy). Synthesizing the results delivers a larger picture and provides more (or less) confidence in the findings.

Step 7: Clinical Application

The application of empirical research findings occurs after you have determined that the research is important and was done validly and the extent to which the research you found is relevant to the issue you are trying to address (Williams et al. 2006). Therefore, did you find empirical information in the literature that helped you determine which was the most effective treatment to implement for Timothy? If the answer is no, then application of the information would not make sense for working with Timothy. If the answer is yes, the next step is to determine whether you can gain more information about the actual treatment. This may occur by looking at the citations and references provided by the authors of the study, if they cited a particular treatment and provided you the reference of how to access it. Conversely, you may need to contact the authors to gain more information about the treatment.

Application also pertains to the degree to which you use the treatment specified. For example, if the treatment is a manualized treatment that was found to work with 14-year-old boys who have been dually diagnosed with ODD and ADD who live within the United States, then you may decide that it is appropriate to apply the treatment as is; however, if the treatment was developed for youth with these diagnoses who live in Australia, you may decide that a few things in the treatment need to be altered to be culturally appropriate to youth, such as Timothy, in the United States. This is where empirical knowledge or research that uses the scientific method combines with your experience as a clinician.

Step 8: Evaluation

The final step in the scientist-practitioner model is to evaluate your performance (Schardt & Mayer, 2010). Many clinicians discuss the need to evaluate one's effectiveness with clients (e.g., ACA, 2005; Duncan, Miller, & Sparks, 2004; Wampold, 2006). There are many ways in which to determine your effectiveness, but it depends on what you want to know. For example, do you want to know if you are effective with one client (e.g., Timothy), if your practice is effective, or if a program works? These three questions lead to different types of evaluative designs. For example, the research design used to assess one client would be a case study or single subject, whereas to look at your practice as a whole with all clients might be more of a repeated measures design, and finally to assess a program would be a program evaluation. In this chapter we highlight case study, single-subject designs, and program evaluation. More information on repeated-measures designs can be found in Heppner and colleagues (2008) or Shadish, Cook, & Campbell (2002).

The first step in determining your effectiveness depends on your outcome goal (Heppner et al., 2008). In other words, what does *effectiveness* mean to you? Does it mean that your clients are satisfied? Would you define it as the reduction of client symptoms or the increase in client wellness or daily functioning? Or is it that clients do not terminate counseling early? It may actually be a combination of these items for you, but before you measure effectiveness you need to determine what you mean by *effective*.

In the case of Timothy, your original question was what treatment would be most effective in working with him. In this instance, effective might be defined as a decrease in problematic behaviors at home and school (i.e., based on reports from his mom and teacher), a decrease in suicidal ideation as reported by Timothy, and an increase in grades. If these are the ways in which you would determine if counseling was working for Timothy, then these are the ways in which you would want to evaluate treatment for him. Two simple ways to explore whether you were effective in applying the new treatment you found and applied in Steps 1 through 7 of the scientist-practitioner process are to conduct a case study or a single-subject design. However, keep in mind that simple does not equate to waking up one morning, deciding to collect data, and merely doing it. There are steps to creating a well-designed, quality study that will provide useful answers to your questions. The implications of a study are only as strong as its weakest point (Sink & Mvududu, 2010; Wampold, 2006), whether that point is the research question, data collection, procedures you set up, or analyses. All are important in the process of conducting research (Wester & Borders, 2011). Both single-subject and case study designs are highlighted here.

Single-Subject and Case Study Designs

Single-subject and case study designs are research methodologies that can be applied with one person or one group (Heppner et al., 2008; Yin, 2003). Whereas both designs have a sample size of one, or evaluate change in one client, they both serve slightly different purposes. Let's first discuss single-subject design.

The main purpose of single-subject design is to establish causation (Horner et al., 2005). For example, in the case of Timothy, a single-subject design would help you determine if the treatment you implemented was the *cause* of Timothy's behavioral change or if his behavior changed due to something else (e.g., developmental maturation, changes to parenting styles). Single-subject designs are used to evaluate behavioral change in an individual, where you follow the individual across a period of time to gauge the treatment performance, impact, and client behavioral change. You would still measure the outcome variables (e.g., for Timothy we established that this was an increase in school grades, a decrease in problematic behaviors at home and school based on his teacher's and mom's report, and a decrease in frequency of suicidal ideations based on Timothy's self-report), but you would do so multiple times to see when and how change occurred. For example, you might measure behavior when Timothy's mother called to schedule an intake appointment, then reassess behavior at intake, followed by multiple assessments at specified time points (e.g., every 3 weeks) until termination. In order to see long-term implications of the treatment, you could even conduct a follow-up with Timothy for assessment at a designated time point once he is no longer a client (e.g., 1 or 2 months posttreatment).

Using single-subject design language, "A" would be considered no treatment, and "B" would be considered treatment or counseling. Taking a look at one outcome measure (i.e., his mom's report of problematic and defiant behavior at home), what you would hope for is that when treatment was implemented, behavioral change occurred with the defiant behavior decreasing while in treatment. Figure 13.3 provides an example of what this might look like.

Figure 13.3 reveals how Timothy's defiant behavior changed while in counseling. If the measure you used for defiant behavior was scored on a scale of 1 (not defiant) to 10 (extremely defiant) you can see that when Timothy's mother called and during intake, she rated his defiant behavior high (i.e., 7 or 8). However, during the subsequent weeks while Timothy was in treatment (B) you can see that his defiant behavior decreased (from 7 at intake to 4 at termination). This indicates that counseling was effective in decreasing Timothy's defiant behavior. In order to see if counseling had long-term effects, you might assess Timothy's behavior at time points after treatment. In this case, in Figure 13.3, it reveals that behavior was assessed at 1 and 2 months after counseling was completed (Posttreatment A). Figure 13.3 reveals that Timothy's defiant behavior remained lower than it was at pre-counseling (Baseline A) and at a rate similar to that of termination. This reveals that for Timothy, counseling had a positive impact and was effective. If Timothy's behavior did not decrease, but stayed consistently high around 7 to 9, this would indicate no treatment effect, or that counseling was not effective. In an opposite scenario, where his behavior, while in or after counseling, increased from a 7 at intake to a 9 or 10 and remained there, this would indicate that counseling had an opposite effect (i.e., increased defiant behavior). For more information on single-subject designs, see Kazdin (2010).

Figure 13.3   Single-Subject Design Graph Revealing Timothy's Defiant Behavior Change as Reported by His Mom

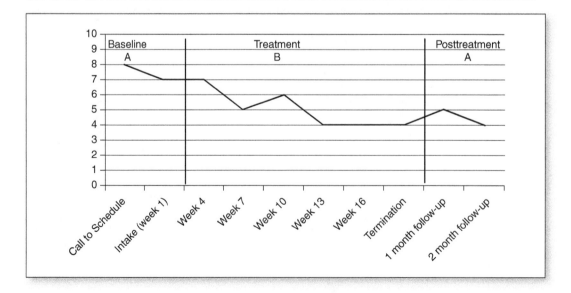

Case study design is another way to evaluate Timothy's progress in treatment and the effectiveness of counseling. Case study, similar to single-subject design, is about explaining why and how a behavior occurred. The goal is to understand what causes change, what aspects of the clients, behaviors, thoughts, and/or feelings have changed, as well as to describe the intervention and other contextual aspects of the case. Case studies contribute to the knowledge of evidence-based practices as well as theory (Yin, 2003). In case study, you may conduct similar assessment time points such as you did earlier in the single-subject design. You may even have a similar graph as presented for single subjects in Figure 13.3. However, case study explores more of the how and why questions, so rather than solely assuming that it was counseling as a whole that impacted Timothy's behavior, case study design might want to know how counseling worked and/or why the behavior decreased. Therefore, you may explore with Timothy what was working or why he felt it was working; you may also describe counseling and the stage process more in depth (Yin, 2003) in order to figure out why Timothy's behavior was a 7 at intake and Week 4 but decreased to a 5 in Week 7. Therefore, what occurred between Week 4 and Week 7 that contributed to the decrease? Was it that a therapeutic relationship was established by this point, or was it something specific that occurred in the counseling process during this time (e.g., Week 5 began looking at cognitions). Case study can evaluate this information by collecting quantitative data (e.g., survey, instrument, measures) or by using qualitative data (e.g., your case notes, conversations with his mother, information provided by Timothy). For more information on how to design a case study, see Yin (2003).

Program Evaluation

Whereas single-subject and case study designs specifically answer questions about causation, such as what is working, why it is working, and how it is working with one client (or one group), the purpose of program evaluation is to determine the effectiveness of one particular program with a particular group of people. For example, returning to the earlier case of Sam and the grief he is experiencing, you may decide that grief is currently a need that is not being met in your agency or in the surrounding community. You may decide, after reading about it, that you would like to implement the 16-week complicated grief disorder treatment discussed by Zhang and his colleagues (2006). In a program evaluation, you have to consider what you want to know about a program (e.g., its effectiveness in minimizing symptoms of grief and bereavement), how the program is implemented (e.g., think manualized treatment or treatment protocol), and when data need to be collected and from whom (Heppner et al., 2008).

In evaluating the effectiveness of the complicated grief disorder treatment program, you would have to select the population you believe it is most appropriate for (e.g., individuals experiencing symptoms of grief related to a family member diagnosed with a chronic illness), determine what interventions occur each week during the 16-week program, and when you want to collect data (e.g., intake, 8 weeks, 16-week termination). The first step is the design of the program. In this case, the structure and implementation of the 16-week program is already in existence (see Zhang et al., 2006). The second step is to determine when and how to collect data. In this case, to assess for grief symptoms you could collect data from a client report, but you may also collect data from other sources (e.g., work or school report on attendance and functioning; partner report). In addition to collecting outcome data at the designated time points, program evaluators should collect data on the quality of program implementation (Heppner et al., 2008). Is the 16-week program being implemented as was specified in the manual? If the protocol required Week 3 of treatment to focus on work-related behaviors and Week 4 to focus on intimacy, were these the topics covered that week? If not, then quality of implementation is brought into question, and the results of the program evaluation could not necessarily be applied to the complicated grief disorder treatment program as specified in the protocol.

Many factors need to be considered in program evaluation, specifically the stakeholders of the program (e.g., who designed the program or wants to implement the program; Heppner et al., 2008). Usually whoever has put money into the implementation of a program, whether it is through program development or staff training, typically does not want to find that the program is ineffective. Therefore, conducting a program evaluation can be difficult at times. More information on conducting and designing program evaluation can be found in Royse (2009) or Fitzpatrick, Sanders, and Worthen (2011).

CONCLUSION

This chapter highlights the importance of research in counseling, specifically discussing the scientist-practitioner model, which includes the consumption, application, and engagement of research. Whereas only a few aspects of research and research design are provided here, resources are provided for more information. The research competencies for the counseling profession, endorsed by ACES, state that the learning of research is a continual process and counselors need to engage in continued education in research to maintain knowledge and skills, as well as gain new knowledge and skills (Wester & Borders, 2011). Training and education typically impact self-efficacy (Wester et al., 2006), and counselor research self-efficacy has been found to be important in the engagement in research (Phillips & Russell, 1994; Wester et al., 2006). Therefore, in order to contribute to the counseling profession, assist in the development of counseling evidence-based practices, and provide support to yourself and others that what you are doing in counseling is working for your clients, it is important that you continue to learn aspects of the research process and engage in research (consumption, application, and evaluation).

REFERENCES

American Counseling Association. (2005). *ACA Code of Ethics*. Alexandria, VA: Author.

Boote, D. N., & Beile, P. (2005). Scholars before researchers: On the centrality of the dissertation literature review in research preparation. *Educational Researcher, 34,* 3–15.

Carmine, E. G., & Zeller, R. A. (1979). *Reliability and validity in assessment.* Thousand Oaks, CA: Sage.

Cohen, J. (1988). *Statistical power analysis for the behavioral sciences* (2nd ed.). Mahwah, NJ: Lawrence Erlbaum.

Duncan, B. L., Miller, S. D., & Sparks, J. (2004). *The heroic client: A revolutionary way to improve effectiveness through client directed outcome informed therapy* (Rev. ed.). San Francisco: Jossey-Bass.

Fitzpatrick, J. L., Sanders, J. R., & Worthen, B. R. (2011). *Program evaluation: Alternative approaches and practical guidelines.* Upper Saddle River, NJ: Pearson Education.

Fong, M. L., & Malone, C. M. (1994). Defeating ourselves: Common errors in counseling research. *Counselor Education and Supervision, 33,* 356–362.

Fonagy, P., & Target, M. (1994). The efficacy of psychoanalysis for children with disruptive disorders. *Journal of the American Academy of Child & Adolescent Psychiatry, 33,* 45–55.

Gambrill, E. (2005). *Critical thinking in clinical practice: Improving the quality of judgments and decisions.* Hoboken, NJ: Wiley.

Hadley, R. G., & Mitchell, L. K. (1995). *Counseling research and program evaluation.* Boston: Brooks Cole.

Hancock, G. R., & Mueller, R. O. (2010). *The reviewer's guide to quantitative methods in the social sciences.* New York: Routledge.

Hays, D. G., & Singh, A. A. (2012). *Qualitative inquiry in clinical and educational settings.* New York: Guilford Press.

Heppner, P. P., Wampold, B. E., & Kivlighan, D. M. (2008). *Research design in counseling.* Belmont: CA: Thomson.

Horner, R. H., Carr, E. G., Halle, J., McGee, G., Odom, S., & Wolery, M. (2005). The use of single-subject research to identify evidence-based practice in special education. *Exceptional Children, 71,* 165–179.

Karam, E. A., & Sprenkle, D. H. (2010). The research informed clinician: A guide to training the next generation MFT. *Journal of Marital and Family Therapy, 36,* 307–319.

Kazdin, A. E. (2010). *Single-case research designs: Methods for clinical and applied settings.* New York: Oxford University Press.

Kennedy, S. H., Lam, R. W., Cohen, N. L., & Ravindran, A. V. (2001). Clinical guidelines for the treatment of depressive disorders. *Canadian Journal of Psychiatry, 46,* 38S–58S.

King, J. H., & Otis, H. (2004). Bridging the research-practice gap: Using applied inquiries to promote client advocacy. *Counseling Outfitters Vistas, 28,* 259–269.

Kraemer, H. C., Morgan, G. A., Leech, N. C., Gliner, J. A., Vaske, J. J., & Harmon, R. J. (2003). Measures of clinical significance. *Journal of the American Academy of Child and Adolescents Psychiatry, 42,* 1524–1529.

Lebow, J. (2006). *Research for the psychotherapist: From science to practice.* New York: Routledge.

Manber, R., Edinger, J. D., Gress, J. L., San Pedro-Salcedo, M. G., Kuo, T. F., Kalista, T. (2008). Cognitive behavioral therapy for insomnia enhances depression outcomes in patients with comorbid major depressive disorder and insomnia. *Sleep, 31,* 489–495.

Phillips, J. C., & Russell, R. K. (1994). Research self-efficacy, the research training environment, and research productivity among graduate students in counseling psychology. *The Counseling Psychologist, 22,* 628–641.

Royse, D. (2009). *Program evaluation: An introduction.* Belmont, CA: Brooks Cole.

Sackett, D. L., Rosenberg, W. C., Gray, J. M., Haynes, R. B., & Richardson, W. S. (1996). Evidence based medicine: What it is and what it isn't. *British Medical Journal, 312,* 71–72.

Sahebi, A., & Mirabdollahi, E. S. (2004). Effectiveness of a new social/cognitive therapeutic model for aggressive children. *Journal of Iranian Psychologists, 1.*

Salkind, N. J. (2000). *Statistics for people who think they hate statistics.* Thousand Oaks, CA: Sage.

Schardt, C., & Mayer, J. (2010). *Introduction to evidence-based practice.* Retrieved from http://www.hsl.unc.edu/Services/Tutorials/EBM/welcome.htm.

Sexton, T. L., Whiston, S. C., Bleuer, J. C., & Walz, G. R. (1997). *Integrating outcomes research into clinical practice and training.* Alexandria, VA: ACA.

Shadish, W. R., Cook, T. D., & Campbell, D. T. (2002). *Experimental and quasi-experimental designs for generalized causal inference.* Boston: Houghton Mifflin.

Sink, C. A., & Mvududu, N. H. (2010). Statistical power, sampling, and effect sizes: Three keys to research relevancy. *Counseling Outcome Research and Evaluation, 1,* 1–18.

Stoltenberg, C. D., & Pace, T. M. (2007). The scientist-practitioner model: Now more than ever. *Journal of Contemporary Psychotherapy, 37,* 195–203.

Thompson, B. (2002). "Statistical," "practical," and "clinical": How many kinds of significance do counselors need to consider? *Journal of Counseling & Development, 80,* 64–71.

Wampold, B. E. (2006). Designing a research study. In F. T. L. Leong & J. T. Austin (Eds.), *The psychology research handbook* (pp. 91–102). Thousand Oaks, CA: Sage.

Wester, K. L., & Borders, L. D. (2011). *Research competencies for the counseling profession.* Lake Worth, FL: Association for Counselor Educators and Supervisors.

Wester, K. L., Borders, L. D., Boul, S., & Horton, E. (2013). Research quality: Critique of quantitative articles. *Journal of Counseling & Development, 91,* 280–290.

Wester, K. L., Mobley, K., & Faulkner, A. (2006, September). *Evidence-based practices: Building a bridge between researchers and practitioners.* Orlando, FL: Southern Association for Counselor Education and Supervision.

Williams, L. M., Patterson, J. E., & Miller, R. B. (2006). Panning for gold: A clinician's guide to using research. *Journal of Marital and Family Therapy, 29,* 29–32.

Yin, R. K. (2003). *Case study research: Design and methods.* Thousand Oaks, CA: Sage.

Zhang, B., El-Jawahri, A., & Prigerson, H. G. (2006). Update on bereavement research: Evidence-based guidelines for the diagnosis and treatment of complicated bereavement. *Journal of Palliative Medicine, 9,* 1188–1203.

Current and Future Trends in Clinical Mental Health Practice

The Applications of Neuroscience to Clinical Mental Health Counseling

Jane E. Myers and Laura Jones

Upon completion of this chapter, you will be able to do the following:

1. Understand the function of key areas in the brain

2. Describe how the brain structure and connections change in response to internal and external factors

3. Explain how neuroscience applies to the therapeutic relationship

4. Identify techniques for working with clients that arise from principles of neuroscience

5. Understand what neurofeedback is and how it works

6. Explain the evidence base for the effectiveness of neurofeedback

7. Identify the training required to practice neurofeedback, certification processes, and ethical standards for practice

8. Explore strategies for integrating neurofeedback into counseling practice

There are numerous ways, both subjective and objective, to measure change and improvement as a counselor. Language or behavior may change. Clients may become less or more emotionally reactive. They may report more positive thoughts or improvements in interpersonal relationships. Regardless of how you measure change, all of these changes have something in common. They all represent underlying changes in the brain. Even the foundation of counseling, the therapeutic relationship, induces changes in the brain. As a counselor, you have an opportunity to understand the power of counseling from an entirely new, yet fundamental, perspective and to use the principles of neuroscience to help clients make longer-lasting beneficial changes toward improved well-being.

Merriam-Webster's Medical Dictionary (2011) defines **neuroscience** as "a branch (as neurophysiology) of science that deals with the anatomy, physiology, biochemistry, or molecular biology of nerves and nervous tissue and especially their relation to behavior and learning." Once viewed as the scientific, biological study of the brain and nervous system primary of interest to medical researchers, neuroscience has evolved to become an interdisciplinary science of critical interest to mental health practitioners. In support of this change, the most recent strategic plan of the National Institute of Mental Health (2010) includes four strategic objectives for the immediate future, one of which is to "promote discovery in brain and behavior sciences to fuel research on the causes of mental disorders" (p. 6). More specific to counseling, the standards of the Council for Accreditation of Counseling and Related Educational Programs (CACREP, 2016) require an understanding of the "biological, neurological, and physiological factors that affect human development, functioning, and behavior" as a core curricular area required of all counseling students (p. 10).

Our goal in this chapter is to provide an overview of essential concepts of neuroscience for counselors, followed by strategies for applying this information in clinical settings. We start from the premise that "it's all in your head" and move from there to the mind-body connection and the need to address neurobiology from a holistic perspective. We introduce neuroscience and provide an overview of **brain anatomy** and key aspects of **neural functioning** and **plasticity**, followed by a discussion of neuroscience as a critical part of the therapeutic relationship. We also discuss the implications and applications of this information to the counseling process in hopes that this will become influential in your work as a future counselor.

NEUROSCIENCE IN COUNSELING

The brain is a highly complex organ, and a basic understanding of the brain's structure and how various parts communicate with one another is essential to understanding how and why this organ regulates and responds to the work of counselors and the therapeutic process. Applying concepts about the brain to clinical practice without having this fundamental knowledge is akin to using techniques from a particular theory without understanding the theory itself (Jones, 2015).

The question of "What does the brain do?" has eluded scientists and philosophers for centuries. Recent advancements in brain imaging and recording technology have allowed scientists to better answer this question. Prior to this technology, scientists relied on examining brains postmortem, investigating other vertebrate animals (e.g., rats and monkeys), and lesioning (i.e., removing) certain areas of the brain and observing the outcomes.

One prominent example is the case of Phineas Gage, a railroad worker who was impaled by a railroad spike and survived. The spike entered underneath Phineas's left cheekbone, passing straight through the front part of his brain, and exited through the top, right frontal region of his skull. Remarkably, not only did Phineas survive, but he was talking and walking around even minutes after the accident. The spike, however, destroyed much of his frontal cortex and Phineas was said to never be himself again. Other than becoming blind in his left eye, he experienced no other physical impairments, nor any impairment to his sensory perception, intellectual capacities, or language comprehension abilities. However, the damage significantly altered his personality and behavior. Before the accident, Phineas was known to be an even-tempered and likeable guy, but after damage to his frontal cortex he was angry and violent and had difficulties with impulse control, including uncontrollable bouts of swearing (see Macmillan, 2002, for a comprehensive account of Phineas Gage). Although they only provided rough estimates of the function of certain brain regions, the famous case of Mr. Gage, the use of postmortem autopsies, and animal studies served as gateways to understanding this mysterious and remarkable organ. Modern technology and medicine, however, have refined theories and begun creating clear images and detailed models of the working brain. From such pictures, counselors now have tangible evidence of how therapeutic relationships and interventions actually alter the function and even structure of the mind.

Neural Anatomy

There are a number of ways to think about the anatomy of the brain, such as the distinction between structural and functional anatomy. **Functional anatomy** refers to the key functions and processes that are regulated by particular brain areas, whereas **structural anatomy** refers to its actual physically distinct areas. From both an evolutionary and simply developmental standpoint, the brain, both structurally and functionally, develops from the inside out. As presented by Siegel (2006), a quick and easy way you can model the brain and its development is by making a loose fist with your hand with your thumb folded inside your fist. The most evolutionarily and developmentally primitive part of the brain would be your wrist and lower part of your forearm. This area of the brain regulates basic survival functions (e.g., heart rate, breathing, body temperature, and balance) and comprises the spinal cord (arm), brain stem (very base of the palm, where your wrist and hand meet), and your cerebellum (just across from your brainstem on the back of your hand). The **limbic system** is the second layer of the brain to develop and can be visualized as your thumb sitting in the space just beneath your fingers. The main brain structures of the limbic system include the amygdala, hippocampus, cingulated gyrus, and the hypothalamus, all of which work together to regulate emotional awareness and processing, memory formation and retrieval, motivation, and one's unconscious responses to such information. The neocortex, evolutionarily and developmentally the most recent layer of the brain, consists primarily of the cerebral cortex (i.e., the folded layers of tissue that make up the outermost portion of the brain) and is responsible for abstract and rational thought, language, sensory perception, planning, consciousness, and attention. The back of your hand and your fingers represent the neocortex, which encases the deeper limbic areas of the brain. Now that you have this useful visual for the brain, the structural and functional anatomy of the human brain is explored in greater detail.

Cerebral Cortex

The cerebral cortex (i.e., your fingers and the upper back part of your fist) comprises the majority of the brain's volume and is the pink, folded tissue that you likely picture when you imagine a brain. When it is preserved it becomes gray and hence is often referred to as the gray matter of the brain. The folded nature of this tissue allows for a greater volume of cortex to develop within the skull, with each ridge of cortex termed a **gyrus**, and each crevice between gyri termed a **sulcus**. The human brain is structurally divided into two hemispheres, the left and right, which are connected by a long, thick band of nerve fibers known as the **corpus callosum**. Each hemisphere controls sensory information (i.e., sight, sound, touch) and movement from the contralateral (i.e., opposite) side of the body. This means, for example, that the left hemisphere of the brain processes the sight, sound, touch, and movement on the right side of the body. Although the hemispheres can function independently of one another, the corpus callosum and a related structure, the anterior commissure, aid the integration of information processed in the separate hemispheres and create a more holistic picture of the body, space, experience, and knowledge of the individual.

The gyri and sulci of the cortex further subdivide the two hemispheres into the following four major **lobes** (i.e., anatomical divisions) of the brain: the frontal, parietal, occipital, and temporal lobes. Each lobe controls different brain functions, and each can be further subdivided based on the specificity of those functions. The **occipital lobe**, the smallest of the four lobes, encompasses the very back (i.e., posterior) portion of the brain. This roughly circular area of the brain contains the primary visual cortex responsible for visual processing. As an individual opens his or her eyes, the visual input is directed from the retina into the brain and is routed to the occipital cortex. The occipital cortex, with the help of other brain regions, then makes sense of what the individual is seeing, including the recognition of color.

The temporal lobes extend from the bottom (i.e., inferior), front (i.e., anterior) portion of the occipital lobe and continue horizontally toward the front of the brain up above the ear. These two lobes are responsible for an array of functions, most notably auditory perception. Although both hemispheres contain primary auditory processing cortex, within the left temporal lobe sits **Wernicke's area**, a specialized area of the temporal cortex responsible for language comprehension, in other words how you understand the sounds that make up a human voice. Due to the positioning of the temporal lobe it also contains subcortical structures associated with the limbic system (described in the next section) and plays a role in memory formation, emotional processing, and olfaction (i.e., smell).

The parietal lobe, located superior to (i.e., above) the temporal lobes and anterior to (i.e., in front of) the occipital lobe, is situated in the middle band of the brain and extends across both hemispheres. This area of cortex, separated from the frontal lobe by the central sulcus, is responsible for somatosensory perception (including both the sensation of touch as well as **proprioception**, or the awareness of the body in space), the integration of sensory information from the different sensory modalities, and hosts a spatial coordinate system of sorts that details the world around you. The postcentral gyrus located in the most anterior (i.e., frontal) portion of the parietal cortex contains the primary somatosensory cortex, a strip of cortex responsible for the perception of touch. Every part of the body, from the tongue to the toes, is mapped out along this gyrus, with the left hemisphere mapping the right side of the body and the right hemisphere mapping the left side of the body. Just posterior to (i.e., behind) this gyrus is an association area of cortex that regulates fine sensory perception such as texture, weight, shape, temperature, and size. Another primary function of the parietal lobe is spatial awareness (both of the self and objects) and spatial navigation, although research has likewise implicated involvement of the temporal lobe in this process (see Karnath, Ferber, & Himmelbach, 2001, for a review).

The frontal lobe, located at the frontalmost region of the brain and extending approximately to the back of the jawline (i.e., your knuckles and fingers on your hand model), is the largest lobe of the brain and the most complex in terms of its function. Generally speaking, the frontal lobe, as demonstrated by the famous case of Phineas Gage, is responsible for executive control and higher-order mental processing. It plays a role in problem solving; moral reasoning and value judgments; determining similarities and differences between situations and objects; initiating action and impulse control; regulating emotions; determining appropriate social responses; foreseeing the consequences of actions; and even language, movement, and memory. The precentral gyrus or primary motor cortex, the area of frontal cortex adjacent to the parietal lobe, contains a similar map of the human body as that found on the sensorimotor cortex, yet this map regulates the movement of body parts as opposed to sensation perception. Furthermore, the left frontal cortex contains a segment of cortex called **Broca's area**, which neighbors the left temporal lobe and is responsible largely for language production. The **prefrontal cortex** (PFC; i.e., the most anterior portion of the frontal cortex, just above the eyes) is considered the director of the brain, managing executive control and serving as a primary means of emotional and social regulation.

Although not considered an actual lobe of the brain, the **cerebellum** is the cauliflower-shaped ball that sits at the back of the brain tucked under the cerebral cortex. This most dorsal (i.e., upper) area of the brainstem was originally thought to only control gross motor movement coordination, precision, timing, and balance. However, sometimes termed the "little brain," the cerebellum has been found to play a role in many functions outside of motor control, such as cognition, attention, memory, sensory perception, language, emotional processing, and possibly addiction (Strick, Dum, & Fiez, 2009).

Subcortical Anatomy

Beneath the cerebral cortex, in the center of the brain, sits a complex network of subcortical structures. The **limbic system** is one of the primary subcortical networks in the brain, which functions in the processing and responding to emotional stimuli, motivation, memory formation, social cognition, and dreaming, among others. Although composed of numerous structures, for the purposes of this text, only the core components of the limbic system are reviewed. The **amygdala** is the seat of emotional (i.e., affective) processing, particularly related to survival, generating emotional responses such as fear, pleasure, and anger. It is also responsible for allied autonomic responses induced by this emotional arousal, namely the fight-flight-or-freeze reactions experienced in the face of danger. The **cingulate cortex**, part of the limbic cortex, wraps on either side of the corpus callosum and also plays a prominent role in emotion, reward, empathy, and social cognition. This affective (i.e., emotion) input influences the functioning of the **hippocampus**, the chief job of which is the formation of new memories, specifically declarative (i.e., fact and event based) and spatial memories, converting short-term into long-term memories, a process called memory consolidation, and in memory retrieval. An interesting feature of the limbic system is the presence of the **olfactory bulbs**, or the primary sensory organs for smell. This means that unlike all other sensory information, direct connections exist between the olfactory bulbs and the amygdala, and thus the sense of smell may influence emotional responding (Kang, Baum, & Cherry, 2009). The thalamus and hypothalamus are two additional vitally important subcortical structures often associated with the limbic system but have functions that extend beyond limbic control. The **thalamus** serves as the central relay station of the brain, coordinating nearly all sensory functions and regulating sleep, wakefulness, consciousness, and movement. All sensory input with the exception of olfaction (i.e., smell) is channeled through the thalamus before being sent to applicable cortical areas. The **hypothalamus** sits just below the thalamus. This critical brain structure regulates body temperature, food and water intake, sexual behavior and reproduction, and sleep-wake cycles and controls the release of key hormones in the body.

Now that the key cortical and subcortical areas of the brain have been discussed, the next step is understanding how the areas communicate with one another.

Communication in the Brain

The various areas of the brain communicate by way of chemical messengers and electrical signals. Neurons are the cells in the brain that carry these messages from one area to another. The neuron is composed of the cell body (i.e., the **soma**), the **dendrites** (i.e., small branchlike projections) that connect to the cell body, the axon (i.e., the long, slender projections from the soma), and the axon terminal (i.e., where the axon connects to the dendrites of neighboring neurons). Dendrites on the cell body contain receptor sites for chemical messengers (i.e., **neurotransmitters**). In order for a neuron to fire, the neurotransmitters must be absorbed into the cell body by appropriate receptors (e.g., certain chemicals can only be absorbed through certain receptor sites, much like puzzle pieces). Once in the soma, the neurotransmitters cause the neuron to fire (i.e., an electrical impulse is generated), by which the chemical message is sent down the axon to be released by the axon terminal into a synaptic cleft (i.e., space between two neurons) where it can be absorbed by the neighboring neuron. If the chemical messengers are not absorbed into the dendrites of the neighboring neuron, they are reabsorbed by the axon terminal, a process known as **reuptake**. Thus, for the class of psychotropic drugs known as selective serotonin reuptake inhibitors, the reuptake of the serotonin (i.e., one class of neurotransmitters) is prohibited, and as a result the serotonin stays in the cleft longer, increasing its chances of being absorbed by the neighboring dendrites. Alterations in brain functioning are largely made by way of alterations to the firing patterns of neurons.

Taking a step back, what do these neuronal connections look like in the brain? The cerebral cortex is composed of both gray matter and white matter. If conceptualized as a computer network, the **gray matter**, predominantly made up of nerve cell bodies, is the actual computers that process information, and the **white matter**, composed mainly of the long, slender axons, can be considered the network cables that connect the various processing areas. The white matter of the cortex is given the white appearance by the **myelination** (i.e., formation of a fatty cell covering) of the axon, which acts as a conductor, allowing the chemical messages to move quickly along the axon. This contributes to the speed at which processing can occur, a critical feature given that some axons can extend as far as 1 meter in length in humans. The number of neurons and neuronal connections present in the human brain fluctuate most prominently as a function of age.

The Developing and Aging Mind

The developmental trajectory of the human brain follows a lengthy process, a process that has implications for the work of a counselor, namely in developing developmentally appropriate goals and choosing apposite therapeutic interventions. Just a few days after conception, the underpinnings of the brain start to arise. From this foundation, the brain grows and forms rapidly, demonstrating its most marked development through the first few years of life. Yet structural and functional brain changes continue into adulthood and later adulthood when such changes can actually lead to cognitive decline and functional impairment.

During this early critical period of development from the third trimester of pregnancy to the third year of life neurons are quickly being formed, migrating to their appropriate locations, creating dendrites, and connecting with other neurons. The number of neuron-to-neuron connections that a child has at age 3 is nearly twice the number in adults. An individual's experiences during childhood and adolescence will determine which of these connections will be reinforced and remain and which will be extinguished (i.e., pruned). The development and connections of these neurons also occurs in relation to the maturation of certain areas of the brain. As suggested previously, the human brain develops from the bottom up or from the brainstem to the cortex, with this developmental process extending into late adolescence and early adulthood. Adolescence represents a second critical period in brain development that underscores the onset of many mental health disorders, including addiction (Crews, He, & Hodge, 2007). The prefrontal cortex and hippocampus in particular follow a slow developmental course and late maturation, representing some of the last cortical regions and connections to develop. This has notable consequences on a child's memory, executive control, attention, and social functioning (Casey, Giedd, & Thomas, 2000; Geuze, Vermetten, & Bremner, 2005). For example, individuals are considered to have two different memory systems, one explicit and one implicit (LeDoux, 1996). Implicit memories are largely unconscious, emotional, or sensory based and present at birth. They represent sensory memories and automatic responses and are reflections of procedural and conditioned learning. Explicit or declarative memories on the other hand are conscious, language-based memories, the formations of which are heavily dependent on the prefrontal cortex and hippocampus development. Children under the age of 18 months, however, have not yet developed their declarative, episodic memory system (Fishbane, 2007), and up until the first 5 years of life their information processing and memory systems are still becoming fully integrated (Siegel, 2006).

Ironically, those areas that are some of the last to develop are also some of the most vulnerable to aging. The prefrontal cortex and hippocampus are the most prone to experience decreases in volume, number of neurons, and number of neuronal connections as an individual ages and can explain the cognitive declines that can be experienced in later adulthood (Burke & Barnes, 2006). The decrease in hippocampal volume relates to decreases in spatial memory and accessing contextual and concrete details of events associated with explicit memory. Furthermore, deficits in working memory and executive functioning that can be seen in later adulthood are reflective of decreases in prefrontal cortex volume and connectivity. The elderly, however, are not destined to experience such structural and functional impairments as they age. Just as in youth, the organization of the brain's many neurons is heavily influenced by environment and overall mental and physical well-being.

Neuroscience and the Therapeutic Relationship

From the moment a client walks into the counseling room and begins to develop a therapeutic relationship with a counselor, before changes ever become palpable at the behavioral, cognitive, or even emotional level, the client's brain begins to transform. Synaptic connections and the firing patterns between neurons can be influenced by the rapport established between client and counselor, similar to the influence of early attachment bonds (Fuchs, 2004; Gabbard, 2000). Science now underscores what Rogers (1956) emphasized early on, that a strong therapeutic relationship serves as the foundation for therapeutic success and lasting change.

Therapeutic Relationships as Attachment Bonds

In infancy, children form attachment bonds to caregivers that can have considerable implications on the ability of the individual to form healthy interpersonal bonds later in life (Ainsworth, 1989; Bowlby, 1988a). Research has shown that the attachment relationship serves as the basis for self and emotional regulation and influences the development of the right hemisphere of the brain, particularly areas of the limbic system and prefrontal cortex (Schore, 2001). The therapeutic relationship can be conceptualized as a secondary attachment relationship that serves to activate the similar neural structures that promote a sense of security, acceptance, comfort, and self-regulation in clients (Amini et al., 1996; Bowlby, 1988b; Fuchs, 2004). Furthermore, research suggests that a strong therapeutic relationship can actually help to repair early detrimental attachment patterns (Pearlman & Courtois, 2005). Just as with early attachment bonds, therapeutic presence and connection made obvious by gestures, expressions, and voice tone can actually create a physical sense of safety in a client by helping to regulate a client's physiological arousal as discussed later in this chapter (Geller & Porges, 2014).

Empathic Resonance and Mirror Neurons

The basis of this attachment process is an emotional attunement and resonance between caregiver and child, or in cases of the therapeutic attachment relationship, the counselor and client. A dynamic interconnection exits between social relationships and the development, functioning, and plasticity of the brain that is driven by the colocalization of social and emotional networks in the brain, namely the communication between the prefrontal cortex and limbic system (Siegel, 2006). The preponderance of interpersonal functioning is hypothesized to occur outside of conscious awareness, operating from *brain-to-brain* connections (Goleman, 2006). This direct neural relationship induces a *visceral sense of resonance* that embodies an empathic connection (Fishbane, 2007). Thus, the ability to express and receive empathy is at the core of social bonds.

This felt sense of resonance is facilitated in part by a system of neurons known as mirror neurons (Carr, Iacoboni, Dubeau, Mazziotta, & Lenzi, 2003; Gallese, Eagle, & Migone, 2007; Siegel, 2001). Located in areas of the frontal lobe, parietal lobe, cingulated cortex, and insula (i.e., a pyramid-shaped area of deep cortex adjacent to the temporal, frontal, and parietal lobes), mirror neurons in one individual fire in the exact same pattern when observing another complete a task as if the observer was completing the action himself or herself (Gallese, 2001; Iacoboni & Mazziotta, 2007; Rizzolatti & Craighero, 2004; Uddin, Iacoboni, Lange, & Keenan, 2007). These neurons were first discovered in macaque monkeys in the early 1990s (Rizzolatti & Craighero, 2004) but have since been the subject of considerable investigation in humans and considered critical to language development, social learning, social cognition, and empathy. As such, the brain-to-brain connections established in the therapeutic relationship and the empathy expressed by the counselor can activate the client's mirror neurons, which in turn engender a felt sense of connection and social bond between the client and counselor. The activation of mirror neurons and the resonance created between client and counselor can likewise enhance the integration of neural functioning between cortical and subcortical areas and lead to improved self-regulation in the client (Fuchs, 2004; Siegel, 2006).

Social Engagement, Autonomic Arousal, and the Therapeutic Relationship

The enhanced self-regulation engendered by the therapeutic relationship likewise results from the regulation of the client's autonomic nervous system (ANS). The ANS originates in the brain stem and spinal cord and is composed of two branches, the sympathetic and parasympathetic nervous systems. This network of systems controls unconscious survival functions of the body such as heart rate, respiration, and digestion, which have a strong influence on an individual's emotional and behavioral regulation. Social engagement and feelings of attachment have been found to influence the arousal of the autonomic nervous system (Porges, 2011). Therefore, within the counseling context, the counselor, just by establishing a social bond with the client, can help to regulate a client's heart rate, breathing, sense of safety, and even emotional responses.

The deterioration in a client's ability to effectively regulate emotions and actions, which is the hallmark of many clinical disorders and client challenges, can be directly related to disruptions in the client's physiological states of arousal. The **polyvagal theory** asserts that the nervous system developed through evolution in such a way as to regulate autonomic arousal and in doing so facilitate and enhance social behavior. When clients are hyper-aroused, such as in states of extreme stress and anxiety, they experience increased heart rate; shorter, more rapid breathing; and a sympathetic nervous system preparing the individual for fight or fight. On the other end of the spectrum, clients who are experiencing dissociative episodes, emotional numbing, or a freeze response are hypoaroused. Neither of these states of arousal allows for optimal social interactions. When in a balanced state of arousal, however, an individual functions from the **social engagement system (SES)**, a branch of the parasympathetic nervous system, which promotes behaviors that enhance social bonds (Porges, 2011). For example, when functioning from the SES, one can optimally regulate eye gaze, facial expressions, tone of voice, social gestures, and even the ability to extract the human voice from background noises in a way that allows for and strengthens the connection experienced between individuals. Therefore, the presence of the counselor can serve to calm a client's level of autonomic arousal, promoting the client's ability to engage in the therapeutic process and be receptive to social cognitive cues such as the verbal and nonverbal empathy expressed by the counselor. Although other techniques, such as mindfulness and relaxation practices, may help clients regulate the sympathetic and parasympathetic nervous systems, the therapeutic relationship is the first step in facilitating lasting change in a client that is made possible through neuroplasticity or the reorganization of neural connections.

Therapeutic Process and Neuroplasticity

The human brain is constantly changing. Even as you read the words printed in this book and learn new concepts, your brain is undergoing neuroplasticity. **Neuroplasticity** is the process by which the brain adapts and reorganizes when presented new information, events, or experiences, either internal or external. Such changes can occur in many ways, such as the growth of new neurons (i.e., **neurogenesis**), the development of new connections between neurons (i.e., **synaptogenesis**), enhancing the strength of the connections between neurons, or the extinction (i.e., **pruning**) of neuronal connections.

Learning and memory are the primary source of neuroplasticity. When an individual is learning, she or he is making new associations between concepts or creating a new concept all together. In the brain, this is translated into changes in the association between neurons, which is made possible through a process called **long-term potentiation** (LTP). First discovered in the hippocampus, LTP is the process of enhancing the connections between neurons. Following a principle put forth by Hebb (**Hebbian learning**; 1949) and refined by Shatz (1992), neurons that fire simultaneously will tend to continue firing in similar patterns, or more simply, neurons that *fire together wire together*. This simultaneous firing in turn is the basis of memory formation. Memories, from a very reductionist standpoint, can simply be thought of as complex patterns of neuronal firing. All of early neural development, therefore, can be conceptualized as neuroplasticity, yet these neuroplastic shifts continue to occur throughout life.

The primary aim of counseling is learning and reinforcing adaptive emotions, behaviors, and cognitions and creating new pictures of the self. In this way, neuroplasticity serves as the neural foundation of counseling. Without neuroplasticity, there can be no enduring change in a client's behaviors, emotions, or cognitions. Along with a strong therapeutic relationship, there are several mechanisms by which counselors can further enhance neural responses and adaptive plasticity within the client (Meyer, Young, & Jones, 2011, n.d.).

Setting the Stage for Counseling

Have you ever noticed that after you exercise, you feel better? Or that you do better on tests if you eat certain foods or get a good night's sleep before your exam? Physical well-being and lifestyle factors such as diet, exercise, and sleep are critical to enhancing neurological functioning across the life span. Counselors can use this information to optimize the benefits of counseling.

The foods that people eat provide the energy source and chemicals that the brain uses to create and alter synaptic connections and generate the chemical messengers (i.e., neurotransmitters) that cause neurons to fire. Without an optimal diet, the brain will not have the fuel it needs to optimally do its work. Research has shown that diets high in saturated fat and refined sugar actually reduce the functioning of neurotrophins and impair neural plasticity in the hippocampus, which results in impaired cognitive performance (Molteni, Barnard, Ying, Roberts, & Gómez-Pinilla, 2002). Additional studies found that food-derived or supplemental sources of dietary compounds such as omega-3 fatty acids and vitamin E can serve to protect neurotrophins in this process and facilitate brain plasticity in the prefrontal cortex, hippocampus, and additional limbic areas (Dyall, Michael, & Michael-Titus, 2010; Wu, Ying, & Gómez-Pinilla, 2004). As a result of its neuroprotective factors, omega-3 has been recommended as a beneficial dietary supplement for individuals with certain mood disorders, such as anxiety, stress responses, depression, and bipolar disorder (Balanz et al., 2011). These results are underscored by research detailing the direct connections between the gut and the brain, a system termed the microbiota-gut-brain access. Largely by way of the vagus nerve, there is a strong reciprocal relationship between the functioning of the brain and the gastrointestinal (GI) tract. Changes in the concentration of beneficial bacteria in the GI have been found to influence sleep cycles, stress responses, mood and mood disorders, sexual behavior, executive functioning, and emotional awareness (Cryan & Dinan, 2012; Forsythe & Kunze, 2013; Mayer, 2011). It is clear that a well-balanced nutritionally rich diet can enhance mental health functioning and possibly support the therapeutic process. Similar to diet, exercise also has been found to prolong life and optimize brain functioning. A significant body of research underscores the benefits of aerobic exercise to cognitive performance, executive functioning, and emotion regulation (Hillman, Erickson, & Kramer, 2008; Oaten & Cheng, 2006). Functional magnetic brain imaging (fMRI) studies have shown that aerobic activity enhances functioning and plasticity of the prefrontal cortex, cingulate cortex, insular cortex (i.e., an area between the frontal and temporal lobes responsible for self-awareness, cognition, and interpersonal functioning), and the hippocampus (Colcombe et al., 2004; Giuliani, Drabant, Bhatnagar, & Gross, 2011; van Praag, Kempermann, & Gage, 1999). This is made possible by an increased production of the neurotrophins following vigorous physical activity (Knaepen, Goekint, Elsa Marie, & Meeusen, 2010).

Sleep is a third physiological factor that enhances change in clients. Everyone understands the difficulties that follow a night of tossing and turning or the effects of staying up all night to finish a paper or cram for an exam. The next day you feel not only physically but mentally drained, struggle to focus, and may be forgetful. Restful and restorative sleep is essential for physical and mental well-being. A lack of sleep has been shown to serve as a physiological stressor that impairs brain functioning. Both moderate and prolonged sleep deprivation disrupts neurogenesis specifically in the hippocampus, which significantly impairs memory and learning (Meerlo, Mistlberger, Jacobs, Craig Heller, & McGinty, 2009). A lack of sleep also has been shown to contribute to the development of mood disorders, and disrupted sleep is a symptom of nearly every mental health disorder. Surprisingly, chronic sleep deprivation actually mimics the neurological effects of depression (Novati et al., 2008). As such, promoting sleep, optimal nutrition, and physical activity in clients will set the foundation for further changes to occur and persist as a result of clinical interventions. These are some of the practices termed therapeutic lifestyle changes, as discussed by Walsh (2012).

Using Neuroscience to Enhance Client Outcomes

Imagine yourself sitting in the counseling room across from your client. You know that she or he has a cortex, subcortical structures, and neurons, the connections between which are malleable. You also know a series of theoretical models of counseling, all of which promote various interventions and techniques to enhance client well-being. Yet when faced with an individual client, how do these two bodies of knowledge come together to benefit the individual looking to you for help? The following techniques draw from knowledge of the brain and can be integrated into any theoretical framework of psychotherapy to enhance the therapeutic process.

Regulating Autonomic Arousal. Many times when clients come into therapy, they are experiencing high levels of anxiety and stress or may exhibit increased stress and anxiety in response to a certain topic that surfaces in the session. Although minimal stress and arousal can benefit functioning and learning, moderate to high levels of stress impede attention and memory and disrupt the LTP process. When an individual experiences stress, a steroid hormone called cortisol is sent throughout the body. In low quantities and transient periods, it can enhance learning, emotion, and physical performance, yet in high quantities and under situations of chronic stress it has been shown to decrease plasticity in the hippocampus, decrease the size of the hippocampus, disrupt the functioning of the autonomic nervous system, and play a role in symptoms of depression and anxiety. As such, not only can pronounced stress significantly impair the cognitive, physical, and emotional well-being of clients, it can also derail the benefits of counseling. Whether destructive stress is your client's presenting concern or is preventing other clinical work from being accomplished, focusing on ways of coping with and moderating stress can greatly benefit clients. As with the therapeutic relationship, techniques to reduce stress also regulate the autonomic nervous system and thus lead to better self and emotional regulation and interpersonal functioning.

One such technique that has extensively been studied and incorporated into psychotherapeutic approaches, such as dialectical behavior therapy and acceptance and commitment therapy, is mindfulness. **Mindfulness** is considered the moment-to-moment nonjudgmental awareness and acceptance of internal or external events as they are occurring in the present moment (Kabat-Zinn, 2005). Mindfulness practices, discussed more fully in Chapter 15, have been shown to markedly decrease subjective feelings of psychological stress and related cortisol levels. Mindfulness also has immediate effects on brain activity, namely increased prefrontal activation (i.e., increased attention) and decreased activation of the amygdala (i.e., less emotional reactivity), substantiating its role in improving emotion regulation. Because mindfulness involves the self-regulation of sustained attention to the present moment (as is demonstrated by the activation of the prefrontal cortex), it can also help clients learn to volitionally control and direct their attention to different aspects of the environment. For example, clients who are experiencing symptoms of depression or post-traumatic stress, who often have a bias toward paying attention to the negative or fearful aspects of a situation, their internal experience, or their social environment, may be able to develop control over their attention and begin noticing the overlooked positive and innocuous aspects of the situation.

Working With Traumatic Stress. Some clients may come to counseling for more acute and pervasive stress following a trauma. Those individuals experiencing acute or posttraumatic stress responses often experience a breakdown in the connection between the amygdala and the prefrontal cortex and hippocampus. This means not only that they frequently experience considerable difficulty in regulating arousal and emotions but also that their memory of the traumatic event is often fractured into two distinct memories: (1) a visceral and emotional implicit memory of the event and (2) a concrete, factual-based declarative or explicit memory. Another interesting neurological outcome of traumatic stress is that in these individuals, both during the event and when reexperiencing the event, Broca's area, the center for speech production, shuts down. Accordingly, during those moments a client literally cannot talk about the event. With such individuals, considerable time and attention must be allocated to helping the client regulate his or her autonomic arousal and emotions, both through the therapeutic relationship and mindfulness- and relaxation-based activities. Trying to work with the traumatic memories and facilitate an integrated narrative of the event can be harmful to clients without first developing this affective and autonomic control. Shapiro (2010) also provides additional preparation exercises for traumatized clients.

Addressing the Whole. The neurological interrelationship between cognitions, emotions, and behavior suggests that all three components of an individual and individual experience must be addressed within the clinical setting. As described in the earlier description of trauma, intense emotion (fear) can disrupt memory storage and language production and influence behavioral responses. Such an integration, however, occurs not just in extreme cases but in everyday functioning. The amygdala plays a role in the production of neurotransmitters that influence cognition, attention, and memory consolidation.

Furthermore, although the terms *feelings* and *emotions* often are used interchangeably, they actually represent different processes. Feelings are cognitive conceptualizations, the words and mental representation of an emotional response, whereas emotions are the actual felt physiological changes in the body (Damasio, 2001). Feelings and emotions are even processed in different areas of the brain. Emotions evoke activation of the limbic system, and feelings are processed by cortical structures of the frontal and temporal lobes. Interestingly, even naming an emotion can suppress the functioning of the limbic system and lead to greater emotional regulation. In fact, researchers have found that when individuals mimicked an expression of fear seen in a photo, the amygdala became significantly more active. When those same individuals verbally labeled the emotion seen in the photo, however, the amygdala actually became less active and the right prefrontal cortex was engaged (Hariri, Bookheimer, & Mazziotta, 2000).

Therefore, exploring with clients their experiences of physiological emotions and explaining the nature of those reactions can create new ways of interpreting bodily responses and visceral sensations. This discussion helps the client learn a new relationship with her or his sensations and, as such, helps to build or strengthen cortico-limbic connections between the sensation and the meaning applied to that sensation. In turn, this influences executive control and attention in the prefrontal cortex, disrupting maladaptive, automatic thoughts; improving decision making; and ultimately leading to the modification of unhealthy behaviors (Cappas, Andres-Hyman, & Davidson, 2005). The process of influence could potentially also flow in reverse. Due to the elaborate cortico-limbic associations, counselors have an opportunity to concurrently induce change in the cognitions, emotions, and behavior of clients.

Priming the Brain. Have you ever smelled a certain smell or heard a particular song that had an immediate effect on your emotions, cognitions, or even behaviors? Often, the brain's unconscious system of processing is a forgotten component in traditional talk therapies. Capitalizing on the concepts of implicit memory and Hebbian learning, however, counselors can actually ***prime* a client's brain** (or more specifically the client's neurons) for future change. **Priming** occurs when an initial response to an internal or external event modifies later responses to those same or similar events by increasing the speed or nature of the response (LeDoux, 1996). Often, priming is discussed with respect to trauma and substance abuse when clients are unconsciously triggered into automatic behaviors as a result of perceiving a particular sight, sound, smell, or even taste. Working with clients to recognize these unconscious triggers and creating new neural connections between the sensory perception and the client's response will disrupt the automatic behaviors associated with the triggers.

Research also has underscored the effect of priming on self-esteem. Vallacher, Nowak, Froehlich, and Rockloff (2002) found that individuals who disclosed a positive life story later expressed higher self-esteem than individuals who shared a negative life event. Taking this into consideration, having a client recount a moment in which he or she felt empowered, competent, and effective prior to discussing the client's presenting concern may facilitate client self-efficacy and assist clients in discovering how they can also feel empowered and effective in the troubling situation.

Getting the Client's Attention. In order to enhance the effectiveness of counseling, clients can benefit from allocating and **increasing attention** (i.e., consciously focusing mental energy) to the therapeutic process and associated interventions. Although learning can occur unconsciously or implicitly, as is the case with priming and the benefits of the therapeutic relationship, much learning is explicit or intentional learning. This type of learning, such as when a client participates in thought stopping, for example, actually engages a different pathway in the brain from that of implicit learning and is strongly facilitated by increased attention. Attention helps to increase both the connections between neurons and the firing rates of those neurons in the prefrontal and cingulate cortices and thus can improve not only learning and memory but also emotional and self-regulation (Banfield, Wyland, Macrae, Münte, & Heatherton, 2004; Posner & Rothbart, 2005).

Appling the previous example of thought stopping, saying the word *stop* out loud serves as a means to increase the client's attention to her or his thoughts and presents an opportunity to change those thoughts. As a counselor, you are helping the client to bring attention back to what had become an automatic and habituated mental process and increase his or her attention to the possibility of modifying maladaptive thought patterns. A second way of increasing a client's attention to change is through the use of **novelty or unexpectedness** (Corbetta & Shulman, 2002). This parallels the premise that exposing children to brightly colored and enriched environments will enhance learning and brain development. Novelty increases attention and augments neuroplasticity across the life span. It can take the form of creative interventions, such as the use of music, art, or dance, or it can be an activity or environmental change novel to that particular client. Additionally, novelty can be encouraged by introducing new perspectives of a situation, such as the use of techniques like paradox and metaphors or even the Adlerian technique known as "spitting in the soup," all of which inspire a consideration of unexpected and novel perspectives. By creating novelty and grabbing and sustaining the client's attention to the therapeutic process and change, the counselor increases the likelihood that new and lasting therapeutic changes will occur.

Creating an Optimal Challenge.   The difficulty of an experiment or goal a counselor develops with a client can have marked consequences on the ability of the client to make lasting change. In order for positive change to occur, the counselor needs to provide clients with an **optimal level of challenge**. Task difficulty directly impacts the level of arousal and motivation experienced by the client (Green & Bavelier, 2008).

As discussed earlier, the level of arousal or stress that a client experiences can influence learning and therapeutic outcomes. Following Yerkes and Dodson's (1908) classic bell-shaped learning curve, arousal or stress improves learning up to a certain critical point, after which additional stress impairs functioning and disrupts learning. At this optimal level of arousal, just enough cortisol is released into the system to enhance plasticity within the hippocampus. If the task is too difficult, however, arousal will surpass the critical point of effectiveness and thus decrease the potential for learning and hippocampal memory formation. Furthermore, Vygotsky's (1978) *zone of proximal development*, instrumental in the field of education, reinforces the need for creating optimal challenges for clients stating that a task that is too difficult or too easy will cause an individual to lose motivation to complete the task. This theory posits that the difficulty of an optimal learning task should be just one step further than the individual's current level of functioning. The concept of scaffolding has been applied to Vygotsky's theory, suggesting that when assisting someone in learning a new task, the steps to achieving that goal should be optimally manageable and the person assisting the learner should provide the necessary support to the individual so that the individual can eventually complete the task independently. This epitomizes the counseling process. Interestingly, there is a comparable theory of scaffolding in neuroscience that suggests that to acquire a novel skill, earlier neural networks must be accessed. These earlier networks function as a scaffold from which to construct new synaptic connections (Reuter-Lorenz & Park, 2010). Incremental changes in learning difficulty lead to analogous incremental changes in neural connectivity. For example, when one learns to ride a bike, most individuals first learn with training wheels. This action creates connections between the visual image of the bike and the various sequential motor areas that together produce the needed movements to understand what one needs to do to power the bike and then do so. Once the training wheels are removed, however, new cortical associations are made between the spatial orientation areas of the brain that allow one to balance while concurrently making all of the movements needed to power the bike.

Within counseling, the concepts of task difficulty and scaffolding play an important role in goal setting with clients. Defining goals and experiments (e.g., a Gestalt two-chair technique) that optimally challenge the client will enhance changes in clients that correlate with the increased ability to develop new thoughts, behaviors, and emotional responses. This underscores the benefit of breaking larger goals down into manageable parts and following a SMART (i.e., specific, measurable, attainable, realistic, and timely) model when coconstructing a client's therapeutic goals. Identifying what is optimally challenging for clients is also involved in clinical interventions such as systematic desensitization and exposure therapy. In gradually reducing the level of arousal a client experiences when confronted with an anxiety-producing stimulus, the counselor also is gradually restructuring the client's neural connections between stimulus and the ensuing behavioral and emotional reaction.

The neuroscientific theory of scaffolding can also be understood as the neural basis for why exploring and using what is already working for a client is often effective in counseling. By investigating similarities between current thoughts, behaviors, or emotional responses and desired thoughts, behaviors, or emotional responses, the counselor is accessing already established neural networks from which to create change and further learning. Therefore, client success with applying a behavior or thought pattern to ease the presenting problem will be enhanced if the client has some degree of familiarity with that behavior, such as having previously applied that thought or behavior in another context.

Vicarious Learning and Visualization. The same mirror neurons that allow for an empathic connection in the therapeutic relationship also can be exploited to benefit client change through the techniques of vicarious learning and visualization. As suggested, mirror neurons in one individual are activated in the exact same way when watching another individual complete a task as if she or he were completing the task himself or herself. Mirror neurons then can be seen as the neural basis of vicarious learning. By watching another complete a task or respond in a certain manner, the network of neurons needed for completing that task or response are being activated in the observer, and in a sense the neural connections are being primed for future firing, increasing the potential that the observer can independently complete the task or response. As such, often the use of role models can be helpful in counseling. For example, watching someone exhibit assertiveness during an interpersonal conflict may very well prime the client's brain to be able to exhibit assertive behavior as well. Although the counselor can serve as a role model, modeling healthy thoughts, emotions, and behaviors to the client, the counselor also can suggest that the client find other individuals outside the therapeutic relationship to serve as models.

Interestingly, **visualization** alone can activate mirror neurons. When having the client imagine himself or herself exhibiting desired behaviors, the brain is responding in the exact same manner as if he or she were actually engaging in those behaviors (Decety & Grèzes, 2006). Therefore, having clients visualize desired behaviors will activate the neural network needed for those behaviors to actually take place. Going back to the assertiveness example, visualizing the assertive behavior will increase the likelihood that the client will be able to respond assertively during times of interpersonal conflict. The power of imagery to activate mirror neurons likewise explains why imagined exposure can be just as effective as in vivo exposure in exposure therapies. In order for any of these changes to be lasting, however, the thoughts, emotions, and behaviors (and thus the associated synaptic connections) must be repeated and reinforced.

Reinforcing Positive Change. The premise of "practice makes perfect" is underscored by neuroscience and the principles of neuroplasticity. Once a new synaptic connection has been formed, reinforcing that synaptic connection is necessary for the connection to survive. Therefore, creating opportunities for the client to repeatedly apply or exhibit the new thoughts, behaviors, or emotional responses will enhance the long-term retention of and ease with which the client can access this desired change. In addition to repetition, another means of reinforcing positive change and facilitating the maintenance of new neuronal connections is by providing feedback to clients (Green & Bavelier, 2008). This is the basis behind evaluation and giving credit in educational settings. Feedback allows clients to fine-tune their learning and associated adaptive changes and gain confidence in their new abilities. Therefore, acknowledging strengths and positive change and working with clients to recognize when a change is not effective will optimize synaptic plasticity and lead to enduring client change. Another way to optimize plasticity is through the use of operant conditioning to help the brain choose to change. In clinical practice, this is the essence of neurofeedback, a cost-effective, often brief intervention that promotes permanent, positive change.

NEUROFEEDBACK: ONE APPLICATION OF NEUROSCIENCE IN PRACTICE

Combining neuroscience with counseling leads quickly to a discussion of neurofeedback (NF), or neurotherapy. It is impossible in a short space to explain how to do neurotherapy. Our goal is to provide a basic working knowledge of what neurofeedback means, how it works, and how you can get future training in this area.

What Is Neurofeedback and How Does It Work?

Neurofeedback is a subset of biofeedback, "a process that enables an individual to learn how to change physiological activity for the purposes of improving health and performance" (Association for Applied Psychophysiology and Biofeedback [AAPB], 2011). Biofeedback teaches individuals to **self-regulate** basic body functions, such as breathing and heart rate, as a means of enhancing stress management, reducing feelings of anxiety and stress, enhancing immune system functioning, and creating greater health and wellness. Neurofeedback teaches individuals to monitor, self-regulate, and change their brain wave patterns in order to change their behavior.

Brain Waves

Brain waves can be measured by way of **electroencephalograms** (EEG), hence neurofeedback is often referred to as EEG biofeedback. The spectrum of brain wave activity includes bandwidths associated with specific wavelengths, shapes, amplitudes, and frequencies. The four primary waves of NF are delta, theta, alpha, and beta waves. **Delta and theta** are referred to as slow waves. They have lower frequencies (fewer cycles per second, or hertz) and higher amplitudes. Delta waves (1–3.5 hertz) predominate during sleep, whereas theta waves (4–8 hertz) occur during the transition from waking to sleep, during which time one is drowsy or daydreaming. **Alpha** and **beta** waves are called fast waves. Alpha waves (8–12 hertz) occur when the brain is idling and ready for action. Beta waves (12–20 hertz) are associated with sustained attention, thinking, and focusing. A special wave frequency, the sensorimotor rhythm (12–15 hertz), occurs in a specific part of the brain and is associated with relaxation and mental alertness.

QEEG: Brain Mapping

NF begins with an assessment of delta, theta, alpha, and beta brain wave activity at each of 19 locations specified through the **internationally accepted 10–20 system** of electrode placement (Schomer & da Silva, 2010). Quantitative electroencephalography, or **QEEG**, requires that a cap with electrodes be placed over the head and connected to a computer. Using a conductive gel, the electrical activity of the brain is assessed as it transmits through the scalp in a noninvasive manner. Tracings of electrical activity at each of the 19 sites for each of the four brainwaves is interpreted through graphical and numerical depictions of the data compared to information in one of several proprietary **normative databases**, resulting in a multicolored brain map depicting brain activity or deviations from what is considered typical activity at each site.

Interpreting Brain Maps

Interpretation of the brain map leads to recommendations for specific intervention protocols to address **dysregulation** of brain functioning. The QEEG is typically one of a series of assessments, including clinical interviews, that help determine the reasons for underlying biological and behavioral problems and inform possible intervention plans. QEEG brain maps are not stand-alone diagnostic measures but rather are used to verify diagnoses and are interpreted in relation to reported symptoms. Although some EEG patterns have been associated with specific disorders (e.g., ADHD, mood disorders such as depression and anxiety), multiple possible patterns may be related to specific symptoms or symptom clusters. At the same time, numerous studies have verified common EEG patterns related to specific diagnoses (see Hammond, 2007), and certain wave forms have been clearly associated with specific behaviors and diagnoses. For example, high beta wave activity in the right hemisphere of the brain is associated with anxiety, whereas high alpha activity in the left hemisphere is associated with depression. High or elevated theta-beta ratios in the anterior cortex are evident in persons with attention-deficit/hyperactivity disorder (ADHD).

Neurofeedback Protocols

Neurofeedback interventions are noninvasive and selected based on client-reported symptoms, clinician assessment, interpretation of psychosocial information, and QEEG results. Though many practitioners provide interventions in the absence of brain mapping, national organizations in the field have established QEEG-based protocols as an ethical imperative (Hoffman, 2007). Neurotherapy uses an operant conditioning paradigm to help clients recognize when their brain wave activity is normal and begin to seek a healthier balance as the brain is reinforced for movement toward normal. Brain waves that are too slow are up-trained, and those that are too fast may be down-trained; slower waves thus become faster and move toward a normal range and faster waves become slower while moving toward a normal range. Reported **side effects and contraindications** are minimal and usually transient (Soutar & Longo, 2011). It is important to note that NF in many instances reduces the need for medications; hence, medication side effects may be exaggerated if doses are not reduced during and following interventions.

The **number of sessions** required for successful NF treatment varies depending on symptoms and diagnosis. Many practitioners recommend 20–40 sessions as optimal, with conditions such as ADHD potentially requiring 4–6 times that many sessions for relief of presenting symptoms. Clients may experience change in only a few sessions, but because NF works through a learning paradigm, additional sessions are needed to reinforce the learning experience and make changes permanent. The brain is a system, and change in one area results in compensatory changes in other areas; compensation may be positive or negative. A repeated brain map following the intervention is likely to reveal changes that support symptom reduction.

Training, Certification, and Ethics

Numerous **training opportunities** exist for those wanting to learn more about neurofeedback. Both the AAPB and the International Society for Neurofeedback and Research (ISNR; www.isnr.org) offer annual training conferences, and many states have biofeedback society conferences that include NF training sessions.

The Biofeedback Certification International Alliance (bcia.org) provides voluntary national certification in biofeedback and neurofeedback, with academic, clinical, and technician options. **Certification** requires (a) a degree in a health care field; (b) completion of a course in human anatomy, biological psychology, or neuroscience; (c) completion of a 36-hour didactic education program; (d) 25 contact hours of supervision with a BCIA-approved mentor; (e) 100 client sessions; (f) 10 case conference presentations; (g) personal practice; and (h) successful completion of a national examination. Certification is valid for 5 years. Certified practitioners adhere to the BCIA's professional standards and ethical principles.

The ISNR offers an extensive bibliography of neurofeedback research on its website, easily organized so that practitioners can search based on symptoms and diagnoses. The ISNR also offers training, conferences, and publications to help researchers and practitioners learn about the science and practice of brain regulation through neurofeedback.

Integrating Neurofeedback Into Counseling Practice

There are at least four ways to integrate neurofeedback into one's counseling practice. First, by being aware of the nature and benefits of neurofeedback, counselors can be prepared to refer potential clients to a certified neurofeedback practitioner. Finding a qualified practitioner in a particular geographic area may be challenging. Online directories are provided at websites of national and international professional associations mentioned earlier as well as through certification organizations. Through recommendations of other professionals, experience, and client feedback, a working relationship with a NF practitioner may evolve. A second way to integrate NF into a counseling practice is for one or more members of the practice to become certified and offer NF interventions to clients throughout the practice.

The third way to integrate NF into one's practice is to become nationally certified. Training and completion of requirements may take 1–2 years and may cost up to $10,000, including the purchase of equipment and supplies. A number of companies offer equipment for neurofeedback training as well as training in the use of their equipment. Those interested in purchasing equipment are advised to talk to practitioners and search for providers through the Internet because the array of equipment possibilities is large and choices are typically made based on intended uses, clientele, costs, and reliability. The fourth way to integrate NF into counseling is through the use of audio-visual entrainment (AVE). AVE is a combination of flashes of light and auditory feedback used to "gently and safely guide the brain into various brain wave patterns . . . it is an effective, inexpensive alternative therapy for many disorders such as ADD, seasonal affective disorder, fibromyalgia, and chronic pain . . . also used successfully to boost physical performance . . . academic performance . . . and cognitive performance" (Mind Alive, n.d.).

NF may be applied to a broad spectrum of clients of any age. Results will vary based on client symptoms, compliance with treatment recommendations, and family and social support. Like any mental health intervention, taking a holistic approach and considering the impact of socioenvironmental factors is important. In addition, physical factors, including nutrition and medications, are critical for successful NF outcomes. The following case study illustrates the integration of NF into counseling practice.

CASE STUDY

Tracey, a 21-year-old female, was referred by her mother after being diagnosed with a major anxiety disorder and prescribed SSRIs by a psychiatrist. She reported feeling sad because she was unable to live independently on her salary as a waitress and had given up her apartment to move home. She had been diagnosed with a learning disability and had always been a poor student who did not enjoy school. After several attempts at college with failing grades, she was thinking about trying again in a 2-year occupational therapy program.

Tracey's QEEG brain map supported the diagnosis of a learning disability, but no signs of anxiety were present. Depression was suspected due to high alpha activity in the left hemisphere, along with sleep issues and a pattern of excessive rumination. The map suggested cognitive issues related to an inability to focus or sustain attention, difficulty problem solving, and problems with short-term memory. The map also reflected a possible severe head injury, which the client validated by explaining she had run into a pole during a sporting event and been knocked unconscious, also hitting the back of her head when she fell.

Traumatic brain injury is known to cause or exacerbate a wide range of physical and psychological symptoms. For Tracey, both cognitive symptoms and her learning disability could have been exacerbated by the injury. She readily validated all of the findings from the map and did not disagree with any of the possibilities raised.

Tracey received 40 sessions of neurofeedback designed to reduce her high alpha activity and increase her ability to focus and concentrate. Her response was very positive and most readily observed in her mood and cognitions. It was necessary to work with the psychiatrist to reduce her medication dosage, which was done over a period of 5 months. During this time, she reported fewer depressed feelings, fewer feelings of low self-worth, a better ability to concentrate, and improved short-term memory. She started back to school and found herself abler to pay attention, especially when the subject matter was boring or uninteresting to her, and her first-semester grades were all B- or better. Additional neurofeedback sessions were recommended, combined with counseling, to solidify her gains and encourage her continued positive growth.

During counseling the distinctions between anxiety and depression were discussed. From a neurofeedback perspective, chronic anxiety overwhelms the brain's defenses, resulting in a shift toward depression with resultant asymmetry and high alpha activity in the left hemisphere, with beta, normally high in the right hemisphere with anxiety, shifted to the left as a consequence. As Tracey's depression began to decrease, her anxiety once again began to increase. As she was helped to understand her anxiety, it became possible to teach coping strategies for anxiety reduction. Cognitive behavioral therapy approaches were implemented, including thought stopping for automatic thoughts, challenging irrational beliefs and expectations for perfection, learning to cope with stress, and eventually strategies for enhancing self-acceptance and self-esteem.

CONCLUSION

The human brain is infinitely complex, and our understanding of how the brain and nervous systems function is changing daily due to advances in applied and theoretical neuroscience. We are challenged to apply what we know in the areas of holistic health and wellness, such as the importance of nutrition and mindfulness for optimum functioning, and as we do so we will begin to see parallels and overlap between the science of the brain and the art of counseling interventions. Continued professional development will lead us to better understand how we can integrate advancing neuroscience knowledge and research in a manner that continues to honor and enhance our current holistic, wellness-based approaches. Ultimately, clients of all ages and diagnoses will benefit as counselors join other mental health professionals in intervening with clients based on our growing understandings of the neurobiological bases of behavior.

REFERENCES

Ainsworth, M. D. (1989). Attachments beyond infancy. *American Psychologist, 44*(4), 709–716.

Amini, F., Lewis, T., Lannon, R., Louie, A., Baumbacher, G., McGuinness, T., et al. (1996). Affect, attachment, memory: Contributions toward psychobiologic integration. *Psychiatry, 59*(3), 213–239.

Association for Applied Psychophysiology and Biofeedback. (2011). *Biofeedback*. Retrieved from www .aapb.org.

Balanza-Martinez, V., Fries, G. R., Colpo, G. D., Silveira, P. P., Portella, A. K., Tabarés-Seisdedos, R., et al. (2011). Therapeutic use of omega-3 fatty acids in bipolar disorder. *Expert Review of Neurotherapeutics, 11*(7), 1029–1047. doi:10.1586/ern.11.42

Banfield, J. F., Wyland, C. L., Macrae, C. N., Münte, T. F., & Heatherton, T. F. (2004). The cognitive neuroscience of self-regulation. In R. F. Baumeister & K. D. Vohs (Eds.), *Handbook of self-regulation: Research, theory, and applications* (pp. 62–83). New York: Guilford Press.

Bowlby, J. (1988a). *A secure base: Parent-child attachment and healthy human development*. New York: Basic Books.

Bowlby, J. (1988b). *A secure base: Clinical applications of attachment*. London: Routledge.

Burke, S. N., & Barnes, C. A. (2006). Neural plasticity in the ageing brain. *Nature Reviews Neuroscience, 7*(1), 30–40.

Council for Accreditation of Counseling and Related Educational Programs. (2016). *2016 CACREP Standards*. Alexandria, VA: Author.

Cappas, N. M., Andres-Hyman, R., & Davidson, L. (2005). What psychotherapists can begin to learn from neuroscience: Seven principles of a brain-based psychotherapy. *Psychotherapy: Theory, Research, Practice, Training, 42*(3), 374–383. doi:10.1037/0033–3204.42.3.374

Carr, L., Iacoboni, M., Dubeau, M.-C., Mazziotta, J. C., & Lenzi, G. L. (2003). Neural mechanisms of empathy in humans: A relay from neural systems for imitation to limbic areas. *Proceedings of the National Academy of Sciences, 100*(9), 5497–5502. doi:10.1073/pnas.0935845100

Casey, B. J., Giedd, J. N., & Thomas, K. M. (2000). Structural and functional brain development and its relation to cognitive development. *Biological Psychology, 54*(1–3), 241–257. doi:10.1016/ s0301–0511(00)00058–2

Colcombe, S. J., Kramer, A. F., Erickson, K. I., Scalf, P., McAuley, E., Cohen, N. J., et al. (2004). Cardiovascular fitness, cortical plasticity, and aging. *Proceedings of the National Academy of Sciences of the United States of America, 101*(9), 3316–3321. doi:10.1073/pnas.0400266101

Corbetta, M., & Shulman, G. L. (2002). Control of goal-directed and stimulus-driven attention in the brain. *Nature Reviews Neuroscience, 3*(3), 201–215.

Crews, F., He, J., & Hodge, C. (2007). Adolescent cortical development: A critical period of vulnerability for addiction. *Pharmacology, Biochemistry, and Behavior, 86*, 189–199.

Cryan, J. F., & Dinan, T. G. (2012). Mind-altering microorganisms: The impact of the gut microbiota on brain and behaviour. *Nature Reviews Neuroscience, 13*(10), 701–712.

Damasio, A. (2001). Fundamental feelings. *Nature, 413*(6858), 781.

Decety, J., & Grèzes, J. (2006). The power of simulation: Imagining one's own and others' behavior. *Brain Research, 1079*(1), 4–14. doi:10.1016/j.brainres.2005.12.115

Dyall, S. C., Michael, G. J., & Michael-Titus, A. T. (2010). Omega-3 fatty acids reverse age-related decreases in nuclear receptors and increase neurogenesis in old rats. *Journal of Neuroscience Research, 88*(10), 2091–2102. doi:10.1002/jnr.22390

Fishbane, M. D. (2007). Wired to connect: Neuroscience, relationships, and therapy. *Family Process, 46*(3), 395–412. doi:10.1111/j.1545-5300.2007.00219.x

Forsythe, P., & Kunze, W. A. (2013). Voices from within: Gut microbes and the CNS. *Cellular and Molecular Life Sciences, 70*(1), 55–69.

Fuchs, T. (2004). Neurobiology and psychotherapy: An emerging dialogue. *Current Opinion in Psychiatry, 17*(6), 479–485. doi:10.1097/00001504-200411000-00010

Gabbard, G. O. (2000). A neurobiologically informed perspective on psychotherapy. *British Journal of Psychiatry, 177*(2), 117–122.

Gallese, V. (2001). The shared manifold hypothesis. From mirror neurons to empathy. *Journal of Consciousness Studies, 8*(5–7), 33–50.

Gallese, V., Eagle, M. N., & Migone, P. (2007). Intentional attunement: Mirror neurons and the neural underpinnings of interpersonal relations. *Journal of the American Psychoanalytic Association, 55*(1), 131–175. doi:10.1177/00030651070550010601

Geller, S. M., & Porges, S. W. (2014). Therapeutic presence: Neurophysiological mechanisms mediating feeling safe in therapeutic relationships. *Journal of Psychotherapy Integration, 24*(3), 178.

Geuze, E., Vermetten, E., & Bremner, J. D. (2005). MR-based in vivo hippocampal volumetrics: 2. Findings in neuropsychiatric disorders. *Molecular Psychiatry, 10*(2), 160–184. doi:10.1038/sj.mp.4001579

Giuliani, N. R., Drabant, E. M., Bhatnagar, R., & Gross, J. J. (2011). Emotion regulation and brain plasticity: Expressive suppression use predicts anterior insula volume. *NeuroImage, 58*(1), 10–15. doi:10.1016/j.neuroimage.2011.06.028

Goleman, D. (2006). *Social intelligence: The new science of human relationships*. New York: Bantam Books.

Green, C. S., & Bavelier, D. (2008). Exercising your brain: A review of human brain plasticity and training-induced learning. *Psychology and Aging, 23*(4), 692–701.

Hammond, C. (2007). Comprehensive neurofeedback bibliography: Update 2007. *Journal of Neurotherapy, 11*(3), 45–60. doi:10.1080/10874200802126241

Hariri, A. R., Bookheimer, S. Y., & Mazziotta, J. C. (2000). Modulating emotional responses: Effects of a neocortical network on the limbic system. *NeuroReport, 11*(1), 43–48.

Hebb, D. O. (1949). *The organization of behavior*. New York: Wiley.

Hillman, C. H., Erickson, K. I., & Kramer, A. F. (2008). Be smart, exercise your heart: Exercise effects on brain and cognition. *Nature Reviews Neuroscience, 9*(1), 58–65.

Hoffman, D. A. (2007). "First, do no harm": A basic tenet in jeopardy? *Journal of Neurotherapy, 10*, 53–61. doi:10.1300/J184v10n04_06

Iacoboni, M., & Mazziotta, J. C. (2007). Mirror neuron system: Basic findings and clinical applications. *Annals of Neurology, 62*(3), 213–218. doi:10.1002/ana.21198

Jones, L. K. (2015). *Thriving in a new era of neuroscience: Understanding how brain science can inform clinical practice*. Alexandria, VA: American Mental Health Counselors Association.

Kabat-Zinn, J. (2005). *Full catastrophe living: Using the wisdom of your body and mind to face stress, pain, and illness* (15th anniversary ed.). New York: Delta Trade Paperback/Bantam Dell.

Kang, N., Baum, M. J., & Cherry, J. A. (2009). A direct main olfactory bulb projection to the "vomeronasal" amygdala in female mice selectively responds to volatile pheromones from males. *European Journal of Neuroscience, 29*(3), 624–634. doi:10.1111/j.1460-9568.2009.06638.x

Karnath, H.-O., Ferber, S., & Himmelbach, M. (2001). Spatial awareness is a function of the temporal not the posterior parietal lobe. *Nature, 411*(6840), 950–953. doi:citeulike-article-id:1218762

Knaepen, K., Goekint, M., Elsa Marie, H., & Meeusen, R. (2010). Neuroplasticity exercise-induced response of peripheral brain-derived neurotrophic factor: A systematic review of experimental studies in human subjects. *Sports Medicine, 40*(9), 765–801.

LeDoux, J. E. (1996). *The emotional brain: The mysterious underpinnings of emotional life.* New York: Simon & Schuster.

Macmillan, M. (2002). *An odd kind of fame: Stories of Phineas Gage.* Cambridge, MA: MIT Press.

Mayer, E. A. (2011). Gut feelings: The emerging biology of gut–brain communication. *Nature Reviews Neuroscience, 12*(8), 453–466.

Meerlo, P., Mistlberger, R. E., Jacobs, B. L., Craig Heller, H., & McGinty, D. (2009). New neurons in the adult brain: The role of sleep and consequences of sleep loss. *Sleep Medicine Reviews, 13*(3), 187–194. doi:10.1016/j.smrv.2008.07.004

Merriam-Webster Medical Dictionary. (2011). *Neuroscience.* Retrieved from http://www.merriam-webster.com/medlineplus/neuroscience.

Meyer, D., Young, J. S., & Jones, L. K. (2011, October). *Maximizing the impact of counseling: Neuroplasticity and the process of therapeutic change.* Paper presented at the Association for Counselor Education and Supervision National Conference, Nashville, TN.

Meyer, D., Young, J. S., & Jones, L. K. (n.d.). *The application of neuroplasticity to clinical practice: Maximizing counseling outcomes.* Unpublished manuscript, Department of Family and Community Medicine, Saint Louis University, St. Louis, Missouri.

Mind Alive. (n.d.). *Welcome to audio-visual entrainment.* Retrieved from www.mindalive.com.

Molteni, R., Barnard, R. J., Ying, Z., Roberts, C. K., & Gómez-Pinilla, F. (2002). A high-fat, refined sugar diet reduces hippocampal brain-derived neurotrophic factor, neuronal plasticity, and learning. *Neuroscience, 112*(4), 803–814. doi:10.1016/s0306-4522(02)00123-9

National Institute of Mental Health. (2010). *The National Institute of Mental Health Strategic Plan.* Washington, DC: Author.

Novati, A., Roman, V., Cetin, T., Hagewoud, R., den Boer, J. A., Luiten, P. G. M., et al. (2008). Chronically restricted sleep leads to depression-like changes in neurotransmitter receptor sensitivity and neuroendocrine stress reactivity in rats. *Sleep, 31*(11), 1579–1585.

Oaten, M., & Cheng, K. (2006). Longitudinal gains in self-regulation from regular physical exercise. *British Journal of Health Psychology, 11*(Pt 4), 717–733. doi:10.1348/135910706x96481

Pearlman, L. A., & Courtois, C. A. (2005). Clinical applications of the attachment framework: Relational treatment of complex trauma. *Journal of Traumatic Stress, 18*(5), 449–459. doi:10.1002/jts.20052

Porges, S. W. (2011). *The polyvagal theory: Neurophysiological foundations of emotions, attachment, communication, and self-regulation.* New York: W. W. Norton.

Posner, M. I., & Rothbart, M. K. (2005). Influencing brain networks: Implications for education. *Trends in Cognitive Sciences, 9*(3), 99–103. doi:10.1016/j.tics.2005.01.007

Reuter-Lorenz, P. A., & Park, D. C. (2010). Human neuroscience and the aging mind: A new look at old problems. *Journals of Gerontology. Series B, Psychological Sciences and Social Sciences, 65*(4), 405–415.

Rizzolatti, G., & Craighero, L. (2004). The mirror-neuron system. *Annual Review of Neuroscience, 27*(1), 169–192. doi:10.1146/annurev.neuro.27.070203.144230

Rogers, C. R. (1956). The necessary and sufficient conditions of therapeutic personality change. *Consulting Psychology, 21*, 95–103.

Schomer, D. L., & da Silva, F. L. (Eds.). (2010). *Niedermeyer's electroencephalography: Basic principles, clinical applications, and related fields.* Hagerstown, MD: Lippincott Williams & Wilkins.

Schore, A. N. (2001). Effects of a secure attachment relationship on right brain development, affect regulation, and infant mental health. *Infant Mental Health Journal, 22*(1–2), 7–66. doi:10.1002/1097–0355

Shapiro, R. (2010). *The trauma treatment handbook: Protocols across the spectrum.* New York: W. W. Norton.

Shatz, C. J. (1992). The developing brain. *Scientific American, 267*(3), 60–67.

Siegel, D. J. (2001). Toward an interpersonal neurobiology of the developing mind: Attachment relationships, "mindsight," and neural integration. *Infant Mental Health Journal, 22*(1–2), 67–94. doi:10.1002/1097–0355

Siegel, D. J. (2006). An interpersonal neurobiology approach to psychotherapy: Awareness, mirror neurons, and neural plasticity in the development of well-being. *Psychiatric Annals, 36*(4), 248–256.

Soutar, R., & Longo, R. (2011). *Doing neurofeedback: An introduction.* San Rafael, CA: International Society for Neurofeedback and Research Foundation.

Strick, P. L., Dum, R. P., & Fiez, J. A. (2009). Cerebellum and nonmotor function. *Annual Review of Neuroscience, 32,* 413–434.

Uddin, L. Q., Iacoboni, M., Lange, C., & Keenan, J. P. (2007). The self and social cognition: The role of cortical midline structures and mirror neurons. *Trends in Cognitive Sciences, 11*(4), 153–157. doi:10.1016/j.tics.2007.01.001

Vallacher, R. R., Nowak, A., Froehlich, M., & Rockloff, M. (2002). The dynamics of self-evaluation. *Personality and Social Psychology Review, 6*(4), 370–379. doi:10.1207/s15327957pspr0604_11

van Praag, H., Kempermann, G., & Gage, F. H. (1999). Running increases cell proliferation and neurogenesis in the adult mouse dentate gyrus. *Nature Reviews Neuroscience, 2*(3), 266–270.

Vygotsky, L. (1978). *Mind and society: The development of higher psychological processes.* Cambridge, MA: Harvard University Press.

Walsh, R. (2012). Lifestyle and mental health. *American Psychologist, 66,* 579–592.

Wu, A., Ying, Z., & Gómez-Pinilla, F. (2004). The interplay between oxidative stress and brain-derived neurotrophic factor modulates the outcome of a saturated fat diet on synaptic plasticity and cognition. *European Journal of Neuroscience, 19*(7), 1699–1707. doi:10.1111/j.1460–9568.2004.03246.x

Yerkes, R., & Dodson, J. (1908). The relation of strength of stimulus to rapidity of habit-formation. *Journal of Comparative Neurology and Psychology, 18,* 459–482.

Emerging Approaches to Clinical Mental Health Counseling

Amanda L. Giordano, Philip B. Clarke, Cheryl L. Fulton,
and Tammy H. Cashwell

Learning Goals

Upon completion of this chapter you will be able to do the following:

1. Describe the basic components of the motivational interviewing approach and how these are applied in a clinical setting

2. Articulate the steps of the emotion-focused therapy model and explain how it is used in clinical mental health (CMH) counseling

3. Describe the elements of dialectic behavioral therapy and its use to treat clinical conditions

4. Explain the components of the interpersonal psychotherapy approach and how it might be used in clinical practice

5. Define the foundational components of trauma-focused cognitive behavioral therapy and apply the model to a client

6. Convey the use of mindfulness as an adjunctive clinical intervention

7. List the foundational components of the acceptance and commitment therapy and describe how the model is applied clinically

8. Describe the unique role that spirituality in counseling can play in working with clients who hold religious and/or spiritual beliefs

Counseling theories are continuously in flux. Just as some theoretical orientations lose their relevance in today's culture and begin to fade out of practice, new approaches are emerging in the literature and clinical settings. This chapter describes the basic tenets of several approaches in the counseling field that often are not covered in introductory theories courses but have relevance for mental health counselors.

This chapter includes descriptions of contemporary approaches for facilitating client change in CMH counseling practice. The authors discuss several contemporary approaches, including motivational interviewing, emotionally focused couple therapy, dialectical behavior therapy, interpersonal psychotherapy, and trauma-focused cognitive behavioral theory. Although the specifics are relatively novel, it is important to note that each approach remains grounded in traditional counseling theories. For example, motivational interviewing stems from Carl Rogers's person-centered theory; emotionally focused couple therapy includes elements of Fritz Perls's Gestalt theory; and dialectical behavior therapy, interpersonal psychotherapy, and trauma-focused CBT are built on a cognitive-behavioral orientation.

In addition to contemporary theoretical approaches, two broad constructs are detailed, namely mindfulness and spirituality, including their application to clinical work. Several mindfulness programs are described, such as mindfulness-based stress reduction and mindfulness-based cognitive therapy. In addition, acceptance and commitment therapy, a mindfulness approach representing the third generation of behavioral theory, is outlined. Spirituality is addressed by providing an operational definition of the construct, identifying obstacles to the integration of spirituality in counseling, and outlining methods for assessing client spirituality.

As evidenced by the previous list, this chapter includes a wide variety of emerging approaches. In each section, a brief introduction is provided in order to outline the basic constructs of the method. Readers are encouraged to consult additional sources and trainings pertaining to approaches of interest in order to gain competency in that approach.

MOTIVATIONAL INTERVIEWING

Motivational interviewing (MI) is a style of counseling used to strengthen a client's motivation to change (Miller & Rollnick, 2013). MI was initially developed by William Miller and Stephen Rollnick as an approach for increasing motivation to change in alcohol abusing clients (Miller, 1983; Miller & Rollnick, 1991). Since its development, MI has been applied more broadly to such issues as lifestyle management in persons with diabetes (West, DiLillo, Bursac, Gore, & Greene, 2007), spiritual concerns (Clarke, Giordano, Cashwell, & Lewis, 2013), and depression (Zuckoff, Swartz, & Grote, 2008). Miller and Rollnick (2013) define MI as "a person-centered counseling style for addressing the common problem of ambivalence about change" (p. 21). Ambivalence, or wanting and not wanting something at the same time, is a common experience on the journey toward change. From an MI perspective, counselors are tasked with addressing ambivalence by eliciting intrinsic motivation, or change talk, from the client, thereby empowering her or him to move toward desired positive change (Rollnick, Miller, & Butler, 2008). The following section provides an overview of MI; interested readers are encouraged to consult Miller and Rollnick (2013) for a detailed description of the approach.

The Basics of MI

More than a series of techniques and processes, MI is a communication style with a distinct spirit directing the counseling interaction. Miller and Rollnick (2013) described the spirit of MI, consisting of four elements, as the heart and foundation of the approach. First, the spirit of MI involves a *partnership* between the counselor and the client. This collaborative effort toward making positive change entails the client's expertise regarding her or his own life as well as the counselor's expertise regarding the process of resolving ambivalence. The second element of the MI spirit is *acceptance*, which involves acknowledging a client's absolute worth as a human being, respecting autonomy, conveying accurate empathy, and affirming strengths and efforts. Directly related to working for the good of the client, *compassion* is the third element of the MI spirit. MI is used in order to support the well-being of clients and stems from a commitment to enhance their best interests. Any other motivation, such as using MI techniques to manipulate the client to change, has diverged from the intent of MI. Finally, the MI spirit comprises *evocation*. Rather than imposing reasons to change, MI counselors believe that ambivalent clients "already have both arguments within them—those favoring change and those supporting status quo" (Miller & Rollnick, 2013, p. 21). Therefore, counselors work to elicit, or draw out, a client's own reasons for change and thereby strengthen intrinsic motivation to make positive changes.

With the spirit of MI in mind, counselors use several core skills throughout the counseling process in order to elicit intrinsic motivation to change. The four primary MI skills include asking *open questions, affirming, reflective listening,* and *summarizing* (OARS; Rosengren, 2009). These skills are basic counseling techniques but are unique within the MI context because the primary focus is to elicit client speech regarding change and thereby increase the client's perceived importance of change, confidence in change, and readiness to change (Arkowitz & Miller, 2008). In the third edition of the text, Miller and Rollnick (2013) added a fifth core skill to the previously established OARS—*informing and advising.* In accordance with the spirit of MI, this skill is used in such a way as to emphasize the partnership between the counselor and client and include elements of evocation. Information is offered with the client's permission in the format of elicit-provide-elicit. The provided information is preceded by eliciting the client's current knowledge and interest in the information and followed by asking for the client's interpretation or understanding. The core MI skills are used throughout the MI interaction consisting of four overlapping processes.

The first process of MI is *engaging* the client in the partnership. As with other counseling approaches, the formation of a collaborative relationship between counselor and client is a necessary requirement for attaining treatment goals. In MI, engagement involves the use of powerful reflections to convey interest and understanding. One type of reflection used in the process is *continuing the paragraph*. Rather than reflecting the client's last statement, the counselor posits a reasonable guess as to the next sentence in the client's paragraph. As the counselor reflects understanding of the client's concerns, perspectives, values, and goals, the client becomes engaged in the process of MI. The MI elements of compassion and acceptance are especially salient during the process of engagement.

The next MI process, *focusing,* is the determination of an agreed-on direction for the counselor and client's work together. At times, the direction of counseling is clear and supported by both the client and the counselor from the onset (such as a client who voluntarily enters a substance abuse treatment facility with the goal of abstaining from drug use). Other instances, however, require investigation and collaboration to identify the focus of counseling. The skill of *agenda mapping* is used during the focusing process and consists of identifying potential options for the direction of counseling and collaboratively determining which option is most beneficial for the client.

Once the client is engaged and a focus has been determined, MI counselors begin the process of *evoking*. This process is most unique to MI because it demonstrates the foundational belief that clients have within themselves the expertise and motivation to move toward positive change. During the evoking process, counselors skillfully draw out this motivation from within clients so that they are essentially talking themselves into making change. Clients who are stuck in ambivalence about making a change (e.g., I want to stop drinking so I do not do further damage to my body, but I don't want to stop drinking because it helps me cope) already have internal reasons for and against change. MI counselors refer to reasons supporting change as *change talk* and reasons supporting the status quo as *sustain talk*. Through the MI dialogue, counselors listen for client change talk and strategically choose to reflect and summarize these statements. The opposite of MI occurs when a counselor is giving the client reasons to make changes and the client is giving the counselor reasons why change is not possible. Instead, the counselor uses the core skills of MI (OARS and informing/advising) to elicit and strengthen the client's own reasons for change. Throughout the evoking process, clients speak from both sides of ambivalence. Counselors use a variety of tools to respond to client sustain talk in such a way as to invite change talk. One such tool is *agreeing with a twist*. This strategy entails validating the client's sustain talk and ending with a reframe that offers a new perspective to consider. For example, a client shares that despite her diabetes diagnosis she does not think she will change her eating habits because it is what she has always known. The counselor responds by saying, "You feel comfortable eating the way you do—it is familiar. Eating differently would be like setting out on an adventure into new terrains." The process of evoking involves guiding the client through his or her ambivalence and strengthening the client's own motivation for moving in the direction of change.

The final process of MI is *planning*. When the client is committed to making change and has resolved his or her ambivalence issue, the next step is to develop a plan detailing how change can be successfully carried out. Before planning begins, the counselor must gauge the client's readiness to construct a change plan. Indicators that the client may be ready for the process of planning are increased change talk and decreased sustain talk, instances in which the client begins to envision making the change, or client questions about the process of change. At the point in which the client is ready to plan for change, the counselor continues to work from the spirit of MI and rely on the core skills. Counselors evoke change plans from clients, believing that clients' expertise of their own experiences includes ideas about how to make the desired changes. Counselors also elicit *mobilizing change talk*, which refers to client speech indicating commitment, movement toward action, and taking steps toward change. The planning process consists of confirming the change goal, summarizing the change plan, evoking mobilizing change talk, and troubleshooting. The four processes of MI build on each other in that during the planning process the client must be engaged, the focus of the plan remains clear, and the plan is evoked from the client (Miller & Rollnick, 2013).

Support for MI

Whereas MI has become an increasingly popular theory incorporated with rising variability in treatment populations, it also has strong empirical support. Meta-analyses of 119 studies indicate that MI is, in fact, an evidence-based practice (Lundahl, Kunz, Brownell, Tollefson, & Burke, 2010) with behavioral changes maintained at various follow-up intervals. Moreover, MI interventions result in higher levels of motivation for treatment and change (Lundahl et al., 2010). Miller and Rose (2009) conducted a review of the literature on MI and noted that the MI spirit, in conjunction with change talk, is a key mechanism of change that underlies this approach. Indeed, researchers have found evidence that change talk correlates with behavior change (Baer et al., 2008). Specifically, in a sample of 54 adolescent substance abuse clients, counterchange talk regarding confidence and motivation to change was related to increased substance use, whereas expressing reasons for change correlated with decreased use. The continued development of MI as an effective approach will benefit from research evaluating both its efficacy and change-inducing elements.

MI in Practice

Miller and Rollnick (2009) described several things that MI is not, one of which is a coercive way of tricking clients into doing something they do not want to do. MI works by eliciting the client's own motivation for change stemming from her or his unique goals and values (Miller & Rollnick, 2013). Therefore, MI cannot override client autonomy because it is the client who provides the momentum and reasons for making a change. This notion is captured in the spirit of MI, which highlights the partnership, acceptance, compassion, and evocation embedded within the approach (Miller & Rollnick, 2013). Therefore, whether the MI counselor is addressing medication compliance, substance abuse, physical health considerations, or mental illness, the MI counselor works to draw out clients' internal reasons for change aligning with their personal goals and values. As the client begins to speak about change and the benefits of changing, the MI counselor uses reflections and summaries to highlight this language until the ambivalence issue is resolved. Using the MI approach, clients are empowered to make informed decisions pertaining to the change issue and take ownership of their progress.

CASE STUDY

Jamal is a college sophomore who has been referred to the counselor by the university due to poor academic performance.

Counselor: What brings you here today, Jamal? (*open question*)

Jamal: I'm here because I have to be. I got put on academic probation. I know you're probably going to lecture me about how I need to study harder. I don't. I just had a bad semester.

(Continued)

(Continued)

Counselor: You do not want to be here right now and feel that your study habits are not something you want to change (*reflection skill used to enhance engagement*). As a counselor, I try to let my clients make their own decisions. It's going to be up to you whether you make any changes in your life (*demonstrating acceptance through emphasizing autonomy*).

Jamal: OK. I just figured you'd be another person trying to tell me what I need to do (*engaging process continues*). I already have to meet with you for 5 sessions in order to stay enrolled here.

Counselor: You're right. We do have to meet for 5 sessions for you to stay enrolled and we do have to talk about your life and maybe even explore why you feel you had a bad semester (*beginning the process of focusing*). We have some different options, though. We can talk about your thoughts about being here, we can explore your experience in your classes this past semester, we can discuss what your goals might be for yourself and your future, or we can discuss something else (*counselor uses agenda mapping to support client autonomy as they determine the direction of the session*).

Jamal: I would be OK talking about goals. I've actually been thinking a lot about them lately (*client engages in focusing process*).

In this scenario, Jamal enters counseling with some reservations, and it is not difficult to imagine how a counselor could get involved in a power struggle with Jamal from the outset. As the conversation related to Jamal's goals develops, the counselor uses OARS skills to begin evoking change talk. The counselor strategically reflects and summarizes Jamal's statements related to his desire and ability to change as well as reasons for considering change. These reflections evoke more change talk as Jamal expresses a willingness to reflect on his study habits in light of his vocational goals. As the interaction continues, Jamal's change talk increases, as does his commitment and motivation to make change.

EMOTIONALLY FOCUSED COUPLE THERAPY

Emotionally focused couple therapy (EFT) emerged in the 1980s as a result of the work of Susan Johnson and Leslie Greenberg. This experiential approach offers an innovative means for attending to attachment needs, expressing emotions, and creating change in negative interaction cycles (Johnson, 2004). EFT is grounded in theory, synthesizing elements of humanistic, systems, and adult attachment theoretical orientations. It has been supported empirically as an effective treatment approach for distressed couples (Baucom, Shoham, Mueser, Daiuto, & Stickle, 1998; Johnson, 2003; Wood, Crane, Schaalje, & Law, 2005).

This section provides an overview of EFT. Interested readers are encouraged to consult Johnson's (2004) work for a more thorough description of the approach.

The Basics of EFT

A primary hallmark of EFT is the recognition that emotions serve to organize behaviors and interactional patterns. Thus, the experiential expression of attachment-oriented emotions is the mechanism for change within this approach. The process of EFT is composed of three stages consisting of nine steps and generally requires 8–20 sessions, although it may require longer where one or both people have a history of trauma. Through the EFT process, a safe therapeutic alliance is created, emotional responses are accessed and defined in the context of attachment, and interactions are restructured.

The aim of Stage 1 is to identify and assess the negative interaction cycle underlying the couple's distress and to unite the couple in their desire to change these patterns. The negative cycle consists of behavioral reactions to unacknowledged feelings and attachment needs. Further, each partner within the couple assumes a particular position in the relationship and interactional cycle. Common types of cycles include those in which one partner is pursuing while the other is withdrawing, one partner is attacking while the other is defending, or both partners are withdrawing or attacking. Depending on the assumed relational positions, the EFT counselor is able to hypothesize the underlying emotions each partner is experiencing.

Stage 1: Deescalation of Negative Cycles of Interaction

During the first stage, assessments are made with regard to interactional patterns, unspoken attachment needs and emotions, and the relational positions of each partner.

Step 1. Creating an alliance and delineating conflict issues in the core attachment struggle.

Step 2. Identifying the negative interactional cycle where these issues are expressed.

Step 3. Accessing the unacknowledged emotions underlying interactional positions.

Step 4. Reframing the problem in terms of the negative cycle, underlying emotions, and attachment needs. The cycle is framed as the common enemy and the source of the partners' emotional deprivation and distress.

Stage 2: Changing Interactional Positions

The steps of Stage 2 are designed to provide experiences that serve to restructure interactions to deepen the engagement of both partners. The EFT counselor works to engage the more withdrawn partner (withdrawer engagement) as well as invite the pursuing partner to express her or his attachment needs (blamer softening) during this stage. In this way, changes in relational positions begin to transpire. As each partner becomes more emotionally engaged and identifies her or his own attachment needs, the other partner responds with acceptance and affirmation.

Step 5. Promoting identification with disowned attachment emotions, needs, and aspects of self and integrating these into relationship interactions.

Step 6. Promoting acceptance of the partner's experience and new interactional responses.

Step 7. Facilitating the expression of needs and wants and creating emotional engagement and bonding events that redefine the attachment between partners.

Stage 3: Consolidation and Integration

Finally, Stage 3 consists of acknowledging and reflecting on the new relational positions assumed by each partner. As a result of the previous two stages, couples are able to respond to issues with new solutions as their attachment needs are now known and emotions are more freely expressed. The EFT counselor draws the couple's attention to new responses and interactional patterns to solidify the changes that have been made.

Step 8. Facilitating the emergence of new solutions to old relationship problems.

Step 9. Consolidating new positions and new cycles of attachment behaviors.

The EFT counselor uses several important skills and interventions during the three stages of the process to accomplish the tasks involved with each step. Specifically, the EFT counselor uses the skill of tracking to monitor the couple's emotional sequences and, in this way, identify and describe the negative cycle. By reflecting the elements of the negative cycle, the interactional process becomes the problem, rather than either partner. EFT counselors also facilitate enactments (i.e., dialogue between the partners) and choreograph experiences in session to both help couples become more aware of the negative cycle in which they are involved and experience new interaction patterns. Enactments are typically used in Stage 1 to "own" the emotional response (e.g., "I know I get angry and use a harsh tone with you sometimes" rather than blaming statements such as "You make me angry when you . . ."). In Stage 2, enactments are used as a means to assume new relational positions and elicit changed responses from each partner. Another skill used by the EFT counselor is empathic conjecture, the counselor's attempts to expand the partner's experience with tentative inferences of deeper meanings. These conjectures are grounded in attachment theory and serve to address unspoken or unowned components of the relationship. Finally, an important skill in EFT is the use of disquisitions. These short narratives or fables are delivered by the counselor to illuminate a particular relational issue that the couple may be experiencing (Millikin & Johnson, 2000). When used effectively, disquisitions promote greater levels of understanding as each partner relates to elements of the story.

Support for EFT

Since the development of EFT, researchers have examined the effectiveness of the approach. Not only has EFT been found to be effective for distressed couples (Johnson, 2003) and for resolving attachment injuries (Makinen & Johnson, 2006), the gains made by using EFT also have been found to endure even 3 years after treatment

(Halchuk, Makinen, & Johnson, 2010). Further, EFT has been found to be effective even with inexperienced counselors (Denton, Burleson, Clark, Rodriguez, & Hobbs, 2000). When compared to other forms of couple counseling, such as behavioral marital therapy (BMT), EFT has been identified as a superior treatment method (Baucom et al., 1998).

In light of the empirical support for the effectiveness of EFT, the approach has been applied to specific populations and couples with relational distress as well as co-occurring diagnostic issues. In a study of couples in which one partner was a survivor of childhood sexual abuse, EFT was found to be an effective treatment approach in that half of the couples experienced significant gains in relationship satisfaction (MacIntosh & Johnson, 2008). Further, in a research study of couples in which one partner met criteria for depression, support was found for the effectiveness of EFT in reducing depressive symptoms (Dessaulles, Johnson, & Denton, 2003).

In addition to being used in couple counseling, EFT also has been applied to both individuals (Greenberg, Warwar, & Malcolm, 2008) and families (Johnson, 2004). EFT for individuals includes experiential techniques (such as a two-chair technique) to foster dialogue and change for those who have been emotionally injured by an important person. In a study comparing the outcomes of individual EFT to a psychoeducation group, those who engaged in EFT were found to demonstrate higher levels of forgiveness and greater gains in symptom reduction (Greenberg et al., 2008). Additionally, EFT has expanded to family counseling (EFFT) and uses the same stages, steps, and attachment perspectives as EFT for couples (Johnson, 2004). EFFT typically spans 10–15 sessions, beginning with 1–2 sessions in which the entire family is present, followed by subsequent sessions composed of only subsystems within the family unit. Although empirical support for EFFT is limited, researchers have found support for the approach in the treatment of families in which a child has a diagnosis of bulimia nervosa (Johnson, Maddeaux, & Bloin, 1998).

EFT in Practice

EFT counselors assume neither the role of expert nor teacher in session; rather they are consultants on the interactional process between partners (Johnson, 2004). Sessions consist of movement through the stages and steps of EFT, as the counselor tracks patterns and choreographs emotional experiences. The presentation of the EFT counselor in session is central to the process. The counselor's process is guided by the acronym RISSSC, which stands for the following:

- *Repeat*—repeat client statements to deepen emotional contact

- *Images*—use visual images, especially those created by the client

- *Soft*—use a soft tone of voice to create emotional safety

- *Slow*—slow the client process down to deepen contact with emotions

- *Simple*—avoid lengthy explanations that tend to move clients away from their present-moment experience

- *Client words*—match key language of the client, particularly when the phrases are attachment related

In this way, the EFT counselor creates an environment conducive to taking risks, becoming vulnerable, and engaging in new emotional experiences (Johnson, 2004).

CASE STUDY

Miguel and Tricia come to counseling as a result of increasing distress within their marriage. Miguel reports that since their wedding, things have been different. Tricia is more demanding and critical and seems dissatisfied with his efforts to provide them with a comfortable home. Tricia agrees that she has been dissatisfied in the relationship and wants Miguel to pursue her like he did when they were dating. From Tricia's perspective, Miguel seems more focused on the house, plans for the future, and finances than on her. She questions whether he is in love with her anymore whereas Miguel cannot understand why she would doubt his affections. After an initial assessment, the EFT counselor begins to track and reflect the negative cycle in which Miguel and Tricia are engaging. Tricia feels undesirable and fears being rejected by Miguel. As a result of these feelings, she pursues him actively and makes demands to elicit a closer connection. Miguel feels as though he is not measuring up as a husband and not good enough for Tricia. He is ashamed of his perceived shortcomings and responds by withdrawing and hiding behind his focus on their home and financial future. Using an attachment frame, the EFT counselor highlights the unspoken attachment needs between Miguel and Tricia. Whereas Tricia seeks to know if she can count on Miguel, Miguel is longing to know if he matters to Tricia. As the negative cycle is identified, underlying emotions are named, and attachment needs are assessed, the EFT counselor can begin moving through Stage 2. During this stage, the counselor will choreograph enactments to engage Miguel (withdrawing partner) and create a space in which he can own his attachment needs. Next, Tricia (pursuing partner) will be invited to respond to Miguel's expression of needs with acceptance and affirmation. As Tricia softens and tells Miguel of her own attachment needs from a less demanding and more vulnerable position, the relational positions of the couple begin to shift. These enactments are essential to the process and lay the foundation for the work in Stage 3.

DIALECTICAL BEHAVIOR THERAPY

Dialectical behavior therapy (DBT) was developed by psychologist Marsha Linehan as a model for the treatment of persons with borderline personality disorder. Since its inception, however, its clinical utility has expanded to a variety of populations, including suicidal adolescents (Miller, Rathus, & Linehan, 2007), substance abusing individuals (Linehan et al., 2002), and the treatment of eating disorders (Linehan & Chen, 2005).

The Basics of DBT

In practice, DBT combines cognitive-behavioral skill-based interventions with a foundation in Eastern philosophy, specifically the dialectical nature of the human experience (Koerner & Dimeff, 2007). The importance of dialectics implies that a major goal of DBT is helping clients increase their ability to be mindful of their experiences and thereby make daily cognitive-behavioral choices that reflect *walking the middle path*. The *middle path* refers to cultivating a balance of multiple perspectives at one time, such as simultaneously subscribing to both change and acceptance (Miller et al., 2007). Because DBT incorporates both skills and awareness-enhancing approaches, one of the hallmarks of DBT is the counselor and client's navigation of the dialectics of acceptance and change in the counselor-client relationship and the client's life outside of session. For instance, a DBT counselor conveys acceptance of the client whether or not he or she completes a between-session homework task but might also confront the client regarding not following through on the agreed assignment. Acceptance of emotions and situations is paramount because clients often harshly judge their own inner and external experiences in addition to the negative evaluations they might receive from significant others. By implementing an attitude of acceptance, the person may react more effectively and is thus more capable of instigating cognitive-behavioral change.

Another hallmark of DBT is the concepts of *wise mind, emotion mind*, and *reasonable mind* (Linehan, 1993). These constructs refer to different states of being experienced by individuals. A person in *emotion mind* is experiencing thoughts based on her or his emotions, rendering the individual to make decisions solely on an affective basis. Someone in *reasonable mind* makes decisions exclusively via factual information. *Wise mind* has been described as the amalgamation of *emotion mind* and *reasonable mind* yet also existing as greater than the sum of its parts. Linehan (1993) noted that "wise mind adds intuitive knowing to emotional experiencing and logical analysis" (p. 214). In the skills portion of DBT, clients are encouraged to learn about these mental states and their corresponding value, in particular the use of *wise mind* (Choate, 2012).

DBT uses a stage structure that focuses on behavioral targets beginning with the highest-risk behaviors and progressing to life enhancement skills as clients improve (Swales, 2009). The client must first be oriented to the structure and goals of DBT and commit to this mode of treatment. The goal of Stage 1 is to address client suicidal behaviors, therapy-interfering behaviors (e.g., not completing between-session tasks), and behaviors that compromise quality of life, such as substance abuse. Additionally, the aim of this stage is to improve behavioral skills. The second stage involves attending to posttraumatic stress through exposure and skills therapies. Finally, Stage 3 goals center on increasing self-respect, which often is low due to the shame-based surroundings in which the client was raised (Linehan, 1993). In order to ascertain key information on the client's weekly behavioral targets, the DBT counselor uses diary cards that the client completes between sessions and then reviews with the counselor. The diary card is used by the client to tally information including substance use, adherence with taking prescribed medication, suicidal ideation, mood, self-harm behaviors, and skill usage (Linehan, 1993).

Four categories of strategies are used by the DBT counselor to address the client's behavioral targets. Dialectical strategies include skills such as the use of metaphor to provide psychoeducation on behavioral targets (Linehan, 1993). In one dialectical intervention, *making lemons out of lemonade*, the counselor uses skills similar to reframing in order to motivate the client to view different crises as opportunities for rehearsing methods of coping. The second strategic category is validation. This approach is in line with the dialectic of acceptance (Swales, 2009). A counselor working in this mode attempts to understand and reflect the client's thoughts, feelings, and behaviors in a nonjudgmental manner, validating the person's experience and need rather than the behavior itself. Clients who improve their ability to identify thoughts and feelings are then better prepared for problem-solving interventions, the third strategic category (Linehan, 1993). This approach incorporates the use of interventions such as behavior chain analysis to clarify thought, emotion, and behavioral triggers. Another phase of this strategy entails identifying and selecting from a range of possible solutions. The final category of skill-based strategies is change procedures. Change procedures are specific methods to ensure that the counselor reinforces target behaviors and provides negative consequences for behaviors that detract from goal progress. Further, change procedures include a DBT framework for addressing problematic thoughts as well as an exposure therapy protocol to help clients cope with painful emotions without avoidance and behavioral reactivity (Lynch, Chapman, Rosenthal, Kuo, & Linehan, 2006).

Support for DBT

As the use of DBT has become more widespread, an increasing number of treatment trials have been conducted to assess its efficacy in reducing suicidal and nonsuicidal behaviors, substance use, and eating disorders. Kliem, Kroger, and Kosfelder (2010) examined 16 random and nonrandom controlled trials of DBT with persons diagnosed with borderline personality disorder (BPD) using meta-analysis and discovered a moderate positive impact overall and specifically with regard to suicidal and self-injurious behaviors. These positive treatment effects were significantly higher than that of treatment as usual but equivalent to other treatments specifically for clients with BPD (Kliem et al., 2010). An efficacy study of DBT with 23 women diagnosed with both BPD and substance dependence revealed reductions in substance use 1 year posttreatment in participants receiving DBT compared to persons receiving comprehensive validation therapy plus 12-step attendance, although reductions in other mental health symptoms were equivalent across treatment groups (Linehan et al., 2002). Finally, a study of 101 women with BPD indicated that DBT not only positively impacts target behaviors, it also fosters a more constructive view of self, which corresponds with less self-injurious behaviors (Bedics, Atkins, Comtois, & Linehan, 2012).

DBT in Practice

The DBT counselor uses four sets of skills modules: core mindfulness skills, interpersonal effectiveness skills, emotion regulation skills, and distress tolerance skills. Linehan (1993) developed a skills manual complete with handouts to add further specificity and utility. The core mindfulness skills are guidelines for how to *observe* one's experience, *describe* what one is experiencing, and then to *participate* in one's experience with awareness

(Miller et al., 2007). The goal of these skills is to practice acceptance of one's experience while also empowering clients to act in a way that will help them be successful in the moment. Similarly, interpersonal effectiveness skills offer a rubric for being both mindful and assertive in social situations. Emotion regulation skills training extends the client's ability to use mindfulness to observe and describe emotions and further how to alter painful emotions and raise the frequency of pleasant feelings. In *taking opposite action* (Linehan, 1993), clients are taught to engage in behaviors in the opposite direction of the current negative emotion. Distress tolerance skills were designed to help clients navigate crises and extreme stressors that can arise frequently in clients with significant problems with emotion regulation (Robins & Chapman, 2004). These include multiple cognitive-behavioral acceptance and change skills, including distraction, self-soothing, and improving the moment.

DBT services are delivered in several modalities. A client participating in a DBT program agrees to engage first in both individual counseling and skills training groups. Linehan (1993) noted that the urgent needs of the client preclude sole reliance on psychoeducation in DBT skills. Accordingly, clients attend both individual counseling and group DBT skills sessions from the outset. Telephone consultation is available to provide clients who isolate themselves and suppress feelings an option for reaching out in a healthy manner. Further, if emergencies arise, the consultation can ensure safety and offer an opportunity for the counselor to coach the client in using acceptance and change skills in the moment (Koerner & Dimeff, 2007).

CASE STUDY

The counselor and the client, Kathy, are reviewing Kathy's diary card when she comments that she has been experiencing strong cravings to drink alcohol all day. Kathy confirms she has not acted on the cravings but appears significantly distressed and confused by the experience, because she has not drunk alcohol for the past 2 months. Kathy and her counselor complete a behavior chain examining each thought, behavior, and feeling she experienced leading up to the alcohol cravings. Behavior chain analysis revealed that Kathy had felt moody before going to work and then identified thoughts and feelings of failure when she did not approach her boss for a raise at work as she had planned. Furthermore, on the way home, Kathy encountered a former drinking buddy with whom she had reluctantly severed ties to support her recovery.

The DBT counselor then used emotion validation by reflecting meaning that Kathy's morning irritability mixed with disappointment, loneliness, and frustration may have led her to want to seek emotional relief through alcohol. The counselor engaged Kathy in a brainstorming (solution analysis) process in which she elected to use the cravings of her emotion mind as information for the wise mind. Upon doing some deep breathing to focus on her wise mind, Kathy decided to use distraction skills both in the session (which resulted in decreased craving) and identified additional emotion regulation and distress tolerance skills to use after the session to prevent relapse.

INTERPERSONAL PSYCHOTHERAPY

Interpersonal psychotherapy (IPT) was developed as a treatment for clinical depression through the work of the New Haven–Boston Collaborative Depression Research Project (Klerman, Weissman, Rounsaville, & Chevron, 1984). The first IPT manual was compiled by Klerman et al. in 1984 and has since been empirically validated as an effective treatment modality for depressive symptoms (Cuijpers, van Straten, Andersson, & van Oppen, 2008; de Mello, de Jesus Mari, Bacaltchuk, Verdeli, & Neugebauer, 2005; Mufson et al., 2004). IPT is a time-limited, systematic approach used to alleviate depression by resolving interpersonal struggles (Weissman, Markowitz, & Klerman, 2007). This section provides a brief overview of IPT. For a more thorough depiction of the approach and details pertaining to the implementation of the theory, readers are encouraged to consult the work of Weissman et al. (2007).

The Basics of IPT

The process of IPT follows a sequence of three phases and typically lasts 12–16 sessions. Each phase consists of a specific task to be completed in order to reach treatment goals. The aim is to foster change in relational patterns within one area of interpersonal difficulty, including grief, interpersonal disputes, role transitions, and interpersonal deficits. Grief refers to complicated bereavement in which the client struggles with the loss of a significant other. Interpersonal disputes include conflict between the client and a spouse, family member, friend, coworker, or other important individual. Role transitions signify the client's struggle to adapt to life changes such as retirement, relocation, illness, divorce, or changes within the family. Finally, interpersonal deficits refer to relational difficulties that are not triggered by a life event such as loneliness, isolation, and lack of social support.

The initial phase of IPT consists of assessing the symptoms of depression as well as conducting an inventory of current interpersonal relationships. The IPT counselor begins by providing psychoeducation related to depression and describes the client as being "sick," thus minimizing shame or self-deprecation. During this initial phase, the counselor and client select a focus for their work from the four interpersonal problem areas. The selection of a focal area and development of treatment goals is a collaborative process between the counselor and client. By the end of the initial phase, the IPT counselor has assessed the client's clinical history, established a diagnosis of depression, provided psychoeducation about depression, and collaborated with the client to determine the primary focus of treatment.

The intermediate phase of the IPT process consists of addressing the selected interpersonal problem area. With regard to the issue of grief, the IPT counselor creates cathartic opportunities for the client to experience a range of grief-related emotions. Rather than allowing the fear of being overwhelmed to hinder clients' process, IPT counselors encourage clients to accept and experience emotions as they come. Additionally, clients working on the area of grief are supported in developing or resuming personal interests and meaningful relationships.

If the selected focus area is interpersonal disputes, treatment strategies consist of exploring the problematic relationship, identifying the components of the disagreement, and considering available options to restore or renegotiate the relationship. The client may believe that he or she is in a stalemate and may have difficulty considering options for change. Thus the IPT counselor facilitates the exploration of possible action plans and modifications of expectations for the relationship. In this way, the counselor and client collaboratively work to resolve the relational issue.

In the event that the problem area is role transitions, the IPT counselor has two aims: to process the loss associated with the old role as well as acknowledge the potential for positive experiences associated with the new role. To accomplish these tasks, the client is encouraged to explore feelings of loss and sadness related to the end of the old role. Next, the client is supported in developing skills and forming relationships associated with the new role. In this way, the role transition becomes more manageable to the client.

Finally, the category of interpersonal deficits becomes the focus area only in the absence of the other three interpersonal problems. Treatment strategies include increasing client confidence, encouraging the development of relationships, improving social and communication skills, and identifying both problematic relational patterns and interpersonal strengths. Due to the more ambiguous nature of this category, progress or goal attainment may be more challenging. Therefore, IPT counselors are encouraged to evaluate progress at the end of the IPT sequence and provide clients with additional treatment options, if necessary.

Upon completion of the intermediate phases, IPT counselors transition to the termination phase. This phase consists of celebrating the progress made during the counseling process and defining steps to maintain positive gains. IPT counselors create opportunities for clients to experience a sense of competence in their abilities to resolve interpersonal struggles. Additionally, clients may struggle with the ending of the therapeutic relationship, and thus ample time should be devoted to processing feelings associated with termination.

Effective IPT counselors use many skills in their work within the three phases of the process, including the elicitation and processing of client affect. In that a key component of IPT is the link between current emotional states and interpersonal relationships, affect is an essential element to address with clients. IPT counselors help clients access, experience, express, and process emotions more fully. Additionally, IPT counselors exercise skills in both role-plays and communication analysis. Role-plays are used to help clients explore alternative relational patterns and develop confidence in their skills. Communication analysis consists of deconstructing reports of meaningful conversations between the client and significant others to identify both strengths and areas for growth. Through communication analysis, clients are able to make meaning of their communication style as well as determine ways to enhance their verbal interactions.

Support for IPT

Much empirical support exists for the usefulness of IPT in the treatment of clinical depression. A meta-analysis of randomized clinical trials confirmed that IPT is more effective for clients diagnosed with depression than placebo only, with some support for the superiority of IPT compared to cognitive behavioral therapy (CBT; de Mello et al., 2005). Additionally, in the meta-analysis of treatment outcomes between multiple approaches for depression, IPT was found to be more effective than approaches such as CBT, psychodynamic, behavioral activation, and problem solving or social skills improvement strategies (Cuijpers et al., 2008).

In light of its effectiveness with depressed populations, researchers have examined the impact of IPT with other presenting concerns such as social anxiety disorder (SAD) (Bohn, Aderka, Schreiber, Stangier, & Hofmann, 2013; Stangier, Schramm, Heidenreich, Berger, & Clark, 2011). Researchers found both IPT and CBT to be more effective in the treatment of SAD than a wait-list control group with sustained changes at a 1-year follow-up, although IPT was less effective than CBT (Stangier et al., 2011). Empirical efforts also have supported the effectiveness of IPT in relation to specific types of depression such as postpartum depression (Weissman, 2007) and adolescent depression (Mufson et al., 2004). Finally, a modified version of IPT has been employed with clients diagnosed with bulimia nervosa with promising findings (Arcelus et al., 2009).

Beyond individual counseling, IPT also has been applied to group counseling. The basic structure for IPT group counseling is the same as individual IPT (Weissman et al., 2007). The potential benefit of group IPT is the formation of a social setting and opportunities for interpersonal encounters. Research supporting the utility of group IPT is in the initial stages, yet a randomized controlled trial of group IPT with clients presenting with depression in Uganda found the modality to be effective in alleviating symptoms (Bolton et al., 2003).

IPT in Practice

IPT counselors serve as guides to facilitate the process of identifying clients' interpersonal problem areas and employing strategies to improve the issues. Rather than addressing childhood experiences, attempting to understand the development of the client's personality, or exploring transference issues within session, the focus of IPT is on current interpersonal relationships in the client's life (Weissman et al., 2007). Sessions are typically active as the counselor and client engage in a partnership to enhance and develop the client's focal area. By conceptualizing depression as an illness, the counselor is able to speak of social deficits as symptoms rather than character flaws inherent in the client. The IPT process is relatively brief, with the goal of facilitating the identification and execution of strategies to better the client's social situation. As a result of IPT, clients can feel a sense of efficacy and accomplishment in their interpersonal skills as well as a decrease in their depressive symptoms.

CASE STUDY

Darrel comes to counseling due to persistent feelings of depression coupled with a lack of interest in the things he used to enjoy such as his current job as a mechanical engineer, golfing, and volunteering at his local community soup kitchen. Upon their first meeting, the IPT counselor engages in an assessment of Darrel's depressive symptoms and his life stressors. The counselor learns that Darrel began experiencing depression shortly after his youngest son left for college 8 months ago.

Darrel discloses that his marriage is stable and satisfying and he has several significant relationships that he describes as meaningful and supportive. Darrel continues to feel overwhelmingly sad, has experienced a loss of appetite, has difficulty sleeping at night and is fatigued during the day, and has trouble concentrating on tasks and assignments at work. After confirming a diagnosis of depression and gaining information related to Darrel's interpersonal relationships, the counselor collaborates with Darrel to select a problem area as the focus of their work together. Darrel is quick to identify his struggle with the role transition from a father of children living at home to an empty nester who is now parenting from a distance. During the second phase of IPT, the counselor facilitates strategies to improve Darrel's situation by focusing on easing his transition into this new role. Darrel is first encouraged to identify and experience his emotions related to the loss of his old role. As counseling progresses, Darrel is encouraged to consider the potential positive aspects related to his new role as an empty nester and to identify the skills necessary to feel confident in his new role. In the final phase of IPT, the counselor highlights Darrel's accomplishments to cultivate his sense of accomplishment and self-reliance.

TRAUMA-FOCUSED COGNITIVE BEHAVIORAL THERAPY (TF-CBT)

It is estimated that from 60% to 90% of children and adolescents who present for mental health treatment have experienced some type of trauma, and up to 43% of children and adolescents will experience at least one traumatic event in their lifetime (Ford et al., 1999). Further, researchers have determined that virtually all people who witness a sexual assault or a parent being murdered will develop post-traumatic stress disorder (PTSD; Hamblen & Barnett, 2009). Similarly, approximately 90% of those sexually abused, 77% of those who witness a shooting at school, and 35% of those who experience violence in their neighborhoods will ultimately develop PTSD (Hamblen & Barnett, 2009). One of the most widely used and well-supported treatments for child or adolescent trauma is trauma-focused cognitive behavioral therapy (TF-CBT) (Cohen, Mannarino, & Deblinger, 2006; Lang, Ford, & Fitzgerald, 2010; Saxe, MacDonald, & Ellis, 2007). Although TF-CBT also may be used with adults, it was developed primarily for use with children and adolescents. Interested readers should consult the work of Cohen et al. (2006) for a complete overview of TF-CBT.

The Basics of TF-CBT

As its name might suggest, TF-CBT includes cognitive-based elements but also incorporates aspects of family therapy, humanist, attachment, and empowerment modalities (Cohen et al., 2006). TF-CBT is designed for use with children and adolescents ages 3 to 18 as well as their parents or caregivers. Although it was originally designed for young people who had experienced sexual abuse and trauma, it has since been proven effective with trauma-related problems such as depression and PTSD (Lang et al., 2010; Seidler & Wagner, 2006), anxiety and fear (Deblinger, Mannarino, Cohen, Runyon, & Steer, 2011), grief (Cohen et al., 2006; Cohen, Mannarino, & Knudsen, 2004), terrorism (Hoagwood et al., 2006), and childhood refugee trauma (Schottellcorb, Doumas, & Garcia, 2012).

TF-CBT has several core values that define the approach. First, it is based on a series of trauma-focused components that are typically addressed in order (Cohen et al., 2006). Second, TF-CBT counselors recognize cultural values and diversity and, accordingly, are adaptable and flexible in their approach to be culturally responsive. Third, TF-CBT counselors have a focus on the family system as a potential source of both healing and retraumatization. Fourth, TF-CBT counselors prioritize the therapeutic relationship to create a safe space for healing trauma. Finally, TF-CBT counselors emphasize self-efficacy in clients (Cohen et al., 2006).

The acronym *PRACTICE* is used to describe the trauma-focused components of TF-CBT.

- *Psychoeducation* and *parenting skills* often are employed initially to normalize both the child and caretaker's response to the traumatic event and provide information related to trauma, diagnoses, and how parents or caregivers can respond to their child after the traumatic event.

- *Relaxation* provides strategies to manage the physiological symptoms of PTSD, including focused breathing, mindfulness, and meditation techniques.

- *Affective expression and modulation* is used to help the child identify and express feelings. Further, affect dysregulation is addressed by building social skills, encouraging problem-solving skills, cultivating positive self-talk, and practicing ways in which to manage distress.

- *Cognitive coping and processing* allows TF-CBT counselors to address both the general thoughts of their clients as well as trauma-related cognitions in order to modify unhelpful thoughts and beliefs.

- *Trauma narrative* is a central component to TF-CBT in which the client is supported in writing a narrative of his or her trauma experience. The purpose of this component is to desensitize the client to triggers corresponding to the trauma as well as process the thoughts and feelings associated with the narrative.

- *In vivo mastery of trauma reminders* is the component in which the child client is exposed to innocuous cues related to the trauma and thus builds tolerance to the associated fear.

- *Conjoint child-parent sessions* allow the TF-CBT counselor to facilitate open dialogue between the parent and child related to the trauma narrative and elements of psychoeducation.

- Finally, *enhancing future safety and development* is the component in which the client learns skills related to safety in order to enhance feelings of confidence and resourcefulness. The trauma-focused components (*PRACTICE*) support the client in processing his or her experience of trauma to prepare her or him to engage in the associated grieving process (Cohen et al., 2006).

Support for TF-CBT

Researchers have studied the effectiveness of TF-CBT through randomized clinical trials and state and national distribution efforts. Generally, results of these investigations reveal that TF-CBT provides quicker and better outcomes than other trauma-based interventions, and, additionally, results are maintained at 1- to 2-year follow-ups (Lang et al., 2010). Further, parents and caregivers experienced improvements in depression and trauma-related stress, abilities to support their children, and successful parenting methods (Cohen, Deblinger, Mannarino, & Steer, 2004; Deblinger, Lippman, & Steer, 1996; Deblinger et al., 2011).

To explore the efficacy of TF-CBT, Cohen, Deblinger, et al. (2004) conducted a large randomized clinical trial with 229 children and adolescents ranging in age from 8 to 14 who had experienced sexual abuse; over 90% also had experienced other trauma. Involvement in TF-CBT lowered PTSD symptoms, depression, and feelings of shame and increased levels of trust. Parents and caregivers reported fewer symptoms of depression and emotional upset in their children and heightened confidence in their parenting practices and support. A follow-up study (Deblinger, Mannarino, Cohen, & Steer, 2006) found that TF-CBT appears to work more quickly in easing emotional distress and decreasing clients' feelings of shame compared to other treatments.

Other researchers have found similarly promising results. In a study of 445 children and adolescents ages 6 to 21 who experienced trauma due to the terrorist attacks of September 11, 2001, Hoagwood et al. (2006) found improvements in symptoms of depression, PTSD, and anxiety as a result of TF-CBT. Similarly, Lyons, Weiner, Schneider, Martinovich, & McClelland (2008) found a decrease in PTSD symptoms and engagement in risky behaviors, as well as improvements in overall psychosocial functioning and anger control, after using TF-CBT with 69 children and adolescents who experienced a distinct traumatic event.

TF-CBT in Practice

This approach can be used with children of varied backgrounds and ethnicities in multiple settings, including homes, residential treatment facilities, clinical sites, schools, foster care, and inpatient sites (Child Sexual Abuse Task Force and Research & Practice Core, 2004). The approach is brief and has been found to be effective in as few as 8 sessions (Deblinger et al., 2011) yet typically involves at least 12 (Child Sexual Abuse Task Force and Research & Practice Core, 2004). Although it is organized to be used in conjunction with parents and caregivers, it has been found to be effective solely with the child or adolescent in situations where the parent or caregiver is not available (Cohen et al., 2006). Although TF-CBT consists of individual sessions with the child and parent or caregiver, and conjoint sessions with the child and parents or caregivers together, the approach is child focused (Cohen et al., 2006). Therefore, the TF-CBT counselor will use the skills of flexibility and creativity and rely on her or his clinical judgment to determine the best course of treatment for each child's unique experience. In addition to training in TF-CBT, the knowledgeable counselor must have a solid understanding of child development (Cohen et al., 2006).

Throughout the sequence of addressing the trauma-focused components, TF-CBT counselors must prioritize the therapeutic relationship (Cohen et al., 2006). Because children exposed to trauma often struggle with issues related to trust, a strong therapeutic relationship is necessary to effectively work through the treatment sequence as well as help clients reestablish trust in others. Therefore, the TF-CBT counselor works to express empathy for the uniqueness of each client's experience and convey genuine understanding. Further, TF-CBT directly involves parents or caregivers in the treatment process, so counselors must possess both child and adult counseling skills. Parent interventions are designed to parallel the work with the child client, and by working in conjunction with parents or caregivers, the TF-CBT counselor has the opportunity to strengthen the relationship between the client and her or his immediate social support (Cohen et al., 2006).

CASE STUDY

David, a 13-year-old client, and his counselor have been working through the trauma-focused components of TF-CBT for several sessions. David's mother brought him to counseling after he witnessed his older brother get shot outside of their apartment. Initially, David would not speak about the incident, began to withdraw socially, and became increasingly resistant to leaving his room. The counselor began treatment by engaging in psychoeducation with David about how people respond to tragic events like shootings and affirming that David's response (withdrawing) was normal. After individual sessions with David, the counselor also met with David's mom to provide psychoeducation on how to manage PTSD symptoms and parenting skills she could employ at home, such as providing praise when David ventures out of his room. In subsequent sessions, the counselor and David began learning relaxation techniques. David became skilled at "belly breathing" in which he focused on taking deep breaths, filling up his lungs and diaphragm. David practices the relaxation techniques between sessions, particularly when he is reminded of the shooting and begins to feel distress. After advancing through the next two components in which David learns skills related to labeling his emotions and talking about them openly, as well as understanding the connection between how he thinks, feels, and behaves, the counselor asks David to begin writing his trauma narrative. Over the course of several sessions, David writes down details of his experience, beginning with minimal statements about his brother. With the support of the counselor, and use of the relaxation techniques, David begins to share more details related to the sequence of events leading up to the shooting. Once completed, the counselor and David read through the narrative and David identifies his thoughts and feelings related to each segment. The counselor praises David for his courage and hard work in writing the narrative. In future sessions, the counselor will process David's cognitions pertaining to the trauma and correct unhelpful or distorted thoughts, begin the process of in vivo exposure to triggers related to the shooting, and conduct several joint sessions with David and his mother to process the trauma narrative and enhance safety skills.

MINDFULNESS

There is a large and rapidly growing body of literature to support the use of mindfulness training for improved physical and mental health. Mindfulness is generally defined as "paying attention in a particular way: on purpose, in the present moment, and non-judgmentally" (Kabat-Zinn, 1994, p. 4). Mindfulness not only involves paying attention but also considers *how* to pay attention. Thus, mindfulness consists of attending characterized by an attitude of openness, acceptance, trust, curiosity, compassion, kindness, equanimity, and patience (Germer, 2006; Kabat-Zinn, 1994). Mindfulness meditation dates back 2,500 years in Buddhist history, although most world traditions also include some form of meditation (e.g., Christian contemplative prayer, Jewish meditation, Hindu transcendental meditation). Stripped of its Buddhist roots, however, mindfulness training has been increasingly used in Western medicine since the 1970s. Further, it has been incorporated into several "third wave" counseling approaches such as dialectical behavior therapy (DBT; Linehan, 1993), acceptance and commitment therapy (ACT; Hayes, Strosahl, & Wilson, 1999), and mindfulness-based cognitive therapy (MBCT; Segal, Williams, & Teasdale, 2002). Although there are several mindfulness-based approaches, this section focuses on mindfulness-based stress reduction (MBSR; Kabat-Zinn, 1990) because it has been widely researched, has been adapted for diverse client concerns, has mindfulness as its primary focus, and is the basis for many other approaches.

The Basics of Mindfulness

The MBSR program, created by Kabat-Zinn (1990), is conducted as an 8- to 10-week structured course for heterogeneous groups of up to 30 participants who meet weekly. Classes include education and discussion regarding stress and coping, instruction and practice in mindfulness meditation skills, and gentle yoga movements. Homework assignments, such as meditation practice or mindfulness awareness during daily activities such as walking and eating, constitute a large component of the program. In fact, participants are instructed to practice mindfulness skills outside of class time for at least 45 minutes, 6 days per week. Audio recordings are provided to guide initial practice efforts. Over time, however, participants are instructed to transition to self-directed mindfulness practice. Silence, yoga, meditation, and mindful eating are included in the program. Mindfulness exercises teach participants to focus their attention (e.g., on the breath) and to nonjudgmentally observe any emotions, sensation, or thoughts that arise without trying to change, avoid, or make meaning of them. These experiences are viewed merely as events that come and go like clouds passing by, and when distracted, participants are guided to gently bring their focus back to the present moment. The program is designed to help participants regain their sense of health and well-being by increasing nonjudgmental awareness of their whole experience.

MBCT is very similar to, and based on, MBSR. It is an 8-week program that teaches mindfulness skills. It was designed, however, specifically for individuals with recurrent depression. It is delivered as a method to prevent, not treat, depression. Unlike MBSR, MBCT incorporates aspects of cognitive therapy, and therefore, mindfulness training is more focused on thoughts (Baer, 2003). Specifically, in MBCT participants learn to "distance" thoughts by viewing them as mental events rather than representations of reality or one's identity. Teasdale Segal, and Williams (1995) found that cultivating this type of attitude and awareness with depression-related cognitions can prevent ruminative thinking that facilitates depression relapse.

Support for Mindfulness

Mindfulness-based training and interventions have been shown to help individuals attend to aversive stimuli, including sensations, cognitions, and emotions, with open, nonreactive, nonjudging, present-moment awareness (Baer, 2003, Cardaciotto, Herbert, Forman, Moitra, & Farrow, 2008). Increasing one's ability to observe experiences with such an attitude has been shown to improve both physical and mental health (Baer, 2003). Specifically, mindfulness has been associated with improvements in physical activity, self-esteem, empathy, self-acceptance, ability to cope with pain (Baer, 2003; Rothaupt & Morgan, 2007), heart disease, cancer, AIDS, stress (Kabat-Zinn, 1994), depression (Teasdale et al., 2000), substance abuse (Marlatt & Gordon, 1985), and disordered eating (Kristeller & Hallett, 1999). In a recent and extensive review of the mindfulness literature, Greeson (2009) found that mindfulness interventions have been empirically associated with less emotional distress such as anxiety, worry, anger, and depression. The author also found that higher innate levels of mindfulness have been directly associated with positive mental states such as joy, hope, well-being, and life satisfaction and the ability to repair negative mood states. Additionally, both "manualized" mindfulness training programs and brief meditation practices have been found to influence areas of the brain involved in regulating attention, awareness, and emotion. Mindfulness also has been associated with improvements in many health behaviors such as eating and sleeping and can positively impact the immune system (Baer, 2003; Greeson, 2009). In a recent systematic review of the MBSR and MBCT literature, Fjorback, Arendt, Ørnbøl, Fink, and Walach (2011) found that MBSR was useful for improving mental health and quality of life in medical disease management and reducing stress, anxiety, and depression, whereas MBCT was effective as a means of relapse prevention for those in recovery for recurrent depression.

Mindfulness in Practice

Skills and interventions will vary depending on the way that mindfulness is incorporated into counseling. It can be imparted through a structured program such as MBSR, through direct mindfulness work with a client, or through the counselor's own mindfulness. To date, the preponderance of mindfulness research has been conducted on MBSR and other manualized approaches, most commonly enacted in a class or group format. Consequently, there is little empirical literature to inform practitioners in the application of mindfulness to individual counseling. Mindfulness-informed therapy (Germer, 2006), however, has been proposed as a framework for integrating mindfulness into the counseling process by incorporating Buddhist and Western psychology with the practical experience of the practitioner. Counseling informed by mindfulness, however, does not include explicitly teaching mindfulness meditation practice to clients (Germer, 2006). Formal mindfulness practice is not necessarily appropriate for all individuals, although it is unclear when it is contraindicated. Although encouraging formal meditation may be productive for some clients, it is often difficult for clients to adhere to, so informal mindfulness activities are more readily integrated into counseling (Germer, 2006). Present-moment awareness and acceptance, a mindful approach to daily activities, or mindfulness exercises can be used as appropriate for a particular client and situation. Breath awareness, mindfulness of certain experiences or activities, a body scan (lying down and noticing each part of the body with intention), and in-session present-moment awareness of experience are all examples of mindfulness in counseling.

Another way that counseling can be infused with mindfulness is through the counselor's own mindfulness practices. Counselor mindfulness has been associated with increased empathy (Aggs & Bambling, 2010; Fulton & Cashwell, 2015; Lesh, 1970), reduced stress and anxiety (Fulton & Cashwell, 2015), positive affect (Aggs & Bambling, 2010), positive client outcomes (Grepmair, Mitterlehner, Loew, & Nickel, 2007), and attention and self-efficacy (Greason & Cashwell, 2009). Although there is not agreement as to the extent to which a counselor needs to practice mindfulness to use it in session, these findings amplify the prevailing belief that a counselor should practice mindfulness if using it with clients (Baer, 2003). The ability to bring mindfulness to the counseling session, therefore, will be determined, in part, by the extent to which the counselor can engage in these mindfulness skills.

CASE STUDY

Anita, a generally well-functioning 29-year-old female, has presented with increased stress, overeating, and weight gain. She has recently encountered many life changes, including starting a new job and relationship. The counselor assesses that she is employing an avoidant strategy that is unproductive and distressing. Anita would benefit from gaining greater contact with her experience to determine what feelings, thoughts, or sensations might be behind her reflexive eating. The counselor's mindfulness work with Anita includes encouraging a curious, open, compassionate awareness of her anxiety as it presents in sessions. Further, the counselor may instruct Anita to perform a "3-minute breathing exercise" (Segal et al., 2002; a brief mindfulness exercise involving attention to the present moment, i.e., what feelings or thoughts am I having right now?), pay attention to her breath to anchor her in the present moment, and expand awareness to her whole body (Germer, 2006). Anita would be encouraged to do this several times a day when she felt stressed or anxious. In time she may notice that fear of failure in her new job and relationship were creating anxiety that led to eating. When she learns to directly access these feelings and greet them with compassion as well as view them as temporary mental events with no truth or meaning, she will eventually be able to reduce her anxiety and overeating.

ACCEPTANCE AND COMMITMENT THERAPY

One specific approach that integrates mindfulness is acceptance and commitment therapy (ACT; Hayes et al., 1999), a behavioral **approach** rooted in the development of mindfulness and acceptance. ACT (pronounced "ACT" rather than A-C-T) is philosophically linked to functional contextualism (FC) and theoretically based on relational frame theory (RFT), a theory of human language and cognition (for a thorough discussion of FC and RFT, see Hayes, Strosahl, & Wilson, 2012). Since its debut in 1999, ACT has gained support, including hundreds of scholarly articles and 60 books worldwide (Hayes et al., 2012), and has been used to address a wide variety of concerns, including depression, addiction, smoking, and diabetes (Ciarrochi & Bailey, 2008; Dewane, 2008).

The Basics of ACT

Client: "I want to do 'X,' BUT I'm too anxious."

Counselor: "You want to do 'X,' AND you feel anxious about it."

The difference between these two statements, although subtle, represents the core of ACT. Rather than seek to eliminate or alter thoughts, feelings, and sensations to produce client change, from the ACT perspective, the counselor seeks to cultivate the client's willingness to experience them *and* change behavior (Dewane, 2008; Hayes et al., 2012). In this view, unpleasant thoughts and feelings and values-driven behavioral change can simultaneously coexist. Although ACT is a member of the larger cognitive behavioral therapy (CBT) orientation, this difference represents a departure from traditional CBT approaches that emphasize behavior modification and cognitive restructuring as the impetus for change (Dewane, 2008).

Using an ACT lens, human suffering results from the way language and cognition interact with life circumstances such that individuals are unable to function in ways that serve long-term valued goals (Luoma, Hayes, & Walser, 2007). Clients are not "broken" but rather are using unworkable strategies and need help gaining greater psychological flexibility (Luoma et al., 2007). Further, human suffering is not the result of unhealthy thoughts and feelings that are symptoms needing to be cured, but rather suffering occurs as a natural consequence of normal thinking processes. Therefore, clients are not conceptualized as possessing syndromes with symptoms to be eliminated but have "loose collections of unknown utility" (Hayes, Levin, Plumb-Vilardaga, Villatte, & Pistorello, 2011, p. 9). In other words, any thought, feeling, behavior, or memory is not inherently pathological; it is only evaluated based on its utility in a particular context.

Psychological rigidity is the root of suffering, and there are six overlapping and interrelated processes that cause, or at least contribute to, this inflexibility: *experiential avoidance*; *cognitive fusion*; *inflexible attention*; *attachment to the conceptualized self*; *disruption of chosen values*; and *inaction, impulsivity, or avoidant persistence* (Hayes et al., 2012; Luoma et al., 2007). There are six corresponding therapeutic processes that produce *psychological flexibility* and are the core of ACT: *acceptance, defusion, flexible attention to the present moment, self as context, chosen values,* and *committed action.* According to Hayes et al. (2012), the absence of one or more of these processes will increase one's vulnerability to psychological rigidity and potential suffering. At its core, ACT is designed to undermine psychological rigidity.

Experiential avoidance is a key source of inflexibility and occurs when there are attempts to control internal or private psychological experiences, such as thoughts, feelings, sensations, and memories, even when doing so causes behavioral harm (Hayes et al., 2012; Luoma et al., 2007). Experiential avoidance stems from the innate ability to evaluate, predict, and avoid events that are determined to be a threat. These problem-solving capabilities evolved over thousands of years so that humans could survive environmental threats to existence. They remain useful for situations in the material world (e.g., how to escape a burning building) but are less effective when applied to the inner experience. If experiencing anxiety, for example, individuals may determine ways to avoid the anxiety that, in the long term, are either unhelpful (e.g., suppress or medicate) or self-fulfilling (i.e., attempts to avoid thinking of anxiety produces more thoughts of it). Experiential avoidance will frequently succeed in the short term, which, regrettably, leads to perpetuating the act, even though, over time, these avoidant strategies will become unproductive. *Acceptance* is the corresponding ACT process to address experiential avoidance. Clients are helped to "make room" for uncomfortable thoughts and feelings rather than trying to suppress or control them (Harris, 2008). The long-term workability of current avoidance strategies is compassionately examined and the counselor cultivates the client's willingness to be open to the whole of his or her experience.

Cognitive fusion is another process that contributes to psychological inflexibility and suffering. Cognitive fusion is one's tendency to get caught up in the content of thinking so that it dominates over other useful sources of behavioral regulation. The problem is not about *what* one thinks but *how* one relates to what he or she thinks. When thoughts become seamless representations of reality and contact is lost with the actual events of reality, the result is cognitive fusion. In other words, if a client is fused with her or his verbal content, then that content can dominate her or his behavior, narrowing the range of possible influences and actions.

Defusion is the corresponding ACT process to address cognitive fusion. Metaphors, paradoxes, and stories are used to help disentangle clients from the automaticity of their thoughts.

Experiential avoidance and cognitive fusion both decrease one's ability to be in contact with the present moment, which supports a third process, *inflexible attention*. When thoughts and feelings related to the past and the future dominate, then one's access to the present moment is muted, making way for rumination, anxiety, and depression. This inflexible attention limits an individual's access to potential new ways of responding. Instead, previously cemented thoughts and reactions prevail. *Flexible attention to the present moment* involves experiential activities that help the client come into contact with present-moment experience in a mindful and accepting manner. Clients increase their willingness and ability to contact present-moment experience so that narrow, persistent avoidance is supplanted with a more open, accepting, choice-filled stance.

A fourth process, *attachment to the conceptualized self*, occurs when an individual overidentifies with her or his own self story. The story encompasses all aspects of the individual, including what has been done and how to function. Even if the entire story is true, a rigid attachment to it limits the ability to access solutions outside of it. Thus, only solutions that exist within the narrow frame of the self story are considered to be options, and these solutions may be unhelpful or even harmful. The corresponding ACT process, *self as context*, is geared toward helping clients learn to be observers of the self. In this regard, the self is a grounded place from which to observe experience and also invites the opportunity to renegotiate one's relationship to experience. For example, a person in pain with cancer can *become* "a sick person" who struggles to control persistent pain (increasing their sense of suffering), or he or she can be a person who has cancer in the body and who acknowledges, experiences, and accepts that pain is a part of the experience. In the latter view, the pain and cancer are unchanged, but their relationship to the experience is altered.

Experiential avoidance also inhibits a person's ability to connect with deeply held values. Behaving in ways that live out values contributes to a meaningful life. If a person's behavior is consumed by control efforts to avoid unpleasant and unwanted thoughts, feelings, sensations, and memories, there will be a *disruption of chosen values*. For example, if a person values friendship and connection but has developed anxiety in social situations, avoiding those situations may temporarily control the anxiety at the cost of spending time with friends. Identifying one's *chosen values* is necessary in determining meaningful, purposeful action.

Finally, cognitive fusion, experiential avoidance, inflexible attention, and the conceptualized self can lead to rigid and persistent control efforts rather than flexible responding that is in concert with deeply held values. Because these control efforts eventually dominate a person's way of coping, a pattern of *inaction, impulsivity, or avoidant persistence* emerges such that an individual appears to lack direction or a meaningful existence. *Committed action* based on chosen values is an essential aspect to a complete ACT intervention. *Mindfulness and acceptance* processes help reduce rigid, persistent avoidance strategies, opening the door for the *commitment and behavioral change* process that leads to a values-oriented, fulfilling life.

Support for ACT

Although the literature is still young, ACT has shown promise as an effective approach for a variety of psychological concerns, including psychosis; depression; anxiety; work stress; stigma and burnout; agoraphobia; social phobia; substance abuse; and health concerns such as smoking, chronic pain, and diabetes (Hayes, Luoma, Bond, Masuda, & Lillis, 2006). Additionally, when compared with clients of non-ACT-trained counselors, clients of ACT-trained counselors reported greater postcounseling coping and were more likely to complete counseling and to share their clinician's perspective regarding treatment progress (Hayes, Masuda, Bissett, Luoma, & Guerrero, 2004). More recently, researchers (Forman, Herbert, Moitra, Yeomans, & Geller, 2007) found that ACT was equivalent to cognitive therapy in producing large improvements in depression, anxiety, quality of life, life satisfaction, and clinician-rated functioning. The authors also reported that ACT has shown promise as an intervention for obsessive-compulsive disorder.

ACT in Practice

ACT is a comprehensive treatment approach that has been delivered in both individual and group counseling formats. Hayes et al. (2004) found that the length of the intervention has varied greatly in published studies, from 48 sessions over 16 weeks to 4 sessions over 3 weeks. Although there are ACT methods specific to certain problems in living (e.g., drug addiction), it is considered a general model that can be used by counselors to address a wide variety of client concerns. Further, because ACT is used to help clients undermine the literality of language that keeps them bound to unproductive control efforts, the counselor will need to use culturally sensitive and relevant metaphors, stories, paradoxes, and experiential exercises as interventions to support clients to connect more directly with psychological processes. The goal of any technique deployed within the ACT model is to help clients relate to their experience in a more fluid, flexible, voluntary way and to identify and enact values-based goals and behaviors.

Although behavioral techniques dominate the model, any technique, including those developed from other therapeutic approaches, can be used within the ACT model as long as it supports movement toward greater psychological flexibility (Hayes et al., 2011). Finally, the ACT counselor's therapeutic stance is one of equality, genuineness, compassion, and belief in the client's intrinsic ability to shift toward more workable strategies. The counselor models acceptance of difficult content as it occurs in sessions without a need to determine resolutions. ACT interventions are flexible and customized to fit the needs of the client.

CASE STUDY

Tara, a 32-year-old woman, is presenting with anxiety related to conflict with a coworker. She is intimidated by her coworker and fears their interactions. Tara has been strategizing to find ways to avoid direct interactions, which is impacting her work and social relations in the office. In this scenario, the ACT counselor would respond to Tara's expression of fear in session by encouraging her to be in contact with the emotion in the present moment (*acceptance* and *flexible attention*). The counselor might refer to the fear metaphorically as a "visitor" to help disentangle Tara from her seamless identification with her feelings and thoughts (*cognitive defusion*). Mindfulness exercises would be used to help Tara gain awareness of herself as an observer (*self as context*). This could then be used to walk Tara through a scenario of interacting with her coworker where she can both experience the fear as well as see herself experiencing the fear as an observer. In this process, bodily sensations related to the fear would be noticed (*contact with the present*) and willingness to change would be cultivated by elevating her sense that she can experience an emotion (i.e., fear) but also renegotiate her relationship with it. Further, Tara's values associated with her work life (e.g., open communication and doing a job well) would be elicited and highlighted, and committed action related to that value would be identified (e.g., practice contact with fear and increase proximity to coworker). Ultimately, Tara would learn to be in contact with her full experience in a kind and accepting way but also take steps toward values-driven behavior.

SPIRITUALITY IN COUNSELING

Although not a specific approach per se, the awareness of spirituality in the counseling process has gained attention in recent years. People seek counseling for a broad range of reasons and presenting issues, and for many people, it seems clear that religion and spirituality serve as potential sources of comfort during times of distress (Zinnbauer et al., 1997). Researchers have found that 96% of Americans believe in a higher power; more than 90% pray; 69% are members of a religious community; and 43% have attended a service at their church, synagogue, temple, or mosque within the past 7 days (Princeton Religion Research Center, 2000). Simply stated, religion and spirituality are core aspects of identity for many people and warrant attention in the counseling process.

Many counselors appear hesitant, however, to assess and address the religious and spiritual life of a client. This is most likely due to the counselor's own discomfort due to personal history or lack of knowledge, or a fear of imposing values on the client that would be unethical (Cashwell et al., 2013). Such a stance, however, may lead some counselors to make errors of omission, that is, to minimize or ignore information about the spiritual or religious life of the client that is critically important to her or his core identity. Spirituality and religion are vital aspects of a person's culture and developmental experiences. This is important because culture and human development are two key curricular foci of counselor training (CACREP, 2016). In short, it is important for counselors to be able to assess and work with client spiritual and religious beliefs, practices, and experiences.

The Basics of Spirituality in Counseling

Early theorists, such as Freud, and more contemporary theorists, such as Ellis, tended to pathologize religion and viewed it as a crutch for weak people. Other early theorists, such as William James and Carl Jung, tended to view the religious and spiritual lives of people as extremely valuable and a source of important information about clients. Accordingly, religion/spirituality and mental health were largely compartmentalized and separated for much of the early history of the counseling profession, with religion and spirituality largely considered the domain of clergy and taboo ground for mental health professionals. Although there certainly are circumstances in which referral to, or consultation with, a clergy member is in order, and it remains vital to distinguish between counseling and such activities as spiritual direction, this compartmentalization of the spiritual life and the psychological life of the client is unfortunate because the two are inextricably linked.

Part of what makes integrating spirituality and religion into counseling so complicated is that spirituality is difficult to operationally define. Some scholars have estimated that there are more than 300 interpretations in the professional literature of what spirituality means (Zinnbauer et al., 1997). Spirituality is difficult to define because it is developmental, contextual, and personal. That is, one's personal definition of spirituality will almost surely evolve over time (developmental) and life circumstance (contextual) and be at least somewhat private (personal). It is difficult, then, to have a single definition that applies to all people, in all contexts, and in all life stages. These caveats notwithstanding, spirituality is the universal human capability to move primary awareness beyond the self, to an awareness of the sacred, with outcomes of increased compassion, acceptance, and love

(Young & Cashwell, 2011). This definition broadly characterizes spirituality as an innate longing in all people, although some people clearly attend to this longing more than others. Also, the spiritual journey involves movement from self as center (ego) to awareness beyond the self. This includes belief in a higher power but also beliefs that are more social justice oriented but not necessarily inclusive of a higher power. It is important to note the requisite outcomes of true spirituality of increased compassion (including self-compassion), acceptance, and love. Unfortunately, unhealthy religious communities sometimes promulgate the opposite of these attributes (judgment, rejection, and hate). Healthy religious and spiritual communities, on the other hand, will provide communal support for the development of compassion and acceptance (of both self and others) and an increased capacity to love (Young & Cashwell, 2011).

In comparison, religion is easier to define. Compared to spirituality, researchers describe religion as more institutional and composed of a system of ideas (Hill & Pargament, 2003). Thus, religion provides the social context within which the spiritual journey can be supported, including narratives, symbols, beliefs, and practices (Young & Cashwell, 2011). Although the counseling profession has clearly distinguished between religion and spirituality, and asserted that people can be spiritual or religious, neither, or both (Young & Cashwell, 2011), it is important to highlight that many people do not make such a distinction. For example, some clients may grow up participating in organized religion and have this remain a vital aspect of their lives into adulthood. For these clients, their spiritual life may be fully intertwined with their religious life. Such a client actually may be confused by the distinction between religion and spirituality. Because it is the counselor's job to meet the client where he or she is, it is important to assess how the client thinks about religion and spirituality and match language to demonstrate respect for the client's belief system.

The Association for Spiritual, Ethical, and Religious Values in Counseling (ASERVIC) is a division of the American Counseling Association that is focused, in part, on the competent and ethical integration of spirituality and religion into counseling. In support of this effort, ASERVIC has developed a set of competencies for integrating spirituality and religious issues into counseling (see Cashwell & Watts, 2010). Although aspirational, with the knowledge that counselors will not excel in all areas, the competencies provide solid guidelines on the knowledge and skills needed to work effectively with spiritual and religious issues in the counseling process.

Support for Spirituality in Counseling

There is a growing body of literature empirically examining the relationship between spirituality in counseling and client treatment outcomes. Researchers have found a connection between client wellness (mental, physical, and emotional) and client spiritual and/or religious beliefs and practices (Koenig & Valliant, 2009; Myers & Sweeney, 2008). In addition, researchers have determined that the use of spiritual interventions in counseling is beneficial for clients (Smith, Bartz, & Richards, 2007). Specifically, spirituality has been found to be an important part of treatment outcomes for substance abusing clients (Heinz, Epstein, & Preston, 2007) as well as adult survivors of childhood sexual abuse (Gall, Basque, Damasceno-Scott, & Vardy, 2007). In an analysis examining the efficacy of spiritual and religious treatment efforts, researchers found that Christian accommodative cognitive therapy, which uses cognitive therapy within a religious context including biblical teaching and religious imagery, was an efficacious treatment for clients with depression (Hook et al., 2010). Additionally, support groups such as Alcoholics Anonymous, which emphasize a spiritual component through 12-step work, have been shown to be helpful for clients with alcoholism (Hook et al., 2010). Therefore, support exists for the effectiveness of incorporating spirituality into counseling practices.

Spirituality in Counseling in Practice

In order to determine whether spirituality and/or religion are important topics for clients, it is important for counselors to infuse spiritual assessment into their work. There are a number of specific quantitative and qualitative methods for assessing spirituality (see Gill, Harper, & Dailey, 2011) as well as several broad guidelines to guide assessment. First, it is important to communicate via professional documents, such as professional disclosure statements and marketing materials, that spirituality and religion are topics that may be talked about in counseling, thereby giving the client permission to broach these subjects. Similarly, questions on an intake form about religion and spirituality communicate to the client that the counselor is open to these topics. A Likert-type question assessing, *How important is religion and spirituality to you?* coupled with a follow-up item asking clients, *Do you want to talk about your religion or spirituality in counseling?* provide counselors with important information for client conceptualization and treatment goals. Clients who indicate that religion and spirituality are very important and they do want to talk about these topics in counseling have invited additional inquiry from the counselor. Similarly, clients who report that religion and spirituality are not important and they do not want to talk about these issues have indicated clearly that they do not wish to devote time in counseling to religion or spirituality. The counselor should respect these requests. Other clients may have a more complex response pattern. For example, some clients will indicate that religion and spirituality are not important but specify that they do want to talk about the topics. This may suggest that religion and spirituality have not been important to them historically, but now they are starting to consider the spiritual or religious components of their struggle. Another interesting response combination occurs when clients indicate that religion and spirituality are important but they do not want to talk about this content in counseling. This request should be honored initially but likely should be gently explored as the therapeutic relationship is established. One possibility is that these clients are stating that they do not believe that the counselor will be accepting of their religious or spiritual beliefs. In many cases, spirituality and religion are integrated in the counseling process only when the counselor provides a structure, initially through the assessment process, in which it becomes safe to talk about this highly personal content. Counselors routinely address sensitive topics such as sexuality and suicidality, and the gentle exploration of the spiritual and/or religious life of the client is another potentially sensitive topic that the counselor may need to respectfully help the client explore.

Throughout the counseling process, counselors may integrate spirituality and religion into counseling by listening for spiritual themes in the client's narrative. In some cases, this is explicitly stated by the client. For example, a client may state that he or she does not believe that forgiveness from God is possible. In other cases, however, the client may not explicitly identify the spiritual theme. By attending closely to the presence of these themes, however, the counselor can gently make these themes more explicit in the client's narrative. Common spiritual themes that emerge may include suffering, control/surrender, meaning and purpose, compassion (including self-compassion), forgiveness, and mindfulness/acceptance.

CASE STUDY

Jani seeks counseling due to feelings of sadness that have amplified over the last several months. In the initial assessment, the counselor asks Jani about her religious/spiritual life. Jani responds that it is no longer important to her and she does not want to talk about it in counseling. The counselor responds by validating Jani's feelings and stating that she is welcome to discuss the religious and/or spiritual aspects of her story at any time, should she find it helpful. Jani describes her difficult transition from her childhood home in a small suburb to her new residence in a major metropolitan area. Although she relocated to pursue her satisfying career, the transition has left her feeling "invisible" even to herself. As counseling progresses, Jani recounts that she had a greater "sense of who she is" when she lived in her hometown. When asked about contributing factors to her understanding of herself, Jani identified her religious belief system as being a foundational component of her self-concept. However, since her move to the city, she felt that her Hindu beliefs were no longer relevant and detached herself from the religion. The counselor gently explores Jani's experience with leaving her religious community as well as her spiritual beliefs. Through this dialogue, Jani gains the awareness that although she is no longer participating in her religious traditions, she has maintained her spirituality, although she believes it has been neglected. Over the course of counseling, Jani begins to identify her spiritual beliefs and brainstorms ways to nurture this part of herself and integrate it more fully into her experience. As she attends to her spiritual self, Jani's feelings of sadness begin to dissipate and her self-concept is strengthened. At the conclusion of counseling, Jani has reestablished herself in a religious community that supports her expression of her spiritual beliefs and reports feeling more "whole."

CONCLUSION

The counseling field continues to evolve through research efforts and clinical experiences. The result of this continuous growth is the development of novel strategies to assist in the client change process as well as extensions of preexisting theories to new populations. This chapter underscores several examples of emerging approaches; however, counselors and counselors in training are encouraged to use counseling journals, conferences, and additional resources to stay informed of new and innovative methods as they develop. In light of the myriad theoretical orientations and counseling styles in practice today, it is clear that there are many ways to help clients reach their goals. Counselors are charged with maintaining awareness of emerging approaches in order to offer the best services available to the clients entrusted to their care.

REFERENCES

Aggs, C., & Bambling, M. (2010). Teaching mindfulness to psychotherapists in clinical practice: The mindful therapy programme. *Counselling & Psychotherapy Research, 10,* 278–286. doi:10.1080/14733145.2010.485690

Arcelus, J., Whight, D., Langham, C., Baggott, J., McGrain, L., Meadows, L., et al. (2009). A case series evaluation of the modified version of interpersonal psychotherapy (IPT) for the treatment of bulimic eating disorders: A pilot study. *European Eating Disorders Review, 17,* 260–268.

Arkowitz, H., & Miller, W. R. (2008). Learning, applying, and extending motivational interviewing. In H. Arkowitz, H. A. Westra, W. R. Miller, & S. Rollnick (Eds.), *Motivational interviewing in the treatment of psychological problems* (pp. 1–25). New York: Guilford.

Baer, R. (2003). Mindfulness training as a clinical intervention: A conceptual and empirical review. *Clinical Psychology: Science and Practice, 10,* 125–143.

Baer, J. S., Beadnell, B., Garrett, S. B., Hartzler, B., Wells, E. A., & Peterson, P. L. (2008). Adolescent change language within a brief motivational intervention and substance use outcomes. *Psychology of Addictive Behaviors, 22,* 570–575.

Baucom, D. H., Shoham, V., Mueser, K. T., Daiuto, A. D., & Stickle, T. R. (1998). Empirically supported couple and family interventions for marital distress and adult mental health problems. *Journal of Consulting and Clinical Psychology, 66,* 53–88.

Bedics, J. D., Atkins, D. C., Comtois, K. A., & Linehan, M. M. (2012). Treatment differences in the therapeutic relationship and introject during a 2-year randomized controlled trial of dialectical behavior therapy versus nonbehavioral psychotherapy experts for borderline personality disorder. *Journal of Consulting and Clinical Psychology, 80,* 66–77.

Bohn, C., Aderka, I. M., Schreiber, F., Stangier, U., & Hofmann, S. G. (2013). Sudden gains in cognitive therapy and interpersonal therapy for social anxiety disorder. *Journal of Consulting and Clinical Psychology, 81,* 177–182.

Bolton, P., Bass, J., Neugebauer, R., Verdeli, H., Clougherty, K. F., Wickramaratne, P., et al. (2003). Group interpersonal psychotherapy for depression in rural Uganda: A randomized controlled trial. *Journal of the American Medical Association, 289,* 3117–3124.

Cardaciotto, L., Herbert, J. D., Forman, E. M., Moitra, E., & Farrow, V. (2008). The assessment of present-moment awareness and acceptance: The Philadelphia Mindfulness Scale. *Assessment, 15,* 204–223.

Cashwell, C. S., Young, J. S., Fulton, C., Willis, B. T., Giordano, A. L., Wyatt, L. L., et al. (2013). Clinical behaviors for addressing religious/spiritual issues: Do we "practice what we preach"? *Counseling and Values, 58,* 45–58.

Cashwell, C. S., & Watts, R. E. (2010). The new ASERVIC competencies for addressing spiritual and religious issues in counseling. *Counseling and Values, 55,* 2–5.

Child Sexual Abuse Task Force and Research & Practice Core, National Child Traumatic Stress Network. (2004). *How to implement trauma-focused cognitive behavioral therapy.* Durham, NC, and Los Angeles: National Center for Child Traumatic Stress. Retrieved from http://www.nctsnet.org/nctsn_assets/pdfs/TF-CBT_Implementation_Manual.pdf.

Choate, L. H. (2012). Counseling adolescents who engage in nonsuicidal self-injury: A dialectical behavior therapy approach. *Journal of Mental Health Counseling, 34,* 56–71.

Ciarrochi, J. V., & Bailey, A. (2008). *A CBT-practitioner's guide to ACT: How to bridge the gap between cognitive behavioral therapy and acceptance and commitment therapy.* Oakland, CA: New Harbinger.

Clarke, P. B., Giordano, A. L., Cashwell, C. S., & Lewis, T. F. (2013). The straight path to healing: Using motivational interviewing to address spiritual bypass. *Journal of Counseling and Development, 91,* 87–94.

Cohen, J. A., Deblinger, E., Mannarino, A. P., & Steer, R. A. (2004). A multisite randomized controlled trial for children with sexual abuse-related PTSD symptoms. *Journal of the American Academy of Child & Adolescent Psychiatry, 43,* 393–402.

Cohen, J. A., Mannarino, A. P., & Deblinger, E. (2006). *Treating trauma and traumatic grief in children and adolescents.* New York: Guilford Press.

Cohen, J. A., Mannarino, A. P., & Knudsen, K. (2004). Treating childhood traumatic grief: A pilot study. *Journal of the American Academy of Child & Adolescent Psychiatry, 43,* 1225–1233.

Council for Accreditation of Counseling and Related Educational Programs. (2016). *CACREP 2016 Standards.* Alexandria, VA: Author.

Cuijpers, P., van Straten, A., Andersson, G., & van Oppen, P. (2008). Psychotherapy for depression in adults: A meta-analysis of comparative outcome studies. *Journal of Consulting and Clinical Psychology, 76,* 909–922.

de Mello, M. F., de Jesus Mari, J., Bacaltchuk, J., Verdeli, H., & Neugebauer, R. (2005). A systemic review of research findings on the efficacy of interpersonal therapy for depressive disorders. *European Archives of Psychiatry and Clinical Neuroscience, 255,* 75–82.

Deblinger, E., Lippman, J., & Steer, R. A. (1996). Sexually abused children suffering posttraumatic stress symptoms: Initial treatment outcome findings. *Child Maltreatment, 1,* 310–321.

Deblinger, E., Mannarino, A. P., Cohen, J. A., Runyon, M. K., & Steer, R. A. (2011). Trauma-focused cognitive behavioral therapy for children: Impact of the trauma narrative and treatment length. *Depression and Anxiety, 28,* 67–75.

Deblinger, E., Mannarino, A. P., Cohen, J. A., & Steer, R. A. (2006). A follow-up study of a multisite, randomized, controlled trail for children with sexual abuse-related PTSD symptoms. *Journal of the American Academy of Child & Adolescent Psychiatry, 45,* 1474–1484.

Denton, W. H., Burleson, B. R., Clark, T. E., Rodriguez, C. P., & Hobbs, B. V. (2000). A randomized trial of emotion-focused therapy for couples in a training clinic. *Journal of Marital and Family Therapy, 26,* 65–78.

Dessaulles, A., Johnson, S. M., & Denton, W. H. (2003). Emotion focused therapy for couples in treatment of depression: A pilot study. *American Journal of Family Therapy, 31,* 345–353.

Dewane, C. (2008). The ABCs of ACT: Acceptance and commitment therapy. *Social Work Today.* Retrieved from http://www.socialworktoday.com/archive/090208p36.shtml.

Fjorback, L. O., Arendt, M., Ørnbøl, E., Fink, P., & Walach, H. (2011). Mindfulness-based stress reduction and mindfulness-based cognitive therapy—A systematic review of randomized controlled trials. *Acta Psychiatrica Scandinavica, 124,* 102–119. doi:10.1111/j.1600-0447.2011.01704.x

Ford, J., Racusin, R., Daviss, W. B., Ellis, C. G., Thomas, J. K., Rogers, K., et al. (1999). Trauma exposure among children with oppositional defiant disorder and attention deficit-hyperactivity disorder. *Journal of Consulting and Clinical Psychology, 67,* 786–789. doi:10.1037/0022-006X.67.5.786

Forman, E. M., Herbert, J. D., Moitra, E., Yeomans, P. D., & Geller, P. A. (2007). A randomized controlled effectiveness trial of acceptance and commitment therapy and cognitive therapy for anxiety and depression. *Behavior Modification, 31,* 772–799. doi:10.1177/0145445507302202

Fulton, C., & Cashwell, C. S. (2015). Mindfulness-based awareness and compassion: Predictors of counselor empathy and anxiety. *Counselor Education and Supervision, 54,* 122–133.

Gall, T., Basque, V., Damasceno-Scott, M., & Vardy, G. (2007). Spirituality and the current adjustment of adult survivors of childhood sexual abuse. *Journal for the Scientific Study of Religion, 46,* 101–117.

Germer, C. (2006). *You gotta have heart.* Retrieved from http://www.mindfulself compassion.org/articles/YouGottaHaveHeart.html.

Gill, C. S., Harper, M. C., & Dailey, S. F. (2011). Assessing the spiritual and religious domain. In C. S. Cashwell & J. S. Young (Eds.), *Integrating spirituality and religion into counseling: A guide to competent practice* (pp. 141–162). Alexandria, VA: American Counseling Association.

Greason, P. B., & Cashwell, C. S. (2009). Mindfulness and counseling self-efficacy: The mediating role of attention and empathy. *Counselor Education and Supervision, 49,* 2–18.

Greenberg, L. J., Warwar, S. H., & Malcolm, W. M. (2008). Differential effects of emotion focused therapy and psychoeducation in facilitating forgiveness and letting go of emotional injuries. *Journal of Counseling Psychology, 55,* 185–196.

Greeson, J. M. (2009). Mindfulness research update: 2008. *Complementary Health Practice Review, 14,* 10–18. doi:10.1177/1533210108329862

Grepmair, L., Mitterlehner, F., Loew, T., & Nickel, M. (2007). Promotion of mindfulness in psychotherapists in training: Preliminary study. *European Psychiatry, 22,* 485–489.

Halchuk, R. E., Makinen, J. A., & Johnson, S. M. (2010). Resolving attachment injuries in couples using emotionally focused therapy: A three-year follow-up. *Journal of Couple and Relationship Therapy, 9,* 31–47.

Hamblen, J., & Barnett, E. (2009). *PTSD in children and adolescents.* Retrieved from http://www.ptsd.va.gov/professional/pages/ptsd_in_children_and_adolescents_overview_for_professionals.asp.

Harris, R. (2008). *The happiness trap.* New York: Shambala.

Hayes, S. C., Levin, M. E., Plumb-Vilardaga, J., Villatte, J. L., & Pistorello, J. (2011). Acceptance and commitment therapy and contextual behavioral science: Examining the progress of a distinctive model of behavioral and cognitive therapy. *Behavior Therapy, 44,* 180–198. doi:10.1016/j.beth.2009.08.002

Hayes, S. C., Luoma, J. B., Bond, F. W., Masuda, A., & Lillis, J. (2006). Acceptance and commitment therapy: Model, processes and outcomes. *Behaviour Research and Therapy, 44,* 1–25.

Hayes, S. C., Masuda, A., Bissett, R., Luoma, J., & Guerrero, L. (2004). DBT, FAR and ACT: How empirically oriented are the new behavior therapy technologies? *Behavior Therapy, 35,* 35–54. doi:10.1016/S0005–7894(04)80003–0

Hayes, S. C., Strosahl, K. D., & Wilson, K. G. (1999). *Acceptance and commitment therapy: An experiential approach to behavior change.* New York: Guilford.

Hayes, S. C., Strosahl, K. D., & Wilson, K. G. (2012). *Acceptance and commitment therapy: The process and practice of mindful change* (2nd ed.). New York: Guilford.

Heinz, A., Epstein, D. H., & Preston, K. L. (2007). Spiritual/religious experiences and in-treatment outcome in an inner-city program for heroin and cocaine dependence. *Journal of Psychoactive Drugs, 39,* 41–49.

Hill, P. C., & Pargament, K. I. (2003). Advances in the conceptualization and measurement of religion and spirituality: Implications for physical and mental health research. *American Psychologist, 58,* 64–74.

Hoagwood, K., Radigan, M., Rodriquez, J., Levitt, J., Fernandez, D., & Foster, J. (2006). *Final report on the Child and Adolescent Trauma Treatment Consortium (CATS) Project.* Albany: New York State Office of Mental Health.

Hook, J. N., Worthington, E. L., Davis, D. E., Jennings, D. J., II, Gartner, A. L., Hook, J. P. (2010). Empirically supported religious and spiritual therapies. *Journal of Clinical Psychology, 66,* 46–72.

Johnson, S. M. (2003). The revolution in couples therapy: A practitioner-scientist perspective. *Journal of Marital and Family Therapy, 29,* 365–385.

Johnson, S. M. (2004). *The practice of emotionally focused couple therapy: Creating connection* (2nd ed.). New York: Brunner-Routledge.

Johnson, S. M., Maddeaux, C., & Blouin, J. (1998). Emotionally focused family therapy for bulimia: Changing attachment patterns. *Psychotherapy: Theory, Research, Practice, Training, 35,* 238–247.

Kabat-Zinn, J. (1990). *Full catastrophe living: Using the wisdom of your body and mind to face stress, pain, and illness.* New York: Delacorte.

Kabat-Zinn, J. (1994). *Wherever you go, there you are: Mindfulness meditation in everyday life.* New York: Hyperion.

Klerman, G. L., Weissman, M. M., Rounsaville, B. J., & Chevron, E. S. (1984). *Interpersonal psychotherapy of depression.* New York: Basic Books.

Kliem, S., Kroger, C., & Kosfelder, J. (2010). Dialectical behavior therapy for borderline personality disorder: A meta-analysis using mixed effects modeling. *Journal of Consulting and Clinical Psychology, 78,* 936–951.

Koenig, L. B., & Valliant, G. E. (2009). A prospective study of church attendance and health over the lifespan. *Health Psychology, 28,* 117–124. doi:10.1037/a0012984

Koerner, K., & Dimeff, L. A. (2007). Overview of dialectical behavior therapy. In L. A. Dimeff & K. Koerner (Eds.), *Dialectical behavior therapy in clinical practice: Applications across disorders and settings* (pp. 1–18). New York: Guilford.

Kristeller, J. L., & Hallett, C. B. (1999). An exploratory study of a meditation-based intervention for binge eating disorder. *Journal of Health Psychology, 4,* 357–363.

Lang, J. M., Ford, J. D., & Fitzgerald, M. M. (2010). An algorithm for determining use of trauma-focused cognitive-behavioral therapy. *Psychotherapy: Theory, Research, Practice, Training, 47,* 554–569. doi:10.1037/a0021184

Lesh, T. (1970). Zen meditation and development of empathy in counselors. *Journal of Humanistic Psychology, 10,* 39–74.

Linehan, M. M. (1993). *Skills training manual for treating borderline personality disorder.* New York: Guilford.

Linehan, M. M, & Chen, E. (2005). Dialectical behavior therapy for eating disorders. In A. Freeman, S. Felqoise, A. M. Nezu, C. M. Nezu, & M. A. Reinecke (Eds.), *Encyclopedia of cognitive behavior therapy* (pp. 168–171). New York: Plenum.

Linehan, M. M., Dimeff, L. A., Reynolds, S. K., Comtois, K. A., Welch, S. S., Heagerty, P., et al. (2002). Dialectical behavior therapy versus comprehensive validation therapy plus 12-step for the treatment of opioid dependent women meeting criteria for borderline personality disorder. *Drug and Alcohol Dependence, 67,* 13–26.

Lundahl, B. W., Kunz, C., Brownell, C., Tollefson, D., & Burke, B. L. (2010). A meta-analysis of motivational interviewing: Twenty-five years of empirical studies. *Research on Social Work Practice, 20,* 137–160.

Luoma, J. B., Hayes, S. C., & Walser, R. D. (2007). *Learning ACT.* Oakland, CA: New Harbinger.

Lynch, T. R., Chapman, A. L., Rosenthal, M. Z., Kuo, J. R., & Linehan, M. M. (2006). Mechanisms of change in dialectical behavior therapy: Theoretical and empirical observations. *Journal of Clinical Psychology, 62,* 459–480.

Lyons, J. S., Weiner, D. A., Schneider, A. Martinovich, Z., & McClelland, G. (2008). *Evaluation of the implementation of three evidence-based practices to address trauma for children and youth who are wards of the State of Illinois, final report.* Evanston, IL: Northwestern University.

MacIntosh, H. B., & Johnson, S. (2008). Emotionally focused therapy for couples and childhood sexual abuse survivors. *Journal of Marital and Family Therapy, 34,* 298–315.

Makinen, J. A., & Johnson, S. M. (2006). Resolving attachment injuries in couples using emotionally focused therapy: Steps toward forgiveness and reconciliation. *Journal of Consulting and Clinical Psychology, 74,* 1055–1164.

Marlatt, G. A., & Gordon, J. R. (1985). *Relapse prevention: Maintenance strategies in the treatment of addictive behaviors.* New York: Guilford.

Miller, A. L., Rathus, J. H., & Linehan, M. (2007). *Dialectical behavior therapy for suicidal adolescents.* New York: Guilford Press.

Miller, W. R. (1983). Motivational interviewing with problem drinkers. *Behavioural Psychotherapy, 11,* 147–172.

Miller, W. R., & Rollnick, S. (1991). *Motivational interviewing: Preparing people to change addictive behavior.* New York: Guilford Press.

Miller, W. R., & Rollnick, S. (2009). Ten things motivational interviewing is not. *Behavioural and Cognitive Psychotherapy, 37,* 129–140.

Miller, W. R., & Rollnick, S. (2013). *Motivational interviewing: Helping people change* (3rd ed.). New York: Guilford Press.

Miller, W. R., & Rose, G. S. (2009). Toward a theory of motivational interviewing. *American Psychologist, 64,* 527–537.

Millikin, J. W., & Johnson, S. M. (2000). Telling tales: Disquisitions in emotionally focused therapy. *Journal of Family Psychotherapy, 11,* 75–80.

Mufson, L., Dorta, K. P., Wickramarathe, P., Nomura, Y., Olfson, M., & Weissman, M. M. (2004). A randomized effectiveness trial of interpersonal psychotherapy for depressed adolescents. *Archives of General Psychiatry, 61,* 577–584.

Myers, J. E., & Sweeney, T. J. (2008). Wellness counseling: The evidence base for practice. *Journal of Counseling & Development, 86,* 482–493.

Princeton Religion Research Center. (2000). Americans remain very religious, but not necessarily in conventional ways. *Emerging Trends, 22,* 2–3.

Robins, C. J., & Chapman, A. L. (2004). Dialectical behavior therapy: Current status, recent developments, and future directions. *Journal of Personality Disorders, 18,* 73–89.

Rollnick, S., Miller, W. R., & Butler, C. C. (2008). *Motivational interviewing in health care: Helping patients to change behavior.* New York: Guilford Press.

Rosengren, D. B. (2009). *Building motivational interviewing skills: A practitioner workbook.* New York: Guilford.

Rothaupt, J. W., & Morgan, M. M. (2007). Counselors' and counselor educators' practice of mindfulness: A qualitative inquiry. *Counseling and Values, 52,* 40–54.

Saxe, G., MacDonald, H., & Ellis, H. (2007). Psychosocial approaches for children with PTSD. In M. J. Friedman, T. M. Keane, & P. Resick (Eds.), *Handbook of PTSD: Science and practice* (pp. 359–375). New York: Guilford Press.

Schottellcorb, A. A., Doumas, D. M., & Garcia, R. (2012). Treatment for childhood refugee trauma: A randomized controlled trial. *International Journal of Play Therapy, 21*(2), 57–73. doi:10.1037/a0027430

Segal, Z. V., Williams, J. M. G., & Teasdale, J. D. (2002). *Mindfulness-based cognitive therapy for depression: A new approach to preventing relapse.* New York: Guilford.

Seidler, G. H., & Wagner, F. E. (2006). Comparing the efficacy of EMDR and trauma-focused cognitive-behavioral therapy in the treatment of PTSD: A meta-analytic study. *Psychological Medicine, 36*(11), 1515–1522.

Smith, T. B., Bartz, J., & Richards, S. P. (2007). Outcomes of religious and spiritual adaptations to psychotherapy: A meta-analytic review. *Psychological Research, 17,* 643–655.

Stangier, U., Schramm, E., Heidenreich, T., Berger, M., & Clark, D. M. (2011). Cognitive therapy versus interpersonal psychotherapy in social anxiety disorder: A randomized controlled trial. *Archives of General Psychiatry, 68,* 692–700.

Swales, M. A. (2009). Dialectical behaviour therapy: Description, research, and future directions. *International Journal of Behavioral Consultation and Therapy, 5,* 164–177.

Teasdale, J. D., Segal, Z. V., & Williams, J. M. G. (1995). How does cognitive therapy prevent depressive relapse and why should attentional control (mindfulness training) help? *Behaviour Research and Therapy, 33,* 25–39.

Teasdale, J. D., Segal, Z. V., Williams, J. M. G., Ridgeway, V. A., Soulsby, J. M., & Lau, M. A. (2000). Prevention of relapse/recurrence in major depression by mindfulness-based cognitive therapy. *Journal of Consulting and Clinical Psychology, 68,* 615–623.

Weissman, M. M. (2007). Recent non-medication trials of interpersonal psychotherapy for depression. *Interpersonal Journal of Neuropsychopharmacology, 10,* 117–122.

Weissman, M. M., Markowitz, J. C., & Klerman, G. L. (2007). *Clinician's quick guide to interpersonal psychotherapy.* New York: Oxford University Press.

West, D. S., DiLillo, V., Bursac, Z., Gore, S. A., & Greene, P. G. (2007). Motivational interviewing improves weight loss in women with type 2 diabetes. *Diabetes Care, 30,* 1081–1087.

Wood, N. D., Crane, D. R., Schaalje, G. B., & Law, D. D. (2005). What works for whom: A meta-analytic review of marital and couples therapy in reference to marital distress. *American Journal of Family Therapy, 33,* 273–287.

Young, J. S., & Cashwell, C. S. (2011). Integrating spirituality and religion into counseling: An introduction. In C. S. Cashwell & J. S. Young (Eds.), *Integrating spirituality and religion into counseling: A guide to competent practice* (pp. 1–24). Alexandria, VA: American Counseling Association.

Zinnbauer, B. J., Pargament, K. I., Cole, B., Rye, M. S., Butter, E. M., Belavich, T. G., et al. (1997) Religion and spirituality: Unfuzzying the fuzzy. *Journal for the Scientific Study of Religion, 36,* 549–564.

Zuckoff, A., Swartz, H. A., & Grote, N. K. (2008). Motivational interviewing as a prelude to psychotherapy of depression. In H. Arkowitz, H. A. Westra, W. R. Miller, & S. Rollnick (Eds.), *Motivational interviewing in the treatment of psychological problems* (pp. 109–144). New York: Guilford.

Index

Printed in the USA
CPSIA information can be obtained
at www.ICGtesting.com
BVHW021824030823
668089BV00003B/6